MW00743675

STRATEGIC MARKETING MANAGEMENT CASES AND APPLICATIONS

The Irwin Series in Marketing

Consulting Editor

Gilbert A. Churchill, Jr.
University of Wisconsin–Madison

STRATEGIC MARKETING MANAGEMENT CASES AND APPLICATIONS

Third Edition

David W. Cravens
Charles W. Lamb, Jr.
M. J. Neeley School of Business
Texas Christian University

1990

Homewood, IL   60430
Boston, MA   02116

© RICHARD D. IRWIN, INC., 1983, 1986, and 1990

The two previous editions of this book were titled
Strategic Marketing Cases and Applications.

Developmental editor: Andy Winston
Project editor: Karen Smith
Production manager: Irene H. Sotiroff
Compositor: Bi-Comp, Incorporated
Typeface: 10/12 Century Schoolbook
Printer: R. R. Donnelley & Sons Company

Library of Congress Cataloging-in-Publication Data

Cravens, David W.
    Strategic marketing management: cases and applications / David W.
Cravens, Charles W. Lamb, Jr.—3rd ed.
        p.   cm.
    Rev. ed. of: Strategic marketing cases and applications. 2nd ed.
1986.
    Includes index.
    ISBN 0-256-07898-X
    1. Marketing—Case studies.   I. Lamb, Charles W.   II. Cravens,
David W.   Strategic marketing cases and applications.   III. Title.
HF5415.C6944   1990
658.8′02—dc20   89–33001
                                                                    CIP

Printed in the United States of America
1 2 3 4 5 6 7 8 9 0 DO 6 5 4 3 2 1 0 9

To M. J. Neeley

PREFACE

Gaining a competitive advantage in marketing is a demanding challenge. An important part of this challenge is analyzing and strategically responding to rapidly changing environmental opportunities and threats. This requires marketing professionals to develop effective strategic analysis, planning, implementation, and control skills.

Marketing is the responsibility of everyone in an organization, not just those in marketing and sales positions. Business advantage is gained through customer satisfaction. Marketing strategy provides the basis for assembling an organization's customer influencing capabilities.

External pressures are adding new demands to marketing strategy:

- The needs and wants of buyers are becoming fragmented and increasingly complex.
- Major changes are taking place in consumer markets due to demographic shifts, geographical movement of people, and new lifestyles.
- Deregulation of financial services, transportation, and telecommunications has created new marketing requirements in these industries.
- Slow growth and excess capacity exist in many industries; explosive change is taking place in others.
- High performance strategies have become essential due to escalating costs and declining productivity in many businesses.
- Intensive global competition for market position exists in many industries such as automobiles, consumer electronics, appliances, steel, apparel, and construction equipment.
- Strategic restructuring (industry consolidation, downsizing) is occurring in many companies to cope with pressures for change from customers and competitors.

Cases and strategy applications provide an effective way to place students in business situations requiring marketing analysis and action recommendations. These cases, representing a wide variety of business and nonprofit organization situations, should enable the student to expand his or her understanding of marketing strategy concepts and their application.

Using Strategic Marketing

This book can serve as a teaching-learning resource in several ways. It can be used with a marketing management book to create a text and applications combination for use in undergraduate advanced marketing management and strategy courses, and in MBA marketing management and strategy courses. Three chapters, which cover a step-by-step approach to marketing analysis and planning, financial analysis, and case analysis, provide useful foundation materials. These chapters are particularly helpful in the absence of a companion text.

Alternatively, this book can be used as the primary text for advanced or capstone marketing management and strategy courses. In addition to helping meet the needs of instructors developing new courses in strategic marketing, it offers instructors a way to expand the strategic emphasis of marketing management courses beyond the coverage in traditional marketing management texts and casebooks. We have purposely avoided focusing primarily on decisions facing large corporations. Many of the cases in this book concern decisions facing small and medium-sized organizations. Of course, *Strategic Marketing Management Cases and Applications* also contains numerous cases that focus on traditional marketing management areas.

Changes For This Edition

The third edition of *Strategic Marketing Management Cases and Applications* is the result of a major revision based on feedback from users and nonusers of the second edition. Many new cases have been added to increase the topical coverage and to provide material for both undergraduate and graduate strategy and management courses. The combined portfolio of cases and applications (short cases) offer the instructor a valuable resource for flexible course development. The instructor's manual has also been substantially revised and expanded.

The Text's Components

Cases. As editors, we have made a comprehensive effort to obtain the best possible cases to illustrate the various aspects of marketing strategy and management. Over one-half of the cases and three-quarters of the applications are new to this edition. Rather than relying only on our experiences, many other sources were utilized to assure complete coverage of topics and representation of different sizes and types of domestic and international consumer and industrial product and service firms. To insure strong student interest, every case was evaluated on interest and difficulty by a student team.

Applications. Several short application cases are included at the end of each group of regular-length cases. We have found these strategy applications particularly useful for class discussion, student presentation, projects, and scenarios for test questions. The applications substantially expand the teaching-learning utility of the book. Detailed suggestions for using the applications are provided in the Instructor's Manual.

Computer Analysis. Personal computer analysis has also been added to this third edition. The various financial analysis and graphics capabilities available provide impressive tools for case analysis. Their use is discussed in Chapters 2 and 3, and extensive analyses are provided in the Instructor's Manual for those cases in which such analyses are appropriate.

Instructor's Manual. The Instructor's Manual provides detailed analyses and supporting materials for each case and application. Suggestions are included for course design, and a topic index is provided. Transparency masters are also included to aid in class discussion of the cases. Information updating several case situations is provided in the manual.

ACKNOWLEDGMENTS

In addition to the important contribution made to the book by the authors of the cases, we want to acknowledge several others whose assistance and support were invaluable. Gilbert A. Churchill, Jr., University of Wisconsin–Madison, as consulting editor, provided many helpful suggestions during the development of the book. Professor Max Lupul, California State University–Northridge; Professor Scott Alden, Purdue University; and Professor Betsy Gelb, University of Houston, offered useful guidelines for improving various editions of this book, as did Carol A. Scott, University of California–Los Angeles; Lawrence P. Feldman, University of Illinois–Chicago; and Benny Barak, CUNY, Bernard Baruch College. We were also fortunate to have the benefit of detailed reviews by the following instructors in developing this edition:

Seymour T. R. Abt	McGill University
E. Wayne Chandler	Eastern Illinois University
Jack R. Dauner	Fayetteville State University
Thomas J. Page, Jr.	Michigan State University
Charles R. Patton	Pan American University at Brownsville
A. M. Pelham	University of Northern Iowa
William N. Rodgers	University of San Francisco
Patrick L. Schul	Memphis State University
R. Viswanathan	University of Northern Colorado

Several of our graduate assistants have made essential contributions to this edition of the book: Ramona Baker, Jan Van DeWalker, Blair Kuhnen,

Michele Neblock, Steve Okland, Sonja Ridgway, and Susan Tate. Special thanks are due Jerilyn White and Barbara Snell for typing the manuscript and for their assistance in other aspects of the project. We are greatly appreciative of the support and encouragement provided by our dean, H. Kirk Downey, without whose help the development of this book would not been possible. Finally, we want to express our appreciation to Eunice West and her late husband James L. West and to M. J. Neeley and his late wife Alice for the endowments that help support our positions and enable us to work on projects like this book.

We are indebted to all of these people and to the many authors and publishers who gave us permission to use their materials. We also appreciate the support and suggestions we have received from adopters of previous editions of this book. While the final result is our responsibility, the assistance provided was essential in completing the project.

David W. Cravens
Charles W. Lamb, Jr.

CASE CONTRIBUTORS

Kenneth Beck, University of Kansas
Roger C. Bennett, McGill University
Thomas M. Bertsch, James Madison University
Harper Boyd, University of Arkansas at Little Rock
Victor P. Buell, The University of Massachusetts
Arnold C. Cooper, Purdue University
Terry H. Deutscher, The University of Western Ontario
Peter Doyle, Bradford University
Maureen Fanshawe, University of Michigan
Susan Fleming, The University of Western Ontario
John Fornier, University of Arkansas at Little Rock
Christopher Gale, University of Virginia
James Graham, University of Calgary
Holly Gunner, Management Analysis Center, Inc.
Robert W. Haas, San Diego State University
Kenneth G. Hardy, The University of Western Ontario
Steven W. Hartley, University of Denver
H. Michael Hayes, University of Colorado–Denver
D. Joseph Irvine, University of Ottawa
Jim Kerlin, University of Alabama
Jay E. Klompmaker, University of North Carolina
Thomas Kosnik, University of Virginia
Charles M. Kummel, University of North Carolina
Peter J. LaPlaca, University of Connecticut
David S. Litvack, University of Ottawa
Philip McDonald, Northeastern University

James C. Makens, Wake Forest University
Stewart C. Malone, University of Virginia
Joseph R. Mills, American Safety Razor Co.
Roger More, The University of Western Ontario
James E. Nelson, University of Colorado
Valerie Pandak, James Madison University
John A. Quelch, Harvard University
Bonnie J. Queram, University of Wisconsin at Madison
James Brian Quinn, Dartmouth College
Stuart U. Rich, University of Oregon
Ray B. Robbins, University of Arkansas at Little Rock
William Rudelius, University of Minnesota
Lawrence M. Rumble, University of Virginia
Adrian B. Ryans, The University of Western Ontario
Earl R. Sage, University of North Carolina at Charlotte
Don E. Schultz, Northwestern University
Shannon Shipp, Texas Christian University
Thomas H. Stevenson, University of North Carolina at Charlotte
Marilyn L. Taylor, University of Kansas
Mark Traxler, Northwestern University
Ulrich Wesche, Howard University
Gary E. Willard, Purdue University
William R. Wooldridge, University of Colorado
Thomas R. Wotruba, San Diego State University

CONTENTS

PART 2
COORDINATING BUSINESS AND MARKETING STRATEGIES

CASES

APPLICATIONS

PART 3
TARGET MARKET STRATEGY

PART 4
MARKETING PROGRAM POSITIONING STRATEGY

PART 5
DEVELOPING MARKETING PLANS

PART 6
ORGANIZING, IMPLEMENTING AND CONTROLLING MARKETING STRATEGY

STRATEGIC MARKETING MANAGEMENT CASES AND APPLICATIONS

PART 1

STRATEGIC MARKETING

CHAPTER 1

GAINING MARKETING ADVANTAGE*

Marketing advantages can be achieved in various ways; finding them is not all that easy, however. Gaining a strategic edge takes time and demands perceptive analysis.

Consider these companies: The Limited (women's apparel retailer), American Airlines (air transportation), Snap-on-Tools (mechanics' hand tools), Lens Crafters (eyeware chain), and Daimler-Benz AG (Mercedes automobiles). They differ according to markets served, products, size, corporate culture, and marketing strategy. But they share one characteristic: Each company has developed an important marketing advantage. The Limited targets promising women's apparel segments, using innovative positioning strategies. American Airlines, under an aggressive marketing strategy, provides customer-responsive services, aided by a highly effective information system. Snap-on-Tools has built an important competitive advantage by using its dealer-in-a-van distribution network to add value to the buyer/seller relationship. Lens Crafters offers convenient locations and fast response to customers' eyeware needs. Daimler-Benz commands an impressive position in the luxury-car market by providing quality automobiles that meet buyers' wants. The marketing strategy selected by each corporation is logically matched to the strategic factors that are important in its competitive arena.

Marketing strategy helps determine whether a business can survive and grow in today's highly competitive business environment. A marketing advantage is essential for all firms. Customer satisfaction is the responsibility of everyone on the corporate team, not just those assigned to marketing positions. Accordingly, we must examine marketing strategy from the point of view of the business, not that of the marketing function.

Gaining strategic marketing advantage involves much more than a solution for success out of some strategy handbook. Although each firm's

---

* A shorter version of this chapter was published in David W. Cravens, "Gaining Strategic Marketing Advantage," *Business Horizons*, September–October 1988, pp. 44–54. Copyright 1988 by the Foundation for the School of Business at Indiana University. Used with permission.

marketing strategy is unique, if a logical sequence of analyses and decisions is followed, corporate and marketing management will be able to better select winning strategies. The final choice is often the result of penetrating assessments of marketing advantage, analysis of market needs and competitive threats, and management's intuitive sense of the strategic fit of the various strategies being considered.

Analysis of a business's strategic situation is the first step toward gaining strategic marketing advantage (see Exhibit 1–1). Situational analysis identifies the relevant strategic forces, including organizational, market, competitive, and environmental factors. In the next step, consideration of these important factors helps management determine the firm's unique advantages. The formulation of key strategic objectives follows this appraisal of the situation. Management must then screen, and critically evaluate, feasible strategic options. The choice and implementation of a marketing strategy begins the process of gaining competitive advantage. Performance

EXHIBIT 1–1
Steps in Gaining Strategic Marketing Advantage

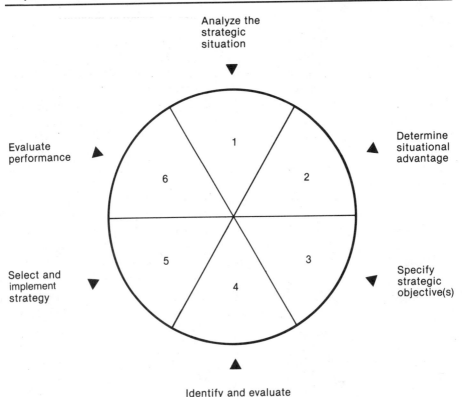

Analyze the
strategic
situation

Evaluate
performance

Determine
situational
advantage

Select and
implement
strategy

Specify
strategic
objective(s)

Identify and evaluate
strategic options

assessment gauges the effectiveness of the strategy and identifies the need for possible strategy alterations.

ANALYZING THE STRATEGIC SITUATION

Minolta Corp. lost the top position in the United States 35 mm camera market to Canon Inc. in the early 1980s. Minolta's management used a new-product strategy to regain the number one position. A major engineering effort resulted in a state-of-the-art 35 mm single-lens-reflex camera, the computerized Maxxum. It was introduced in early 1985 with the theme, "Only the human eye focuses faster." By 1986 it was clear that the new strategy had gained a major marketing advantage for the firm. The camera's innovative features helped Minolta regain its market position. Nikon introduced a camera with similar features in 1986, and other manufacturers followed in 1987. By 1988 several competitors offered features similar to those introduced by Minolta.

Strategic Forces

The strategic forces in the marketplace create an array of marketing strategy situations. Minolta's need to regain its dominant position in the camera market is illustrative. Opportunities are identified by assessing organizational factors, market structure dynamics, industry and competition, and the environmental forces.

The Organization. Reviewing the organization's strengths and weaknesses is an important part of situational analysis. The organization's influences on a marketing strategy situation include the corporate culture (shared values and style), the stage in the firm's development, organizational structure, and operating policies. The size, performance, capabilities, and resources (including people) of an organization also affect its strategy selection. For example, a company's power and influence through its distribution channels can be a marketing advantage. The Limited has a corporate-owned vertical marketing system, from producer to end user. Its Mast Industries works with more than 200 production facilities in 30 countries to supply The Limited's vast retail distribution network.

Market Structure Dynamics. The structure and characteristics of markets—and the changes that occur in them—create various marketing strategy situations. Market maturity often intensifies competition and limits growth and profit opportunities. The product life cycle is widely recognized as an influence on marketing strategy. Minolta's management responded to the maturity of the 35 mm camera market and the need to alter its product line by using a new-product strategy. Differences in what buyers in a market want create opportunities for market specialization. Each market segment is a competitive arena with specific strategic requirements and opportunities for marketing advantage.

The Industry and the Competitive Arena.   Industry structure and the key competitors must be included in the situation assessment.[1] A firm's position and capabilities relative to its competitors' create important marketing advantages and strategic weaknesses. Variations in industry structure create different strategic situations. Compare, for example, the competitive situation of a pioneering firm in an emerging industry (such as Guest Supply in hotel bathroom amenities) and the intense competition present in a mature global industry (such as automobiles).

Environmental Forces.   External influences, largely uncontrollable, affect the marketing situations of specific firms and industries. The effect may be favorable or unfavorable; opportunities or threats may be created. Relevant economic, political, social, technological, and natural forces should be identified and evaluated. Forecasts assess the future effect of these forces on marketing strategy. Often the influences alter the attractiveness of market opportunities. The strategic situations created by the deregulation of industries such as transportation services, financial services, and telecommunications illustrate this point dramatically.

Diamler-Benz AG dominates the high-priced luxury European-style automobile market with its Mercedes line. To gain additional growth opportunities, management decided to target the lower-priced luxury European-style car segment that was dominated by BMW. Exhibit 1–2 shows the situation assessment. Management correctly assessed the strategic situation as a differential-advantage opportunity. Mercedes' advantage was an established luxury image in the automobile market. This perception helped position the 190 in the lower-priced luxury segment. A successful entry into this segment would generate additional sales and profits for Daimler-Benz, but resource requirements were high—an estimated $1 billion to develop the baby Benz. The marketing strategy positioned the 190 to attract younger people than those buying the current Mercedes lines. A successful appeal to the young affluent could also favorably alter the company's existing conservative image. Daimler-Benz implemented the strategy through the existing marketing and distribution system. Introduced in 1982, the 190 was a success; sales from introduction through late 1986 totaled nearly 700,000.[2] Perhaps more importantly, the baby Benz attracted a substantial number of first-time Mercedes buyers.

---

[1] See Michael E. Porter, "How Competitive Forces Shape Strategy," *Harvard Business Review*, March–April 1979, pp. 137–145; and Michael E. Porter, *Competitive Advantage* (New York: The Free Press, 1985).

[2] Thomas F. O'Boyle, "Small Luxury Car Is Success for Daimler," *The Wall Street Journal*, September 19, 1986, p. 24.

EXHIBIT 1–2
Daimler-Benz's Strategic Situation in the Lower-Priced Luxury European-Style Car Segment

Organizational Factors

   Favorable. Competence and experience in successfully developing and marketing luxury automobiles. Strong brand image. Extensive resources. Established worldwide distribution network.
   Unfavorable. Mercedes automobiles are perceived as conservative, appealing more to older people. Possible cannibalization of the higher-priced segment sales.

Market Structure and Dynamics

   The lower-priced luxury European-style car segment offers a promising growth opportunity in the United States. Consumer preferences are clearly differentiated from other automobile segments. Buyers are willing (and able) to pay substantial prices for products that meet their preferences. Image is important. Future demographic and other environmental changes should favorably affect this segment. Attracting the buyers in the segment will increase Mercedes' opportunity to eventually attract them to the high-priced luxury segment dominated by Mercedes' other product lines.

The Competitive Arena

   This market segment is served by BMW, Volvo, Audi, and others. BMW, the leading competitor, has been very successful. Surprisingly, BMW did not attempt to strengthen its position through product innovation until 1987. This apparent complacency gave Mercedes a potential source of advantage through innovative product design and aggressive marketing.

Environmental Forces

   The lower-priced luxury European-style car segment was expected to expand substantially from 1980–90 in the United States due to large population growth in the 25-to-44 age group.

DETERMINING THE SITUATIONAL ADVANTAGE

The strategic forces operating in the marketplace create many specific situations. Strategic analysis is facilitated by identifying a small set of typical situations that occur in many different industries and markets.[3] The types are: market development, market domination, market selectivity, differential advantage, and no advantage (see Exhibit 1–3). They are defined by the stage of industry development, the competitive position of the enterprise, the existence of a competitive advantage, and the extent of differentiation of

---

   [3] David W. Cravens, "Strategic Forces Affecting Marketing Strategy," *Business Horizons,* September–October 1986, pp. 77–86.

EXHIBIT 1–3
Illustrative Marketing Strategy Situations

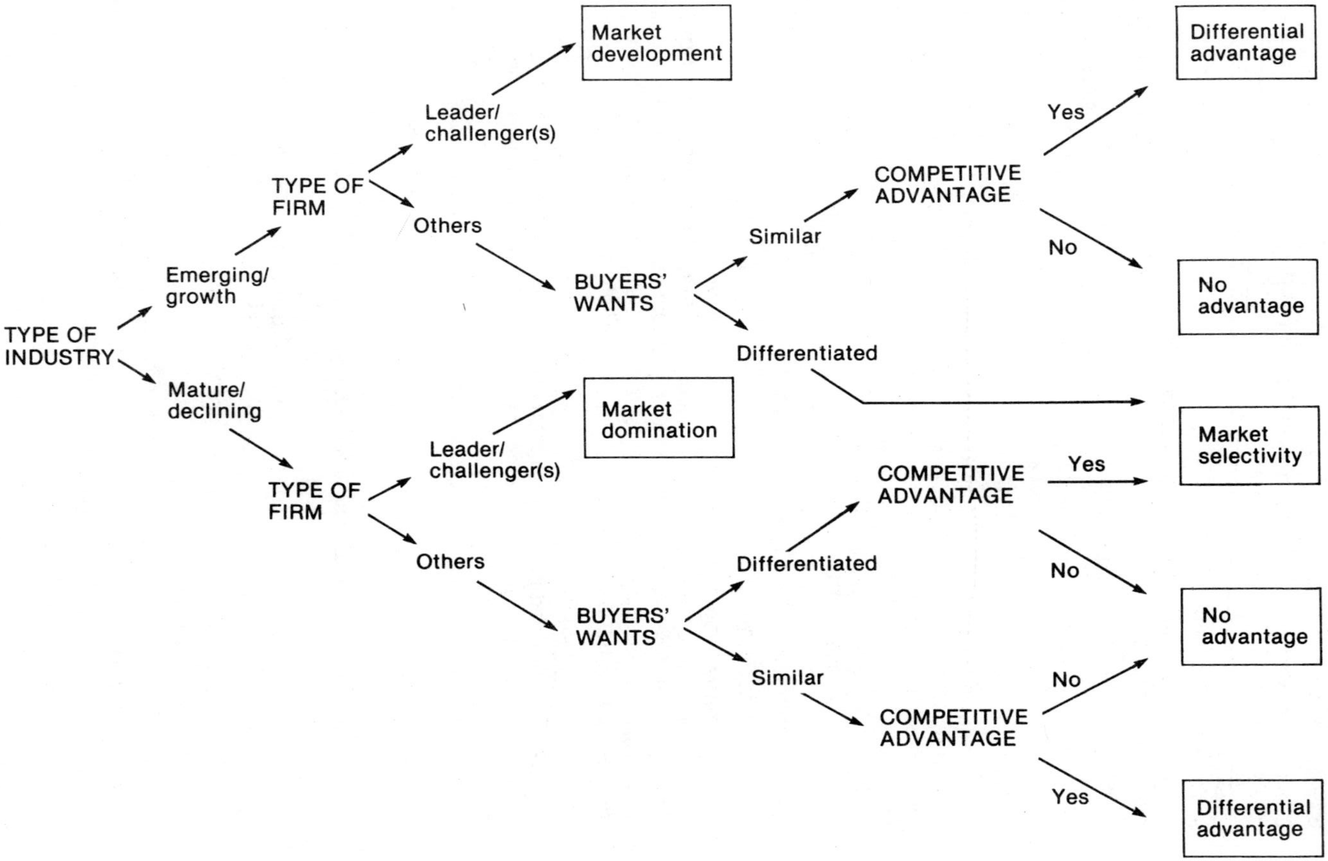

buyers' wants. The effects of other strategic forces, such as organizational capabilities, environmental influences, and market structure, are described within each situational category.

Market Development

The first firm to enter a new market has the opportunity to play a leadership role in that market's development. Other early entrants also occupy market development positions. The microcomputer-software industry emerged in the 1970s as a cottage industry and expanded rapidly in the 1980s. Lotus Development Corporation was one of the pioneers. Founded in 1982, Lotus led the industry in 1986 with revenues of $283 million. The market pioneer has an important chance to gain a sustainable competitive advantage.[4] A competent firm with an advantage can enter the market at a later stage and still gain the lead position from the pioneer. The late entries of IBM into the personal-computer market and Gallo into the wine-cooler market are examples. A market development situation can also occur in a fragmented industry that has no market leader.

The market development situation presents an interesting strategic challenge. Management can influence the direction of market development, but it faces the risk of creating a future competitive disadvantage. Sony pioneered the videocassette recorder market with the Betamax system but eventually lost market position to competitors offering the VHS format. The firm that finds itself in a market development situation has several marketing strategy options; a central consideration in selecting the correct strategy is building a sustainable competitive advantage.

Market Domination

Market domination is the position occupied by the market leader in an established market and one or two major challengers. Companies in this situation include Goodyear (tires), The Limited (women's apparel), and Anheuser-Busch (beer). A firm may gain a dominant position through early market entry, low costs, product advantages, marketing capabilities, customer franchise, and other strengths.

The Limited is the dominant women's-apparel firm. Its powerful marketing advantage has been gained through targeting multiple market segments and developing highly effective product, distribution, price, and promotion strategies. The Limited's management knows how to satisfy customers. The marketing positioning strategy aimed at each target is carefully analyzed, selected, and implemented, using an integrated combination

---

[4] William T. Robinson and Claes Fornell, "Sources of Market Pioneer Advantages in Consumer Goods Industries," *Journal of Marketing Research*, August 1985, pp. 305–17.

of strategic actions. The result is a very favorable and difficult-to-duplicate positioning of The Limited in the eyes and minds of the buyers in each target market. Management adjusts targeting and positioning strategies over time to respond to market dynamics.

Differential Advantage

The differential-advantage situation occurs when a firm possesses one or more sustainable advantages. It may develop in any industry for firms other than the market leader and perhaps for a few other large firms. Advantage may be caused by patent protection, special capabilities and experience, low costs, innovative products, favorable brand perception, product specialization, a strong sales force, or distribution strengths. Importantly, the advantages held by an organization are often central components of its marketing strategy.

Examples of firms in the differential-advantage situation include Tandy in personal computers (cost and distribution advantages); Tootsie Roll Industries in candy (product-specialization advantage); and Maytag in kitchen appliances (favorable brand image gained from high-quality products and service-free performance). This type of advantage is often critical to the survival of small firms in a commodity-type market.

Market Selectivity

Market selectivity describes the situation of many small firms when buyers' wants are differentiated. This occurs in various industries. Market selectivity is created by market forces (differences in buyers' wants); whereas the differential-advantage situation is the consequence of an organization's unique capabilities. Differences in buyers' preferences provide an opportunity for market segmentation. Buyers with similar requirements form each segment. Segments that are not dominated by large competitors offer the small firms a way to gain a marketing advantage. The leading companies in the market may not target certain small niches because other more attractive market segments are available.

Snap-on-Tools' market position and financial performance in the mechanics' hand-tool market are impressive. Selective targeting of professional mechanics has helped the company avoid direct competition with mass merchandisers and producers of low-priced imported tools. Snap-on's customers benefit from on-location contact, quality products, product innovation, liberal replacement, and responsive service. The firm's independent dealers, operating in vans, have strong financial incentives for adding value to the buyer/seller relationship, since satisfied customers continue buying tools. The dealers also obtain useful customer feedback on product performance and new product ideas.

No Advantage

A company may not have a competitive advantage. This is characteristic of the small firms in an industry where suppliers offer similar products because buyers' wants are not differentiated. Examples of no-advantage situations include various single-outlet specialty retailers that have short life spans. Depending upon industry structure and competition, the no-advantage situation may lead to low performance and even business failure unless

EXHIBIT 1–4
Strategic Situation Characteristics and Strategy Implications

Strategic Situation	Characteristics	Strategy Implications	Examples
Market development	Market leader/ challenger in an emerging or growth market	Strengthen market position and advantage to discourage new competitors	Lotus Development Corp. (software) Guest Supply (hotel amenities)
Market domination	Market leader/ challenger in mature or declining market	Strengthen position with multiple strategies in various market segments	Citicorp (banking) Merrill Lynch (financial services)
Market selectivity	Smaller firm(s) in markets where buyers' needs are differentiated	Dominate one or a few market segments	Twentieth Century Insurance (targets low-risk drivers)
Differential advantage	Firm(s) in any market that possess a competitive advantage	Exploit and protect competitive edge	Tandy Corp. (personal computers) Honda (Acura)
No advantage	Firm(s) in any market in which buyers' needs are *not* differentiated and/or the firm(s) does/do not have a competitive advantage	Create advantage through segmentation and/ or special skills. If not feasible, harvest/divest	Small retailers in highly competitive metromarkets

Source: David W. Cravens, "Developing Marketing Strategies for Competitive Advantage," in *Handbook of Business Strategy*, ed. H. E. Glass (New York: Warren, Gorham and Lamont, Inc., 1989), p. 16-7.

management finds a way to gain advantage. Opportunities for competitive leverage may be difficult to achieve. Industry shakeouts involving the exit or consolidation of firms are evidence of no advantage. A number of small oil-field service firms and other energy-related businesses were unable to survive the huge drop in oil prices in 1986 because they had no unique advantages compared to stronger competitors.

Several characteristics of these strategic situations are outlined in Exhibit 1–4. Implications of each situation are also shown. The analysis of

EXHIBIT 1–5
Outline for the Situational Profile

I. Organizational Profile
  A. Mission statement/objectives
  B. Review of past performance
  C. Current operations
    1. Products
    2. Markets
II. Strategic Situation
  A. Define and describe the strategic situation(s) (e.g., market domination, market selectivity) that applies to the business.
  B. Strategy implications
III. Market Definition and Analysis
  A. Market definition
    1. Generic product–market
    2. Product type, product–market
    3. Brand product–market
  B. Market analysis
    1. Market size and projections
    2. Description of buyers
    3. Industry structure
    4. Distribution channels
IV. Segmentation and Targeting Analysis
  A. Market segmentation analysis
  B. Targeting opportunities
V. Competitive Situation
  A. Analysis of key competitors' positioning approaches
  B. Positioning strategy implications
VI. Competitive Advantage Assessment
  A. Unique advantages
  B. Competitive threats
  C. Advantage gaps
  D. Generic strategy implications
  E. Financial considerations

Source: David W. Cravens, "Developing Marketing Strategies for Competitive Advantage," in *Handbook of Business Strategy*, ed. H. E. Glass (New York: Warren, Gorham and Lamont, Inc., 1989), pp. 16-6–16-8.

action strategies should be expanded in assessing a particular situation. Determining the situation (e.g., market domination or market selectivity) is the first part of diagnosing marketing advantage.

Developing the Situational Profile

A situational profile completes the advantage assessment. A checklist of information that is often included in the profile, is provided in Exhibit 1–5. The purpose of the profile is to clearly and completely portray the specific marketing advantages that correspond to the situation being analyzed. Such a profile should indicate the generic strategy that provides the best fit for the organization's strategic situation. The generic strategy (e.g., growth, turnaround) indicates a broad direction or objective that must be achieved by one strategy or a combination of specific action strategies—such as developing and marketing a new product.

EXAMINING STRATEGIC OBJECTIVES AND STRATEGY ALTERNATIVES

The identification of the organization's strategic situation allows top management to determine the strategic objectives that are appropriate (and feasible) for the particular situation. Objectives indicate the performance expectations for each business area of the corporation. Marketing strategy should contribute to meeting these expectations.

Strategic Objectives

Objectives should be feasible given the strategic situation of the firm. For example, market-share gains may be difficult in certain intensely competitive situations. Price competition may limit profit opportunities. Slow market growth may constrain sales. Objectives are of two major types: market position and performance.

Market Position.   The purpose of this objective may be to maintain an existing market position, increase market share, or regain a lost position. An important objective of Coca-Cola's 1985 introduction of "New Coke" was to regain the market share lost to Pepsi during the previous few years.

Performance.   Various financial measures are used to gauge performance, including profit contribution, return on assets, and return on net worth. Management's objective may be to improve current performance, maintain an established level of performance, or achieve a performance turnaround. If a company is in financial trouble, short-term survival may be the primary objective. Increasing the productivity of marketing resources is often included in the performance objectives. Areas of marketing productivity improvement include sales per salesperson, sales per square foot of retail space, sales-to-expense ratios, distributor performance, and advertising productivity.

These objectives are designated to be generic objectives since they provide broad guidelines or directions for change. They indicate what management wants to happen rather than what to do to make it happen. Examples include growth, turnaround, differentiate, retrench, or divest.

Identifying the Strategic Alternatives

The range of possible marketing strategy options that can be used to achieve objectives is shown in Exhibit 1–6. Unless a new venture is involved, a firm's existing marketing strategy provides the base for future action. The important issue is what new or revised actions should be taken to achieve, build, or protect a marketing advantage. Continuing a successful marketing

EXHIBIT 1–6
Identifying the Strategic Options

strategy is one option. If changes are needed, the options shown in Exhibit 1–6 indicate strategy alternatives.

New Product. The characteristics of the product life cycle normally force an organization to introduce new and improved products and phase out old products that no longer contribute to business objectives. Managing the product portfolio is thus an ongoing responsibility of business and marketing managers. A major new-product introduction can provide an important strategic advantage. The introduction in 1986 of Ford's Taurus and Sable lines contributed to its gaining an advantage in the world automobile market.

Market Targeting. A company that dominates market segments (niches) can gain an important marketing advantage. Identifying segments that provide a good strategic fit is a major challenge. Markets can be divided in various ways. Determining a segmentation scheme that yields attractive targets is an important strategic activity. The existence of differentiated buyer needs is an essential requirement for market segmentation. Targeting options include selective targeting of one segment or a few segments or multiple targeting of several segments. Hartmarx Corp., a major manufacturer of men's clothing, has gained a strategic marketing advantage by using a multiple targeting strategy. The company produces and markets 12 brands designed to appeal to various price and style segments. Included are Hickey-Freeman in the high-price contemporary-style category, Henry Grethel in the medium-price forward-fashion category, and Kuppenheimer in the discount-price contemporary-style category. Hartmarx uses a more selective targeting approach in the women's executive clothing market.

Marketing Program Positioning. Positioning is how buyers perceive the brands that are available in the marketplace. The concept of positioning a product or service recognizes that the buyer is influenced by the marketing programs of the various companies serving a particular market. Positioning of a particular brand is relative to competing brands. Thus, a brand is really positioned in the mind of the buyer or prospect.[5] Positioning typically results from several attributes that are considered by the buyer. These vary in importance. Marketing advantage is gained if a company's brand is positioned favorably, relative to competing brands, in the combination of attributes that buyers consider important when making purchases.

Various product, distribution, price, and promotion strategies can be used to achieve a desired position in a particular target market. Management may decide to strengthen an existing position or attempt to reposition

---

[5] Al Ries and Jack Trout, *Positioning: The Battle for Your Mind* (New York: Warner Books, 1982).

the company's offering. American Airlines has developed a strong customer franchise by using a combination of quality services, service availability, multiple distribution channels (travel agents, groups, company retail offices), innovative and competitive pricing, and effective promotion programs (including the very successful American Advantage program).

Productivity Improvement.   Improving marketing productivity is an important means of gaining competitive advantage. Productivity can be improved by increasing results from a given level of expenses or obtaining the same results at a lower cost. Improvement in sales-force productivity is one way to accomplish productivity improvement. Telemarketing programs have reduced selling expenses. Firms have made gains in the productivity of marketing and sales operations.

Organizational Design.   Companies targeting multiple markets and segments within each market are faced with complex organizational-design tasks. Development of an effective organizational structure can contribute to the effective implementation of marketing strategy. Design can contribute to the effectiveness of such strategies as marketing program positioning, and, for example, selling and advertising programs can be more effectively integrated through a good organizational design.

Exploit Special Advantage.   A company may possess an important strategic advantage over competitors. This advantage must be used and strengthened for its benefits to be realized. Examples include low production costs, patents, a strong consumer franchise, a government monopoly, or other special capabilities. An important strategic-analysis activity is identifying and evaluating a firm's special advantages. Polaroid's monopoly position in the instant camera and film market and its new Spectra camera gave the company a major sales increase in 1986. Some companies fail to use their existing advantages. In 1980, microwave ovens were in 20 percent of U.S. households; by 1986 penetration had reached 50 percent. The microwave-cookware market expanded rapidly during this period to $500 million in annual sales.[6] Corning Glass Works' blue-flower casserole dishes and its marketing and distribution network gave management a key edge at the beginning of the microwave expansion. The Corning brand was widely recognized by consumers as a quality product, and it was microwave-safe. Distribution channels were in place, and the company had experience in serving cookware buyers. Surprisingly, Corning did not aggressively promote its microwave-safe feature until early 1985. By that time competitors such as Anchor Hocking and Nordic Ware had gained important positions in a market that Corning could have dominated with aggressive marketing and new-product development.

---

[6] Leslie Pittel, "Too Little, Too Late," *Forbes*, March 24, 1986, pp. 172–73.

Acquisition/Merger/Strategic Alliance.   Combining the strengths of two or more organizations may provide marketing and other advantages. This strategy has been popular in the airline industry. Texas Air Corp. (Continental Airlines, Eastern Airlines, and New York Air) became the largest carrier in the industry through an acquisition strategy. Similar consolidations have occurred in other mature and highly competitive industries, such as trucking, kitchen appliances, and food processing. The strategic alliance is used to combine the capabilities of two or more organizations. Japan Air Lines established cooperative agreements with Delta Airlines in 1986. These arrangements include placing Japanese-speaking flight attendants on certain Delta flights, frequent-flyer cross credits, and cooperative promotional programs. The strategic and operating value of such strategic alliances is not yet clearly established.

Exit.   The contemporary business environment contains many examples of managements who have decided to exit from a particular business area because of an unattractive market opportunity and poor performance. Greyhound's sale of its bus operations in 1987 is one. Exit may be through the sale of the business or some other means of recovering value. Some business units have been sold to the existing management team. Top management decided to liquidate American Safety Razor (owned by Philip Morris) but accepted a buyout proposal made by top management. Several insider buyouts have proven successful for the insider management groups.

MOVING FROM STRATEGY TO ACTION

A good marketing strategy is a combination of penetrating analyses, sound judgment, and an intuitive sense of what is appropriate for the situation. Strategy selection is facilitated if one divides the task into two parts. First, the strategic fit of the options under consideration is determined. Second, important selection criteria are used to identify alternatives that appear the most promising.

Determining Strategic Fit

Strategy evaluation begins with a comparison of each alternative to the strategic situation (see Exhibit 1–3). Is the strategy appropriate, given the important forces that are present (organization, market structure and dynamics, competition, and environmental influences)? Within a particular situational category (such as market selectivity) unique strategic forces may alter an option's feasibility and attractiveness. The situation/action matrix shown in Exhibit 1–7 identifies the strategy options that correspond to each of five situational categories.[7]

---

[7] David W. Cravens, "Conceptualizing the Marketing Strategy/Performance Relationship," 1987 Winter AMA Proceedings.

EXHIBIT 1-7
Using the Situation/Action Matrix to Determine Strategic Fit

Strategy Options	Strategic Situation				
	Market Development	Market Selectivity	Differential Advantage	Market Domination	No Advantage
New product	Determine future needs	Determine future needs	Evaluate new-product opportunities	Develop product portfolio strategy	Questionable
Market targeting	Priority targeting of multiple segments	Evaluate focus of existing strategy	Evaluate focus of existing strategy	Extensive targeting of segments	Focus targeting efforts
Marketing program positioning	Determine mix priorities	Evaluate existing position effectiveness	Highlight advantage(s)	Evaluate effectiveness and integration opportunity	Evaluate cost effectiveness
Productivity improvement	Delay	Pursue	Pursue	Pursue	Consider
Organizational design	Evaluate	Evaluate	Evaluate	Consider	Evaluate
Exploiting special advantage	Capture opportunity	Capture opportunity	Capture opportunity	Capture opportunity	Not applicable
Acquisition/merger/ Strategic alliance	Questionable	Evaluate future threats	Consider	Consider	Pursue
Harvest/Divest strategy	Not applicable	Evaluate future threats	Questionable	Not applicable	Pursue

Strategy Selection Criteria

Determining the outcome of one or more strategy options under consideration by management is a complex and sometimes impossible task. One approach is to eliminate the options that are the least promising. The situation/action matrix (Exhibit 1–7) indicates where a good strategic fit does not exist. The feasible options should then be evaluated to determine their relative attractiveness. Several screening criteria can be used for this purpose.[8]

Sustainable Advantage.   One assessment area is an option's competitive vulnerability. Certain strategic actions are more vulnerable than others. Pricing actions can easily be duplicated by competitors. For example, the price strategies of low-fare airlines have been matched by major national carriers in many U.S. markets. Once the price is matched, the competitive advantage is eliminated. In contrast, low production costs, strong brand images, and efficient distribution networks are difficult for competitors to duplicate without substantial investment in time and resources.

Impact on Performance.   Coca-Cola's top management believed that the introduction of New Coke and the withdrawal of old Coke from the market in 1985 would have a favorable impact on Coke's market share. But the new Coke failed to give the company the strategic edge that management had anticipated. Management quickly recognized that the strategy/results linkage was not favorable. Within a few weeks, old Coke was reintroduced as Coca-Cola Classic. It seems clear that management was convinced that other possible methods of strengthening Coke's dominant market position, such as aggressive advertising, could not deliver the results management wanted. The experience is a dramatic example of the difficulty of predicting buyers' responses to strategic marketing actions.

Each strategy offers a specific set of risks and rewards. Management should determine the likelihood that each strategy will produce the desired results. An important part of the assessment is estimating the potential impact on performance if a strategy is not successful. If the strategy fails, what are the estimated consequences?

Feasibility.   Typically, resource needs for the strategy options vary. The requirement for some options may be prohibitive. Proposed strategies should be ranked by the estimated costs and returns. When management is not certain that a strategy will achieve a desired result, and if it represents

---

[8] For a more complete discussion of strategy option evaluation see George S. Day, *Strategic Market Planning: Pursuit of Competitive Advantage* (St. Paul, Minn.: West Publishing Co., 1984), chap. 7.

a large expenditure, caution is appropriate. An attempt to reduce the uncertainty through marketing research should be considered.

Realism in the evaluation is essential. Are the results that management hopes to achieve feasible given the strategic situation? The experience of a large regional financial-services institution whose primary market target consists of household consumers is instructive. Management learned from buyer-research studies and service-cost analyses that the marketing costs of attracting customers away from competitors' institutions were too high to justify the effort. Instead, management targeted its marketing strategy to consumers who had to change their banking relationship because of marriage, relocation, divorce, or leaving home.

Strategy Design/Implementation Complexity. Two strategy options may promise similar results while differing substantially in the complexity of their design or implementation. Minolta's innovative development of the Maxxum camera presented a major product-design challenge. Complexity may be caused by a difficulty in identifying market segments, coordinating business and marketing functions, or determining the proper combination of positioning components, changes in distribution patterns, and other strategic actions. Complexity of strategy designs and implementation demands high levels of professional expertise and the participation of various organizational units within the company. One important issue is whether a company has the requisite skills and experience to develop and successfully implement a proposed strategy, even if it is otherwise appropriate for the strategic situation.

Adaptability. The business environment will change over time and this fact should be considered in the strategy selection. Strategies that can be adapted to changing conditions should be favored over other alternatives. The major changes that occurred in the personal computer market during the 1980s demonstrate the rapidly changing environment. The initial market focus of the personal computer in the mid-1970s was the use of the PC as a hobby. Less than a decade later the market had experienced explosive growth, and business applications represented the major growth area.

Strategy Selection

There are two important stages in marketing strategy selection as shown in Exhibit 1–8. First, a strategy must be selected which has a reasonable chance of achieving the desired effect. Second, management must determine if the organization can successfully implement the strategy.

Stage One of the selection process should identify one or more feasible strategy options based on how the strategy matches the situation (strategic fit), its estimated competitive advantage, and the impact it is likely to have

EXHIBIT 1–8
Two-Stage Evaluation of Strategy Alternatives

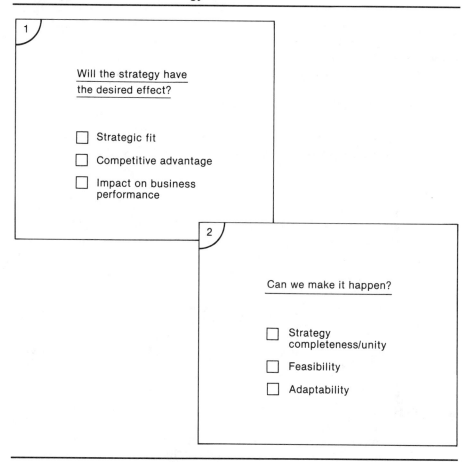

Source. David W. Cravens, "Developing Marketing Strategies for Competitive Advantage," in *Handbook of Business Strategy*, ed. H. E. Glass (New York: Warren, Gorham and Lamont, Inc., 1989), pp. 16-15.

on the performance of the organization. The failure of any one of these evaluation factors to match management's expectations may cause a strategy alternative to be eliminated from further consideration.

Stage Two considers the capacity of the organization to implement the strategy. For example, an industrial products firm might find it very difficult to introduce a new consumer product due to the lack of marketing experience in this area. Complex strategies involving several business functions create major implementation hurdles. The adaptability of the strategy to changing conditions must also be considered.

MARKETING STRATEGY AND BUSINESS PERFORMANCE

A marketing strategy is influenced by three factors: how well the strategy fits the situation; the effectiveness of the strategy implementation; and how much the environmental situation changes during implementation. Performance may depend on any one or a combination of these influences.

Strategy Selection and Performance

Some useful guidelines for understanding how marketing strategy affects business performance are provided by strategy-research findings, the concept of "strategic windows," and the diagnosis of strategic successes and failures.

Strategy Research.   Examining the relationship between marketing strategy and performance is complex because many potential performance determinants must be evaluated simultaneously. The Profit Impact of Marketing Strategy (PIMS) studies of over 2,000 businesses, conducted by the Strategic Planning Institute, are examples of such efforts. Other strategy-research programs are under way. The Marketing Science Institute, founded by a group of corporate members, conducts research on marketing strategy performance. Electronic scanner technology can help quantify the effects of targeting positioning strategies through the use of household panels in selected test cites. Information Resources Inc. pioneered this concept for grocery and drug products.

Strategic Windows.   A strategic window is an optimal match of market requirements with the particular competencies of the firm that is serving the market.[9] The timing of entry is important. Taking action when the window is open (a good match exists) can gain marketing advantage. Five strategic-window situations are shown in Exhibit 1–9. Three of the companies timed their strategic actions to benefit from the open window, while two moved too late to take advantage of the opportunity. The importance of finding open strategic windows and avoiding closed windows emphasizes the role of environmental scanning, understanding market dynamics, and competitor analysis.

Strategy Diagnosis.   Study of past marketing successes and failures is useful in strategy selection, particularly if consistent guidelines emerge from the analysis. Consider Honda's attempt with the Acura Legend to enter the same market segment targeted by the Mercedes 190. Honda had no established differential advantage in the luxury European-style automo-

---

[9] Derek F. Abell, "Strategic Windows," *Journal of Marketing*, July 1978, pp. 21–26.

EXHIBIT 1–9
Strategic Window Situations

Company	Window Opportunity	Opportunity Seized	Marketing Strategy
ChemLawn, Inc. (lawn care)	A fragmented industry comprising many small competitors coupled with an opportunity to expand a market that was substantially underdeveloped.	Yes	Targeting of consumers interested in quality lawn care, responsive services, and guaranteed results.
Corning Glass Works (microwave cookware)	The microwave oven boom created a major need for "safe" cookware. Corning could immediately meet the needs of this emerging market.	No	Delayed aggressively marketing existing products and developing new products until after competitors had gained important market positions.
Domino's Pizza (home-delivered pizza)	Recognition of consumers' needs for rapid and reliable home delivery of pizza. No major competitive force was present at the time Domino's entered the market.	Yes	Responsive home delivery of pizza from a network of retail outlets. The company emphasizes quality, speed of delivery, courteous employees, and hot pizza.
Lens Crafters (eyeware chain)	Opportunity to develop customer-responsive services in an industry dominated by practicing optometrists.	Yes	Launched a chain of retail shops conveniently located in malls, offering eye exams and one-hour glasses.
United Airlines (air travel)	Deregulation, industry restructuring, and an opportunity for marketing leadership due to a dominant position. Held a strong market position at the time of deregulation.	No	Did not expand services and marketing capabilities to strengthen position and gain advantage. United lost market position to more aggressive competitors.

bile market, although it had experience and competence in serving lower-priced segments of the market. Management decided to market the Legend through a new dealer network to position the car as a more expensive and prestigious automobile than the existing Honda lines. This required creating a new image for the Legend instead of building on an existing image, as Daimler-Benz did with the 190. Introduced in 1986, initial market response was less then predicted by Honda's management. Honda's marketing challenge is more complex than Mercedes was. Nevertheless, by early 1988 it was clear that Honda had proven its critics wrong. The Acura Legend was the unit sales leader in the import luxury segment. Facing a tough competitive challenge, Honda launched a customer-driven strategy that gave the firm marketing advantage. The features of the car were aggressively marketed. The Acura Legend coupe was named the *Motor Trend* Import Car of the Year in 1987 and was top rated in customer satisfaction. The success encouraged other Japanese auto producers to develop products for the luxury import segment.

Implementation Issues

The importance of effective strategy implementation in achieving high performance is clearly established.[10] Faulty implementation can cause a sound strategy to falter or even fail.

Linked Planning and Implementation.   Planning and implementation are so closely related that it is essential that participants in the two activities work together closely. Planning and implementation can be effectively coupled by assigning responsibility for planning activities to line management. Dividing these responsibilities often hampers implementation. Decision makers should develop plans and participate in implementation. An important contributing factor to the successful implementation of American Airlines' marketing strategy has been the active participation of top and middle management. Analysis of many other marketing successes points to the critical role of implementation in achieving high performance.

Strategy Integration.   A major management challenge in marketing strategy implementation is the coordination and integration of each strategic component. As a company grows in size, and its product and market portfolio becomes complex, strategy integration is difficult. Fragmented strategic actions will contaminate performance. Innovative organizational design can facilitate strategy integration during implementation. Procter & Gamble's brand-management system was altered in the mid-1980s to respond to a changing market and competitive environment.

---

[10] Thomas V. Bonoma, "Making Your Marketing Strategy Work," *Harvard Business Review*, March–April 1984, pp. 69–76.

Environmental Vulnerability

Environmental factors may affect strategies in different ways. The potential impact of environmental forces on a firm's strategy may be specific to the firm or common to the industry group. The vulnerability of the Southwest's financial institutions in 1987 to low oil prices is one example. Banks and savings institutions were adversely affected because of loans to energy firms, service companies, and real-estate developers.

Contingency analysis helps a firm evaluate the nature and extent of environmental vulnerability. By identifying possible future scenarios, the company can evaluate the strategic impact of alternative environmental situations. For example, oil prices of $10 to $15 a barrel should have been included in the contingency planning of Southwestern banks in the early 1980s. While environmental vulnerability should not dictate strategy selection, it is an important consideration in choosing between alternative options. Moreover, by evaluating the potential strategic impact of a possible future event, management is better prepared to cope with the situation if it does occur.

Achieving excellence in marketing is a demanding challenge in today's business environment. Although an important part of the task is understanding and strategically responding to the opportunities and threats that are unique in the specific business arena, several strategic requirements cut across different businesses. Following a step-by-step approach of strategic analysis and action to gain marketing advantage has proven to be effective in a wide range of businesses. Central to the approach is selecting the marketing strategy that corresponds best to situational forces that are present in the firm's business environment.

A strategic marketing advantage does not create one winner and many losers. Winning depends on deciding in what strategic arenas to compete and how to do so. There is no better example of this than Nucor Corp., a small mini-mill steel producer in an industry dominated by giants and threatened by global competition. Efficient production, high productivity from motivated employees, and product specialization have given this firm a strategic edge for more than a decade. Nucor is a high performer in a tough industry.

Successful marketing strategy implementation cuts across the entire enterprise, involving everyone in the organization. Customer satisfaction is a business responsibility. Gaining strategic marketing advantage requires the commitment and effort of each person whose job responsibilities influence customer satisfaction.

CHAPTER 2

FINANCIAL ANALYSIS FOR MARKETING DECISIONS

Accounting is the scorecard of business, portraying the activities of a company by using a set of objective numbers which indicate how the firm is performing.[1] The finance function interprets the accounting scorecard in assessing performance and planning for the future. An understanding of the use of basic financial analysis methods is required of marketing executives. Consider, for example, the poor financial performance of Volkswagen AG in the late 1980s. Unit sales in the United States fell from 300,000 in 1980 to about 210,000 in 1988.[2] The company had a 1987 pretax loss in the United States of 572 million German marks ($341 million). VW's group net income in 1987 was 598 million marks. The most serious problem affecting these sales was the negative impact of sudden acceleration charges concerning the Audi 5000. The 1988 unit sales were about 30 percent of 1985 sales. Audi faced a major marketing challenge. The product marketing problems experienced by Volkswagen highlight the close link between marketing strategy and the firm's financial performance. Financial performance is clearly a high priority consideration for VW's marketing strategists.

Several kinds of financial analyses are needed for marketing planning and control activities. Sales and cost information is used in various kinds of financial analyses for marketing management. Such analyses represent an important part of your case preparation activities. In some instances it will be necessary for you to review and interpret the financial information provided in the cases. In other instances you may actually prepare analyses to support your recommendations.

This chapter considers several financial analysis activities and methods that are used to: (1) gauge how well marketing strategy is working, (2) evaluate marketing decision alternatives, and (3) develop plans for the future. We shall also discuss some special considerations that may affect marketing financial analyses. The methods covered in this chapter represent a

---

[1] Robert C. Higgins, *Analysis for Financial Management* (Homewood, Ill.: Dow Jones-Irwin, 1983), p. 3.

[2] Bradley A. Stertz and Thomas F. O'Boyle, "Volkswagen Aims to Halt Skid in U.S.," *The Wall Street Journal*, May 6, 1988, p. 6.

group of tools and techniques for use in marketing financial analysis. Throughout the discussion we are assuming that you have a basic understanding of accounting and finance fundamentals.

ANALYSIS ACTIVITIES

While many kinds of financial analyses underlie marketing operations, most of these financial analyses fall into the four categories shown in Exhibit 2–1. The *financial situation analysis* is intended to determine how well marketing activities are doing. It involves the study of trends, comparative

EXHIBIT 2–1
Marketing Financial Analysis Activities

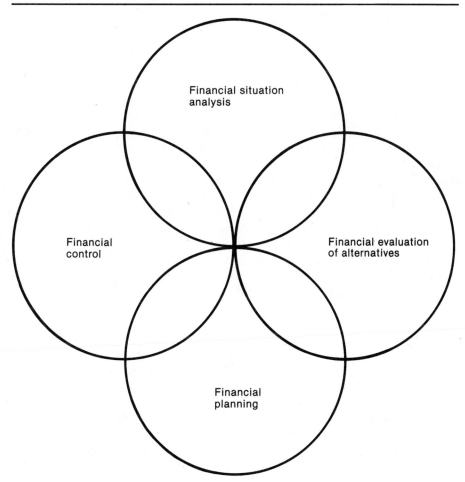

EXHIBIT 2–2
Financial Analyses

Situation analysis:
   Sales and cost analyses
   Profit contribution and net profit analyses
   Liquidity analysis

Evaluation of alternatives:
   Sales and cost forecasts
   Break-even analyses
   Profit-contribution and net profit projections
   Return on investment

Financial planning:
   Sales and cost forecasts
   Budgets
   Pro forma income statement

Financial control:
   Sales and cost analyses
   Actual results to budgets
   Profit performance

---

analyses, and assessments of present financial strengths and limitations for the entire business or a unit, brand, or some other component of the business. *Financial evaluation of alternatives* involves the use of financial information to evaluate such alternatives as whether to introduce a new product, expand the sales force, eliminate a mature product, or move into a new market. *Financial planning* involves projections concerning activities that marketing management has decided to undertake. For example, if it has been decided to introduce a new product on a national basis, management must prepare sales and cost forecasts, budgets, and other financial planning and control tools. Finally, in *financial control*, actual results are compared to planned results. The objective is to keep the gap between actual and planned results as narrow as possible. Several illustrative financial analyses are shown in Exhibit 2–2.

Unit of Financial Analysis

Various units that can be used in the financial analysis of marketing are shown in Exhibit 2–3. Two factors often influence the choice of a unit of analysis: (1) the purpose of the analysis and (2) the costs and availability of the information needed to perform the analysis. We shall briefly examine each influence to see how it affects the choice of each unit used for the analysis activities shown in Exhibit 2–1.

In a marketing situation assessment, more than one unit of analysis is often needed. Marketing management may be interested in examining the financial performance of several of the units shown in Exhibit 2–3. In con-

EXHIBIT 2–3
Alternative Units for Financial Analysis

Market	Product/Service	Organization
Total market	Industry	Company
Market niche(s)	Product mix	Segment/division/unit
Geographic area(s)	Product line	Marketing department
Customer groups	Specific product	Sales unit
Individual customers	Brand	Region
	Model	District/branch
		Office/store
		Salesperson

trast, the unit used in the financial evaluation of alternatives should correspond to the alternative under consideration. For example, if an expansion of the sales force is being analyzed, the salesperson is a logical basis of analysis. If a product is a candidate for elimination by a firm, an analysis should be performed to assess the revenue and cost impact of dropping the product. The analysis should include the drop candidate plus other products that would be affected. Finally, in financial planning and financial control, the unit or units of analysis often correspond to products and/or organizational units (branches, departments, business units, etc.) since budgeting and forecasting analyses are typically prepared for these units.

The most readily available sales and cost information for financial analysis is that which corresponds to the formal financial reporting practices in the given firm. Units that are used for internal reporting often include product categories, business units, and subparts of the sales organization (regions, districts, etc.). When the desired unit of analysis does not correspond to one that is included in the firm's information system, both the cost and the difficulty of obtaining information increase significantly. For example, if the cost accounting system has not tabulated costs by individual products, obtaining such information may require a substantial effort. Fortunately, the information needed for marketing analysis can often be estimated at accuracy levels suitable for that purpose.

Sales and Cost Information

The data base for marketing financial analysis is obtained by accumulating historical sales and cost data for the various units shown in Exhibit 2–3. The data base can be used in forecasting future sales and costs. In addition to the sales and cost data, marketing management often wishes to examine sales and cost trends. Among the widely used bases for the analysis of such trends are dollar and unit sales, percentage growth rates, and market share. Note, for example, the competitor sales analysis for Dillard Department Stores Inc., shown in Exhibit 2–4. Sales trends can be examined for each of

EXHIBIT 2–4
Dillard Department Stores on the Move

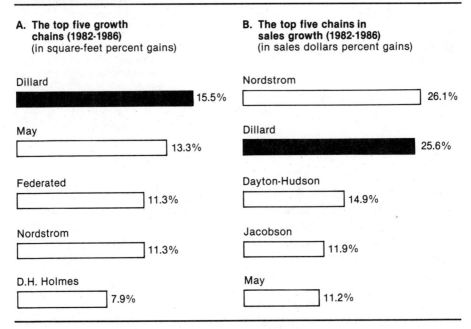

A. The top five growth
chains (1982-1986)
(in square-feet percent gains)

Dillard
15.5%

May
13.3%

Federated
11.3%

Nordstrom
11.3%

D.H. Holmes
7.9%

B. The top five chains in
sales growth (1982-1986)
(in sales dollars percent gains)

Nordstrom
26.1%

Dillard
25.6%

Dayton-Hudson
14.9%

Jacobson
11.9%

May
11.2%

Source: Michael Totty, "Growth-Minded Dillard Draws Notice," *The Wall Street Journal*, March 16, 1988, p. 6.

the retailer's key competitors. The chart illustrates the trends in total sales and sales per square foot.

Cost information is not very useful for marketing financial analysis unless it is combined with revenue (sales) data to perform various kinds of profit analyses. While in some instances we can analyze historical costs such as the average cost required to close a sale, the analysis is incomplete unless we compare costs to what they have accomplished.

EVALUATING FINANCIAL PERFORMANCE

Several factors are involved in evaluating financial performance. The discussion begins by examining some accounting fundamentals. This is followed by a review of the basic financial reports. Next, several important financial ratios are defined. Finally, a financial analysis model is presented, and some additional marketing performance measures are indicated.

Some Fundamentals

Costs. As we move through the discussion of financial analysis, be sure to recognize the type of costs being used in the analysis. Using accounting terminology, costs can be designated as fixed or variable. From basic

EXHIBIT 2–5
Break-Even Analysis

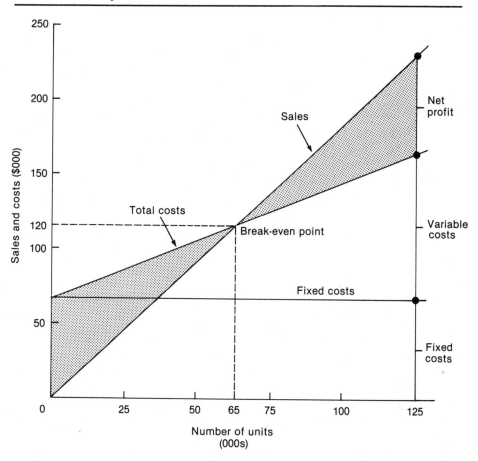

accounting you will recall that a cost is *fixed* if it remains constant over the observation period, even though the volume of activity varies. In contrast, a *variable* cost is an expense that varies with sales over the observation period. Costs are designated as semivariable in instances when they contain both fixed and variable components.

Break-Even Analysis[3].   This is a technique for examining the relationship between sales and costs. An illustration is given in Exhibit 2–5. Using sales and cost information, you can easily see from a break-even analysis how many units of a product must be sold in order to break even. In

---

[3] This illustration is drawn from David W. Cravens, Gerald E. Hills, and Robert B. Woodruff, *Marketing Decision Making: Concepts and Strategy*, rev. ed. (Homewood, Ill.: Richard D. Irwin, Inc., 1980), pp. 335–36.

this example 65,000 units at sales of $120,000 are equal to total costs of $120,000. Any additional units sold will produce a profit. The break-even point can be calculated in this manner:

$$\text{Break-even units} = \frac{\text{Fixed costs}}{\text{Price per unit} - \text{Variable cost per unit}}$$

Price in the illustration shown in Exhibit 2–5 is $1.846 per unit, and variable cost is $0.769 per unit. With fixed costs of $70,000, this results in the break-even calculation:

$$\text{Break-even units} = \frac{\$70,000}{\$1.846 - \$0.769} = 65,000 \text{ units}$$

You should note that this analysis is not a forecast. Rather it indicates how many units of a product at a given price and cost must be sold in order to break even. Some important assumptions that underlie the above break-even analysis should be recognized:

1. We have assumed that fixed costs are constant and that variable costs vary at a constant rate.
2. We have assumed that all costs are either fixed or variable.
3. The analysis considered only one selling price. A higher price would yield a lower break-even point, and a lower price would yield a higher break-even point.

When the above assumptions do not apply, the analyst must modify the basic break-even model shown in Exhibit 2–5. The model can be expanded to include nonlinear sales and costs as well as alternative price levels.

Used in conjunction with traditional break-even analysis, estimates of market demand can approximate profit-maximizing decisions. An example is presented in Exhibit 2–6 in which the fixed costs are $200,000, the unit variable costs are $2.50, and demand forecasts are given for prices of $5, $10, $15, and $20. Of the four prices considered, the $15 price yields the highest profits ($360,000). You may find it useful to review these calculations.

Contribution Analysis. When the performance of products, market segments, and other marketing units is being analyzed, an examination of the profit contribution generated by a unit is often useful to management. Contribution margin is equal to sales (revenue) less variable costs. Thus contribution margin represents the amount of money available to cover fixed costs, and the excess available is net income. For example, suppose a product is generating a positive contribution margin. If the product is dropped, the remaining products would have to cover fixed costs that are not directly traceable to it. An illustration of contribution margin analysis is given in Exhibit 2–7. In this example, if Product X were eliminated, $50,000 of product net income would be lost. If the product is retained, the $50,000 can be used to contribute to other fixed costs and/or net income.

EXHIBIT 2–6

Break-Even Analysis with a Market Demand Schedule

Unit Price	Market Demand (units)	Total Revenue	Total Costs	Break-Even Points (units)	Expected Profits
$ 5	65,000	$325,000 (d')	$362,500	80,000 (d)	$ (37,500)
10	55,000	550,000 (c')	337,500	26,667 (c)	212,500
15	45,000	675,000 (b')	314,500	16,000 (b)	360,500
20	30,000	600,000 (a')	275,000	11,429 (a)	325,000

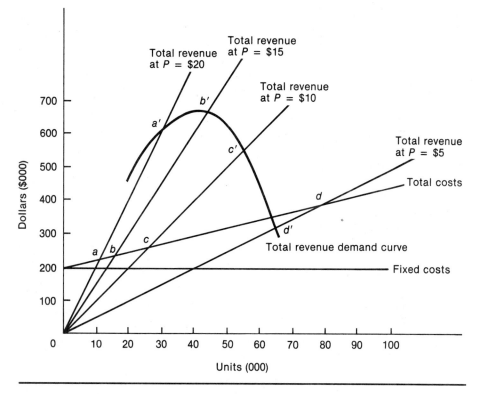

EXHIBIT 2–7

Contribution Margin Analysis for Product X ($000)

Sales	$300
Less:	
Variable manufacturing costs.	100
Other variable costs traceable to Product X.	50
Equals: Contribution margin	150
Less: Fixed costs directly traceable to Product X.	100
Equals: Product net income.	$ 50

EXHIBIT 2–8
Profit and Loss Statement ($000)

Sales revenue	$752
Less: Cost of goods sold	492
Equals: Gross profit margin	260
Less: Selling and administrative expenses.	140
Equals: Net profit before taxes	120
Less: Taxes.	50
Equals: Net profit.	$ 70

Gross and Net Profit Margins.   Gross and net profit margins are used to gauge company and business unit financial performance and to budget for future operations. Gross and net profit are shown on the profit and loss or income statement. Margins on sales can be calculated by dividing gross or net profit amounts by sales in dollars. The income statement is used to report financial performance to stockholders and to compute taxes. An illustrative statement is shown in Exhibit 2–8.

Basic Financial Reports

These reports are typically prepared for a company and its major subdivisions:

1. *Balance sheet:* A statement of financial position at a particular time (e.g., December 31, 1990), indicating total assets by category, short- and long-term liabilities, and stockholders' equity.
2. *Income statement:* This report covers a period of time (e.g., year ending December 31, 1990). It indicates sales minus all relevant costs, and the difference is net income (see Exhibit 2–8).
3. *Cash flow statement:* Sometimes referred to as the sources and uses of funds, this report starts with a beginning cash balance for a period (e.g., a quarter) plus all cash receipts minus all cash expenditures. It ends with a net cash balance for the period.

Since these reports and future forecasts (pro forma projections) are prepared for a company and its major parts or segments, the reports are normally not part of the marketing plan. Nevertheless it is important that marketing executives understand the composition and relationships among major financial reports for the enterprise.

Several of the ratios discussed in the next section utilize information from the balance sheet; you will need to review its composition. An example is shown in Exhibit 2–9.

EXHIBIT 2–9
Composition of the Balance Sheet ($000)

Cash	$ 100	Current liabilities	$ 75
Accounts receivable	200	Short-term debt	125
Inventory	150	Long-term debt	1,000
Total current assets	450	Total liabilities	1,200
Property and equipment	1,500	Net worth	1,050
Other assets	300	Total liabilities	
Total assets	$2,250	and net worth	$2,250

Key Financial Ratios

Financial information will be more useful to management if it is prepared so that comparisons can be made. James Van Horne comments upon this need:

> To evaluate a firm's financial condition and performance, the financial analyst needs certain yardsticks. The yardstick frequently used is a ratio or index, relating two pieces of financial data to each other. Analysis and interpretation of various ratios should give an experienced and skilled analyst a better understanding of the financial condition and performance of the firm than he would obtain from analysis of the financial data alone.[4]

As we examine the financial analysis model in the next section, note how the ratio or index provides a useful frame of reference. Typically, the ratio is used to compare historical and/or future trends within the firm or to compare a firm or business unit with an industry or specific firms.

Several financial ratios that are often used to measure business performance are shown in Exhibit 2–10. Note that these ratios are primarily useful as a means of comparing:

1. Ratio values for several time periods for a particular business.
2. A firm to its key competitors.
3. A firm to an industry or business standard.

There are several sources of ratio data.[5] These include data services such as Dun & Bradstreet, industry and trade associations, government agencies, and investment advisory services.

---

[4] James C. Van Horne, *Fundamentals of Financial Management*, 4th ed. (Englewood Cliffs, N.J.: Prentice-Hall, 1980), pp. 103–4.

[5] A useful guide to ratio analysis is provided in Richard Sanzo, *Ratio Analysis for Small Business* (Washington, D.C.: Small Business Administration, 1977).

EXHIBIT 2–10
Summary of Key Financial Ratios

Ratio	How Calculated	What It Shows
Profitability ratios:		
1. Gross profit margin	$\dfrac{\text{Sales} - \text{Cost of goods sold}}{\text{Sales}}$	An indication of the total margin available to cover operating expenses and yield a profit.
2. Operating profit margin	$\dfrac{\text{Profits before taxes and before interest}}{\text{Sales}}$	An indication of the firm's profitability from current operations without regard to the interest charges accruing from the capital structure.
3. Net profit margin (or return on sales)	$\dfrac{\text{Profits after taxes}}{\text{Sales}}$	Shows after-tax profits per dollar of sales. Subpar profit margins indicate that the firm's sales prices are relatively low or that its costs are relatively high or both.
4. Return on total assets	$\dfrac{\text{Profits after taxes}}{\text{Total assets}}$ or $\dfrac{\text{Profits after taxes} + \text{Interest}}{\text{Total assets}}$	A measure of the return on total investment in the enterprise. It is sometimes desirable to add interest to after-tax profits to form the numerator of the ratio, since total assets are financed by creditors as well as by stockholders; hence it is accurate to measure the productivity of assets by the returns provided to both classes of investors.
5. Return on stockholders' equity (or return on net worth)	$\dfrac{\text{Profits after taxes}}{\text{Total stockholders' equity}}$	A measure of the rate of return on stockholders' investment in the enterprise.
6. Return on common equity	$\dfrac{\text{Profits after taxes} - \text{Preferred stock dividends}}{\text{Total stockholders' equity} - \text{Par value of preferred stock}}$	A measure of the rate of return on the investment which the owners of common stock have made in the enterprise.
7. Earnings per share	$\dfrac{\text{Profits after taxes} - \text{Preferred stock dividends}}{\text{Number of shares of common stock outstanding}}$	Shows the earnings available to the owners of common stock.

36

Liquidity ratios:

1. Current ratio
$$\frac{\text{Current assets}}{\text{Current liabilities}}$$
Indicates the extent to which the claims of short-term creditors are covered by assets that are expected to be converted to cash in a period roughly corresponding to the maturity of the liabilities.

2. Quick ratio (or acid-test ratio)
$$\frac{\text{Current assets} - \text{Inventory}}{\text{Current liabilities}}$$
A measure of the firm's ability to pay off short-term obligations without relying upon the sale of its inventories.

3. Cash Ratio
$$\frac{\text{Cash \& Marketable securities}}{\text{Current liabilities}}$$
An indicator of how long the company can go without further inflow of funds.

4. Inventory to net working capital
$$\frac{\text{Inventory}}{\text{Current assets} - \text{Current liabilities}}$$
A measure of the extent to which the firm's working capital is tied up in inventory.

Leverage ratios:

1. Debt-to-assets ratio
$$\frac{\text{Total debt}}{\text{Total assets}}$$
Measures the extent to which borrowed funds have been used to finance the firm's operations.

2. Debt-to-equity ratio
$$\frac{\text{Total debt}}{\text{Total stockholders' equity}}$$
Provides another measure of the funds provided the creditors versus the funds provided by owners.

3. Long-term debt to equity ratio
$$\frac{\text{Long-term debt}}{\text{Total stockholders' equity}}$$
A widely used measure of the balance between debt and equity in the firm's overall capital structure.

4. Times-interest-earned (or coverage ratios)
$$\frac{\text{Profits before interest and taxes}}{\text{Total interest charges}}$$
Measures the extent to which earnings can decline without the firm's becoming unable to meet its annual interest costs.

5. Fixed charge coverage
$$\frac{\text{Profits before taxes and interest} + \text{Lease obligations}}{\text{Total interest charges} + \text{Lease obligations}}$$
A more inclusive indication of the firm's ability to meet all of its fixed-charge obligations.

EXHIBIT 2–10 (concluded)

Ratio	How Calculated	What It Shows
Activity ratios:		
1. Inventory turnover	$\dfrac{\text{Cost of goods sold}}{\text{Inventory}}$	When compared to industry averages, it provides an indication of whether a company has excessive inventory or perhaps inadequate inventory.
2. Fixed-assets turnover*	$\dfrac{\text{Sales}}{\text{Fixed assets}}$	A measure of the sales productivity and utilization of plant and equipment.
3. Total-assets turnover	$\dfrac{\text{Sales}}{\text{Total assets}}$	A measure of the utilization of all the firm's assets; a ratio below the industry average indicates the company is not generating a sufficient volume of business given the size of its asset investment.
4. Accounts receivable turnover	$\dfrac{\text{Annual credit sales}}{\text{Accounts receivable}}$	A measure of the average length of time it takes the firm to collect the sales made on credit.
5. Average collection period	$\dfrac{\text{Accounts receivable}}{\text{Total sales} \div 365}$ or $\dfrac{\text{Accounts receivable}}{\text{Average daily sales}}$	Indicates the average length of time the firm must wait after making a sale before it receives payment.

* The manager should also keep in mind the fixed charges associated with noncapitalized lease obligations.

Source: Adapted from Arthur A. Thompson, Jr., and A. J. Strickland III, *Strategy and Policy* (Plano, Tex.: Business Publications, 1981), pp. 216–18.

EXHIBIT 2–11
Financial Analysis Model

Profit margin	Asset turnover	Return on assets	Financial leverage	Return on net worth
↓	↓	↓	↓	↓
$\dfrac{\text{Net profits (after taxes)}}{\text{Net sales}}$ ×	$\dfrac{\text{Net sales}}{\text{Total assets}}$ →	$\dfrac{\text{Net profits (after taxes)}}{\text{Total assets}}$ ×	$\dfrac{\text{Total assets}}{\text{Net worth}}$ =	$\dfrac{\text{Net profits (after taxes)}}{\text{Net worth}}$

Financial Analysis Model

The model shown in Exhibit 2–11 provides a useful guide for examining financial performance and identifying possible problem areas. The model combines several important financial ratios into one equation. Let's examine the model, moving from the far right to the left. Assuming that our performance target is return on net worth, the product of return on assets and financial leverage determines performance. Increasing either ratio will increase return on net worth. This can be accomplished by increasing leverage (e.g., greater debt) or by increasing profits. Next, note that return on assets is determined by the product of profit margin and asset turnover. Thus, greater expense control or faster asset turnover (e.g., inventory turnover) can improve return on assets. The values of these ratios will vary considerably from one industry to another. In grocery wholesaling, for example, profit margins are typically very low, whereas asset turnover is very high. Through efficient management and high turnover a wholesaler can stack up impressive returns on net worth.

Note how the equation incorporates the major parts of the balance sheet and the income statement. An illustration using the model ratios plus other financial ratios is provided in Exhibit 2–12. The variations by type of wholesaler highlight the importance of comparative analysis of ratios. For example, comparisons between grocery wholesalers is more appropriate than comparing a grocery wholesaler to an industrial distributor.

An interesting comparison of the financial performance of several kinds of retailers is shown in Exhibit 2–13. An example of the use of the model to analyze one of the retailers in the home decorating specialty store group is shown in Exhibit 2–14. Color Tile, Inc., had a net profits/net worth ratio substantially below the industry group in 1982.

Productivity Measures

Various units of analysis can be used as the basis of measuring the productivity of marketing activities. Examples include sales per square foot of retail floor space, occupancy rates of hotels and office buildings, and sales

EXHIBIT 2–12
Median and Upper Quartile Financial Ratios for Six Types of Wholesalers, 1980

Median and Upper Quartile Financial Performance by Type of Wholesaler

Financial Ratios	Drug Wholesalers		Grocery Wholesalers		Hardware Wholesalers		Electrical Distributors		Plumbing and Heating Wholesalers		Industrial Distributors	
	Median	Upper Quartile	Median	Upper Quartile	Median	Upper Quartile	Median	Upper Quartile	Median	Upper Quartile	Median	Upper Quartile
Strategic profit model ratios*												
Net profits/net sales (percent)	1.7%	3.4%	0.9%	1.5%	2.8%	4.4%	2.7%	5.1%	2.6%	4.7%	3.2%	5.0%
Net sales/total assets (times)	3.3×	3.0×	5.6×	7.3×	2.7×	3.3×	2.9×	3.0×	3.0×	3.0×	2.7×	3.2×
Net profits/total assets (percent)	5.6%	10.3%	5.0%	10.9%	7.5%	14.6%	7.9%	15.2%	7.8%	14.3%	8.6%	15.9%
Total assets/net worth (times)	2.3×	1.7×	2.1×	1.5×	1.6×	1.3×	1.9×	1.5×	1.7×	1.4×	1.7×	1.4×
Net profits/net worth (percent)	12.8%	17.5%	10.5%	16.3%	12.0%	19.0%	15.1%	22.8%	13.2%	20.0%	14.6%	22.3%
Liquidity/capital structure ratios												
Current assets/current liabilities (times)	1.9×	2.7×	2.0×	3.2×	2.7×	4.2×	2.2×	3.4×	2.5×	3.7×	2.6×	3.6×
Current liabilities/inventory (percent)	101.7%	70.5%	84.1%	51.7%	70.1%	44.0%	102.9%	64.1%	83.8%	51.1%	89.4%	56.0%
Current liabilities/net worth (percent)	103.1%	49.8%	78.4%	36.5%	50.5%	27.9%	75.2%	35.6%	59.9%	34.2%	56.4%	32.2%
Total liabilities/net worth (percent)	128.7%	67.3%	111.2%	45.9%	60.9%	33.5%	91.4%	45.4%	74.7%	37.3%	66.2%	36.4%
Productivity ratios												
Net sales/accounts receivable (times)	10.7×	17.4×	26.1×	45.6×	9.4×	12.2×	8.1×	10.1×	8.9×	11.1×	8.9×	11.1×
Collection period (days)	34.0	21.0	14.0	8.0	39.0	30.0	45.0	36.0	41.0	33.0	41.0	33.0
Net sales/inventory (times)	7.1×	9.1×	12.3×	17.6×	5.5×	8.1×	7.2×	10.3×	5.9×	8.4×	6.8×	11.5×
Working capital ratios												
Net profits/net working capital (percent)	15.2%	23.3%	11.8%	22.2%	13.5%	21.6%	17.5%	25.7%	15.4%	23.2%	18.0%	27.0%
Net sales/net working capital (times)	8.1×	14.4×	14.1×	25.4×	4.6×	7.1×	5.9×	9.2×	5.2×	7.8×	5.5×	8.0×

* The strategic profit model ratios may not multiply to the totals indicated because the ratios are median and upper quartile ratios rather than weighted averages.

Source: Dun & Bradstreet and Distribution Research Program, University of Oklahoma.

EXHIBIT 2–13
Performance Profile of New-Wave Retailers, 1982

	Strategic Profit Model Ratios				
	Net Profits	Net Sales	Net Profits	Total Assets	Net Profits
Type of Retailer	Net Sales (percent)	Total Assets (times)	Total Assets (percent)	Net Worth (times)	Net Worth (percent)
Hobby and craft centers	7.2%	2.2×	15.8%	1.8×	28.5%
Home decorating specialty stores	7.0	1.8	12.6	2.1	26.5
Paint and home decorating supermarkets	7.4	1.8	12.6	1.8	24.0
Super hardware stores	5.8	2.7	15.7	1.6	25.1
Super drug stores	3.6	4.0	14.4	1.8	25.9
Combination stores	2.5	5.1	12.8	2.1	26.8
Upscale discounters	3.2	4.1	13.1	2.0	26.2

Source: Distribution Research Program, University of Oklahoma.

per salesperson. As an illustration, K mart had 1987 sales per square foot of $183 compared to Wal-Mart's $213 and Target's $193.[6] Interestingly, 75 percent of the adults in the United States shop at K mart at least once every three months. The key to increasing K mart's sales is to sell these buyers more merchandise. Space productivity measures can be obtained for individual departments in retail stores that offer more than one line, such as department stores.

Another widely used productivity measure is inventory turnover (net sales divided by inventory). Exhibit 2–12 indicates inventory turnover for six types of wholesalers. Note, for example, the high turnover rate for grocery wholesalers (25.4 × upper quartile). Exhibit 2–13 shows a performance profile for several types of retailers. A detailed analysis of Color Tile, Inc., is shown in Exhibit 2–14.

FINANCIAL PLANNING

Financial planning involves two major activities: (1) forecasting revenues and (2) budgeting (estimating future expenses). The actual financial analyses and forecasts that are included in the strategic marketing plan vary considerably from firm to firm. Those that are often placed in the financial analysis section of the plan include:

- Sales and market-share analyses and forecasts by product, market segment, areas, and other categories.

---

[6] Francine Schwadel, "K mart Is Trying to Put Style on the Aisle," *The Wall Street Journal*, August 9, 1988, p. 6.

EXHIBIT 2–14
Financial Profile of Color Tile, Inc.

Strategic Profit Model Ratios
(1982)

$$\frac{\text{Net profits}}{\text{Net sales}} \times \frac{\text{Net sales}}{\text{Total assets}} = \frac{\text{Net profits}}{\text{Total assets}} \times \frac{\text{Total assets}}{\text{Net worth}} = \frac{\text{Net profits}}{\text{Net worth}}$$

| 5.4% | × | 1.2× | = | 6.3% | × | 2.0× | = | 12.6% |

Current Size
($ millions)
(1982)

| Net sales | $222.7 |
| Net profits | $ 11.9 |

Compound annual growth rates
(1978–1982)

Net sales	19.0%
Net profits	15.6
Earnings per share	8.0

Composition of Balance Sheet
(1982)

Current assets		Current liabilities	
Cash	16.3%	Notes payable	.9%
Accounts receivable	.7	Accounts payable	2.8
Inventory	29.3	All other	7.6
All other	1.6	Total	11.3
Total	47.9%	Long-term liabilities	38.6
Fixed assets	50.4%	Net worth	50.1
All other assets	1.7	Total liabilities and	
Total assets	100.0%	net worth	100.0%

Liquidity Ratios
(1982)

Current assets/current liabilities (times)	4.2×
Current assets (minus inventory)/Current liabilities (times)	1.7×
Cash/Current liabilities (percent)	143.5%
Net profits (before interest and taxes)/Interest (times)	13.8×

Growth Potential Ratios
(1982)

Net profits (after dividends)/Net working capital (percent)	17.2%
Net profits (after dividends)/Net worth (percent)	12.6%
Net profits (before interest and taxes)/Total assets (percent)	11.7%
Accounts payable/Inventory (percent)	9.7%

Source: Distribution Research Program, University of Oklahoma, 1983.

- Budget projections for marketing operations.
- Break-even and profit contribution projections by marketing planning unit (e.g., market target, product line, market area).
- Return on investment projections by marketing planning unit.
- Capital requirements.

Examples of marketing financial planning forms used by the R. T. French Company, a food-processing firm, are shown in Exhibit 2–15. As is

EXHIBIT 2-15
Sales—Marketing—Profit Summary

	ACTUAL YEARS PAST			CURRENT YR (EST)	NEXT YR PLAN	ESTIMATE—FUTURE YEARS		
	19	19	19	19	19	19	19	19
FACTORY SALES IN UNITS (DOZEN OR OUNCES) INCLUDING NEW PRODUCTS								
PERCENT INCREASE OVER PREVIOUS YEAR %								
FACTORY SALES DOLLARS, INCLUDING NEW PRODUCTS (A) ($000)								
PERCENT INCREASE OVER PREVIOUS YEAR %								
INCOME BEFORE MARKETING ($000)								
PERCENT OF SALES %								
MARKETING EXPENDITURE (B) INCLUDING NEW PRODUCTS ($000)								
PERCENT OF SALES %								
ADVERTISING EXPENDITURE ($000)								
MERCHANDISING EXPENDITURE ($000)								
PROFIT AFTER MARKETING (BEFORE ALLOCATIONS) (C) ($000)								
PERCENT OF SALES %								
PROFIT PERCENT INCREASES OVER PREVIOUS YEAR %								

(A) NEW PRODUCTS FACTORY SALES DOLLARS   (Included Above)   PRODUCTS INTRODUCED THIS YR   ($000)
(LIST ITEMS BELOW)   PRODUCTS PROPOSED NEXT 5 YRS   ($000)
TOTAL NEW PRODUCTS   ($000)

(B) EXCLUDE MARKETING RESEARCH, PACKAGING DESIGN, PUBLICITY.
(C) PROFIT AFTER MARKETING: INCOME BEFORE MARKETING LESS MARKETING (EXCLUDES ALLOCATIONS AND CORPORATE ADJUSTMENTS).

43

EXHIBIT 2–15 (concluded)

MARKETING BUDGET PROPOSAL FOR _____

SUMMARY		19__ ACTUAL	19__ ACTUAL	19__ ORIGINAL VOTE	19__ ESTIMATED	19__ PROPOSED	19__ APPROVED
Sales	$						
Income Before Marketing	$						
Income before Marketing to Sales	%						
Marketing (A)	$						
Marketing to Sales	%						
Marketing including Allocations (B)	$						
Operating Income before Adj. (D)	$						
Operating Income to Sales	%						
Population	M						
Sales Milex ($/ 1000 pop.)	$						
Marketing Milex ($/ 1000 pop.)	$						

MARKETING BUDGET CATEGORIES

1 Magazines
2 Newspaper Rop
3 Newspaper Supplements
4 Radio
5 Television
6 Posters
7 Special Media
8 Agency Fees
9 Trade Media

11 Consumer Non-Price Incentive					
13 Consumer Price Incentives					
14 Sales Conferences					
15 Merchandising Materials					
17 Trade Allowances					
18 Trade Free Goods					
19 Sundries					
MARKETING (A)					
Allocations of Publicity					
Alloc. of Fgt. on Un-indent. Merch. Mat.					
Alloc. of Military Food Marketing					
MARKETING INCLUD. ALLOC. (B)					
Package Development (C)					
Market Research (C)					

(A) Marketing—Total of Budget Categories
(B) Marketing including Allocations—Marketing plus Allocations of Publicity, Freight on Unidentified Merchandising Materials, and Military Food Marketing.
(C) Already deducted via Administration Expense in arriving at Income before Marketing.
(D) Operating Income Before Adjustments—"Income before Marketing" less "Marketing including Allocations," before Corporate Adjustments.

PER _____ DATE _____

Source: David S. Hopkins, *The Marketing Plan*, Report No. 801 (New York: Conference Board, 1981), pp. 94–95.

often the case in financial planning, the past, present, and future results and forecasts are included. Note how the profit summary compares marketing's impact on the bottom line. The budget proposal illustrates the budget categories accounted for by marketing. The internal financial reporting and budgeting procedures vary widely among companies, so you should consider French's approach as one example rather than a norm.

The choice of the financial information to be used for marketing planning and control will depend upon its relationship with the corporate or business unit strategic plan. Another important consideration is the selection of performance measures to be used in gauging marketing performance. Our objective is to indicate the range of possibilities and to suggest some of the more frequently used financial analyses.

IMPORTANT FINANCIAL ANALYSIS ISSUES

Selecting Performance Criteria

Companies vary considerably as to how they gauge marketing performance. Consider these five examples of profitability measures used by different firms:[7]

1. A diversified manufacturing company currently expects an operating margin on sales of at least 5 percent for all products.
2. Management in a chemicals company now looks for return on investment (ROI) of at least 15 percent from each product line, and considers an ROI figure of less than 11 percent as calling for close review and possible divestment.
3. A consumer packaged-goods company has the general objective that any product's marginal profit before advertising and promotional expenditures should be a minimum of 20 percent higher than fixed and variable costs.
4. A manufacturer of capital equipment demands at least 25 percent ROI from each product or operating unit.
5. Another capital goods producer, employing the ratio of direct costs to sales price as a means of measuring relative profit performance, classes a ratio of 60 percent as satisfactory and one over 70 percent as unsatisfactory.

How exactly should management measure the financial performance of marketing operations? What criteria should be used: return on investment, sales, profit contribution, or what? Many firms use volume attainment and profitability as criteria although, surprisingly, those using ROI seem to be

---

[7] David S. Hopkins, *Business Strategies for Problem Products* (New York: Conference Board, 1977), p. 11.

in the minority.[8] This may be due to several difficulties in attempting to apply the technique to gauge marketing performance:

> Because there are innumerable variations of profit levels, a proper question initially is, "*What return* is being used for the measure?" Examples of profit levels are profit before royalties (including or excluding interest payments), profit before taxes, cash flow, division profit contribution, factory contribution, or sales region or district contribution.
>
> Any of the above are useful, depending upon the investment base being used.
>
> Again, one could ask, "Return on *what investment?*" It may be total parent company investment, total investment of subsidiary, total assets, manipulative assets (excluding intangibles), funds employed (tangible working capital), or selected bases (receivables, inventories, cash, etc.).
>
> The remaining question is, "*Whose investment?*" The investment of the stockholder differs in concept with the operating investment of the firm. Use of each may give startlingly different results, especially in the case where tangible funds employed in a firm are contrasted with the stockholder's investment if large amount of goodwill has been capitalized.[9]

Once these questions are answered, ROI measures provide an important gauge of marketing performance.

Marketing's decision-making information needs often do not correspond to traditional managerial accounting reporting procedures, so some give-and-take negotiations may be necessary between top management, marketing, and accounting. Issues as to how to allocate revenues and costs, the extent of disaggregation of both revenues and costs, and many other questions must be resolved in order to obtain relevant information for financial analysis. Revenue and cost information has two dimensions, the past and the future. Accumulating and analyzing past information are necessary in order to measure the effectiveness of past strategies. Developing future estimates is needed to evaluate proposed strategies.

Finally the time period of analysis must be selected. Most strategic marketing decisions extend from a few to several years into the future, so financial analysis must take into account the time value of money and the flows of revenue and costs over the relevant time horizon. The high rate of inflation expected during the next decade adds another complicating factor to financial projections.

Marketing's Influence on Financial Performance

Marketing strategy, once it is implemented, affects the financial performance of the corporation by generating sales and by incurring costs. An examination of a basic financial analysis system widely known as the

---

[8] Sam R. Goodman, *Financial Analysis for Marketing Decisions* (Homewood, Ill.: Dow Jones-Irwin, 1972), p. 88.

[9] Ibid., pp. 102–3.

Du Pont investment model will place marketing's impact upon financial performance into perspective. This model is shown in Exhibit 2–16. The heavy-lined boxes indicate that marketing has some effect upon the area. Note that ROI in Exhibit 2–16 corresponds to net profits (after taxes) divided by investment, measured by total assets. By following the arrows, you can trace marketing's influence upon revenues and costs all the way to return on investment. Exhibit 2–16 can be expanded to include more details. For example, the investment box can be broken down into fixed assets (cash, marketable securities, accounts receivable, and inventories). Likewise, selling, general, and administrative expenses can be divided into specific expense components.

Eliminating Information Gaps

You will rarely find all the information that you would like to have for use in financial analysis in a case. This parallels the state of affairs in business practice. Marketing management must often eliminate information gaps by estimating the values of information needed in an analysis. You should proceed in a similar manner when necessary (and appropriate) in performing various kinds of financial analyses for the cases in this book.

EXHIBIT 2–16
ROI Model

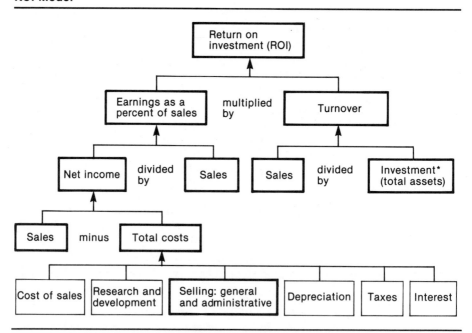

* Other measures of investment can be used.

An example will be useful in illustrating how information gaps can be eliminated. Suppose you have a company with three products: A, B, and C. You want to perform break-even analysis for Product B, but the fixed-cost information provided is for the entire company. Since you have sales for each product, one way to proceed is to assume that fixed costs can be allocated to each product based on the percentage of total sales accounted for by that product. For example, if Product B represents 20 percent of sales, then it would be assigned 20 percent of fixed costs. Using this fixed-cost estimate and per unit selling price and variable cost, break-even for Product B can be estimated. While the fixed-cost estimate may not be exact, it is probably adequate to give a close approximation of break-even.

You should note that other bases for allocating fixed costs may be appropriate in a given situation. The important consideration is that the assumptions underlying your estimating procedure be logical and, if possible, supported by facts provided in the case.

In estimating needed information, you should proceed with caution. A key requirement is that you have some basis for what you do. You should not make unrealistic guesses about the values of the information you need. In general, a good rule to follow is to be conservative with your estimates. It is sometimes helpful to estimate a range of values of the unknown factor. For example, if you are projecting the sales of a new product for the next three years, you might make three estimates: an optimistic estimate, a pessimistic estimate, and a most-likely estimate of sales for each of the three years.

Finally, it may be helpful to determine how sensitive your analysis is to the information you are estimating. Referring again to Product B, if the break-even level is not affected very much by different assumptions about how to allocate fixed costs, then any reasonable assumption about allocation should be acceptable. Alternatively, if the outcome of the financial analysis is affected significantly by small changes in the value you are estimating, then you should carefully assess the probable accuracy of your estimates.

Impact of Inflation

The double-digit inflation rates of the late 1970s and early 1980s signal the importance of proper treatment of the impact of inflation on marketing financial analysis. Conventional financial reporting using historical cost accounting suffers from two inadequacies during inflationary periods: (1) the dollar does not represent a constant or stable measuring unit over time; and (2) prior to sale, no recognition is given to changes in the prices of the assets held by a firm.[10] Some alternative methods of inflation accounting are shown in Exhibit 2–17.

---

[10] Frederick E. Webster, Jr., James A. Largay III, and Clyde P. Stickney, "The Impact of Inflation Accounting on Marketing Decisions," *Journal of Marketing*, Fall 1980, p. 10.

EXHIBIT 2–17
Alternative Inflation Accounting Methods

	Nominal Dollars*	Constant Dollars
Historical cost	1. Method used in conventional financial reporting	2. Dollars restated to dollars of constant general purchasing power
Current cost	3. Dollar amounts reported in terms of current replacement cost of specific assets	4. Same as 3 except that all amounts in 3 are restated to a constant-dollar basis

* Actual dollars received at sale of product and expended when inventory and equipment were acquired.

Source: Adapted from Frederick E. Webster, Jr., James A. Largay III, and Clyde P. Stickney, "The Impact of Inflation Accounting in Marketing Decisions," *Journal of Marketing*, Fall 1980, pp. 9–17.

Perhaps the most significant implication is the apparent emphasis by top management on the total level of asset commitment to specific products and markets. This, of course, will have its greatest impact on products and markets requiring heavy capital investments in fixed assets and working capital.[11]

Time Value of Money

The time value of money represents another influence on the evaluation of the financial performance of marketing operations. Since several sources provide extensive coverage of this topic, we shall only note its importance in marketing financial analysis, particularly when dealing with uneven cash flows over long time periods.[12]

SPREADSHEET ANALYSIS—USING PERSONAL COMPUTERS

The increased availability of computers has provided us with a powerful tool of analysis. With the most basic of personal computers, the business student has the capability to simplify lengthy and repetitive analyses and evaluation of multiple alternatives. Customized programs and graphing features are widely used by businesses, along with electronic spreadsheet software.

---

[11] Ibid., p. 14.

[12] An excellent discussion of evaluating investment opportunities is provided in Higgins, *Analysis for Financial Management*, chaps. 8 and 9.

Spreadsheet Capabilities

The electronic spreadsheet—marketed under names such as Lotus 1-2-3®, Borland Quattro, and others—provides the basic tools of analysis in an easy-to-use software program. Text, formulas, and numbers can be fed into the computer to develop ratio analyses, sales forecasts, reconciliations, accounting statements, and cost data. The major advantage of the spreadsheet is the ability to conduct analysis while changing various assumptions and to arrive at an answer or conclusion without manually repeating the calculations.

Some software packages, including Lotus 1-2-3, have computer graphics capabilities. Graphs, pie charts, bar charts, and other visual comparisons can be prepared. For example, the analysis shown in Exhibit 2–18 was prepared in only a few minutes on an IBM XT computer, using Lotus 1-2-3. The analyst needs only to type in the ranges for each product group, the range for time periods, and appropriate titles. A graphic comparison of the sales projections is shown in Exhibit 2–19.

How Spreadsheet Analysis Is Set Up

To illustrate its features, a more detailed description of the mechanics of spreadsheet analysis is necessary. The spreadsheet is a matrix of cells which can be filled with text, formulas, or numbers. Data can be manipulated by referencing a cell. This includes the row and column location denoted by numbers and letters respectively. It is this feature that allows formulas to be calculated based upon whatever number is entered in a cell and not just relying upon a number that may need to be replaced should an assumption or key figure be changed.

For example, assume that a firm produces Products A and B and that the firm wishes to calculate the total revenue from these products. For each product, one cell would contain the price of a product and another the amount sold. The cell that would display the total revenue would contain the formula: number of units of A sold times the price, added to the number

---

EXHIBIT 2–18

Estimated annual sales by product group

Product group	Annual growth rate	Annual sales 1988	Projected annual sales 1989	1990	1991	1992
A	5.0%	$870,000	$913,500	$959,175	$1,007,134	$1,057,490
B	-2.0%	$767,000	$751,660	$736,627	$721,894	$707,456
C	12.0%	$583,000	$652,960	$731,315	$819,073	$917,362

EXHIBIT 2–19

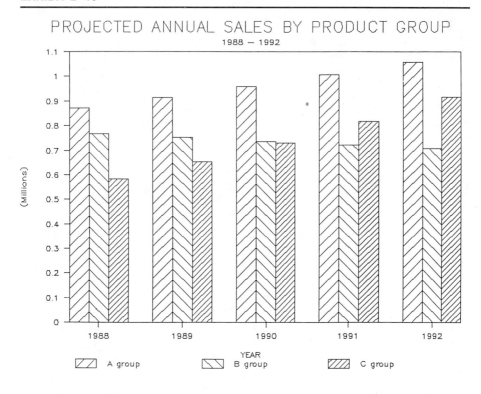

PROJECTED ANNUAL SALES BY PRODUCT GROUP
1988 – 1992

of units of B sold times the price. If the formula was entered using the numerical values of the prices and units sold, then if any of these values should change, the formula would have to be reentered in the cell to display the correct total revenue accounting for the changes. However, if the formula was entered using the cell location for the values of the number of units of A and B sold and the prices of A and B, the total revenue figure would be changed automatically. Any change in the price or amount sold of A or B would be entered in the appropriate cell. The computer would recalculate the total revenue based upon this change and display the answer in the cell for total revenue. Setting up the formulas based upon cell locations rather than values is especially useful where there are complex, lengthy formulas and when conditions are likely to change or there is a desire to see the proposed effect of certain changes in variables.

Using the Spreadsheet in Case Analysis

The electronic spreadsheet is very useful in case analysis. Ratios, break-even points, or forecasts can be determined from balance sheet and income statement data entered on the spreadsheet from the case information. The analyst can change key assumptions or figures in the balance sheet or income statement and immediately see the effect of these changes on any calculations. A standard financial analysis format can be established, and data from any case can be entered on the spreadsheet. The possibilities are endless, limited only by your imagination and the data provided in the case.

CONCLUDING NOTE

This chapter develops a foundation for marketing financial analysis. A variety of financial analysis methods were examined. Emphasis has been on application rather than method, since we have assumed that you already have an understanding of basic managerial accounting and finance. To supplement the coverage in the chapter, several sources are cited in the footnotes.

It is clear that marketing executives' financial analysis responsibilities are expanding rapidly, demanding a capability in using new concepts and techniques as well as interpreting financial analyses provided by others:

> To respond to these pressures positively, marketing managers will need a better understanding of accounting and financial management than that of their predecessors. The characteristic marketing manager's emphasis in analysis and action on sales volume, gross margin, and market share must be replaced by a more general management focus on bottom-line profitability and return on investment. Top management will think increasingly in terms of total resource allocation across products and markets, assessing the total product portfolio in terms of complex trade-offs between business growth opportunities in markets requiring additional investment for future profitability versus cash generation now in markets with limited or negative investment. Heightened awareness of the impact of inflation on measures of corporate financial performance will undoubtedly sharpen management concern on this dilemma. Marketing management must adopt new attitudes, what might be called "a general management orientation," as well as make use of the sophisticated measurements, analytical techniques, and strategic planning approaches that are available to help cope with the new pressures and complexities.[13]

As you move through the analysis of the various cases, you may find it helpful to refer to this chapter when you analyze financial information provided in a case or prepare your own financial analyses. Building upon the materials discussed in this chapter, Chapter 3 considers various aspects of case analysis.

---

[13] Webster et al., "The Impact of Inflation Accounting," pp. 16–17.

CHAPTER 3

GUIDE TO CASE ANALYSIS

A case presents a situation involving a managerial problem or issue that requires a decision. Typically, cases describe a variety of conditions and circumstances facing an organization at a particular time. This description often includes information regarding the organization's goals and objectives, its financial condition, the attitudes and beliefs of managers and employees, market conditions, competitors' activities, and various environmental forces that may affect the organization's present or proposed marketing strategy. Your responsibility is to carefully sift through the information provided in order to identify the opportunity, problem, or decision facing the organization; to carefully identify and evaluate alternative courses of action; and to propose a solution or decision based on your analysis.

This chapter provides an overview of the case method. It begins with a discussion of the role that cases play in the teaching/learning process. This is followed by a series of guidelines for case analysis. After carefully reading this material, you should be prepared to tackle your first case analysis. Even if you have had previous experience with cases, this chapter will provide a useful review.

WHY CASES?

The case method differs substantially from other teaching/learning approaches such as lecture and discussion. Lecture- and discussion-oriented classes provide students with information about concepts, practices, and theories. In contrast, cases provide an opportunity to *use* concepts, practices, and theories. The primary objective of the case method is to give you a hands-on opportunity to apply what you have learned in your course work.

Consider this analogy: Suppose that you want to learn to play a musical instrument. Your instruction might begin with several classes and reading assignments about your particular instrument. This could include information about the history of the instrument and descriptions of the various parts of the instrument and their functions. Sooner or later, however, you would actually have to play the instrument. Eventually you might become an accomplished musician.

Now suppose you want to become a marketing professional, instead of a musician. You started with classes or courses that introduced you to the foundations of marketing management. Your prior studies may have also included courses in areas of specialization such as marketing research, buyer behavior, and promotion, as well as other business disciplines such as management, finance, accounting, economics, and statistics. You need practice and experience to become a professional. This is precisely the purpose of the case method of instruction. The cases in this book will give you opportunities to apply your knowledge of marketing and other business subjects to actual marketing situations.

Case studies help to bridge the gap between classroom learning and the practice of marketing management. They provide us with an opportunity to develop, sharpen, and test our analytical skills at:

- Assessing situations.
- Sorting out and organizing key information.
- Asking the right questions.
- Defining opportunities and problems.
- Identifying and evaluating alternative courses of action.
- Interpreting data.
- Evaluating the results of past strategies.
- Developing and defending new strategies.
- Interacting with other managers.
- Making decisions under conditions of uncertainty.
- Critically evaluating the work of others.
- Responding to criticism.

In addition, cases provide exposure to a broad range of situations facing different types and sizes of organizations in a variety of industries. The decisions that you encounter in this book will range from fairly simple to quite complex. If you were the managers making these decisions, you would be risking anywhere from a few thousand to several million dollars of your firm's resources. And you could be risking your job and your career. Obviously the risk, or the cost of making mistakes, is much lower in the classroom environment.

A principal difference between our earlier example of learning to play a musical instrument and the practice of marketing lies in what might be called consequences. A musician's expertise is based on his or her ability to perform precisely the same series of actions time after time. The outcome of perfect execution of a predetermined series of actions is the sought consequence: a beautiful melody. Marketing, on the other hand, is often described as a skillful combination of art and science. No two situations ever require exactly the same actions. Although the same skills and knowledge may be required in different situations, marketing executives must analyze and diagnose each situation separately and conceive and initiate unique strategies to produce sought consequences. Judgment, as opposed to rote memory and repetition, is one key to marketing success. When judgment and a basic understanding of the variables and interrelationships in marketing situations are coupled, they form the core of an analysis and problem-solving approach that can be used in any marketing decision-making situation.

THE CASE METHOD OF INSTRUCTION

The case method of instruction differs from the lecture/discussion method that you have grown accustomed to since you began your formal education 14 or more years ago. It is only natural that you are a bit anxious and apprehensive about it. The methods of study and class preparation are different, your roles and responsibilities are different, and the "right" answers are much less certain. The case method is neither better nor worse than alternative methods; it is just different.

The case method is participative. You will be expected to take a more active role in learning than you have taken in the past. The case method is based on a philosophy of learning by doing as opposed to learning by listening and absorbing information. Case analysis is an applied skill. As such it is something you learn through application, as opposed to something someone teaches you. The more you practice, the more proficient you will become. The benefit you receive from case analysis is directly proportional to the effort you put into it.

Your Responsibilities

Your responsibilities as a case analyst include active participation, interaction, critical evaluation, and effective communication.

Active Participation. We have already noted that the case method is participative. It requires a great deal of individual participation in class discussion. Effective participation requires thorough preparation. This entails more than casually reading each case before class. The guidelines in the next section of this chapter will assist you in preparing case analyses. Also, keep in mind that there is a difference between contributing to a class discussion and just talking.

Interaction. Interaction among students plays an important role in the case method of instruction. Effective learning results from individual preparation and thinking combined with group discussion. Whether you are assigned to work independently or in groups or teams, most instructors encourage students to discuss cases with other students. This, of course, is common practice among managers facing important business decisions. Case discussions, in and out of class, are beneficial because they provide immediate feedback regarding individual perspectives and possible solutions. Other important benefits of case discussions are the synergism and new insights produced by group brainstorming and discussion.

Critical Evaluation.   One of the most difficult responsibilities of student case analysts is learning to critique their peers and to accept criticism from them. Typically, students are reluctant to question or challenge their classmates or to suggest alternatives to the perspectives proposed by others in the class. Students find this difficult because they are generally inexperienced at performing these functions, and are also unaccustomed to being challenged by their peers in the classroom. However, the case method of instruction is most effective when all parties engage in an open exchange of ideas. Good cases do not have one clear-cut superior solution. Don't be shy about expressing and defending your views. Moreover, the reasoning process you use and the questions you raise are often more important than the specific solution that you recommend.

Effective Communication.   Each of the three responsibilities discussed above requires effective communication. It is important that you organize your thoughts before speaking out. You will develop and refine your communication skills by making class presentations, participating in case discussions, and writing case analyses. Furthermore, the focus of the case method is the development and sharpening of quantitative and qualitative analytical skills. Your analytical skills will improve as you organize information, diagnose problems, identify and evaluate alternatives, and develop solutions and action plans.

Case analysis plays an important role in your overall education. What you learn in a course that utilizes the case method may be your best preparation for securing your first job and launching your career. If you ask a sample of recruiters to assess the students who are completing undergraduate and graduate programs in business administration today, you will probably hear that these students are extremely well-trained in concepts and quantitative skills but that they lack verbal and written communication skills and decision-making skills. The case method offers students an excellent opportunity to enhance and refine those skills.

A GUIDE TO CASE ANALYSIS

There is no one best way to analyze a case. Most people develop their own method after gaining some experience. As with studying, everybody does it a little bit differently. The following suggestions are intended to give you some ideas regarding how others approach cases. Try these suggestions and make your own adjustments.

Begin by reading each case quickly. The purpose of the first reading should be to familiarize yourself with the organization, the problem, or the decision to be made, the types and amount of data provided, and in general to get a feel for the case. Your second reading of the case should be more careful and thorough. Many students find it helpful to underline, highlight, and make notes about symptoms, potential problems and issues, key facts, and other important information.

Now you should be in a position to investigate the tabular and numerical data included in the case. Ask yourself what each figure, table, or chart means, how it was derived, whether or not it is relevant, and whether further computations would be helpful. If calculations, comparisons, or consolidations of numerical data appear useful, take the necessary action at this time.

A large part of what you will learn from case analysis is how to define, structure, and analyze opportunities and problems. The following information is intended to provide you with a general framework for problem solving. In essence, it is the scientific method with some embellishment. If your instructor does not assign a preferred analytical framework, use the approach shown in Exhibit 3–1. A discussion of each step follows, and a detailed outline of analytic issues and questions is provided in the appendix to this chapter.

Step 1: Situation Audit

The situation audit phase of the problem-solving process is basically a synopsis and evaluation of an organization's current situation, opportunities, and problems. The primary purpose of the audit is to help you prepare for problem definition and subsequent steps in the problem-solving process. Thus, much of the material in the audit should be in worksheet form rather than formal discussion that is handed in with a written case. You should not simply restate material included in the case. The purpose of this step is to interpret and show the relevance of important case information. Thus it is important that your situation audit be diagnostic rather than descriptive.

It is descriptive to simply report that, "Company A's current and quick ratios are 1.03 and 0.64, respectively." A diagnostic look at these figures indicates that Company A may not be able to meet maturing obligations. The poor quick ratio shows that without inventory, the company's least liquid asset, short-term obligations could not be met. In other words, Company A is insolvent. If you have information about a number of different problems or challenges facing Company A, knowing that the company is insolvent helps you to focus your attention on those that affect the firm's short-term survival needs.

The breadth and depth of an appropriate situation audit are determined by the nature and scope of the case situation, and your instructor's format preference. In this book, you will find cases that deal with both corporate and business-unit decisions. Some case situations focus on major corporate strategic decisions, and others focus on individual marketing mix decisions at the brand level. Each case will require a situation audit that is a little

EXHIBIT 3–1
An Approach to Case Analysis

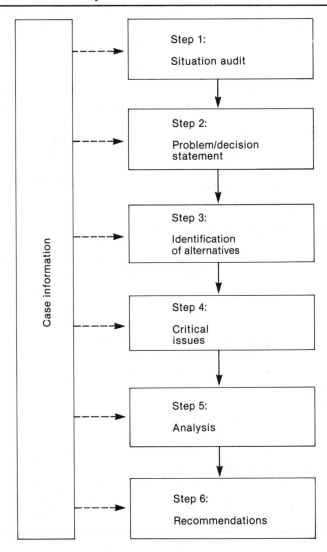

different from any of the others because of the information available and the decision to be made.

There are at least two philosophies regarding the appropriate depth and scope of a situation audit. One philosophy holds that the situation audit should include a thorough and comprehensive assessment of the organization's mission and objectives; each business unit of interest; present and potential customers and competitors; the organization's market-target objectives and strategies; its marketing program positioning strategy; its product, distribution, pricing and promotion strategies; current planning, implementation and management activities; its financial condition, and an overall summary of the organization's situation. If your instructor favors a thorough and comprehensive situation audit, you will find the outline for case analysis in the appendix to this chapter quite helpful in organizing your work.

Some instructors, however, feel that the situation audit need not be a thorough and comprehensive study, but rather a short, concise analysis of the organization's major strengths, weaknesses, opportunities, and threats—reserving the comprehensive effort for the analysis step. Some call this a SWOT analysis, and recommend including only information that is crucial in preparing to analyze the case. The emphasis here is on *analysis*, *diagnosis*, *synthesis*, and *interpretation* of the situation. In a written assignment you should be able to present this in less than two pages.

A Note on Gathering More Data and on Making Assumptions. Students often feel that they need more information in order to make an intelligent decision. Decision makers rarely, if ever, have all the information they would like to have prior to making important decisions. The cost and time involved in collecting more data are often prohibitive. Decision makers, like you, therefore have to make some assumptions. There is nothing wrong with making assumptions as long as they are explicitly stated and reasonable. Be prepared to defend your assumptions as logical. Don't use lack of information as a crutch.

For example, an assumption that Company A, mentioned previously, cannot borrow large sums of money is both reasonable and defensible. To assume that it could borrow large sums of money would require a clear explanation of why some lender or investor would be willing to loan money to, or invest money in, a firm with a quick ratio of 0.64.

Step 2: Problem/Decision Statement

Identification of the main problem, opportunity, or issue in a case is crucial. To paraphrase from *Alice In Wonderland*, if you don't know where you are going, any solution will take you there. If you don't properly identify the central problem or decision in a case, the remainder of your analysis is not likely to produce recommendations necessary to solve the organization's main problem.

You may become frustrated with your early attempts at problem/decision identification. Don't feel alone. Most students and many experienced managers have difficulty with this task. Your skill will improve with practice.

A major pitfall in defining problems/decisions occurs in confusing symptoms with problems. Such things as declining sales, low morale, high turnover, or increasing costs are symptoms that are often incorrectly identified as problems. You can frequently avoid incorrectly defining a symptom as a problem by thinking in terms of causes and effects. Problems are causes, and symptoms are effects. The examples cited above are the effects or manifestations of something wrong in the organization. Why are sales declining? Why is morale low? Why is turnover high? Why are costs increasing? The key question is why. What is the cause? Sales may be declining because morale is low and turnover is high. Why is morale low, and why is turnover high? These effects may be caused by an inadequate compensation plan, which in turn may be caused by inadequate profit margins. Profit margins may be low because products have been incorrectly priced or because the distribution system is outdated. As you can see, symptoms may appear in one part of the overall marketing program, and the true problem may lie elsewhere in the program. Keep asking why, until you are satisfied that you have identified the problem (cause) and not just another symptom (effect).

Think about this analogy. You are not feeling well, so you make an appointment to see your physician. The physician will ask you to describe what is bothering you. Suppose you say you have a headache, a sore throat, chills, and a fever. The physician will probably take your temperature, look in your throat, and perhaps examine you in other ways. The goal, of course, is to diagnose your problem so that a remedy can be prescribed.

How does this relate to case analysis? Your headache, sore throat, chills, and fever are symptoms of something wrong. They are signals to you to seek help. This information also assists your physician in making his or her diagnosis. These symptoms are similar to the declining sales, poor morale, high turnover, and increasing costs that we discussed earlier. They are the effects of some underlying cause. Your role in case study, like the role of your physician, is to analyze the combination of symptoms that can be identified, and then to determine the underlying problem.

Let's carry the analogy a bit further. Suppose the physician's diagnosis is that you have a common cold. Since there is no cure for a cold, all he or she can do is prescribe medication to treat the symptoms. The cold will cure itself in a matter of days.

Now suppose the diagnosis of the cause is incorrect. Instead of just a common cold, you contracted malaria during a recent vacation in Southeast Asia. If the physician treats the symptoms or effects, they will be temporarily reduced or eliminated, but they will soon reappear. Each time they reappear they will be more severe, until the ailment is properly diagnosed or you die. This is precisely what will happen in an organization if a symptom is incorrectly identified as a problem. Treating the symptom will temporarily reduce its dysfunctional impact on the organization, but sooner or later it will reappear. When it reappears it will probably be more severe than it was previously. This is why carefully identifying the root problem, decision, or issue in your case analysis is so important.

When you identify more than one major problem or decision in a case, ask yourself whether or not the problems or decisions are related enough to be consolidated into one problem/decision statement. You may not yet have reached the central problem. If, however, you have identified two or more problems that are not directly associated with one another, we recommend that you rank them in the order of their importance and address them in that order. You may find that although the problems do not appear to be closely linked, the solutions are related. One solution may solve multiple problems.

A final suggestion regarding defining problems or decisions is to state them concisely and, if possible, in the form of a question. Try to write a one-sentence question that is specific enough to communicate the main concern. For example:

- Should Brand A be deleted from the product line?
- Should General Mills implement a cents-off campaign, or should it use coupons to stimulate trial of its new cereal Gold Rush?
- Which two of the five candidates should be hired?
- How should Magic Chef define its marketing planning units?
- What is the best marketing program positioning strategy for Agree creme rinse?

In addition to your problem/decision statement, you may find it useful to provide a brief narrative describing the main parameters of the problem/decision. This is helpful when you have a compound problem/decision that can be subdivided into components or subproblems.

Step 3: Identification of Alternatives

Alternatives are the strategic options or actions that appear to be viable solutions to the problem or decision situation that you have determined. Often, more than two seemingly appropriate actions will be available. Sometimes these will be explicitly identified in the case, and sometimes they will not.

Prepare your list of alternatives in two stages. First, prepare an initial list of alternatives which includes all the actions that you feel might be appropriate. Group brainstorming is a useful technique for generating alternatives. Be creative, keep an open mind, and build upon the ideas of others. What may initially sound absurd could become an outstanding possibility.

After you have generated your initial list of alternatives, begin refining your list and combining similar actions. Use the information that you organized in your situation audit regarding goals, objectives, and constraints, to help you identify which alternatives to keep and which to eliminate. Ask yourself whether or not an alternative is feasible given the existing financial, productive, managerial, marketing, and other constraints and whether or not it could produce the results sought. That is, does the alternative directly address the problem or decision you identified in Step 2? If your problem/decision statement and your alternatives are inconsistent, you have erred in one step or the other. To help avoid this mistake, be explicit in showing the connections between the situation audit, the problem/decision statement, and the final set of alternatives.

Doing nothing and collecting more data are two alternatives often suggested by students with limited case experience. These are rarely the best actions to take. If you have identified a problem or a decision that must be made, ignoring the situation probably will not help. Likewise, recommending a survey, hiring a consultant, or employing some other option associated with gathering more data is rarely a viable solution to the central problem or issue. In some cases, a solution may include further study, but this will normally be part of the implementation plan rather than part of the solution. Most cases, at least those included in this book, are based on real business situations. You have the same information that was available to the decision maker when the decision was made. The major difference is that your data are already compiled and organized. If complete information were available, decisions would be easy. This is not the case in business situations, so it may help you to become familiar with making decisions under conditions of uncertainty. Executives, like case analysts, must rely on assumptions and on less-than-perfect information.

Step 4: Critical Issues

Next you should develop a list of critical issues. These are the main criteria that you will use to evaluate your strategic options. By expressly stating the critical issues you intend to use in evaluating alternatives, you make clear the criteria you plan to use in assessing and comparing the viability of your alternative courses of action.

Perhaps the best place to start in identifying critical issues is to ask yourself what factors, in general, should be considered in making a strategic decision regarding this particular problem. For example, assume that your task is to identify the most attractive product-market niche. Your alternatives are niches X, Y, and Z. Your question then would be: What criteria should be employed in assessing the choices of product-market niches? An appropriate set of criteria might include (for each niche) potential sales volume, variable costs, contribution margins, market share, total niche sales, business strength, and niche attractiveness. This will provide an evaluation relative to the market and to competition.

The single most important critical issue in many decisions is profitability. Since profits are a principal goal in all commercial organizations, nearly every marketing decision is influenced by monetary considerations that ultimately affect profits (or expected profits). Sometimes several profit-oriented critical issues are involved. These may include future costs and revenues, break-even points, opportunity costs, contribution margins, taxes, turnover, sales, and market share, for example.

Many critical issues are only indirectly linked to profits. Such things as the impact of a decision on employees, the local economy, the environment, suppliers, or even customer attitudes may not directly affect profits. Because profits are almost always the overriding critical issue, all factors bearing on them, directly or indirectly, must be considered.

Step 5: Analysis

Analysis is the process of evaluating each alternative action against the issues that were identified in Step 4. Often, analysis includes assessment of advantages and limitations associated with each issue. A tendency exists when first starting a case analysis to identify important issues carefully and then to analyze each issue superficially. The consequence is a weak analysis. Your analysis will be much more penetrating and comprehensive if you use the same criteria in assessing each alternative.

One way of assuring that you assess each alternative in terms of each critical issue is to organize your analysis in outline form as follows:

Step 5:   Analysis
    Alternative A: (Specify the alternative)
      1.   Identify the *critical issue* and thoroughly discuss Alternative A in terms of critical issue number 1.
      2.   For the remaining critical issues, follow the same procedure.
    Alternative B: (Specify the alternative)
      1.   *Critical issue 1.* Thoroughly discuss Alternative B in terms of critical issue number 1.
      2.   *Critical issue 2–n.* Follow the same procedure.

Following is a brief, unedited example from a student paper. The problem/decision was whether Wyler Foods, a powdered soft-drink subsidiary of Borden, should introduce a new line of unsweetened powdered drink mixes to compete with the market leader, Kool-Aid. One alternative was to introduce the product and attempt to compete head-to-head with Kool-Aid. Critical issues identified by the student were:

1. Projected profit impact.
2. Long-term growth implications.
3. Competitor reactions.
4. Resource requirements.
5. Competitive advantages and/or disadvantages.

Analysis of the alternative in terms of each critical issue follows. (*Note that exhibits identified in the analysis are not included.*)

Step 5:   Analysis

Alternative A.   Head-to-head competition with Kool-Aid

1.1 *Projected profit impact.*   The profit potential for head-to-head competition with Kool-Aid does not seem promising. Assuming that the product will perform nationally as it did during test marketing, it should achieve a 4 percent share of the $143.51 million unsweetened powdered drink mix (UPDM) market (see Exhibit 1).

This represents sales of $5.74 million. Long-term share could be as low as 2.5 percent of the overall market. A retail price of 12 cents per packet, and cost of goods sold of 9.4 cents per packet will produce a contribution margin of approximately $1.24 million (see Exhibit 2). This level of contribution margin will not be sufficient to cover advertising and sales promotion expenditures, which will exceed $4 million, and could rise to $8–10 million.

Quantity allowances to stimulate grocer acceptance will have to be in the $800,000 area. Adopting this alternative would lead to substantial first-year losses, minimally in the $4–5 million range, and possibly much higher (see Exhibit 3).

1.2 *Long-term growth implications.*   Long-term corporate growth factors are dependent upon how deeply the new product can penetrate the Kool-Aid-dominated UPDM market. If the product performs no better than the test market results indicate, this strategy would be a long-term money loser. The product will have to capture roughly 15.4 percent of the UPDM market to break even (see Exhibit 4).

1.3 *Competitor reactions.*   Kool-Aid can be expected to spend $10–12 million more on advertising and sales promotion than is proposed for the new product in its first year. Kool-Aid can also be expected to emphasize its traditional position as the favored UPDM. The leading brand is able to exercise considerable influence in established distribution channels to keep the new product line off the grocers' shelves, necessitating huge quantity allowances to achieve penetration. Through 50 years of acclimation, the consumer is now at the point of utilizing the Kool-Aid product as the taste benchmark; this imperils the new product line even before the contest starts. Perhaps of greatest importance, Kool-Aid may opt for price competition. Because of sales volume considerations, Kool-Aid can cut prices and maintain profitability. Wyler simply could not afford to match Kool-Aid's potential price cuts. To do so would further darken its bleak profit outlook (see Exhibit 5).

1.4 *Resource requirements.*   Wyler seems to be short on financial resources necessary to implement this alternative (see Exhibit 5). Substantial cash infusions would be needed for some time before any cash outflows would be generated. Wyler's personnel seem to be capable of executing the strategy.

1.5 *Competition advantages and/or disadvantages.*   Implementation of this alternative involves doing battle with Kool-Aid on Kool-Aid's home ground. Rather than exploiting a key Wyler strength, this alternative seems to favor Kool-Aid's strengths and Wyler's weaknesses. Wyler will be playing by Kool-Aid's rules, which isn't likely to produce a successful outcome.

Although this is a fairly simple example without any financial comparisons, it illustrates a useful approach for evaluating alternative actions. Note that each alternative should be evaluated in terms of each critical issue. After the alternatives are analyzed against each issue, you should complete your analysis with a summary assessment of each alternative. This summary will provide the basis for preparing your recommendations.

One approach that students sometimes find useful in preparing their summary analyses is illustrated in an exhibit labeled *Summary Assessment ABC Company*. It entails five steps.

Step 1: List critical issues on one axis and alternative actions on the other axis.

Step 2: Assign a weight to each critical issue reflecting its relative importance on the final decision. For convenience, assign weights that add up to one.

Step 3: Review your analysis and rate each alternative on each critical issue using a scale of one to five with one representing very poor and five representing very good.

Step 4: Multiply the weight assigned to each issue by the rating given to each alternative on each issue.

Step 5: Add the results from Step 4 for each alternative.

ABC COMPANY
Summary Assessment

Critical Issues	Relative Weights	Alternatives (ratings)		
		(1)	*(2)*	*(3)*
Corporate mission & objectives	(.2)	(5)	(2)	(3)
Market opportunity	(.3)	(2)	(3)	(5)
Competitive strengths/weaknesses	(.2)	(2)	(3)	(2)
Financial considerations	(.3)	(1)	(1)	(4)
Index: Relative weight × Rating		2.3	2.2	3.7

It is important to understand that this type of analytical aid is *not* a substitute for thorough, rigorous analysis, clear thinking, and enlightened decision making. Its value is in encouraging you to assess the relative importance of alternatives and critical issues, and helping you to organize your analysis.

Step 6: Recommendations

If your analysis has been thorough, the actions you recommend should flow directly from it. The first part of your recommendations section addresses what specific actions should be taken and why. State the main reasons you believe your chosen course of action is best, but avoid rehashing the analysis section. It is important that your recommendations be specific and operational. The following example of a recommendation deals with whether a manufacturer of oil field equipment should introduce a new product line.

> The key decision that management must make is whether viscosity-measurement instrumentation represents a business venture that fits into the overall mission of the firm. The preceding analysis clearly indicates that this would be a profitable endeavor. If AOS concentrates on the high-accuracy and top end of the intermediate-accuracy range of the market, sales of $500,000 appear feasible within two to four years, with an estimated contribution to overhead and profits in the $145,000 range. This is assuming that manufacturing costs can be reduced by 20 to 25 percent, that effective marketing approaches are developed, that further product development is not extensive, and that price reductions per unit do not exceed 10 percent.

The second part of your recommendations section addresses implementation. State clearly who should do what, when, and where. An implementation plan shows that your recommendations are both possible and practical. For example:

> AOS should initially offer two instruments. One should provide an accuracy of 0.25 percent or better; the second should be in the accuracy range of 0.1 to 0.5 percent. Top priority should be assigned to inland and offshore drilling companies. Next in priority should be R&D laboratories in industry, government, and universities, where accuracy needs exist in the range offered by AOS. Based on experience with these markets, other promising targets should be identified and evaluated.
>
> AOS needs to move into the market rapidly, using the most cost-effective means of reaching end-user markets. By developing an original-equipment-manufacturer (OEM) arrangement with General Supply to reach drilling companies and a tie-in arrangement with Newtec to reach R&D markets, immediate access to end-user markets can be achieved. If successful, these actions will buy some time for AOS to develop marketing capabilities, and they should begin generating contributions from sales to cover the expenses of developing a marketing program. An essential element in the AOS marketing strategy is locating and hiring a person to manage the marketing effort. This person must have direct sales capabilities in addition to being able to perform market analysis and marketing program development, implementation, and management tasks.

The last part of your recommendations section should be a tentative budget. This is important because it illustrates that the solution is worth the cost and is within the financial capabilities of the organization. Too often, students develop grandiose plans that organizations couldn't possibly afford even if they were worth the money. Budgeting and forecasting are discussed in Chapter 2.

Your instructor realizes that the numbers used in your tentative budget may not be as accurate as they would be if you had complete access to the records of the company. Make your best estimates and try to get as close to the actual figures as possible. The exercise is good experience, and it shows that you have considered the cost implications.

Students often ask how long the recommendations section should be and how much detail they should go into. This question is difficult to answer because each case is different and should be treated that way. In general it is advisable to go into as much detail as possible. You may be criticized for not being specific enough in your recommendations, but you are not likely to be criticized for being too specific.

APPENDIX: AN OUTLINE FOR CASE ANALYSIS

The outline shown here is an expanded version of the approach to case analysis discussed in this chapter. Although reasonably comprehensive, the guide can be shortened, expanded, and/or adapted to meet your needs in various situations. For example, if you are analyzing a business unit that does not utilize channels of distribution, section VIII B of the outline will require adjustment. Likewise, if the salesforce represents the major part of the marketing program, then section VIII E should probably be expanded to include other aspects of salesforce strategy.

This guide is not intended to be a comprehensive checklist that can be applied in every case. Instead, it is illustrative of the broad range of issues and questions you will encounter in analyzing the strategic decisions presented in this book and elsewhere. The key is to *adapt the outline to the case*, not the case to the outline.

Step 1. Situation Audit

  I. Corporate mission and objectives
     A. Does the mission statement offer a clear guide to the product-markets of interest to the firm?
     B. Have objectives been established for the corporation?
     C. Is information available for the review of corporate progress toward objectives, and are the reviews conducted on a regular (quarterly, monthly, etc.) basis?
     D. Has corporate strategy been successful in meeting objectives?
     E. Are opportunities or problems pending that may require altering marketing strategy?
     F. What are the responsibilities of the chief marketing executive in corporate strategic planning?
 II. Business unit analysis
     A. What is the composition of the business (business segments, strategic planning units, and specific product-markets)?
     B. Have business strength and product-market attractiveness analyses been conducted for each planning unit? What are the results of the analyses?
     C. What is the corporate strategy for each planning unit (e.g., growth, manage for cash)?
     D. Does each unit have a strategic plan?

    E. For each unit, what objectives and responsibilities have been assigned to marketing?

III. Buyer analysis

    A. Are there niches within the product-market? For each specific product-market and niche of interest to the firm, answer items B through I.

    B. What are estimated annual purchases (units and dollars)?

    C. What is the projected annual growth rate (five years)?

    D. How many people/organizations are in the product-market?

    E. What are the demographic and socioeconomic characteristics of customers?

    F. What is the extent of geographic concentration?

    G. How do people decide what to buy?

      1. Reason(s) for buying (What is the need/want?).

      2. What information is needed (e.g., how to use the product)?

      3. What are other important sources of information?

      4. What criteria are used to evaluate the product?

      5. What are purchasing practices (quantity, frequency, location, time, etc.)?

    H. What environmental factors should be monitored because of their influence on product purchases (e.g., interest rates)?

    I. What key competitors serve each end-user group?

IV. Key competitor analysis. For each specific product-market and each niche of interest to the firm, determine:

    A. Estimated overall business strength.

    B. Market share (percent, rank).

    C. Market share trend (five years).

    D. Financial strengths.

    E. Profitability.

    F. Management.

    G. Technology position.

    H. Other key nonmarketing strengths/limitations (e.g., production cost advantages).

    I. Marketing strategy (description, assessment of key strengths and limitations).

      1. Market-target strategy.

      2. Program positioning strategy.

      3. Product strategy.

      4. Distribution strategy.

      5. Price strategy.

      6. Promotion strategy.

V. Market-target strategy

    A. Has each market target been clearly defined and its importance to the firm established?

    B. Have demand and competition in each market target been analyzed, and key trends, opportunities, and threats identified?

    C. Has the proper market-target strategy (mass, niche) been adopted?

    D. Should repositioning or exit from any product-market be considered?

VI. Market-target objectives

    A. Have objectives been established for each market target, and are these consistent with planning-unit objectives and the available resources? Are the objectives realistic?

B. Are sales, cost, and other performance information available for monitoring the progress of planned performance against actual results?

C. Are regular appraisals made of marketing performance?

D. Where do gaps exist between planned and actual results? What are the probable causes of the performance gaps?

VII. Marketing program positioning strategy

A. Does the firm have an integrated positioning strategy made up of product, channel, price, advertising, and salesforce strategies? Is the role selected for each mix element consistent with the overall program objectives, and does it properly complement other mix elements?

B. Are adequate resources available to carry out the marketing program? Are resources committed to market targets according to the importance of each?

C. Are allocations to the various marketing mix components too low, too high, or about right in terms of what each is expected to accomplish?

D. Is the effectiveness of the marketing program appraised on a regular basis?

VIII. Marketing program activities

A. Product strategy

1. Is the product mix geared to the needs that the firm wants to meet in each product-market?

2. What branding strategy is being used?

3. Are products properly positioned against competing brands?

4. Does the firm have a sound approach to product planning and management, and is marketing involved in product decisions?

5. Are additions to, modifications of, or deletions from the product mix needed to make the firm more competitive in the marketplace?

6. Is the performance of each product evaluated on a regular basis?

B. Channels of distribution strategy

1. Has the firm selected the type (conventional or vertically coordinated) and intensity of distribution appropriate for each of its product-markets?

2. How well does each channel access its market target? Is an effective channel configuration used?

3. Are channel organizations carrying out their assigned functions properly?

4. How is the channel of distribution managed? What improvements are needed?

5. Are desired customer service levels reached, and are the costs of doing this acceptable?

C. Price strategy

1. How responsive is each market target to price variation?

2. What roles and objectives does price have in the marketing mix?

3. Does price play an active or passive role in program positioning strategy?

4. How do the firm's price strategy and tactics compare to those of competition?

   5. Is a logical approach used to establish prices?
   6. Are there indications that changes may be needed in price strategy or tactics?
D. Advertising and sales promotion strategies
   1. Are roles and objectives established for advertising and sales promotion in the marketing mix?
   2. Is the creative strategy consistent with the positioning strategy that is used?
   3. Is the budget adequate to carry out the objectives assigned to advertising and sales promotion?
   4. Do the media and programming strategies represent the most cost-effective means of communicating with market targets?
   5. Do advertising copy and content effectively communicate the intended messages?
   6. How well does the advertising program meet its objectives?
E. Salesforce strategy
   1. Are the roles and objectives of personal selling in the marketing program positioning strategy clearly specified and understood by the sales organization?
   2. Do the qualifications of salespeople correspond to their assigned roles?
   3. Is the salesforce the proper size to carry out its function, and is it efficiently deployed?
   4. Are salesforce results in line with management's expectations?
   5. Is each salesperson assigned performance targets, and are incentives offered to reward performance?
   6. Are compensation levels and ranges comparable to those of competitors?
IX. Marketing planning
A. Strategic planning and marketing
   1. Is marketing's role and responsibility in corporate strategic planning clearly specified?
   2. Are responsibility and authority for marketing strategy assigned to one executive?
   3. How well is the firm's marketing strategy working?
   4. Are changes likely to occur in the corporate/marketing environment that may affect the firm's marketing strategy?
   5. Do major contingencies exist that should be included in the strategic marketing plan?
B. Marketing planning and organization structure
   1. Are annual and longer-range strategic marketing plans developed and used?
   2. Are the responsibilities of the various units in the marketing organization clearly specified?
   3. What are the strengths and limitations of the key members of the marketing organization? What is being done to develop employee skills? What gaps in experience and capability exist on the marketing staff?
   4. Is the organizational structure for marketing appropriate for implementing marketing plans?

X. Financial analysis
   A. Sales and cost analyses and forecasts
   B. Profit contribution and net profit analyses and projections
   C. Liquidity analyses
   D. Break-even analyses
   E. Return on investment
   F. Budget analyses
   G. Pro forma statements
XI. Implementation and management
   A. Have the causes of all performance gaps been identified?
   B. Is implementation of planned actions taking place as intended? Is implementation being hampered by marketing or other functional areas of the firm (e.g., operations, finance)?
   C. Has the strategic audit revealed areas requiring additional study before action is taken?
XII. Summary of the situation
   Has the situation audit revealed opportunities which would enable the organization to gain a competitive advantage based upon its distinctive competencies?
   A. What are the major opportunities available to the organization?
   B. What are the major threats facing the organization?
   C. What are the requirements for achieving success in selected product-markets?
   D. What are the organization's and the principal competitors' distinctive competencies regarding these requirements? Do these areas of strength complement a given opportunity, or do strategic gaps exist that serve as barriers to pursuing the opportunity?
   E. What strategic gaps, problems, and/or constraints relative to competitors appear?
   F. What time and resources are required to pursue an opportunity or close a strategic gap?
   G. Does the organization's mission (or objectives) need to be redefined?
XIII. Opinions and assumptions
   A. Are opinions or assumptions provided by others? Are they reasonable, given the source?
   B. Is it necessary to make assumptions about the organization's objectives, competition, the environment, or something else?

Step 2. Problem/Decision Statement

A. What are the symptoms that suggest a problem exists?
B. What is the major problem or decision that must be addressed?
C. Are there secondary problems or decisions?

Step 3. Identification of Alternatives

A. What actions might provide viable solutions to the problem or decision?
B. Can actions be combined?
C. Can actions be eliminated without further consideration?

Step 4. Critical Issues

What criteria should be used to evaluate the strategic options? Any of the items listed in the situation audit may be relevant issues in analyzing the alternatives.

Step 5. Analysis

A. Examine each alternative in terms of each critical issue.
B. What are the relative advantages and disadvantages of each choice in terms of each of the critical issues?

Step 6. Recommendations

A. What specific actions, including the development of marketing or other plans, should be taken and why?
B. Who should do what, when, and where?
C. What are the expected costs and returns associated with your recommendations?
D. What contingencies may alter the attractiveness of your recommendations?

PART 2

COORDINATING BUSINESS AND MARKETING STRATEGIES

The importance of developing market-driven business strategies became clear during the 1980s. Slow growth in many industries, intensive global competition, and scarce financial resources spelled out the challenge facing corporate managements. Strategic planning with a market-centered focus has become essential to survival in turbulent economic environments.

Strategic planning for the enterprise demands perceptive insights about customers' needs and wants, as well as ways of achieving customer satisfaction through the firm's marketing offer (product, distribution, price, and promotion strategies). Thus a close working relationship between marketing strategists and executives responsible for the strategic planning of the enterprise is essential.

Unfortunately, the glamour and mystery often associated with strategic planning may mask what should be viewed as a demanding yet logical process: deciding the mission and objectives of the enterprise and then devising strategies for reaching those objectives.

WHAT IS STRATEGIC PLANNING?

An overview of business planning is shown in Exhibit 1. The process is a continuing one, beginning with an assessment of the situation faced by a corporation. This leads to an examination of corporate mission and objectives which may over time be changed to respond to the findings of the situation assessment. Strategies are required to accomplish mission and objectives. These strategies are developed for the product and market areas

EXHIBIT 1
Business Planning Overview

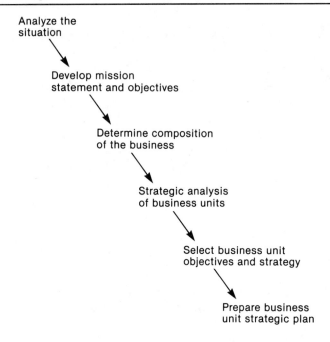

that determine the composition of the business. An important part of planning in a firm that is made up of more than one product-market area is regular evaluation of the different business areas. These business units often have different objectives and strategies, representing a portfolio of businesses. The strategic plan for each unit spells out what its assigned role is in the corporation and how that role will be fulfilled. Underlying the plan are strategies for marketing, finance, operations, and other supporting areas. Strategies are implemented and managed. Regular assessment of the strategic situation completes the cycle.

SITUATION ASSESSMENT

A corporate situation assessment provides a foundation for developing the strategic plan. The analysis should clearly describe the present situation faced by the organization, and should include the following information:

1. Analysis of external forces that do (or will) influence the corporation. These include economic, technological, social, governmental, and natural factors.
2. Analysis of demand, customers, industry, and distribution structure.

3. Evaluation of key competitors.
4. Objective assessment of corporate capabilities and limitations, high-lighting key differential advantages over competition.
5. Identification of strategic opportunities and threats.

A useful format for combining this information is a situation assessment *summary* that includes the strategic implication of each item in the summary. It should be specific, pointing to areas that may affect the corporate mission and objectives, business composition, strategic analysis of business units, and business unit strategies (Exhibit 1).

CORPORATE MISSION AND OBJECTIVES

The path(s) that management chooses to follow in the development of the firm establishes key guidelines for strategic planning. The choice of mission and objectives should spell out where the company is going and why:

> Management must initially establish the nature and scope of a firm's operations and adjust these decisions as necessary over time. Strategic choices about where the firm is going in the future, taking into account company capabilities and resources and opportunities and problems, establish the mission of the enterprise.[1]

The Mission Statement

A useful means for communicating business purpose and objectives is the mission statement. The following are examples of its contents.[2]

1. The reason for the company's existence and the responsibilities of the company to stockholders, employees, society, and various other stakeholders.
2. The customers' needs and wants to be served with the firm's product or service offering (areas of product and market involvement).
3. The extent of specialization within each product-market area (e.g., deciding to offer just Tootsie Rolls rather than a variety of candies).
4. The amount and types of diversification of product-markets desired by management.
5. Management's performance expectations for the company.
6. Other general guidelines for overall business strategy, such as the role of research and development in the corporation.

---

[1] David W. Cravens, *Strategic Marketing* (Homewood, Ill.: Richard D. Irwin, 1987), p. 37.
[2] Ibid.

An overriding influence upon the mission decision is: What does management want the business to be? Acknowledging the constraining nature of capabilities, resources, opportunities, and problems, management is left with much flexibility in making the decision as well as changing it in the future. Uncontrollable factors may create the need for alteration of mission. Peter Drucker has noted that:

> Defining the purpose and mission of the business is difficult, painful, and risky. But it alone enables business to set objectives, to develop strategies, to concentrate its resources, and go to work. It alone enables a business to be managed for performance.[3]

In addition to a mission statement, long-range objectives should be indicated so that the performance of the enterprise can be gauged. Objectives for the corporation are often set in the following areas: marketing, innovation, resources, productivity, social, and financial.[4] Examples include sales growth and market-share expectations, human resources training and development, new-product targets, return on invested capital, earning growth rates, debt limits, energy reduction objectives, and pollution standards. Objectives should be realistic and specific so that management can measure progress toward achieving them.

Corporate Development Alternatives

Most companies start business operations in some core business area. Success often leads to expanding into related areas and sometimes into entirely new product-market areas. The major corporate development options are shown in Exhibit 2. There are, of course, many specific strategies and combinations of these options. We shall examine each alternative to gain a better understanding of corporate expansion activities.

Core Business. Many firms start out serving one product-market. The product or service may be a single product or a line of products. The initial venture is the core business, as food products were in the case of General Mills, and women's apparel was in the case of The Limited. This strategy, when it involves a single product-market, offers the advantages of specialization but contains the risks of being dependent upon one set of customer needs. As a corporation grows and prospers, management often decides to move into other product and market areas as shown in Exhibit 2.

New Markets for Existing Products. One way to expand away from the core business is to serve other needs and wants, using the same product or a similar product. The Maytag Company is a leading manufacturer of

---

[3] Peter F. Drucker, *Management* (New York: Harper & Row, 1974), p. 94.
[4] Ibid., p. 100.

EXHIBIT 2
Corporate Development Options

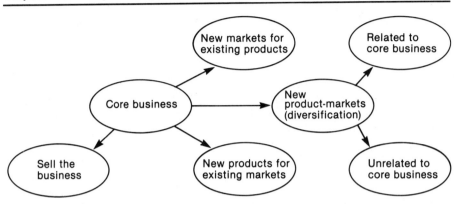

home *and* commercial laundry equipment. A. T. Cross markets its line of writing instruments to consumers—and to organizations for incentives, employee recognition, and other uses. For many companies, this is a natural line of development. The strategy reduces the risks of depending upon a single market, yet it allows the use of existing technical and production capabilities. The major demands arising from this strategy are adequate resources for expansion and the capabilities for developing a new marketing strategy. Since it may be difficult to acquire a marketing capability or to turn it over to a marketing intermediary, the requirements for internal marketing strategy development should be recognized when adopting this alternative. The primary caution to be exercised is to be sure the new market opportunity is carefully evaluated as to its feasibility and attractiveness.

New Products for Existing Market. Another strategy for shifting away from dependence upon one product-market is to expand the product mix offered to the firm's market target. This can be achieved either by acquiring companies or products or by internal new-product development. A disadvantage of this strategy is the continued dependence upon a particular market area.

Diversification. Diversification has become a popular option for corporate development by many firms. The distinction between diversification and product or market expansion is that the former involves movement into a new product-market area by either internal development or acquisition. Often the riskiest and costliest of the options shown in Exhibit 2, it may be attractive if existing product-market areas face slow growth, if resources for diversification are available, and if good choices are made. Diversification, once it has been successfully implemented, offers the advantage of spreading business risks over two or more segments of business. Diversification may follow one of two avenues: (1) movement into different, yet related, product-market areas or (2) building the corporation into a conglomerate consisting of unrelated product-market areas.

BUSINESS COMPOSITION

Understanding the composition of a business is essential in both corporate and marketing planning. When firms serve multiple markets with multiple products, grouping similar business areas together facilitates planning. Several guidelines to use in forming business planning units are shown in Exhibit 3. Management, of course, has some flexibility in deciding how to divide the business into planning units. Building up from specific product-market categories offers a more useful scheme in forming planning units than starting from the top and breaking it down. A note of caution is in order: Forming too many planning units can be more harmful than useful. A large number of units will require a correspondingly large number of strategies and management structures which are expensive and probably not cost effective.

BUSINESS UNIT STRATEGY

Management must decide whether: (1) to maintain or strengthen position, (2) to attempt to shift into a more desirable position, or (3) to exit from a business unit. Of course, as a product-market matures, strategic position may be altered due to a decline in the attractiveness of the product-market.

EXHIBIT 3
Guidelines for Forming Business Units

Inventory the products offered by the corporation to identify specific products, product lines, and mixes of product lines. Determine the end-user needs that each product is intended to satisfy.

Identify which products satisfy similar needs (e.g., foods for main meals). Also determine which products satisfy the needs of more than one user group.

Form units composed of one or more products or product lines that satisfy similar needs (e.g., food preparation appliances). The products that form a planning unit should have major strategic features in common, such as distribution channels, market target, technology, and/or advertising and salesforce strategies.

Determine if there are management, market, operating, or other advantages to combining two or more planning units into a division, group, or business segment.

Review the proposed scheme to determine if it offers both operational and strategic advantages. Do the potential benefits of the scheme exceed the costs?

EXHIBIT 4
Strategic Planning Guide

Business mission/objectives/capabilities
  Business mission definition and description
  Objectives*
  Summary of business position (strengths and limitations)*

*Complete the following for each unit of the business
and each major product-market within the unit.*

Situation analysis
  Product-market analysis
    Market size and growth
    Describe existing/potential customers
    How do customers decide what to buy?
    What factors influence buying?
  Industry/distribution analysis
    Industry characteristics and trends
    Operating practices in the industry
    Competition from other industries
  Analysis of key competitors
    Estimated overall business strength
    Market position
    Financial strengths and performance
    Management capabilities (and limitations)
    Technical and operating advantages
    Marketing strategy evaluation
    Other key strengths/limitations
  Analysis of our strengths/limitations
    Same factors as for key competitors
Summary of strategic opportunities and threats in the product-market
Key assumptions underlying our strategic plan
Major contingencies to be considered in the strategic plan

Market target(s) description
  The market target decision is the choice of the people or organizations in a
    product-market toward which a firm will aim its marketing program strategy.
  Describe each major customer/prospect group toward which a specific mar-
    keting strategy will be directed.

Strategic plan for the business unit
  Objectives
  Strategies for achieving objectives
  Key plans
    Business development
    Marketing strategy
    Operations
    Finance
    Human resources
    Other
Financial analysis and summary
Contingency plans

* Determined after completion of the situation analysis.

Management must select a strategic plan for each strategies' business unit (SBU), taking into account strategic position, available resources, forecasts of future competitive and market conditions, and the relative attractiveness of available opportunities.

Selecting a Strategy

After completing the analysis of an SBU, the following questions should be answered:

- What is the strategic situation of the business unit in terms of product and market maturity?
- How has the business unit performed during the past three to five years?
- How attractive will the product-market opportunities be in the next three to five years?
- How strong is our business unit position compared to that of competition?
- What should be the future strategy of the business unit over the next three to five years?

The use of a three- to five-year time span will vary among firms, depending upon the planning horizon used. The decision will depend on the rate of change in markets, competition, and other external factors.

The strategy options for an SBU range from an aggressive growth strategy to maintaining market position to exiting from the business area. In a multiunit corporation, the strategies for SBUs will normally be determined as a part of the corporation's total portfolio strategy.

The Business Unit Plan

Top management should establish guidelines for long-term strategic planning. In a business that has two or more strategic business units, decisions must be made at two levels. Top management must first decide what business areas to pursue, and then establish priorities for allocating resources to SBUs. Decision makers within SBUs must determine the appropriate strategies for delivering the results that management expects.

Most businesses that have multiple SBUs have specific guidelines for business units to use in developing strategic and tactical plans. The strategic planning guide shown in Exhibit 4 covers the major issues commonly addressed in business unit plans.

CONCLUDING NOTE

We have examined the major steps in developing business plans shown in Exhibit 1. Business planning begins with the corporate situation assessment and is followed by consideration of the adequacy of corporate mission and objectives, determination of business composition, analysis of business units, setting objectives and selecting strategies for business units, fitting these strategies into plans, and then implementing and managing the strategic plans.

The planning process shown in Exhibit 1 generally corresponds to the approaches used in business firms and other goal-directed organizations. It demonstrates marketing's rapidly increasing role in business planning, and it provides essential guidelines to marketing management.

CASES AND APPLICATIONS
FOR PART 2

The eight cases and five applications in Part 2 focus on corporate and marketing planning issues.

Cases

The first case, Rockingham Memorial Hospital, describes a regional hospital considering whether or not to develop and implement a sports medicine program. Local population statistics and anticipated expense and revenue data are provided.

Case 2–2, World View Travel Agency, Inc., presents an organization trying to decide how to meet increased competition, deal with the effects of deregulation in the travel industry, and take advantage of emerging market opportunities. One of the company owners observed, "We have the organization, the know-how, and the desire to grow. It's just a matter of setting our objectives, deciding upon a strategy, and getting on with the task."

MacTec Control AB (Case 2–3) is a rapidly growing Swedish firm that markets computer hardware and software for the monitoring and control of pressurized water flows. Municipal water departments and industrial firms represent the primary target markets for MacTec's Aqualex System. The case focuses on a decision facing Georg Carlsson, president of MacTec, regarding whether or not to enter the U.S. market, and if so, how.

Case 2–4, Kinder-Care, is about a chain of preschool education centers in the United States and Canada that has experienced phenomenal growth in its 12-year history. The national director of marketing considers how to continue growing, and the possible impact of changing demographics on Kinder-Care's marketing strategy.

Marion Laboratories (Case 2–5) is an ethical drug and health-care products company. At issue is whether to retain or divest a subsidiary that produces specialty agricultural chemicals. Analysis requires considering the trade-off between stated long-range planning goals and potential profitability.

Case 2–6, Simons Lumber Company, describes a small, family-owned business that has been successful for over 100 years. The president, Stephen Simons, is trying to decide on a future direction and a strategy for the company. The case closes with the following observations: "The future of the Simons Lumber Company is highly dependent on the choices made in the next year. Given the fairly stable nature of the company's products and personnel, Simons is reasonably confident that the company can continue to earn satisfactory profits over the next five years with minimal supervision on his part. On the other hand, expansion would dictate many major changes in personnel and the way the company currently operates."

Webber Manufacturing Company, Inc. (Case 2–7), concerns a firm that manufactures and markets environmental test chambers for industrial product testing and evaluation. The company's two managers differ in their view of its future prospects and the strategy to follow. The case analysis focuses upon these issues.

The final case in Part 2, Rogers, Nagel, Langhart (RNL PC), Architects and Planners (Case 2–8), describes business and marketing strategy in a professional services organization. The firm's challenge is to maintain and strengthen its competitive advantage in the market for architectual services. The changing environment requires attention to be given to marketing strategy issues.

Applications

The Kimberly-Clark Corp. application (2–9) describes a diversification strategy and the firm's search for competitive advantage. Daimler-Benz AG (2–10) examines the issues and risks involved in moving beyond the core automobile business. Fisher-Price Toys (2–11) describes a brand extension strategy designed to capitalize on the firm's established position in the toy market. Campbell Soup Company (2–12) is an interesting example of managing a portfolio of products and markets. Pier 1 Imports (2–13) provides a look at a rapid-growth specialty retailer's strategy and corporate culture.

CASE 2–1

Rockingham Memorial Hospital

Rockingham Memorial Hospital has made patient care its primary objective. Through practical application of this philosophy, the Physical Therapy Department has provided education, treatment, and rehabilitation of patients. To fulfill this goal more effectively, the department is considering expansion into a sports medicine program. This particular service would

---

This case was prepared by Valerie Pandak, Research Associate, and Thomas Bertsch, Professor of Marketing at James Madison University.

provide education, treatment, and rehabilitation for injuries resulting from sports and fitness-related activities.

Research measures have been started, to check into the feasibility of starting a full department for sports medicine. The supervisor of the Physical Therapy Department, the hospital President, and the Vice President of Operations and Planning contacted various individuals to determine interest in such a program and facility. The hospital's organizational structure is illustrated in Exhibit 1.

In-depth discussions with the local county school superintendents, coaches, and athletic directors revealed a sincere interest in this type of program. The hospital administrators also attended conferences concerning the development of sports medicine clinics. In addition, they visited a few successful sports medicine clinics to discuss issues involved in the formation of such a facility.

A portion of Rockingham Memorial Hospital's service area was selected to survey. The total service area includes seven counties plus three cities.

EXHIBIT 1
Organizational Structure

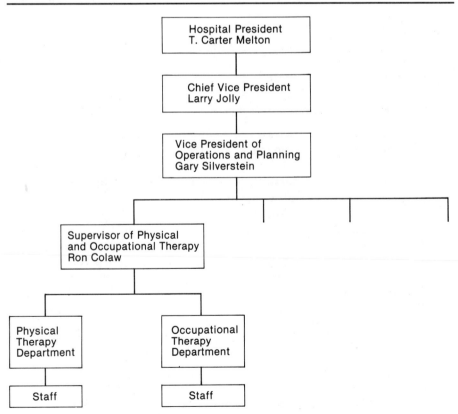

However, the City of Harrisonburg plus Rockingham County were selected because they seemed to be the best serviced areas. Within the survey area are five high schools, five junior high schools, three colleges, and two recreation departments.

Information regarding the possibility of a sports medicine clinic was presented initially to the superintendents of schools, then to the coaching staffs. During this informational process, data was obtained from the schools concerning their knowledge and need for sports medicine. Since the early reactions were favorable and more information was requested, meetings were conducted with various principals and athletic directors. As a result of the positive feedback, interviews were also conducted with coaching staffs and trainers. The schools were able to identify seven areas considered important enough to include in the educational services of such a facility:

1. Preseason screenings and evaluations to include flexibility and strength, and functional tests to augment the routine physicals by physicians.
2. Assistance with conditioning programs.
3. Equipment evaluations, plus assistance in purchasing new equipment.
4. Student trainer programs.
5. Assistance with specific rehabilitations, plus guidelines to follow for sports injuries.
6. Seminars on immediate care of injuries, first aid, and safety considerations.
7. Specific testing plus assistance with criteria for returning to play.

The results of the research revealed frustrations encountered by coaches regarding prevention, care, and treatment of their athletes. Each school has some form of conditioning or rehabilitating equipment, but many of the facilities were neither well equipped nor properly monitored. All in all, the coaches involved in the survey were extremely enthusiastic, as well as supportive of a sports medicine facility opening in the area.

Other information provided by the survey is shown in Exhibit 2. The 10 percent market share excludes minor injuries, which would not require a physician's care and ultimately would not require the care given in a sports medicine rehabilitation program. The data seemed to indicate a significant population size for the types of services being considered.

The Sports Medicine Center would provide educational services in addition to actual treatment. The educational programs include: ongoing educational opportunities for health professionals involved with sports medicine, seminars for scholastic coaches plus trainer visits to sports events; community education regarding aspects of injury prevention relating to sports; and the ongoing education of injured athletes, during their progression through rehabilitation. The center's staff members serve as consultants regarding conditioning programs and equipment purchases by schools.

EXHIBIT 2
Local Population Statistics

Schools*	Number of Athletes	Estimated 30% Injury Rate	10% Market Share of Injuries
Harrisonburg High School and Thomas Harrison Junior High	408	122.4	12.2
Broadway High School and J. C. Myers Junior High	300	90.0	9.0
Spotswood High School and Montevideo/Elkton Junior High	342	102.6	10.2
Turner Ashby High School and John Wayland Junior High	320	96.0	9.6
Eastern Mennonite High School	240	72.0	7.2
Bridgewater College	200	60.0	6.0
Eastern Mennonite College	185	55.5	5.5
Totals	1,995	598.5	59.7

Service Area	Total Population	30% of Recreation Athletes	15% of Estimated Injuries	10% Market Share of Injuries
Rockingham County	54,000	16,200	2,430.0	243.0
Harrisonburg	25,700	7,710	1,156.5	115.65
Surrounding area	44,300	13,290	1,993.5	199.35
Totals	124,000	37,200	5,580.0	558.0

Organized Recreational Populations

Rockingham County	5,844
Harrisonburg	1,612
Totals	7,456

* The populations of students and athletes from the area's university are not included due to the already existing athletic training program there.

The actual treatment of the patient at the sports medicine center can be broken down into five areas: evaluations; acute treatment of injury; subacute/chronic treatment; rehabilitation postsurgery; and testing capabilities. Within each of these areas, the services to the patient will depend on the type and extent of injury.

To provide the forementioned services, a variety of equipment would be required. A list of the equipment and prices is provided in Exhibit 3. However, the list does not include the costs of renovating the facility area needed to provide an adequate setting for the program. These projected renovation costs are listed in Exhibit 4.

EXHIBIT 3
Projected Equipment Expenses

Equipment Item	Price
Computer—software	$ 250
Computer—IBM PC	4,000
Ortho Tron II	8,495
Filtron	1,095
UBE	1,995
Eagle Equipment	
Chest press	2,345
Shoulder press	2,195
Lateral pulldown	1,945
Leg extension	2,395
Leg curl	2,295
Multi-hip	2,295
Leg press	4,295
Ice machine	3,000
Whirlpool—large 46 × 24 × 25	1,800
Whirlpool—small 25 × 13 × 15	1,575
Whirlpool table 47 × 43	295
Ultrasound/electrical stimulation (2 machines)	6,290
Hot packs	945
Hot pack rack	215
Treatment tables 3 @ $376 each	1,128
Small treatment table	286
Wall pulleys	615
Cryotemp	1,000
Multi-ankle-exerciser	500
Hand weights	
Dumbell—weights & rack	400
Velcro—wrist and ankle with rack	335
Rowing machine	2,000
Universal Exercise Equipment	8,000
Treadmill	11,000
Television, VCR and VCR camera	2,000
Shoe insert fabrication machine	*
Miscellaneous items	3,016
Total	$78,000

* No estimate available.

The initiation of the sports medicine program would necessitate hiring the following staff:

1. Physical therapist experienced in the treatment of athletic injuries.
2. Athletic trainer with experience as well as current knowledge of sports-related injuries.
3. Attendant to assist both the therapist and the trainer.

EXHIBIT 4
Renovation Expenses

Expense Item	Projected Amount
Baseboard	$ 153
Floor covering 24 × 82	3,500
Floor covering 24 × 18	589
Ceiling and labor	2,700
Wall and door	2,000
Light fixture and labor	750
Ceiling fixture	2,000
Desk work area	400
Wall covering	700
Cubical curtain	400
Curtain rods	400
Heating connectors, other fixed equipment, and miscellaneous costs	46,408
Total	$60,000

The evaluation and development of specific therapeutic programs by the physical therapist coupled with the taping, screening, and prevention program skills of the athletic trainer would provide a well-rounded program of care and rehabilitation. The salary expenditures are listed in Exhibit 5.

For the Sports Medicine Center to be successful, it would have to be highly visible in the early stages of development. In order to educate poten-

EXHIBIT 5
Salary Expenses

Next year	One full-time licensed physical therapist for ½ year: $10,800
	One full-time athletic trainer for ½ year: $8,850
Following year	Licensed physical therapist: $21,800
	Athletic trainer: $17,700
Yearly	Licensed physical therapist: $21,800
	Athletic trainer: $17,700
	Physical therapist/athletic trainer: $20,000
	Part-time secretary/aide: $7,300

Notes: Salary expenses include 8 percent pay increases each year on January 1.

Employee benefits are projected at 26 percent of total salary cost. This forecast assumes that when employees are on vacation, it will be necessary to provide additional coverage.

Training and travel expenses are projected to increase 5 percent annually.

Utilities, housekeeping, and maintenance are budgeted at the Hospital's cost of $17.84 per square foot. The sports medicine program area will require approximately 2,400 square feet. These costs will increase at 5 percent per year.

Medical supplies are projected at $1,000 for the first full year.

Depreciation is projected with a 10-year life on equipment.

tial users, the staff members would visit schools in the area on a frequent basis to further promote awareness of the program. During these visits, the staff would establish the groundwork for a good relationship with the coaches and athletes of these schools. Programs for the general public would include speeches to area Boosters' Clubs, community organizations, and recreational groups. A list of recreational organizations is provided in Exhibit 6. Participants of the recreational organizations would be sent a promotional brochure along with an invitation to visit the sports medicine facility shortly after its completion. Physicians of all specialities and medically related staff would also be sent a brochure and invited to an open house. Other individuals that would be invited to visit the facilities on different occasions would include: Hospital Auxiliary members, church leagues, high school boosters, county and city school boards, athletic coaches, and school principals.

The local news media would be invited during the initial week of service to encourage publicity coverage. Advertisements would be placed in the local newspapers in addition to school publications. Later, radio ads would be used to promote special events involving the Sports Medicine Center. T-shirts would be given to patients on their initial visit to the Center.

The program's success would rely heavily on its visibility with physicians. Each patient would have to have a physician's referral, before he or she could receive treatment at the clinic.

The projected market share figures for the first seven years of operation are listed in Exhibit 7. In Exhibit 8, a projected income statement for these initial seven years of the Sports Medicine Center of Rockingham is illustrated. The figures in Exhibits 7 and 8 have been projected by Rockingham Memorial Hospital's finance department. However, the figures would require a revision each year as more experience was gained with the program.

EXHIBIT 6
Recreational Organizations

Valley Wellness Center—over 2,100 members
2 golf courses
3 dance studios
Track/running club
Bicycle club
Bowling alley
Tennis leagues
2 fitness centers
2 baseball leagues
Swim team
Competitive ski team
Summer sports camps at 2 colleges
Roller skating club
Bowhunters club

EXHIBIT 7 Market Share Analysis

Market Features	Program Year						
	1	2	3	4	5	6	7
Recreational athletes							
Population of area served	124,000	124,000	124,000	124,000	124,000	124,000	124,000
Percentage of recreational athletes	30%	30%	30%	30%	30%	30%	30%
Estimated recreational athletes	37,200	37,200	37,200	37,200	37,200	37,200	37,200
Injury rate	15%	15%	15%	15%	15%	15%	15%
Annual estimated injured recreational athletes	5,580	5,580	5,580	5,580	5,580	5,580	5,580
Estimated market share (percent)	10%	15%	25%	30%	30%	30%	30%
Recreational athletes participating in sports medicine program	558	837	1,395	1,674	1,674	1,674	1,674
Visits/Athlete	7	7	7	7	7	7	7
Total recreational athlete visits	3,906	5,859	9,765	11,718	11,718	11,718	11,718
Scholastic athletes							
Estimated scholastic athletes	1,995	1,995	1,995	1,995	1,995	1,995	1,995
Injury rate	30%	30%	30%	30%	30%	30%	30%
Annual estimated injured scholastic athletes (total recreational athlete visits)	599	599	599	599	599	599	599
Estimated market share (percent)	10%	15%	25%	30%	30%	30%	30%
Scholastic athletes participating in sports medicine program	60	90	150	180	180	180	180
Visits/Athlete	7	7	7	7	7	7	7
Total scholastic athlete visits	420	630	1,050	1,260	1,260	1,260	1,260
Total scholastic and recreational athlete visits	4,326	6,489	10,815	12,978	12,978	12,978	12,978

EXHIBIT 8 Projected Income Statement

Financial Issues	1*	2	3	4	5	6	7	Total of Years 1–7
Revenue								
Price per visit	$ 30.00	$ 31.50	$ 33.08	$ 34.73	$ 36.47	$ 38.29	$ 40.20	$ 244.27
Number of visits	2,163	6,489	10,815	12,978	12,978	12,978	12,978	71,379
Total revenue (price × visits)	$64,890	$204,404	$357,760	$450,726	$473,308	$496,928	$521,716	$2,569,732
Bad debts	$ 3,245	$ 10,220	$ 17,888	$ 22,536	$ 23,665	$ 24,846	$ 26,086	$ 128,486
Net revenue	$61,645	$194,184	$339,872	$428,190	$449,643	$472,002	$495,630	$2,441,166
Expenses								
Salaries	$19,750	$ 39,500	$ 69,960	$ 75,557	$ 81,602	$ 88,130	$ 95,180	$ 469,679
Employee benefits	5,135	10,270	18,190	19,645	21,217	22,914	24,747	122,118
Training and travel	1,600	1,600	1,764	1,852	1,945	2,042	2,144	12,947
Marketing	7,000	1,000	1,000	1,000	1,000	1,000	1,000	13,000
Utilities, housekeeping, and maintenance	21,408	44,058	47,205	49,565	52,043	54,645	57,377	326,301
Medical supplies	500	1,000	1,050	1,103	1,158	1,216	1,277	7,304
Miscellaneous expenses	1,000	1,000	1,000	1,000	1,000	1,000	1,000	7,000
Depreciation—equipment and renovation	5,650	12,300	13,600	13,600	13,600	13,600	13,600	85,950
Total expenses	$62,043	$110,808	$153,769	$163,322	$173,565	$184,547	$196,325	$1,044,379
Net income	($398)	$ 83,376	$186,103	$264,868	$276,078	$287,535	$299,305	$1,396,867
Discounted annual cash flows								
Cash inflows present value @ 10%	($377)	$ 71,538	$144,506	$186,212	$175,667	$165,640	$156,106	$ 899,292
Less start-up cash outflow								
Equipment								(78,000)
Renovation								(60,000)
Total cash outflow								(138,000)
Net present value								761,292
Break-even charge	14.35	15.07	15.82	16.61	17.44	18.31	19.23	
Break-even volume	1,035	3,104	5,173	6,208	6,208	6,208	6,208	

Program Year

* The first-year data is for only six months.

CASE 2–2

World View Travel Agency, Inc.

In January 1983 the president and the general manager of World View Travel Agency, Inc., were discussing the possible need for new strategies to meet increased competition and the effects of deregulation of the industry, and to take advantage of a market they both regarded as unsaturated.

HISTORY OF THE COMPANY

World View Travel was located in a southwestern city of 150,000 people and was owned by Rene Townsend and her husband, Bob. Although Bob was a full partner, he continued to work full-time in his career as a pathologist and did not participate in the active management of the company. Rene served as president and shared management responsibilities with Sylvia Franklin, the general manager.

After 10 years of operation, World View had become the largest travel agency in town, with $5 million in gross billings and 16 employees. Prior to establishing World View, Rene had worked two years for a competitive travel agency. At that time there were only two travel agencies in town, each with eight or nine employees. By 1983, the competition had grown to 11 agencies, including an in-house firm within a large electronics company that served as the area's largest employer.

The growth of World View had been fairly consistent, and some in the industry regarded it as extraordinary. In the first year of operation, World View recorded over $1 million in billings. Growth occurred each subsequent year, despite two recessions in the 10 years. However, the percentage of growth in recession years was less than in years when the economy was stronger. The years 1981 and 1982 had proven to be ones in which little growth had occurred. The corresponding U.S. recession had undoubtedly been a major contributing factor to the leveling in sales, but Rene and Sylvia were concerned that the plateau might also signal a need for new marketing strategies.

CITY LOCATION

The southwestern city in which World View was located consisted of approximately 150,000 residents, with approximately 30 percent classified as mi-

---

This case was prepared by James C. Makens, The Babcock Graduate School of Business, Wake Forest University, Winston-Salem, North Carolina, as a basis for class discussion. Reprinted by permission.

nority. The largest part of the minority population was Mexican American; blacks represented approximately one-fourth of the minority group.

The city was heavily middle class, and although there were lower-income areas, there were surprisingly few areas that could be regarded as slums. This was due to a combination of the city's good industrial base and good public administration, and its residents' civic pride. There were four major employers in the area and many smaller ones. The city was corporate headquarters for one company listed on the New York Stock Exchange and one listed on the American Exchange. (These were involved in electronics and pharmaceuticals.)

The predominant industries in the city were banking-finance, insurance, pharmaceuticals, and electronics. The city also boasted a large medical complex that attracted many patients from outside the area, and two universities.

The city was located on a major interstate highway and was served by three major airlines and two commuters. Two national hotel chains operated downtown properties, and several chains operated motels along the interstate highway. Three or four of the restaurants in town could be regarded as good, but none were known for consistent excellence in service or food. There were many fast-food establishments offering the normal mix of hamburgers, pizza, and chicken. The city had an attractive shopping mall and a small convention center that was to be markedly improved in size and quality within the next four years. It was felt that the addition of a new convention center would enable the city to attract visitors from a wider area and would also attract new visitor services. A major hotel had expressed interest in entering the city.

The mayor had recently called for the formation of a blue-ribbon council to study tourism. This council included representatives from several segments of the city with a good mixture of industrial and cultural interests. The city had grown as a commercial crossroads rather than as a result of nearby natural attractions such as seashore or mountains. Nevertheless, there was a strong consensus that the number of travelers to the city could be increased through a combination of attractive facilities and events.

The recession currently affecting the nation had created a national unemployment rate of over 10 percent. This city had witnessed a 5.5 percent rate of unemployment. Although the city was not considered a "boom city," it had enjoyed growth during the past 10 years and was located in a region of the nation that was generally regarded as a growth area.

COMPETITION

Eleven travel agencies existed in the city. One of these was an in-house agency for the largest employer in town. Consequently, very little direct business was generated by this company for any of the 10 independent agencies. Among these, one had originally intended to specialize in group travel but had soon become a full-service agency and did not specialize in groups to any greater degree than the others. All the agencies offered a mixture of services and were not particularly distinguishable in terms of product offering or market segments served.

The two agencies that had been the only competitors in the city when World View began operation continued to serve as strong competitors, even though they were now smaller than World View. Both firms had suffered the death of their owners, had undergone considerable turnover in personnel, and seemed to be currently lacking in direction.

The largest increase in numbers of travel agencies had occurred three or four years earlier, and there currently seemed to be relative stability in the industry. There were no rumors of new firms opening in the city or of major expansion by competitors, but this was subject to change at any time.

A major effect of the increased competition had been a heightened public awareness of the benefits of using a travel agency. One of the major airlines serving the area reported that the volume of tickets that came from travel agencies had risen from 40 percent in 1975 to nearly 80 percent in 1982. Despite an increase in awareness on the part of the traveling public, there were still many individuals and smaller companies who did not consistently use the services of a travel agent. There were also many clients who were unfamiliar with the multiple service offerings of a travel agency. Rene and Sylvia mentioned that clients sometimes expressed surprise upon learning that World View could make hotel and auto rental reservations.

DESCRIPTION OF WORLD VIEW TRAVEL

After establishing World View Travel, Rene personally called on companies in the area and asked for their travel business. This approach proved to be so successful that after only three years of operation, her agency was as large as that of any competitor. Most of the calls were made to individuals Rene or her husband knew through prior business or social settings. Rene admitted to having a distaste for making "cold calls" to organizations and firms unknown to her; she preferred to call persons with whom a prior contact of some kind had been established. In several cases these were referrals by friends or satisfied clients. Time after time she was told by prospective clients that this was the first time the owner or manager of a travel agency had ever asked them for their business.

Location

The location of World View was not conducive to walk-in traffic nor to good visual exposure. World View leased space in a new office building located on a side street in a light industrial park. The street was not a thoroughfare and ended in a cul-de-sac. A sign in front identified World View Travel but was neither larger than nor particularly distinct from the signs of neighboring businesses. There was little reason for anyone to visit the building unless they had specifically come to see someone at World View or one of the neighboring tenants.

Client Mix

The mix of billings in 1982 for World View was approximately 56 percent commercial and 44 percent group and individual. Of the commercial accounts, six clients had billings of $500,000 or more. These were the larger companies in town. World View did most of the travel business for the second largest employer in town. However, Rene said that this business was not evenly distributed among all departments within the company. She was certain there were two or three major departments within the client company that did not deal with World View.

The rest of the commercial business came from a mixture of small and medium-sized companies. Rene and Sylvia emphasized that they had purposely tried to obtain a large mix of commercial clients. Rene stated that she felt it was likely that on a time-per-client basis, the firm's sales productivity and earnings were less for small clients than for large ones. She felt that from the standpoint of the bottom line, her agency would probably be better off with fewer of the smaller commercial clients and more of the larger ones. For instance, she said, "We probably could get every bit of the business of the second largest employer in town. However, that frightens us, since we would then have too many of our eggs in one basket. At this point, we feel we're better off with a larger number of corporate clients even if some are relatively unproductive."

An analysis of revenues for 1982 indicated that 40 percent resulted from corporate business, 45 percent came from personal and vacation billings, and 15 percent were listed as group. When corporate travel was excluded and group was compared only to personal and vacation revenue, the ratio was 1 to 4 in favor of personal and vacation travel. Revenue comparisons between international and domestic billings revealed that revenue from all international billings contributed 15 percent, whereas domestic contributed 85 percent. This occurred despite the fact that commissions from international billings averaged 9.8 percent as opposed to 8.8 percent from domestic ones.

Nearly all the services performed by World View in 1982 could be considered "outbound." A small percentage consisted of making local reservations for corporate clients and helping with inbound events such as sales meetings and seminars in which corporate clients brought visitors to the local area.

In reviewing the current customer and product mix, Rene commented that she felt commercial business would be significantly more important in the future. The failure of other agencies to gain reputations as strong corporate service firms meant that World View could strengthen its relationship with the area's major employers, resulting in more travel billings. Rene also expressed interest in moving toward the meeting and convention-planning business on both an inbound and outbound basis. She believed that corporate clients were receptive to professional outside assistance in this area and that in the future, professional fees could be charged for this service. If a decision was made to expand in this area, changes or additions to the number of sales personnel would be needed.

Personnel

World View employed 15 full-time female employees and one part-time employee who worked half-days. Of these, five were involved in non-sales functions, including one bookkeeper, Rene, Sylvia, one person to double-check fares and do general office work, and one errand runner. This left 11 employees with direct sales responsibilities. Of these, four were assigned to corporate sales, one to group sales, and six to "front office" sales. The six known as front-office sales personnel handled a mix of group and personal-vacation and business travel. The percentage mix of group and personal travel varied among the six saleswomen and depended upon a variety of factors, including their experience, interests, and contacts. For example, one of these with 20 years' experience in travel demonstrated a strong interest in group sales (see Exhibit 1). She was not afraid to follow up leads and to

EXHIBIT 1
World View Travel: December 1982 Sales Records

	Years Experience as Travel Agent	Billings
Corporate Sales		
Melanie Lamb	10	$69,000
Virginia Fare	5	60,000
Carol Gifford	1.5	55,000
Nancy Senate	*	
Personal and Group Sales		
Arlene Felton	20	$61,000
Janice Grant	5	38,000
Marian Terple	4	44,000
Gloria Barrett	*	
Glenda Riggins	NA	
Kristine Fraser	†	
Amy Clarke	†	

* These members of the sales force have less than six months' experience.
† On maternity leave.
NA = Not available.

aggressively seek this business. Rene and Sylvia had been considering asking her to specialize in group sales. Others seemed far more comfortable with personal travel. None of the sales force spent much time out of the office. None had an expense account, and unless they specifically requested to entertain a client for lunch, all business entertainment was conducted by Rene.

The educational backgrounds of the corporate and personal saleswomen were quite different. The four in corporate sales did not hold college degrees. The typical educational background of this group was a high school diploma or one year in a junior college or trade school. All but one of the saleswomen who specialized in personal sales held college degrees. The individual without a degree had attended several years of specialized trade school and had a background as assistant manager of a savings and loan institution prior to working for World View.

Rene explained that the difference in backgrounds were the result of the nature of each position. Corporate saleswork tended to be routine and repetitive. It demanded someone who enjoyed working with details and doing clerical tasks, and who was very thorough so that few errors were made and nothing was left to chance. Although personal travel work also required precision, it offered a wider variety of challenges to the salesperson and allowed more creativity than did corporate work.

Different compensation systems existed for those in corporate and personal sales. Those who had responsibility for corporate sales were paid a salary plus an end-of-month bonus. The bonus was determined using a formula that called for a dollar sales productivity four times in excess of gross salary. Once the productivity level had been reached, a salesperson would obtain 20 percent of the excess revenue above the 4X salary. The addition of a support-staff person meant that each corporate salesperson was relieved of certain clerical chores, which left more time for sales. It was felt that the addition of the support-staff person increased sales productivity and that the formula for a bonus should reflect the change. Prior to the change, those in corporate sales were realizing more from their bonus than from their salary.

A corporate salesperson would begin with an annual salary of $9,000 to $10,000 per year. After a period of six months to a year, those in corporate sales realized incomes of from $14,000 to $20,000, including the bonus. The personal (front-office) salesperson also started at $9,000 to $10,000 per year and worked on a salary-plus-bonus basis. The formula used for this group called for sales productivity of three rather than four times gross salary. This was felt to be equitable, as this group received less staff support. The annual income of experienced salespeople in this area ranged from $14,000 to $22,000.

In addition to monetary compensation, all members of the sales force were eligible for "fam" trips throughout the year. ("Fam" or familiarization trips are provided free or at a greatly reduced cost to travel agents by airlines or destination areas as a means of acquainting travel agents with travel services and destinations.) Those in corporate sales generally obtained two short fam trips per year; those in personal sales averaged two to two-and-one-half longer ones per year. The typical fam trip for those in corporate sales was domestic. Individuals in personal sales were more likely to obtain international fam trips.

Fam trips were regarded by Townsend and Franklin as more than nonmonetary motivating tools. They were seen as professionally desirable and necessary for persons who sold travel. After visiting a new destination on a fam trip, the salesperson was expected to make a brief presentation to the rest of the sales force. This individual was also expected to share expertise concerning destination areas with other members of the sales force when the need occurred.

Advertising and Promotion

Advertising was not regarded as an activity that deserved a heavy budget appropriation. Rene confined advertising to the Yellow Pages. Advertisements were purchased in high school annuals and theater programs, but these were regarded as contributions in terms of their effect upon sales. A limited number of baggage tags and flight bags printed with the name of World View were purchased, but these were given only to selected clients. Rene felt that the best advertising a travel agency could acquire was word-of-mouth referrals based on professional service for clients.

A special corporate relations program existed that seemed to have been very successful. It consisted of the following:

1. A $100,000 automatic free flight-insurance policy for corporate clients who flew on tickets issued by World View.
2. A corporate-rate hotel program in which a handbook of nearly 350 pages, containing names of hotels and the best corporate rates available, was given to all corporate clients.
3. An emergency 800 number that could be used in case of a travel problem anywhere in the United States.
4. A special training seminar for executive secretaries to acquaint them with the basics of business travel. This seminar was conducted at the offices of World View and had been popular with executive secretaries.
5. A regular newsletter that was sent to clients.
6. The addition of a special staffperson to recheck all fares to ensure the lowest cost to the client.
7. A computer-generated statistical capability to assist major clients in analyzing their travel expenditures and trends.

THE FUTURE

The past 10 years had been rewarding ones for World View. Rene and Sylvia were confident that their travel agency was as well equipped to meet future opportunities and challenges as any in town. In assessing the agency's present strengths, Townsend stated there were five factors that she felt would be invaluable in terms of planning future strategies. First, World View was automated beyond the levels of all its competitors. This had begun five years ago when the agency purchased a stand-alone minicomputer to assist in bookkeeping. Since then, Rene had added a computer system available through United Airlines, known as the Apollo system. Rene felt that automation had been the principal factor allowing World View to efficiently serve commercial accounts; it had made this sector of the agency the most profitable. Rene said that the agency was committed to automation and would continue to use new technology as it became available.

The second factor was the strength of the sales force. Sylvia emphasized that World View's sales force was the most committed of any agency she had seen. Turnover was comparatively low, and there was a good *esprit de corps* among the employees.

The third factor was that the agency had developed a good reputation in the community. This was particularly important in the case of corporate clients, who seemed to regard World View as the most professional agency in town.

The company's good financial condition was the fourth factor. Rene pointed out that bankers had told her they would be happy to consider loan requests from World View at any time.

The management team of Rene and Sylvia was the final factor. It had worked well. "If a buyer ever took us over, the new owner would probably ask one of us to leave to cut administrative costs," Rene said. "We understand that working as a team we increase administrative costs, but there is a terrific symbiotic relationship here that works well and just can't be measured in dollars and cents. We honestly feel we are one of the few agencies in town giving much thought to future strategies. Most seem to think in terms of the short run only."

Despite their optimism, Rene and Sylvia admitted that there were outside variables that had to be considered which could dramatically affect the entire travel agency industry. A worsening in the U.S. and world economy would certainly affect the travel market. Only a week earlier, *The Wall Street Journal* had carried a front-page article describing the fears of many that a worldwide depression was going to occur in 1983 or 1984. Although it appeared that the bottom of the recessionary trough had been reached and that recovery was at hand, there were simple economic warnings to feed a pessimistic appraisal of the future.

Another consideration was a possible change in travel habits within the corporate and personal travel sectors. Articles had been written describing a future reduction in business travel as a result of advances in communications technology. Holiday Inns had installed satellite disks at several of their properties and were encouraging corporations to hold meetings on a regional level with satellite communication hookups between several Holiday Inns. This would permit corporations to hold national meetings without the expense of flying large numbers of personnel to a central meeting site. New telephone companies were offering discount rates and improved technologies to businesses and individuals. It was impossible to predict what the effect of a communications breakthrough such as Phonavision might have upon the travel industry.

During the recession year of 1982, many international vacation destinations had reported a poor year. At the same time, many states had reported an excellent year for tourism. This seemed to be particularly true for resort areas that could be reached within a few hours. Gasoline prices had actually dropped, and employed Americans could seriously plan for summer vacation trips. Airlines and buses were aware of this change and were fighting for market share in a depressed economy. Greyhound offered a transcontinental fare for $99 from coast to coast. Airlines were also offering discounted fares between major markets such as New York and Los Angeles or New York and Miami. Rates as low as $69 between New York and Miami were being advertised. Virtually all air carriers other than commuters were offering some form of discount fare. It was almost impossible for the average traveler to keep track of these offerings or in many cases to clearly understand them. Manufacturers such as Kodak, Polaroid, and Chevrolet had offered travel discounts on certain airlines to the public as incentives for purchasing their products. Airlines were offering travel clubs in which discounts or free flights could be obtained after flying a specified number of miles on a particular carrier.

One of the outside variables presenting the greatest uncertainty to travel agents was the continuing effect of deregulation in air transportation. The movement toward less government regulation had begun during President Carter's administration and had continued under President Reagan. The purpose of deregulation had been to encourage greater competition within the travel industry and reduce the importance of the federal government in the establishment of air fares, selection of routes, arbitration of disputes, and other areas that affected the structure and conduct of the air transportation industry. One of the eventual aims of deregulation was to disband the Civil Aeronautics Board (CAB).

The effects of deregulation had been dramatically attested to in 1982 by the bankruptcy of Braniff International Airlines. This was followed by the bankruptcy of Altair, a small East Coast airline. At the same time new airlines, such as People Express and Muse Air, had sprung up. These and others entered by serving a specific market and offering discount fares.

Deregulation had affected travel agents by increasing the complexity of the numbers of fares available from airlines. The effect had also been quite evident surrounding the bankruptcy of Braniff. Now a new aspect of deregulation looked as though it could present travel agents with a direct challenge to traditional methods of doing business. A ruling known as the Maximum Tariff Rule, issued by the CAB in October 1981, had still not greatly affected travel agents, but it and successive CAB rulings created the potential for drastic change.

Prior to October 1981, all domestic airlines were required to file each of their fares with the CAB. After filing, neither the airline nor travel agents were permitted to sell tickets at prices above or below these prices. Under the new rule, carriers were required only to file their standard coach fare in any market as the maximum fare to be charged. Airlines were not required to file discount fares or other special prices. This essentially meant that airlines and agents could cut prices. It was felt that this would lead to large discounts for large organizations such as corporations.

Despite the ruling, generally there was not a great deal of price cutting or shared commissions by travel agents with large corporate clients. This was partially forestalled by the fact that the major airlines continued to file all their fares with the CAB. The airlines also advised travel agents not to engage in price cutting for preferred customers.

Nevertheless, a few travel agents in the United States, including one in Indianapolis, did cut prices. TWA and American Airlines responded by removing ticketing validation plates from that travel agency. In spite of the fact that widespread discounting or commission sharing by travel agents had not occurred, the possibility now existed and could not be discounted for the future. The ruling had also opened the door for airlines to bypass travel agents and offer discount prices to large groups such as conventions and corporations.

The Maximum Tariff Rule was not the only legal change emanating from Washington. Changes in two other rules were also under serious consideration by the CAB. These were known as the Exclusivity Rule and the 20 Percent Rule. The Exclusivity Rule stated that only appointed travel agents were eligible to receive commissions from the carriers for the sale of air transportation. In January 1983, the entire U.S. travel agent industry was concerned with the end of the Exclusivity Rule. Various scenarios for the future were being predicted, including supermarket chains and department stores directly selling airline tickets at discount prices.

The 20 Percent Rule stated that a travel agency owned by a larger corporation could not do more than 20 percent of its total air ticketing volume for the needs of the parent corporation without becoming ineligible for commissions. Otherwise, airlines would consider the agency an in-house travel department and not an independent travel agency.

It seemed apparent that changes in the rules governing the methods of operation of travel agencies and in the competitive environment would be forthcoming. The effects of these changes on travel agencies and on World View in particular were not apparent.

In spite of changes that might occur, Rene and Sylvia spoke very encouragingly of the future. Both felt that the most difficult years were behind them and that the future offered excellent opportunities for growth. Rene summarized her feelings by saying, "World View may look quite different 10 or even 5 years from now, but we intend to remain the leading travel agency in this area. In fact, there is no reason we have to confine our plans to this area. We proved we were capable of success in this market, and there is no reason we can't think in far broader terms. We have the organization, the know-how, and the desire to grow. It's just a matter of setting our objectives, deciding upon a strategy, and getting on with the task."

CASE 2–3

MacTec Control AB

Georg Carlsson is president of MacTec Control AB, a Swedish firm located in Kristianstad. Georg began MacTec in 1980 with his wife, Jessie. MacTec grew rapidly and now boasts of 30 employees and annual revenues of about $2.8 million. Since 1985, MacTec has been partly owned by the Perstorp Corporation whose headquarters are located nearby. Perstorp is a large manufacturer of chemicals and chemical products, with operations in 18 countries and annual revenues of about $600 million. Perstorp has provided MacTec with capital and managerial advice, as well as chemical analysis technology.

MACTEC's AQUALEX SYSTEM

MacTec's product line centers around its Aqualex system: computer hardware and software designed to monitor and control pressurized water flow. The water flow consists mostly of potable water or sewage effluent as these liquids are stored, moved, or treated by municipal water departments.

The system employs MacTec's MPDII microcomputer (see Exhibit 1) installed at individual pumping stations where liquids are stored and moved. Often these stations are located quite far apart, linking geographically dispersed water users (households, businesses, etc.) to water and sewer systems. The microcomputer performs a number of important functions. It

---

This case was written by Professor James E. Nelson, University of Colorado. © 1989 by the Business Research Division, College of Business and Administration and the Graduate School of Business Administration, University of Colorado, Boulder, Colorado, 80309-0419.

EXHIBIT 1

The Aqualex System is based on the MPDII which controls and monitors the pumping stations

An MPDII microcomputer is installed at a pumping station and works as an independent, intelligent computer. When required, it can go online with the central computer and report its readings there.

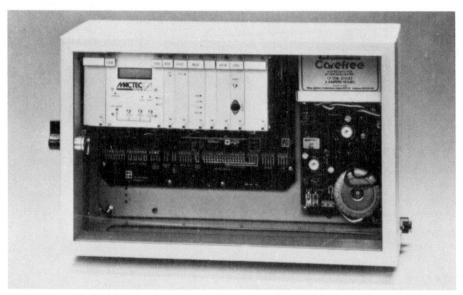

Here are some of the functions of the MPDII:

— It governs the starts, stops, and alarms of up to four pumps, controlled by an integrated piezo-resistive pressure-level sensor.

— It checks the sump level.

— It checks pump capacity and changes in pump capacity.

— It activates an alarm when readings reach preset deviation limits.

— It registers precipitation and activates an alarm in case of heavy rain.

— It constantly monitors pump power consumption and activates an alarm in case of unacceptable deviation.

— It registers current pump flow by means of advanced calculations of inflow and outfeed from the sump.

— It can register accumulated time for overflow.

— It switches to forward or reverse action, even by remote command.

— It stores locally the last nine alarm instances with time indications. These may be read directly on an LCD display.

— It can be remotely programmed from the central computer.

An MPDII does a great job, day after day, year after year.

controls the starts, stops, and alarms of up to four pumps, monitors levels and available capacities of storage reservoirs, checks pump capacities and power consumptions, and records pump flows. It even measures the amount of rainfall entering reservoirs and adjusts pump operations or activates an alarm as needed. Each microcomputer can also easily be connected to a main computer to allow remote control of pumping stations and produce a variety of charts and graphs useful in evaluating pump performance and scheduling needed maintenance.

The Aqualex system provides a monitoring function that human operators cannot match in terms of sophistication, immediacy, and cost. The system permits each individual substation to: control its own pumping operations; collect, analyze, and store data; forecast trends; transmit data and alarms to a central computer; and receive remote commands. Alarms can also be transmitted directly to a pocket-size receiver carried by one or more operators on call. A supervisor can continually monitor pumping operations in a large system entirely via a computer terminal at a central location and send commands to individual pumps, thereby saving costly service calls and time. The system also reduces the possibility of overflows that could produce disastrous flooding in nearby communities.

MacTec personnel work with water and sewage engineers to design and install the Aqualex system. Personnel also train engineers and operators to work with the system and are available 24 hours a day for consultation. If needed, a MacTec engineer can personally assist engineers and operators if major problems arise. MacTec also offers its clients the option of purchasing a complete service contract whereby MacTec personnel provide periodic testing and maintenance of installed systems.

An Aqualex system has several versions. In its most basic form, the system is little more than a small "black box" that monitors two or three lift station activities and, when necessary, transmits an alarm to one or more remote receivers. An intermediate system monitors additional activities, sends data to a central computer via telephone lines and receives remote commands. An advanced system provides the same monitoring capabilities but has forecasting features, maintenance management, auxiliary power back-up, and data transmission and reception via radio. Prices for the three different types in early 1989 are $1,200, $2,400, and $4,200.

AQUALEX CUSTOMERS

Aqualex customers can be divided into two groups—governmental units and industrial companies. The typical application in the first group is a sewage treatment plant having 4 to 12 pumping stations, each station containing one or more pumps. Pumps operate intermittently and, unless an Aqualex or similar system is in place, are monitored by one or more operators who visit each station once or twice each day for about half an hour. Operators take reservoir measurements, record running times of pumps, and sometimes perform limited maintenance and repairs. The sewage plant and stations are typically located in flat or rolling terrain, where gravity cannot be used in lieu of pumping. If any monitoring equipment is present at all, it typically consists of a crude, on-site alarm that activates when fluid levels rise or fall beyond a preset level. Sometimes the alarm activates a telephone dialing function that alerts an operator away from the station.

Numerous industrial companies also store, move, and process large quantities of water or sewage. These applications usually differ very little from those in governmental plants except for their smaller size. On the other hand, there are considerably more industrial companies with pumping stations and so, Georg thinks, the two markets often offer close to identical market potentials in many countries.

The two markets desire essentially the same products, although industrial applications often use smaller, simpler equipment. Both markets want their monitoring equipment to be accurate and reliable, the two dominant concerns. Equipment should also be easy to use, economical to operate, and require little regular service or maintenance. Purchase price often is not a major consideration. As long as the price is in an appropriate range, customers seem more interested in actual product performance than in initial cost outlays.

Georg thinks worldwide demand for Aqualex systems and competing products will continue to be strong for at least the next 10 years. While some of this demand represents construction of new pumping stations, many applications are replacements of crude monitoring and alarm systems at existing sites. These existing systems depend greatly on regular visits by operators, visits that often continue even after new equipment is installed. Most such trips are probably not necessary. However, many managers find it difficult to dismiss or reassign monitoring personnel that are no longer needed; many are also quite cautious and conservative, desiring some human monitoring of the new equipment "just in case." Once replacement of existing systems is complete, market growth is limited to new construction and, of course, replacements with more sophisticated systems.

Most customers (and noncustomers) consider the Aqualex system the best on the market. Those knowledgeable in the industry feel that competing products seldom match Aqualex's reliability and accuracy. Experts also believe that many competing products lack the sophistication and flexibility present in Aqualex's design. Beyond these product features, customers also appreciate MacTec's knowledge about water and sanitation engineering. Competing firms often lack this expertise, offering products somewhat as a sideline and considering the market too small for an intensive marketing effort.

The market is clearly not too small for MacTec. While Georg has no hard data on market potential for Western Europe, he thinks annual demand could be as much as $9 million. About 40 percent of this figure represents potential, the rest is demand for replacing existing systems. Industry sales in the latter category could be increased by more aggressive marketing efforts on the part of MacTec and its competitors. Eastern European economies represent additional potential. However, the water and sewer industries in these countries seem less interested in high-technology equipment to monitor pumping operations than do their Western counterparts. Additionally, business is often more difficult to conduct in these countries. In contrast, the U.S. market looks very attractive.

MACTEC STRATEGY

MacTec currently markets its Aqualex system primarily to sewage treatment plants in Scandinavia and other countries in northern and central Europe. The company's strategy could be described as providing technologically superior equipment to monitor pumping operations at these plants. The strategy stresses frequent contacts with customers and potential customers to design, supply, and service Aqualex systems. Superior knowledge of water and sanitation engineering with up-to-date electronics and computer technology is also important. The result is a line of highly specialized sensors, computers, and methods for process controls in water treatment plants.

The essence of MacTec's strategy is demonstrating a special competence that no firm in the world can easily match. MacTec also prides itself on being a young, creative company, without an entrenched bureaucracy. Company employees generally work with enthusiasm and dedication; they talk with each other regularly and openly. Most importantly, customers—as well as technology—seem to drive all areas of the company.

MacTec's strategy in its European markets seems fairly well-decided. That is, Georg thinks that a continuation of present strategies and tactics should continue to produce good results. However, one change is the planned creation of a branch office conducting sales and manufacturing activities somewhere in the European Community (EC), most likely the Netherlands. The plan is to have such an office in operation well before 1992, when the 12 countries in the EC (Belgium, Denmark, France, Greece, Ireland, Italy, Luxembourg, the Netherlands, Portugal, Spain, United Kingdom, and West Germany) would mutually eliminate national barriers to the flow of capital, goods, and services. Having a MacTec office located in the EC would greatly simplify sales to these member countries. Moreover, MacTec's presence should also avoid problems with any protective barriers the EC itself might raise to limit or discourage market access by outsiders.

Notwithstanding activities related to this branch office, Georg is considering a major strategic decision to enter the U.S. market. His two recent visits to the United States have led him to conclude that the market represents potential beyond that for western Europe and that the United States seems perfect for expansion. Industry experts in the United States agree with Georg that the Aqualex system outperforms anything used in the U.S. market. Experts think many water and sewage engineers would welcome

MacTec's products and knowledge. Moreover, Georg thinks U.S. transportation systems and payment arrangements would present few problems. The system would be imported under U.S. Tariff Regulation 71249 and pay a duty of 4.9 percent.

Entry would most likely occur in the form of a sales and service office located in Philadelphia. The Pennsylvania and New York state markets seem representative of the United States and appear to offer a good test of the Aqualex system. The two states together probably represent about 18 percent of total U.S. market potential for the system. The office would require an investment of $200,000 for inventory and other balance sheet items. Annual fixed costs would total close to $250,000 for salaries and other operating expenses; Georg plans to employ only a general manager, two sales technicians, and a secretary for at least the first year or two. Each Aqualex system sold in the United States would be priced to provide a contribution of about 30 percent. Georg wants a 35 percent annual return before taxes on any MacTec investment, beginning no later than the second year. The issue is whether Georg can realistically expect to achieve this goal in the United States.

MARKETING RESEARCH

Georg had commissioned the Browning Group in Philadelphia to conduct some limited marketing research with selected personnel in the water and sewage industries in the city and surrounding areas. The research had two purposes: To obtain a sense of market needs and market reactions to MacTec's products, and to calculate a rough estimate of market potential in Pennsylvania and New York. Results were intended to help Georg interpret his earlier conversations with industry experts and perhaps facilitate a decision on market entry.

The research design employed two phases of data collection. The first consisted of five one-hour, tape-recorded interviews with water and sewage engineers employed by local city and municipal governments. Questions included:

1. What procedures do you use to monitor your pumping stations?
2. Is your current monitoring system effective? Costly?
3. What are the costs of a monitoring malfunction?
4. What features would you like to see in a monitoring system?
5. Who decides on the selection of a monitoring system?
6. What is your reaction to the Aqualex system?

Interviewers listened closely to the engineers' responses and probed for additional detail and clarification.

Tapes of the personal interviews were transcribed and then analyzed by the project manager at Browning. The report noted that these results described typical industry practices and viewpoints. A partial summary from the report appears below:

> The picture that emerges is one of fairly sophisticated personnel making decisions about monitoring equipment that is relatively simple in design. Still, some engineers would appear distrustful of this equipment because they persist in sending operators to pumping stations on a daily basis. The distrust may be justified because potential costs of a malfunction were identified as expensive repairs and cleanups, fines of $10,000 per day of violation, lawsuits, harassment by the Health department, and public embarrassment. The five engineers identified themselves as key individuals in the decision to purchase new equipment. Without exception, they considered MacTec features innovative, highly desirable, and worth the price.

The summary also noted that the primary purpose of the interview results was for construction of a questionnaire to be administered by telephone.

The questionnaire was used in the second phase of data collection, as part of a telephone survey that contacted 65 utility managers, water and sewage engineers, and pumping station operators in Philadelphia and surrounding areas. All respondents were employed by governmental units. Each interview took about 10 minutes to complete, covering topics identified in questions 1, 2, and 4 above. The Browning Group's research report stated that most respondents were quite cooperative, although 15 people refused to participate at all.

The telephone interviews produced results that could be considered more representative of the market because of the larger sample size. The report organized these results under the topics of monitoring procedures, system effectiveness and costs, and features desired in a monitoring system:

> All monitoring systems under the responsibility of the 50 respondents were considered to require manual checking. The frequency of operator visits to pumping stations ranged from monthly to twice daily, depending on flow rates, pumping station history, proximity of nearby communities, monitoring equipment in operation, and other factors. Even the most sophisticated automatic systems were checked because respondents "just don't trust the machine." Each operator was responsible for some 10 to 20 stations.
>
> Despite the perceived need for double-checking, all respondents considered their current monitoring system to be quite effective. Not one reported a serious pumping malfunction in the past three years that had escaped detection. However, this reliability came at considerable cost—the annual wages and other expenses associated with each monitoring operator averaged about $40,000.
>
> Respondents were about evenly divided between those wishing a simple alarm system and those desiring a sophisticated, versatile microprocessor. Managers and engineers in the former category often said that the only feature they really needed was an emergency signal such as a siren, horn, or light. Sometimes they would add a telephone dialer that would be automatically activated at the same time as the signal. Most agreed that a price of

around $2,000 would be reasonable for such a system. The latter category of individuals contained engineers desiring many of the Aqualex System's features, once they knew such equipment was available. A price of $4,000 per system seemed acceptable. Some of these respondents were quite knowledgeable about computers and computer programming while others were not. Only four respondents voiced any strong concerns about the cost to purchase and install more sophisticated monitoring equipment. Everyone demanded that the equipment be reliable and accurate.

Georg found the report quite helpful. Much of the information, of course, simply confirmed his own view of the U.S. market. However, it was good to have this knowledge from an independent, objective organization. In addition, to learn that the market consisted of two, apparently equal-size segments—of simple and sophisticated applications—was quite worthwhile. In particular, knowledge of system prices considered acceptable by each segment would make the entry decision easier. Meeting these prices would not be a major problem.

An important section of the report contained an estimate of market potential for Pennsylvania and New York. The estimate was based on an analysis of discharge permits on file in governmental offices in the two states. These permits are required before any city, municipality, water or sewage district, or industrial company can release sewage or other contaminated water to another system or to a lake or river. Each permit showed the number of pumping stations in operation. Based on a 10 percent sample of permits, the report estimated that governmental units in Pennsylvania and New York contain approximately 3,000 and 5,000 pumping stations for waste water, respectively. Industrial companies in the two states were estimated to add 3,000 and 9,000 more pumping stations, respectively. The total number of pumping stations in the two states (20,000) seemed to be growing at about 2 percent per year.

Finally, a brief section of the report dealt with the study's limitations. Georg agreed that sample was quite small, that it contained no utility managers or engineers from New York, and that it probably concentrated too heavily on individuals in larger urban areas. In addition, the research told him nothing about competitors and their marketing strategies and tactics. Nor did he learn anything about any state regulations for monitoring equipment, if indeed any existed. However, these shortcomings came as no surprise, representing a consequence of the research design proposed to Georg by the Browning Group six weeks ago, before the study began.

THE DECISION

Georg's decision seems difficult. The most risky option is to enter the U.S. market as soon as possible; the most conservative is to stay in Europe. The option also exists of conducting additional marketing research.

Discussion with the Browning Group had identified objectives of new research as rectifying limitations of the first study and providing more accurate estimates of market potential. (The estimates of the numbers of pumping stations in Pennsylvania and New York were accurate to around plus or minus 20 percent.) This research was estimated to cost $40,000 and take another three months to complete.

CASE 2–4

Kinder-Care Learning Centers, Inc.

INTRODUCTION

"Good morning, Rob." Rob Hartley looked up from his desk. Perry Mendel, the president and founder of Kinder-Care Learning Centers walked in the office carrying two cups of coffee. "I thought you could use some coffee after last night," Mr. Mendel said. "Congratulations!"

"Thanks," Rob said as he reached for the cup. Mr. Mendel always took time to praise an employee for a job well done. Rob had gotten home late the night before from an out-of-town awards ceremony. At 33, Rob was Kinder-Care's national director of marketing. He had been honored to accept *Sales and Marketing Management's* "1982 Outstanding Achievement Award for Service Marketing" for the new Kindustry program he had developed.

Rob had joined Kinder-Care in April 1981. He remembered sitting in Mr. Mendel's office and hearing the Kinder-Care story. Mr. Mendel had recalled, "Right from the start I expected it to be big, like Holiday Inns. I would not have gone into it unless I thought I would have an opportunity to accomplish the *vastness* of what I dreamed about." Now Mr. Mendel's dream had turned into 723 child-care centers in 36 states and in one Canadian province, as shown in Exhibit 1.

J. Barry Mason and Morris L. Mayer, *Modern Retailing: Theory and Practice,* 3d ed. (Plano, Tex.: Business Publications, 1984), pp. 922–33. This case was prepared by Jim Kerlin.

EXHIBIT 1
Number of Centers in Each State

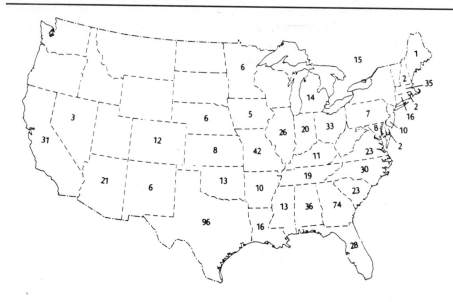

Mr. Mendel sat down with a warm smile on his face. "Rob," he began slowly, "I've asked a few of the board members to set up a meeting with you next week. I really value your judgment. I would like you to put forward your ideas for our marketing program over the next five years." Rob felt buoyant, and then he felt distressed. He sensed what was about to be said.

"We have quite a challenge ahead of us," Mr. Mendel continued. "The demographics may start to turn against us by then. I want us to be in a position to meet that challenge head-on."

After a brief pause, Rob managed to say, "You can count on me, Mr. Mendel." "I have a lot of confidence in you, Rob," Mr. Mendel countered as he stood to leave, "and once again, congratulations!" Rob felt relieved as Mr. Mendel left the office. He leaned back in his swivel chair and took a sip of coffee.

"Donna," Rob called to his secretary, "bring me my marketing development file please." He spun around and peered out the window. It was beautiful outside, and he began to muse about Kinder-Care: how it came so far so fast, what it was now, and where it was going. Donna brought in the file and laid it on his desk. "Thanks, Donna," he said as he opened it.

GROWTH AND FINANCIAL HIGHLIGHTS

The first thing Rob noticed was the importance that demographics had played in the founding of Kinder-Care. After World War II, Perry Mendel had joined his three brothers-in-law in the family auto parts business. Several years later one of the three went into real estate development, building shopping malls and 250 homes a year. Later Perry Mendel switched to the more profitable real estate business with Aaron as it began to prosper from the population migration to the Sun Belt. In studying population demographics as part of his new job, Mendel began to realize that women's liberation, a soaring divorce rate, and economic necessity were sending mothers back into the work force in record numbers.

Excited by an article he had read on the potential of child care, Mendel and eight business associates raised the first $200,000 to start Kinder-Care. The first center opened in July 1969. By the end of the first year, seven centers were operating. Early in 1970, after franchising proved to be an unprofitable means of financing development, Mendel sold 40 percent of the equity for $2.8 million to go public. It was not enough. By October Mendel sold out reluctantly to Warner National Corporation for $1.5 million in stock.

With his financing worries out of the way, Mendel began to concentrate his efforts on the real estate aspect of Kinder-Care. Soon he began using a sale/leaseback method to get local investors to finance expansion. Kinder-Care guaranteed the investor a nice income on a 20-year lease. The investor earned about 15 percent pretax on his investment, and Kinder-Care grew. By 1973 there were 48 centers in 10 states. In 1974 the present corporate office was built. By year-end, Kinder-Care had 4,250 children enrolled in 62 centers.

By 1976 Mendel wanted Warner National to relinquish its 72 percent interest in Kinder-Care. He borrowed $2.25 million from banks and raised $2.25 million from 19 individuals. Armed with $4.5 million cash, he cinched the deal by throwing in all of his Warner stock. In 1977 Taft Broadcasting bought a 20 percent interest for $3.6 million. Kinder-Care later managed to obtain a $5 million mortgage loan commitment to develop 20–25 centers over the next two years. In August 1977 Kinder-Care acquired 15 day-care centers from AID, Inc. for $2.7 million. Its year-end earnings were nearly $750,000 on $12.8 million in sales. Sales and earnings history of the firm is shown in Exhibit 2.

By 1978 Kinder-Care's stock had grown so much that the board voted a 2-for-1 stock split. It also formed a subsidiary, Kinder Life Insurance Company, to provide life insurance to children enrolled in the centers and to employees. Recent stock and dividend data are shown in Exhibit 3.

Kinder-Care's expansion continued in 1979 with the acquisition of Mini-Skools Limited of Canada for $16 million in cash and stock. It gained 88 centers in the United States and Canada. The next year, it entered the New England states when it bought Living and Learning Centers for $3.6 million in cash and notes. It acquired 87 centers for $10 million in cash and notes from American Creative Schools and Creative Day Schools of North Augusta, Georgia. It added 33 centers in the Southwest with the purchase of American Pre-Schools for an undisclosed amount. All of this growth was partially financed by a 450,000-share offering in March at $9.13 per share

EXHIBIT 2
Sales and Earnings History

Year	Revenues	Net Income	Earnings per Share
1973	$ 2,268,551	$ 216,800	$0.15
1974	4,663,346	346,516	0.24
1975	6,088,993	369,247	0.26
1976	9,108,769	509,787	0.35
1977	12,820,884	745,180	0.18*
1978	19,744,208	1,320,761	0.29*
1979	28,591,345	2,173,226	0.46
1980	56,577,767	3,499,495	0.55†
1981	87,037,734	4,290,743	0.56
‡	23,326,538	(2,737,979)	—
1982	116,467,200	6,654,637	0.66

Note: The actual loss was $1,797,856 for the period, with an accounting debit of $940,133 due to a cumulative-effect accounting change. Comparable year-earlier results are $14,196,954 in sales and $311,111 net income, or $0.05 earnings per share after stock-split adjustment.
* Adjusted for 2-for-1 stock split.
† Adjusted for 5-for-4 stock split.
‡ Results of a 13-week "short year" caused by the changing of the fiscal year-end from the last Friday in May to the last Friday in August. The new year-end is in harmony with the beginning of the fall enrollment period and employee incentive programs.

Source: *The Wall Street Journal*, Earnings Digests.

and a 750,000-share offering at $16.25 per share in October. The May year-end net was nearly $3.5 million.

Taft Broadcasting offered 1,422,217 shares of Kinder-Care at $12.50 in late 1981. The board decided to change the year-end to the last Friday in August at that time. By then Kinder-Care had over 700 centers. In May 1982 a $32 million convertible debt offering which paid 11 percent interest was issued to allow even more expansion. Further, in August 1982 a three-year, $25 million revolving credit facility was established with Bank of America for long-term or sale/leaseback financing. It included a five-year term loan.

As Rob Hartley looked at the previous two years' financial statements he felt confident of Kinder-Care's position. The common stock had traded over-the-counter at a red-hot 25 times earnings. Return on equity was 12.4 percent last year and 18.3 percent in 1980. The debt-equity ratio had fallen from a 3.64 high in 1980 to a moderate 2.33 : 1 in 1981. Kinder-Care anticipated earnings to be $8.6 to $8.9 million in 1983 or earnings per share of $0.84 to $0.88 after a 25 percent stock dividend in November. The number of centers was expected to continue its nearly 30 percent growth rate to over 950 centers by year-end.

EXHIBIT 3

Recent stock and dividend data

Year	Price Range	Dividends
1977	$12.75–$11.00*	$0.02
1978	18.25– 9.00†	0.03
1979	15.25– 7.75	0.07
1980	20.00– 8.37‡	0.09
1981	17.50– 10.25	0.10

Note: 8,081,878 shares outstanding at 1981 end.
* After 100 percent stock dividend, previously a range of $18.25–$13.25.
† After 100 percent stock dividend, previously a range of $29.25–$11.75.
‡ After 25 percent stock dividend, previously a range of $17.75–$8.37.

Source: *Moody's OTC Industrial Manual 1982*, p. 1515.

Consolidated Income Account
($000)

	Year ended		
	5/29/81‡	5/30/80†	6/1/79
Operating revenues	$ 87,038	$ 56,578	$ 28,591
Direct operating expenses	74,625	46,808	23,883
General and administrative expenses	1,749	1,184	718
Operating profit	10,664	8,586	3,990
Other income	1,220	665	586
Total.	1,883	9,251	4,575
Interest	6,468	4,654	1,473
Income taxes	1,415	1,295	1,040
Equity earnings	291	117	111
Net income	4,291	3,449	2,173
Previous retained earnings.	8,323	5,281	3,390
Dividends	711	407	283
Retained earnings	11,902	8,323	5,281
Earnings, common share*.	$0.56	$0.55	$0.37
Year-ending common shares	8,081,878	5,632,458	4,713,520

* As reported on 7,702,948 (1980, 6,274,099; 1979, 5,889,765) average common shares adjusted for 25 percent stock dividend 12/80.
† Reflects change in accounting for interest capitalization and includes Mini-Skools Limited acquired as of August 31, 1979, on purchase basis.
‡ Includes Living and Learning Centers, Inc. (acquired August 31, 1980), 41 day-care centers (acquired August 1, 1980), and 11 day-care centers (acquired May, 1981) from dates of acquisition.

EXHIBIT 3 (*concluded*)

Subsidiaries (wholly owned): Kinder Care–Eagle Properties, Inc.; Kinder-Care Merchandise, Inc.; Kinder Life Insurance Co.; Kinder Canada Ltd.

Officers
Perry Mendel, president
R. J. Grassgreen, executive vice president, secretary, and treasurer
F. E. Montgomery, vice president
Emanuel Kulbersh, vice president
H. L. Cohen, vice president

Directors

Perry Mendel	L. E. Wallock	W. L. Gauntt
R. J. Grassgreen	Fred Berman	E. L. Lowder
A. M. Aronov	Mark Sabel	C. S. Mechem, Jr.

Auditors: Peat, Marwick, Mitchell & Co.

Consolidated Balance Sheet
($000)

	5/29/81	5/30/80
Assets		
Cash	$ 4,966	$ 3,840
Certificate of deposit	8,092	3,450
Receivables	1,520	523
Prepays	1,709	671
Total current	$ 16,288	$ 8,483
Property, etc., net	85,924	70,928
Excess cost acquired	1,458	2,138
Equity in subsidiary†	2,572	2,281
Other assets	9,101	3,544
Total	$115,345	$87,375
Liabilities		
Notes, etc., pay	4,018	2,032
Accounts, etc., pay	3,543	3,180
Total current	$ 7,561	$ 5,212
Long-term debt	58,172	49,157
7½s, convertible debentures	9,985	10,000
Deferred rent	1,017	376
Deferred income taxes	3,944	3,217
Common stock ($0.50)	4,041	3,057
Additional paid-in capital	18,721	7,972
Retained earnings	11,902	8,323
Reacquired stock*	—	dr 540
Total	$115,345	$87,375
Net current assets	8,727	3,271

Note: Above statements include accounts of company's Canadian subsidiaries which have been translated to U.S. dollars.
* 481,389 shares at cost.
† Equity in Kinder Life Insurance Company, a wholly owned subsidiary formed in May 1978.

Source: *Moody's OTC Industrial Manual 1982*, p. 1515.

MARKETING STRATEGY

Next, Hartley reviewed Kinder-Care's marketing strategy. He realized that one key to Kinder-Care's success was its location decisions. Two board members were experienced real estate developers. Many Kinder-Care centers were located on land adjacent to shopping malls which they developed. Naturally Kinder-Care benefited from the marketing research and land development expertise offered by the firms. Locations were on a side street not far from the McDonald's-type locations, but near a neighborhood and less expensive. Kinder-Care's construction teams built centers according to the latest prototype layout as shown in Exhibit 4. They also dealt with equipment manufacturers to purchase swing sets, seesaws, and other playground equipment. Some centers in warmer climates even had small swimming pools in a separate fenced-in area.

The second aspect of the strategy was the prepackaged educational plans. Consultants in nutrition, physical fitness, early childhood education, and health helped develop Kinder-Care's exclusive GOAL program (Growth Opportunities for Achievement and Learning). The program had various "discovery areas" within each center: library, home living, construction, math, music, creative arts, manipulations, science, sound table, and woodworking. All teachers were given a monthly guide with materials for each day's activities. The material covered was consistent throughout the nation. It was shipped approximately one month in advance, with two months of material to a shipment. Parents were given a three-month "Kinder Calendar" of the upcoming activities, a sample of which is shown in Exhibit 5. Among the professional packages offered in the program were the respected Lippincott "Beginning to Read, Write, and Listen" for five-year-olds and Rowland's "Happily Ever After" series of children's tales for four-year-olds.

The final aspect of the strategy was the center itself, a prototype of which is shown in Exhibit 4. Many promotional image-building services were offered, including early education, life insurance, and mail-order catalog merchandise. Staff was paid the minimum wage. Center directors received a modest salary. Consequently turnover was high. Teacher-pupil ratios were kept at a low 1 to 10. Each state had regulations to control pupil ratios, building codes, discipline, and the like. The centers were designed to hold a capacity of either 80, 100, or 120 children. Kinder-Care's enrollment now was over 50,000. Rob was pleased his fall enrollment campaign had increased occupancy. Over 500 centers had achieved their base or better from last spring. Rates were competitive for comparable services offered elsewhere. The rates are shown in Exhibit 6.

Rob knew that Kinder-Care was three times larger than its nearest competitor, La Petite Academies of Kansas City, Missouri. He did not consider churches or other tax-exempt places which simply baby-sat to be real competition. He was proud that Kinder-Care had become known as "the child-care centers for children of schoolteachers." He believed this gave

EXHIBIT 4
Latest Prototype Design

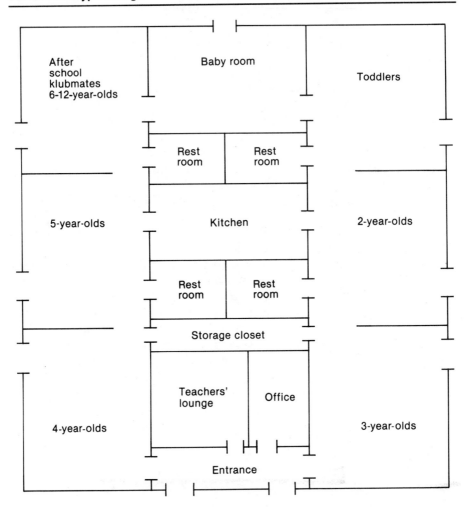

credence to the educational programs. In order to improve Kinder-Care's competitive position, the Kindustry program was developed.

Kindustry was designed to help corporations solve two growing problems: (1) valuable employees were quitting to raise a family, and (2) working couples were complaining they did not know what to do with youngsters before and after school. Kinder-Care's solution was to have a staff member pick up a child in the morning and take him to school and after school to deliver him to the nearest center where he could be taught such things as

EXHIBIT 5

February '83
Scents, Cents, and Senses

WEEKS:	Monday	Tuesday	Wednesday	Thursday	Friday
Jan 31–Feb. 4 They Number 5 "E"	1 Nose · 2 Ears · 2 Eyes · 2 Hands · 1 mouth = 5 ? ? ? ? ? ? ? ? ? ? Sniff. Sniff. the ROSE — Wouldn't it be terrible if we didn't have a nose?	A pair of ears . . . better to hear you with, my dear	Groundhog Gala Seeing is Believing Brush up on dental care! Children's Dental Health Month	Hands There are things that hands do that feet never can Did you know? Winter is half over on February 6th?	Mouth I wish I had two Little mouths just like my 2 little feet — One to talk with and one just to eat!
February 7–11 Let's Play Store "M" Review	What Shall it Be? A donut shop The supermarket A toy store or better yet a place to eat	It Pays to Advertise Coupon Power Coin Display	Label Fun Penny Power (Making change)	Resource Person (Sharing of Coin Collection) Cents. Cents. and more Cents (Make play money for Trade Day)	TRADE DAY
February 14–18 Love Makes the World Go Round "L"	Cupids. Candies. Flowers and Cards VALENTINE'S DAY	Making flowers for someone we LOVE February is American Heart Month	Everything is Coming Up Rosy! Discover pink Make someone happy — send a Happy Gram	Bottle Music Make lovable Characters	Candy Making And would you believe it's even healthy?
February 21–25 Imagination and Me "I"	What Would Happen if . . . CREATIVE EXPRESSIONS	Inside. outside. upside down (Spatial concepts) Looby Lou will teach me right and left.	Wacky Wednesday Artful Me Tin Can Band	Mystical Magnets Backwards Day	Chef's See & Do Using my Thinking Cap

Kinder Care

first aid until his parent took him home. Kinder-Care introduced a red schoolhouse logo for the program, dubbed the youngsters (ages 6 to 12) "Klubmates" and created special areas within the centers for them alone.

Next, Kinder-Care organized a sales force and designed a pilot program. First, a sales force was set up with three zone marketing managers

EXHIBIT 6
Rates

Infants and toddlers	$46 per week
Age 2	$40 per week
Age 3 and older	$36 per week
"Klubmates" (age 6–12)	$12 per week after school
Optional transportation	$6–8 per week

Note: Klubmates are part of the Kindustry program.

(one each in California, Texas, and North Carolina), 16 regional managers, and 65 district managers (each assigned to about 12 centers). No one had sales experience except the zone managers. Training skills were taught. The Equitable Life Assurance company began testing the program in Atlanta, Albuquerque, and Columbus, Ohio. The employer paid 20 percent of the cost for 1,200 eligible employees. Kinder-Care billed the company, which in turn deducted the remainder of the cost from paychecks. The new tax law helped encourage this program even further. It expanded the tax credit to 20–30 percent of the costs of child care. For a family with income over $28,000, for example, as much as $480 for one child or $960 for two or more children could be deducted.

After its initial success, Kinder-Care expanded the program to include a dozen hospitals, several insurance companies, and a dozen industrial firms. A major development was the opening of a center at Walt Disney World. It provided care for the children of the 13,000 employees and the children of the theme park guests. The Klubmates now made up about 20 percent of total enrollment.

Another service offering was life insurance. Kinder Life Insurance offered two policies which were underwritten by Republic National Life. Kinder-Care developed promotional literature to explain the policies. Kinder-Care pays the first year's premium. One policy is $5,000 whole life paid up at 80. Semiannual premiums are $10.50 to age 21 and $32.50 thereafter. The other policy is a 17-year convertible term policy for $16,000. Rates vary depending upon the parent's age. For example, a mother of age 23–26 would pay $18.01 semiannually.

Yet another service was the mail-order catalog. Kinder-Care marketing had expanded this to include items such as T-shirts, watches, tote bags, sportswear, and huggable "Kinderoo" kangeroo dolls. Kinderoo had been Kinder-Care's answer to Ronald McDonald: a giant, dressed-up kangaroo to open each new center and to serve as a goodwill ambassador. A song was even developed by Perry Mendel called "Let's All Be Little Kinderoos" to rival Mickey Mouse's theme song. Other promotional literature given with the catalog included magazine subscription forms for parents, bumper stickers, and a brochure explaining Kinder-Care programs like Kinder-Camp, a summer camp program for children through age five. In addition Kinder-Care had started fund-raising projects to help "Jerry's Kids" at MDA. The 1980 contribution was over $126,000, and in 1981 over $104,000 was raised. Overall Rob felt Kinder-Care had a very good marketing mix.

CHANGING DEMOGRAPHICS

Now Rob Hartley turned his attention to the problem at hand. He wanted to be ready for his meeting, so he began to browse through various demographic and kindergarten enrollment data he had accumulated as shown in Exhibits 7, 8, and 9. He was looking for trends and implications. He tried to think of ways his present marketing mix could be improved or which aspects he should emphasize. New ideas also began to come to mind: Kinderoo

EXHIBIT 7
Demographic Data on Location, Age, and Unit Size

	1970	1980
U.S. resident population (in millions)		
Total persons	203.2	226.5
Urban	149.3	167.0
Rural	53.9	59.5
In SMSAs	153.7	169.4
Percentages	(75.6%)	(74.8%)
Central cities	67.9	67.9
Suburbs	85.8	101.5
In nonmetro areas	49.6	57.1
Age of population (in millions):		
Under 5	17.2	16.3
5–9	n.a.	16.6
10–14	n.a.	18.4
15–19	n.a.	21.1
20–24	n.a.	21.3
25–29	24.9	19.4
30–34	n.a.	17.7
Median age	28.0	30.0
Unit size		
Persons per household	3.14	2.75
Persons per family	3.58	3.28

n.a. = Not available.

EXHIBIT 8
Demographic Data on Projections, Participation Rates, and Miscellaneous

U.S. Population Projection (in millions)*

	Fertility Rate Assumed		
	2.7	2.1	1.7
1980	224	222	221
1985	239	233	229
1990	255	244	236
1995	269	253	242
2000	283	260	246

	1970	1980
Miscellaneous data		
One-person households	17.0%	22.5%
Female householder	26.8%	36.6%
Birth rate per 1,000	18.4	16.2
Marriages per 1,000	10.6	10.9
Divorces per 1,000	3.5	5.3
Labor force participation rates		
Married men, spouse present	86.9%	81.0%
Married women, spouse present	40.8	50.2
With children under 6	30.3	45.0

* Based on base year 1976, population 215 million.

EXHIBIT 9
Various Child-Care Data

	1970	1980
Enrollment (in millions)*		
Nursery school	4.3	2.4
Elementary school	32.7	28.3

	1983	1985
Projected enrollment (in millions)*		
Elementary and kindergarten	31.2	31.4
Public	27.6	27.8
Private	3.6	3.6

Number of Establishments	Receipts ($000)	Annual payroll ($000)	Employees
14,172	$759,554	$338,781	87,510

* 1977 Census of Service Industries, SIC 835 Child Care

camps with retreats for his Klubmates to pick up summer enrollment, Kinder-Care computer centers for adults after work hours, and shopping services for single-parent households. He knew he must be careful in any diversification strategy. He felt that if he moved too far from his prime target market—14 million working women of childbearing age in middle- to upper-income households—that Kinder-Care might not reach its occupancy goals.

CASE 2–5

Marion Laboratories, Inc.

Michael E. Herman, senior vice president of finance for Marion Laboratories, had just received word that the board of directors was planning to meet in three days to review the company's portfolio of subsidiary investments. In particular, he and his senior financial analyst, Carl R. Mitchell, were to prepare an in-depth analysis of several of the subsidiaries so the board could be better positioned with respect to these subsidiaries' compatibility with Marion's overall strategic objectives. The analysis was part of a continuing process of self-assessment to assure future growth for the company. At the upcoming meeting, the board was interested in a review of Kalo Laboratories, Inc.,[1] a subsidiary that manufactured specialty agriculture chemicals.

Kalo was profitable and in sound financial shape for the fiscal year just ended. (See Exhibit 1—Sales, profit, and assets of major industry segments.) But Kalo, in the agricultural chemical industry, was unique for Marion, and Mr. Herman knew that Kalo's long-term status as a Marion subsidiary would depend on more than just profitability.

Marion's future had been the subject of careful study following the first two years of earnings decline in the company's history. In fiscal 1975, net earnings for the company were 12 percent lower than in 1974. In fiscal 1976 Marion faced a more serious problem as earnings fell 30 percent below 1974 levels while sales decreased 4 percent and cost of goods sold rose by 12 percent above 1974 levels.

As a result of the interruption in the earnings' growth pattern, Marion has sought to reexamine its corporate portfolio of investments. By fiscal

---

This case was prepared by Professor Marilyn L. Taylor and Kenneth Beck of the University of Kansas. Copyright © 1981.

[1] Kalo Laboratories, Inc., was utilized as the case subject due to the singular nature of the segment information available in Marion Laboratories' SEC submissions, and does not reflect Marion's intentions as to its investment in Kalo or any of its other subsidiary operations. Materials in this case were generally gathered from publicly available information.

EXHIBIT 1

MARION LABORATORIES, INC.
Sales Profits and Identifiable Assets
by Industry Segments
($000)

	Year Ended June 30				
	1978	*1977*	*1976*	*1975*	*1974*
Sales to unaffiliated customers					
Pharmaceutical and hospital products	$ 84,223	$ 72,299	$59,236	$64,613	$54,165
Specialty agricultural chemical products	9,302	5,227	2,880	4,522	4,044
Other health care segments	23,853	22,605	18,722	14,961	13,569
Consolidated net sales	$117,378	$100,131	$80,838	$84,096	$71,778
Operating profit					
Pharmaceutical and hospital products	$ 27,900	$ 23,439	$18,941	$28,951	$25,089
Specialty agricultural chemical products	905	382	(328)	881	620
Other health care segments	929	1,251	(593)	686	871
Operating profit.......	29,734	25,072	18,020	30,518	26,580
Interest expense	(1,546)	(1,542)	(898)	(97)	(83)
Corporate expenses	(5,670)	(4,474)	(3,106)	(2,795)	(2,475)
Earnings before income taxes................	$ 22,518	$ 19,056	$14,016	$27,626	$24,022
Identifiable assets					
Pharmaceutical and hospital products	$ 75,209	$ 69,546	$60,376	$43,658	$35,103
Specialty agricultural chemical products	3,923	3,805	1,801	1,942	1,790
Other health-care segments	14,635	14,875	13,902	14,229	12,217
Corporate	5,121	3,424	4,518	3,928	3,770
Discontinued operations .	—	—	—	3,370	6,865
Consolidated assets.......	$ 98,888	$ 91,650	$80,597	$67,127	$59,745

Source: 1978 Annual Report.

year 1977 some results from the reappraisal were seen, as earnings rose 28 percent from the previous year. Although sales continued to climb, earnings had not yet recovered to the 1974 level by the end of fiscal year 1978. Marion's long-range planning was an attempt to define what the company was to become in the next 10-year period. Current performance of subsidiaries and investments was analyzed within this 10-year framework. As part of this long-range planning, a statement of Marion's corporate mission was developed.

Statement of Corporate Mission

1. Achieve a position of market leadership through marketing and distribution of consumable and personal products of a perceived differentiation to selected segments of health-care and related fields.
2. Achieve long-term profitable growth through the management of high risk relative to the external environment.
3. Achieve a professional, performance-oriented working environment that stimulates integrity, entrepreneurial spirit, productivity, and social responsibility.

In addition to these more general goals, Marion also set a specific sales goal of $250 million. No time frame was established to achieve this goal, as the major emphasis was to be placed on the stability and quality of sales.

Mr. Herman realized, however, that even though there was no written timetable for earnings growth, it was well understood that to meet stockholder expectations, the company must grow fairly rapidly.

On June 8, 1978, in a presentation before the Health Industry's Analyst Group, Fred Lyons, Marion's president and chief operating officer, emphasized Marion's commitment to growth. In his remarks he stated:

> We expect to grow over the next 10 years at a rate greater than the pharmaceutical industry average and at a rate greater than at least twice that of the real gross national product. Our target range is at least 10–15 percent compounded growth—shooting for the higher side of that, of course. Obviously we intend to have a great deal of new business and new products added to our current operations to reach and exceed the $250 million level.
>
> Our licensing activities and R&D expenditures will be intensified. . . . At, the same time, we'll undertake some selective in-house research business into Marion through the acquisition route. It is our intention to keep our balance sheet strong and maintain an "A" or better credit rating, to achieve a return on investment in the 12–15 percent range, and to produce a net after tax compared to sales in the 8–12 percent range.

To finance this growth in sales, Marion was faced with a constant need for funds. Most of these funds in the past had come from the company's operations. To finance a $25 million expansion in its pharmaceutical facilities, the company in fiscal year 1976 found it necessary to borrow $15 million in the form of unsecured senior notes. The notes were to mature on October 1, 1980, 1981, and 1982, with $5 million due on each of those dates.

In regard to possible future financing, Mr. Herman made the following comments before the Health Industry's Analyst Group: "Most of you realize that industrial companies have a debt–equity ratio of 1 : 1, and if we so desired to lever ourselves to that level, we could borrow $66 million. However, we would keep as a guideline the factor of always maintaining our A or better credit rating, so we would not leverage ourselves that far."

Although Marion was fairly light on debt, the potential for future borrowing was not unlimited. Besides maintaining an A credit rating, it was felt that a debt–equity ratio greater than 4 : 1 would be inconsistent with the pharmaceutical industry.

To analyze Kalo's future as well as the futures of the other nonpharmaceutical subsidiaries, Mr. Herman realized that he and his analysts would have to consider the impact of these financing constraints on Marion's future growth. With unlimited financing in the future he would have only had to make a "good" investment decision. However, to balance the goals of a strong balance sheet and a high growth rate, Mr. Herman was faced with making the optimal investment decision. It was with these constraints that Mr. Herman would eventually have to make his recommendation to the board of directors.

COMPANY HISTORY

In 1979 Marion Laboratories, Inc., of Kansas City, Missouri, was a leading producer of ethical (prescription) pharmaceuticals for the treatment of cardiovascular and cerebral disorders. (See Exhibit 2—Marion's major ethical products.) Marion also owned subsidiaries which manufactured hospital supplies, proprietary (nonprescription) drugs, eyeglasses, optical accessories, electrical home-stairway elevators, and specialty agricultural chemicals.

Marion Laboratories was founded in 1950 by Ewing Marion Kauffman. Prior to establishing his own company, Mr. Kauffman held a job with a field sales force of a Kansas City pharmaceutical company. After four years on the job Kauffman's sales efforts were so successful that he was making more money in commissions than the company president's salary. When the company cut his commission and reduced his sales territory, Kauffman quit to establish his own firm.

In its initial year of operation the new company had sales of $36,000 and a net profit of $1,000. Its sole product was a tablet called OS–VIM, and was formulated to combat chronic fatigue. The company's three employees, counting Mr. Kauffman, worked from a 13 × 15-feet storeroom that served as manufacturing plant, sales office, warehouse, and headquarters.

From the company's inception, the major emphasis for Marion was on sales and marketing. Mr. Kauffman was successful in developing an aggressive, highly motivated sales force. During the mid-1960s the company's

EXHIBIT 2
Major Ethical Pharmaceutical Products

Product	Product Application	Estimated Market Size ($ millions)	Marion's Product	Share of Market
Cerebral and peripheral vasodilators	Vascular relaxant to relieve constriction of arteries	$90–100	PAVABID®	22%
Coronary vasodilators	Controlled-release nitroglycerin for treatment of angina pectoris	90–100	NITRO–BID®	12
Ethical and OTC plain antacids	Tablets for relief of heartburn	37	GAVISCON®	26
Androgens-estrogens	Product for treatment of calcium deficiencies	12	OS–CAL®	46
Topical burn antimicrobials	Ointment for prevention of infection in third-degree burns	8	SILVADENE®	57
Urologic antispasmodics	Product for treatment of symptoms of neurogenic bladder	10	DITROPAN®	10

Source: Smith, Barney, Harris, Upham and Co. research report (January 19, 1978).

sales effort was concentrated on developing Pavabid, introduced in 1962, into the leading product in the cerebral and peripheral vasodilator market.

While other drug companies were spending large amounts on research and development, hoping to discover new drugs, Marion concentrated on the sales effort, spending very little on basic research. Nearly all of its research expenditures were directed at improving its current products or further developing products licensed from other drug companies. This particular approach to product development was still being followed in 1979.

Beginning in the late 1960s Marion decided to reduce its dependence on Pavabid, which accounted for more than half of Marion's sales. In the pharmaceutical area, the company continued to minimize basic research and worked to develop new drug sources. Marion also began diversifying into the hospital and health products sector primarily by acquiring existing firms in those areas. (See Exhibit 3 for a summary of Marion's acquisition

EXHIBIT 3

Summary of Subsidiary Acquisitions and Divestitures

Name of Subsidiary	Type of Product(s)	Date Acquired	Date Divested
Marion Health Safety	First aid and hospital products	1968	—
American Stair Glide	Manufacturer of home stairway lifts and products to aid the handicapped	1968	—
Kalo Laboratories	Manufacturer of specialty agricultural chemicals	1968	—
Rose Manufacturing	Industrial fall-protection devices	1969	Sold: 1978
Mi-Con Laboratories	Manufacturers of ophthalmic solutions	1969	Merged into MH&S: 1973
Pioneer Laboratories	Manufacturer of sterile dressings	50 percent in 1970	Sold out: 1971
Signet Laboratories	Vitamin and food supplements	1971	Discontinued operations, selling some assets: 1975
Optico Laboratories	Eyeglasses, hard contact lenses, and related products	1973	—
Certified Laboratories	Manufacturer IPC products	1969	Sold: 1978
IPC	Marketer IPC products	1969	Merged into Pharmaceutical Division: 1979
Marion International	Distributor of pharmaceutical products	Incorporated 1971	—
Inco	Industrial creams	1972	Merged into MH&S: 1974
Occusafe	Consulting services, re OSHA regulation and compliance	Incorporated 1972	Discontinued operations: 1973
Nation Wide	Specialty AG–Chem products	1973	Merged into Kalo
Marion Scientific	Manufacturer and distributor	Acquired by MH&S: 1973	—
Colloidal	Specialty agricultural products	1973	Merged into Kalo: 1974
WBC	Holding company for IPC	Incorporated 1976	Sold: 1978
SRC	Specialty AG–Chem products	1977	Merged into Kalo

and divestiture activities.) Taking advantage of the high market value of its common stock,[2] the company acquired several subsidiaries engaged in businesses other than pharmaceuticals.

ORGANIZATION

Marion's operations in 1979 were divided into two separate groups, the Pharmaceutical Group and the Health Products Group. (See Exhibit 4, Marion organizational chart.) The Pharmaceutical Group's operations were a continuation of the original ethical drug line of the company. The Health Products Group was composed of subsidiaries purchased by Marion in hospital and health-related fields.

Fred W. Lyons, 41, was president, chief executive officer, and member of the board of directors. As president, Lyons was responsible for the total operation and performance of the corporation. This responsibility included the company's pharmaceutical operating group as well as all subsidiary operations, corporate planning functions, and corporate supportive activities.

Lyons joined Marion in 1970 as vice president and general manager, and director. He came to Marion from a similar position with Corral Pharmaceuticals, Inc., a subsidiary of Alcon Laboratories, Inc. Lyons was a registered pharmacist and had received an MBA from Harvard University in 1959.

Also serving on the board of directors was Senior Vice President and Chief Financial Officer Michael E. Herman, 37, who joined Marion from an investment banking firm of which he was a founding partner. Herman started with Marion as vice president of finance in 1974 and in 1975 was named director of the company. His responsibilities were financial planning, financial control of operations, the management information systems, the treasury functions, product development, and strategic long-range planning. Mr. Herman was also chairman of the company's New Business Task Force Committee which was responsible for the financial review, planning, evaluation, and negotiation of acquisitions. Herman earned a bachelor of science degree in metallurgical engineering from Rensselaer Polytechnic Institute and an MBA from the University of Chicago.

Gerald W. Holder, 48, was the senior vice president in charge of administrative functions for Marion. Holder was responsible for all corporate administrative functions, including Marion's legal, personnel, facilities and engineering services, public relations, and risk management staffs. He joined the company in 1973, rising to the senior vice president level in March 1978.

---

[2] Price-earnings ratios for Marion in 1968 and 1969 were 46 and 52, respectively.

EXHIBIT 4
Organization Chart

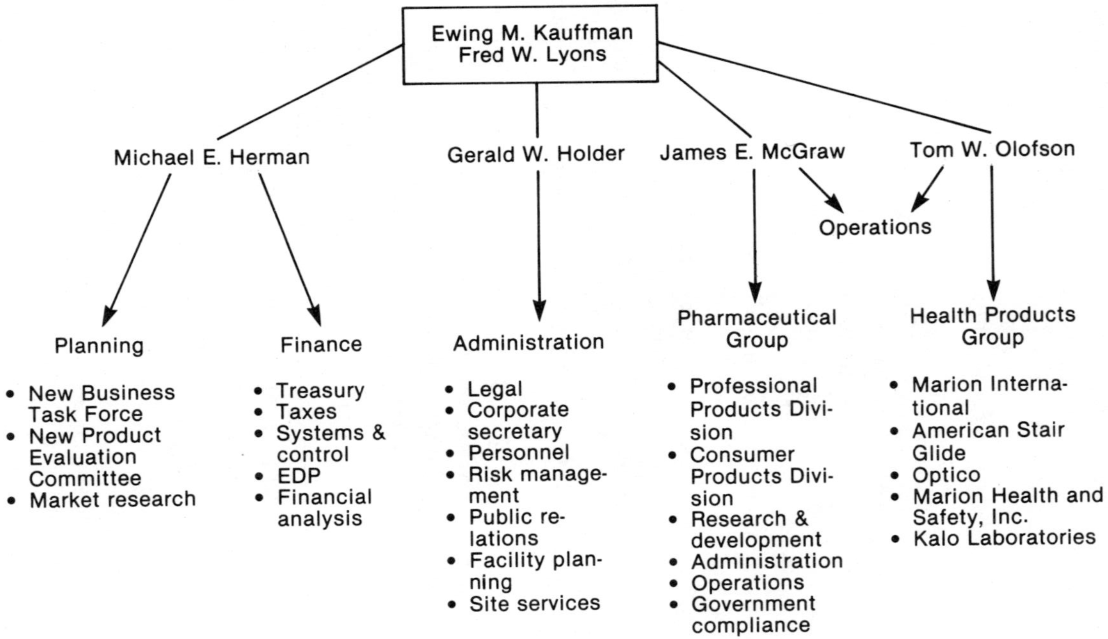

Source: Organization chart as rendered by authors.

James E. McGraw, 46, was senior vice president of Marion Laboratories, Inc. and president of the company's Pharmaceutical Group. He was responsible for the manufacturing, marketing, quality control, and accounting functions within the two operating units of the Pharmaceutical Group: the Professional Products Division and the Consumer Products Division. McGraw joined Marion in 1974 from a position as president of the General Diagnostics Division of Warner-Lambert Company.

Tom W. Olofson, 36, was a senior vice president and president of the Health Products Group. His responsibilities included financial and planning aspects for each of the subsidiaries in the Health Products Group.

Within the described organization, Marion made some of its operating decisions in small group or task force settings that brought together corporate personnel from several different disciplines. The process of approving certain capital expenditures was an example of the review and analysis process.

Marion had a formal capital expenditure review program for expenditures on depreciable assets in excess of $10,000. At the option of the group president, the review program could also be applied on expenditures of less than $10,000, with the modification that in these cases only the group president was involved in the review process.

A form that forced the requesting individual to discount the cash flows of the project was required to be completed and submitted, if the net present value of cash flows was positive, to a corporate planning group. This group consisted of corporate accounting and facilities planning personnel who, since the company was operating with limited funds, decided which projects, based on financial and strategic considerations, should be forwarded to Fred Lyons for final approval or rejection. This process occurred after the planning period and prior to the purchase of the asset. The capital expenditure review program was used for expenditures in both the Pharmaceutical Group and the Health Products Group.

PHARMACEUTICAL GROUP

Marion's ethical and over-the-counter drug operations were the major components of the Pharmaceutical Group. These operations were split into two divisions, the Professional Products Division and the Consumer Products Division. James E. McGraw headed the Pharmaceutical Group, which also was made up of the functions of research and development, administration, operations, and government compliance. Although Marion had been exclusively an ethical drug maker prior to diversification efforts, the company had recently increased its operations in the proprietary drug area.

In 1978 Marion formed the Consumer Products Division from what had been International Pharmaceutical Corp. (IPC) to market its growing non-prescription product line. This market area, previously untapped for Marion, was expected to be a major ingredient for near-term growth. To aid in the marketing of its nonprescription line, Marion hired a full-scale consumer advertising agency for the first time in the company's history.

Sales for the Consumer Products Division were boosted when, in fiscal 1978, Marion purchased the product Throat-Discs from Warner-Lambert's Parke-Davis division. In addition, Marion also purchased two Parke-Davis ethical products, Ambenyl cough-cold products and a tablet for the treatment of thyroid disorders. Because of the timing of the acquisition, most of the sales and earnings were excluded from that year's earnings results. Sales for these three lines were expected to be nearly $8 million in 1979.

Marion's ethical pharmaceutical products were marketed by its Professional Products Division. The company sold its ethical product with a detail sales force of about 200 that called on physicians, pharmacists, and distributors within their assigned territories. The sales force was very productive by industry standards and was motivated by intensive training and supervision and an incentive compensation system. There was very little direct selling to doctors and pharmacists, the main purpose of the salesman visits being promotion of Marion's products. In addition, Marion had an institutional sales force that sold directly to hospitals, institutions, and other large users.

In fiscal 1978, 80 percent of Marion's pharmaceutical products were distributed through 463 drug wholesalers. All orders for ethical drug products were filled from the Kansas City, Missouri, manufacturing plant. Marion's pharmaceutical distribution system is diagrammed below.

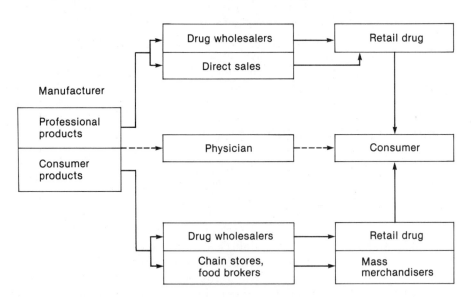

During 1978 the company decided to use its improved liquidity position to aid its wholesale drug distributors. Many wholesalers used outside financing to purchase their inventory and were unable to maintain profit margins when interest rates rose. By extending credit on key products, Marion helped its distributors maintain higher inventories and gave the company a selling edge over competitors.

One of Marion's major goals for each of its products was for the product to hold a market leadership position in the particular area in which it competed. This goal had been accomplished for most of the company's leading products. (See Exhibit 2.)

Capturing a large share of a market had worked particularly well for Marion's leading product, Pavabid, which in 1978 accounted for 18 percent of the entire company's sales. Marion was decreasing its reliance on Pavabid (see Exhibit 5), which since its introduction in 1962 had been the company's most successful product. Through the 1960s Pavabid had been responsible for almost all of Marion's growth. In recent years, as the product's market matured, sales growth had slowed, forcing the company to become less dependent on Pavabid. The decrease in sales of 3.9 percent in fiscal year 1976 was due primarily to previous overstocking of Pavabid and the subsequent inventory adjustments at the distributor level.

In April 1976 the Food and Drug Administration (FDA) had requested that makers of papaverine hydrochloride (sold by Marion as Pavabid) submit test data to support the safety and efficacy of the drug. Many small manufacturers were not able to submit the data and dropped out of the market. Marion complied with the request and had not yet been notified by

EXHIBIT 5
Changing Product Mix

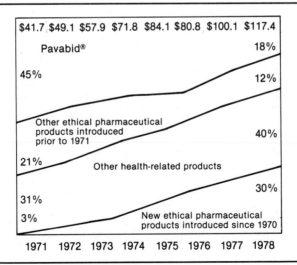

Source: 1978 Annual Report.

the FDA of the outcome of the review by early 1979. A negative action by the FDA was not expected since it had taken so long for a decision, and papaverine had been used safely for decades. However, if the FDA ruled that compounds such as Pavabid could not be marketed because they either were not safe or were not effective, Marion would lose its leading product.

In August 1977, the FDA requested that manufacturers of coronary vasodilators, including nitroglycerin compounds such as Marion's Nitro-Bid, submit test data to prove product safety and efficacy. This review was the same process that Pavabid was subject to, and a negative ruling, although not expected, would adversely affect the company.

Proving its products to be safe and effective was only one area in which the company dealt with the FDA. Before any ethical drug product could be marketed in the United States, Marion had to have the approval of the FDA. Under the system effective at that time, the company was required to conduct extensive animal tests, file an investigational new drug application, conduct three phases of clinical human tests, file a new drug application, and submit all its data to the FDA for final review. With the FDA's approval, the drug firm could begin marketing the drug.

The approval process, from lab discovery and patent application to FDA approval, took from 7 to 10 years. Often a company had only seven or eight years of patent protection left to market its discovery and recover the average $50 million it had taken to fully develop the drug from the initial discovery stages.

To avoid the R&D expenses necessary to fully develop a new drug entity into a marketable product, Marion's source for new products was a process the company called "search and development." Marion licensed the basic compound from other drug manufacturers large enough to afford the basic research needed to discover new drugs. Generally the licensors, most notably Servier of France and Chugai of Japan, were companies lacking the resources or expertise necessary to obtain FDA approval and marketing rights in the United States. Marion's R&D effort then concentrated on developing a product with an already identified pharmacological action into a drug marketable in the United States. By developing existing drug entities, Marion was able to shorten the development time required to bring a new drug to market at a lower cost than discovering its own drugs. This enabled Marion to compete in an industry dominated by companies many times its own size. (See Exhibits 6 and 7 for drug industry information.)

In addition to the FDA, the federal government was also affecting the drug industry with its activities that promoted generic substitution. In early 1979, 40 states had generic substitution that allowed nonbranded drugs to be substituted for branded, and often more expensive, drugs. The U.S. Department of Health, Education and Welfare and the Federal Trade Commission had also recently proposed a model state substitution law and a listing of medically equivalent drugs. Under other federal programs, the maximum allowable cost (MAC) guidelines, reimbursement for medicaid

EXHIBIT 6
Selected Ethical Drug Companies, 1977 ($000)

	Net Sales	Cost of Goods Sold	R&D Expenses	Net Income*
Pfizer, Inc.	$2,031,900	$978,057	$ 98,282	$174,410
Merck & Co.	1,724,410	662,703	144,898	290,750
Eli Lilly & Co.	1,518,012	571,737	124,608	218,684
Upjohn, Inc.	1,134,325	—	102,256	91,521
SmithKline Corp.	780,337	299,338	61,777	89,271
G. D. Searle & Co.	749,583	345,224	52,645	(28,390)
Syntex Corp.	313,604	132,710	27,648	37,643
A. H. Robbins Co.	306,713	122,374	16,107	26,801
Rorer Group, Inc.	186,020	59,606	5,174	18,143
Marion Laboratories	100,131	37,330	5,907	10,652

* After tax.

Source: Drug and cosmetic industry (June 1978).

and medicare prescriptions was made at the lowest price at which a generic version was available.

Generics accounted for 12 percent of new prescriptions being written and were likely to increase in relative importance. To combat the decreasing profit margins that were expected, the industry was looking to its ability to develop new drugs to offset the expected shortfall that was expected in the 1980s caused by a loss of patent protection on many important drug compounds.

The effect that generic substitution laws would have on Marion was unclear. The company had always concentrated on products with a unique pharmacological action rather than those that were commodity in nature. Generic substitution required an "equivalent" drug be substituted for the brand-name drug, and there were uncertainties about how equivalency would be defined.

EXHIBIT 7
Ethical Drug Industry Composite Statistics

	1978	1977	1976	1975
Sales ($ millions)	$12,450	$10,859	$10,033	$9,022
Operating margin (%)	22.5%	22.2%	21.9%	22.1%
Income tax rate (%)	36.5	36.4	36.2	36.7
Net profit margin (%)	11.8	11.7	11.7	11.6
Earned on net worth (%)	18.5	17.9	18.2	18.4

Source: *Value Line Investment Survey.*

Marion's pharmaceutical operations had not produced a major new product for several years. Products that were in various stages of development were diltiazen hydrochloride, an antianginal agent; sucralfate, a nonsystematic (does not enter the bloodstream) drug for the treatment of ulcers; and benflourex, a product that reduces cholesterol levels in the blood.

HEALTH PRODUCTS GROUP

Subsidiaries selling a wide range of products used in health-care and related fields made up Marion's Health Products Group. The company had bought and sold several subsidiaries since beginning to diversify in 1968 (see Exhibit 3). By 1978 the group of subsidiaries was responsible for 39 percent of total company sales and 22 percent of earnings before taxes.

Several times after purchasing a company, Marion had decided to sell or discontinue operations of a subsidiary. The divestment decision in the past had been based on considerations such as a weak market position, low-growth position, excessive product liability, or a poor "fit" with the rest of Marion.

In his presentation before the Health Industry's Analyst Group, Fred Lyons noted the importance of a subsidiary fitting in with the rest of Marion when explaining the company's decision to sell Rose Manufacturing.

> You may have noticed that during this past year we determined through our strategic planning that Rose Manufacturing, in the fall-protection area of industrial safety, did not fit either our marketing base or our technology base. Therefore we made a decision to spin Rose off, and we successfully culminated its sale in November 1977. Rose, like Signet Laboratories three years ago, just did not fit.

In adjusting its corporate profile, Marion was always searching for companies that provided good investment potential and were consistent with the company's goals. To provide a framework within which to evaluate potential acquisitions and to avoid some of the mistakes made in past purchases, Marion developed a set of acquisition criteria to be applied to possible subsidiary investments.

Search Criteria for Acquisitions

Product area	Health care
Market	$100 million potential with 8 percent minimum growth rate
Net sales	$3 to 30 million
Tangible net worth	Not less than $1 million
Return on investment	Not less than 20 percent pretax
Method of payment	Cash or stock

The board of directors made the ultimate decision on the acquisitions and divestment of Marion's subsidiaries. At the corporate level, Mr. Herman was responsible for evaluating changes in the corporate portfolio and, based on his analysis, making recommendations to the board. Since Mr. Herman was also on the board of directors, his recommendations were heavily weighted in the board's final decision.

In early 1979 Marion had four subsidiaries in its Health Products Group: Marion Health and Safety, Inc., Optico Industries, American Stair Glide, and Kalo Laboratories. Following is a brief description of each:

Marion Health and Safety, Inc., sold a broad line of hospital and industrial safety products through its Marion Scientific Corp. and Health and Safety Products Division. Recently introduced Marion Scientific products (a consumer-oriented insect bite treatment and a device for transporting anaerobic cultures) showed good acceptance and growth in their respective markets. Distribution is generally through medical/surgical wholesalers and distributors who in turn resell to hospitals, medical laboratories, reference laboratories, etc. Health and Safety Division manufactures and/or packages primarily safety-related products (hearing protection, eyewash, etc.) and first-aid kits and kit products, such as wraps, bandages, and various OTC products. Sale of these products is made to safety-equipment wholesalers/distributors who resell to hospitals, industry, institutions, etc. Sales of Marion Health and Safety, Inc., were estimated by outside analysts to have increased about 17 percent, to a level estimated at $19.0 million. Pretax margins were about 10 percent in this industry. Marion Health and Safety, Inc., was headquartered in Rockford, Illinois.

Optico Industries, Inc., participated in the wholesale and retail optical industry. Its main products were glass and plastic prescription eyeglass lenses and hard contact lenses. Outside analysts estimated this subsidiary recorded sales gains of about 26 percent for 1978 for sales estimated to be about $8 million. Optico had reduced profitability during 1978 due to expansion of its retail facilities. Pretax margins for 1978 were estimated at 6 percent, but this was expected to improve when the expansion program was completed. Optico's headquarters were located in Tempe, Arizona.

American Stair Glide Corp. manufactured and marketed home stairway and porch lifts and other products to aid physically handicapped individuals. These products were principally sold to medical/surgical supply dealers for resale or rental to the consumer. In some instances distribution is through elevator companies. Sales were estimated at about $5 million annually by outside analysts. This subsidiary was expected to grow slowly and steadily, and it had a very stable historical earnings pattern. The trend for greater access to buildings for the handicapped was expected to impact favorably on this Grandview, Missouri–based subsidiary.

EXHIBIT 8
Kalo Laboratories: Sales, Investment, and Expense Information ($ millions)

	1978	1977	1976	1975	1974	1973
Sales	$9.0	$5.0	$2.0	$4.0	$3.0	$2.0
Total assets	5.0	4.0	2.0	2.0	2.0	1.0
Total investment*	3.0	3.0	1.0	1.0	1.0	.5
Expenses (as percent of sales):						
Cost of goods sold	43%	54%	61%	53%	55%	48%
R&D expense	8	7	7	5	5	3
Marketing, selling, and general and adminis- trative expenses	37	31	42	23	24	27

* Includes Marion's equity in Kalo and funds lent on a long-term basis.

Source: Authors' estimates.

KALO LABORATORIES, INC.

Kalo Laboratories operated in the specialty agricultural chemical market and provided products to meet specialized user needs. In the past, Kalo had been successful in marketing its line of specialty products. (See Exhibit 8— Kalo's past earnings information.) In assessing Kalo's future, there were many risks to consider. These risks included competition from large chemical companies, governmental regulatory actions, and uncertain future product potential.

Competition and Industry

The United States and Canadian agricultural chemical market was estimated to be $3.2 billion in 1978 and growing at more than 15 percent a year.[3] The industry was dominated by large chemical manufacturers, including Dow Chemical, Du Pont, Stauffer Chemical, and Gulf Oil. The market was also shared by large ethical drug manufacturers including Eli Lilly, Pfizer, and Upjohn. (See Exhibit 9 for agriculture-related sales.) Economies of scale allowed the larger companies to produce large amounts of what might be perceived as a commodity product (herbicides, insecticides, and fungicides) at a much lower cost per unit than the smaller companies. Diversification of, and within, agricultural product lines assured the larger manufacturers even performance for their agricultural divisions as a whole.

---

[3] 1979 Du Pont Annual Report and 1979 Upjohn Annual Report.

EXHIBIT 9
Total and Agriculture-Related Sales of Selected Companies, 1979 ($ millions)

| | | Agriculture-Related | |
	Total Sales	Sales	Earnings (before tax)
Eli Lilly	$2520	$920*	28.6%
Pfizer	3030	480*	9.8
Upjohn	1755	280*	9.2
Marion (1978)	100	9	9.0

* Includes international sales.

Source: *Value Line Investment Survey.*

Since smaller chemical companies like Kalo could not afford to produce large enough amounts of their products to match the efficiency and prices of the large companies, these firms concentrated on specialty markets with unique product needs. By identifying specialty chemical needs in the agricultural segment, Kalo was able to produce its products and develop markets that were very profitable but weren't large enough to attract the bigger firms.

Products

Since the larger chemical companies dominated the large product segments, Kalo's products were designed to meet the specialized needs of its agricultural users. Kalo's product line was divided into four major classes: seed treatments, adjuvants, bactericides, and herbicides.

Seed treatments for soybeans accounted for the majority of Kalo's sales. One product in this area was Triple Noctin. Products in the seed treatment class were intended to act on soybean seeds to increase their viability once in the ground. Kalo manufactured seed treatments for soybeans only.

Adjuvants were chemicals that, when added to another agricultural product, increased the efficacy of the product or made it easier to use. For instance, Biofilmo prevented liquid fertilizer from foaming, which made it easier to apply, and Hydro-Wet enhanced the soil's receptiveness to certain chemicals, which reduced runoff into surrounding areas.

The newest product for Kalo was the adjuvant EXTEND, a chemical compound added to fertilizer that made it bind chemically with the soil or the plant. The binding process helped retain the fertilizer where it was applied, making each application longer lasting and more effective. EXTEND was only recently introduced, and its success was difficult to assess at such an early stage. Kalo's management was planning to build a family of products around EXTEND. Sales projections showed EXTEND contributing between 60 and 70 percent of Kalo's future growth through 1987.

Bactericides and herbicides were the final two product classes at Kalo. Bactericides were applied to the soil to either inhibit or encourage the growth of selected bacteria. One product, ISOBAC was used to control boll rot in cotton. Herbicides, mainly for broadleaf plants, were used to control or kill unwanted weeds, leaving the desirable crop unharmed.

In the past, Kalo had acquired several of its products by acquiring the company that manufactured the product. When it purchased a going concern intact, Kalo was able to gain both manufacturing facilities and an existing distribution system. In the future, Kalo expected to diversify its product line in a similar fashion. To enlarge its existing product lines, Kalo was planning to use both internal and contract R&D. An example of enlarging the product family was the planned adaptation of its products to numerous different crop applications.

Because Kalo did not have a well-diversified product line, its operations were more cyclical than the overall agricultural sector. Two major factors beyond Kalo's control made its annual performance extremely unpredictable: the weather and spot prices for commodities.

Kalo's operating results were seasonal, as its products were primarily intended to be applied in the spring months. It was not unusual for the subsidiary to show a net loss from operations for the nine months from July until March and show a large profit in the three months April, May, and June when the products were being purchased for immediate application. If the spring months were particularly rainy, Kalo's profitability was adversely affected. Heavy farm equipment couldn't operate on wet fields without getting stuck, and application was impossible until the fields dried out. Once the fields were dry, Kalo's agricultural users often did not have time to apply the herbicides or other products, even though it would have been economically advantageous to do so.

The other factor that affected the demand for Kalo's products was the spot pricing of commodities. The price of commodities relative to each other had a large effect on the total amount of each type of crop planted. Because the producer was free to switch crops yearly, based on the spot prices, Kalo's demand for the upcoming planting season was uncertain and variable. Kalo was particularly vulnerable to swings in demand caused by the substitutability of crops, since many of their products were applicable only to soybeans.

Distribution and Marketing

The end user of Kalo's products was usually the individual farmer. Kalo and the rest of the agricultural chemical industry had a distribution system like the one that follows.

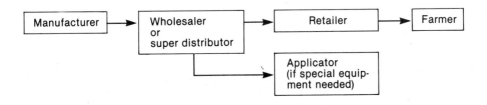

Kalo promoted its products with a sales force of about 30 salesmen. The main task of these salesmen was to call on and educate wholesalers/distributors on the advantages, unique qualities, and methods of selling Kalo's products. In addition some end-user information was distributed to farmers, using "pull" advertising to create demand. A limited amount of promotion was done at agricultural shows and state fairs, but because of the expense involved, this type of promotion was not used often.

Kalo's Future

Sales forecasts prepared by the staff analysts for Mr. Herman looked very promising as they predicted sales gains of $4–6 million in each of the next nine years (see Exhibit 10). There were, however, some important assumptions on which the forecasts were based.

As mentioned earlier, 60–70 percent of the forecasted growth was to come from a product family based on the new product EXTEND. A great deal of uncertainty surrounded the product, however. Since it was new, the current success of EXTEND was difficult to measure, particularly in determining how current sales translated into future performance. If the market evaluation for EXTEND and related products was correct, and if a family of products could be developed around EXTEND, then the sales potential for the proposed product family was very promising, provided Kalo was able to exploit the available sales opportunities.

Additional growth projected in the sales forecasts was to come from existing products and undefined future products that were to be developed

EXHIBIT 10
Kalo Laboratories: Forecasted Sales and Asset Turnover ($ millions)

	1979	1980	1981	1982	1983	1984	1985	1986	1987
Net sales (current dollars)	$12	$16	$20	$25	$30	$35	$40	$45	$50
Asset turnover	1.8×	1.8×	1.9×	1.9×	1.9×	1.9×	1.9×	1.9×	1.85×

Note: After-tax margin expected to increase to 7 percent by 1984.

Source: Authors' estimates.

or acquired. Approximately 20 percent of the growth was to come from the existing products in the next four to five years. Ten to 20 percent of the growth in the later years of the forecast was expected to come from currently unknown products.

For Kalo to realize the forecasted growth, it was going to be necessary for Marion to provide financing. It was going to be impossible for Kalo to generate all the required funds internally. Kalo had been a net user of cash provided by Marion since 1976. (See Exhibit 8—Kalo's sales and earnings information, Exhibit 11—Kalo's balance sheets at 6/30/78, Exhibit 12—Balance sheets, and Exhibit 13—Ten-year financial summary, for information about Marion's investment in Kalo.) Marion's management did not consider the amount of cash provided through the first part of 1979 to be excessive so long as Kalo maintained adequate profitability and steady growth rates. In addition to the long-term funds provided by Marion, Kalo also required short-term financing of inventory during each year, due to the seasonality of its sales.

Government Regulation

Another major uncertainty in Kalo's future was an unpredictable regulatory climate. Regulation of agricultural chemicals was under the jurisdiction of the Environmental Protection Agency (EPA). Compliance with the EPA was a similar process as with the FDA. The process of developing and introducing a new chemical product took 8 to 10 years, which included the 2 to 5 years necessary to obtain EPA approval. The costs of developing and bringing a new product to market were generally $5 to 10 million.

Once a product was on the market, the EPA had powers of recall similar

EXHIBIT 11

KALO LABORATORIES
Balance Sheet
6/30/78
($ millions)

Assets		Liabilities	
Current assets.	$2.5	Current liabilities	$1.4
PP&E (net)	1.9	Long-term debt	1.0
Other	.2	Capital	2.2
Total.	$4.6	Total.	$4.6

Source: Authors' estimates.

to the FDA and could require the company to do additional research after the product was introduced. The prospect of having a product removed from the market was an added element of risk for Kalo if any of its products were affected. No problems were expected for Kalo, although several of the subsidiary's products (particularly its herbicides and bactericides) had a relatively high potential for environmental problems if not applied correctly.

EXHIBIT 12

MARION LABORATORIES INC.
Consolidated Balance Sheet
1977 and 1978

	June 30	
	1978	1977
Assets		
Current assets:		
Cash....................................	$ 381,116	$ 961,588
Short-term investments, at cost which approximates market...........................	2,561,660	10,028,297
Accounts and notes receivable, less allowances for returns and doubtful accounts of $1,845,466 and $2,305,793.................	28,196,199	20,576,412
Inventories......................	19,640,945	15,568,170
Prepaid expenses........................	2,305,403	1,461,367
Deferred income tax benefits	757,585	895,110
Total current assets	53,842,908	49,490,944
Property, plant, and equipment, at cost:		
Land and land improvements................	2,832,588	2,935,671
Buildings.......................	24,458,746	25,224,652
Machinery and equipment...................	19,671,607	18,110,907
Aircraft and related equipment...............	1,670,904	1,670,904
Construction in progress....................	365,311	357,338
	48,999,156	48,299,472
Less accumulated depreciation	10,725,533	8,585,190
Net property, plant, and equipment	38,273,623	39,714,282
Other assets:		
Intangible assets..........................	4,774,055	2,042,762
Notes receivable (noncurrent)	890,692	11,589
Marketable equity securities, at market value....	688,914	—
Deferred income tax benefits (noncurrent)......	318,434	249,647
Miscellaneous...........................	99,597	141,232
Total other assets.......................	6,771,692	2,445,230
Total assets.............................	$98,888,223	$91,650,456

EXHIBIT 12 *(concluded)*

	June 30	
	1978	1977
Liabilities and Stockholders' Equity		
Current liabilities:		
Current maturities of long-term debt...........	$ 82,102	$ 95,004
Accounts payable, trade	3,979,341	4,224,105
Accrued profit-sharing expense	1,752,515	243,096
Other accrued expenses	3,864,168	3,008,238
Dividends payable	1,260,612	1,198,938
Income taxes payable	4,391,252	5,030,219
Total current liabilities....................	15,329,990	13,799,600
Long-term debt, excluding current maturities	15,580,072	15,661,399
Deferred income taxes payable	1,107,000	733,000
Deferred compensation.......................	177,975	172,889
Stockholders' equity:		
Preferred stock of $1 par value per share		
Authorized 250,000 shares; none issued	—	—
Common stock of $1 par value per share		
Authorized 20,000,000 shares; issued		
8,703,346 shares	8,703,346	8,703,346
Paid-in capital..............................	3,474,358	3,475,443
Retained earnings	58,358,925	51,604,550
	70,536,629	63,783,339
Less:		
293,153 shares of common stock in treasury,		
at cost (189,500 shares in 1977)	3,819,243	2,499,771
Net unrealized loss on noncurrent marketable		
equity securities	24,200	—
Total stockholders' equity..................	66,693,186	61,283,568
Commitments and contingent liabilities		
Total liabilities and stockholders' equity..........	$98,888,223	$91,650,456

Source: 1978 Annual Report.

EXHIBIT 13

MARION LABORATORIES, INC.
Ten-Year Financial Summary
(Years Ended June 30)

	1978	1977	1976	1975	1974	1973	1972	1971	1970	1969
Sales ($000):										
Net sales	$117,378	$100,131	$80,838	$84,096	$71,778	$57,937	$49,066	$41,692	$35,322	$30,188
Cost of sales	43,177	37,330	29,315	26,078	21,715	18,171	14,932	12,262	10,622	8,985
Gross profit	74,201	62,801	51,523	58,018	50,063	39,766	34,134	29,430	24,700	21,203
Operating expenses	51,718	43,397	37,292	31,699	26,991	21,155	19,164	17,181	13,828	12,453
Operating income	22,483	19,404	14,231	26,319	23,072	18,611	14,970	12,249	10,872	8,750
Other income	1,581	1,194	683	1,404	1,033	722	709	599	630	328
Interest expense	1,546	1,542	898	97	83	109	116	88	198	260
Earnings ($000):										
Earnings from continuing operations before income taxes	22,518	19,056	14,016	27,626	24,022	19,224	15,563	12,760	11,304	8,818
Income taxes	10,804	8,404	5,628	13,295	11,791	9,297	7,730	6,364	5,899	4,493
Earnings from continuing operations	11,714	10,652	8,388	14,331	12,231	9,927	7,833	6,396	5,405	4,325
Earnings (loss) from discontinued operations	—	—	—	(3,617)	(120)	76	488	—	—	—
Net earnings	$ 11,714	$ 10,652	$ 8,388	$10,714	$12,111	$10,003	$ 8,321	$ 6,396*	$ 5,405	$ 4,325
Common share data:										
Earnings (loss) per common and common equivalent share:										
Continuing operations	$ 1.38	$ 1.23	$ .96	$ 1.65	$ 1.40	$ 1.14	$ .90	$ .76	$ .65	$ .52
Discontinued operations	—	—	—	(.42)	(.01)	.01	.06	—	—	—
Net earnings	$ 1.38	$ 1.23	$ .96	$ 1.23	$ 1.39	$ 1.15	$ .96	$ .76*	$ .65	$ .52
Cash dividends per common share	$ .59	$ .53	$ .52	$ .48	$ .28	$ .21	$ .20	$ .16	$ .12	$ .12
Stockholders' equity per common and common equivalent share	$ 7.87	$ 7.09	$ 6.63	$ 6.29	$ 5.52	$ 4.16	$ 3.16	$ 2.52	$ 2.01	$ 1.47
Weighted average number of outstanding common and common share equivalents	8,475	8,640	8,707	8,708	8,689	8,715	8,651	8,396*	8,377	8,354

* Before extraordinary charge of $916,000, equal to $.11 per common share resulting from the disposition of investment in affiliated companies.

Source: 1978 Annual Report.

THE DECISION

Mr. Herman knew that in making his recommendation he would have to balance the immediate and long-term resource needs and the goals of Marion. Although Kalo looked promising from the forecasts, there were many uncertainties surrounding these subsidiaries' futures that had to be considered. Among these uncertainties was the price Marion would obtain for Kalo. Mr. Herman felt that a subsidiary of the nature of Kalo might sell for 8 to 15 times earnings, depending on the estimated growth rate, the uncertainty of the estimate, and the haste with which Marion wanted to sell the subsidiary.

Since Marion had no new drug products ready to be introduced soon, the company would have to rely on other areas of the company to reach its growth goals. Kalo was growing, but it was also requiring a constant input of funds from its parent.

One possibility for growth was to purchase another drug manufacturer and add its products to Marion's, taking advantage of any distribution synergies that might exist. To make such a purchase, the company would need more resources. To sell a subsidiary could provide needed resources, but to do so quickly under less than optimum conditions would surely result in a significantly lower price than could be realized under normal conditions. The income and cash flow impact of this approach would be undesirable.

With the board meeting so soon, Mr. Herman was faced with analyzing the complex situation quickly. In three days he would have to make his recommendation to the board of directors.

CASE 2–6

The Simons Lumber Company

"I guess we are in a predicament that many of our competitors would envy," said Stephen Simons. "Our company's reputation is among the best in the industry, we make a respectable profit in both good and bad economic times, and we know our business, but it is very difficult to enlarge our niche without running into competition from a national wholesaler or manufacturer."

Simons had spent the past 16 years of his life in this company, although in the past four years he spent only 20 percent of his time at the business, having started an unrelated venture in 1982. Now, as this new venture was taking more of his time, Simons was trying to decide the best course of action for the lumber business. Whereas his father had focused on managing the "top line" of the income statement, Stephen Simons had focused primarily on the "bottom line." Stephen Simons now wondered whether his emphasis had been carried too far and if it was time for a change in focus. Should he try to plot a course of planned expansion or should he be content to continue dominating the niche the company now occupies? Given the difficulty of obtaining market information on a narrow product line in a limited geographic area, Simons is not even sure that his firm is dominating its selected niche. He thought his company still had the largest market share in its products, but he suspected that position may be eroding.

THE WHOLESALE LUMBER INDUSTRY

Wholesale lumber companies provide the linking pin between the lumber producer and retailer or end-user of the lumber. These wholesale companies are generally small, family-owned businesses, although the past 20 years have seen the rise of larger national or regional wholesalers. Even the larger wholesalers tend to be privately owned, and currently only one lumber wholesaler's stock is traded publicly.

There are at least two dimensions on which lumber wholesalers may differ (Exhibit 1). The first dimension is the breadth of product line handled. Full-line wholesalers carry the entire spectrum of lumber and building products. Studs, plywood, and dimension lumber for building are major

EXHIBIT 1

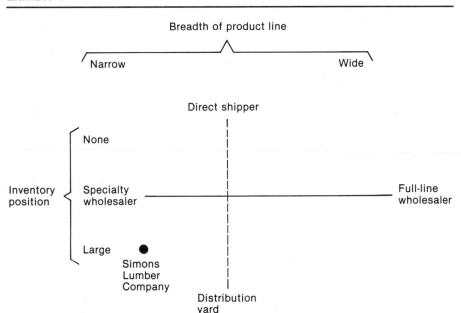

product lines for these firms. These products are often regarded as commodities, and the profit margin per unit may be extremely small; but the market for these products is large, and they tend to sell in large blocks. Given the financial resources and exposure in this type of business, full-line wholesalers tend to be larger than average in size.

As opposed to the full-line wholesaler, the specialty wholesaler has an extremely narrow product line, often only one or two products. Specialty wholesalers are generally found where there is a high degree of product or market knowledge required. Sales volumes are usually smaller for a specialty wholesaler, but markups are generally higher.

A second dimension that distinguishes wholesalers is their inventories. Direct shippers are wholesalers that seldom take physical possession of the products they sell. Their function is to obtain and order from a customer, place it with a mill for production, and the mill then ships it directly to the wholesaler's customer. A distribution yard wholesaler, however, maintains a physical inventory of the product line, in the geographic market where business is conducted. Because of the financial risk and requirements of maintaining a physical inventory, profit margins are generally considerably higher for a distribution yard wholesaler.

Some wholesalers (primarily distribution yards) add additional value to their products by remanufacturing or altering the size, shape, finish, and so on of certain products. It is much easier to enter the wholesale business as a direct shipper than as a distribution yard, because the requirements for entry are limited to mill and customer contacts, as well as credit line for working capital. Many wholesale lumber businesses are started by a sales representative leaving an established firm to start his own direct-shipper company. Often, if the new venture is successful, the new wholesaler will then add distribution yard facilities to his company.

In actual practice, the distinctions between direct shippers and distribution yards should be considered a continuum since many companies may have both direct and distribution yard sales. The 1982 Census of the Wholesale Trade showed 1,317 lumber wholesalers without a yard (direct shippers) and 1,950 wholesalers with a yard (distribution yards).

The North American Wholesale Lumber Association reported that a survey of its members for 1983 showed that average sales per distribution yard were approximately $6.5 million, a 26 percent increase over the previous year. The average sales of the membership companies (both direct and distribution yards) were approximately $21 million in 1983.

The industry still depends heavily on person-to-person contact for developing relationships between customers and suppliers. Wholesalers maintain lists of active, inactive, and potential customers, which are then used by their sales representatives to solicit orders. While face-to-face contact was once the most prevalent method of soliciting business, telephone contact is now far more prevalent, given the cost of travel. One wholesale trade association survey estimated the average lumber wholesaler's telephone expense during 1983 was $84,000. Obviously, the telephone expense is de-

EXHIBIT 2
New Housing Units Started 1977–1984 (in thousands)

1978	1979	1980	1981	1982	1983	1984
2,036	1,760	1,313	1,100	1,072	1,712	1,753

pendent on the intensity of the firm's marketing area and its geographic trading area.

Inasmuch as lumber is an undifferentiated product, suppliers in this industry compete heavily on price and service (product expertise, advantageous delivery schedules, etc.). Those products which are regarded as commodities, such as 2×4s and plywood, are exceedingly price sensitive, and most customers have little loyalty to a particular manufacturer or wholesaler. Specialty items are somewhat more differentiated, and a customer may be dependent on a wholesaler for highly technical information. Brand or supplier loyalty is somewhat greater in this class of product.

The major market for lumber in the United States is the housing industry, and the wholesale lumber industry shares many characteristics with it. First, housing demand is highly interest-rate sensitive. Generally, when mortgage rates increase, the demand for new housing falls. Thus, given the swings in interest rates, both the housing and lumber markets are highly cyclical. (See Exhibit 2.)

While demand for lumber may be cyclical, there have been certain changes in the industry in the past 10 years that have affected competition. With energy costs increasing through the 1970s and freight carriers deregulated in the 1980s, the cost of transportation became a significant portion of the lumber cost. Many wholesalers, especially those dealing in price-sensitive commodity items, found it necessary to add a traffic manager to their staffs in order to remain competitive. Increased transportation costs also led wholesalers to focus on species of lumber that were geographically closer to the consuming market. In the last 20 years, the amount of lumber from the Pacific Northwest shipped to markets east of the Rockies declined dramatically, while southern pine and eastern Canadian woods increased their market share in the eastern half of the United States.

COMPANY HISTORY

In 1894 Robert Simons joined with partner Bernard Taylor to open a lumberyard in downtown Baltimore. With a small inventory and two delivery wagons, the two men soon prospered. After 15 years of successful operation, Simons bought out Taylor to establish Robert Simons & Sons. The company followed a typical growth path for a lumberyard; that is, serving a wider and larger range of customers. Individual consumers, building contractors, and, later, industrial accounts were sought. As the company entered the 1920s, its customer base was centered around the building contractor and industrial trade. This period of prosperity led to profitable years at the company, but Simons' son, who was now president, followed the same conservative financial methods as his father. Thus, the Great Depression was a serious, but not catastrophic, event for the company.

By World War II, the company entered its fastest growth period, supplying material for the war effort. Its largest single customer was the federal government, with large contractors and shipbuilders making up the balance. As the war ended, the nation's attention turned to home building. The pent-up demand during the Depression and the war years produced a huge surge in building, and, by this time, the company had evolved into a large, full-line retailer, carrying the inventory of plywood, studs, roofing materials, etc., as well as a wholesale supplier of timbers to other retail lumber companies within a 50-mile radius.

As the 1950s ended, the third Simons to manage the company was facing increasing competitive pressure from much larger retail lumber companies. Sales volume was at a record high for the company, but profits were down due to margins eroding under competitive price cutting. Since Simons was well known and respected by the lumber retailers (he had just completed a three-year term as president of their national trade association), he decided to eliminate the high-volume, high-exposure retail business and concentrate on wholesaling or supplying the needs of his former competitors. A year after the switch was made, annual sales had dropped 70 percent, with profits down 10 percent.

The business continued basically unchanged through the 1960s until 1969, when the fourth Simons joined the company as a salesman. The difference between the two generations was apparent by the approach each took to the company. The elder Simons focused on sales and customer relations, even though many of the sales were not very profitable. The younger Simons concentrated on smaller, high-profit segments of the market. Profit, not total sales, was the emphasis of the young Simons. At that time, the company's customer base was approximately 40 percent retail yards and 60 percent large contractors and industrials. Throughout the early 1970s, the company focused on developing the higher-margin retail lumber customer and deemphasizing the contractor business, where sales were always subject to competitive bidding. The geographic trading area was expanded to a 200-mile radius of Baltimore. Products were added that were more architectural and less industrial in nature.

ORGANIZATION/MANAGEMENT

The company is currently managed by the fourth generation of the Simons family, Stephen Simons. Simons had spent his entire adult life in the business, with the exception of the period he was away working toward a graduate degree. The small size of the company prevented even a functional organization, since each employee had to be able to do several jobs, which might have been unrelated. The office was located in suburban Baltimore, and at this location were the president, the two inside salespeople, and a secretary. Simons handled all of the purchasing and financial duties as well as those sales calls which required engineering or technical information. Karen Welsh and Jane Watson, the two salespeople, handled the more routine orders and inquiries as well as shipping details. Mrs. Welsh and Mrs. Watson had both started with the company as secretaries approximately six years ago. As they became increasingly familiar with the company's customers and products, they began to assume increasing sales responsibilities. The secretary/bookkeeper took care of general office work and the operation of the company's minicomputer.

The yard and sawmill were located on an eight-acre site in an industrial section of Baltimore. Over the years, the market value of this property had increased dramatically, and Simons wondered whether it was still economically feasible to operate a lumber company from this site. The property consisted of the building where the millwork machines were housed and another small storage building where some of the finished lumber was stored. Most of the lumber was stored outside, and the lack of inside storage had limited the types of products which the company could consider carrying in its inventory.

The yard foreman and six workers were employed at this location. Joe David, the yard foreman, had been employed by the company for 10 years, having taken over from a predecessor who had been there for 40 years. David was given a great deal of discretion in the operation of the yard. Unless there was a special requirement, David scheduled all production as well as maintained the elderly and specialized sawmill machines. He was generally responsible for the hiring, management, and discipline of six subordinate employees.

The company enjoyed a high degree of loyalty from most of its employees. The office salespeople and the yard foreman received annual bonuses based on the company's profit, and, in good years, these bonuses were in the range of 25 percent of base salary. Unlike a large number of its competitors, the company did not lay off its yard employees during the slow winter months, and Simons believed this steady employment policy helped maintain the workers' loyalty. The company also contributed a certain amount to a qualified profit-sharing trust for the employees' retirement.

CORPORATE PHILOSOPHY

In its long history, the company had gone through several expansions/contractions, yet its objective had always been to focus on high-profit and fairly small types of markets, where its flexibility and ability to provide specialized service allowed it to compete successfully. Simons' philosophy had been to avoid marketing wars with major wholesalers and manufacturers and to compete in those market segments which appeared too small or unattractive to its bigger competitors. When Simons Lumber shifted from a retailer to a wholesaler in the late 1950s, the company adopted a policy of not competing with its customers. This policy, which had earned it a high degree of customer loyalty, had also had its costs. On a number of occasions, Simons had lost orders to other wholesalers who bid the job direct to the contractor (thus eliminating the retailer). During the 1960s, Stephen Simons had considered buying a treating plant, which chemically preserved the lumber. Simons correctly believed that this field was a high-growth area but did not follow through with the acquisition because it would have meant competing with one of the company's largest customers at the time. As it turned out, this customer was later lost, and Simons regretted not having entered the treating business.

In terms of financial philosophy, Simons had always followed a conservative path. For the past several years, the company had carried no long-term debt, and generally has retained almost all of its current earnings each year.

Through its philosophy of operating in sheltered niches, as well as its highly conservative financial posture, Simons Lumber had always generated a profit and seldom, if ever, incurred a loss.

PRODUCT LINE

The company marketed three main types of products: timbers, laminated beams, and roof decking. As of 1984, timbers, laminated beams, and decking accounted for 50 percent, 35 percent, and 15 percent of total sales, respectively. These products were used on expensive single-family construction as well as commercial buildings. The timbers were generally used for structural purposes, such as exposed beam ceilings. Simons bought this material from lumber mills in the Pacific Northwest and often remilled the lumber to the customers' specifications. Although the timbers carried a high profit margin, they also had high handling and manufacturing costs associated with them. Demand for this product had been fairly stable over the past 10 years and had shown very little growth.

The laminated beams were used in applications very similar to that of the solid-sawn timbers, but the laminated beams (or glulams) offered significantly greater strength than a solid-sawn timber and had greater dimensional stability and aging characteristics. These advantages had a price, however, in that a laminated beam was about 50 percent more expensive than a comparable piece of solid-sawn timber. Generally speaking, glulams were used in more contemporary types of architecture, whereas solid-sawn timbers were seen in more rustic or traditional structures. The market for laminated beams had grown steadily over the past five years, even with the entry of new competitors.

Roof decking was a product that was generally applied over exposed beams to form the ceiling of the structure. After the decking was nailed down, insulation and roofing shingles were applied to complete the roof of the structure. Decking was produced in a variety of sizes and grades, but Simons carried only the premium grades since the appearance of the ceiling was so critical in these applications.

MARKETING PROMOTION

The marketing effort of Simons Lumber Company was concentrated in the Middle Atlantic area of the United States. Because lumber had a fairly high weight-to-value ratio, freight costs made it difficult for the company to be competitive much more than 250 miles from its distribution yard. The company's primary customers were retail lumber dealers. While chain retailers bought from the company, approximately 80 percent of the company's sales were to independently owned retail lumber dealers. When a builder needed a timber-type product, he generally contacted the lumber retailer who was supplying the other construction lumber on the job. This retailer then asked for quotations from suppliers like Simons.

Up until the 1960s, the geographic scope of the business was limited enough that personal sales calls were the main thrust of the company's marketing effort. As the geographic area expanded, customers were seen personally on a less frequent basis and increasing emphasis was placed on telephone sales. The bulk of the telephone contacts consisted mainly of order taking; that is, quoting price and availability to customers. Technical or large jobs were handled either by Stephen Simons or the senior salesperson. Simons was worried that too much of the telephone contact was coming in from the customers, rather than being initiated by his sales personnel. While he had sent the two salespeople to several telemarketing seminars sponsored by the telephone company, outgoing calls generally increased for a time and then subsided.

Advertising the company and its products had been frustrated by the lack of an effective medium for this effort. Until very recently, there was no publication for the wholesale trade that focused on the company's geographic area. The use of a national publication was judged too costly to be effective. For these reasons, the company had relied on exhibiting at the one annual trade show that was located in the Middle Atlantic market as well as using direct mail. The direct-mail efforts, undertaken on a somewhat sporadic basis, had generally been successful in temporarily increasing the sales of existing products, but Simons realized that these efforts must be more consistent and regular if they were to have a major and long-lasting effect. At the current time, Simons had initiated a program of a direct mailing to retail lumber dealers on a once-a-month level of frequency. Additionally, the two salespeople had been assigned a number of accounts, which they were to contact and solicit on a regular basis.

A LOOK AT COMPETITORS

While competition was keen in the wholesale lumber industry, the niches in which the Simons Company operated were somewhat protected. The company did, however, face different competitors in each of its product lines.

Over the past 15 years, the number of competitors in the timber portion of the business had declined. Major competitors in New York and Washington failed in the last housing recession. While some benefit accrued to the company from the failings of its competitors, direct shippers and new products prevented this occurrence from being a major windfall. The increasing popularity of treated yellow pine timbers had resulted in the loss of market share in certain very small timber sizes. Likewise, a large national wholesaler had started to carry a small inventory of popular-size timbers that cost significantly less than Simons'. While the quality of the competitor's timber was so much lower that they could not be used for exposed applications, the competitor's cost advantage had resulted in the loss of a certain amount of business where the appearance of the lumber was not important. Finally, packaged home kits which featured exposed beams had also increased competition for Simons since some homebuyers opted for a packaged home, which did not contain Simons beams, rather than a custom-built home, which Simons might have been able to supply.

In the laminated sector of the market, the company had competed with several of the largest wholesalers in the country who operated in the Baltimore area over the past 15 years, only to see these wholesalers exit the market in disarray. While laminated beams carried a high profit margin, this product normally sold in fairly small quantities (compared to the commodity products these wholesalers were used to) and required a substantial amount of technical expertise and advice. The most successful competitor, Rogers Supply, was another small (but larger than Simons) wholesaler located approximately 60 miles away. Like Simons, this wholesaler supplied a quality product and technical information; but, unlike Simons, Rogers distributed the product to anyone, retailer or builder. While Rogers' distribution technique angered retailers who may have been eliminated from a sale, these retailers often continued to buy from Rogers if the price was advantageous.

Competition in the decking market depended on the size and grade of decking being considered. Of the three products that Simons handled, decking had less value added than any of the other products and was considered by some to be almost a commodity product. For this reason, profit margins were about half of what Simons received on its other two product classes.

Two-inch-thick decking constituted the majority of decking sales in the Simons' market area, and this product was carried by a number of small and large competitors. Especially in the lower grades, competition was fierce, and price alone often determined which supplier got the order. Simons concentrated on the premium appearance grade of decking, which highly complimented the timbers and beams that it sold. The competition was somewhat less rigorous than in the lower grades, and profit margins were better, although total sales volume was smaller.

A smaller portion of the total decking market was 3-inch-thick decking, which was used on very large residential jobs as well as commercial construction. Simons was one of the few wholesalers in the area to stock this product, and when small quantities were needed or the material was needed rapidly, Simons had little competition. On larger jobs (a truckload or more) when the material was not needed immediately, Simons faced competition from direct-shipment wholesalers and from the lumber manufacturers themselves. Whereas a sale from inventory carried a markup of 15 to 20 percent, a direct sale often carried a markup of 5 percent or less, depending on the order size. Simons often quoted the larger jobs on a direct-shipment basis, but the main focus had been on the smaller orders where little competitive pressure exists.

FINANCIAL INFORMATION

The stock of the company was owned by Stephen Simons (33 percent) and his father (67 percent). While the elder Simons had not been active in the company since his retirement 13 years ago, he controlled the majority of the stock and still came to the office every day. Any major changes in the company's operations had to meet with his approval.

Stephen Simons had found it difficult to assess the company's performance relative to its competitors. Since most of its competitors were closely held, there were few financial comparisons available, and much of the data published in secondary sources were based on companies that are very different in size, geographical scope, and product specialization. During the late 1970s, the industry trade association collected information from member companies and published averages that Simons found very useful. These reports showed that, compared to industry averages, Simons Lumber had lower total sales per employee, a lower growth rate, and among the highest gross margin per employee and the highest return on sales. Simons found this data very useful, but the reports were discontinued in 1982 because so few wholesalers were willing to release sensitive financial information.

The company had always followed a conservative financial policy. Suppliers had always valued their relationship with the company, since it had discounted every invoice since its founding. At the present time, the conservative financial posture had become dysfunctional. The company, like other closely held firms, had seldom paid a dividend. Until 1975, earnings were small enough that this did not pose a problem. However, the past 10 years had seen a large increase in the level of earnings without a corresponding increase in cash usage. Now, the IRS was suggesting that the amount of cash retained was unreasonable and wanted the company to pay a sizable dividend.

Balance sheets and income statements for the past five years are pre-

EXHIBIT 3

SIMONS LUMBER COMPANY
Balance Sheet
For the Years 1981–1985

	1981	1982	1983	1984	1985
Assets					
Current assets:					
Cash	$ 148,213	$ 250,524	$ 599,944	$ 695,267	$ 418,391
Marketable securities	423,102	401,362	135,645	180,006	1,048,743
Accounts receivable/trade ..	154,242	220,227	146,880	161,234	189,082
Accounts receivable/other ..	14,366	23,741	94,688	95,638	100,825
Inventory.................	529,948	582,436	427,128	515,288	505,727
Life insurance	120,777	141,824	166,546	296,334	313,962
Total current assets......	1,390,648	1,620,112	1,570,831	1,943,767	2,567,731
Fixed assets (net):					
Land	158,460	158,460	85,500	85,500	85,500
Buildings.................	0	0	0	0	0
Machinery and equipment ..	54,857	61,617	47,150	37,797	36,072
Transportation	70,999	64,192	12,067	7,148	0
Office fixtures............	17,301	13,384	16,944	4,830	6,264
Total fixed assets........	301,617	297,652	161,662	135,274	127,836
Total assets	$1,692,265	$1,917,765	$1,732,492	$2,079,041	$2,704,566
Liabilities and Stockholders' Equity					
Current liabilities:					
Accounts payable—trade ...	$ 300,711	$ 359,026	$ 15,861	$ 28,624	$ 284,939
Accrued salaries	52,060	33,964	0	121,410	220,362
Federal and state taxes payable	11,353	(276)	42,839	27,090	26,344
Accrued profit-sharing pay..	34,200	34,200	11,400	57,000	45,600
Total current liabilities:...	398,324	426,915	70,101	234,124	577,245
Stockholders' equity:					
Preferred stock (2,394 shares 7% cumulative— $100)	239,400	239,400	239,400	239,400	239,400
Common stock (978 shares outstanding)	185,820	185,820	185,820	185,820	185,820
Retained earnings	868,722	1,065,630	1,237,172	1,419,697	1,702,102
Total stockholders' equity.	1,293,942	1,490,850	1,662,392	1,844,917	2,127,322
Total liabilities and stockholders' equity...............	$1,692,265	$1,917,765	$1,732,492	$2,079,041	$2,704,566

EXHIBIT 4

SIMONS LUMBER COMPANY
Income Statement
For the Years 1981–1985

	1981	1982	1983	1984	1985
Sales.	$2,441,559	$2,478,704	$2,115,194	$2,808,037	$3,124,242
Cost of goods sold	1,576,373	1,614,939	1,241,359	1,734,360	1,998,253
Gross profit	865,186	863,765	873,835	1,073,677	1,125,989
Yard expenses:					
Payroll and payroll taxes . . .	175,750	176,700	176,493	185,820	193,840
Maintenance.	38,243	25,095	18,445	20,340	51,619
Delivery expenses	8,370	11,558	12,470	2,544	4,590
Gas and oil.	14,343	19,492	16,205	16,958	16,931
Electricity	6,998	6,205	6,283	8,402	9,893
Depreciation.	30,997	50,287	31,445	26,408	22,813
Total yard	274,700	289,338	261,341	260,471	299,687
Administrative expenses:					
Payroll and payroll taxes . . .	198,489	218,198	218,717	267,803	267,030
Group insurance	19,521	22,215	26,963	22,048	16,942
Office rent.	10,501	12,369	13,994	15,650	16,255
Office supplies.	16,781	11,290	15,324	13,631	21,307
Advertising	3,350	3,002	1,395	1,132	1,845
Insurance	38,663	40,157	38,293	33,953	24,229
Professional expenses	3,040	3,059	8,797	5,206	10,606
Local taxes.	7,877	8,170	8,512	8,989	10,784
Travel and entertainment . . .	23,839	16,199	10,456	2,504	1,628
Dues and subscriptions	7,230	5,974	6,625	5,273	5,666
Contributions	276	243	190	8,398	846
Pension expense	70,161	78,181	83,706	87,231	90,223
Profit-sharing expense	34,200	34,200	11,400	57,000	45,600
Interest expense.	5,200	5,210	5,341	5,105	0
Telephone.	15,130	17,961	20,281	21,709	22,637
Bad debts	1,102	10,406	950	561	1,353
Miscellaneous expense.	4,342	0	0	0	0
Total administrative	459,701	486,833	470,942	556,193	536,950
Operating profit.	130,785	87,594	141,552	257,013	289,353
Other income:					
Interest income	65,092	83,249	67,097	80,186	99,058
Rental income	25,080	23,370	18,240	1,520	0
Purchase discounts.	29,826	31,160	26,828	0	0
Miscellaneous	2,784	5,159	(2,831)	5,360	3,612
Total other income.	122,782	142,937	109,334	87,066	102,670
Net profits before taxes	253,566	230,531	250,886	344,079	392,023
Federal and state taxes	39,900	42,231	51,602	44,916	47,500
Net profits after taxes	$ 213,666	$ 188,300	$ 199,283	$ 299,163	$ 344,523

sented in Exhibits 3 and 4. Several facts should be noted about the financial statements:

1. Starting in 1984, purchase discounts were netted against the company's purchases, rather than presented separately.

2. The pension expense represents payments to employees who retired prior to the inception of the current pension plan.
3. Federal and state taxes are not a constant percentage of profits due to various credits and adjustments.
4. Inventory values are calculated on a LIFO basis.
5. The life insurance figure is the cash surrender value of policies on the officers.

FUTURE OUTLOOK

The future of the Simons Lumber Company is highly dependent on the choices made in the next year. Given the fairly stable nature of the company's products and personnel, Simons is reasonably confident that the company can continue to earn a satisfactory profit over the next five years with minimal supervision on his part. On the other hand, expansion would dictate many major changes in personnel and the way the company currently operates. (An organization chart is shown in Exhibit 5.)

EXHIBIT 5
Organization Chart

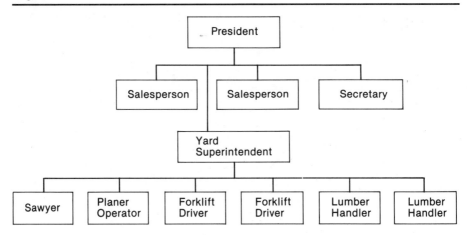

CASE 2–7

Webber Manufacturing Company, Inc. (A)

In April 1979 Richard Dirlam, general manager of Webber Manufacturing Company, was considering the future of his company in the environmental test chamber industry. Although he would not have financial statements until July, first-quarter shipments were up over the same period last year. If the present trends continued to the end of the year, sales would reach the 1974 high of $1.4 million, and it was possible that Webber would finish the year in the black. If that happened, it would be the first profit the company had earned since he became general manager in 1975. Perhaps all the long hours, difficult decisions, and changes he had made over the last four years were beginning to pay off.

"Now that we seem to have our internal systems under control," Dirlam said thoughtfully, "we need to grow—not by 10 percent or 20 percent a year, but dramatically. We need to get up there to $6 or $7 million in sales."

"The thing that concerns us most right now is that there seems to be a definite trend toward segmentation in the industry. By this I mean all our competitors are developing their product segments and polishing them, and we haven't done that. Oh, we've talked about it and we've seen opportunities, but other people seem to be there just ahead of us, or after we really understood it, they've been there for a long time. The biggest thing it takes to succeed in our industry is low price. We came in with the notion that you could sell quality. You cannot sell quality in volume. The only thing you can sell in volume is low price; and to get a true low price with profitability, you've got to have a real niche. We're not at all sure there are any niches left for us to assume."

On this somewhat pessimistic note, Richard Dirlam, general manager, and Paul Richardson, manager of marketing for Webber Manufacturing Company, concluded a meeting at which the future of the environmental test chamber industry in general, and Webber Manufacturing Company in particular, had been the topic of discussion.

ENVIRONMENTAL TEST CHAMBER INDUSTRY

Environmental test chambers (ETCs) were enclosures of various dimensions which ranged from approximately 1 cubic foot of interior volume to 12,000

This case was prepared by Gary Willard under the direction of Professor Arnold C. Cooper, Purdue University. © Copyright 1981 Purdue Research Foundation. All rights reserved.

cubic feet of interior volume in which certain environmental conditions could be produced and maintained for product testing and evaluation purposes. Prices ranged from a few hundred dollars to several hundred thousand dollars. The great majority, however, sold for between $5,000 and $50,000 each. Temperatures could be ranged from −200°F to 350°F, relative humidity levels could be varied from 10 percent to 95 percent, and pressures could be ranged from atmospheric pressure at sea level to the equivalent of an altitude of 200,000 feet or more.

The product line included temperature chambers, temperature and humidity chambers, temperature and altitude chambers, thermal shock cabinets, AGREE chambers, industrial freezers, and biological freezers.[1]

Purchasers of these products represented an international cross section of industrial, governmental, medical, and educational institutions. See Exhibit 1 for Webber's sales. Industrial demands for ETCs were for use in research labs, as a part of many production line processes and in quality control and product testing procedures. Primary governmental uses were for weapons testing programs, aeronautical and space research projects, and for low-temperature storage of biomedical specimens. Medical and educational uses were commonly in research labs and for low-temperature processing and storage of biological specimens. The demand for ETCs was not dependent on the economic conditions of any particular industry but tended to come from the current growth segments of the general economy.

Major industrial purchasers of the ETCs included steel manufacturers, various divisions of the leading automakers, aerospace manufacturers, solid-state and industrial electronics firms, biomedical and pharmaceutical companies, chemical producers, and consumer product manufacturers. Many major users of ETCs required more than one type. A major auto manufacturer, for example, might require industrial freezers for the hardening of certain engine parts, thermal shock cabinets for testing electronic subassemblies before installation, and temperature and humidity chambers for various tests on completed engines. Although it was not always the case, many users of different types of ETCs tended to favor purchasing additional units of one type from their previous source for that type chamber.

---

[1] *Thermal shock cabinets* are enclosures in which the product being tested can be subjected to the stresses of repeated cycling under rapid and extreme temperature fluctuations.

AGREE chambers derive their name from the Advisory Group for Reliability of Electronic Equipment and are a special type of ETC designed specifically for reliability testing of airborne electronic equipment. Performance requirements include variable-frequency vibration, temperature, humidity, and altitude and are rigorously controlled by military specifications.

Industrial freezers are chest-type enclosures used in hardening metals after heat treating and in many production applications where molecular structures of materials must be modified.

Biological freezers are chest, cabinet, or walk-in enclosures with precise temperature and humidity capabilities used in preparation and storage of biomedical specimens.

EXHIBIT 1
Classification of Sales of Purchaser

Purchaser	Approximate Percentage of Total Sales	
	1970–1974	*1977–1979**
U.S. government		
Military-related	20%	8%
Nonmilitary-related	4	1
Total U.S. government	24	9
Nonprofit organizations	2	3
Industrial sales†	‡	
Automotive industry		15
Electronics industry		33
Heat-treating industry		24
Other		14
Total industrial sales	63	86
Foreign sales	11	2
	100%	100%

* 1979 figures are projected year-end figures based on first-quarter shipments and firm orders scheduled for shipment in 1979.
† Classification of industrial sales by industry is somewhat arbitrary due to multiple needs for which various customers purchase chambers.
‡ Breakdown of industrial sales not available for years 1970–1974.

Source: Webber Company records and case writer's classification.

ETC manufacturers were basically assemblers who purchased more or less standard industrial supply components ranging from sophisticated programmable microprocessors to mechanical refrigeration compressors, controls, and accessories to ordinary steel sheets and angle iron. Then they assembled these into the various combinations and configurations necessary to meet the needs of the purchasers. Most of the work was performed by semiskilled workmen using general-purpose tools in a job shop-type operation. Skilled workmen were required for the installation and adjustment of the refrigeration equipment, electrical wiring, and in the final testing and adjusting of the completed chamber. The time required for final testing and adjusting before shipment varied from 24 hours to two weeks depending on the complexity of the specifications and the nature of any problems encountered. The completed product was customarily shipped to the purchaser completely assembled, requiring only electrical power connections (and in some cases, water and drain connections) to be made in the field.

The ETC industry was fragmented and had no industry association or spokesman. Approximately 40 relatively small firms, the largest of which had sales of $11.3 million in 1978, comprised the industry. In 1978 the three largest firms accounted for 52 percent of industry sales. Most ETC manufacturers did not make the full product line but chose to compete only in particular segments of the market. Only the two largest firms in the industry competed aggressively in all segments of the market.

Industry sales,[2] which totaled approximately $25 million in 1975, $31 million in 1976, $34 million in 1977, and $38 million in 1978, were expected to reach $50 million in 1979.

ETCs were usually purchased on the basis of competitive bids or negotiated design-bid-build contracts for larger and more specialized needs or "catalog shopping" for smaller, standardized models.

When purchased by competitive bids, the purchaser would prepare a specification establishing the minimum performance requirements for the chamber. These specifications established the temperature, humidity, and pressure levels to be maintained, the product load which had to be handled, the time constraints for reaching the design conditions after the product was added, and the allowable fluctuation in parameter levels. In addition, the specifications defined the instrumentation and control devices desired, the degree of programmability required, and the construction techniques and materials to be incorporated in the chamber. The completed specification was then submitted to interested firms for the preparation of bids. Bidders would then perform whatever design and engineering work was necessary to prepare their bid. Depending on the nature of the product application and the specification, preparation of the bid might involve up to 80 man-hours. On the date set to receive bids, the purchaser determined which of the several bidders had submitted the lowest bid in accordance with the specification and normally awarded the contract for the chamber to the lowest bidder. For most governmental purchases, the opening of bids was public; that is, the bids were opened and read in the presence of the interested parties. Many, if not most, industrial bid openings were private; that is, the bidders were not permitted to be present at the opening. In private biddings the bidder was usually advised only that his bid was accepted or rejected but was not told how his bid compared with those of the other bidders.

In a negotiated design-bid-build situation, the purchaser would contact one or more ETC manufacturers to discuss the purchaser's requirements and constraints. The manufacturer would then design and price whatever product he felt best met these requirements and submit to the purchaser his proposal for solving the purchaser's problem. The purchaser would then evaluate the proposals to determine which best met his needs. Two or more personal contacts between the purchaser and the ETC manufacturer were required for almost every proposal. Since different manufacturers might

---

[2] Industry sales estimates are by Webber Manufacturing Company and are for that portion of the market in which Webber competes.

propose different solutions to the problem, price was not always the determining factor in making the award. Time lags of a year or more between the initial contact with the purchaser and delivery of the completed chamber were not uncommon.

For small, relatively standardized chambers, the purchaser frequently selected from a manufacturer's catalog the model which seemed best suited to his particular need. Then after some comparison shopping between manufacturers who cataloged similar products, he simply placed the order with the firm whose product seemed to offer the best buy.

WEBBER MANUFACTURING COMPANY

Webber Manufacturing Company (WMC) was incorporated in Indianapolis, Indiana, in 1948. Robert C. Webber, who developed and patented eight inventions relating to mechanical refrigeration and freezing, was the founder and president. Webber's wife was secretary-treasurer and managed the accounting and financial affairs of the company.

From 1948 through 1973, Webber, in addition to his duties as president, was responsible for product design, engineering, production management, and all sales efforts. By 1973, sales had grown to $1.2 million (approximately 200 chambers), almost 20 percent of which were foreign sales. As the demand for ETCs grew, the selling function demanded more and more of Webber's time, requiring his frequent absence from the factory for extended periods. In 1973, responsibility for product design and production management was delegated, but Webber continued to direct the sales efforts of the company.

WMC's Marketing (under R. C. Webber)

The marketing efforts under Webber were a combination of personal selling, directed advertising, and competitive bidding for government installations.

Personal selling by Webber accounted for the majority of the orders received by the company. It was felt that the technical nature of the product, and the fact that 90 percent of all orders were "custom built" to a specification, required the expertise, attention, and technical knowledge of a trained salesperson. Except for a full-time sales agent in India whom Webber had personally trained, all selling was done by Webber.

Advertising in selected trade journals directed to the automotive and heat-treating industries and to the quality control function was felt to be a primary source of new inquiries.

A government bidding service, to which WMC subscribed, provided plans, specifications, and bidding documents, permitting the company to submit bids on many government agency purchases of ETCs. In addition to the prebid services, after each bidding WMC was furnished a tabulation of the bids on all such jobs, indicating which competitors had bid and what their bids were.

All sales were the result of written quotations prepared and priced under Webber's direction. Prices quoted were based on historic costs of similar jobs completed over the previous three years, plus or minus some factor intended to compensate for differences between the job being quoted and the previous similar jobs. Quoted prices did not change significantly between 1972 and 1975, a point which Webber emphasized in many of his proposals.

WMC's Production (under R. C. Webber)

The production techniques used could best be described as a team approach. When an order was released for production, a group of employees would be assigned to it, and those individuals would then build the enclosure, install the mechanical system, perform all electrical wiring, test the completed unit, paint the unit, and crate up the shipment. Total responsibility for a particular order was thus "fixed" in a particular team of employees. Very few construction drawings of any kind were used in the manufacturing process. Problems regarding construction were resolved on an ad hoc basis, usually by consensus of the team members. The average time for an order to be in the shop, from release to shipping date, was 105 days.

Components, materials, and supplies were ordered on a job basis, but no materials requisition system or purchase order system was used. A few basic supplies and materials, common to most orders, were kept in stock, but there was no stockroom or inventory control system. No cost accounting system was used.

By early 1975 Webber and his wife, then in their early 60s, had accumulated a number of interests outside the company and were frequently absent for periods of several weeks. On several occasions Webber had expressed a willingness to sell the company.

WMC's New Management Team

Richard Dirlam and Paul Richardson were recent graduates of Purdue University's Krannert Graduate School of Management. Both were approximately 30 years old and had previous leadership experience as military officers, but had no previous business management experience. During their final year in the M.S.[3] program in Krannert, they became acquainted with a successful Indianapolis businessman who suggested they consider starting their own business or buying an existing business as an alternative to the placement interview routine graduating masters students usually followed.

---

[3] Master of science in management.

They began the search for a suitable company, and it was soon learned that WMC was for sale. After an initial three-month investigation by Dirlam, negotiations were begun, and a purchase agreement was completed. Forty-nine percent of the outstanding common stock was reacquired by WMC for cash, and the remaining stock was acquired by an Indianapolis manufacturing firm. An unsecured $250,000 line of credit for working capital was arranged with an Indianapolis bank, and an immediate loan of $100,000 was obtained from the parent company. Webber's relationship to the parent company was one of a wholly owned but autonomous subsidiary. No profit criteria were imposed by the parent, and profits would not be remitted to the parent company. Webber could not draw upon the parent for engineering or financial resources and would be required to repay the $100,000 loan at a rate of $21,450 per year.

In July 1975 Dirlam was appointed general manager in charge of production, internal controls, financial matters, and company policy. Richardson became marketing manager, responsible for all sales work, product promotion, advertising, and new-product development. Although not originally anticipated, product promotion, advertising, and new-product development responsibilities required nearly 70 percent of Richardson's time during the first three years. Webber agreed to remain with the new management team as a marketing consultant for one year to acquaint Richardson with WMC's customers, procedures, and products. After three months, Dirlam and Richardson felt they had no further need for Webber's counsel. Mrs. Webber retired from the business. No other personnel changes were made. The existing facilities were leased from the former owners.

Dirlam related his perception of the job that lay ahead when he became general manager.

> There was simply no system for doing anything. There were no books, no records, no order control system. We didn't know how many orders we had, how long we had them, or when they would be shipped. We couldn't tell what was on order or for what job. It was a major accomplishment in August when we got our first bank statement, so we knew what the cash balance was.

Richardson described the product and marketing problems he encountered.

> It was obvious we had some product problems. Our control system was cam-operated,[4] which was really rather primitive—since our competition was using tape-controlled programmers and were known to be working on a control system even more sophisticated than that. We had a catalog of "standard" models, many of which we had *never* built. Our products were overdesigned

---

[4] *Cam-operated* control systems used plastic discs cut to the shape of a desired control sequence to physically open and close control contacts as the discs rotate. Necessarily, the control sequences must be relatively simple for this type of actuating system to work.

and underpriced. Our design was not competitive—we simply built a better, heavier-duty product than the specifications called for. That made it difficult for us to get a competitive bid job; and if we did get one, it meant we weren't likely to make any money on it. What we really did well was to build what the competition couldn't build, the really special units that couldn't just be thrown together off the shelf. I suppose you could say we were just a big job shop. We could build anything you asked for—as long as we could build it one at a time.

The foreign sales were discouraging, too. Not only were sales terribly competitive, but there were all the delays and paperwork involved in letters of credit and foreign exchange. The first year's warranty service could really get to be expensive. We really never should have been in the foreign market to begin with.

During the first three years, the new management team instituted several important changes. An order control system was developed to process incoming customer orders to assure that necessary parts and components were ordered and expedited and that delivery dates could be scheduled and met. A materials requisition–purchase order system was established to complement the order control system, to aid in identifying materials when deliveries were made, and to eliminate duplicate orders of components for jobs. A stockroom was established, and components and materials which were frequently used were ordered in quantity for stock. A stockroom clerk was named, and an inventory control system was established.

Standardized drawings and materials lists were developed for many products and introduced into the production process. The "team construction" concept was abolished, and production employees were assigned to one of three departments (welding, cabinetmaking, or refrigeration) on the basis of their skills. Orders entering the shop for production would now pass from department to department in the production process, and problems would be resolved by reference to the standard drawing or the appropriate design technician.

Between 1975 and 1978 nearly 80 percent of the original production employees left the company. Only one individual was terminated. The production staff declined from 43 persons to 21.

Dirlam cited the rate of change as the reason for the high employee turnover.

> We had to change a lot of things. In fact, we had to change most of the things we were doing, or at least the way we were doing them. We didn't try to get rid of anyone, but those who could not adapt to the changes just left. We hated to lose some of them, but we felt the changes we were making were absolutely necessary.

A cost accounting system was introduced which was designed to allow current prices to flow into the job cost records. Components and materials ordered for particular jobs were charged directly to those jobs at invoiced costs. Materials could be drawn from the stockroom for jobs in process only on a material requisition which was charged to that particular job. Careful records of production time were instituted with each job being charged daily with the hours spent on it. The new job cost records provided weekly comparisons between budgeted and actual expenditures for every job in process. Engineering costs, however, were not charged to specific jobs but were considered to be general and administrative costs.

In addition to efforts to install procedural systems covering every function in WMC's operation, the new management was also faced with a sizable backlog of previously accepted but clearly unprofitable orders. There also were a number of partially completed orders which had stalled at some stage in the production process because of the technological problems, and a considerable number of outstanding quotations for which orders could be placed at prices quoted by the previous owner.

"We had to decide," Dirlam related, "whether we would bite our lip and finish those orders, knowing we would lose money, or whether we would try to get out of them. Our lip got awfully sore, but we thought it would be better in the long run—better for our reputation if we lived up to the bargain—even though we didn't make it, we just inherited it. I think there was only one order we got out of, and that was by mutual agreement with the customer. I think he wanted out of it almost as badly as we did."

Early in 1976 WMC announced a substantial price increase. Following the increase, WMC was less and less successful in winning foreign contracts. In July 1978, partially because of this lack of success but also in view of the increasing complexity of fluctuating rates of exchange and the cost of performing warranty service, the decision was made to withdraw from active pursuit of the foreign market. WMC concentrated its sales efforts in the United States, generally east of the Mississippi plus Louisiana and Texas, and in Canada. Marketing emphasis was placed on the automotive, electronics, and heat-treating industries. About 40 percent of Richardson's sales calls were directed to the heat-treating industry. The remainder were divided equally between the automotive industry, the electronics industry, and "all other" potential purchasers. Approximately 25 percent of the ETCs Webber submitted prices on were competitive bid, plan, and specification jobs.

Product-line adjustments made during these years resulted in dropping industrial freezers, temperature and altitude chambers, and AGREE chambers. Value engineering[5] studies were implemented on the remaining products to improve WMC's competitive position and profit margin. See Exhibits 2, 3 and 4 for production and product data. A decision to change compressor

---

[5] *Value engineering* is a process by which manufacturers identify and correct instances of overdesign in existing products to achieve a better match between customer expectations and product performance. A major emphasis of VE is cost reduction without performance impairment.

EXHIBIT 2
Summary of Annual Production

	1975‡	1976	1977	1978	1979*
Number of chambers†	100	115	102	62	66
Total chamber dollars	$1,144,000	$1,177,000	$993,000	$740,000	$1,291,000
Average number of employees	37	43	32	26	30
Average revenues					
Dollars per chamber	$11,400	$10,235	$ 9,735	$11,935	$19,560
Dollars per employee	$31,000	$27,000	$31,000	$28,000	$43,000

* 1979 figures are projected year-end figures based on first-quarter shipments and firm orders scheduled for shipment in 1979.
† Figures shown here are for chambers only. Income statement sales include chambers, parts, and services.
‡ June–December; annualized.

Source: Company records.

EXHIBIT 3
Average Gross Margin by Product Type

Product Type	1977	1978	1979*
Standard industrial freezers	0.244	0.234	0.197
Special industrial freezers	0.348	0.277	0.363
Standard test chambers	0.278	0.151	0.215
Standard biological freezers	0.327	0.203	
Special biological freezers		0.333	

* 1979 figures are projected year-end figures based on first-quarter shipments and firm orders scheduled for shipment in 1979.

Source: Company records.

manufacturers was made to improve the reliability of the refrigeration system. That decision resulted in a dramatic reduction of compressor problems from a "failure"[6] rate of 30 percent to 3 percent. This change was soon copied by WMC's competitors. "In this business, you don't have a competitive advantage for long, but value engineering is and will continue to be an important part of our product-line strategy," Richardson explained.

---

[6] Webber Manufacturing Company defines a failure as "any problem which results in the interruption of a planned sequence and requires a service technician to correct."

EXHIBIT 4
Analysis of Product Mix

Proportion of Total Annual Chamber Revenues by Product Type and Market

Market	1977						1978						1979					
	Std. Ind. Freezers	Spec. Ind. Freezers	Std. Test Chambers	Spec. Test Chambers	Std. Bio. Freezers	Spec. Bio. Freezers	Std. Ind. Freezers	Spec. Ind. Freezers	Std. Test Chambers	Spec. Test Chambers	Std. Bio. Freezers	Spec. Bio. Freezers	Std. Ind. Freezers	Spec. Ind. Freezers	Std. Test Chambers	Spec. Test Chambers	Std. Bio. Freezers	Spec. Bio. Freezers
U.S. government, military-related				.10			$<.01$	.01		.07	.01				.03	.02		
U.S. government, nonmilitary-related			.02	.01						.01		.01			.01	.01		
Nonprofit institutions			.10	.09					.04	.01						.01		
Automotive applications			.10	.18					.14	.01						.12		
Electronics applications									.11	.17					.05	.37		
Heat-treating applications		.08	.04	.11	.01			.12					.07	.17				
Other applications				.03					.01	.11					.06	.06		
Foreign sales	.13															.02		
Totals	.13	.08	.26	.52	.01		.17	.13	.30	.38	.01	.01	.07	.17	.15	.61		

EXHIBIT 4 (concluded)

Proportion of Total Annual Chamber Output in Units by Product Type and Market

Market	1977						1978						1979					
	Std. Ind. Freezers	Spec. Ind. Freezers	Std. Test Chambers	Spec. Test Chambers	Std. Bio. Freezers	Spec. Bio. Freezers	Std. Ind. Freezers	Spec. Ind. Freezers	Std. Test Chambers	Spec. Test Chambers	Std. Bio. Freezers	Spec. Bio. Freezers	Std. Ind. Freezers	Spec. Ind. Freezers	Std. Test Chambers	Spec. Test Chambers	Std. Bio. Freezers	Spec. Bio. Freezers
U.S. government, military-related				.04			.02	.02		.06	.02	.02			.04	.02		
U.S. government, nonmilitary-related			.01	.01						.02						.02		
Nonprofit institutions			.08	.08					.02	.02					.02	.02		
Automotive applications									.10	.02						.10		
Electronics applications			.13	.16					.12	.10					.07			
Heat-treating applications	.27						.29	.08					.22			.10		
Other applications			.05	.12	.01				.04	.06					.11	.04		
Foreign sales		.04												.22		.02		
Totals	.27	.04	.27	.41	.01		.31	.10	.28	.28	.02	.02	.22	.22	.24	.32		

In October 1975 Richardson began working with a major electronic control manufacturer to develop a more accurate, versatile, and reliable control system to replace the cam-operated controller used on all Webber products. The cam controller lacked many of the capabilities of the competitors' control systems and was completely unsuitable for certain types of ETCS, thus effectively preventing WMC from bidding on some jobs. It was not until late 1978 that these efforts were successful.

WMC's new control system, called Total Control, eliminated the need for constant supervision during operation of the ETC and provided a keyboard through which the user could enter and store as many as 20 control programs. When activated, a microprocessor would call up the program selected and execute that sequence through as many as 80 steps. If required the controller could "loop back" to repeat a previous step or series of steps. Auxiliary loads, such as cycling the product being tested, could also be controlled by the new system. The controller was "interactive" in that it could proportionately increase or decrease system capacity to compensate for deviations from specified conditions in response to signals from multiple sensors located in the chamber and attached to the product under test.

In addition to a continuous digital display, the complete record of a test sequence—including time, program step number, parameter levels within the chamber, and product status—was kept by local recorders and could be transmitted to a remote quality control information system. A separate alarm system would signal when parameter limits were exceeded. A manual override system permitted an operator to interrupt the programmed sequence and to substitute his own instructions for those of the program. Control could then be returned to the programmed sequence when desired. A battery-operated power source protected the microprocessor memory and kept timers and recorders operating for up to 96 hours in the event of a power failure.

Although the new system was developed specifically for use on WMC's new ETCs, Richardson visualized a sizable retrofit[7] market and an application in controlling other industrial processes such as heat-treating and industrial drying furnaces. Richardson estimated this market for Total Control at 30 units per year, priced at $6,000 to $8,000 each. By April 1979 one had been sold, but WMC had received nearly 200 inquiries regarding Total Control.

Advertising, which had been run in several specialty trade magazines, was discontinued in 1976 to permit Richardson time to determine that the proper publications were being used and that the proper markets were being covered. In 1977 advertising was resumed in four monthly publications

---

[7] Retrofit is a trade term which refers to modifying existing equipment by installing a more recently developed control system or mechanical equipment. In this case it is a later-model control system.

directed to the automotive and electronics industries and to the quality control function. The new advertising plan called for increasing ad size from one-sixth to one-fourth page black and white ads to one-half and full-page ads placed in at least three consecutive issues. Some full-page four-color ads were planned for new product introductions. WMC's advertising budget grew from $6,000 in 1975 to $8,000 in 1977 to $15,000 in 1978 and to nearly $30,000 in 1979. It was expected to remain at that level, adjusted for inflation, for the next few years.

Early in 1979 Richardson contracted with an Indianapolis refrigeration service company to provide after-sale service on Webber's ETCs. The new contract-service company, owned by a former WMC employee, would dispatch a repairman from Indianapolis to the customer's installation site, usually arriving at the site within 72 hours of the receipt of the call.

"We gained three ways in this move," Richardson explained. "We no longer disrupt the production process by pulling someone off the floor to do this; we realize a little additional revenue; and we benefit from increased customer satisfaction because it has improved our response time."

PROFILE OF WMC'S MAJOR COMPETITORS

Thermotron Industries (see Exhibit 5)

Thermotron, the largest manufacturer of ETCs, was founded in 1963 by Charles Conrad, who had begun manufacturing ETCs in 1951. When his original company was purchased in 1962 by Gulf & Western,[8] Conrad formed the new company specifically to manufacture AGREE chambers. From 1962 through 1974 AGREE chambers constituted most of Thermotron's sales, and as late as 1978 the company claimed to have manufactured 90 percent of all AGREE chambers in existence.

In 1975 the company began a major program of market expansion. They aggressively sought competitive bid contracts for installations other than AGREE chambers, entered the market for negotiated contract installations, began development work on a new programmable control system, and began developing a line of standardized catalog models of ETCs in commonly used sizes.

In late 1976 Thermotron introduced the industry's first microprocessor-controlled programmer for ETCs and in early 1977 brought out their first line of standardized, cataloged, in-stock temperature chambers in sizes up to 32 cubic feet. In late 1977 a complementary line of temperature and humidity chambers was announced, permitting Thermotron to cover a significant

---

[8] Gulf & Western liquidated their environmental test chamber business in 1967.

EXHIBIT 5

THERMOTRON INDUSTRIES, INC.
Condensed Comparative Financial Statements
For Fiscal Years Ended March 31, 1974 and 1976–1978

	1974	1976	1977	1978
Assets				
Cash	36,378	61,436	78,959	63,813
Accounts receivable	934,310	1,288,819	1,759,252	2,592,176
Inventory.	806,133	1,290,676	1,919,700	2,444,123
Prepaid expenses	13,493	2,657	116,445	102,872
Total current assets. . . .	1,790,314	2,643,588	3,874,356	5,202,984
Fixed assets	462,531	439,192	324,296	530,874
Note receivable	—	179,721	154,392	147,491
Other assets	143,960	58,537	125,032	130,478
Total assets	2,396,805	3,321,038	4,478,076	6,011,827
Liabilities				
Accounts payable	523,457	594,855	1,207,913	1,498,911
Notes payable	1,024,830	1,146,700	1,626,949	2,016,700
Accrued expenses	302,645	505,039	709,824	1,028,405
Taxes payable (except income)	— *	228,854	—	—
Income taxes payable	— *	—	—	113,654
Total current liabilities .	1,850,932	2,475,448	3,544,686	4,657,670
Long-term debt	129,860	110,215	—	—
Reserves	25,200	61,700	—	—
Other long-term liabilities.	—	—	—	20,000
Total liabilities	2,005,992	2,647,363	3,544,686	4,677,670
Common stock.	33,000	33,000	33,000	33,000
Retained earnings	357,812	640,670	900,390	1,301,157
Total liabilities and equity	2,396,804	3,321,033	4,478,076	6,011,827
Net sales.	n.a.	5,655,763	7,523,230	11,339,000
Net profits.	(156,422)	161,155	228,891	400,767

* Not reported separately prior to 1976.

Source: Webber Manufacturing Company.

part of industry demand with nine models which could be delivered from stock in 5 to 10 days rather than the industry standard of 90 days or more.

In mid-1978 Thermotron introduced a sophisticated vibration table of their own design, coinciding with a change in the military specification governing AGREE chamber testing. The revised military specs were such that virtually no manufacturer's current production model vibration table except Thermotron's would comply. As a result, several of its competitors

EXHIBIT 6

TENNEY ENGINEERING, INC.
Condensed Income Statements
For Fiscal Years Ended December 31, 1974–1977

	1974	1975	1976	1977
Net sales	5,925,396	5,882,096	5,319,469	7,474,729
Cost of goods sold.	4,504,879	4,374,776	3,864,184	5,244,582
Gross margin on sales. . . .	1,420,517	1,507,320	1,455,285	2,230,147
General sales and admin-				
istrative expenses	1,326,611	1,290,986	1,386,738	1,662,156
Income (loss) from sales . .	93,906	216,334	68,547	567,991
Other income	—	7,013	14,281	9,593
Other expenses.	(11,233)	—	—	—
Earnings before taxes	82,673	223,347	82,828	577,584
Federal income tax	32,600	88,000	26,000	275,000
Extraordinary items	32,600	(65,927)	26,000	163,000
Net income (loss)	82,673	69,420	82,828	465,584

Source: Webber Manufacturing Company.

withdrew from that market rather than buy the table from Thermotron or attempt to bid their chamber without the vibration table.[9]

In late 1978 Thermotron announced a standardized line of walk-in chambers which featured field-assembled prefabricated wall, ceiling, and floor panels with separate self-contained mechanical systems which merely rolled into place in one of the panel openings. The advantages claimed for the new line included reduced delivery time, lower delivery charges, and fewer on-site modifications required for installation.[10]

Thermotron marketed its product line through technically competent manufacturers' representatives and factory application engineers. After-sale service was provided through a regional network of repair parts inventories and factory-trained service technicians.

Tenney Engineering Company (see Exhibits 6 and 7)

Founded in 1945, Tenney was one of the oldest and, until 1977, the largest manufacturer of ETCs. Since the early 1960s Tenney had refined its product line into a standardized, cataloged offering which was marketed through

---

[9] *Vibration tables* are specially designed supports for the electronic equipment being tested in the AGREE chambers. These must be capable of generating the variable-frequency vibrations and other physical simulations of aircraft-induced stress. Price tags for the vibration table alone of $200,000 were not uncommon.

[10] Not infrequently, one or more walls must be removed and replaced to permit installation of a factory-assembled ETC. The field-assembled type mentioned here required no such building modifications, since the individual parts were all small enough to pass through a standard door.

EXHIBIT 7

TENNEY ENGINEERING, INC.
Condensed Comparative Financial Statements
For Fiscal Years Ended December 31, 1974–1977

	1974	1975	1976	1977
Assets				
Cash	92,198	176,495	190,519	597,053
Accounts receivable	1,374,791	856,539	1,319,324	943,899
Inventory	984,421	928,084	1,057,972	1,406,955
Prepaid expenses	19,728	49,256	64,153	39,529
Total current assets	2,471,138	2,010,374	2,631,968	2,987,436
Fixed assets	480,476	483,200	502,234	496,270
Deferred charges	—	—	6,259	4,819
Other assets	142,378	66,077	16,812	19,886
Total assets	3,093,992	2,559,651	3,157,273	3,508,411
Liabilities				
Accounts payable	979,098	632,451	967,191	944,469
Notes payable	95,444	—	210,000	—
Accrued expenses	106,804	75,978	120,287	125,803
Current portion, long-term debt	377,095	130,087	146,315	32,518
Other current liabilities	14,433	9,668	37,103	42,217
Total current liabilities	1,572,874	848,184	1,480,896	1,145,007
Long-term debt	659,628	784,546	677,574	765,017
Deferred taxes	14,935	10,946	—	112,000
Total liabilities	2,247,437	1,643,676	2,158,470	2,022,024
Common stock	62,493	62,493	72,953	94,953
Additional paid-in capital	1,649,114	1,649,114	1,733,968	1,733,968
Retained earnings	(865,052)	(795,632)	(808,118)	(342,534)
Total liabilities and equity	3,093,992	2,559,651	3,157,273	3,508,411

Source: Webber Manufacturing Company.

technically trained manufacturers' representatives to a broad range of commercial, industrial, and institutional users. Nonstandard requirements were handled by factory application engineers working with the rep and the user. Tenney was also very active in both the competitive bid market and the negotiated contract market.

After many months of development work, the company introduced its first microprocessor-based control system for ETCs in early 1977. Despite a limited range of program steps and number of functions it could control, the new system was seen as a significant improvement over the company's previous control system and was actively promoted in the sales of new ETCs and as a retrofit item for existing installations.

Tenney's sales were worldwide, with approximately 11 percent of its

1978 sales being foreign. No one customer accounted for more than 10 percent of sales in 1978, but contracts with various U.S. governmental agencies traditionally averaged between 20 percent and 25 percent of total sales.

Cincinnati Sub-Zero Products (see Exhibit 8)

The company was founded in 1940 as a manufacturer of low-temperature chest-type storage cabinets. Over the years, CSZP had added to its product line, which in 1978 included biological and industrial freezers, temperature chambers, temperature and humidity chambers and a line of hypo-hyperthermia systems used in surgical and nursing areas of hospitals.

EXHIBIT 8

CINCINNATI SUB-ZERO PRODUCTS, INC.
Condensed Comparative Financial Statements
For Fiscal Years Ended March 31, 1975–1978

	1975	1976	1977	1978
Assets				
Cash	166,562	212,588	103,388	254,439
Marketable securities	75,000	75,000	40,000	—
Accounts receivable	202,845	256,745	367,623	438,811
Inventory	259,564	295,833	472,620	694,905
Prepaid expense	15,531	13,751	10,527	—
Total current assets	719,502	853,917	994,158	1,388,155
Fixed assets	130,601	203,876	280,162	333,116
Investments	33,087	26,905	27,856	27,856
Other assets	46,289	49,715	53,522	194,615
Total assets	929,479	1,134,413	1,355,698	1,943,742
Liabilities				
Accounts payable	55,148	73,803	128,004	161,000
Accrued expenses	84,894	113,519	163,619	305,000
Taxes (except for income) . . .	—	—	—	—
Income taxes payable	8,520	40,908	11,832	237,000
Current portion of long-term debt	12,000	12,000	12,000	12,000
Total current liability	160,562	240,230	315,455	715,632
Long-term debt	37,000	25,000	13,000	1,000
Total liabilities	197,562	265,230	328,455	716,632
Common stock	5,594	5,594	5,594	5,594
Addition paid-in capital	2,124	2,124	2,124	2,124
Retained earnings	724,199	861,545	1,024,156	1,219,392
Security loss	—	—	(4,631)	—
Total liabilities and equity . . .	929,479	1,134,493	1,355,698	1,943,742

Source: Webber Manufacturing Company.

CSZP marketed their product line worldwide through direct factory sales efforts, primarily in the negotiated contract market. Approximately 5 percent of sales were to foreign customers. CSZP did not compete strongly in the competitive bid market and had not been a major product innovator in the industry.

WMC CONSIDERS THE FUTURE

"We need to grow." Richard Dirlam repeated a comment he had made earlier. "We need to leapfrog the competition to stay within range of Thermotron. If they continue to grow like they have been doing, they'll have such a commanding lead, we won't be able to gain at all. I think we have the organization. I think we have the people. I think we have the systems in place right now for dramatic growth. This year we should hit $1.4 million, and we'll do it with fewer people than it took in the past. With the changes we've made, I think we could double that figure in our present layout. What we need is, maybe, to buy Thermotron, or maybe we could figure a way to get them to buy us with the condition that our management take over their operation. I think we are better managed than they are. Maybe it couldn't be done, but then, maybe it could." (See Exhibits 9, 10, and 11 for organization and financial position of Webber.)

EXHIBIT 9
Organizational Structure Planned for July 1979

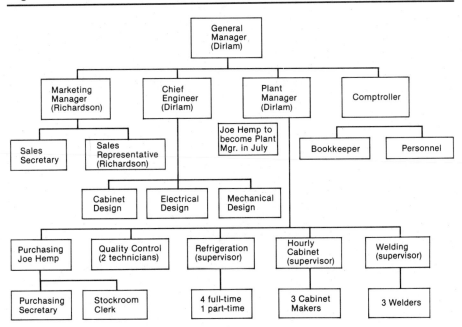

EXHIBIT 10

WEBBER MANUFACTURING COMPANY
Condensed Income Statements
For the Years 1972–1978

	1972*‡	1973*‡	1974*	1975†	1976	1977	1978
Net sales	1,352,223	1,269,811	1,439,563	631,567	1,246,351	1,085,856	794,561
Cost of goods sold	661,666	533,356	1,054,225	478,529	1,151,590	894,363	735,098
Gross margin on sales	690,557	736,455	385,338	153,038	94,761	191,493	59,463
General sales and administrative expenses	669,973	723,191	347,318	139,007	261,156	199,914	198,690
Income (loss) from sales	20,584	13,264	38,020	14,031	(166,395)	(8,421)	(139,227)
Other income	3,013	6,752	—	6,810	7,856	6,519	733
Other expenses	—	—	(71)	(2,539)	(14,564)	(12,583)	(14,969)
Earnings before taxes	23,597	20,016	37,949	18,302	(173,103)	(14,485)	(153,643)
Federal income tax	4,962	3,219	11,642	6,460	—	—	—
Extraordinary items	—	—	—	—	79,909§	12,887§	—
Net income (loss)	18,635	16,797	26,307	11,842	(93,194)	(1,598)	(153,463)

* For fiscal year ended July 31.
† Figures for July 9–December 31 only.
‡ Cost of goods sold and general sales and administrative expenses are not directly comparable with other years.
§ Federal and state income-tax refund due to loss carryback.

Source: Webber Manufacturing Company.

EXHIBIT 11

WEBBER MANUFACTURING COMPANY
Condensed Balance Sheets
For the Years 1972–1978

	1972*	1973*	1974*	1975†	1976	1977	1978
Assets							
Cash	98,217	48,786	86,572	22,915	4,978	2,239	560
Accounts receivable	270,369	285,867	140,481	166,583	304,773	191,284	112,537
Inventory	16,078	99,537	219,920	263,560	262,814	181,489	257,249
Investments	6,000	6,000	6,000	—	6,000	6,000	6,000
Prepaid expenses	—	25	525	10,293	2,049	7,025	8,976
Total current assets	390,664	440,215	453,498	463,351	580,614	388,037	385,322
Fixed assets	53,135	53,496	37,548	15,931	30,420	29,689	35,401
Other assets	—	—	—	165,986	139,417	111,191	82,966
Total assets	443,799	493,711	491,046	645,268	750,451	528,917	503,689
Liabilities							
Notes payable	89,876	105,764	—	—	125,000	50,000	125,000
Accounts payable	6,445	24,642	82,880	52,407	169,616	61,019	134,417
Accrued expenses	1,863	1,377	9,840	22,437	30,375	21,019	27,505
Taxes (except income)	3,702	3,219	2,548	38,348	7,107	4,331	4,491
Income taxes payable	—	—	10,762	21,450	21,456	21,456	21,456
Current portion of long-term debt	—	—	—	—	—	—	5,814
Other current liabilities	—	—	—	—	4,749	11,168	—
Total current liabilities	101,886	135,002	106,030	134,642	358,303	168,993	318,683
Long-term debt	59,149	59,149	59,149	226,798	145,366	123,910	102,454
Total liabilities	161,035	194,151	165,179	361,440	503,669	292,903	421,137
Capital stock	161,500	161,500	161,500	161,500	161,500	161,500	161,500
Additional paid-in capital	496	496	496	496	59,645	59,645	59,645
Retained earnings	120,768	137,564	163,871	258,832	162,637	151,869	(1,593)
less treasury stock	—	—	—	(137,000)	(137,000)	(137,000)	(137,000)
Total owner's equity	282,764	299,560	325,867	283,828	246,782	236,014	82,552
Total liabilities and equity‡	443,799	493,711	491,046	645,268	750,451	528,917	503,689

* For fiscal year ended July 31.
† Figures based on July 9–December 31 only.
‡ Some totals may not add due to rounding error.

Source: Webber Manufacturing Company.

When questioned about the prospect for rapid growth, Paul Richardson related a number of "elements" which he claimed must be present before rapid growth could occur in the ETC industry:

1. A technological breakthrough, which Richardson felt the microprocessor control system represented.
2. A well-defined market, product line, and price structure.
3. A well-developed sales contact system.
4. Efficiently operating internal systems.

"We have all of these elements necessary for rapid growth in place," Richardson stated.

> But so far as dramatic growth is concerned, I'm not convinced and I never have been. Our bottleneck is still the production capacity. We've tried to increase it, but the results have never been especially encouraging. I doubt that we could double our production. The constraint is the skilled labor—refrigeration, electrical wiring, and final testing. That's the bottleneck.
>
> I've always told Rich I could sell all he could produce, and I have. He has always said he could produce all I could sell, and he has—but not in a time frame acceptable to the customer. Right now, we're quoting 90–120 days delivery, and it is taking every bit of that. Sure, we've cut down the time on the floor, but the way we did it was by stretching out the time between receipt of order and release for production. The total time hasn't changed much. We just don't release the order for production until all the parts are on hand. If Rich says he can double capacity—do $2.8 million with this setup—maybe he's right. Maybe I'm that far out of it, but I don't think so.

CASE 2–8

Rogers, Nagel, Langhart (RNL PC), Architects and Planners

It was August 1984. John B. Rogers, one of the founders and a principal stockholder in RNL, had just completed the University of Colorado's Executive MBA program. Throughout the program John had tried to relate the concepts and principles covered in his courses to the problems of managing a large architectural practice. In particular, he was concerned about the marketing efforts of his firm. As he put it, "Marketing is still a new, and some-

---

This case was prepared by H. Michael Hayes, Professor of Marketing and Strategic Management, University of Colorado at Denver, as the basis for class discussion rather than to illustrate either effective or ineffective handling of an administrative situation. Copyright © 1985 by H. Michael Hayes.

times distasteful, word to most architects. Nevertheless, the firms that survive and prosper in the future are going to be those which learn how to market as effectively as they design. At RNL we are still struggling with what it means to be a marketing organization, but we feel it's a critical question that must be answered if we're going to meet our projections of roughly doubling by 1989, and we're giving it lots of attention."

RNL

In 1984, with sales (design fees) of approximately $3,300,000, RNL was one of the largest local architectural firms in Denver and the Rocky Mountain region. The firm evolved from the individual practices of John B. Rogers, Jerome K. Nagel, and Victor D. Langhart. All started their architectural careers in Denver in the 1950s. The partnership of Rogers, Nagel, Langhart was formed from the three individual proprietorships in 1966, and became a professional corporation in 1970.

In 1984 the firm provided professional design services to commercial, corporate, and governmental clients, not only in Denver but throughout Colorado and, increasingly, throughout the western United States. In addition to basic architectural design services, three subsidiaries had recently been formed:

Interplan, which provides pre-architectural services, programming, planning, budgeting, scheduling, and cost projections, utilized in corporate budgeting and governmental bond issues.

Denver Enterprises, formed to hold equity interests in selected projects designed by RNL and to take risk by furnishing design services early in a project and by participating in the capital requirements of a project.

Space Management Systems, Inc. (SMS), which provides larger corporations with the necessary services (heavily computer system supported) to facilitate control of their facilities with respect to space, furnishings, equipment, and the cost of change.

In 1984, the firm had 72 employees. John Rogers served as chairman, and Vic Langhart served as president. Nagel had retired in 1976 (see Exhibit 1 for an organization chart). Development of broad-based management had been a priority since 1975. The firm had seven vice presidents. Two of these vice presidents, Phil Goedert and Rich von Luhrte, served on the board of directors, together with Rogers and Langhart.

Growth was financed through retained earnings. In addition, a plan to provide for more employee ownership, principally through profit sharing (ESOP in 1984), was initiated in 1973. Rogers and Langhart held 56 percent of RNL stock, and 10 percent was held by the other two board members. The Colorado National Bank Profit Sharing Trust held 12 percent in its name.

EXHIBIT 1
Corporate Organization

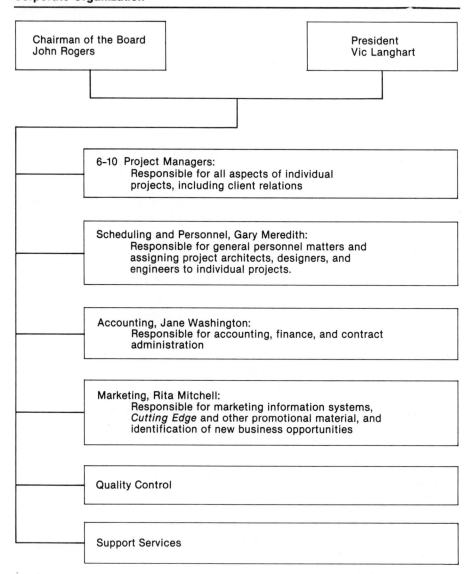

Chairman of the Board
John Rogers

President
Vic Langhart

6–10 Project Managers:
Responsible for all aspects of individual projects, including client relations

Scheduling and Personnel, Gary Meredith:
Responsible for general personnel matters and assigning project architects, designers, and engineers to individual projects.

Accounting, Jane Washington:
Responsible for accounting, finance, and contract administration

Marketing, Rita Mitchell:
Responsible for marketing information systems, *Cutting Edge* and other promotional material, and identification of new business opportunities

Quality Control

Support Services

Note: RNL does not have a formal organization chart, as such. This exhibit was developed by the case writer to portray the general nature of work assignments and reporting relationships in the firm. As a general rule, project managers report to either John Rogers or Vic Langhart. Most administrative staff functions report to Vic Langhart. At the operational level, Interplan and SMS projects are handled similarly to RNL projects.

The remaining 22 percent was controlled by 23 other employees, either personally or through their individual profit sharing accounts. It was a goal of the firm to eventually vest stock ownership throughout the firm, in the interest of longevity and continuity.

The firm's principal assets were its human resources. Rogers and Langhart, however, had significant ownership in a limited partnership that owned a 20,000-square-foot building in a prestigious location in downtown Denver. In 1984, RNL occupied 15,000 square feet there. Use of the remaining 5,000 square feet could accommodate up to 30 percent growth in personnel. By using automation and computers, RNL felt it could double its 1984 volume of work without acquiring additional space.

ARCHITECTURAL SERVICES

> Architecture: the profession of designing buildings, open areas, communities, and other artificial constructions and environments, usually with some regard to aesthetic effect. The professional services of an architect often include design or selection of furnishings and decorations, supervision of construction work, and the examination, restoration, or remodeling of existing buildings.
>
> *Random House Dictionary*

Demand for architectural services is closely tied to population growth and to the level of construction activity. The population in the Denver metropolitan area grew from 929,000 in 1960 to 1,620,000 in 1980, and it is estimated to grow to 1,958,000 by 1990. Denver's annual population change of 3.4 percent in the decade 1970–80 ranked 10th for major American cities (Dallas and Phoenix ranked 1 and 2). The projected population growth for the Denver metropolitan area from 1978 to 1983 ranked third in the nation, and Colorado was predicted to be one of the 10 fastest-growing states during the 1980s.

Commercial construction permits grew from 340 in 1970 with an estimated value of $70,818,000, to 1,235 in 1980 with an estimated value of $400,294,000. This growth was not steady, however. Year-to-year changes in dollar value of commercial construction varied from 0.2 percent to 91.6 percent, and the number of permits dropped from a high of 2,245 in 1978 to 1,235 in 1980. Similar patterns of growth and variation characterized industrial construction.

Translating construction growth into estimates of demand for architectural services is difficult. One rule of thumb holds that each additional person added to the population base requires 1,000 square feet of homes, schools, churches, offices, hospitals, manufacturing facilities, retail and shopping facilities, and transportation facilities. In the Denver metro area alone, this could mean 338 million square feet. At $50 average per square foot, total construction expenditure over the decade could reach $16.9 billion, involving as much as $845 million in design fees during the 1980s.

The past and projected growth in demand for architectural services was accompanied by a significant growth in the number of architects in Colorado. From 1979 to 1982, the number of state registrations of individual architects grew from 1,400 to 3,381, an increase of 141.5 percent. Over 100 architectural firms competed actively in the Denver market. (Over 500 architects are listed in the Yellow Pages of the Denver metro area phone directory.) In recent years, a number of national firms (e.g., Skidmore, Owens and Merrill) opened offices in Denver. Other major firms came to Colorado to do one job and then returned to their home offices (e.g., Yamasaki for the Colorado National Bank Office Tower, TAC for Mansville World Headquarters). Of the 26 major firms working on 38 selected jobs in Denver in 1983, 16, or 61.5 percent, were Denver based. Of the other 10, which have headquarters offices elsewhere, all but 2 had offices in Denver.

Major categories of customers for architectural services include:

Industrial	Government
Commercial	Federal
Owner	State
Developer	Municipal

Residential (Note: RNL did not compete in this market.)

Within these categories, however, not all architectural work is available to independent firms, and not all architectural work on a project is awarded to one architect. A recent Denver survey, for example, indicated that of 49 commercial jobs under construction with a known architect, 11 were handled by an "inside" architect. Of the remaining 38 jobs, 20 included shell and space design, whereas 18 involved space design only. In the 18 space designs, only 50 percent were actually done by architects.

The rapid growth in the construction market in Denver came to an abrupt halt in February 1982. Triggered by the broad realization that the oil boom was over, or had at least slowed significantly, project after project was put on hold. Construction of office space literally came to a halt. Of particular concern to RNL, which had just completed negotiations for a $1 million contract with Exxon, was the Exxon announcement of the closure of its Colorado Oil Shale activities at Parachute, Colorado.

It was against the backdrop of these changes that RNL felt the pressing need to review its marketing activities.

MARKETING OF ARCHITECTURAL SERVICES

The basis of competing for architectural work has changed dramatically over the past several decades. As John Rogers recalled:

> At the beginning of my practice in 1956, you could establish an office, put a sign on your door, print calling cards, and have a "news" announcement with

your picture in the *Daily Journal* that you had established a new practice of architecture. Beyond that, it was appropriate to suggest to friends and acquaintances that I was in business now and I hoped that they might recommend me to someone they knew. The Code of Ethics of the American Institute of Architects, like many other professions at the time, prohibited any kind of aggressive marketing or sales effort as practiced in recent times.

In fact, after convincing one school board member (an artist) in Jefferson County that design was important, and then being awarded a commission to design an elementary school, which led to another and another, it was not surprising to read in the *Daily Journal* that the school board had met the previous evening and had elected me to design a new junior high school, one that I hadn't even known about. I called and said, "Thank you." Marketing expense was zero with the exception of an occasional lunch or courtesy call here and there.

Today, the situation is vastly different. We have to compete for most jobs, against both local firms and, increasingly, large national firms. Clients are becoming more sophisticated regarding the purchase of architectural services [see Exhibit 2 for a brief description of buyer behavior]. Promotion, of some kind, and concepts such as segmentation have become a way of life.

During the 1960s, development of an architectural practice was a slow process, characterized by heavy reliance on word-of-mouth regarding professional experience and expertise. Overt communication about an architect's qualifications was limited to brochures. Personal acquaintances played a significant role in the development of new clients. Personal relations between principals and clients were an important part of continuing and new relations. This method of practice development tended to favor local firms, whose reputation could be checked out on a personal basis, and small firms, whose principals could provide personal management and design of client projects.

As Denver grew, the market changed. The advantage of being a successful, local architect and knowing the local business community diminished. Newcomers to Denver tended to rely on relationships with architects in other cities. For local architects there wasn't time to rely on traditional communication networks to establish relationships with these newcomers. The size of projects grew, requiring growth in the size of architectural staffs. Personal attention to every client by principals was no longer possible.

Concomitantly, there was a growing change in the attitude toward the marketing of professional services. New entrants in the fields of medicine and law, as well as architecture, were becoming impatient with the slowness of traditional methods of practice development. A Supreme Court decision significantly reduced the restrictions that state bar associations could impose on lawyers with respect to their pricing and advertising practices. In a similar vein, the American Institute of Architects signed a consent decree with the Justice Department, which prohibited the organization from publishing fee schedules for architectural services.

Perhaps of most significance for architects, however, was the start of

EXHIBIT 2
Buyer Behavior

Purchase of architectural services is both complex and varied. Subject to many qualifications, however, there seems to be a number of steps that most buying situations have in common:

Development of a list of potential architects.

Identification of those architects from whom proposals will be solicited for a specific job (usually called the short list).

Invitations to submit proposals.

Evaluation of proposals and screening of final candidates.

Selection of a finalist, based on proposal evaluation, or invitations to finalists to make oral presentations to an evaluation group.

From a marketing standpoint, the focus of interest is the process of getting on the short list and the process by which the final selection is made.

The Short List

Prospective clients find out about architects in a variety of ways. Those who are frequent users of architectural services will generally keep a file of architects, sometimes classified as to type or practice. Additions to the file can come from mailed brochures, personal calls, advertisements, press releases, or, in fact, almost any form of communication. When a specific requirement develops, the file is reviewed for apparent fit. With many variations, a short list is developed and proposals are solicited.

Those who use architects infrequently tend to rely on various businesses of social networks to develop what is in essence their short list. In either case, a previously used architect is almost always on the short list, provided the past experience was satisfactory.

As the largest single customer for architectural services, agencies of the federal government follow a well-defined series of steps, including advertisements in the *Commerce Business Daily* and mail solicitation of local firms.

The Selection Process

The selection process is significantly influenced by the nature and scope of the work and its importance to the firm. Architect selection on major buildings is usually made at the highest level in the organization: by a principal or the president in a private organization or by various forms of boards in not-for-profit organizations such as churches. In some instances, the principal, president, or board are actively involved in all phases of the process. In others, the management of the process is delegated to others who develop recommendations to the decision makers. On smaller jobs, and those of an ongoing nature (e.g., space management), the decision is usually at lower levels and may involve a plant engineer or facilities manager of some kind.

Regardless of the level at which the selection process is made there seem to be two well-defined patterns to the process. The first, and predominant one, evaluates the firms on the short list, taking into prime consideration nonprice

EXHIBIT 2 (concluded)

factors such as reputation, performance on previous jobs, and current work-load. Based on this evaluation, one firm is selected and a final agreement is then negotiated as to the scope of the work, the nature of the working relation-ship, the project team, and specific details as to price. The second pattern, of limited but growing use, attempts to specify the requirements so completely that a firm price can accompany the proposal. In some instances, the price and the proposal are submitted separately. Evaluation of the proposals includes a dollar differential, and these dollar differentials are applied to the price quotation to determine the low evaluated bidder.

Regardless of the process, there appear to be three main criteria on which firms are evaluated:

1. *The ability of the firm to perform the particular assignment.* For standard work this assessment is relatively easy and relies on the nature of past work, size of the organization, current backlogs, and so forth. For more creative work the assessment becomes more difficult. Much importance is put on past work, but the proposal starts to take on additional importance. Sketches, drawings, and, sometimes, extensive models may be requested with the proposal. In some instances, there may actually be a design compe-tition. Much of this evaluation is, perforce, of a subjective nature.
2. *The comfort level with the project team that will be assigned to do the work.* For any but the most standard work there is recognition that there will be constant interaction between representatives of the client's organization and members of the architectural firm. Almost without exception, therefore, some kind of evaluation is made of the project team, or at least its leaders, in terms of the client's comfort level with the personalities involved.
3. *Finally, the matter of cost.* While direct price competition is not a factor in most transactions, the cost of architectural services is always a concern. This has two components. First, there is concern with the total cost of the project, over which the architect has great control. Second, there is growing concern with the size of the architect's fee, per se.

At least some assessment of the reputation of the architect with respect to controlling project costs is made in determining the short list. Once final selec-tion is made, there is likely to be much discussion and negotiation as to the method of calculating the fee. The traditional method of simply charging a per-centage of the construction price seems to be on the wane. Increasingly, clients for architectural services are attempting to establish a fixed fee for a well-de-fined project. The nature of architectural work, however, is such that changes are a fact of life and that many projects cannot be sufficiently defined in the initial stages to allow precise estimation of the design costs. Some basis for modifying a basic fee must, therefore, be established. Typically this is on some kind of direct cost basis plus an overhead adder. Direct costs for various classes of staff and overhead rates obviously become matters for negotiation. In the case of the federal government, the right is reserved to audit an architect's books to determine the appropriateness of charges for changes.

the so-called proposal age. Investigations in Maryland and Kansas, among other states, had revealed improper involvement of architects and engineers with state officials. Financial kickbacks were proven on many state projects. Formal proposals, it was felt, would eliminate or reduce the likelihood of contract awards made on the basis of cronyism or kickbacks. Starting in the government sector, the requirement for proposals spread rapidly to all major clients. In 1984, for example, even a small church could receive as many as 20 detailed proposals on a modestly sized assignment.

MARKETING AT RNL

In 1984, RNL was engaged in a number of marketing activities. In addition to proposal preparation, major activities included:

- Professional involvement in the business community by principals, which provides contacts with potential clients. This included memberships in a wide variety of organizations such as the Downtown Denver Board, Chamber of Commerce, and Denver Art Museum.
- Participation in, and appearances at, conferences, both professional and business oriented.
- Daily review of *Commerce Business Daily* (a federal publication of all construction projects) along with other news services that indicate developing projects.
- Maintenance of past client contacts. (RNL found this difficult but assigned the activity to its project managers.)
- Development of relationships with potential clients, usually by giving a tour through the office plus lunch.
- VIP gourmet-catered lunches for six invited guests, held once a month in the office. These involved a tour of the office and lively conversation, with some attempt at subsequent follow-up.
- Participation in appropriate local, regional, or national exhibits of architectural projects.
- Occasional publicity for a project or for a client.
- The *Cutting Edge*.[1]
- An assortment of brochures and information on finished projects.
- Special arrangements with architectural firms in other locations to provide the basis for a variety of desirable joint ventures.

RNL participated in a number of market segments, which are identified in Exhibit 4, together with its view of the required approach.

---

[1] The *Cutting Edge* is an RNL publication designed to inform clients and prospects about new developments in architecture and planning and about significant RNL accomplishments (see Exhibit 3 for an example of an article on a typical issue).

EXHIBIT 3

The Cutting Edge

Planning for Parking

The recent boom in downtown Denver office building has resulted in tremendous increases in population density in Denver's core, bringing corresponding increases in the number of vehicles and their related problems as well.

Auto storage, or parking, is one of the major resulting problems. Most building zoning requires parking sufficient to serve the building's needs. Even building sites not requiring parking are now providing parking space to remain competitive in the marketplace.

RNL's design for this above-grade parking structure at 1700 Grant aided in facilitating lease of the office building.

Parking solutions can range from a simple asphalt lot to a large multi-floor parking structure; the decision is based on many factors including site access, required number of spaces, land costs, budget and user convenience.

For many suburban sites, where land costs are sufficiently low to allow on-grade parking, design entails mainly the problems of circulation and landscaping. Circulation includes issues of easy site access and optimal efficient use of the site. Landscaping, including landforming, can visually screen automobiles and break up ugly seas of asphalt common to poorly designed developments.

At the opposite end of the parking spectrum are downtown sites where high land costs necessitate careful integration of parking into the building concept. This is often accomplished by building parking underground, below the main structure. Parking design, in this case, becomes a problem of integrating the circulation and the structure of the building above. While building underground eliminates the need for

acceptable outer appearance, the costs of excavation, mechanical ventilation, fire sprinklering and waterproofing make this one of the most expensive parking solutions.

Between on-grade parking and the underground structure is the above-grade detached or semi-detached parking structure. This solution is very common in areas of moderate land cost where convenience is the overriding factor.

Site conditions do much to generate the design of an above-grade parking structure, but where possible the following features should ideally be included:

1. Parking is in double loaded corridors, i.e. cars park on both sides of the circulation corridor to provide the most efficient ratio of parking to circulation area;

2. Parking at 90 degrees to circulation corridors rather than at angles, once again the most efficient use of space;

3. Access to different garage levels provided by ramping the parking floors, efficiently combining vertical circulation and parking;

4. A precast prestressed concrete structure (this structure economically provides long spans needed to eliminate columns which would interfere with parking circulation and the fireproof concrete members have a low maintenance surface that can be left exposed).

5. Classification as an "open parking garage" under the building code, meaning that the structure has openings in the walls of the building providing natural ventilation and eliminating the need for expensive mechanical ventilation of exhaust fumes;

6. A building exterior in a precast concrete finish, allowing the designer to combine structure and exterior skin into one low cost element.

RNL recently completed work on the $20,000,000 1700 Grant Office Building for Wickliff & Company. The inclusion of a 415 car parking garage in the 1700 Grant project provided one of the amenities necessary for successful leasing in a very depressed leasing market.

A Publication of **RNL**/Inception   •   by Richard T. Anderson   •   Vol. II No. I   •   1576 Sherman Street Denver, Co. 80203 (303) 832-5599

EXHIBIT 4

Segment	Approach
Government	
City and county governments	Personal selling, political involvement.
School districts	Personal selling (professional educational knowledge required).
State government	Political involvement, written responses to RFPs (requests for proposals, from clients), personal selling.
Federal government	Personal selling, very detailed RFP response, no price competition in the proposal stage.
Private sector	Personal selling, social acquaintances, referrals, *Cutting Edge,* preliminary studies, price competition.
Semiprivate sector (includes utilities)	Personal selling, *Cutting Edge,* referrals, continuing relationships, some price competition.

Net fee income and allocation of marketing expenses by major segments are given in Exhibit 5. The general feeling at RNL was that there is a lapse of 6 to 18 months between the marketing effort itself and tangible results such as fee income.

Salient aspects of budgeted marketing expense for 1985, by segment, were:

1. *Government.* Heavy emphasis on increased trips to Omaha (a key Corps of Engineers location), Washington, and other out-of-state (as well as in-state) locations plus considerable emphasis on participation in municipal conferences.
2. *Private.* Personal contact at local, state, and regional levels with corporations, banks, developers, and contractors plus local promotion through Chamber of Commerce, clubs, VIP lunches, *Cutting Edge,* promotion materials, and initiation of an advertising and public relations effort.
3. *Semiprivate.* Increased level of personal contact and promotional effort.
4. *Interiors.* Major allocation of salary and expenses of a new full-time marketing person to improve direct sales locally plus other promotional support.
5. *Urban design.* Some early success indicates that land developers and urban renewal authorities are the most likely clients. Planned marketing expense is primarily for personal contact.

EXHIBIT 5

	1982		1983		1984 (estimated)		1985 (estimated)	
	Net Fee	Marketing Expense	Net Fee	Marketing Expense	Net Fee	Marketing Expense	Net Fee	Marketing Expense
Government	$ 800	$104	$1,220	$101	$1,012	$150	$1,200	$140
Private	1,376	162	1,261	140	1,200	195	1,616	220
Semiprivate	88	11	118	24	100	25	140	30
Interiors	828	40	670	30	918	100	1,235	110
Urban design	95	20	31	10	170	30	220	40
Total	$3,187	$337	$3,300	$305	$3,400	$500	$4,411	$540

Note: All amounts are in $000s.

193

Additional marketing efforts being given serious consideration included:

- A more structured marketing organization with more specific assignments.
- Increased visibility for the firm through general media and trade journals; paid or other (e.g., public relations).
- Appearances on special programs and offering special seminars.
- Use of more sophisticated selling tools such as videotapes and automated slide presentations.
- Increased training in client relations/selling for project managers and other staff.
- Hiring a professionally trained marketing manager.
- Determining how the national firms market (i.e., copy the competition).
- Expansion of debriefing conferences with successful and unsuccessful clients.
- Use of a focus group to develop effective sales points for RNL.
- Training a marketing MBA in architecture versus training an architect in marketing.

RNL CLIENTS

RNL described its clients as:

1. Having a long history of growing expectations with respect to detail, completeness, counseling, and cost control.
2. Mandating the minimization of construction problems, including changes, overruns, and delays.
3. Having an increased concern for peer approval at the completion of a project.
4. Having an increased desire to understand and be a part of the design process.

Extensive interviews of clients by independent market researchers showed very favorable impressions about RNL. Terms used to describe the firm included:

Best and largest architectural service in Denver.

Innovative yet practical.

Designs large projects for "who's who in Denver."

Long-term resident of the business community.

Lots of expertise.

Designs artistic yet functional buildings.

RNL's use of computer-aided design systems was seen as a definite competitive edge. Others mentioned RNL's extra services, such as interior systems, as a plus, although only 35 percent of those interviewed were aware that RNL offered this service. In general, most clients felt that RNL had a competitive edge with regard to timeliness, productivity, and cost consciousness.

Two major ways that new clients heard about RNL were identified. One was the contact RNL made on its own initiative when it heard of a possible project. The other was through personal references. All those interviewed felt advertising played a minor role, and, in fact, several indicated they had questions about an architectural firm that advertises.

Clients who selected RNL identified the following as playing a role in their decision:

Tours of RNL's facilities.

Monthly receipt of *Cutting Edge.*

Low-key selling style.

RNL's ability to focus on their needs.

Thoroughness in researching customer needs and overall proposal preparation and presentation.

RNL's overall reputation in the community.

Belief that RNL would produce good, solid (not flashy) results.

Clients who did not select RNL identified the following reasons for their decision:

RNL had less experience and specialization in their particular industry.

Decided to stay with the architectural firm used previously.

Decided to go with a firm that has more national status.

Other presentations had more "pizazz."

Overall, clients' perceptions of RNL were very positive. There was less than complete understanding of the scope of RNL services, but its current approach to clients received good marks.

MARKETING ISSUES AT RNL: SOME VIEWS OF MIDDLE MANAGEMENT

Richard von Luhrte joined RNL in 1979, following extensive experience with other firms in Chicago and Denver. In 1984, he led the firm's urban design effort on major projects, served as a project manager, and participated actively in marketing. He came to RNL because the firm "fits my image." He preferred larger firms that have extensive and complementary skills. He commented on marketing as follows:

RNL has a lot going for it. We have a higher overhead rate, but with most clients you can sell our competence and turn this into an advantage. I think RNL is perceived as a quality firm, but customers are also concerned that we will gold-plate a job. I'd like to be able to go gold-plate or inexpensive as the circumstances dictate. But it's hard to convince a customer that we can do this.

For many of our clients continuity is important and we need to convey that there will be continuity beyond the founders. RNL had done well as a provider of "all things for all people," and our diversification helps us ride through periods of economic downturn. On the other hand, we lose some jobs because we're not specialized. For instance, we haven't done well in the downtown developer market. We're starting to do more, but if we had targeted the shopping center business we could have had seven or eight jobs by now. One way to operate would be to jump on a trend and ride it until the downturn and then move into something else.

There's always the conflict between specialization and fun. We try to stay diversified, but we ought to be anticipating the next boom. At the same time, there's always the problem of overhead. In this business you can't carry very much, particularly in slow times.

I like the marketing part of the work, but there's a limit on how much of it I can, or should, do. Plus, I think it's important to try to match our people with our clients in terms of age and interests, which means we need to have lots of people involved in the marketing effort.

Oral presentations are an important part of marketing, and we make a lot of them. You have to make them interesting, and there has to be a sense of trying for the "close." On the other hand, I think that the presentation is not what wins the job, although a poor presentation can lose it for you. It's important that the presentation conveys a sense of enthusiasm and that we really want the job.

As comptroller, Jane Washington was involved extensively in the firm's discussions about its marketing efforts. As she described the situation:

There is little question in my mind that the people at the top are committed to developing a marketing orientation at RNL. But our objectives still aren't clear. For instance, we still haven't decided what would be a good mix of architecture, interiors, and planning. Interiors is a stepchild to some. On the other hand, it is a very profitable part of our business. But it's not easy to develop a nice neat set of objectives for a firm like this. Two years ago we had a seminar to develop a mission statement, but we still don't have one. This isn't a criticism. Rather, it's an indication of the difficulty of getting agreement on objectives in a firm of creative professionals.

One problem is that our approach to marketing has been reactive rather than proactive. Our biggest marketing expenditure is proposal preparation, and we have tended to respond to RFPs as they come in, without screening them for fit with targeted segments. From a budget standpoint we have not really allocated marketing dollars to particular people or segments, except in a pro forma kind of way. As a result, no one person is responsible for what is a very large total expenditure.

Another problem is that we don't have precise information about our marketing expenditures or the profitability of individual jobs. It would be impractical to track expenditures on the 500 to 1,000 proposals we make a year, but we could set up a system that tracks marketing expenditures in, say, 10 segments. This would at least let individuals see what kind of money we're spending for marketing, and where. We also could change from the present system, which basically measures performance in terms of variation from dollar budget, to one that reports on the profitability of individual jobs. I've done some studies on the profitability of our major product lines, but those don't tie to any one individual's performance.

Rita Mitchell, who has an MS in library science and information systems, joined RNL in 1981. Originally her assignment focused on organizing marketing records and various marketing information resources. In her new role as new-business development coordinator she had a broader set of responsibilities. According to Rita;

> We definitely need some policies about marketing, and these ought to spell out a marketing process. In my present job, I think I can help the board synthesize market information and so help to develop a marketing plan.
>
> I do a lot of market research based on secondary data. For instance, we have access to Dialog and a number of other online databases, using our PC. Based on this research, and our own in-house competence, I think I can do some good market anticipation. The problem is what to do with this kind of information. If we move too fast, based on signals about a new market, there is obviously the risk of being wrong. On the other hand, if we wait until the signals are unmistakably clear, they will be clear to everyone else, and we will lose the opportunity to establish a preeminent position.
>
> With respect to individual RFPs, our decision on which job to quote is still highly subjective. We try to estimate our chances of getting the job, and we talk about its fit with our other work, but we don't have much hard data or policy to guide us. We don't, for instance, have a good sense of other RFPs that are in the pipeline and how the mix of the jobs we're quoting and the resulting work fits with our present work in progress. The Marketing Committee [consisting of John Rogers, Vic Langhart, Phil Goedert, Rich Von Luhrte, Dick Shiffer, Rita Mitchell, and, occasionally, Bob Johnson] brings lots of experience and personal knowledge to bear on this, but it's not a precise process.
>
> We have a number of sources of information about new construction projects: the *Commerce Business Daily* [a federal government publication], the *Daily Journal* [which reports on local government construction], the Western Press Clipping Bureau, Colorado trade journals, and so forth. Monitoring these is a major activity, and then we have the problem of deciding which projects fit RNL.

Bob Johnson, a project manager and member of the Marketing Committee, commented:

> The way the system works now, we have 4 board members and 12 project managers, most of whom can pursue new business. They bring these opportunities before the Marketing Committee, but it doesn't really have the clout to say no. As a result, people can really go off on their own. I'd like to see the committee flex its muscles a little more on what jobs we go after. But there's a

problem with committing to just a few market segments. Right now we're involved in something like 30 segments. If we're wrong on one it's not a big deal. But if we were committed to just a few then a mistake could have really serious consequences.

For many of us, however, the major problem is managing the transfer of ownership and control to a broader set of individuals. Currently the prospective owners don't really have a forum for what they'd like the company to be. My personal preference would be to go after corporate headquarters, high-tech firms, speculative office buildings, and high-quality interiors. But there probably isn't agreement on this.

MARKETING ISSUES: THE VIEWS OF THE FOUNDERS

Vic Langhart started his practice of architecture in 1954 and has taught design in the architecture department of the University of Colorado. He was instrumental in developing new services at RNL, including Interplan and SMS, Inc., and was heavily involved in training the next level of management. In 1984, he supervised day-to-day operations and also served as president of Interplan and SMS, Inc. Looking to the future, Vic observed:

> Our toughest issue is dealing with the rate of change in the profession today. It's probably fair to say there are too many architects today. But this is a profession of highly idealistic people, many of whom feel their contribution to a better world is more important than dollars of income and so will stay in the field at "starvation wages." We wrestle with the question of "profession or business?" but competition is now a fact of life for us. The oil boom of the 1970s in Denver triggered an inrush of national firms. Many have stayed on, and we now have a situation where one of the largest national firms is competing for a small job in Durango. We're also starting to see more direct price competition. Digital Equipment recently prequalified eight firms, selected five to submit proposals that demonstrated understanding of the assignment, and asked for a separate envelope containing the price.
>
> Our tradition at RNL has been one of quality. I think we're the "Mercedes" of the business, and in the long haul an RNL customer will be better off economically. A lot of things contribute to this—our Interplan concept, for instance—but the key differentiation factor is our on-site-planning approach.
>
> From 1966 to 1968, we were almost 100 percent in education. Then I heard that they were closing some maternity wards, and we decided to diversify. Today we have a good list of products, ranging from commercial buildings to labs and vehicle maintenance facilities. In most areas, the only people who can beat us are the superspecialists, and even then there's a question. Our diversification has kept our minds free to come up with creative approaches. At Beaver Creek, for example, I think we came up with a better approach to condominium design than the specialists. Plus, we can call in special expertise, if it's necessary.
>
> Over the past several years we've had a number of offers to merge into national, or other, firms. We decided, however, to become employee owned.

Our basic notion was that RNL should be an organization that provides its employees a long-time career opportunity. This is not easy in an industry that is characterized by high turnover. Less than 10 percent of architectural firms have figured out how to do it. But we're now at 35 percent employee ownership.

I'm personally enthusiastic about Interplan. It has tremendous potential to impact our customers. In Seattle, for instance, a bank came to us for a simple expansion. Our Interplan approach, however, led to a totally different set of concepts.

We've had some discussion about expansion. Colorado Springs is a possibility, for instance. But there would be problems of keeping RNL concepts and our culture. We work hard to develop and disseminate an RNL culture. For example, we have lots of meetings, although John and I sometimes disagree about how much time should be spent in meetings. A third of our business comes from interiors, and there is as much difference between interior designers and architects as there is between architects and mechanical engineers.

In somewhat similar vein, John Rogers commented:

In the 1960s, RNL was primarily in the business of designing schools. We were really experts in that market. But then the boom in school construction came to an end, and we moved into other areas. First into banks and commercial buildings. We got started with Mountain Bell, an important relationship for us that continues today. We did assignments for mining companies and laboratories. In the late 1960s, no one knew how to use computers to manage office space problems, and we moved in that direction, which led to the formation of Interplan. We moved into local and state design work. One of our showcase assignments is the Colorado State Judicial/Heritage Center.

In the 1980s, we started to move into federal and military work, and this now represents a significant portion of our business.

We have done some developer work, but this is a tough market. It has a strong "bottom-line orientation," and developers want sharp focus and expertise.

As we grow larger we find it difficult to maintain a close client relationship. The client wants to know who will work on the assignment, but some of our staff members are not good at the people side of the business.

Currently we're still doing lots of "one-of-a-kind" work. Our assignment for the expansion of the *Rocky Mountain News* building, our design of a condominium lodge at Beaver Creek, and our design of a developer building at the Denver Tech Center are all in this category. A common theme, however, is our "on-site" design process. This is a process by which we make sure that the client is involved in the design from the start and that we are really tuned in to his requirements. I see this as one of our real competitive advantages. But I'm still concerned that we may be trying to spread ourselves too thin. Plus, there's no question that there is an increased tendency to specialization: "shopping center architects," for example.

We need to become better marketers, but we have to make sure that we don't lose sight of what has made us the leading architectural firm in Denver: service and client orientation.

APPLICATION 2–9

Kimberly-Clark Corp.

Forty minutes into the hit movie "Raising Arizona," protagonist Herbert McDunnough races down a grocery-store aisle, dodging a spray of bullets, in search of diapers for a baby he kidnapped. He tears past Pampers and Luvs and snatches a sack of Huggies-brand disposable diapers.

So far, some five million Americans have viewed the scene in which Kimberly-Clark Corp.'s Huggies triumph over the competing brands. Priceless publicity—and it was free. The film's writer and producer, Ethan Cohen, says he chose Huggies because the name "sounded funnier than any other brand name."

Go ahead and laugh, says Kimberly-Clark—as long as Huggies keep disappearing from the store shelves. Today, 3 out of 10 disposable diapers sold in America are Huggies. Kimberly-Clark's success in the highly profitable, ultracompetitive diaper business has amazed people in the consumer-product industry. Huggies have dealt a blow to competitor Pampers and their maker, Procter & Gamble, which in fiscal 1985 reported its first operating earnings decline in 33 years; the drop was due partly to its so-called diaper wars with Kimberly-Clark.

And the triumph clinched Kimberly-Clark's evolution from a staid paper company to a plucky consumer-product competitor, selling such durable name brands as Kleenex and Kotex and such successful newcomers as Lightdays panty liners. In 1970, Kimberly-Clark was a lumbering manufacturing company with headquarters in poky Neenah, Wisconsin. Today, it has shiny offices in Neenah, Dallas, and Atlanta, with squadrons of marketing executives and million-dollar research and development labs, where babies crawl about with temperature and humidity sensors trailing from their tails. Last year consumer products accounted for 78 percent of the company's $4.3 billion in sales and 70 percent of its operating profit.

"People don't smile anymore when they hear Neenah, Wisconsin, says Jerry DellaFemina, the chairman of DellaFemina, Travisano & Partners, a big New York ad agency, which has never handled a Kimberly-Clark account. "It used to be, 'God, they're behind the times. The big guys [in consumer products] will come in and clean their clocks.'"

Kimberly-Clark's goal in the 1970s and 1980s, to soften the wild swings of the commodities business by diversifying, was a common one in American industry and yet uncommonly tricky. Many corporations failed in similar attempts.

Source: Cynthia F. Mitchell, "Paper Tiger: How Kimberly-Clark Wraps Its Bottom Line in Disposable Huggies," *The Wall Street Journal,* July 23, 1987, pp. 1, 12.

Kimberly-Clark succeeded with a slow and careful diversification into the fiercely competitive consumer-product industry. It focused on products linked to its core industry. Much of the filling inside a Huggies diaper, for example, comes from a Kimberly-Clark pulp mill in Coosa Pines, Alabama. The linings are produced in plants in North Carolina, Mississippi, and Wisconsin.

Added to that was the company's doggedness, even when a product faltered, and its trailblazing use of media. Television ads for Kimberly-Clark's Kotex sanitary napkins in the 1970s ended the taboo on advertising feminine products. The company hopes to duplicate its success with its advertising of Depend undergarments for incontinent adults. Its flops, which include a germ-killing facial tissue that consumers sneezed at, not into, have been relatively few.

The transformation of Kimberly-Clark is largely the work of Darwin E. Smith, the amiable, 61-year-old chairman since 1971. When Mr. Smith took control of the company, management was gliding along on past successes. Kimberly-Clark was a major supplier of newsprint to such companies as New York Times Inc. Its Kleenex brand controlled one-third of the market for facial tissues, and Kotex had more than half of the sanitary-napkin market, which it pioneered in 1920.

Mr. Smith decided that future growth could come only from new businesses, and he began a restructuring program that shook the company's very foundations. He closed four large mills that produced coated paper, which was not always profitable, and laid off 3,000 workers in the process. He sold the paper mill that Kimberly-Clark's founders had opened in the 1880s, 323,000 acres of prime timberland and two sawmills in Northern California. "We were striking at some very deep-running traditions," says Mr. Smith.

The various divestments saved the company money and earned it more than $250 million in cash, which Mr. Smith used as a diversification war chest.

The battle Mr. Smith envisioned was with Procter & Gamble, the king of consumer-products. He used his war chest to raid the marketing and research staffs of his competitors, to beef up the company's research and development efforts, and to spend on extensive advertising. In 1980, he supplemented Neenah with a 98-acre operating headquarters north of Atlanta, increasing the company's ability to recruit white-collar staff.

The arena in which Mr. Smith decided to fight Procter & Gamble was disposable diapers. The market was relatively new—the first disposable diapers were introduced in the early 1960s—enormous and, with a new baby boom beginning, poised to explode. (Current studies show that each child under the age of two goes through 2,300 diapers a year, which makes a market of $3 billion in the United States alone.)

Kimberly-Clark had already achieved some success in the diaper business, but it was short-lived. In 1968, the company introduced a disposable diaper designed to compete with Pampers. Called Kimbies, the diapers within a year snared 20 percent of the market in each city in which they were introduced. But management rested on its laurels. It shifted its focus away from keeping Kimbies as the market's innovation leader—the very aspect that had enabled the brand to so quickly snag Pampers' market share—and sales declined. By the mid-1970s, many of the company's executives had concluded the brand was a failure. They recommended the company withdraw from the business.

Mr. Smith rejected the idea. He felt disposable diapers were the embodiment of Kimberly-Clark's strengths: its expertise in paper and its growing marketing flair. In 1978, he brought out Huggies—virtually the same diapers as Kimbies but with a new hourglass shape, a new, more absorbent filling, a fresh name and extensive marketing support. The brand took off and now accounts for 26 percent of the company's sales. Recently, it replaced Kleenex as the flagship brand of the company.

Turning the corner into consumer products was tricky, and a key element of Mr. Smith's strategy was blending the old operations with the new. Kimberly-Clark's profit margins on diapers and other paper-based products are generally higher than its competitors, thanks to the integration of the two sides of the business.

For this reason, Mr. Smith makes sure the paper-product managers and workers don't feel inferior to their counterparts at the more glamorous marketing divisions.

"It's a fine, fine line you've got to walk," says Mr. Smith, a down-to-earth executive who tours plants in blue jeans and running shoes. When he visits the huge Coosa Pines, Alabama, pulp mill, he reminds workers there would be no diaper sales without the efficient production of fluff pulp, the diapers' absorbent. The theme recurs in the four "fireside chats" he has videotaped for the company's 19,000 domestic employees this year. (Kimberly-Clark spends large sums modernizing its football-field-length paper machines, having spent $150 million on the Coosa Pines mill alone in the past five years.)

After a few near-tumbles, the company has learned to be vigilant with its marketing successes. In the late 1970s, sales of Kleenex tissues stagnated, and the brand was having trouble maintaining a third of the market. Research showed that consumers preferred competing brands because they were softer. (In fact, the company had gradually increased the level of recycled wood pulp in the tissues to about 50 percent, which made them cheaper to produce but cardboard-like.)

"It's kind of like horsefeed. You can keep stretching it with sawdust and it doesn't seem like the horse cares," says James D. Bernd, the president of the company's household-products sector. "Then one day, you look up and the horse is dead." The company gave Kleenex back its soft texture, and market share quickly jumped. Last year, an even softer Kleenex was introduced, incorporating expensive eucalyptus pulp. Kleenex now commands about half the market.

By early 1986, Kimberly-Clark's resilience was being tested again. P&G had beaten the company to the market with an extra-thin diaper called "Ultra Pampers." Kimberly-Clark possessed the necessary technology—super-absorbent polymers which replaced some of the bulky fluff—and was even using it in its adult incontinence products. But the company delayed its plans for thin baby diapers when research showed that parents didn't think diapers were absorbent unless they doubled the size of baby's bottom.

The research was wrong, and Huggies' market share dropped sharply. The company hustled to put a thin diaper on the market—it took six months to retool its old machines—and Huggies regained their one-third market share, which had fallen to 25 percent in 1986.

One of the most intriguing new products invented by Kimberly-Clark was a germ-killing tissue, nicknamed Killer Kleenex by company employees and marketed under the name Avert. The product was an impressive blend of the old and the new. In 1980, company scientists discovered that disposable tissues treated with citric acid actually stopped the spread of germs. The tissue was tested in an experiment undertaken at the University of Wisconsin, during which poker-playing students were given germ-killing tissues to wipe their hands and noses. They managed to avoid catching colds from the sneezing, sniffling card player planted in each game. Kimberly-Clark began marketing Avert tissues in 1985.

But the product had two serious drawbacks: Avert's selling price per tissue was roughly four times that of regular Kleenex. And in practice, the tissues were good at preventing the spread of colds when used by a sick person. But they were no protection for a consumer who bought the tissues to *avoid* catching a cold.

"Intellectually, it's a good idea," Mr. Bernd says. "But the consumer said, 'No way. I'm not going to pay that price for something I have to use so my friend doesn't get my cold.'"

To try to salvage the product, Kimberly-Clark is attempting to sell Avert to institutions like schools, hospitals, and offices, where the higher price might pay off through reduced levels of illness and absenteeism. The company has also cut the price in half.

The next test for Kimberly-Clark is maintaining its 50 percent stake in the market for adult incontinence products, which some analysts say will grow to $500 million by 1991 from its present $150 million. Kimberly-Clark's dominance is largely the result of its aggressive television advertising campaign, which the company launched when it introduced the product in 1980. For the past two years, actress June Allyson has appeared on television ads for Depend adult incontinence products, frankly confronting viewers with the problem. Competing brands have only recently begun TV advertising.

Getting the advertisements on network television was a feat. Only recently did two of the three networks allow advertisements for adult incontinence products during prime time, after heavy lobbying by Kimberly-Clark. (NBC still restricts the ads to daytime or after 9 P.M.)

The company's success with a sensitive product like Depend mirrors its earlier efforts to strip the brown wrapping from sanitary napkins. "They're almost Oriental in their attitude toward marketing," says Mr. Della-Femina, whose agency is renowned for creating tasteful advertisements for condoms. "They're so patient. They'll figure a way to prevail, and sooner or later they win."

Analysts of the consumer-product industry say Kimberly-Clark has embarked on some new projects that bear watching. In 1984, it acquired Spenco Medical Corp., a Waco, Texas, maker of sports and health-care products, including aerobic weights and dressings for wounds. The move was a departure for Kimberly-Clark: For the first time it is producing goods that don't contain any fibers produced at its own factories. But many of the products do feed off Kimberly-Clark's extensive research in chemically based fibers.

The company has a few minor problems, including labor difficulties and currency troubles in Mexico, where it has a minority-owned factory. And in a Dallas federal court, the company is squaring off against its nemesis, Procter & Gamble, which alleges that Kimberly-Clark has unlawfully used P&G's method of elasticizing its diaper waistbands. Kimberly-Clark has countersued, claiming P&G is illegally trying to monopolize the diaper market. (Analysts dismiss the suit as another salvo in the "diaper wars" and say the company could quickly figure out a new way to elasticize its diapers if it loses.)

More interesting is the question of who will succeed Mr. Smith when he retires in four years. But while analysts and Kimberly-Clark watchers say

EXHIBIT 1

Kimberly-Clark's Changing Markets (profit in millions of dollars)

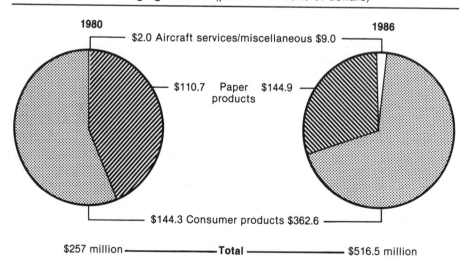

1980 — 1986

$2.0 Aircraft services/miscellaneous $9.0

$110.7 Paper $144.9 products

$144.3 Consumer products $362.6

$257 million ——————— **Total** ——————— $516.5 million

it will be an interesting battle—they each tick off two to four potential successors—they don't fear a new chief will steer Kimberly-Clark off its present course.

"It's a very substantive company; one man doesn't run the whole thing," says Bruce Kirk, a consumer-product analyst with Goldman, Sachs & Co. "I don't look for any cataclysmic, wrenching kind of changes. I put my money on evolution, not revolution."

Discussion Questions

1. Why has Kimberly-Clark apparently been successful in diversification from the core business when many other corporations have not?
2. Discuss the impact of top management's vision and committment on the success of Kimberly-Clark in the disposable diaper market.
3. Examine the role of marketing strategy in gaining competitive advantage for Kimberly-Clark.
4. Discuss how Kimberly-Clark's experiences illustrate the importance of the marketing concept as a basic guide to business success.

APPLICATION 2–10

Daimler-Benz AG

Stuttgart, West Germany—Werner Breitschwerdt dropped his understated manner for a moment last week when he announced Daimler-Benz AG's surprise bid for majority control of AEG AG.

"We are entering a new dimension," Daimler's 58-year-old chairman said.

On the eve of the 100th anniversary of Karl Benz's patent for his first automobile, the West German prestige auto maker that bears his name is taking a revolutionary new road. By gobbling up three West German high-technology companies for the equivalent of about $1 billion this year, the conservative auto maker is seeking to maintain a technological and competitive edge over its rivals.

The company traditionally has concentrated on the automotive business. Its Mercedes cars have earned the company what one competitor calls "an unassailable reputation for excellence." Its trucks have captured a lion's share of the world market.

Source: Peter Gumbel, "Daimler-Benz Seeks Technological Edge over Rivals with Its Takeover of AEG." Reprinted by permission of *The Wall Street Journal.* © Dow Jones & Co., Inc., October 21, 1985. All rights reserved.

But the purchase of AEG, a diversified electrical and electronics group with annual sales of $4.12 billion, will transform Daimler from a narrowly focused automotive company into a sprawling industrial conglomerate with a wide mix of products.

At the heart of Daimler's acquisition policy lies its desire to tap the potential of auto-related technology. Electronic systems that can precisely control functions such as brakes, suspension, steering, and air conditioning are finding new importance in cars and trucks.

Competitors are doing the same thing. General Motors Corp. has paid about $7.5 billion in the past year acquiring Hughes Aircraft Corp. and Electronic Data Systems Corp., a computer-services company. Other major U.S. auto concerns are snapping up aircraft makers and high-tech producers.

Heinz Duerr, AEG's chairman, estimates that half of AEG's business can loosely be defined as high tech, although most of this isn't auto-related. But, for example, AEG's factory-automation division could enable Daimler to build robots for use on its own assembly lines. And, speculates one German banker, "It won't be long before Mercedes cars come with AEG car telephones."

AEG also produces some pure automotive equipment, such as cables and small motors, although this amounts to just 2 percent of its sales. But company officials note that the merger will give Daimler the ability to do a wide range of research with electronic systems, thanks to new economies of scale.

The purchase also means that one of West Germany's biggest corporate successes, Daimler, will join hands with the country's biggest corporate insolvency, AEG.

But while most experts say Daimler's management has the ability to make the venture succeed, some wonder what sleek automobiles have in common with ordinary vacuum cleaners.

"This [change of structure] is the extraordinary thing about the deal," says Margot Schoenen, a companies analyst at Westdeutsche Landesbank Girozentrale. Roger Hornett, an analyst at stockbrokers James Capel & Co. in London adds: "The fit is just not that obvious to me." Mr. Breitschwerdt is quick to reassure. "AEG is a good partner," he says. "If we work together with good partners, I can't see any damage being done to our image."

Even though it will produce turbines and typewriters, refrigerators and radar, Daimler stresses that cars and trucks will remain its core business. And the auto maker says it will leave day-to-day management of AEG activities to the present AEG chairman, Heinz Duerr.

Daimler last week purchased a 24.9 percent stake from AEG for $265 million. A group of banks then offered it a further 30 percent stake for $314.4 million, and Daimler says it will pay other shareholders the same price, $63.48 a share. The takeover is still subject to clearance by the Federal Cartel Office, but that isn't seen as a problem. Once approval is given,

Daimler will become West Germany's largest company, with about 300,000 employees and annual sales of at least $22 billion.

It will also become the country's second largest defense contractor, supplying the military with $1.12 billion of equipment annually. Its engines will be used in the air, on land, and at sea, and its space technology might even play a role in President Reagan's Strategic Defense Initiative.

Investors generally view the expansion as a positive and bold step by Daimler, and the company's stock has risen sharply. Purely as an investment, Daimler seems to have picked up a bargain. It gained a majority stake in AEG for less than $600 million.

Moreover, buying the Frankfurt-based company will enable the auto maker to enter large-scale electronics production. And there are several key areas in which the different arms of the Daimler group will be able to work together. "The synergy effects are considerable," says Mr. Breitschwerdt.

But the moves have raised nagging doubts, too. AEG, which emerged from bankruptcy proceedings in September 1984, remains financially weak. Although Daimler's purchase will wipe out its debts, insiders say AEG's assets are probably overvalued. And although AEG has maintained its reputation for innovative research, it has lost some of its brightest employees during the past few years' financial difficulties.

"One of AEG's weaknesses is that it's into a number of areas where prospects for growth are low or uncertain," such as household goods, says a Frankfurt bank analyst who asks not to be named. "The way it spreads out also makes it cumbersome."

Daimler management has steered the company through other crises. At the start of the decade, when many of its competitors languished in the doldrums of world recession, Daimler increased sales and profits. Its luxury limousines are snapped up as fast as the company can produce them, and the popularity of its boxy new 190 model, the Baby Benz, has helped it grab market share away from its main challengers at home, BMW and Audi.

The company says its commercial vehicles division still is profitable, even though it has been hit by falling worldwide demand in recent years, particularly in the Middle East. Overall, Daimler group sales rose 25 percent to $14.23 billion in the first nine months of this year. No profit figures were given, but in 1984, Daimler's consolidated net income jumped 11 percent to $412 million on sales of $16.29 billion, up 8.8 percent.

"We only have two ways to describe our business, 'generally satisfactory' and 'satisfactory,'" says one Daimler manager. "The first means our profits are up, the second means our profits are way up."

It isn't above making mistakes, though. Its U.S. subsidiary, Euclid Inc., a maker of heavy off-road haulers it bought in 1977, incurred severe losses for a number of years because of a collapse in demand for heavy equipment, falling oil prices, and economic recession. Daimler finally sold the unit last year.

Discussion Questions

1. Discuss some of the reasons why Daimler-Benz's management might feel that it is necessary to diversify the firm from its core business.
2. Evaluate the strategic "fit" of the acquisitions the company has made.
3. Identify several issues that top management must consider in developing a strategy for the company.

APPLICATION 2–11

Fisher-Price Toys

Dressing toddlers can be a frazzling experience. Executives at Fisher-Price Toys had that point hammered home well to them last year. For four hours they peered through a one-way mirror and eavesdropped as a dozen women in Cleveland complained about their battles with the zippers, buckles, buttons, and snaps on kids' clothing.

"These were combat veterans who had five years of experience with two children," says Stephen Muirhead, a manager in Fisher-Price's Diversified-Products Division. "They were talking about things that touch their daily lives very deeply."

Grumpy mothers were just what Fisher-Price hoped to find. The market research convinced the company that with its famous name and a unique design, it could find a niche in the lucrative but increasingly cutthroat children's wear market. This month, the Quaker Oats Co. subsidiary will roll out its first line of preschool playwear, and there isn't a button, zipper, or frill to be found. Nearly all the fasteners are Velcro. "Oshkosh overalls are beautifully designed," says Mr. Muirhead, "but kids being toilet trained need to be Houdini to get out of them."

The Fisher-Price playwear has other features: padded knees and elbows, extra-long shirttails, cuffs that can be unfurled as children grow, and big neck openings to accommodate kids' disproportionately large heads. "Fisher-Price is attacking clothing the way it does everything else," says Ken Wilcox, director of marketing administration at Tonka Corp. "The company identifies an area where kids aren't being served well and then comes up with a nearly indestructible product that's easy to use."

But it won't be an easy jump from toys to playwear. Fisher-Price is trying to break into a splintered industry where style often matters more

---

than durability. "It's very difficult to position yourself on the basis of functionality and performance," says Peter Brown of Kurt Salmon & Associates, a management consulting firm. "Children's wear, blue jeans, and men's underwear are all advertised for their performance characteristics, but it's hard for consumers to see much difference."

And the business is becoming more crowded as other big companies are tempted by what demographers call the "baby-boom echo"—the rising number of births to women of the baby-boom generation. In the past 12 months alone, Gerber Products Co. has acquired three children's clothing companies, including the Buster Brown line. "Incursion of more adult brands into the kids' market is also intensifying the battle on the retail floor," says Terry Jacobs of Walter K. Levy Associates Inc., retail marketing consultants.

Troubled by sagging sales of jeans to adults, Levi Strauss & Co. will introduce baby Levis next spring. The company will sell blue denim pants and diaper covers for infants, as well as tiny knit shirts proclaiming, "My First Levis." Says Bill Oldenburg, general manager of the youthwear division: "We're trying to develop brand loyalty at an earlier age." (But just in case mothers can't picture their newborns clad in Levis, the company will bring out infantwear under both the new Petite Bijou and Little Levis brand names.)

Levi predicts that by 1990 more than 8 million babies will be crawling about, an increase of 11 percent from 1983. Already, the United States has more moppets under five years—17.8 million—than in any year since 1968. What interests marketers most, though, is the growing percentage of births that are first births. That's when parents and doting grandparents tend to make their largest purchases. Kurt Salmon & Associates currently estimates the preschool clothing market at more than $6 billion a year.

"The outlook is tremendous," says Leo Goulet, president of Gerber. "There are more working mothers who have the money to spend and who are going for better-quality merchandise." The baby-food company expects sales of clothing, furniture, and other nonfood products for kids to double to $450 million in five years.

Working mothers in particular are changing the way children's wear companies design and market products. William Carter Co., for instance, is now selling Swifty Change suits that contain more snaps to make diapering babies simpler. Fisher-Price found mothers especially interested in clothing that will enable children to dress themselves at an earlier age.

To make its playwear stand out, Fisher-Price is advertising it as "the children's clothing that mothers helped design." The company is also banking heavily on the strong pull of its brand name and its toys, which it says are in 99 percent of the homes where a child under the age of six lives. Fliers announcing the apparel line will be inserted into toy packages this Christmas season, and from now on, all kids featured in toy ads will be dressed in the playwear.

It became apparent rather quickly to Fisher-Price that fashioning play-wear is a world apart from building plastic and wooden toys. So the company farmed out manufacturing and distribution to a girls' dressmaker. Fisher-Price retains close control over design and marketing, however, and refuses to licence its trademark, as Tonka and the Playskool Division of Milton Bradley Co. have done. Research showed that consumers are fed up with paying a premium for a logo stamped on an otherwise ordinary T-shirt.

Fisher-Price may try to parlay its reputation for durability into kids' underwear and shoes too. "I doubt if we'll ever try to sell party dresses, though," Mr. Muirhead says. "We're not seen as very stylish or avant garde."

Discussion Questions

1. What are the advantages (and limitations) in extending the brand name Fisher-Price from toys to children's playwear?
2. What are some of the marketing problems that Fisher-Price is likely to encounter in moving into the apparel market?
3. Discuss the marketing research used in planning the Fisher-Price line of play-wear.
4. Analyze the demographic and socioeconomic trends from 1985 to 1990 for the playwear line. Do the trends appear favorable or unfavorable for the new product line?

APPLICATION 2–12

Campbell Soup Company

CAMDEN, N.J.—R. Gordon McGovern, the president and chief executive of Campbell Soup Co., was so obsessed with cooking up new products a few years ago that he sent key executives copies of "In Search of Excellence," a primer on corporate innovation. Partly as a result, the company has introduced 334 new products in the past five years—more than any other company in the hotly competitive food industry.

But now Mr. McGovern has decided that Campbell may have done too much innovating too fast. His new reading assignment has a different emphasis. This year, he sent his executives a book about how to improve prod-

---

Source: Francine Schwadel, "Revised Recipe: Burned by Mistakes, Campbell Soup Co. Is in Throes of Change." Reprinted by permission of *The Wall Street Journal.* © Dow Jones & Company, Inc., August 14, 1985, pp. 1, 13. All rights reserved.

uct quality and production efficiency to hold down costs. "Read it carefully," Mr. McGovern wrote in an accompanying memo. "Failure to control costs," he said, "could leave Campbell without enough money to support its new-product strategy."

Indeed, the company's new-product recipe itself is changing. Mr. McGovern wants a more rigorous review of costly new-product ventures and a slower pace of national introductions. Herbert M. Baum, the newly installed president of Campbell's huge U.S. division, says Campbell can no longer afford to run "a new-product boutique."

When Mr. McGovern was promoted from executive vice president and chief operating officer to the Campbell presidency in 1980, his single-minded goal seemed to be turning the stodgy soup maker into a consumer-driven marketing company. In the past, Campbell had concentrated so much on production efficiency that its new products appeared to be designed on the basis of what the company could make easily, rather than what people wanted to buy. So Mr. McGovern focused on consumers by encouraging executives to visit supermarkets, restaurants and people's kitchens.

To foster entrepreneurial attitudes, the new president split the company into 50 autonomous business units divided by such product categories as soup, frozen foods, and beverages. Then he poured money into marketing, increasing expenditures by almost 150 percent between 1980 and 1985.

But the results weren't entirely satisfactory. True, the company says 7 of the 10 major new brands introduced in the McGovern era have been successful, generating at least $25 million in annual sales. What's more, two new Campbell concoctions—Prego spaghetti sauces and Le Menu frozen dinners—became superstars, accounting for more than $450 million of Campbell's $4 billion in annual sales. Lately though, the company has spent heavily to promote new and existing products without reaping the expected rewards.

Some glaring examples: Juice Works, a new line of natural blends for kids, did so poorly initially that Campbell had to reformulate three flavors and revamp its advertising campaign last fall. Pepperidge Farm, a star performer in the 12 years that Mr. McGovern ran the unit, has been slow to recover from disastrous forays into new products that had little to do with the brand's premium image. After three disappointing quarters, Campbell's operating earnings in the fiscal year ended July 28 are estimated to have approximated last year's $5.93 a share—falling far short of Mr. McGovern's goal of 15 percent annual growth.

"I think what happened was the brand managers became so involved in looking at new products that they ignored the base businesses," says one Campbell marketing manager. Mr. McGovern himself concedes that the company has made enough mistakes for him to replace the presidents of both the U.S. division and Pepperidge Farm. But he describes his efforts to tighten control over major new-product introductions as a necessary phase of Campbell's evolution, rather than a response to soft earnings.

Whatever the reason, Laurel Cutler, an advertising executive who helps Campbell and other companies plot new-product strategies, applauds the change. "I feel it is the healthiest possible move," says Mrs. Cutler, vice chairman of Leber Katz Partners in New York. "Nothing that important can be delegated below the most senior management."

Campbell's cost-control efforts might also protect it from the takeover fever that has swept the food industry. Certainly, Campbell's strong brands make it an attractive target. In May, Campbell stock leaped almost $8 to $76.375 a share on news that R. J. Reynolds Industries Inc. and Nabisco Brands Inc. were planning to merge. In late June, Campbell hit $79 on rumors that General Foods Corp. might be the target of a bid by Philip Morris Inc. To make Campbell stock more affordable for small investors, Campbell in June declared a two-for-one stock split that was payable last month. Yesterday, Campbell closed at $38 a share.

A Campbell merger seems unlikely any time soon. The Dorrance family owns 58 percent of the stock, and John T. Dorrance, Jr., who retired last fall as Campbell chairman and who is the sole beneficiary of a family trust that owns 31.5 percent of the stock, has said he doesn't intend to sell. But one line of speculation says the Dorrances could change their minds, especially if earnings don't improve.

Despite the new emphasis on discipline, Campbell hasn't lost its penchant for taking risks. It is testing more new ideas than ever before, among them refrigerated salads, soups in microwavable containers, Pepperidge Farm ice cream and granola bread. And it is beginning an assault on the $290 million dry-soup-mix market dominated by Thomas J. Lipton Inc., a unit of the Anglo-Dutch Unilever Group. The move makes sense, Campbell officials say, because dry-soup sales in the U.S. have been growing faster than sales of canned soups.

"What we're trying to prevent is a quick trigger finger," says Mr. Baum. "We want the products that go national to be well-tested unless there is some competitive reason to go national all at once."

Lipton's aggressive response to test marketing of an early Campbell dry-soup product provided the reason to spring today's six-flavor line of soup mixes into national distribution, starting this summer, Mr. Baum says.

So Campbell committed $16 million to the launch, and Mr. Baum is watching its progress carefully. At his urging, the soup-mix team twice revised its marketing plan, putting more money into advertising aimed at consumers, rather than trade allowances that would lower prices.

In the past, Campbell's racing into the marketplace has produced mixed results. The strategy paid off with Le Menu, the line of premium frozen dinners that Campbell launched in the West in 1982. The company's engineers hadn't yet designed much of the production equipment needed to fill the round dinner plates automatically. So Campbell hired people to fill the plates by hand. They used ice-cream scoops to dish out rice, and they picked

EXHIBIT 1
Campbell's Leading New Products ($600 million in sales for fiscal 1985)

1985 Ranking	Year Introduced
1 Le Menu Frozen Dinner	1982
2 Prego Spaghetti Sauce	1982
3 Chunky New England Clam Chowder	1984
4 Great Starts Breakfasts	1984
5 Prego Plus	1985

Quarterly net income ($ millions)   **Quarterly earnings per share** ($ millions)

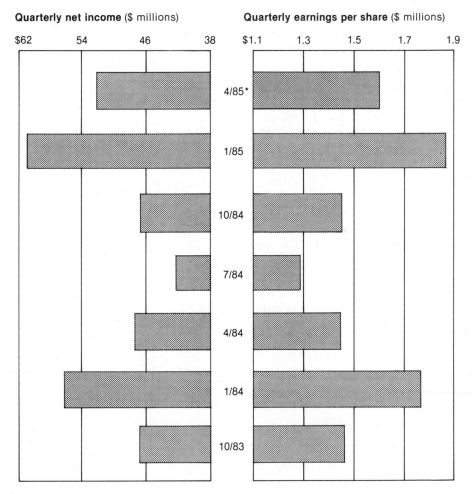

* Includes an after-tax gain of $5 million, or 15 cents a share.

up meats with gloved fingers. The production line was inefficient, but demand for the dinners was strong.

Introducing Juice Works in the Northeast last fall in bottles and single-serving cans, without offering aseptic packages, turned out to be a costly error. Juice blends packed in the lightweight cardboard boxes were added to the Juice Works line in January. But because Campbell misjudged the importance of aseptic packages in the Northeast (it had tested the packages elsewhere), it initially had trouble persuading retailers to carry the products. Competition from juice blends made by Tree Top Inc., Welch Foods Inc., the Libby, McNeill & Libby unit of Nestlé Enterprises Inc. and others made the task tougher.

The false starts, including ingredient problems and an advertising campaign that was scrapped when it failed to produce results, cost Campbell "several million dollars," according to Mr. Baum. In the fiscal year that just ended, Juice Works sales fell an estimated $8 million short of the $32 million Campbell had forecast.

Sales have picked up dramatically in recent months, but Mr. Baum wants to look at the results through December before taking the product national. Juice Works had been scheduled to go national last spring.

Pepperidge Farm suffered $9 million in losses because it rushed Star Wars cookies and apple juice into the marketplace in 1983. By last summer, when Richard A. Shea became the third Pepperidge Farm president in four years, morale had sunk to a low point. Press reports about the cookie and apple-juice flops—both products now are defunct—reinforced the impression that the unit had lost sight of its heritage.

Pepperidge Farm was founded in 1937 by Margaret Rudkin, who baked her first loaf of whole-wheat bread when a doctor recommended its natural ingredients as a treatment for her asthmatic son. Within a few years, Mrs. Rudkin was receiving orders from as far away as India, and the company expanded rapidly. Campbell bought Pepperidge Farm in 1961.

To get Pepperidge Farm back on track, Mr. Shea and 50 marketing managers retreated last fall to a motel to talk about where the company was headed. They listened to presentations about consumer trends. Then they split up into small groups, first to discuss the meaning of the Pepperidge Farm brand and later to brainstorm new-product ideas. "It was amazing to me how each group kept coming up with the same . . . things," says Edith Volino Anderson, marketing manager for frozen new products. "You started to see the company take shape. You started to see a philosophy."

Among the key attributes mentioned over and over at the meeting were premium quality, natural ingredients, meeting a consumer need, and an ability to build on the company's bakery heritage. But some managers were still confused about the types of products Pepperidge Farm should make, suggesting popcorn or snack cakes, for example. Mr. Shea recalls saying that Pepperidge Farm couldn't add anything to popcorn to make it a premium product and that snack cakes, as a children's product, wouldn't support a premium price.

Mr. Shea later boiled down the managers' ideas into new-product standards and priorities. He instituted monthly meetings at which once-autonomous marketing managers must compare the progress of their projects with their forecasts. He also dropped 275 products that weren't up to snuff, including several flavors of Deli's, a line of frozen, pastry-encased meat and cheese sandwiches for which Pepperidge Farm had high hopes a few years ago. The sandwiches will be phased out entirely in the fall because, despite high trial rates, most consumers didn't buy them again.

Beyond the problems of Pepperidge Farm, Mr. McGovern has the bigger picture to contend with. Now 58 years old, he is concentrating on choosing and grooming a successor to Campbell's presidency. He is expected to become chairman within a few years, and last fall, at his suggestion, the board elected William S. Cashel Jr., a retired American Telephone & Telegraph Co. executive, as a transitional chairman.

In his efforts to revitalize Campbell, Mr. McGovern must strike the right balance between disciplining the business units and leaving enough room for innovation. Some marketing managers are bound to be disappointed, since Campbell plans to undertake fewer national launches at a time when it has so many new ideas.

But marketing managers seem to be adjusting. They describe the call for discipline as a dose of reality in an environment where the sky seemed to be the limit. "The plan had been for every unit to work . . . on new products to make successes out of them all," says Patti F. Goodman, marketing manager for Juice Works. "Now we want to put our (money) behind those products that have the greatest chance of success."

Discussion Questions

1. Discuss some of the strategic and operating issues of coordinating corporate and business unit strategies.
2. What business unit implementation guidelines can be used to achieve proper management of existing and new products?
3. Comment on Campbell's use of 50 business units.
4. Evaluate Campbell's approach to new-product planning, suggesting any improvements that are needed.

APPLICATION 2–13

Pier 1 Imports, Inc.

In many places, Pier 1 Imports Inc. still conjures up the image of psychedelic pillows, scented candles, beaded curtains, and other cheap furnishings for counterculture digs.

But yesterday's Sgt. Pepper generation has grown up and, after a time, so has Pier 1. Now its stores are piled to the rafters with pricey wicker settees, French stemware, and decorative Italian tables that appeal to the stores' new customers—college-educated women between the ages of 25 and 44 who earn more than $35,000 a year. With nearly 400 stores in 37 states, the Fort Worth, Texas-based chain is the only specialty home-furnishing outfit that can claim national status.

To remake its image, Pier 1 has turned itself inside out, remodeling its stores, sprucing up its advertising and bringing in tough, corporate management. "They had to wrench themselves into the '80s and they spent the whole '70s doing it," says Chris LaBastille, a growth-company analyst for Shearson Lehman Hutton Inc.

The company is now so Establishment, in fact, that last week the industry was thick with rumors that such All-American retailing giants as Sears, Roebuck & Co., J. C. Penney Co., and K mart Corp. might seek to acquire Pier 1, which racked up about $327 million in sales last year.

Pier 1's stock soared to $11.25 a share from $8.75 in composite trading on the New York Stock Exchange last week after the company announced an unsolicited inquiry from an unnamed retailer seeking to buy it. Pier 1 immediately hired Drexel Burnham Lambert to help it weigh offers. Yesterday, Pier 1 closed at $10.75, up 12.5 cents, giving the company an indicated value of $326.8 million based on 30.4 million shares outstanding.

Pier 1 has approval from its major owner, Intermark Inc., to sell the company, but only if the price is "substantially" above its current market price, says Charles Scott, Intermark's president and chief executive. An offer of $13 "wouldn't even pique our interest," he says.

Sears and the other retailers won't discuss any plans they might have to acquire Pier 1. But last year Sears created a specialty stores division and recently acquired several speciality retailers. A Sears spokesman says the company "is committed to expanding" into specialty retailing, and Sears has compelling reasons to do so. Like most other big retailers, it is finding it tough to increase earnings internally; profit for its merchandise group peaked in 1984 and has slipped since. Pier 1, in contrast, is expected to grow at a heady 25 percent a year clip for at least five years.

Source: Michael Totty, "For Pier 1, the Days of the Counterculture Are Gone," *The Wall Street Journal,* April 27, 1988, p. 6.

"The big retailers don't have that kind of growth out in front of them," says Bo Cheadle, a specialty retailing analyst for Montgomery Securities in San Francisco. "They're all reaching out and looking for some segment of retailing that they can grow in."

In recent months, Sears bought a small chain of women's clothing stores, a Texas-based eye-care company, and is wrapping up its purchase of the Western Auto automotive parts chain. Penney also has ventured into specialty stores, buying a 20 percent stake in the Alcott & Andrews women's apparel outlets.

There's plenty of reasons why Pier 1 is suddenly attracting attention. Since new management took over three years ago, sales have climbed 23 percent and profits 40 percent. Pier 1's gross profit margins, a measure of just how high a retailer can mark up its goods, reached an enviable 57.3 percent in fiscal 1988. And the company is expanding by leaps and bounds, having opened 179 new stores under its new management. Pier 1 plans another 87 new stores this year and expects to have 500 stores across the United States and Canada by 1990. And as an importer, it has buying and manufacturing capabilities in about 60 countries that competitors would be hard pressed to duplicate (see Exhibit 1.)

Pier 1 also dominates a niche it created—exotic imported furniture and housewares that, experts predict, will continue to enjoy rapid growth as baby boomers reach their peak home-furnishing years.

Yesterday's "flower children" are still flocking to Pier 1 because its

EXHIBIT 1
Growth at Pier 1

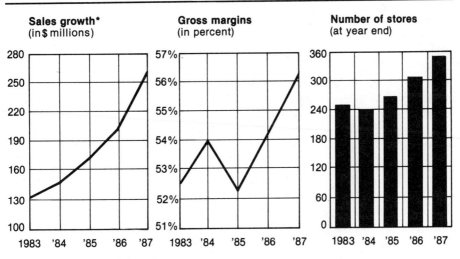

Sales growth* (in $ millions) · Gross margins (in percent) · Number of stores (at year end)

* Fiscal year ending in February.

stores offer the unique and the exotic. The difference is that Pier 1's patrons today own their own homes and have the money to fix them up. "Pier 1 appeals to the innate snobbishness of the group for uniqueness," says Carl Steidtman, chief economist at Management Horizon, a retail consulting unit of Price Waterhouse.

Charles Tandy, founder of Tandy Corp., opened the first Pier 1 in 1962 as an outlet for a little-known San Francisco importer of Far Eastern pottery and housewares. Soon, the stores blossomed as the flower children of the 60s flocked to Pier 1 in search of "far-out" furnishings that reflected their distaste for tradition. By the end of the decade, Pier 1 was the recognized outfitter of college dorms and hippie pads—the Ralph Lauren of the bead-and-incense set.

But as its former customers left college, cut their hair, and climbed the corporate ladder, the company began to founder. From 1971 to 1980, the number of sales dropped by half. In desperation, stores tried to win back shoppers with art supplies, wine and spirits—even tropical fish. All of these retailing experiments failed miserably.

Pier 1's unconventional style extended even to its annual reports. Its 1984 report resembled a National Geographic magazine which informed shareholders of the company's "gypsy team" that scoured such exotic places as Java and Bali in search of ethnic clothing and accessories.

Pier 1 badly needed a new sense of direction—and quickly. Clark A. Johnson, a former president of Wickes Furniture—a company battered by the severe recession in the 1970s—was brought in to turn Pier 1 around. Mr. Johnson instilled a market-driven, by-the-numbers approach to the business, and pushed Pier 1 to upgrade its merchandise and quadruple its size by the end of the century. "We wanted to hurry up and increase our stores so that the company was positioned to take advantage of that growth," says Mr. Johnson.

That was an ambitious undertaking for a company that, like love beads and day-glow posters, had become passé. Pier 1's shoppers, if they remembered Pier 1 at all, recalled dingy stores reeking of incense and crowded with college-dorm furnishings. "It was like visiting a poorly lit bazaar in some Third World country," says Stan Richards of Richards Group, Pier 1's outside advertising agency.

To shed its Third World image, floors were painted red and store layouts were redone to a less-cluttered look. Fluorescent fixtures gave way to focused spots that highlighted merchandise. And candles and incense were relegated to corners of the stores.

In changing its image, however, Pier 1 didn't completely reject its past. The large Japanese paper lanterns still hang prominently from the ceilings, and rattan emperor chairs, albeit with higher price tags, are still popular. Such items "really defined the company in a way that we hoped people would recognize," explains Thomas Christopher, Pier 1's senior vice president for operations.

Pier 1's "new image" advertising highlights merchandise with brightly colored photos of umbrellas, pillows and kitchenware. Black-and-white newspaper advertisements that simply stated "Sale $29.99," were replaced by eye-catching color ads in Sunday supplements that promised "The best swiveling rocker since Elvis."

All the company's efforts aren't lost on former customers who are finding their way back. Joe Crews, a Dallas attorney who used to buy his window shades and bedspreads at the store while in college, now shops for end tables and lampshades while his wife buys cotton clothing.

On a recent visit, they were looking at bedspreads for a new king-size bed. "When I first came back (a few years ago), I had the impression it was cheaper and poorer quality stuff," Mr. Crews recalls as he browses through some bedspreads priced at about $70 at one of Pier 1's Dallas emporiums. In the old days, the bedding selection would have been largely limited to India print spreads that sold for about $5.

Mr. Crews, like a lot of Pier 1 shoppers who used to shop there during his college days, seemed impressed. "I've seen it go from a lot of little baskets and candles to better-quality furniture," he says. "The styles are substantially different."

Discussion Questions

1. Prepare a complete situational assessment of Pier 1, including a discussion of the strategic implications of the situation.
2. Discuss the relationship between Pier 1's business and marketing strategies.
3. Evaluate the retail market opportunity available to Pier 1 during the early 1990s.
4. Assess the appropriateness of Pier 1's targeting and positioning strategies, indicating any recommended changes.

PART 3

TARGET-MARKET STRATEGY

Deciding which people or organizations to serve in the marketplace is one of management's most important and demanding strategic decisions. All operations of the firm revolve around the target-market decision. Target-market alternatives range from serving all (or most) buyers, using a mass strategy, to serving one or more niches (segments), using a differentiated strategy in each niche.

There are clear indications that market niching will become the dominant strategy of successful firms in the 1990s—particularly those that are not market leaders. This is because high market share is often linked to strong business performance. Serving a niche or segment of a product-market may be the only feasible way for a firm to gain and hold market share. While the niche decision alone will not guarantee high performance, it can be the first step in building a high-performance marketing strategy.

Two major activities underlie the target-market decision: (1) defining and analyzing product-markets to gauge present opportunity and growth potential; and (2) deciding which people/organizations to serve and how to target the firm's marketing efforts in each product-market of interest. We shall briefly examine each of these activities.

DEFINING AND ANALYZING PRODUCT-MARKETS

Market opportunity analysis serves two purposes. It enables the firm to understand markets before deciding whether and how to serve them. Equally important, it enables the firm to track product-market trends to determine when shifts in targeted customers, or adjustments in marketing efforts, are needed.

Four kinds of information are normally included in a market opportunity analysis:

1. As much information as possible about the people/organizations that use the product. (These profiles of customers are useful in designing marketing strategy and tactics.)
2. The present size of each product-market and how fast it is growing.
3. The firms that supply products and services at each level, including both similar types of firms (e.g., manufacturers) and those functioning at different levels in channels of distribution (e.g., distributors, retailers).
4. An assessment of major competitors (essential to guiding marketing strategy decisions).

The analysis should help management decide what market-target strategy to adopt and the marketing program positioning strategy to use. (The terms market-target and target-market can be used interchangeably.)

Customer Profiles

Answers to these four questions will supply essential information about customers:

1. Who are the existing/potential customers?
2. What are their characteristics?
3. How do they decide what to buy?
4. What factors, other than customer characteristics and company marketing efforts, influence buying?

Identifying and describing the people or organizations that comprise the market for a product (questions 1 and 2) are the first steps in product-market analysis. Typically, demographic and socioeconomic characteristics are used to identify potential users in product-markets. Characteristics such as family size, age, income, geographical location, sex, and occupation are often useful in identifying customers in consumer markets. A variety of factors can be used to identify end users in industrial markets, including type of industry, size, location, and product application.

Many published sources of information are available for use in identifying and describing customers; for example, United States census data, trade association publications, and studies by advertising media (TV, radio, magazines). The important task is to find those characteristics that will identify potential customers. In some situations, research studies may be necessary.

In examining how customers decide what to buy, it is useful to observe how people move through the sequence of steps leading to a decision to purchase a particular brand. Buyers normally begin by recognizing a need. Next, they seek information. Third, they identify and evaluate alternative products. Finally, they choose a brand. This process varies, based upon a number of factors, including the importance of the purchase, whether it is an individual or group decision, and whether it is a first-time purchase or a repeat purchase. Essential in studying buyer behavior is learning what criteria people use in making decisions. Determining why people buy offers important insights for marketing strategy.

The final step in building customer profiles is to identify external factors that may alter buyers' needs and wants. Environmental influences include the government, social change, economic shifts, technological changes, and other macroenvironmental forces. Typically, these factors cannot be controlled by the buyer or the firms that market the product.

Size and Growth Estimates

Two market-size estimates are often used in product-market analysis. One is a measure of the potential that exists in a market. Since in most instances an opportunity is never fully realized by the firms serving the product-market, a second measure is needed. This is a forecast of what is likely to occur for the time period under consideration. The potential represents an upper limit; the forecast normally is something less than total potential. In addition to size estimates, expected growth rates over the planning period are very useful in planning.

Industry and Distribution Analyses

The ways in which products and services reach end users should be identified and analyzed. Normally an analysis is conducted from the point of view of a particular firm. For example, a department store chain such as Dayton-Hudson would include other retailers in its industry analyses. Two kinds of information are needed:

1. Study of the industry of which the company is a part.
2. Analysis of the distribution channels that link together the various organizations serving end users' needs and wants.

Starting first with the industry analysis, the following information is needed:

- Industry characteristics and trends, such as sales, number of firms, and growth rates.
- Operating practices of the firms in the industry, including product mix, services provided, barriers to entry, and related information.

A knowledge of distribution channels is essential to understanding and serving product-markets:

- When do producers go directly to their end users?
- When do producers work through distribution channels?

Key Competitors

Normally a company does not compete with all firms in an industry, so it is necessary to find out which are key competitors. Also, if specific customer needs can be satisfied by product categories from other industries, potential competitors should be included in the analysis. Information that is obtained from a key-competitor analysis often includes:

- Estimated overall business strength of each key competitor.
- Present market share and past trends.
- Financial strengths and performance.
- Management capabilities (and limitations).
- Technical and operating advantages (e.g., patents, low production costs, new products).
- Description and assessment of marketing strategy.

Keeping up with what the competition is doing is one of management's most important responsibilities. The above information should be obtained and studied on a regular basis.

STEPS IN MARKET TARGETING

The selection of market targets is one of management's most demanding challenges. Should a company attempt to serve all customers that are willing and able to buy, or selectively go after one or more subgroups of customers? An understanding of a product-market is essential in selecting the market-target strategy. The selection steps are:

1. Decide how to form segments in the product-market.
2. Describe the people/organizations in each segment.
3. Evaluate market-target alternatives.
4. Select a market-target strategy.

The possibilities for selecting the firm's target group of customers range from attempting to appeal to most of the people in the market (a mass-market approach) to going after one or more segments within the market. The mass and segment market-target strategies are defined as follows:

Mass-Market Strategy. All potential customers in a product-market are assumed to be sufficiently similar in their responsiveness to a marketing program. Note that *mass* refers not to absolute size but instead to the fact that the firm is aiming one marketing program at all of the people or organizations, rather than going after one or more subgroups within the product-market by using a totally different or modified marketing program for each subgroup.

Market-Segmentation Strategy.   Using this strategy one assumes that people or organizations within a product-market will vary as to their responsiveness to any marketing program. The objective is to identify two or more subgroups within the product-market. Each subgroup represents people or organizations who respond similarly to a marketing offer. A segmentation strategy can be implemented by going after a single segment or by designing a separate marketing program to appeal to each segment of interest.

Finding and Describing Segments

Using a segmentation strategy, a company may gain worthwhile advantages compared to using a mass approach—including higher profitability and strength over competition—through better use of the firm's capabilities and resources. By selecting niches of the product-market, each containing people or organizations that exhibit some degree of similarity, management can gain greater customer responsiveness from effort expended than by directing the same marketing effort to the whole product-market.

Management must somehow identify possible segments and then, for each segment of interest, determine which marketing program positioning strategy will obtain the most favorable profit contribution, net of marketing costs. Since there are many ways to divide a product-market and several marketing program combinations that might be used for each niche, finding the very best (optimal) market target and marketing program strategy is probably impossible. One should first decide whether moving away from a mass strategy is advisable and, if so, what market-target alternative(s) looks attractive to management.

Criteria for Segmentation.   An important question is whether segmentation is worth doing. Since there are many ways to form niches, how does the planner make the choice? Five criteria are useful. First is the responsiveness to a company's efforts. If little or no variation exists between four selected consumer groups, then the way they respond (e.g., amount, frequency of purchase) to any given marketing program should be the same. If four (or any) segments actually exist in this selection, their responses will be different—and a different marketing program strategy will work best for each group.

After meeting the first condition—measuring responsiveness to a company's efforts—the other requirements come into play. Second, it must be feasible to identify two or more different customer groups, and third, a firm must be able to aim an appropriate marketing program strategy at each target segment. Fourth, in terms of revenue generated and costs incurred, segmentation must be worth doing. Fifth, the segments must exhibit adequate stability over time so that the firm's efforts via segmentation will have enough time to reach desired levels of performance.

If we fail to meet the five requirements, use of a niche strategy is questionable. The ultimate criterion is performance. If a niche scheme leads to improved performance (profitability) in a product-market, it is worthwhile. The advantage of meeting the requirements for segmentation is that we are more certain the strategy will lead to improved performance.

Forming Segments

Much of the information obtained from product-market analysis can be used in describing market niches. The starting point in describing niches is the definition and analysis of the product-market (customer profiles) that were discussed previously. The objective is to identify key characteristics that will be useful in distinguishing one niche from another.

Describing the Segments

It is important to identify key characteristics of the people or organizations that occupy each niche. Factors such as those used in dividing product-markets into segments are also helpful in describing the people in the niches. You will recall from the discussion of market analysis that the following information was needed:

- Market profiles of customers.
- Size and growth estimates.
- Distribution channels.
- Analysis of key competitors.
- Product- or brand-positioning strategy.

This same information is needed for each segment of interest to better evaluate its potential value.

Evaluating Market-Target Alternatives

Market-target alternatives range from a mass strategy to a strategy directed toward one, more than one, or all segments. When serving several niches, the marketing program positioning strategy used for a segment may be totally different from that used for other segments, or each program may overlap to some extent programs for other segments. Thus, a firm may use a unique combination of the product offering, distribution approach, price, advertising, and personal selling to serve each segment, or some of the marketing mix components may be used for more than one segment. For example, the same airline services are used to appeal to business and pleasure travelers, although different advertising and sales efforts are aimed at each user group.

Once segments are formed, each one should be evaluated to accomplish three purposes:

1. Since there is often more than one marketing program that can be used for a given segment, a selection of the best alternative is necessary for each candidate.
2. After evaluation is complete, those segments which still look attractive as market-target candidates should be ranked as to their attractiveness.
3. Finally, evaluations will help management decide if a niche strategy is better than a mass-market approach.

SELECTING A MARKET-TARGET STRATEGY

Assuming that segments can be identified, management has the option of selecting one or more niches as market-targets or, instead, of using a mass strategy. Several factors often affect this decision: characteristics of the product-market, company characteristics, and some other considerations.

Product-Market Characteristics

The market that a firm decides to serve has a strong influence upon the choice of a market-target strategy. When buyers' needs and wants are similar there is no real basis for establishing niches. A product-market made up of a small number of end users also argues in favor of a mass strategy, particularly if dollar purchases per buyer are small. Market complexity is another consideration, overlapping to some extent the other factors. The more complex the market situation as to competing firms, variety of product offering, variation in user needs and wants, and other factors, the more likely that a useful niche scheme can be found.

Company Characteristics

A firm's market share is an important factor in deciding what market-target strategy to use. Low market-share firms can often strengthen their position over competition by finding a segment where they have (or can achieve) an advantage over that competition.

The success of some small market-share firms such as Nucor (steel) lends strong support to this position. Also important in choosing a market-target strategy are the resources and capabilities of a firm. With limited resources a niche strategy may be essential, as is also the case when the firm's capabilities are in short supply.

Other Considerations

Selection of an appropriate strategy must also take into account the number of competing firms and the capabilities of each. Intense competition often favors a niche strategy, particularly for low-share firms. Finally, production and marketing-scale economies may influence management in choosing a strategy. For example, large volume may be required to gain cost advantages, and scale of production may also affect marketing and distribution programs. If so, a mass strategy may be necessary in order to reach the sales volume necessary to support large-volume production.

CONCLUDING NOTE

Understanding product-markets is essential to making good marketing decisions. The activity of defining and analyzing product-markets is probably more critical to making sound planning decisions than any other activity in the enterprise. The uses of these analyses are many and varied. Defining and analyzing product-markets includes examining customer profiles, making size and growth estimates for the product-market and industry, conducting distribution analyses, analysis of key competitors, and developing marketing strategy guidelines.

The market-target decision sets into motion the marketing plan. Choosing the right market-target is a most important decision affecting the enterprise. This decision is central to properly positioning a firm in the marketplace. Sometimes a single target cannot be selected for an entire strategic business unit when the SBU contains different product-markets. Moreover, locating the firm's best differential advantage may first require detailed segment analysis. Market-target decisions connect corporate and marketing planning. These decisions establish key guidelines for planning, and the market-target decision provides the focus for the remaining marketing-planning decisions.

When it appears feasible to identify segments in a product-market, management should consider attempting to form niches, evaluate them, and then choose between niche and mass strategies. We have developed several guidelines to assist in segment identification and evaluation. Likewise, important considerations in choosing between mass and niche strategies were discussed. While various promising methods are available for use in segment formation, the task continues to offer management a major challenge.

CASES AND APPLICATIONS
FOR PART 3

The six cases and five applications in Part 3 focus primarily upon market-target decisions and strategies.

Cases

The TenderCare Disposable Diaper case (3–1) concentrates on the planned introduction of a superior diaper. Lawrence Bennett, vice president of marketing at Rocky Mountain Medical Corporation, must quickly decide upon market-target and marketing-program positioning strategies for the new product.

Case 3–2, The Michigan League, concerns a University of Michigan food service operation that has been experiencing a decrease in business. Pat Lawson, manager of the Michigan League for the past six years, is interested in discovering why fewer customers are eating in the League's cafeteria and coffee shop and is making plans to reverse that trend.

Case 3–3, Sungold Cabinets, describes a company that experienced a decline in sales following a fire that destroyed its production and warehouse facilities. Company management has decided to review alternative market opportunities and the firm's marketing strategy.

Algonquin Power and Light Company, a metropolitan gas and electric utility, is considering whether to begin manufacturing compost for sale from tree and shrubbery trimmings (Case 3–4). Management must decide whether to pursue this business opportunity, and if so, whether to target the retail market, the wholesale market, or both.

The Freeman Roller Rink case (3–5) presents the results of a study intended to assess the feasibility of a roller rink/arcade project. The Freeman brothers must decide whether or not to move forward with the endeavor.

The final case in Part 3 focuses on whether or not the Kellogg Company should introduce a new brand, Kellogg Rally Cereal. Test market results seven years earlier comparing Rally to the nutritional ready-to-eat market segment leader, Quaker Oats' Life, were very favorable. A. B. Smith must prepare a recommendation to management.

Applications

The Keithley Instruments application (3–7) illustrates the market-segmentation strategy of a medium-size, high-technology industrial products company. Whittle Communications L. P. (3–8) provides an interesting examination of an innovative media specialist. Toyota Lexus (3–9) describes the market-entry strategy of a Japanese company planning to invade the European-style luxury-automobile market segment. Marriott Corp.'s Courtyard Hotel chain (3–10) describes the company's move into the medium-price segment of the market to compete with Holiday Inn and Ramada Inn. Morning Treat Coffee Bags (3–11) provides an opportunity to evaluate a proposed market research study for a new product.

CASE 3–1

TenderCare Disposable Diapers

Tom Cagan watched as his secretary poured six ounces of water onto each of two disposable diapers lying on his desk. The diaper on the left was a new, improved Pampers, introduced in the summer of 1985 by Procter & Gamble. The new, improved design was supposed to be drier than the preceding Pampers. It was the most recent development in a sequence of designs that traced back to the original Pampers, introduced to the market in 1965. The diaper on his right was a TenderCare™ diaper, manufactured by a potential supplier for testing and approval by Cagan's company, Rocky Mountain Medical Corporation (RMM). The outward appearance of both diapers was identical.

Yet the TenderCare diaper was different. Just under its liner (the surface next to the baby's skin) was a wicking fabric that drew moisture from the surface around a soft, waterproof shield to an absorbent reservoir of filler. Pampers and all other disposable diapers on the market kept moisture nearer to the liner and, consequently, the baby's skin. A patent attorney had examined the TenderCare design, concluding that the wicking fabric and shield arrangement should be granted a patent. However, it would be many months before results of the patent application process could be known.

As soon as the empty beakers were placed back on the desk, Cagan and his secretary touched the liners of both diapers. They agreed that there was no noticeable difference, and Cagan noted the time. They repeated their

---

This case was written by Professor James E. Nelson, University of Colorado. Some data are disguised. © 1986 by the Business Research Division, College of Business and Administration and the Graduate School of Business Administration, University of Colorado, Boulder, Colorado 80309-0419.

"touch test" after one minute and again noted no difference. However, after two minutes, both thought the TenderCare diaper to be drier. At three minutes, they were certain. By five minutes, the TenderCare diaper surface seemed almost dry to the touch, even when a finger was pressed deep into the diaper. In contrast, the Pampers diaper showed little improvement in dryness from three to five minutes and tended to produce a puddle when pressed.

These results were not unexpected. Over the past three months, Cagan and other RMM executives had compared TenderCare's performance with ten brands of disposable diapers available in the Denver market. Tender-Care diapers had always felt drier within a two- to four-minute interval after wetting. However, these results were considered tentative because all tests had used TenderCare diapers made by RMM personnel by hand. Today's test was the first made with diapers produced by a supplier under mass manufacturing conditions.

ROCKY MOUNTAIN MEDICAL CORPORATION

RMM was incorporated in Denver, Colorado, in late 1982 by Robert Morrison, M.D. Sales had grown from about $400,000 in 1983 to $2.4 million in 1984 and were expected to reach $3.4 million in 1985. The firm would show a small profit for 1985, as it had each previous year.

Management personnel as of September 1985 included six executives. Cagan served as president and director, positions held since joining RMM in April 1984. Prior to that time he had worked for several high-technology companies in the areas of product design and development, production management, sales management, and general management. His undergraduate studies were in engineering and psychology; he took an MBA in 1981. Dr. Morrison currently served as chairman of the board and vice president for research and development. He had completed his M.D. in 1976 and was board certified to practice pediatrics in the state of Colorado since 1978. John Bosch served as vice president of manufacturing, a position held since joining RMM in late 1983. Lawrence Bennett was vice president of marketing, having primary responsibilities for marketing TenderCare and RMM's two lines of phototherapy products since joining the firm in 1984. Bennett's background included an MBA received in 1981 and three years' experience in groceries product management at General Mills. Two other executives had also joined RMM in 1984. One served as vice president of personnel; the other as controller.

Phototherapy Products

RMM's two lines of phototherapy products were used to treat infant jaundice, a condition experienced by some 5 to 10 percent of all newborn babies. One line was marketed to hospitals under the trademark Alpha-Lite. Bennett felt that the Alpha-Lite phototherapy unit was superior to competing products because it gave the baby 360-degree exposure to the therapeutic light. Competing products gave less complete exposure, with the result that the Alpha-Lite unit treated more severe cases and produced quicker recoveries. Apart from the Alpha-Lite unit itself, the hospital line of phototherapy products included a light meter, a photo-mask that protected the baby's eyes while undergoing treatment, and a "baby bikini" that diapered the baby and yet facilitated exposure to the light.

The home phototherapy line of products was marketed under the trademark Baby-Lite.™ The phototherapy unit was portable, weighing about 40 pounds, and was foldable for easy transport. The unit when assembled was 33 inches long, 20 inches wide, and 24 inches high. The line also included photo-masks, a thermometer, and a short booklet telling parents about home phototherapy. Parents could rent the unit and purchase related products from a local pharmacy or a durable-medical-equipment dealer for about $75 per day. This was considerably less than the cost of hospital treatment. Another company, Acquitron, Inc., had entered the home phototherapy market in early 1985 and was expected to offer stiff competition. A third competitor was rumored to be entering the market in 1986.

Bennett's responsibilities for all phototherapy products included developing marketing plans and making final decisions about product design, promotion, pricing, and distribution. He directly supervised two product managers, one responsible for Alpha-Lite and the other for Baby-Lite. He occasionally made sales calls with the product managers, visiting hospitals, health maintenance organizations, and insurers.

TenderCare Marketing

Right now most of Bennett's time was spent on TenderCare. Bennett recognized that TenderCare would be marketed much differently than the phototherapy products. TenderCare would be sold to wholesalers, who in turn would sell to supermarkets, drugstores, and mass merchandisers. Tender-Care would compete either directly or indirectly with two giant consumer-goods manufacturers, Procter & Gamble and Kimberly-Clark. TenderCare represented considerable risk to RMM.

Because of the uncertainty surrounding the marketing of TenderCare, Bennett and Cagan had recently sought the advice of several marketing consultants. They reached formal agreement with one, a Los Angeles consultant named Alan Anderson. Anderson had extensive experience in advertising at J. Walter Thompson. He had also had responsibility for marketing and sales at Mattel and Teledyne, specifically for the marketing of such products as IntelliVision,™ the Shower Massage,™ and the Water Pik.™ Anderson currently worked as an independent marketing consultant to several firms. His contract with RMM specified that he would devote 25 percent of his time to TenderCare the first year and about 12 percent the following two years. During this time, RMM would hire, train, and place its own marketing personnel. One of these people would be a product manager for TenderCare.

Bennett and Cagan also could employ the services of a local marketing consultant who served on RMM's advisory board. (The board consisted of 12 business and medical experts who were available to answer questions and provide direction.) This consultant had spent over 25 years in marketing consumer products at several large corporations. His specialty was developing and launching new products, particularly health and beauty aids. He had worked closely with RMM in selecting the name TenderCare, and had done a great deal of work summarizing market characteristics and analyzing competitors.

MARKET CHARACTERISTICS

The market for babies' disposable diapers could be identified as children, primarily below age 3, who use the diapers, and their mothers, primarily between ages of 18 and 49, who decide on the brand and usually make the purchase. Bennett estimated there were about 11 million such children in 1985, living in about 9 million households. The average number of disposable diapers consumed in these households was thought to range from zero to 15 per day and to average about seven.

The consumption of disposable diapers is tied closely to birth rates and populations. However, two prominent trends also influence consumption. One is the disposable diaper's steadily increasing share of total diaper usage by babies. Bennett estimated that disposable diapers would increase their share of total diaper usage from 75 percent currently to 90 percent by 1990. The other trend is toward the purchase of higher-quality disposable diapers. Bennett thought the average retail price of disposable diapers would rise about twice as fast as the price of materials used in their construction. Total dollar sales of disposable diapers at retail in 1985 were expected to be about $3.0 billion, or about 15 billion units. Growth rates were thought to be about 14 percent per year for dollar sales and about 8 percent for units.

Foreign markets for disposable diapers would add to these figures. Canada, for example, currently consumed about $0.25 billion at retail, with an expected growth rate of 20 percent per year until 1990. The U.K. market was about twice this size and growing at the same rate.

The U.S. market for disposable diapers was clearly quite large and growing. However, Bennett felt that domestic growth rates could not be maintained much longer because fewer and fewer consumers were available to switch from cloth to disposable diapers. In fact, by 1995, growth rates for disposable diapers would begin to approach growth rates for births, and unit sales of disposable diapers would become directly proportional to numbers of infants using diapers. A consequence of this pronounced slowing of growth would be increased competition.

COMPETITION

Competition between manufacturers of disposable diapers was already intense. Two well-managed giants—Procter & Gamble and Kimberly-Clark—accounted for about 80 percent of the market in 1984 and 1985. Bennett had estimated market shares at:

	1984	1985
Pampers	32%	28%
Huggies	24	28
Luvs	20	20
Other brands	24	24
	100%	100%

Procter & Gamble was clearly the dominant competitor with its Pampers and Luvs brands. However, Procter & Gamble's market share had been declining, from 70 percent in 1981 to about 50 percent today. The company had introduced its thicker Blue Ribbon™ Pampers recently in an effort to halt the share decline. It had invested over $500 million in new equipment to produce the product. Procter & Gamble spent approximately $40 million to advertise its two brands in 1984. Kimberly-Clark spent about $19 million to advertise Huggies in 1984.

The 24 percent market share held by other brands was up by some 3 percentage points from 1983. Weyerhaeuser and Johnson & Johnson manufactured most of these diapers, supplying private-label brands for Wards, Penneys, Target, K mart, and other retailers. Generic disposable diapers and private brands were also included here, as well as a number of very small, specialized brands that were distributed only to local markets. Some of these brands positioned themselves as low-cost alternatives to national brands; others occupied premium ("designer") niches with premium prices. As examples, Universal Converter entered the northern Wisconsin market in 1984 with two brands priced at 78 and 87 percent of Pampers' case price. Riegel Textile Corporation's Cabbage Patch™ diapers illustrated the premium end, with higher prices and attractive print designs. Riegel spent $1 million to introduce Cabbage Patch diapers to the market in late 1984.

Additional evidence of intense competition in the disposable diaper industry was the major change of strategy by Johnson & Johnson in 1981. The company took its own brand off the U.S. market, opting instead to produce private-label diapers for major retailers. The company had held about 8 percent of the national market at the time and decided that this simply was not enough to compete effectively. Johnson & Johnson's disposable diaper was the first to be positioned in the industry as a premium product. Sales at one point totaled about 12 percent of the market but began to fall when Luvs and Huggies (with similar premium features) were introduced. Johnson & Johnson's advertising expenditures for disposable diapers in 1980 were about $8 million. The company still competed with its own brand in the international market.

MARKETING STRATEGIES FOR TENDERCARE

exper. thru medical / hospital use same channels?

Over the past month, Bennett and his consultants had spent considerable time formulating potential marketing strategies for TenderCare. One strategy that already had been discarded was simply licensing the design to another firm. Under a license arrangement, RMM would receive a negotiated royalty based on the licensee's sales of RMM's diaper. However, this strategy was unattractive on several grounds. RMM would have no control over resources devoted to the marketing of TenderCare: the licensee would decide on levels of sales and advertising support, prices, and distribution. The licensee would control advertising content, packaging, and even the choice of brand name. Licensing also meant that RMM would develop little marketing expertise, no image or even awareness among consumers, and no experience in dealing with packaged-goods channels of distribution. The net result would be that RMM would be hitching its future with respect to TenderCare (and any related products) to that of the licensee. Three other strategies seemed more appropriate.

The "Diaper Rash" Strategy

The first strategy involved positioning the product as an aid in the treatment of diaper rash. Diaper rash is a common ailment, thought to affect most infants at some point in their diapered lives. The affliction usually lasted two to three weeks before being cured. Some infants are more disposed to diaper rash than others. The ailment is caused by "a reaction to prolonged contact with urine and feces, retained soaps and topical preparations, and friction and maceration" (Nelson's *Text of Pediatrics,* 1979, p. 1884). Recommended treatment includes careful washing of the affected areas with warm water and without irritating soaps. Treatment also includes the application of protective ointments and powders (sold either by prescription or over the counter).

The diaper rash strategy would target physicians and nurses in either family- or general-practice and physicians and nurses specializing either in pediatrics or dermatology. Bennett's estimates of the numbers of general or family practitioners in 1985 was approximately 65,000. He thought that about 45,000 pediatricians and dermatologists were practicing in 1985. The numbers of nurses attending all these physicians was estimated at about

290,000. All 400,000 individuals would be the eventual focus of TenderCare marketing efforts. However, the diaper rash strategy would begin (like the other two strategies) where approximately 11 percent of the target market was located—California. Bennett and his consultants agreed that RMM lacked resources sufficient to begin in any larger market. California would provide a good test for TenderCare because the state often set consumption trends for the rest of the U.S. market. California also showed fairly typical levels of competitive activity. *Cal - a good choice?*

Promotion activities would emphasize either direct mail and free samples or in-office demonstrations to the target market. Mailing lists of most physicians and some nurses in the target market could be purchased at a cost of about $60 per 1,000 names. The cost to print and mail a brochure, cover letter, and return postcard was about $250 per 1,000. To include a single TenderCare disposable diaper would add another $400 per thousand. In-office demonstrations would use registered nurses (employed on a part-time basis) to show TenderCare's superior dryness. The nurses could be quickly trained and compensated on a per-demonstration basis. The typical demonstration would be given to groups of two or three physicians and nurses and would cost RMM about $6. The California market could be used to investigate the relative performance of direct mail versus demonstrations.

RMM would also advertise in trade journals such as the *Journal of Family Practice, Journal of Pediatrics, Pediatrics,* and *Pediatrics Digest.* However, a problem with such advertisements was waste coverage because none of the trade journals published regional editions. A half-page advertisement (one insertion) would cost about $1,000 for each journal. This cost would be reduced to about $700 if RMM placed several advertisements in the same journal during a one-year period. RMM would also promote TenderCare at local and state medical conventions in California. Costs per convention were thought to be about $3,000. The entire promotion budget as well as amounts allocated to direct mail, free samples, advertisements, and medical conventions had yet to be decided.

Prices were planned to produce a retail price per package of 12 TenderCare diapers at around $3.80. This was some 8 to 10 percent higher than the price for a package of 18 Huggies or Luvs. Bennett thought that consumers would pay the premium price because of TenderCare's position: the pennies-per-day differential simply would not matter if a physician prescribed or recommended TenderCare as part of a treatment for diaper rash. "Besides," he noted, "in-store shelf placement of TenderCare under this strategy would be among diaper rash products, not with standard diapers. This will make price comparisons by consumers even more unlikely." The $3.80 package price for 12 TenderCare diapers would produce a contribution margin for RMM of about 9 cents per diaper. It would give retailers a per-diaper margin some 30 percent higher than that for Huggies or Luvs.

The Special-Occasions Strategy

The second strategy centered around a "special-occasions" position that emphasized TenderCare's use in situations where changing the baby would be difficult. One such situation was whenever diapered infants traveled for any length of time. Another occurred daily at some 10,000 day-care centers that accepted infants wearing diapers. Yet another came every evening in each of the 9 million market households when babies were diapered at bedtime.

The special-occasions strategy would target mothers in these 9 million households. Initially, of course, the target would be only the estimated one million mothers living in California. Promotion would aim particularly at first-time mothers, using such magazines as *American Baby* and *Baby Talk*. Per-issue insertion costs for one full-color, half-page advertisement in such magazines would average about $20,000. However, most baby magazines published regional editions where single insertion costs averaged about half that amount. Black-and-white advertisements could also be considered; their costs would be about 75 percent of the full-color rates. Inserting several ads per year in the same magazine would allow quantity discounts and reduce the average insertion cost by about one-third.

Lately, Bennett had begun to wonder if direct-mail promotion could instead be used to reach mothers of recently born babies. Mailing lists of some 1 to 3 million names could be obtained at a cost of around $50 per 1,000. Other costs to produce and mail promotional materials would be the same as those for physicians and nurses. "I suppose the real issue is, just how much more effective is direct mail over advertising? We'd spend at least $250,000 in baby magazines to cover California while the cost of direct mail would probably be between $300,000 and $700,000, depending on whether or not we gave away a diaper." Regardless of Bennett's decision on consumer promotion, he knew RMM would also direct some promotion activities toward physicians and nurses as part of the special-occasions strategy. Budget details were yet to be worked out.

Distribution under the special-occasions strategy would have TenderCare stocked on store shelves along with competing diapers. Still at issue was whether the package should contain 12 or 18 diapers (like Huggies and Luvs) and how much of a premium price TenderCare could command. Bennett considered the packaging and pricing decisions interrelated. A package of 12 TenderCare diapers with per-unit retail prices some 40 percent higher than Huggies or Luvs might work just fine. Such a packaging/pricing strategy would produce a contribution margin to RMM of about 6 cents per diaper. However, the same pricing strategy for a package of 18 diapers probably would not work. "Still," he thought, "good things often come in small packages, and most mothers probably associate higher quality with higher price. One thing is for sure—whichever way we go, we'll need a superior package." Physical dimensions for a TenderCare package of either 12 or 18 diapers could be made similar to the size of the Huggies or Luvs package of 18.

The Head-On Strategy

The third strategy under consideration met major competitors in a direct, frontal attack. The strategy would position TenderCare as a noticeably drier diaper that any mother would prefer to use anytime her baby needed changing. Promotion activities would stress mass advertising to mothers, using television and magazines. However, at least two magazines would include a dollar-off coupon to stimulate trial of a package of TenderCare diapers during the product's first three months on the market. Some in-store demonstrations to mothers using "touch tests" might also be employed. Although no budget for California had yet been set, Bennett thought the allocation would be roughly 60:30:10 for television, magazines, and other promotion activities, respectively.

Pricing under this strategy would be competitive with Luvs and Huggies, with the per-diaper price for TenderCare expected to be some 9 percent higher at retail. This differential was needed to cover additional manufacturing costs associated with TenderCare's design. TenderCare's package could contain only 16 diapers and show a lower price than either Huggies or Luvs with their 18-count packages. Alternatively, the package could contain 18 diapers and carry the 9 percent higher price. Bennett wondered if he really wasn't putting too fine a point on the pricing/packaging relationship. "After all," he had said to Anderson, "we've no assurance that retailers or wholesalers would pass along any price advantage TenderCare might have due to a smaller package. Either one or both might instead price Tender-Care near the package price for our competitors and simply pocket the increased margin!" The only thing that was reasonably certain was Tender-Care's package price to the wholesaler. That price was planned to produce about a 3-cent contribution margin to RMM per diaper, regardless of package count.

Summary of the Three Strategies

When viewed together, the three strategies seemed so complex and so diverse as to defy analysis. Partly the problem was one of developing criteria against which the strategies could be compared. Risk was obviously one such criterion; so were company fit and competitive reaction. However, Bennett felt that some additional thought on his part would produce more criteria against which the strategies could be compared. He hoped this effort would produce no more strategies; three were plenty.

The other part of the problem was simply uncertainty. Strengths, weaknesses, and implications of each strategy had yet to be given much thought. Moreover, each strategy seemed likely to have associated with it some surprises. An example illustrating the problem was the recent realization that the Food and Drug Administration (FDA) must approve any direct claims RMM might make about TenderCare's efficacy in treating diaper rash. The chance of receiving this federal agency's approval was thought to be reasonably high; yet it was unclear just what sort of testing and what results were needed. The worst-case scenario would have the FDA requiring lengthy consumer tests that eventually would produce inconclusive results. The best case could have the FDA giving permission based on TenderCare's superior dryness and on results of a small-scale field test recently completed by Dr. Morrison. It would be probably a month before the FDA's position could be known.

"The delay was unfortunate—and unnecessary," Bennett thought, "especially if we eventually settle on either of the other two strategies." In fact, FDA approval was not even needed for the diaper rash strategy if RMM simply claimed (1) that TenderCare diapers were drier than competing diapers and (2) that dryness helps treat diaper rash. Still, a single-statement, direct-claim position was thought to be more effective with mothers and more difficult to copy by any other manufacturer. And yet Bennett did want to move quickly on TenderCare. Every month of delay meant deferred revenue and other postponed benefits that would derive from a successful introduction. Delay also meant the chance that an existing (or other) competitor might develop its own drier diaper and effectively block RMM from reaping the fruits of its development efforts. Speed was of the essence.

FINANCIAL IMPLICATIONS

Bennett recognized that each marketing strategy held immediate as well as long-term financial implications. He was particularly concerned with finance requirements for start-up costs associated with the California entry. Cagan and the other RMM executives had agreed that a stock issue represented the best option to meet these requirements. Accordingly, RMM had begun preparation for a sale of common stock through a brokerage firm that would underwrite and market the issue. Management at the firm felt that RMM could generate between $1 and $3 million, depending on the offering price per share and the number of shares issued.

Proceeds from the sale of stock had to be sufficient to fund the California entry and leave a comfortable margin remaining for contingencies. Proceeds would be used for marketing and other operating expenses as well as for investments in cash, inventory, and accounts receivable assets. It was hoped that TenderCare would generate a profit by the end of the first year in the California market and show a strong contribution to the bottom line thereafter. California profits would contribute to expenses associated with entering additional markets and to the success of any additional stock offerings.

Operating profits and proceeds from the sale of equity would fund additional research and development activities that would extend RMM's diaper technology to other markets. Dr. Morrison and Bennett saw almost immediate application of the technology to the adult incontinent diaper market, currently estimated at about $300 million per year at retail. Underpads for beds constituted at least another $50 million annual market. However, both of these uses were greatly dwarfed by another application, the sanitary napkin market. Finally, the technology could almost certainly be applied to numerous industrial products and processes, many of which promised great potential. All these opportunities made the TenderCare situation that much more crucial to the firm; making a major mistake here would affect the firm for years.

CASE 3–2

The Michigan League

Pat Lawson has been manager of the Michigan League for six years. She is in charge of the operation and maintenance of the League building. She acts as purchasing agent and is in charge of the accounting and financial management of the League's activities. As business manager, Pat Lawson is responsible to a board of governors and to the vice president for finance. She is expected to report regularly to both.

Recently the staff has noticed a continuing decrease in the number of customers in the cafeteria and coffee shop. However, at the same time the other League functions (conferences, banquets, special events) are operating near capacity. Pat is interested in finding the underlying causes of the decrease in the customer count. She would like to develop courses of action to reverse this trend.

BACKGROUND

The Michigan League is one of three University Activity Centers in Ann Arbor. The other two centers are the North Campus Commons and the Michigan Union. The Michigan League was built in 1929 with funds raised by University of Michigan women. At the time of the League's construction,

---

Prepared by Maureen Fanshawe, in James D. Scott, Martin R. Warshaw, and James R. Taylor, *Introduction to Marketing Management*, 5th ed. Copyright © 1985, by Richard D. Irwin. Reprinted by permission of the publisher.

women were not permitted to use the Michigan Union. In response to the women's need, the University alumnae built the Michigan League "for the purpose of promoting the social and recreational welfare of the women students in the university." Through the years the emphasis has shifted, and presently for both men and women the primary student building (receiving the major university funding) is the Michigan Union. Currently the Michigan League serves not only the campus community but also the general public.

The League is centrally located one block from the main street of the campus area. It is situated on a highly trafficked street and is very visible. A large sign near the sidewalk advertises the cafeteria and other services. In addition to the cafeteria and coffee shop, the League building has a gift shop, study rooms, conference rooms, a ballroom, several large banquet rooms, student organization offices, and, on the fourth floor, hotel service consisting of 21 rooms. Over the past four years there has been a significant increase in the use of the building by students for study and meeting space.

CAFETERIA

The cafeteria is open Monday–Saturday, 11:30 A.M.–1:15 P.M. and 5:00 P.M.–7:15 P.M. Dinner is served on Sunday from 11:30 A.M. to 2:15 P.M. A full menu is provided for both lunch and dinner. Meal prices range from approximately $3.00 for lunch to $4.25 for dinner. The cafeteria does not serve alcohol. The League has a limited conference liquor license for scheduled events. A daily special is offered in addition to the other items. The luncheon and dinner entrees are on a three-week cycle and offer a different variety daily. Although there is no table service, the cafeteria maintains a full staff. The cafeteria has a pleasant atmosphere and emphasis is placed on cleanliness.

NATURE OF THE MARKET

The Michigan League is available to the general public as well as the campus community. Throughout the school year the cafeteria serves approximately 388 lunches and 350 dinners daily. The coffee shop serves 800–1,200 people daily. During the summer months the daily totals are considerably lower. Peak seasons are directly associated with the academic year. From May through August there is a steady decline in business (Exhibits 1 and 2). Special functions scheduled at the League are also affected by the "seasonality" factor. During the months of May–August the League facilities for weddings operate at capacity. Hill Auditorium and Powers Center are university cultural performance centers, each within one block of the League. Plays, concerts, and

EXHIBIT 1

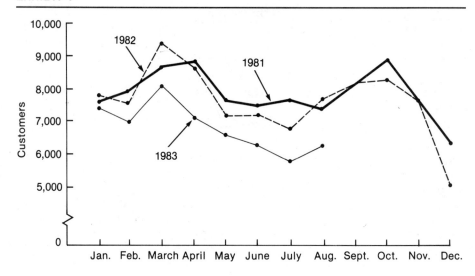

Customer Count: Lunch

	1981	1982	1983
January	7,641	7,648	7,487
February	7,883	7,586	6,989
March	8,725	9,403	8,067
April	8,816	8,780	7,125
May	7,675	7,267	6,610
June	7,440	7,221	6,290
July	7,659	6,795	5,722
August	7,435	7,724	6,236
September	8,144	8,049	*
October	8,900	8,418	*
November	7,667	7,682	*
December	6,422	5,227	*

* Customer count not yet taken for September–December 1983.

ballet are frequently run. On performance nights the League adjusts its regular schedule and menu. There is an increase in the cafeteria customer count on these evenings. This increase is not as high as Pat believes it could be. She has attributed this fact to the large number of area restaurants serving alcohol which are available to the Hill Auditorium and Powers Center patrons.

The results of a 1978 survey performed by the League cafeteria revealed that present customers use the cafeteria on a regular basis and for

EXHIBIT 2

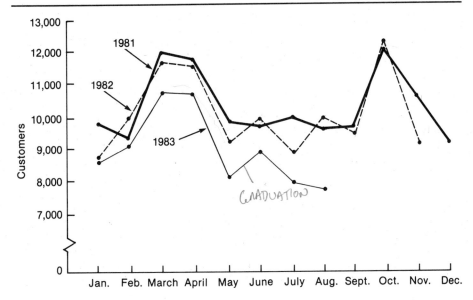

Customer Count: Dinner		
	1981	*1982*	*1983*
January	9,757	8,666	8,635
February	9,265	9,849	9,074
March	11,946	11,636	10,779
April	11,664	11,552	10,718
May	9,894	9,170	8,098
June	9,688	9,838	8,941
July	9,943	8,766	7,925
August	9,628	9,844	7,812
September	9,673	9,572	*
October	12,152	12,164	*
November	10,778	9,168	*
December	9,253	7,555	*

* Customer count not yet taken for September–December 1983.

the following reasons: they enjoy the food, location, no tipping feature, cafe-teria-style service, and atmosphere. Also provided by this survey were posi-tive and negative comments about the cafeteria (Exhibits 3 and 4).

A third and final part of the survey requested customer suggestions. Many of the suggestions were for bigger salads, a salad bar, to expand the variety of vegetarian dishes and specials, and to include a vegetable or salad

EXHIBIT 3
Survey Results for Michigan League (1978)

	Tuesday Noon (170 surveys)	Tuesday Night (128)	Thursday Night (130)	Sunday (140)
How Often				
First time	2	2	2	4
Infrequent	40	19	25	33
Often	125	107	88	102
Enjoy				
Food	128	117	101	132
Location	154	105	85	98
Cafeteria	126	98	86	122
No tipping	117	100	87	116
Atmosphere	91	91	88	117
Music				
Prefer music	41	54	43	37
Prefer no music	41	27	5	46

Cumulative Results (568 surveys)

How Often		*Enjoy*		*Music*	
First time	10	Food	478	Prefer music	175
Infrequent	117	Location	432	Prefer no music	119
Often	422	Cafeteria	432		
		No tipping	426		
		Atmosphere	387		

EXHIBIT 4
Frequent Comments

Positive		*Negative*	
Enjoy the food	74	Dull variety	23
Variety	25	Too much gravy	13
Reasonable price	32	Student special	19
International night	17	Prices too high	28
Service	51	Cold food	25
Atmosphere	18	Service	
		Long, slow lines	38
		Discourteous staff	21
		Small portions	38
		Parking	20

with the student special. Presently the League has comment and suggestion cards available in the cafeteria, coffee shop, and hotel rooms. After each special function, a short rating and suggestion card is sent to the person who made the arrangements.

SPECIAL FEATURES AT THE CAFETERIA

The League cafeteria offers daily specials. These specials are available to the students at a reduced price. A luncheon special costs $2.50, and a dinner student special costs $2.75. The cafeteria sells approximately 125 luncheon and 60 dinner specials daily. The student specials are less than the cost of dormitory dinners. Students find it the "best food for the price in town." Over the years, the board has felt "that providing good food to students at the lowest possible cost in an attractive university setting was an important responsibility of the League." The League has a student tax discount but does not have senior citizen discounts.

From October through July, every Thursday evening at the cafeteria is "International and American Heritage Night." Each Thursday night the menu consists of foods from the featured country or state. International night has been successful. On this night the cafeteria serves an average of 475 customers.

The Michigan League cafeteria "Command Performance dinner" offered the customer a unique dining experience. The customers were encouraged through advertisements to make requests for their favorite foods, to be served at the Command Performance dinner. From these nominations the most requested items were selected to make up the menu for the evening. This special feature has been offered twice and was successful.

Sunday dinner at the cafeteria is served from 11:30 A.M. to 2:15 P.M. White linen cloths and fresh flowers are placed on the tables. The Sunday customer profile at the cafeteria is primarily senior citizens.

COMPETITION

The Michigan League is centrally located on the Michigan campus one block from the campus shopping street and three blocks from downtown Ann Arbor. There are approximately 143 restaurants in the downtown area. Eighty of these restaurants provide full service. The League cafeteria's 1982 share of the Ann Arbor restaurant market was 1.9 percent. In a recent report the board of governors recommended that, "The university administration officially recommend that all university departments use the university centers (League, Union, and North Campus Commons) food services, both within these buildings and for catering wherever needed on the university campus."

In direct competition with the League cafeteria is the Michigan Union. The recent revitalization of the Union is expected to affect the League. Food revenue may decline as Union revenue increases. The Union University Club offers a menu similar to the League's, with prices approximately one dollar higher per meal at lunch and two dollars higher at dinner. The Union has table service and serves alcohol. Every Sunday night at the Union from 5:30 P.M.–8:00 P.M. is an "all-you-can-eat" Italian Festival for $3.99. The Italian Festival night is successful. A recent addition to the Union's lower level, the Michigan Union Grill (MUG), has a variety of food counters and primarily caters to student clientele. The prices are relatively low, to meet the students' budgets, and a student tax discount is offered. Dormitory food service does not operate on Sundays. The other area restaurants have a wide variety of menus but are priced slightly higher than the League. The recent restructuring of dorm food service to include breakfast and flexible hours affected the League's student count adversely.

The recent construction of the Ingalls Street pedestrian mall has drastically decreased parking availability for League patrons. Ingalls Street (which runs adjacent to the League) previously had 45 open-meter parking spaces. More than half of the spaces were destroyed. This loss of parking has been a problem for League patrons. There are two public parking structures, each within one block of the League. It costs two dollars to park in the garage. Across the street from the League is a staff parking lot. Parking is permitted in this lot only after 5:00 P.M. Street parking on North University after 5:00 P.M. has recently been permitted, adding about 12 spaces.

PROMOTION

The League's 1982 advertising budget was $5,500. Of this budget, 91 percent was allocated to the cafeteria. The objective of the cafeteria advertising is to increase awareness in the community. The emphasis of weekly advertisements is usually placed on special-feature nights at the cafeteria. The Command Performance dinner was advertised twice in the *Ann Arbor News*. The League purchased a 2" × 5" ad (space is sold by column inch, $7.50 per inch) and ran the ad the week preceding the event. When the League is not advertising for a feature night, a 1½" × 2" ad is purchased for $22.50 and run once a week.

For several years the League ran a weekly advertisement for the cafeteria, using a limerick theme. Readers would compose an advertising limerick for the cafeteria and mail their suggestions to Julie, Pat Lawson's administrative assistant. She would then select the best limerick entry weekly, to be used in the advertisement. The winning entry received two free dinners at the cafeteria. The League employed this promotional strategy for five years prior to its discontinuance in July 1983. The League staff felt that although they had received a tremendous response, the theme had become overused and repetitive and, as a result, had lost effectiveness.

Presently the League has no measurement of ad effectiveness. In addition, their promotional strategy uses a mass appeal, with minimal attention given to individual market segments. The staff wonders whether the advertising dollars could be more effectively spent by placing emphasis on slow nights rather than on already successful feature nights. To increase the customer count on slow nights, Pat is considering the extension of the feature-night concept to these nights. She also senses a need for an advertising strategy to define her key potential customers and then to target the advertising efforts to this market.

The League also advertises in the *Observer,* a monthly newspaper publication. The cafeteria is listed in the Restaurant Guide section. The price is 6 months for $25 for a four-line listing. The ad is clearly visible but is listed with many other Ann Arbor restaurants. A one-fourth page display advertisement in the *Observer* costs $246 (for a one-month edition). However, the *Observer* offers a frequency rate discount. The League has never purchased display ad space in the *Observer.* Presently they purchase only the service ad in the restaurant guide.

The *Michigan Daily* is a student-run newspaper on the Ann Arbor campus of The University of Michigan. The *Daily* has approximately 5,000 subscribers. Advertising space costs $4.75/inch. Presently the League does not advertise in the *Michigan Daily.*

The remaining balance of the advertising budget is used to purchase flyers for the League cafeteria and coffee shop. These flyers are distributed to all new students and staff. Included on this flyer is a coupon for a free beverage, which is heavily used by students. The International and American Heritage Nights schedule is printed on a 2″ × 3″ card and is available throughout the university.

FINANCIAL RESOURCES

The University Activities Centers—North Campus Commons, Michigan Union, and the Michigan League—are owned by the university. The League uses earned revenue to meet its operating expenses. Financial support from the university is made available through allocations. All improvements have been financed from reserves and university loans. Loans are repaid on schedule, and there is only a small balance outstanding. Presently the student fee allocation to the League is $3.50 per student.

The number of customers served at the cafeteria and coffee shop is declining. A statement of the League's revenues and expenses for the year 1982–83 is shown in Exhibit 5. Revenue for the Michigan League for fiscal year 1982–83 was 6 percent greater than for fiscal year 1981–82. This includes: guest room rentals (up 2 percent), meeting room rentals (up 25 percent), banquets and parties (up 16 percent), catering (up 79 percent), and beverages (up 12 percent). However, despite these growth areas cafeteria revenue is down $25,437 (3 percent) and coffee shop revenue is down $6,145

EXHIBIT 5

MICHIGAN LEAGUE
Statement of Revenue and Expense
June 1983 and Fiscal 1982–83

	June 1983	June 1982	7/1/82–6/30/83	7/1/81–6/30/82
Revenue				
House:				
Guest room rentals	$ 14,368	$ 14,335	$ 194,569	$ 189,848
Meeting room rentals	8,273	9,809	120,757	96,540
Front desk merchandise. . . .	7,976	8,877	113,718	113,372
Sundry	193	2,920	7,316	10,707
Food:				
Cafeteria.	59,191	67,692	725,102	750,539
Coffee shop	18,355	22,178	272,373	278,518
Banquets and parties	38,867	47,081	414,803	357,603
Catering	23,315	4,897	105,701	59,095
Beverage.	6,401	15,487	83,757	74,582
NCC administrative services . .	450	450	5,400	5,400
Total operating revenue	$177,389	$193,726	$2,043,496	$1,936,204
Expense				
House:				
Salaries and wages	$ 22,004	$ 21,360	$ 184,593	$ 174,272
Front desk merchandise. . . .	9,435	6,272	85,585	79,147
Supplies and general	991	1,214	9,893	10,300
Equipment repairs.	1,306	92	4,010	4,327
Laundry.	602	634	11,476	10,268
Food:				
Coffee shop salaries and wages	11,194	11,438	116,170	100,338
Food, salaries, and wages . .	70,128	68,385	652,021	617,413
Food cost	37,276	41,201	533,873	540,594
Transportation	-0-	-0-	2,531	2,452
Supplies and general	4,260	2,187	37,275	35,429
Equipment repairs.	383	704	9,940	9,353
Laundry.	2,182	2,644	35,476	29,638
Beverage.	(293)	5,163	25,692	27,192
General:				
Administrative salaries	11,781	18,599	137,432	131,137
Maintenance wages.	2,198	2,182	20,587	23,316
Office	930	613	7,936	6,002
Telephone.	(82)	(150)	7,722	8,386
Building maintenance.	4,475	4,877	37,901	41,978
Board of Governors.	56	415	712	1,443
Publicity	419	281	4,245	5,970
Sales tax	3,485	4,270	51,312	45,618
Insurance	74	148	9,094	10,626
Unemployment insurance. . .	-0-	-0-	2,107	503
Bad debts	-0-	-0-	17	60
Miscellaneous	2,408	850	17,479	15,243
Total operating expense	185,842	193,379	2,005,079	1,931,005
Net operating income (loss). . .	$ (8,453)	$ 347	$ 38,417	$ 5,199

EXHIBIT 5 *(concluded)*

	June 1983	June 1982	7/1/82– 6/30/83	7/1/81– 6/30/82
Other Income and Expense				
U-M allocation	$ 17,781	$ 48,877	$ 319,761	$ 295,919
Interest on investments	33,898	26,430	33,898	26,430
Development fund	6,376	100	62,707	200
Utilities	(12,486)	(15,255)	(214,863)	(204,080)
Student awards	(629)	-0-	(629)	(549)
Debt retirement	-0-	(4,837)	(58,272)	(58,040)
Equipment reserves	(950)	(397)	(11,393)	(4,761)
Building reserves	(1,570)	(466)	(18,854)	(5,589)
Total other income and expense	42,420	54,452	112,355	49,530
Net income (loss)	$ 33,967	$ 54,799	$ 150,772	$ 54,729
Total salaries and wages	$117,305	$121,964	$1,110,803	$1,046,476

(2 percent). Food costs are in line, but labor costs are 50 percent of total earned income. In a report to the board of governors, Pat Lawson states, "A major staff training program is currently under way to increase productivity, but with an already lean, hard-working staff, it is unrealistic to expect much of a reduction in labor costs because of the AFSCME (union) wage rates."

The staff is presently considering several cafeteria improvement projects. The League is unwilling to borrow additional funds until the current loan is repaid. Alternative sources considered are: "A search for major donors (fund-raising committee and fund drive)" and additional financial assistance from the university. The League's fund raising for 1982 collected $69,000. The League is developing a cookbook for sale. The book will be ready for sale in June 1984 and is expected to earn $50,000–$100,000. Pat Lawson believes that although revenue generated by the cafeteria is the most important source of operating funds, it is not a source of funds for projects that might be undertaken in the future.

FURTHER CONSIDERATIONS

In her report to the board of governors, Pat Lawson stated a need for financial assistance to meet necessary kitchen modernization costs (new appliances). The projected need totals $500,000. However, Pat is considering a complete remodeling of the cafeteria within the next three years. Total costs for complete remodeling are approximately $750,000. The project would include the necessary kitchen equipment, line restructuring, and a complete redecoration of the cafeteria. The plans for the cafeteria line re-structuring are to change it from a straight line to an "open"-style square line (scramble system). This would improve efficiency and provide additional customer convenience by eliminating unnecessary waiting. Customers would be able to proceed directly to the section of items they desired. The development of an "open" line would decrease seating capacity. The cafeteria presently seats 250 persons.

As Pat considers the remodeling plans, she is also hoping to include plans to build a small extension to the cafeteria, which would help to recover the seating lost to the line restructuring. The extension as a "greenhouse"-style design is being considered. She believes that the extension should be built at the same time as the other remodeling is undertaken so that shutdown time is minimized. The greenhouse room is to extend from the front of the League building, which faces the main street.

Pat believes that the new room would provide several benefits: (1) make the League cafeteria more visible, (2) provide a direct entrance from the street to the cafeteria, (3) increase seating, and (4) improve cafeteria attractiveness. If remodeling plans include construction of the greenhouse room, estimated total costs could be approximately $1 million. Pat is interested in determining the feasibility of the League financing the remodeling project. She believes that the League's opportunities are limited to income provided by loans, fund raising, cookbook sales, and increased business at the cafeteria.

Sungold Cabinets

In April 1979 the executives of Keith Homes, a division of the Genstar group, were evaluating the sales and market potential for their organization and were particularly concerned about one division, Sungold Cabinets. In November 1977 a fire had destroyed the manufacturing and warehousing facilities of Sungold. Although temporary facilities were fully operational in less than a month, Sungold experienced a substantial drop in sales. In early 1979, sales slipped below the break-even point for the new plant built to replace the burnt facilities. Mr. Len Reith, marketing manager for Keith Homes, decided it was time to review the available market opportunities to determine if action could be taken for an immediate short-term improve-

---

This case was prepared by James Graham of the University of Calgary, Calgary, Alberta, Canada.

ment in sales. He also wanted to review the company's marketing strategy to ensure that it was appropriate for the changing market environment for kitchen cabinets.

BACKGROUND

Genstar is a large, multinational firm with interests in heavy construction, building materials manufacturing, and residential construction. It has shown a strong growth pattern since 1970. Cash dividends have increased each year, and net income has increased by an average rate of 27 percent. In 1978 Genstar had net assets valued at $1,207.5 million (Exhibits 1 and 2). This growth is attributed to Genstar's policies of acquiring companies which show above-average profit and promoting internal expansion through market development within its divisions.

Sungold was established 20 years ago to manufacture and sell quality kitchen cabinets to builders and distributors. In the months previous to the fire, Sungold sales had been at the plant capacity of 220 units per day. The new plant, built in November 1977 following the fire, cost about a million dollars to equip and was located in a 12,000-square-foot building with a yearly rent of $4 per square foot. Management calculated the break-even volume for the plant at 195 units per day and the plant capacity at 250 units per day. The bulk of Sungold sales were to one distributor and six builders. Two of the six builders were members of the Genstar group. Divisions within the group are free to buy and sell outside the group. Together the six builders produced about 60 percent of the single-family homes in the Sungold primary market area of western Canada. These six companies were formed at about the same time and have maintained close ties while expanding in the Calgary and Edmonton areas. In 1978 the mean number of cabinets sold were 200 units per day, but during the first three weeks of 1979, sales averaged only 155 units per shift per day (Exhibit 3).

EXHIBIT 1
Sungold's Position in the Genstar Group

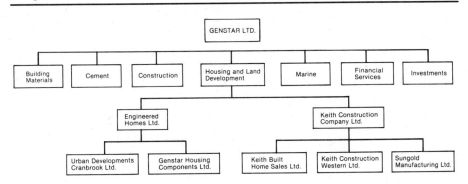

EXHIBIT 2 Summary of Financial Highlights for Genstar for the Five Years Ended December 31, 1978 (millions of Canadian dollars, restated)

	1978	1977	1976	1975	1974
Revenues	$ 1,143.0	$ 981.1	$ 821.5	$ 684.3	$ 578.4
Cost and expenses:					
Cost of sales and services	778.0	677.9	565.1	491.5	418.8
Selling, general, and administrative	116.3	98.2	81.1	59.8	48.6
Depreciation, depletion, and amortization	50.2	34.7	32.3	26.5	24.2
Interest	49.9	49.3	40.2	21.9	17.8
Total costs and expenses	994.4	860.1	718.7	599.7	509.4
Income before income taxes	148.6	121.0	102.8	84.6	69.0
Provision for income taxes	67.0	56.6	47.1	37.4	33.9
Net income	$ 81.6	$ 64.4	$ 55.7	$ 47.2	$ 35.1
Per common share:	*STILL UP?*				
Net income—Canadian method:					
Basic	$ 6.03	$ 5.06	$ 4.63	$ 4.03	$ 3.06
Fully diluted	5.74	4.65	4.18	3.61	2.71
United States method:					
Primary	6.01	5.01	4.58	4.01	3.05
Fully diluted	5.89	4.73	4.23	3.69	2.77
Dividends	1.61	1.42	1.25	1.20	1.05
Return on net assets	9.0%	8.5%	7.5%	10.4%	9.0%
Capitalization ratios:					
Total debt to equity	49.51	62.38	67.33	49.51	49.51
Long-term debt to equity	32.68	50.50	52.48	39.61	33.67
Other statistics ($ millions, except for employees):					
Shareholders' equity	$ 556.1	$ 368.2	$ 315.6	$ 263.6	$ 226.0
Working capital	268.6	108.5	114.7	103.1	44.2
Funds from operations	116.3	108.6	93.8	77.1	64.6
Capital expenditures	52.8	107.1	89.7	67.6	55.8
Fixed assets	626.4	671.8	563.8	490.5	443.8
Net assets	1,207.5	1,064.2	1,034.3	571.8	491.7
Common shares outstanding:					
Actual	13.4	12.9	11.9	11.5	11.1
Average	13.2	12.6	11.7	11.4	11.0
Number of employees	10,428	11,077	10,695	10,125	10,181

Source: 1978 Annual Report.

EXHIBIT 3
Sungold Income and Expenses (thousands of Canadian dollars)

	1978	1977	1976
Revenues..............................	$3,110.0	$2,903.0	$2,933.0
Materials used	1,000.4	900.3	810.3
Direct labor...........................	1,468.7	1,321.8	1,189.6
Supervision...........................	20.0	18.1	16.2
Utilities...............................	28.1	24.7	23.2
Rent..................................	48.0	48.0	46.2
Depreciation machinery.................	80.0	16.0	17.2
Cost of goods manufactured	$2,645.2	$2,328.9	$2,102.7
Gross profit...........................	464.8	574.1	830.3
Sales salaries	90.0	82.8	78.7
Administrative salaries..................	80.0	76.1	71.4
Interest on inventory	31.1	26.6	24.4
Insurance.............................	5.3	5.1	4.9
Shipping, handling, and guarantees	62.3	43.6	41.4
Depreciation, building...................	20.0	0.0	.8
Office supplies	100.4	98.4	96.8
Income taxes..........................	44.9	105.6	194.6
Total operating expenses	$ 454.0	$ 438.2	$ 513.0
Net income	$ 10.8	$ 135.9	$ 317.3

EXHIBIT 4
Dwelling Unit Starts in Calgary

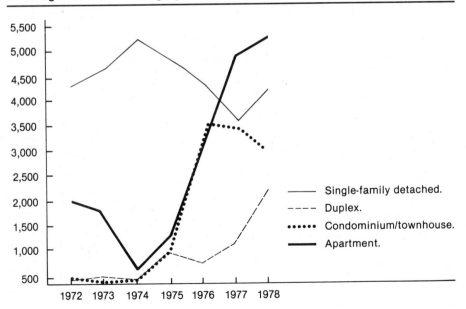

Single-family detached.
Duplex.
Condominium/townhouse.
Apartment.

Sungold had a marketing sales manager and a sales representative in Edmonton, Calgary, and Winnipeg. Calgary and Edmonton had almost equal numbers of housing starts and were among the most active housing markets in North America. Calgary was becoming a financial center for the resource industries and Edmonton was expanding as a result of increasing exploration for oil and gas. Exhibit 4 shows the recent history of dwelling starts by type in Calgary.

The booming housing market in western Canada was attracting large builders from other areas of North America to Calgary and Edmonton. These new large builders offered good market opportunities to Sungold salesmen. Prior to 1977 the plant was producing at capacity, and the salesmen were principally solving problems of existing customers, not working to develop new customer accounts. The additional cabinets available for sale after the new plant was constructed in 1977 put pressure on the sales force to develop new accounts and increase the sales of the company's product.

CHARACTERISTICS OF THE MARKET

In past years approximately 40 percent of Sungold's cabinets were sold at retail through building supply dealers, and 60 percent of sales were direct-to-builder accounts.

Retail Market

Retail sales of kitchen cabinets to individuals building new homes or renovating older homes are made primarily through building supply firms such as Beaver Lumber and Revelstoke Lumber. Sears sells some lower-quality cabinets through its stores and catalog operation. A new development in the market is stores specializing in kitchen cabinets, major appliances, and floorings, that have opened in western Canadian cities in the last few years. Some of these stores appeared quite successful, though Sungold management did not have a good estimate of their sales volume.

In western Canada, Sungold cabinets have been retailed exclusively through the Beaver chain, which includes 139 locations in western Canada and sells Sungold and Kitchen Craft cabinets. Beaver used Kitchen Craft as its main supplier in Manitoba and Saskatchewan, with Sungold its main supplier of cabinets in Alberta. Beaver usually sold between 1,400 and 1,600 kitchens per year.

The other major building supply store that sells kitchen cabinets is Revelstoke Lumber, with 108 stores in western Canada and sales of approximately 1,000 kitchens per year. It uses two preferred suppliers—Gress Kitchens, manufactured in Chambly, Quebec; and Belwood Cabinets, manufactured in Mississippi. Revelstoke's managers did not feel that they were doing an adequate job in the sale of cabinets and had plans to expand their volume to 3,000 kitchens per year. In the past, they reported having had delivery problems with Sungold. As a result, Revelstoke management was reluctant to purchase cabinets from Sungold.

Retailing Skills

Generally the sales of kitchen cabinets by building supply stores such as Beaver and Revelstoke were decreasing. Most store staff had poor design and layout skills, and the store managers were plagued by high employee turnover. Sungold ran a training program for store employees, but rapid turnover of retail salespeople reduced the effectiveness of these programs. The corporate managers of retail chains felt it necessary for the supplier to develop a relationship with individual store personnel, as salespeople promoted whatever product they felt best about. Cabinets require a large amount of floorspace for sales to develop, and often retail store managers are not that dedicated to the product. (An interview with a salesman at the Beaver Home Store in Calgary is included in Appendix A.)

The marketing sales manager for Sungold reported that one or two customers per week dropped in at the manufacturing facilities to purchase cabinets. Customers were told of the various distributors carrying Sungold cabinets, but most customers said they did not want to buy from these outlets because of the poor service they had received. In addition to the kitchen specialty stores selling kitchen cabinets, some of Sungold's competitors had opened their own retail stores. HTH Cabinets Limited had been one of the more recent and successful entries into the retail market.

HTH Cabinets Ltd.

HTH Cabinet sales were approximately 50 percent to small business contractors and 50 percent from walk-in sales. HTH offers a complete service including kitchen design and sells countertops and linoleum along with five lines of cabinets. The cabinets are made of oak or pine and are manufactured in "knockdown" form in Denmark and shipped to Canada for assembly. All units are guaranteed for one year. The units are manufactured in modular sizes of 20, 30, 40, 50, 60, 80, and 100 centimeters. The shelves are made of Nelamine, a type of material resembling arborite. Most kitchen units could be supplied within two weeks of order. Complete installation service could be provided, with the cost varying with the size and type of kitchen ordered. The salesmen are knowledgable about their product and spend a considerable amount of time explaining hinges, rollers, design, and the styles of cabinets. The HTH salesperson has available four brochures explaining basic layout, sizes, and types of cabinets available, a price list, a color brochure of various styles of kitchens using their cabinet lines, and a kitchen planning kit. HTH advertises regularly in the local newspaper and magazines.

Home Builders

Builders use modular cabinets for the low- and medium-price single-family subdivision homes but usually build customized kitchens on site in more expensive models.

The larger builders tend to use one or two preferred suppliers for their single-family homes, selected through a two-step process. First builders tender their requirements once a year. The potential suppliers, using a general layout for each series of homes, bid on all cabinets forecast for the coming year. The general manager's design team (if there is one) and estimators approve one or two cabinet suppliers based on the bids submitted. The second step takes place later when the project manager responsible for a specific project chooses a cabinet supplier from the approved lists. Smaller builders usually use two or more suppliers. They tend to view each group of homes built as an individual project and tender separately for each group of homes.

Builders are not very concerned about the advantages and disadvantages of different cabinets. Past experience indicates that home buyers are more concerned with the appearance of kitchens than with quality. While it may be argued that certain features of Sungold cabinets were better than competitors' products, the builders and most home buyers did not perceive Sungold products as being of higher quality. The factors most important to builders in selection of subcontractors for cabinets were delivery, service, and installation. Builders also looked at the attractiveness of cabinets and their effect on selling the home. Larger builders indicate that if price was within ±10 percent for two tenders, reliable delivery was more important in the selection of a supplier. Smaller builders were more price conscious than major builders and often made their choice of supplier based on price alone.

In early 1979, builders began to reject tenders that didn't include an installation guarantee. Sungold was developing its capacity for installation and had begun to bid separately on cabinet installation. Sungold gained two new builder accounts in 1979 as a result of its installation guarantee. Sungold did not have its own installation crew, and cabinet installation was subcontracted.

In the past, Sungold management did not find it necessary to offer installation, since its largest customers, Nu West, Keith Construction, and Engineered Homes, did not require this service. Keith Construction and Engineered Homes are also members of the Genstar group. These builders, longtime users of Sungold cabinets, accounted for about half of the building starts in Calgary and Edmonton—Sungold's primary market areas. These builders were predicting reductions in their new home starts in 1979 to 90 percent of the 1978 levels because of overbuilding in their primary market areas.

None of the builders planned major revision in their kitchens as a method of increasing sales. The builders expected delivery within three to five weeks, with replacement for defective units being delivered from one to a maximum of two weeks after the order was placed. Although the cost to the builder varies with the cabinets installed, an "average" 16-unit kitchen is priced as follows:

Cabinets	$1,450
Tops (including installation)	250
Subtotal	$1,700
Discount 33 percent	($ 560)
Delivery	50
Installation of cabinets	150
Total	$1,340

Multiple Dwellings

Kitchen cabinets for condominiums and apartments were subcontracted for each project, based on a tender that included a specification of the quality of cabinets to be delivered and the timing of delivery. Most apartments used low-quality, standardized kitchen units 8 feet long. Sungold's entry into this market would require additional salesmen and a new discount structure to secure adequate volume to make entry profitable. A typical apartment kitchen, made up of Sungold's all-wood cabinets from its lowest price line at $680, costs about $150 more than the competitor's particle board with vinyl overlay cabinets.

Competition

The principal competitors of Sungold are listed below. The five main cabinet builders accounted for 80 percent of the kitchen cabinet sales for new housing. Each of the manufacturers offered complete service and were viewed as acceptable suppliers by most buyers.

Manufacturers	Construction
Citation Cabinets	Wood panel doors for single-family housing units— K–3 particle board with melamine overlay for a multifamily unit.
HTH Cabinets	Wood panel doors.
Kitchen Craft	Raised-panel wood door.
Crestwood	Wood panel (ash, elm) particle board overlay.
Merit	Wood panel, oak doors.

A survey of competitors and customers indicated that builder accounts had a low propensity to change suppliers. However, after the fire, some difficulty was experienced by Sungold in redeeming customers who had found satisfaction from other suppliers during the disruption in Sungold's production. Competitors could usually match price, although Sungold was experiencing a slight price advantage because of the stability in the price of maple and elm compared to other materials.

Product Line

Sungold manufactured nine lines of natural wood cabinets in either maple or elm. A recent technological innovation allowed Sungold management to eliminate the lowest models of cabinet made of K–3 board (a material made from pressed wood chips). The change to wood from K–3 board resulted in a better quality all-wood cabinet at an average increase in cost of $30 per kitchen.

Sungold products were approved by the Canadian Standards Association for use in homes financed under the Canada Mortgage and Housing Corporation and were guaranteed for one year. The wood frame cabinets were high quality with dove-tail drawers, adjustable self-closing hinges, and mortised and tenoned frames for extra strength. The wood surfaces received six coats of stain, sealer, lacquer, or paints, and the customer could choose from a wide selection of decorator knobs and pulls.

The cabinets were made with unit sizes of 9 inches, 12 inches, 15 inches, 21 inches, and 27 inches to allow designers a variety of cabinet configurations to fit in different shapes and sizes of kitchens. The gable ends of the separate units could be screwed together, resulting in a strong, continuous-appearing cabinet which was actually made up of a number of different modular units.

FUTURE MARKETS

A new market opportunity developed with another company in the Genstar group—Broadmore Development of California. In 1977, during a strike of local manufacturers, Sungold supplied cabinets to the U.S. market. Broadmore Development and its customers were pleased with the product quality and styling of Sungold products. Sungold management found that at the current rate of 86 cents (U.S.) per Canadian dollar, high-quality cabinets could be shipped airfreight to the U.S. market at a cost of $50,000 and still be competitive with U.S. products. Broadmore Development had suggested Sungold bid on its scheduled production of 700 homes for 1979. In order to service an order that large, Sungold would have to rent warehouse space in California. Warehouse costs in California were comparable to Calgary prices.

Another Genstar company, in Houston, was also interested in Sungold Cabinets. The Houston builders were prepared to guarantee a minimum order of 100 kitchens over the next year and were prepared to supply their own installation and warehousing. Sungold was also considering the possibility of shipping units in a knockdown form to the United States. Knockdown units are unassembled cabinets that require assembly before installation. A semitrailer could carry from 100 to 150 knockdown units versus 10 to 15 assembled units.

Appendix A Interview with Salesman at Beaver Home Sales (Calgary)

This store carried three lines of cabinets: Citation, Kitchen Craft, and Sungold. The store had displays of the nine lines of Sungold cabinets and model kitchens of Citation and Kitchen Craft.

Q: I am interested in finding out about advantages of different lines of cabinets. Of the three lines you carry, which would you recommend?

S: I would recommend Sungold as they are the cheapest, having increased in price only 8 percent over the past year. They are also superior in quality.

Q: What is the price range?

S: Without seeing blueprints of your kitchen, I can give you a rough estimate of $60 a lineal foot for the cheapest model to $110 a foot for the top of the line. If you wanted to add to the number of units purchased, it would not be that difficult to backorder the cabinets.[1]

Q: Are Sungold cabinets guaranteed?

S: Yes, for one year; for something like doors that warp. If anything is likely to go wrong, it will within a year. I'll show you something about Kitchen Craft; the drawers jam and get stuck because they don't have the dovetailed feature of Sungold drawers.

Q: How far ahead would I have to order?

S: About a month in advance. If you bring in your plans I could do a layout in about one-half hour.

Q: What about installation?

S: Normal installation cost is around $800, and I could supply names for you, but it isn't that hard to install your own.

Q: Do you have any brochures I could take with me?

S: No, I don't.

Appendix B Kitchen Design

The kitchen in a new home was usually designed to fit the space remaining after standard features such as bedrooms, bathrooms, entranceways and special treatment such as cathedral ceilings, living, and dining areas had been laid out. After determining the length and width of space available for the kitchen, the location of

---

[1] The sample kitchen with 16 units as an example of Sungold's builder price is 31 linear feet of cabinets.

plumbing lines, stove plugs, and special obstructions such as a chimney, the specialist recommended a sequence of modular units that best meets the customer's needs and produces the most attractive functional kitchen. Other factors that a designer must consider were the location of electrical plugs; the height, size, and space of either side of windows; the appliances wanted by a customer, including built-ins such as garburators, dishwashers, microwave ovens; the type of countertop desired; and the color combination of the cabinetry. Specialist's recommendations for functional kitchen arrangements could save the homeowner many hours of work over the life of the home.

The position of the dining area and the arrangement of cabinets provide the framework for cooking and eating. Flexibility in the arrangement of shelves and specialized features such as wire baskets or rotating shelves as well as room for bulky items can facilitate organization and convenience. A family kitchen that was appropriately planned could include the potential for change and space for new acquisitions. However, many purchasers considered exterior appearance only and ignored the importance of layout and construction quality in their new kitchen. Kitchen sizes expressed in terms of number of cabinet units varied from 10 to 16 units in standard homes and 16 to 23 units in larger custom-built homes.

CASE 3–4

Algonquin Power and Light Company (A)

BACKGROUND

Allan Beacham is the marketing director for the Algonquin Power and Light Company, a large public utility providing gas and electric service to a major metropolitan area whose market is more than 1.5 million people.

Beacham is studying a report sent to him by Donald Orville, the company's forester. Orville is employed by Algonquin Power and Light to manage reforesting and reseeding of company construction projects. Possessing a degree in forestry from Syracuse University, Orville is acknowledged as a real authority in the forestry community.

Like many other public utilities across the country, Algonquin Power and Light Company conducts a maintenance program on its existing power lines. Trees, shrubs, and scrub are cut away from the lines to prevent chances of damage and subsequent power shortages. This maintenance program is directed by Donald Orville, and he estimates that the company's

---

Reprinted by permission from Robert W. Haas and Thomas R. Wotruba, *Marketing Management: Concepts, Practice and Cases* (Plano, Texas: Business Publications, Inc., 1983), pp. 324–32.

maintenance crews collect 100 tons of waste wood residue (cuttings) each week as a result of the line-clearing program.

Orville has developed a compost from these tree and shrub cuttings in his company laboratory. In his mind, this compost provides an organic soil amendment that is in much demand in the county. In his report, Orville states, "Waste wood-chip residue can be converted into a humus material superior in quality to the organic peats, leaf molds, and composted redwood products being marketed in the county. An accelerated composting process will convert this waste material into a marketable soil amendment in a matter of 6 to 10 weeks," The Orville report continues, "Composted trimming wastes have properties superior to the various redwood products. Leafy vegetative matter is included in the chip residue resulting in a more complete composting of the material. This product has a low carbon to nitrogen ratio, which is desirable in composts." Orville firmly believes the compost can be marketed profitably and this is the reason he has submitted his report to Allan Beacham.

PAST COMPANY TREE CUTTINGS DISPOSAL PRACTICES

Environmental push.

Up to this time, the company has simply taken its line maintenance cuttings to county-operated dumps or disposal sites. An average of 50 loads of wood chips is produced each week by the cutting crews, and the county assesses a dump charge against each truckload of waste hauled to the dump. This amounts to an annual disposal charge of $3,000.

In addition, each time a trip is made to the dump, an average of one hour of productive crew time is lost. Based on 50 such trips a week, crew time involved costs the company an additional $55,000 annually.

Orville contends that these costs could be eliminated if the waste wood material was processed into the soil amendment compost. Line-clearing equipment would then be based at the processing site or sites. The company would realize a profit on its sales of such compost.

Reading through Orville's report, Beacham is impressed with the logic of Orville's argument. To date, Algonquin Power and Light Company has paid money to dispose of product components that may be in great demand. In addition, Beacham believes such a program may have ecological advantages to the utility—the company would be converting a previously wasted resource into a valuable soil amendment.

COSTS OF OPERATING A COMPOST OPERATION

In his report, Orville foresees the need for two pieces of equipment to convert the waste wood residue into marketable humus composting material. Equipment required will be: (1) a 75-cubic-yard-per-hour shredder. Waste

too much capacity

materials will pass through the shredder and would then compost in long windrows on a packed earth surface. After composting, the material will be reshredded and screened. Such a shredder costs $15,000; (2) a size 1½-cubic-yard loader will be needed to load the wood chips into the shredder and the compost into waiting trucks. The cost of this loader is $25,000.

Labor studies conducted by Orville indicate that a single man working with the mobile processing equipment can operate the compost program. In his report, Orville outlined what he believes the annual cost of operation to Algonquin Power and Light Company would be. His estimate of $46,786.16 is derived in the manner shown in Exhibit 1.

In his report, Orville estimates that the 100 tons of waste wood residue collected each week will convert into 10,000 to 15,000 cubic yards per year of marketable compost. He also believes that a "virtually unlimited market exists for all locally produced humus material at a bulk price of $8.50 per cubic yard." Using a 10,000 cubic yard forecast, he computes the return to the company from such a program to be $96,000 based on the following:

$ 85,000	10,000 cubic yards of finished compost @ $8.50/yard
−47,000	Operation expenses of a subsidiary operation
$ 38,000	Direct profit from sale of compost
+58,000	Savings in residue hauling and dumping fees
$ 96,000	Return to the company

EXHIBIT 1
Annual Cost of Operation of the Compost Program

Capital Base	Annual Capital Cost Factor*	Equipment Operation Expense	Annual Revenue Requirements
Land			
($60,000) (0.1969)†	$11,814.00		$11,814.00
Loader			
($25,000) (0.3251)†	8,127.50	(1,500 hrs.) ($1.197) = $1,795.50	9,923.00
Shredder			
($15,000) (0.2626)†	3,939.00	(1,000 hrs.) ($1.197) = $1,197.00	5,136.00
Land and equipment revenue requirements			$26,873.00
Labor (special equipment operator)			
Annual labor factor		Overhead (33% of base labor)	
$10,836.96		$3,576.20	$14,413.16
Insurance estimate (from company insurance department)			500.00
Miscellaneous expense factors:			
Supervision, sales, etc.			5,000.00
Total annual return requirements, including return on equity			$46,786.16

* Levelized annual capital cost factors include a return on equity of 15 percent.
† Rates used by the company to compute annualized capital costs.

While Beacham is impressed with Orville's report, he is suspicious of some of the figures. He is particularly concerned with Orville's demand computations. For example, he questions Orville's contention that the compost could be sold at a bulk price of $8.50 per cubic yard. He also wonders if 10,000 cubic yards could in fact be sold in a year. Before he makes any decision regarding the compost program, Beacham wants his concerns to be addressed. He respects Orville's cost and technical expertise, but he questions his market knowledge and expertise. In short, Beacham requires more information before he makes a decision.

power + light vs. Compost?

MARKETING ORGANIZATION

Algonquin Power and Light Company's marketing organization is headed by Allan Beacham who holds the position of director of marketing. Reporting to Beacham are three marketing program managers, Bob Morton, Ed Walton, and Carlos Berlozzi. These marketing program managers function very much like product managers—each is responsible for developing and implementing assigned specific marketing programs. For example, Berlozzi has responsibility for the utility's energy-conservation program while Walton manages the industrial-applications program. In addition to these three marketing program managers, the department includes Marjorie Haskins, the marketing research manager, who supervises a staff of three research analysts, and Edward Robinzes, the advertising manager. Both Haskins and Robinzes provide staff assistance to Beacham and the three marketing program managers. Beacham decides to give the compost project to Bob Morton and calls him to his office.

THE MEETING BETWEEN ALLAN BEACHAM AND BOB MORTON

Allan Beacham briefed Bob Morton on Orville's findings and recommendations and handed him a copy of the forester's report. "Bob," Beacham said, "I would like you to check this out. Orville may have something here, but we need more definitive market information. Look into it, and get back to me with a feasibility report and a strategy recommendation either to enter or not to enter this compost business. Back up your recommendation with some research data so that we will have some facts to fall back on. I will alert Marjorie Haskins so that she knows you need her help. Get with her as soon as you can and then get back to me. In the meantime, I will put Orville on hold." With that, Bob Morton returned to his office to study Orville's report. From the tone of Beacham's conversation, he knew this was a high priority project and that he would have to act soon. After thoroughly studying Orville's report, he scheduled a meeting with Marjorie Haskins, the marketing research manager.

RESEARCH REQUIREMENTS

In his meeting with Haskins, Morton outlined what he thought were his research requirements. Specifically, he wanted to know:

1. The approximate size of the total county compost market, both for commercial and residential users.
2. Competitive prices in both the commercial and residential markets.
3. Present producers of compost sold in the county and their locations.
4. Resellers and/or middlemen involved in marketing compost in the county.
5. The willingness of prospective customers to switch to Algonquin's compost from their present product.

Morton outlined these requirements to Haskins and impressed upon her the need for prompt information. She knew of the project's priority because Allan Beacham had briefed her, too. She promised Morton she would schedule a meeting with her staff immediately and would have information back to him within a month. Morton was pleased with Haskins' cooperation, and he left the meeting with a positive feeling that Haskins would provide him with the type of information he needed.

RESEARCH FINDINGS

About three weeks after their meeting, Haskins called Morton to inform him that the research had been completed by her department. Through the use of a "build-up" research methodology, Haskins had discovered seven basic markets for compost in the county. These are shown in Exhibit 2, which also indicates estimates of annual compost demand for each market. She considered the estimate of 78,641 cubic yards to be conservative yet realistic.

Breaking down the markets into retail and wholesale/user segments, she provided Morton with information showing brands and products presently being purchased, their sources and suppliers, and prices paid. These data may be seen in Exhibits 3 and 4.

From field interviews with prospective customers, Haskins developed a list of product specifications that the compost must meet if customers were to seriously consider Algonquin compost as a substitute for existing competitive products already on the market. These specifications may be seen in Exhibit 5.

EXHIBIT 2
Estimates of County Demand for Compost by Type of Customer

Customer Type	Estimate of Cubic Yards Used per Year
Topsoil companies	36,800
Retail nurseries:	
Specialty nurseries	11,400
Chains and discounters	4,816
Growers: Farms, orchards, etc.	19,200
Landscape contractors and gardeners	6,425
Manufacturers and distributors	Unable to ascertain
Government	Unable to ascertain
Total demand	78,641

Note: A limited number of manufacturers did use compost, but it was often purchased indirectly through landscapers, topsoil companies, etc. Local distributors also handled compost, but since they resold to other demand components (retailers, etc.), much of their demand was also duplicated in the demand of other components. Interviews with government buyers at city, county, and state levels indicated that government did at times purchase quantities of compost from outside suppliers. However, they also composted their own trimmings. Thus reliable estimates of compost purchased from outside suppliers could not be obtained. In view of these considerations, the estimate of 78,641 cubic yards is viewed as a conservative estimate.

The field research also revealed some concerns or fears expressed by potential users. Some of the most commonly expressed fears were:

1. Could Algonquin Power and Light provide compost in the required quantities over time? Many prospective customers were reluctant to switch because they were afraid they might later find that the utility could not provide quantities required. This was a particular concern of large growers and topsoil companies mainly because the utility company's policy of underground power lines in new areas would in the long run reduce the source of compost materials.

2. How good would Algonquin's quality control be? The utility was seen as a novice in the soil amendment business. Many potential buyers expressed a fear concerning the company's production and quality-control capabilities. independent lab cert.

3. How would the Algonquin compost compare to redwood compost? Most of the prospective customers interviewed did not think the compost would be as good as redwood compost, despite Orville's contentions that it was. The major concern was that the Algonquin compost would break down quicker than redwood compost. This was a particularly big point with growers of trees and large ornamental shrubs who use exclusively redwood compost. They argued that redwood compost allowed them to grow their

↓ price get vol. "social good"

EXHIBIT 3 Potential Competition in the Wholesale and/or User Market based on Selected Field Interviews

Business Operation Interviewed	Products Presently Being Purchased	Quantities Purchased Annually	Sources and Locations of Suppliers	Present Price Being Paid
Maynard Sand and Material Company (topsoil company)	Douglas fir wood chips 3/8" or less in size	24,000 cu. yd.	Local county distributor	$2.50 per cu. yd.
	Redwood shavings 3/8" or less in size	3,600 cu. yd.	Local sawdust company (in county)	$4.50 per cu. yd.
Dave Parker Supplies (topsoil company)	Used sawdust	500–1,500 cu. yd.	Stall sweepings from local horse ranches	$1.00 per cu. yd.
	Nitrolized fir compost 1" or less in size	250–750 cu. yd.	Both bought from out-of-county distributor 200 miles away	$5.50 per cu. yd. + $3.00 per cu. yd. freight
	Redwood compost 1" or less in size	250–750 cu. yd.		$6.00 per cu. yd. + $3.00 per cu. yd. freight
Green Thumb Nursery (wholesale nursery grower of small ornamentals)	Redwood compost 1/8" or less in size	100 cu. yd.	Local sawdust company (in county)	$4.50 per cu. yd.
Marlowe's Nursery (wholesale nursery grower of trees and large shrubs)	Redwood compost 1/4" or less in size	1,000 cu. yd.	Local sawdust company (in county)	$3.50 per cu. yd. bought on a 40 cu. yd. basis
Garden Valley Nursery (wholesale nursery grower of 1- and 5-gallon plants)	Nitrolized redwood and fir compost 1/4" or less in size	2,000–3,000 cu. yd.	Local sawdust company (in county)	$4.00 per cu. yd.
County government	Redwood R.S.A. nitrogen-treated compost bulk	Unable to determine	Local county distributor for small orders / Out-of-county sawdust company for large orders	$5.75 per cu. yd. delivered on a 35 cu. yd. basis / $4.90 per cu. yd. delivered on a 60–65 cu. yd. basis

sell here ↑

EXHIBIT 4
Potential Competition in the Retail Nursery Business based on Selected Store Samplings

Type of Store	Brand Name of Competitive Product(s) Presently Stocked	Producer and/or Supplier of Present Products	Form in Which Product Is Sold to Consumers	Retail Price Charged
Discount Store A	Hawaiian Magic (redwood compost)	Out-of-county fertilizer Producer A	70 lb. bags	$1.19 per bag
	Garden Pride redwood soil conditioner	Out-of-county fertilizer Producer B	2 cu. ft. bags	$1.99 per bag
Specialty Nursery A	Garden Humus Bark Compost	Out-of-county fertilizer Producer C	3 cu. ft. bags	$2.49 per bag
Specialty Nursery B	Redwood Garden Mulch	Local fertilizer Producer A (in county)	4 cu. ft. bags	$4.00 per bag
Discount Store B	University Formula Redwood Compost	Out-of-county fertilizer Producer D	60 lb. bags	$2.17 per bag
Department Store A	Redwood Compost	Private brand—no producer listed on bags	60 lb. bags	$2.49 per bag
Chain Drug A	Hawaiian Magic (redwood compost)	Out-of-county fertilizer Producer A	70 lb. bags	$2.29 per bag
	Organic compost	Out-of-county fertilizer Distributor A	65 lb. bags	$2.49 per bag
Specialty Nursery C	Redwood Garden Mulch	Local fertilizer Producer A (in county)	4 cu. ft. bags	$2.97 per bag
Discount Store C	Viva Redwood Compost	Local fertilizer Producer A (in county)	4 cu. ft. bags	$2.99 per bag
Discount Store D	Viva Redwood Compost	Local fertilizer Producer A (in county)	4 cu. ft. bags	$2.99 per bag
Specialty Nursery D	Bandini 101 Redwood Compost	Bandini (National producer and sold through local distributor)	4 cu. ft. bags	$3.79 per bag
Discount Store E	Red Star Redwood Compost	Out-of-county fertilizer Producer E	4 cu. ft. bags	$2.26 per bag

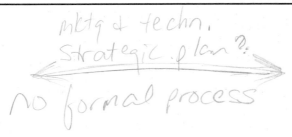

EXHIBIT 5

Required Product Specifications for Compost Soil Amendment

Based on field interviews with such potential customers as topsoil companies, retail nurserymen, growers in the nursery industry, landscaping personnel in city, county, and state governments, and others, the compost produced would have to meet the following specifications if it is to be seriously considered as a substitute for existing competitive products already on the market:

- Its ability to sustain and stimulate plant life must be demonstrated.
- It should contain 1 to 2 percent nitrogen content.
- It should be a dark earthy color.
- It should be fine in content. Nursery customers would like compost to be capable of passing through a 1/4″ screen and preferably through a 1/8″ screen. Topsoil companies require a compost that will pass through a range of 1/2″ to 3/8″ screen, preferably the latter.
- It must be free of weed, seed, dust, and other objectionable materials.
- It must be friable—properties that allow it to be easily crumbled.
- It must be stable over time. Changes in content because processing batches were different would have adverse effects in all markets.
- Its source of supply must be reliable over time.
- It must hold moisture well.
- It must not contain any cuttings that might be harmful to plant life, such as oleander, eucalyptus, and hardwoods.
- It may contain other ingredients, such as peat moss and leaf mold, but it must *not* contain steer manure.
- It must be bagged and labeled for the retail-nursery business but can be sold in bulk for growers and topsoil companies.
- It must be certified by an independent laboratory.

plants in a pot to the desired sale size with a single planting because the break-down period of the redwood was the same as the growing time. If they switched to the Algonquin compost, they would have to replant during the growing period because the new compost's break-down period was considerably shorter. This, of course, meant increased cost to these growers. Growers of small plants expressed no such concerns.

Despite the concerns, most prospective customers who were interviewed were interested. All were concerned about future sources of redwood compost as the supply of redwood is limited, and all were looking for comparable competitive products that could be purchased at lower prices.

In summary, Haskins felt the compost market for Algonquin looked promising and she told that to Morton. After receiving Haskins' research findings, Morton called Donald Orville on the phone. He wanted to hear the forester's reaction to the required product specifications that the research uncovered. Specifically, he wanted to know if Orville's compost could meet those specifications. Orville's reaction was most positive. While the compost's present form did not meet those exact specifications, there was little problem in changing it to meet them. The present compost is light brown but could easily be given a dark earthy color. It could easily be nitrolized to meet the 1 to 2 percent nitrogen content requirement, and it could also be screened to any size desired. Other than that, the present compost could support plant life, and Orville had evidence of that in his laboratory. The certification requirement was no problem, and Orville had already met with a local chemical lab on such certification. Orville believed the compost could meet the required specifications with very little modification.

Armed with the research findings provided him by Haskins' department and Orville's positive reaction, Bob Morton starts to prepare the feasibility report that Beacham requested, and he considers strategy recommendations he would make for Orville's compost. Based on the research findings, Morton believes that any strategy recommendations must consider both the retail and the wholesale-user markets. Advise Bob Morton on what strategy approach is most appropriate.

CASE 3–5

Freeman Roller Rink

In late August 1982, Dr. Garman P. Freeman and his brother Al E. Freeman, Jr., formed a partnership for the possible purchase of a building for the operation of a combination roller rink and video game arcade in Little Rock, Arkansas. The building, located on the corner of 24th and High Streets (see Exhibit 1), was originally a Safeway supermarket. Both men felt that sufficient financing would be available if a feasibility study revealed that a skating rink and arcade could generate reasonable profits.

Dr. Freeman, a dentist who had been in practice since 1949, had built a reputable clientele over the years. Although not retired, he had participated actively in SCORE (Senior Corps of Retired Executives) in past years, but stated that "I think they needed a black to serve, so they asked me even though I didn't quite fit in." He had been active in business, civic, and church affairs for many years. In addition to his dental practice, he had been engaged in real estate work, including the construction and ownership of

Prepared under the supervision of Professor Ray B. Robbins, Department of Management, College of Business Administration, University of Arkansas, Little Rock, by Mr. John Fornier. © 1983 by the College of Business, University of Arkansas, Little Rock. This case is based on a feasibility study.

EXHIBIT 1
Map Showing Freeman's Marketing Area

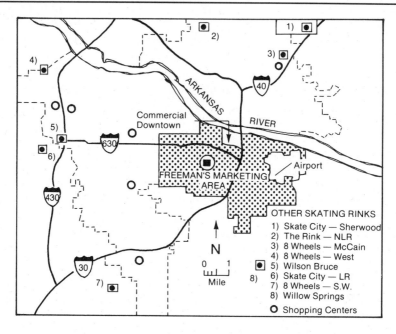

two one-story office buildings. Al Freeman, vice president and sales manager for Bond All Laboratories, Inc., located in Madison, Arkansas, received
his college degree in 1948 and had served as a dental technician in the U.S.
Army during the Korean War. Later he helped establish Bond All Laboratories for the purpose of manufacturing chemically related products, of which
embalming fluid was the leading seller. The brothers did not intend to
manage the new venture themselves; rather they planned to hire a full-
time, experienced rink/arcade manager.

In an effort to determine the feasibility of their rink/arcade project, the
Freeman brothers turned for help to the Small Business Assistance Program housed in the College of Business, University of Arkansas at Little
Rock. The analysts assigned to conduct the study focused first on the market
potential for the proposed services and second on the construction of a simulated profit and loss statement.

The geographical market which could be served was determined primarily on the basis of other skating rinks (see Exhibit 1). A list of these
follows:

1. The Rink, North Little Rock.
2. Skate City, Sherwood.
3. 8 Wheels (McCain Mall), North Little Rock.
4. Willow Springs, Little Rock.

5. 8 Wheels (S.W.), Little Rock.
6. 8 Wheels, Little Rock.
7. Wilson Bruce, Little Rock.
8. Skate City, Little Rock.

The three 8 Wheels franchised rinks were substantially larger than the proposed Freeman operation. All had modern facilities, hardwood floors, and were certified for national competition. The Sherwood Skate City rink was larger than any of the 8 Wheels operations, had modern facilities including a hardwood floor, and was also certified for national competition. It also featured an attached ice skating rink. The other Skate City was similar in size and facilities to the 8 Wheels rinks. The remaining three rinks were "independents" and had approximately the same size operation as was planned by the Freemans. These rinks had artificial flooring and were not certified for national competition.

All of the competitors served food and had pinball and video games. Each of the three 8 Wheels rinks had two game machines; the large Skate City rink had six, and the small Skate City had four. The independents had three to four machines. The extent of the food service operation varied with the size of the rink; i.e., the larger the rink, the more extensive the food service. Two of the three independents provided only food and beverage vending machines.

The skating rink nearest to the proposed enterprise would be four miles away since no skating rinks existed in central Little Rock. The market boundaries were set on the basis of proximity to the nearest rink, natural boundaries, and major streets and highways. It included census tracts 1–14, 25, 26, 28, and 29, which had a combined population of 41,738 individuals and 15,800 households. About 80 percent of the population was black. (For further demographic data see Exhibit 2.) It was estimated that the Freeman rink would attract 90 percent of the prospective skaters in the area; i.e., 10 percent would go to other rinks. Further, it was estimated that the Freeman rink would attract 1 percent of the skating admissions of the remaining area.

According to a survey conducted by National Family Opinion, Inc., a marketing research organization located in Dayton, Ohio, some 39.2 million Americans enjoy roller skating. Nationwide this represented one skater in 23 percent of all households. Another study revealed that 62 percent of all skaters were between the ages of 15 and 18. Only 27 percent were over 18. The study from National Family Opinion, Inc. showed that the head of skater households was younger than the average family head and that 66 percent of skater households had a total annual income above $20,000. In general, skaters came from larger households (four or more members) and lived in smaller metropolitan areas. Nationally the average skater visited a rink 26 times a year. Winter months represented the peak skating period while summer was the off-season, although this varied by geography.

EXHIBIT 2
Freeman Market Area (1980 Census demographic data)

1. Age Distribution

Little Rock

Age	Total	Male	Female
5–9 years	12,559	6,300	6,295
10–14	11,441	5,714	5,727
15–19	12,569	6,120	6,449
20–24	15,766	7,153	8,613
25–34	30,711	14,650	16,061
35 and over	75,415	33,374	42,005
Total	158,461	73,311	85,150

North Little Rock

	Total	Male	Female
5–9 years	4,814	2,439	2,375
10–14	4,593	2,332	2,261
15–19	5,243	2,540	2,703
20–24	5,814	2,700	3,114
25–34	10,623	5,154	5,469
35 and over	33,201	15,307	17,894
Total	64,288	30,472	33,816

Freeman Market Area

	Total	Male	Female
5–9 years	3,483	1,680	1,803
10–14	3,053	1,537	1,516
15–19	3,739	1,796	1,943
20–24	4,627	2,158	2,469
25–34	6,962	3,397	3,565
35 and over	19,874	8,373	11,645
Total	41,738	18,941	22,941

2. Racial Breakdown—Freeman Market Area

White	10,392	Black	31,136	Other	210
Male	4,618	Male	14,226	Male	97
Female	5,774	Female	16,910	Female	113

3. Family Data

	Little Rock	North Little Rock	Freeman Market Area
Total families	40,804	17,603	9,118
Families with children	20,938	8,649	4,893

4. Housing Value and Income Data—Freeman Market Area
   a. Median housing unit value = $25,236 versus $39,950 for Little Rock and North Little Rock.
   b. Average median household income = $9,308 versus $14,375 for Little Rock and $15,190 for North Little Rock.
   c. Households with income over $20,000 = 2,358.
   d. Households with income under $20,000 = 13,442.

Using the data in Exhibit 2, it was possible to estimate the number of skaters who would patronize the Freeman rink during a two-week period. The calculations are shown in Exhibit 3.

The Freeman brothers planned to modernize the building and to use bright colors and eye-catching designs to provide an atmosphere for fun and enjoyment. They also recognized the importance of properly maintaining the building and its parking lot, including the use of adequate lighting and security. A new polyurethane rink floor would be installed at a cost substantially below (50 percent) that of a wooden floor. This type of floor also required less maintenance but did not last as long.

Special programs would be used to attract customers. These would include lessons, clinics, dance sessions, contests, shows, and exhibitions. Prices would vary by the time and day of the week. Competitors typically divided the week into daily sessions from 4 to 7 P.M. and 7 to 10 P.M. The peak periods were Friday and Saturday nights, for which the large competitors charged either $3.50 or $4.00. The Saturday afternoon price was $3.00, and all other sessions were $2.00. The Freemans planned to charge $2.50 for the two peak periods and $2.00 for all other sessions. The average admission was expected to be $2.00, which would take into account price promotions. They hoped to be able to rent the rink at least one weekday night each week at a price of $250 for such special events as birthdays, company parties, and charity-sponsored activities. They planned to investigate the use of special price deals, such as an unlimited-use monthly ticket for $20, group discounts, two back-to-back sessions for the price of one, and the use of dollar-off coupons. A 50-cent fee would be charged for rental skates per session.

In an effort to learn more about the arcade game portion of the business, several distributors were contacted. On the basis of what was learned, it was

EXHIBIT 3
Estimated Number of Skaters

Population:	
Little Rock	158,461
North Little Rock	62,288
Freeman market area	41,738
Average persons per household:	
Little Rock	2.55
North Little Rock	2.57
Freeman market area	2.62
Number of households:	
Little Rock	62,142
North Little Rock	25,015
Freeman market area	15,800
Skaters per 2-week period:	
$90(15,800) + .01(87,157 - 15,800) \times 23\% = 3,435$	

concluded that 12 electronic games could be placed in operation on a commission basis; i.e., the machines would be owned by a local distributor who would not only purchase the machines but maintain them. Distributors typically required a 60 percent take on all receipts. The alternative was to buy such games at a cost of $2,600 to $3,100 each. Based on national data from grocery stores, it was estimated that each game would, on average, provide revenue of $150 per week.

It was not clear whether to install food and beverage machines or to open a snack bar similar to those operating in movie theaters. The latter involved an additional investment and higher fixed costs but had a higher revenue potential if the rink attracted large numbers of skaters. The average skater was expected to spend $1.25 per month on food and beverages.

Considerable time was spent in preparing an estimate of the costs of setting up the rink-arcade venture. These costs are broken down in Exhibit 4.

It was likely that, of the nearly $200,000 investment required, $150,000 could be borrowed from several sources. The expected average interest rate which would have to be paid at that time was 11.5 percent. The land was estimated to be worth $30,000 and the building $36,000. It was anticipated

EXHIBIT 4
Estimated Costs

Land and building	$ 69,000
Remodeling/decorating:	
Furniture/fixtures	28,500
Polyurethane floor ($2 × 8,250 sq. ft.)	16,500
Walls/partitions	2,500
Carpeting ($3 × 916 sq. ft.)	2,750
Lighting, air conditioning, heating, electrical,	
and plumbing	30,000
Enlarged office area	1,500
Snack bar equipment	7,000
Outside lighting	150
Music PA system	4,000
Signs	1,800
Inventory:	
Skates, 300 pair @ $31.95	9,585
Extra wheels and parts	650
Snack bar supplies/inventory	1,000
Office and cleaning supplies	1,000
Other costs:	
Working capital	15,000
Legal and professional fees, licenses/permits,	
utility deposits, and initial advertising	5,000
Total investment	$199,435

EXHIBIT 5
Estimated Monthly Expenditures

	Percent of Sales
Salaries	8%
Wages	12
Advertising	3
Interest/mortgage	22
Supplies/food	12
Telephone/utilities	5
Insurance	2
Maintenance	2
Taxes/licenses	5
Security	7
Repairs	3
All other	5
Total	86%

Source: *Roller Skating Business Fact Book* and Roller Skating Operator Trade Association.

EXHIBIT 6
Estimated Total Sales

1. Admissions:
   6,870 skaters[a]   Price = $2.00 with own skates;
   4,000 with own skates[b] $2.50 with rental skates
   2,870 with rental skates[b]

   $\quad\quad\quad$ 4,000 × $2.00 = $8,000
   $\quad\quad\quad$ 2,870 × $2.50 = $7,175 $\quad\quad\quad\quad\quad\quad$ $15,175.00

2. Arcade games: 12 games × $150/week[c] × .40[d] × 4 weeks $\quad$ 2,880.00
3. Snack bar: Average skater spends $1.25 per 4-week period ×
   6,870[e] $\quad\quad\quad\quad\quad\quad\quad\quad\quad\quad\quad\quad\quad\quad\quad$ 8,587.50

Total sales $\quad\quad\quad\quad\quad\quad\quad\quad\quad\quad\quad\quad\quad\quad\quad\quad\quad\quad$ $26,642.50

[a] From earlier data.
[b] National survey shows 66 percent of skaters are from households with incomes of $20,000 or more. It is assumed that such skaters own their own skates.
[c] Based on national average of machines in grocery stores.
[d] Commission rate charged by suppliers in Little Rock and North Little Rock.
[e] Estimated from data provided by local theater operators.

that a 20-year mortgage of $35,000 could be obtained on a variable interest basis, i.e., the actual interest charged would vary depending on prevailing rates.

From a variety of sources it was possible to put together an estimate of monthly expenditures in the form of percentage of sales ratios for a rink similar in size to the one being considered (see Exhibit 5). Total sales per four-week period were estimated as shown in Exhibit 6.

Based on a profit-before-tax margin of 14 percent, the venture was estimated to yield profits of $3,729.95 per average four-week period or an annual profit before taxes of $48,489.35 without taking into account depreciation which was estimated to be about $20,000 annually. At this level, state and federal income taxes were expected to total about 20 percent. The Freemans recognized that their rink/arcade would not be profitable from the outset, although they did think it would be possible to break even in the first year of operation.

CASE 3–6

Kellogg Rally Cereal

In early 1978 Mr. A. B. Smith sat in his office in Battle Creek, Michigan, evaluating the nutritional portion of the ready-to-eat cereal market. He was particularly concerned about several trade reports he had seen recently about the success of the Quaker Oats Company's Life cereal commercial titled "Mikey." The commercial was being touted as one of the best-remembered commercials on the air.

Mr. Smith was also concerned about the recent trends in the ready-to-eat (RTE) cereal category such as the success of the bran-type products and the declining interest in the so-called natural cereals. The growth in the nutritional RTE category had been strong. Kellogg's product entries in this category, however, had not shown the same growth as the market leader, Life. In addition, Life, through the "Mikey" commercial, had strengthened its position as a "nutritional cereal the whole family will like." Kellogg's two nutritional products, Product 19 and Special K, had both been strongly positioned against the adult market.

In the early 1970s Kellogg had successfully market-tested a new product which was directly competitive to Life under the name of Rally. With the growth of the category, the established position of the present Kellogg brands in the nutritional area, and the present consumer concern about

---

This case was prepared by Professor Don E. Schultz and Mr. Mark Traxler of Northwestern University.

sugar content in RTE cereals, Mr. Smith was reviewing Kellogg's position in the category prior to making a recommendation to management for 1979. Launching a new brand of RTE cereal was a major undertaking involving several million dollars. In addition Mr. Smith was concerned about the potential cannibalization of Kellogg's Special K and Product 19 if another product were introduced.

If Life's all-family appeal was being communicated through the "Mikey" commercial, was that an area Kellogg was missing?

Rally had been market-tested in the early 1970s. Was that test still valid? Could the results of that test be used as a basis for a new product introduction in 1979? All of these questions and more were crossing Mr. Smith's mind as he pondered the problem.

KELLOGG COMPANY

Kellogg Company had grown out of the Western Health Reform Institute, a 19th-century health clinic in Battle Creek, Michigan, affiliated with the Seventh-Day Adventist movement. Dr. John Harvey Kellogg had become head of the institute in 1876. With his younger brother Will, Kellogg became interested in whole-grain cereal products for patients at the clinic. C. W. Post, who had been a patient at the clinic, had the same idea and had developed and promoted some of the foods served at the clinic into successful products.

By 1906, Will Kellogg began producing cereal products developed at the clinic under the Battle Creek Toasted Corn Flake Company name. As the company grew and the cereals were widely accepted, the name was changed to Kellogg Company in 1922.

Kellogg quickly became the market leader in RTE cereals and presently enjoys an approximate 42 percent share of business, followed by General Mills with 19 percent, General Foods Post Division with 16 percent, and Quaker Oats with 8 percent. Kellogg markets some 15 different brands of RTE cereal, including such famous names as Rice Krispies, Corn Flakes, Sugar Frosted Flakes, Fruit Loops, and Raisin Bran. Kellogg cereal sales totaled $726 million out of total corporate sales of $1.385 billion in 1976. In addition, Kellogg has expanded into other food categories, primarily through acquisition of such companies as Salada Foods, Mrs. Smith's Pie Company, and Fearn International.

THE BREAKFAST CEREAL MARKET

In 1977 the RTE cereal industry continued its upward climb in total pound and dollar sales. RTE cereals are now the fifth-fastest-growing consumer product category, averaging nearly a 5 percent annual increase, according to the U.S. Department of Commerce. Sales for the past four years were:

Year	Pounds (billions)	Percent Change
1974	1.63	—
1975	1.69	+4%
1976	1.81	+7
1977	1.85	+2

Retail sales in 1976 amounted to $1.48 billion, which is approximately 1 percent of all retail food store sales. Per capita consumption of RTE cereal is increasing also. Between 1972 and 1973, consumption of RTE cereals increased from 6 to 8 pounds per person. The Cereal Institute estimates "cold cereal" consumption by age as follows:

Age	Pounds per Person per Year
1–2	7.2
3–5	9.4
6–8	12.0
9–11	9.8
12–14	9.8
15–19	5.9
20–54	3.6
55+	5.9

Since 1974 cereal prices have been steadily increasing:

Year	RTE Average Retail Price per Pound	Percent Change
1974	$0.908	—
1975	0.933	+3%
1976	0.951	+2
1977	1.022	+7

Usage of RTE cereals is spread fairly evenly across the country, with nearly 80 percent of all persons using them. Target Group Index (TGI) defines "heavy users" as those consuming six or more individual portions of RTE cereal per week. These "heavy users" comprise nearly 38 percent of all RTE cereal users. There is a slight geographic variance in RTE heavy users. The Mid-Atlantic (110) and East Central (107) areas index the highest, while the Southeast (88) and Southwest (84) areas are the lowest (index average = 100). There is also a slight seasonal sales skew, ranging from a high of 110 in July and September to a low of 88 in November (index average = 100).

The cereal category is broken down into seven categories by Selling-Marketing Areas, Inc. (SAMI). These categories and their approximate percentage of the total are:

Category	Share
Children's	24%
All family	46
High fortified	9
Bran	7
Granola	4
Variety pack	3
Other	5
Granola bars	2

TGI separates RTE cereal into three categories—presweetened, natural, and regular. Based on research data it appears that consumers are even less discriminating, preferring to lump RTE cereals into either presweetened or regular. In spite of this generalization, there is consumer recognition of the various types of products available, with some five to seven "acceptable brands" on most shoppers' lists.

Changes in manufacturer's list prices for RTE cereals are relatively infrequent. The normal retail margin is approximately 18 percent.

There are few middlemen in the RTE cereal channels. Orders flow from the grocery chain buyer or food broker to the sales force to the factory. The goods are shipped to the grocer's warehouse and from there directly to the retail outlet. RTE cereals are fast-moving products, with about one box purchased per family per week. Typical RTE promotion to consumers includes cents-off coupons and self-liquidating premiums. The package is used as a breakfast-time entertainment medium by printing interesting information or games on the back and/or side panels.

While there are certain anticipated trade deals for new products, established brands rely more heavily on consumer advertising and promotion than on promotional programs.

Because of the large number of brands marketed, there is no one dominant brand. Kellogg's Corn Flakes is the largest selling brand, with an approximate 7 percent share, followed by Cheerios, with approximately 5.6 percent. Others range downward, with most in the 1 percent to 1.5 percent share area.

NUTRITIONAL RTE CEREALS

The "nutritional" segment constitutes about 15 percent of the total RTE market when several "all-family" entries are added to the SAMI "adult highly fortified" category. The "adult highly fortified" brands are Life, Product 19, Special K, Buc∗Wheats, Golden Grahams, and Total. Other all-family RTE which appear to be directly competitive are Cheerios, Chex (Rice, Corn, Wheat), Wheaties, Shredded Wheat, and Team. Most of the brands in this segment are long established, with few recent additions. Total RTE brand share ranges from a low of approximately 0.27 percent for Fortified Oat Flakes to approximately 5.6 percent for Cheerios. Kellogg's two entries in this category are Special K, with 2.2 percent share, and Product 19, with 1.2 percent share. The Special K share has been declining slightly over the past two years, while Product 19 has remained steady.

The growth rate of the nutritional segment is much faster than the growth rate of the total RTE cereal market. The following table demonstrates:

	Percent Increase	
Year	Nutritional	RTE
1974	6%	n.a.
1975	13	4%
1976	14	7
1977	16	2

n.a. = Not available.

When new cereals are priced, prices of directly competing products are an important consideration. Typical out-of-store (OOS) pricing for brands in the competitive segment are as follows:

Brand	Size (ounces)	Price
Buc*Wheats	15	$1.11
Cheerios	10	0.83
Life	15	0.93
Product 19	12	1.03
Total	12	1.05
Special K	15	1.21

Note that Product 19 and Total, which are in direct competition, are priced accordingly.

Due to the number of brands offered to the consumer, sales volume requires frequent assessment by grocery chain buyers of which brands to reorder. The decision is based on SAMI and Nielsen data to define the best-selling brands, the grocery's own historical sales data, and in the case of new products, the national advertising and promotional plans. New products are usually given a six-month trial period by most grocery retailers. However, gaining the necessary two-shelf facings to launch the new brand requires several decisions. It is common for the RTE cereal aisle to be set proportionately to the grocer's sales for each brand.

Sales forces in the RTE category are highly trained and motivated. Since cereal is an established category, the sales force is usually a key determinant in a successful new-product introduction.

Brands in the high-nutrition segment invested an average of $6.35 million in measured media in 1977, according to the Leading National Advertisers (LNA) annual summary. In 1976, investments in the directly competitive market ranged from less than $1.9 million for Buc∗Wheats to over $10 million for Cheerios. Expenditures for Life in 1976 were estimated to be approximately $6.4 million compared to the Special K investment of $6.2 million and the Product 19 budget of $2.9 million. With the success of the "Mikey" commercial, Life was expected to increase its advertising expenditures in 1978.

As a rule of thumb, advertisers in the high-nutrition and all-family cereals invested 60 percent of their funds in network television, 33 percent in spot television, and approximately 7 percent in print.

The messages of the major competitors are summarized below:

Special K   An adult cereal with a high-protein high-nutrition campaign stressing weight control and fitness. Copy focuses on the "Special K Breakfast" of less than 240 calories.

Wheaties   Advertising features Bruce Jenner, a current sports celebrity who included Wheaties as part of his winning diet. The brand is known as the "Breakfast of Champions."

Total   Campaign stresses vitamin and nutrition content compared to that of other leading cereal brands. Good taste is a secondary message to reassure the consumer.

Cheerios   A long-running family-oriented campaign which says, "Get a powerful good feeling with Cheerios."

Product 19   Campaign aimed at adults focusing on good nutrition. The copy asks, "Did you forget your vitamins today?"

Life   Uses "Mikey" (described below) as product hero in its long-running campaign.

The essence of the "Mikey" commercial for Life is as follows: The commercial shows two skeptical older children and a younger child, Mikey, in a kitchen setting. Because the older children already know that Life is supposed to be "good for you"—implying that Life could not possibly taste good—they use Mikey as a guinea pig to taste Life cereal. Mikey innocently eats it while the other two eagerly watch for his reaction. Mikey smiles. Amid shouts of "He likes it!" and "He's eating it!" the two skeptics conclude that Life *must* taste good for Mikey to like it.

Life cereal has used trial-size sampling to stimulate interest in the product. The packages included three one-ounce servings of Life and sold for 10 cents in chain grocery outlets. Sales improved slightly as a result.

The heavy media dollars and promotional efforts described above are aimed at the primary purchasers of high-protein/high-nutrition cereals. They are profiled as women 18–49 for products like Life, Cheerios, and Wheaties and as slightly older women (25–54) for Special K, Product 19, Buc*Wheats, and Total. They live in SMSAs, most have at least a high school education, and annual household income is in excess of $10,000. They are married, with three or more individuals in the household and children 6 to 11 years old, according to TGI.

THE PRODUCT

Kellogg's new-product development department describes Rally as a delicately presweetened high-protein cereal for younger adults and children. The actual appearance is a square puffy pillow shape much like that of Ralston-Purina's Chex cereals. Since Rally is a rice-based product it stays crisper in milk than oat- or wheat-based cereals. Rally's delicate presweetening translates into 18 percent sugar by volume as compared to less than 10 percent for nonsweetened brands. Nutritionally, RALLY has 20 percent of the U.S. recommended daily allowance (RDA) of protein with milk and is enriched to 25 percent RDA with eight essential vitamins and iron. Quaker's Life is the only other product with such a high protein level, light presweetening, and a comparable vitamin and mineral content. Rally contains 33 percent of the RDA for vitamins B_1 and B_2, niacin, and iron, compared to Life's 25 percent.

In choosing a package size for Rally, Kellogg looked at the brand's direct competitor, Life cereal. Life markets two sizes, 15 ounces and 20 ounces. The 15-ounce box retails for 93 cents. To compete with Life in the same price range, the largest size Kellogg could offer would be a 13-ounce box at 97 cents because of a difference in the cost of goods. Rally was tested in a 7-ounce box priced at 75 cents in the 1970 market test.

Rally's test-market package design showed the red Kellogg logo, a black sticker stating "High protein," and the name Rally in big black letters at the top. The bottom portion showed a bowl full of cereal. In the midsection was a set of pennants waving above the bowl as if it were a stadium.

CONSUMER TEST

The 1970 consumer panel results for Rally among women and children were very encouraging.

	Preference		
	Rally	*Life*	*None*
General appearance	76%	14%	10%
Shape	54	19	27
Taste	62	20	18
Texture "just right"	83	16	

From the consumer test, the major advantage of Rally over Life appears to be based on the comment, "Life gets soggy too soon."

Rally was preferred 3 to 1 over Life by a consumer panel of children and was rated superior in taste, texture, and sweetness level. Against four leading nutritional brands (Life, Total, Product 19, and Special K), women showed a significant preference for Rally. Consumers also rated Rally as better than the cereals they were presently using.

MARKET TEST

Rally was market-tested in two eastern cities in the early 1970s. It was positioned as an "all-family nutritional cereal with better taste" directed to children and young adults. Rally was able to generate and maintain a sales rate equaling a 1 percent share of the total RTE market pound sales in these tests.

The introductory sell-in used Kellogg's own sales force to acquaint grocery clients with Rally and offered a 75 cent to $1 per dozen introductory case allowance to help defray warehousing and stocking expenses. The media plan included network children's and prime-time programming and spot children's and daytime programming for the 17-week introductory period.

SUMMARY

In reviewing the Rally test case, Mr. Smith was still undecided about a recommendation to introduce Rally nationally. On the positive side, consumer response seven years ago was good. Unlike many presweetened cereals, Rally's sugar content would not stir consumer concern. Every day in the papers, consumers read about the importance of good nutrition, and high protein was certainly an important part of nutrition. And finally Rally seemed to overcome the consumer problem of Life, getting soggy in milk too soon.

However, there were problems to be considered, not the least of which was the product name. Should it still be called Rally? Was Kellogg's target market—young adults and children—correct during the test market? As a new product, could Rally compete with Life in gaining both segments of the target? After 17 years, Life had only recently acquired a strong children's following with the "Mikey" commercial. Are the test market results still valid for a new-product introduction in 1979? What about cannibalization of Kellogg's existing brands?

Finally, if Mr. Smith should make the recommendation to introduce Rally, before giving his final recommendation to management he would have to answer such questions as the following: What package and pricing changes would be necessary; what improvements in the distribution system would be required; and what sort of advertising strategy and promotion should be used to make Rally a viable competitor against Life and its "Mikey" commercial?

APPLICATION 3–7

Keithley Instruments

When IBM researchers won the 1987 Nobel Prize for Physics for discovering electrical superconductivity at a high temperature, the publicity shot of one of the winning scientists gave the folks at Keithley Instruments a happy moment. In the photo, behind the researcher, was a Keithley nanovoltmeter used in superconductivity work.

Keithley equipment had made an equally gratifying appearance in the 1986 Nobel Prize photo. No accident, either. For little Keithley is very much a part of the high-tech picture. From its home in Solon, Ohio, a Cleveland suburb, Keithley turns out gadgets that monitor such electrical phenomena as voltage and resistance, and competes with the likes of Hewlett-Packard and John Fluke Manufacturing. Many researchers prefer Keithley, especially for jobs in Keithley's specialty niches, such as the measurement of very weak voltages. The breakthrough research in today's electronics—such as superconductivity—just happens to require these specialized gadgets.

Keithley's niche expertise, and the falling U.S. dollar, have sparked an average of 20 percent a year growth in sales and earnings over the past decade. In fiscal 1987, ended September, profits rose to 97 cents a share, from 87 cents the previous year.

Although it has been in business for quite a spell, the company has been publicly owned only since 1985. During this span, the shares have traded between 6¾ and 14⅝ and currently are changing hands around 10.

Joe Keithley founded Keithley Instruments over 40 years ago, not long after graduating from the Massachusetts Institute of Technology. An ac-

---

Source: William M. Alpert, "High-Tech Niche Picker," *Barron's,* January 18, 1988, pp. 18, 20.

quaintance complained of the difficulty in measuring very weak electrical currents. Keithley supplied him with a suitable device, and found his calling. For several decades, Keithley's firm was the only place to go when a researcher discovered that a millivolt was too big—when he found himself counting microvolts, or even nanovolts. Another of Keithley's specialties was measuring the impedence of an insulator, to see how good it was at keeping the electrical juice from spilling into where it did not belong.

As the semiconductor industry grew—with corporations and universities studying the electrical properties of exotic semiconductor materials—Keithley Instruments grew as well. By the fiscal year ended September 1979, sales had reached $19.5 million, with earnings of $1.29 million, or 42 cents a share. "If you walked through most labs, you'd almost always see a Keithley catalog," recalls Larry Rubin, who is head of instrumentation and operations at the National Magnet Laboratory at MIT.

Like rivals such as Hewlett-Packard and Tektronics Keithley also sold industrial-grade meters, although not without some disappointments. In the late Seventies, for example, Keithley introduced the first hand-held meters that a serviceman could use for testing electronics equipment in the field. But the idea was easily copied. Keithley soon found itself in a commodity business, and pulled out of that market in 1983.

Most of Keithley's wares, however, were specialty instruments with good margins. In fact, through the toughest times of the electronics industry, Keithley never suffered a loss. Even during the severe semiconductor slump of 1981, Keithley managed a profit of five cents a share. And despite the industry's lean years of 1985 and 1986, Keithley rang up sales of $48 million for the year ended September 1986, and earnings of $2.9 million, or 87 cents a share—on a par with the preceding year's profits.

What has helped tide Keithley over some rough patches are its markets outside the electronics industry, notably the automotive and life-science businesses. But it helped even more to have customers outside the United States. One of the biggest contributors to Keithley's prosperity over the past three years has been the declining dollar. In the year ended September 1987, the instrument maker registered $57.7 million in revenue, a jump of 21 percent over the 1986 period. Some 58 percent of those 1987 sales came from foreign customers. "For a long time after the dollar began its decline," comments Chief Financial Officer Ron Rebner, "the nation's net export position was supposed to improve, but it didn't. You'd read that people were having trouble finding the exporters who were benefiting. Well, all along, it's been our little company in Solon, Ohio. When the dollar moved down, our sales went right up."

Nearly all of Keithley's production is right in Solon, where about 400 of the company's 523 employees work. About one-fourth of those workers are engaged in production, says Rebner, with the rest in technical and professional jobs. Although the company had considered foreign manufacture during the dollar's pre-1985 climb, it decided to stay at home—partly to keep a close watch on product quality. "An important factor in our business," observes Rebner, "is the testing and calibration of our instruments. That's something that you don't want to lose the recipe for."

Most of the growth in international sales has been in Western Europe, where Keithley has gained high market share and where capital spending by electronics firms has been stronger than in the United States or Japan. "The company was pretty smart," boasts Rebner, "when it opened direct sales offices in all the countries of Western Europe a long time ago. So we were in a position to benefit from the growth in the test and measurement business there."

Keithley Instruments has kept up a steady stream of new products. The company spends about 10 percent of its sales revenue on internal research and development. "We are very much a new-product company," says Rebner. "You have to be in this business. Some products last 8 or 10 years, but others only last 3 or 4 years."

Keithley picks its spots in the test and measurement business. "If we can't be No. 1 or No. 2," Rebner says, "then we wonder why we should want to do something at all. If you choose something and do it well, then you can compete against the bigger players. They're good competitors, but they can't afford to spend money on everything."

The best examples of niches where Keithley has excelled are the measurement of tiny voltages and high resistance. "Those are two areas that Keithley has a lock on," notes Rubin at the National Magnet Lab. "It's remarkable—in this day and age—that they've had no competition there in over 20 years."

As computer firms like IBM and Cray Research try to replace the silicon in their computer chips with faster material such as aluminum-gallium-arsenide, their scientists use Keithley devices. Another favorable development is the near panic that has followed IBM's discovery, last year, of a copper-oxide mixture that carries electricity without resistance at temperatures well above absolute zero's minus-460 degrees Fahrenheit. These "high-temperature" superconductors promise to speed up computers and telephone lines, by allowing electrons to zip down superconducting paths. Work with these superconductors calls for plenty of gadgets from Keithley.

When researchers buy Keithley's specialized instruments, they have an incentive to buy Keithley's more routine devices, too. That is because various pieces of equipment made by the same manufacturer usually work best together, even though instrumentation firms all observe a common standard. For this reason, says MIT's Rubin, the National Magnet Lab has fixed on Keithley instruments as the standard.

The company's Radiation Measurements Division tracks the X-ray doses of people working in medicine and nuclear research.

Another successful market for the company is quality control for semiconductor makers. "Yield is the name of the game there," says Rebner. "If you've got good yields, you'll make money. If you've got bad yields, you don't make money."

For this market, Keithley's Systems Division developed the YieldStation S900, a personal-computer-based product that lets small semiconductor foundries test their silicon wafers for electrical defects. In 1987, European chipmakers spent heavily on such products. And toward the end of its September fiscal year, Keithley reported increasing orders from America's recovering chipmakers.

Much of Keithley's new-product stress lately has been directed toward the personal computer. Customers now can collect measurements from various instruments and then analyze the results by PC. On this score, Keithley last summer made a big commitment by acquiring for $9 million the developers and distributors of ASYST software. This Rochester, N.Y.-based firm, along with a marketing unit that Keithley also purchased, had sales of about $4 million in 1986, making it the dominant software supplier in the scientific-instrumentation software field. This market is growing at an annual rate of 20 percent. Keithley hopes to supplement the sales to original-equipment manufacturers by selling ASYST directly to the even large number of individual scientists who are starting to use PCs to run their labs. "Watch how successful we are with ASYST," advises Rebner. "We paid a good buck for it, and we expect good things."

Financially, Keithley seems in good shape to finance growth. At the end of September, current assets amounted to 1.8 times current liabilities. Book value, adjusted for a 3-for-2 split in October 1987, stood at $7.53 a share. And since September, Rebner reports, the company used some of its cash to boost its current ratio to 2-to-1 and reduce total debt to less than 15 percent of capital.

Although the stock market crash has made Keithley's customers jittery about the economic outlook, Rebner says that U.S. semiconductor clients report no slowing of the recovery that began early in 1987. Keithley is looking for continued growth in Europe and in the Far East, where Korea and Taiwan are rising producers. With an expansion of its Japanese offices in 1988, the Ohio company hopes to keep in closer touch with its customers and its competitors in Japan. "If we can do well on the same soil as the Japanese," says Rebner, "then the likelihood of our waking up and finding them in our own backyard is slimmer."

Keithley aims to boost its sales and earnings at a rate of 10 percent to 15 percent a year, while keeping return on equity at over 15 percent. At September's end, backlog stood at a healthy $7.2 million—a 50 percent jump over the year-earlier figure. The company's board recently voted a 14 percent boost in quarterly dividends, to 2.5 cents a share.

Perhaps most important, as a warranty of future growth, the customers seem to be satisfied. "They supply the breadth of things that researchers need," says Rubin at MIT. "I know that if I start with Keithley, I will never be sorry."

Discussion Questions

1. Analyze Keithley Instruments' competitive advantage(s).
2. Evaluate the appropriateness of Keithley's market targeting strategy.
3. Identify and evaluate potential environmental and competitive threats that this small instrument manufacturer may face in the future.
4. What are the targeting and positioning strategy implications of each threat?

APPLICATION 3–8

Whittle Communications L.P.

When media entrepreneurs Phillip Moffitt and Christopher Whittle parted company last July [1986], Mr. Moffitt made off with their most visible property, *Esquire* magazine. He made headlines six months later when he sold it for about $40 million and announced plans to devote himself to a writing career.

Mr. Whittle went home to Knoxville, Tennessee, to run a hodgepodge of lesser-known publishing ventures that were his share of the partners' company, 13–30 Corp. But he may be the bigger winner in the long run. Whittle Communications L.P.—his company's new name—is garnering a lot of attention among advertisers with an innovative formula for reaching consumers.

The Whittle gospel holds that the clutter of advertising on television and in mass-circulation magazines has made most traditional advertising ineffective. To exploit advertisers' concerns about clutter, Whittle Communications has become a specialist in "targeted media"—magazines, posters and other advertising vehicles that are created for a single advertiser or a small group of sponsors and distributed to specialized audiences.

Among the company's 26 media properties are Connections, a posterlike information center in 1,500 high schools that is sponsored by Procter & Gamble Co.; Best of Business magazine, a quarterly digest of business publications distributed to 350,000 Xerox Corp. customers; and Connecticut's Finest, a quarterly magazine for customers of Southern New England Telephone Co.

To get its message to Madison Avenue decision makers, Whittle Communications has been running a series of slick ads in newspapers and media

---

Source: Laura Landro, "Whittle Communications Grabs Innovative Ad Niche." Reprinted by permission of *The Wall Street Journal.* © Dow Jones & Company, Inc., April 22, 1987, p. 6. All rights reserved.

trade journals. "We're wasting a lot of money on this ad," announces a bold headline in one. The point: "Virtually every advertiser in every medium is paying to reach viewers or readers who never become customers."

Whittle Communications is still small—it expects to have revenue of $85 million for the year ending June 30—but industry specialists say the company has struck a nerve with its message. "Advertisers are increasingly saying they want to try different things to get away from the clutter, and there's a tremendous shift to direct, targeted media" says Paul Hale, a publishing specialist at media investment banker Veronis, Suhler & Associates.

Leo Scullin, director of print and new electronic media at advertising agency Young & Rubicam Inc., says Whittle Communications has "created some highly visible media forms." Advertising agencies "usually look for consumer-driven media, then the advertising follows," he says, but Whittle "has managed to flip the formula."

Advertising revenue from Whittle Communications' media properties currently ranges from $2 million to $10 million each. Mr. Whittle now aims to develop properties that can garner revenue of $40 million to $60 million each by featuring noncompeting products from multiple large advertisers. Mr. Whittle recently hired former *Esquire* publisher Alan Greenberg to spearhead the search for big revenue-producing properties. Whittle Communications also will introduce its first video and audio products during the next two years, businesses from which Mr. Whittle expects to generate large revenue.

Mr. Whittle is particularly interested in what he calls the 35-to-50-year-old "aging baby boom group," the business market, and regional consumers. He says the company has "development relationships" in certain food categories, financial services, credit cards, airlines, laundry products, and domestic automobiles. It also is going after retail, fast-food, and beverage advertisers.

New products will be pumped directly through Whittle Communications' national distribution network, which covers 70,000 locations in the largest 100 markets. The company's sales force—which doesn't actually sell anything—persuades such diverse types as obstetricians, veterinarians, school boards, and banks to hand out its magazines or display its wall posters (see Exhibit 1).

"We occasionally get resistance if a doctor doesn't want us on his wall or doesn't like advertisers, or if a school has a policy against advertisers," says Michael McAllister, head of distribution for Whittle Communications. But he adds that the company's health-publishing ventures often have a waiting list, and most high schools like anything that encourages students to read.

For example, one issue of the Procter & Gamble-sponsored *Connections* featured the popular rap music group Run-DMC as "hosts" of "Get Hip to Lit," about poetry and literary classics. The performers are pictured with books by T. S. Eliot and E. E. Cummings; brief articles range from why

EXHIBIT 1
Whittle Communications' Top Media Properties

Property	Format	Distribution
Physician's Weekly	Wall Information Center	1,600 hospitals with 280,000 doctors
Campus Voice	Magazine (three times a year)	400 campuses with 1.2 million students
Pet Care Reports	Wall Information Center (monthly)	7,900 veterinarians' offices
Best of Business	Quarterly magazine	350,000 executives
Dental Health Adviser	Wall Information Center (quarterly)	30,000 dentists' offices

Canterbury Tales and *Beowulf* are classics to why rap is like poetry. P&G ads for Prell shampoo, Crest toothpaste, and Duncan Hines cookies run in a strip across the bottom of posters.

Mr. Whittle emphasizes that the editorial staffs of the various publications are independent; they don't write about sponsors' products or mention product names. Sponsors typically see a publication 10 days before it is distributed, and have the right to withdraw if they don't approve of the subject matter—but they still have to pay for the advertising.

Whittle Communications' editorial staffs work to develop material that serves the needs of the audience the advertiser is targeting. For Johnson & Johnson, for example, Whittle Communications came up with *Pre-Parent Adviser* magazine, distributed through prenatal instructors, and *New Parent Adviser,* distributed by obstetrics nurses in 3,400 hospitals. Parenting Adviser, an information center with free pamphlets, is displayed in 4,700 pediatric offices and pushes such products as Children's Tylenol.

William Egan, director of marketing for Johnson & Johnson's baby products unit, says that while the publications are "expensive," the company is committing a growing portion of its advertising budget to them. The Whittle Communications publications can't be measured by traditional methods used for network and magazine advertising. "What attracted us to them is their ability to target mothers, the audience that is so important to us," Mr. Egan says. "We're competing in a media world that is so cluttered, it's worth paying a premium to establish an exclusive, value-added" advertising vehicle.

Similarly, Whittle Communications designed "Pet Care" information centers and booklets for Ralston Purina Co. that are in veterinarian's offices in the top 100 cities and include booklets on such subjects as caring for an older dog, with ads for Ralston's Fit and Trim food for older dogs. Booklets on cats and puppies, meanwhile, feature ads for the appropriate products.

"Each (booklet) is like a little heat-seeking missile," Mr. Whittle says. "It only goes where it's supposed to go; it's really targeted and there's no competitive message."

Whittle Communications' business isn't without risks. Though the company typically requires a commitment of three to five years before it pours resources into a new editorial product, advertisers sometimes drop out after the initial commitment, for such reasons as a change in management or strategy. For example, the U.S. unit of Bayerische Motoren Werke AG dropped a magazine called *Destinations,* an upscale travel magazine that Whittle Communications distributed to high-income consumers, advertising BMW's most expensive cars. BMW decided to focus instead on promoting its more moderately priced cars, and Whittle Communications had to fold the magazine.

Similarly, RJR Nabisco Inc.'s R.J. Reynolds Tobacco USA unit sponsored a magazine called *Moviegoer,* which advertised the company's cigarette products and was distributed nationally to movie theaters. The company dropped the magazine after deciding it wasn't reaching the right audience—and after Mr. Whittle hired away its chief marketing executive, Nicholas Glover, now chief executive officer of Whittle Communications.

Mr. Whittle has a powerful financial backer in a longtime 13-30 Corp. investor, Associated Newspapers Holdings PLC. The British concern, which also owns *American Lawyer,* controls well over half of Whittle Communications but leaves operating control to the 39-year-old executive. Depending on the company's growth and profitability—Mr. Whittle believes it can post revenue of $500 million by 1992—he could end up owning more than a 40 percent stake. He doesn't disclose the company's exact current ownership.

Industry specialists say Whittle Communications has carved out a unique and profitable niche. Smaller competitors can't match its national distribution network, and Mr. Whittle says he doesn't fear that larger publishing competitors will push single-sponsor publications. "They'd slit their own throats," he says. "Big media companies have trouble competing with us, because it would be heretic when they've got $1 billion in advertising coming in from mass circulation magazines. The big players haven't accepted that this is where the market is going."

Discussion Questions

1. Discuss Whittle Communications' competitive advantage(s).
2. How does the communications firm's market-targeting strategy differ from that of a traditional magazine publisher?
3. What are the market-segmentation strategy implications for a firm such as Johnson & Johnson in using the services of Whittle Communications?
4. Discuss how Whittle's positioning strategy and the positioning strategies of clients are interrelated.

APPLICATION 3–9

Toyota Lexus

The official launch of the 1990 Lexus luxury-car division of Toyota is still some 18 months away, but the presell promotion has already begun. Lexus marketing executives, after studying some competitors' promotional strategies, expect to model their efforts after some of the auto industry's most successful launches. In fact, Lexus' research included talks with Acura dealers.

"Textbook example: Ford's Taurus and Sable launches were the best we've ever seen. The cars were sold out long before they came to market, a great pre-sell," says Janet Thompson, the division's national marketing/operations manager. Ms. Thompson is former national ad manager for Toyota pickup trucks and onetime Chrysler Corp. executive.

Prototype Lexus models will be displayed at the first of the 1989 national auto shows next January. The finalized versions of the factory production units are expected to roll into dealer showrooms in September 1989.

This year marketing strategies for Lexus—the car that Toyota Motor Sales U.S.A, Torrance, Calif., has promised will be "a dramatically new, world-class luxury performance sedan that will establish new standards in technology and performance"—will focus on image-building and name recognition.

According to Ms. Thompson, "We're expecting to do a tremendous presell. By the time of the official launch and dealership grand openings everything with a Lexus name on it will be sold and gone. They're exclusive cars, not mass-market vehicles. Supply will be about one less than demand."

Although Lexus was formally announced late last August, Toyota had the concept of the new division at least since January 1987, when J. Davis Illingworth, previously the company's assistant national sales manager,

EXHIBIT 1
Toyota: Total U.S. Car Sales

1986	641,195
1987	630,052
Percent change	−2%
Projected 1988	Same as 1987

Source: *Automotive News*, Projected 1988 sales from Toyota Motor Sales USA.

Source: Chuck Wingis, "Lexus Learning the Lexis of Luxury," *Advertising Age,* February 29, 1988, pp. S–6, S–10, S–14.

was named corporate manager. Before joining Toyota in 1980, Mr. Illingworth had spent 10 years at Chrysler Corp.

There are currently 40 staff members for the division; the company hopes to have more than 200 people on board by the fall 1989 launch date. Upcoming hirings will include administrators for sales development and auto shows/special events.

Lexus was hastened by the March 1986 entry of American Honda Motor Co.'s luxury-car division, Acura, and by Nissan Motor Corp.'s Infiniti division, which was announced just a month ahead of Lexus.

When Toyota decided to join the other players in the luxury-car segment, it moved quickly, selecting the company's [ad agency] Saatchi & Saatchi DFS, Torrance, California, as the agency for Lexus in early November.

The S&S offspring handling Lexus is known as Team One. Scott Gilbert, senior VP for Team One, had previously worked with Ms. Thompson for nearly a year executing the marketing strategy that established Toyota pickup trucks as a market leader.

The day after its selection, Team One began fine-tuning its research of the luxury-car market and began creative work on a Lexus video presentation for the 1988 auto show season.

Its study found that an estimated 29 new models would enter the market by 1992, bringing the total number of models in that category to 70 or 80.

The Team One videotape was debuted at the Greater Los Angeles Auto Show in January. No Lexus product was shown but the video presentation helped trigger 5,000 consumer inquiries from potential buyers. Repeat performances in Chicago, Atlanta, and New York auto shows were expected to boost the total response to more than 20,000 names, leads Team One will follow up with a direct-mail campaign.

Full-page ads that ran last summer in *Automotive News* and *Ward's Auto Dealer,* have generated more than 1,000 inquiries and 400 applications (as of January) from potential Lexus dealers, according to the company.

The print ad reads, "Lexus is looking for the finest dealers to sell the world's finest motor cars," and carries the names and addresses of the division's area marketing representatives. Besides the auto shows, this one ad represents the only real advertising Lexus has done to date.

The ante for acquiring a dealership is $3 million to $6 million, depending on market location. Both Toyota and non–Toyota dealers are being considered as Lexus dealers. They will be judged on their customer satisfaction records, financial soundness, and business know-how.

About 100 dealers will be in place at launch time; the first dealers will be announced in late March or early April. Dealers will be concentrated in the top 50 U.S. luxury-car markets.

A public relations effort is also polishing the Lexus image. The liaison between Lexus management and the press is Kurt von Zumwalt, public relations manager, a 14-year veteran of the Toyota Motor Sales organization.

Phase one of the promotional effort began in January with the unveiling of the Lexus logo at the Los Angeles Auto Show. Known as the gold "L" design, the logo was the product of three design and advertising agencies over a six-month period.

The new logo was tested with Toyota employees and focus groups made up of luxury-car owners. Nearly 75 percent of the test groups rated the gold "L" as their first or second choice among the eight designs tested. Gold will be the primary color for Lexus logo applications.

In January, Toyota also released an artist's rendering of the Lexus sedan, which will be one of the two 1990 models.

Both models are Japanese-designed and built. Auto shows scheduled for the 1989 season will feature actual prototypes of the Lexus models. The division's primary market will be the United States, although the line will eventually be sold in other major markets throughout the world.

The flagship model, priced from $30,000 to $35,000, will be a 4-door luxury sedan, with a V8 engine and equipped with state-of-the-art electronics. The sedan will compete in the market now dominated by European nameplates—Mercedes-Benz, BMW, Jaguar, Volvo, and Audi—but the majority of buyers are expected to be baby boomers, many of them Toyota owners looking to move upscale.

A second Lexus model, a 4-door sedan powered by a V6 engine, will carry a price tag of about $20,000. The sedan will compete with selected European models as well as the Acura Legend and the Sterling. A sport coupe will be added to the line in 1991.

Toyota's Lexus division and Nissan's Infiniti division each will have three basic model lines by 1991 to compete in the upper $20,000 to mid-$30,000 range.

Infiniti's 1990 V8-powered flagship sedan and Lexus' V8 sedan are expected to try to create a new niche between the big American luxury cars and European cars, such as Mercedes-Benz, Volvo, and BMW's 5 and 7 series.

Lexus executives see the Acura Legend, which sells in the $20,000- to $25,000-range, as being more volume oriented than Lexus models. And, priced at $30,000-plus, the Lexus V8 comes to market at a higher price level than the Acura. "Our $20,000 near-luxury Cressida is more in the range of the Acura and is a nearer competitor," says Ms. Thompson. "With Lexus we're coming in with an exclusive, true luxury car, 'leap-frogging' the Acura, which is more of a mass-market product . . ."

Total sales of the Acura Legend and Integra in 1987 were 109,470 units.

Though the Lexus executives wouldn't discuss advertising budgets, they did say they expect to spend heavily—possibly more than the competition—in order to carve a niche in the crowded, luxury segment. Spot TV, radio, auto-buff magazines, and selected consumer publications will be part of the media mix.

The luxury market is a high stakes game, says Ms. Thompson. "A $50-million, $60-million budget . . . BMW is up to $75 million now . . . and that's just in basic media spending. They can see us coming and they're trying to solidify their markets as much as they can."

While Acura reported total sales gains in 1987, other importers in the luxury category did not.

The Lexus sales forecast for the first four months is 16,000 units. Tentative sales target for calender 1990, its first complete year, is 60,000 units, rising to a goal of 100,000 units in its fifth year.

"You lose exclusivity when you aim for the mass market and a 600,000-unit sales goal," says Mr. Illingworth.

Last fall, at the start of the 1988 model year, Toyota adopted a 3 year/ 36,000 mile comprehensive car warranty, the same as that for Honda's Acura line and some European manufacturers. The same type of warranty is expected to extend to Lexus cars, although Toyota can be expected to tout product quality, not the new warranty.

The launch is proceeding on schedule; however, there are still advertising and marketing questions to be answered, such as sports sponsorship and the use of celebrity spokesmen. The Lexus marketers view sports, both local and national events, as an important part of the luxury-car promotion effort.

"We're still six months away from making a decision in this area. We think the customer we're trying to reach is very focused, so our attention needs to be equally focused on specific media offerings that appeal to . . . the customer's interest." Possible areas may include college basketball and cultural events programming, says Mr. Illingworth.

"Our preliminary research indicates that maybe a celebrity spokesman wouldn't work for us, but we're certainly not going to overrule that possibility," he says.

"We've only begun to work on our creative marketing, and we're not going to eliminate any approach too early in the game."

Discussion Questions

1. Analyze the market opportunity for the luxury European-style segment of the automobile market.
2. Evaluate the key competitors that the Lexus faces in 1990 when entering the market.
3. What are the targeting and positioning implications of the market potential and competitor analyses conducted by Lexus marketing executives?
4. Discuss the appropriateness of Toyota's plan to target this segment of the automobile market.

APPLICATION 3–10

Marriott Corp.

In early 1982, Marriott Corp. started building the prototype of a new mid-priced hotel chain, something more modest than its usual hotels. Sample rooms with movable walls were assembled and furnished in the company's Gaithersburg, Maryland, hotel. Hammers and calculators labored in unison as Marriott executives slid walls back and forth, settling on three possible room shapes.

Then, over several weeks, hundreds of prospective customers were herded through the test rooms and quizzed. They howled at the idea of a room a foot shy on width, but they made nary a peep when length was trimmed 18 inches.

That little discovery should save Marriott more than $80,000 on each hotel property, or at least $24 million over the life of the project. It also says a lot about the changing nature of the hotel industry. In the late 1970s, market research wasn't in such vogue. Marriott, like most hoteliers, had grown easily with one sort of hotel that it duplicated again and again.

But a building boom has left several cities and some market segments saturated. And many hotel companies have spent the last few years researching and retooling in order to develop new growth strategies that are just now becoming clear. The new hotels themselves—and the development of the new systems needed to operate them—portend vast changes for this $33 billion industry.

Holiday Corp., for example, is entering three new market segments. Hyatt Corp., Ramada Inns Inc., Imperial Group PLC's Howard Johnson Co., and Manor Care Inc.'s Quality Inns International have all targeted new groups of customers. "What all of us are trying to do," says Darryl Hartley-Leonard, the executive vice president of Hyatt, "is steal some market share."

No lodging company is more ambitious than Marriott. [Exhibit 1 shows financial information for 1984.] The Bethesda, Maryland, company, which also owns contract food-service businesses and owns and franchises Big Boy and Roy Rogers restaurants, plans to build 300 "Courtyard by Marriott" hotels by the early 1990s in a bid to take market share away from mid-priced mainstays, Holiday Inns and Ramada Inns.

In addition, Marriott is expanding its downtown convention network, launching a line of suites-only hotels and testing the time-share condomin-

---

EXHIBIT 1
Marriott Corp.—1984

Sales	$3.5 billion
Net income	$139.8 million
Employees	140,000
1984 lodging revenue	$1.6 billion
Resort hotels	21
Convention hotels	12
Other hotels	114
Rooms	65,279

ium market. Still on the drawing board: a retirement-community business that would incorporate the features of a nursing home, and a scaled-down model of its regular, full-service hotel aimed at smaller markets.

The stakes are high. The outcome of this segmentation movement could dramatically affect the makeup of this industry for the next decade and beyond. Some chains, such as Howard Johnson and Ramada, have already gone through hard times. Independent operators, who provide about half the hotel rooms in the country, also are feeling the heat as industry giants fight it out. "Some old-line chains will gradually lose market share, and some newer, more aggressive chains are going to gain market share," says J. W. Marriott Jr., the company's president and chief executive officer. "The question for us is: How successful will we be with these new products?"

The biggest question for Marriott is Courtyard, a two-story 150-room suburban hotel aimed at the $45- to $65-a-night market. (A traditional Marriott hotel room rents for $65 to $100 a night.) Analysts say many properties in the midpriced sector are old and could be vulnerable to a new competitor, and success here would vastly broaden Marriott's customer base.

But such an ambitious invasion of new turf has its risks. Marriott is committing more than $2 billion over the next several years to build Courtyard. What's more, Marriott is entering a market with different pricing and marketing strategies, different service labels, and a different clientele.

The company hasn't taken the move lightly. It spent about three years researching Courtyard before a test model was built. "I must have slept in a couple hundred midpriced facilities," says Donald A. Washburn, the vice president for market development.

Marriott's research indicates that room quality and outdoor surroundings matter most to a would-be guest. So Marriott is trying to keep Courtyard's rooms as close as possible in quality to its full-service rooms, while throwing in a landscaped courtyard with serpentine walkways and, of course, a swimming pool.

Most of the cost cutting has come out of public space and service. A

Courtyard hotel has a tiny lobby and lounge, just one restaurant, a couple of small meeting-rooms, and no doorman, bellman or room service. Marriott now has six test-Courtyards in Georgia and boasts of an average occupancy rate of 90 percent. "You get a room that's worth more than you're paying for it," says John J. Rohs, a vice president for research at Wertheim & Co. Adds an executive at a competing chain, "If Bill Marriott builds 300 of those, he could hurt a lot of people."

Marriott spent many years in the highly competitive, low-profit-margin family restaurant business before building its first hotel in 1957. And its aggressive interest in market segmentation stems in part from an intense desire to set itself apart from the rest of the hotel industry. While most hotel chains grow primarily through franchising, Marriott likes to keep to itself by designing, building, financing, and managing (but not owning) its hotels. The hotels usually are sold to limited partnerships or institutions and managed by Marriott. It rarely uses outside consultants, and its doesn't like to hire general managers from competing hotels.

Unions are grudgingly tolerated at most companies, but Marriott fights them on every front. Its only unionized hotel, at San Francisco's Fisherman's Wharf, is neither owned nor managed by Marriott. (It is one of the few hotels Marriott has franchised.) Many chains publicly release occupancy rates; Marriott generally won't, though Courtyard has been an exception. "It's a competitive world we live in," says Mr. Marriott.

Such attitudes have led to allegations of arrogance and union busting, but few disparage Marriott's achievement. The hotel division, which accounted for about half of Marriott's $327.7 million pretax operating profit last year, has increased both revenue and profit at an annual rate of 20 percent for the past 20 years.

Since 1980, the hotel chain has more than doubled in size to 147 properties. More important, it has become the largest single operator of hotel rooms in the United States, and its lucrative management contracts have made Marriott one of the industry's most profitable companies. "Right now," says a rival executive, "they're the darlings of the industry."

The source of drive for the company has always been a workaholic member of the Marriott family. The first was J. Willard Sr., a devout member of the Church of Jesus Christ of Latter-day Saints, who founded the company as a root-beer stand in 1927 and who died [in 1985] at age 84. Also a Mormon, Mr. Marriott's eldest son—known as Bill—became chief executive in 1972. He remembers spending the vacations of his youth with his father in California visiting several family restaurants a day in search of ideas to take back to the East Coast.

Now Bill Marriott . . . emulates his father's practice, visiting about 100 Marriott hotels a year and about that number of competitors' hostelries. While the younger Mr. Marriott is expanding the chain at a much faster pace, the hotels are still run in the same old way: rigidly centralized and with great attention to the bottom line.

Mr. Marriott recalls a visit to a small luxury chain earlier this year. Despite its 10 percent occupancy, the hotel insisted on putting fresh flowers in every room. "The only person who saw [most of] them was the maid who took out the dead ones and put in the fresh ones," he says. "This happens more than you think in this industry."

But it couldn't happen at a Marriott. Marriott hotels are "run by the book, and the book is controlled by central people," says Gary L. Wilson, who recently left his post as Marriott's chief financial officer for a similar job at Walt Disney Productions. "The book" is in fact a dozen or so encyclopedia-like tomes detailing, among other operations, how to remove hair from bathroom sinks. The "central people" are numerous. Hyatt, traditionally Marriott's most direct competitor, estimates that for every two hotel executives it employs, Marriott has seven. No ingredient in hotel food may be changed without the explicit approval of headquarters. "We test our recipes," says Mr. Marriott. "We know what they cost. We won't let anyone mess with the food specs."

While concentrating on operations, however, Marriott, like most of its competitors, historically did little else. Consumer research and extensive marketing were rare. Room decor was chosen according to the personal taste of Marriott's decorators, and with a nod from Bill Marriott. The company got quite a jolt in the early 1980s, when its first forays into consumer research showed those decor decisions weren't going over with guests. Marriott's trademark reds and loud patterns were thereupon scrapped in favor of subtle shades of rust and beige.

"You might say the hotel industry grew in spite of itself," says Mark V. Lomanno, the associate director of research at Laventhol & Horwath, the consulting and accounting firm.

That changed with the onset of the 1980s, however, when many lodging companies began forecasting tough times. Tax incentives, in the form of investment tax credits and accelerated depreciation, lured scores of investors into hotel construction, often in areas where it wasn't needed. Marriott was running out of places to put its standard hotel, a 300- to 400-room, full-service facility located near an airport or a large suburban population center. In search of new markets, "we had to make the shift from a purely operations-driven company to a marketing-oriented company," says Frederic V. Malek, the executive vice president for hotels who had been a White House aide in the Nixon administration.

For Marriott, the move has meant bolstering the marketing staff, altering promotion paths and compensation scales to keep its best people selling, and starting a frequent-guest bonus program that costs $16 million a year to operate, according to a study done by a competing chain. It has also meant automating its hotel operations to allow more efficient tracking of guests, and attempts at jazzing up Marriott's rather staid image.

The company's internally designed hotels, for example, had a reputation for efficiency and consistency, but not for style or chic. So Marriott has been acquiring and building more resort properties, and it has turned to outside architects. John C. Portman, Jr., known for his cavernous atriums, glass elevators and other extravagances, designed the new Marriott Marquis hotels in Atlanta and New York.

Fashion, however, has its price. The Times Square property, which opened this month, cost $400 million and thus is one of the most expensive hotels ever.

But the key change, and the most difficult, has been the development of new operating cultures needed to succeed in new markets. When the first Courtyard was built, for example, Marriott moved the Courtyard management team from the hotel division and put it in a division that includes the company's fast-food chains, hoping to foster more creativity. "We make some decisions without all our flanks covered," says A. Bradford Bryan, Jr., the Marriott vice president in charge of Courtyard. He concedes that such a statement would be heresy in the hotel division.

In fact, none of the hotel division's traditions seems sacred at Courtyard. All-cotton towels, a hallmark of Marriott's hotel chain, have given way at Courtyard to cheaper fabric. Even a biography of the company founder, free for the taking in other Marriott hotel rooms (right beside the Bible), is sold at Courtyard vending machines, for 75 cents.

The hard part for Courtyard executives, however, is just beginning. Marriott plans to open 30 Courtyards in 1986 and about one a week thereafter, for the next several years.

Of course, competitors aren't taking this frontal assault lightly. Holiday Corp. is refurbishing some of its older properties, building about 50 Holiday Inns a year and throwing out an equal number of marginal properties. Says Richard Gonzalez, Holiday's director of new-business planning: "Marriott may find that there's some very, very strong competition in the midscale market."

Some of Marriott's stiffest challenges may be internal. There are some thorny marketing issues. To consumers, "the Marriott name may just mean expensive," says Daniel R. Lee, a senior analyst at Drexel Burnham Lambert Inc. Francis W. Cash, a Marriott executive vice president, acknowledges that the company must condition potential guests to expect fewer frills and less service with Courtyard. "If you think [Courtyard] is the little Marriott," he says, "you're going to be disappointed."

The company is attempting to run the smaller, less complicated hotels with managers who have much less experience than its traditional general managers. And it plans to deviate from tradition by hiring managers from competing chains.

As the time to begin "mass production" approaches, Courtyard executives continue to tinker with the "product." For example, a fully equipped office for guest rental has failed and will be replaced, probably by an exercise room. And a large game room, designed to create a "home away from home" atmosphere, has been shrunk to the size of an extra-large closet. Marriott found that Courtyard guests didn't go for Ping Pong and pool, so a few video games should do nicely.

Discussion Questions

1. Describe the market segments and Marriott's market-target strategy in the lodging product-market.
2. Critically evaluate Marriott's Courtyard venture in terms of market opportunity.
3. Identify and evaluate the key competitors of the Courtyard chain.
4. What strategy options are appropriate for marketing the Courtyard chain? Which do you recommend and why?

APPLICATION 3–11

Morning Treat Coffee Bags

William Brandt, marketing manager to the Morning Treat Coffee Company, was trying to decide if the company's newest product was ready for a test market. The product—real, fresh coffee in a bag similar to a tea bag— had been tested by a consumer panel for several months. The results were encouraging and suggested that the product would have appeal because it offered the convenience of instant coffee combined with the aroma and flavor of fresh coffee. Mr. Brandt was concerned about going into test marketing without a better understanding of the types of coffee drinkers most likely to use the new coffee bag.

Approximately 2 billion pounds of coffee were sold annually through food stores in the United States. About 35–40 percent of total coffee sales were in the instant or freeze-dried form, which was a growing segment of the coffee market. This growth in instant and freeze-dried coffee was due to the increased popularity of convenience foods. The demand for convenience in beverages was reflected in the fact that over 90 percent of the loose tea sold in the United States was packaged in individual bags.

It had taken more than 20 years to develop a process for packaging coffee in individual bags. Tea can be packaged in a cellulose fiber bag placed inside an individual paper bag because it is an organic material that is relatively unaffected by exposure to air. However, coffee is a more complex

---

Source: Harper W. Boyd, Jr., Ralph Westfall, and Stanley F. Stasch, *Marketing Research: Text and Cases,* 5th ed. (Homewood, Ill: Richard D. Irwin, 1981), pp. 576–80.

substance, consisting of oils, solids, and gases that are affected by oxygen. Because of its complex chemical composition, freshly ground coffee cannot be packaged in a tea bag. The newly developed coffee-bagging process used a specially developed synthetic fabric which sealed freshly ground coffee in a bag containing no oxygen. The shelf life of the coffee in the new bag was in excess of one year.

Mr. Brandt and other members of the marketing staff believed that Morning Treat Coffee Bags would appeal to convenience-oriented consumers. It was felt that heavy drinkers of fresh coffee were not likely to be included in this group because of the ingrained habit of brewing a large pot of coffee. The target groups were thought to be moderate and light drinkers of fresh coffee and all drinkers of instant and freeze-dried coffee. The marketing staff believed that many users of instant and freeze-dried coffee liked the convenience but that they were less than satisfied with the flavor, taste, and aroma of that beverage. Heavy users of instant and freeze-dried coffee were considered to be the main market for the new product. Some staff members were concerned, however, that the coffee bags might appeal most to a relatively unimportant market segment—households of only one, two, or three individuals who consumed small quantities of fresh coffee.

Identifying the best market segments for coffee bags and the reasons why some segments would be attracted to coffee bags were thought to be critical issues which had to be resolved before going into test markets. The J. M. South Company, a marketing research firm, was invited to propose the research that would clarify these issues. An abbreviated version of its proposal is shown in Exhibit 1.

EXHIBIT 1
Proposal

Purpose

The purpose is to identify the market segment or segments which include the most potential users of the new coffee bags and also to identify the basic reasons for the product's appeal to those segments. Specific measures of respondent identification will include whether they drink fresh or instant/freeze-dried coffee and the amount of coffee consumed. Because of the convenience aspect, coffee bags may appeal most to single persons and families with two working parents. Therefore, potential users will also be identified relative to the number of adults in the household and their employment status.

Design

The following four-point research design is proposed:

1. Use the U.S. Postal Service to distribute free packages containing three coffee bags to households on selected blocks in selected zip code areas in the same city or cities to be used as test markets. Each package of sample coffee bags will include a cover letter explaining that the product is new, the samples are free, and the respondents are invited to try them at their convenience.
2. Follow-up personal interviews will be made three to six weeks after the sample mailing. Persons selected as respondents will be adults who received and tried the new coffee bags.
3. Respondents will be identified as potential users or potential nonusers, depending upon how they score on the product-attitude rating scale to be used in the proposed questionnaire. (That scale is described below.)
4. All respondents (both potential users and potential nonusers) will be classified according to three descriptive measures: (a) amount of coffee consumed—three or more cups daily (heavy) or less than three cups daily (light); (b) form of coffee consumed—fresh only, instant/freeze-dried only, or both; and (c) number of working adults in the household—single adult, one working parent, two working parents, or others. Thus respondents will be classified according to amount and form of coffee consumed and number of adults in the household and their employment status. Tabulation will consist of counting the number of respondents falling into each category and calculating the percentage of potential coffee-bag users in each category. These findings will identify the most important market segments for coffee bags.

Questionnaire

A four-part questionnaire will be used during the personal interview.

1. Questions will measure the type and amount of coffee consumed and necessary demographic information.

EXHIBIT 1   (continued)

2. Respondents will rate their regular coffee drink on each of the following seven traits. (Figures shown in parentheses are the weights to be given to each rating. The weights are used in the analysis discussed below.)

Coffee Trait	Very Important (+3)	Important (+2)	Slightly Important (+1)	Not Important (0)
Aroma	_____	_____	_____	_____
Convenience	_____	_____	_____	_____
Flavor/taste	_____	_____	_____	_____
Freshness	_____	_____	_____	_____
No messy cleanup	_____	_____	_____	_____
Price	_____	_____	_____	_____
Strength	_____	_____	_____	_____

3. Respondents who tried coffee bags will compare them with their regular coffee drink on each of the above seven traits, using the five-point scale shown in the following table:

	Coffee bags are definitely better (+2)	Coffee bags are slightly better (+1)	Coffee bags are neither better nor worse (+0)	Regular drink is slightly better (−1)	Regular drink is definitely better (−2)
Aroma	_____	_____	_____	_____	_____
Convenience	_____	_____	_____	_____	_____
Flavor/taste	_____	_____	_____	_____	_____
Freshness	_____	_____	_____	_____	_____
No messy cleanup	_____	_____	_____	_____	_____
Price	_____	_____	_____	_____	_____
Strength	_____	_____	_____	_____	_____

4. Respondents will be asked their "intention to buy" coffee bags on a five-point scale: very likely to buy, likely to buy, don't know, not likely to buy, will not buy.

Analysis

1. *For each of the seven traits* measured in questionnaire items 2 and 3, the following weighting system will be used to determine a "score" for each *respondent* relative to each trait. The respondent's "score" is the figure shown at the intersection of the appropriate row and column.

EXHIBIT 1   (continued)

The respondent indicated in questionnaire item 2 that the trait is:	In questionnaire item 3 the respondent rates coffee bags on this trait as:				
	Definitely Better (+2)	Slightly Better (+1)	Neither (0)	Slightly Worse (−1)	Definitely Worse (−2)
Very Important (+3)	+6	+3	0	−3	−6
Important (+2)	+4	+2	0	−2	−4
Slightly Important (+1)	+2	+1	0	−1	−2
Not Important (0)	0	0	0	0	0

Thus, if a respondent indicates freshness is "very important" in questionnaire item 2 (weight of +3) and that coffee bags rate "definitely better" than his/her regular coffee drink (+2), the respondent is given a score of +6 (+3 times +2) on freshness. If aroma is "important" (+2) and the respondent rates coffee bags as "slightly worse" (−1), the respondent is given a score of −2.

2. Respondents will be given a score on each trait. These seven scores will be summed to determine "total score," which will lie somewhere between +42 and −42.
3. The respondent's "total score" and "intention to buy" coffee bags (from questionnaire item 4) will classify her/him as a potential user or not a potential user, according to the following rules:

Potential User	Not Potential User
a. Total "score" is > +12 and respondent *answers* "very likely to buy" or "likely to buy" coffee bags.	c. "Score is > +12 and respondent *does not answer* "very likely to buy" or "likely to buy" coffee bags.
b. Total "score" is between +6 and +12 and respondent *answers* "very likely to buy" coffee bags.	d. "Score" is between +6 and +12 and respondent *does not answer* "very likely to buy" coffee bags.
	e. "Score" is +5 or less.

4. All respondents who tried coffee bags will be classified into one (and only one) of the following cells:

EXHIBIT 1 *(concluded)*

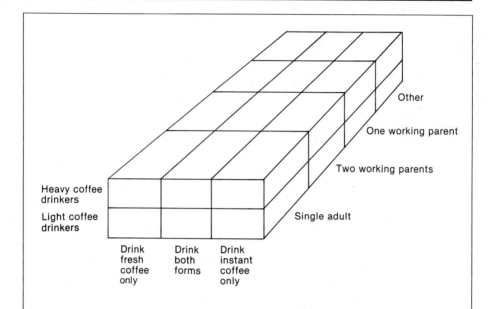

5. Each cell will have a total *number* of respondents and the *percentage* who have been classified as "potential users" of coffee bags. This information will identify the more important market segments which find the new coffee bags appealing.

6. Answers from respondents *in the more important market segments* will then be reanalyzed to identify that aspect, or those aspects, of coffee bags which they find most appealing. This reanalysis will identify the coffee traits which these respondents consider important or very important *and* for which they rated coffee bags as better than their regular coffee drink. Those are the product characteristics which potential users find most appealing.

Discussion Questions

1. Indicate the information needed by the marketing manager to determine if the new coffee bag is ready for a test market.
2. Discuss the pros and cons of conducting research before test marketing.
3. Critique the proposed research study, indicating its strengths and weaknesses.
4. Propose a modified research study which retains the strong points of the research proposal and incorporates the changes needed to overcome the limitations of the original proposal.

PART 4

MARKETING PROGRAM POSITIONING STRATEGY

Marketing strategy consists of:

- Choosing a strategy for each market target to be served by the business unit.
- Setting objectives for each target market.
- Designing a marketing program positioning strategy for each target market.
- Implementing and managing the marketing strategy.

We examined target-market strategy in Part 3. Part 4 is concerned with setting objectives, and with marketing program design. In Parts 5 and 6 we shall consider developing marketing plans and implementing and controlling marketing strategy.

A marketing program positioning strategy consists of more than a product, or even a line of products. Distribution, price, and promotion strategies must be combined with product strategy to form an integrated marketing mix.

SETTING OBJECTIVES

An objective indicates something that marketing management wants to accomplish, such as increasing market share in target market A from 21 percent last year to 28 percent during the next three years. Objectives should address various areas such as sales, expenses, profit contribution, and human resources. Each objective should indicate a desired level of performance, how it will be measured, and who will be responsible for meeting it. We shall examine some characteristics of good objectives and then discuss how to set objectives.

Characteristics of Good Objectives

Well-stated objectives possess several important characteristics. When evaluating objectives, ask the following questions:

- Is each objective relevant to overall results? For example, if market-share gain is an objective, will increasing advertising awareness contribute to the market-share objective?
- Is each objective consistent with the other marketing objectives and with nonmarketing objectives as well? One inconsistent objective may work against another objective.
- Does each objective provide a clear guide to accomplishment? Well-stated objectives should enable management to determine the extent to which the objective has been achieved for it to be of value. Has the objective been quantified and a time frame specified?
- Is the objective realistic? Is there a reasonable chance of meeting the objective? Objectives should represent achievable results.
- Is responsibility for each objective assigned to someone? Are joint responsibilities indicated?

Setting good objectives is one of management's prime responsibilities. The task is demanding, and it requires close coordination among the people in the marketing organization to assure that all objectives correspond to the marketing mission.

Setting Objectives

There are essentially two kinds of objectives:

1. Those that specify end results (e.g., profit contribution).
2. Those that, if accomplished, will (or should) help to achieve end results (e.g., add 10 new retail outlets by January 1, 1993).

Objectives should cover market position, productivity, resources, profitability, and other important end results.

Among the troublesome problems encountered in setting objectives are the interrelationships among objectives and the shared responsibility for achieving objectives. Each objective does not fit neatly into an isolated box. Thus, considerable skill is required in determining a balanced set of objectives for different organizational levels and across different functional areas (e.g., advertising and personal selling).

Marketing objectives are normally set at the following levels:

1. The entire marketing organization within a particular company or business unit in a diversified firm.

2. Each market target served by the company or business unit.
3. The major marketing functional areas such as product planning, distribution, pricing, and promotion.
4. Subunits within particular functional areas (e.g., individual sales-people).

The extent to which the above levels are relevant in a particular firm will depend on the size and complexity of the organization.

MARKETING PROGRAM POSITIONING STRATEGY

A marketing program positioning strategy is how marketing objectives are accomplished in a firm's target markets. Product, distribution, price, and promotion strategies represent an integrated bundle of actions aimed at customers/prospects in the target market. An overview of the decisions that make up a positioning strategy is shown in Exhibit 1. We shall briefly examine each program area, beginning with product/service strategy.

Product/Service Strategy

A product/service strategy consists of:

- Deciding how to position a business unit's product/service offering (specific products and/or services, lines, or mixes) to service its target market(s).
- Setting strategic objectives for the product and/or service offerings.
- Selecting a branding strategy.
- Developing and implementing strategies for managing new and existing products and/or services.

Product Positioning and Objectives.   Product positioning consists of deciding how to compete with a product or line of products against key competitors in the market targets selected by management. Key decisions about quality, price, and features establish guidelines for product development and improvement. Closely associated with positioning decisions are the strategic objectives for the product strategy. Examples of objectives are: market penetration, profit contribution, and establishing a reputation for quality.

Branding Strategy.   The major alternatives in the branding decision by a manufacturer are:

- Make no attempt to establish brand identity, and instead rely on intermediaries to establish brand reputation.
- Produce products which have the private brands of retailers on them.
- Utilize the corporate name (e.g., Deere & Co.) as an umbrella identity for all of the firm's products.

EXHIBIT 1
Positioning-Strategy Overview

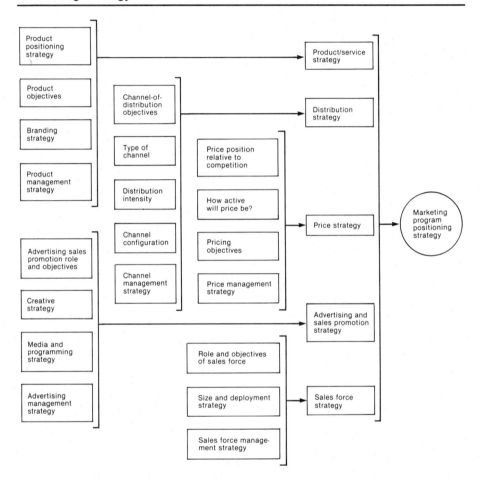

- Establish brand names for lines of products, as with Sears' Craftsman tools.
- Build a strong brand identification for individual products, as in the case of Procter & Gamble.
- Use a combination of the above strategies.

Marketing intermediaries often utilize the company and/or brand identity of manufacturers. Alternatively, if they have the resources, retailers and other intermediaries may choose to establish private brand identities.

Product Planning and Management. Firms are continually faced with the management of their product portfolios. Decisions include new-product development, product improvement, product repositioning, and product elimination. Increasingly, firms are formalizing their product planning and management activities to more closely link product strategies with corporate, business unit, and marketing strategies.

Distribution Strategy

A manufacturer's distribution strategy consists of first deciding whether to go direct to end users, using a company sales force, or to work through marketing intermediaries, such as wholesalers, distributors, dealers, and retailers. The latter strategy requires additional decisions such as the type of channel of distribution to be used, the intensity of distribution, and the types and number of intermediaries to include at each level in the channel.

The channel decision rests heavily on the role of the manufacturer in the channel. If the firm has a strong market position and adequate resources, management may decide to manage the channel. Ethan Allen, in furniture, has built a strong network of independent retailers. These dealers have been instrumental in the success of the company. Small firms with limited resources may be restricted to finding distribution channels to which they can gain access.

Price Strategy

The nature and scope of price strategy will be established by two decisions: the decision on price position relative to competition, and the decision on how active price will be in the marketing program. The first is closely linked to several other aspects of the positioning strategy—including product quality, distribution strategy, and advertising and personal selling programs. The second decision establishes, for example, how price will be used in advertising and personal selling efforts. Once these two decisions are made, guidelines can be established for price objectives and for the management of pricing activities.

Promotion Strategy

Advertising, personal selling, publicity, and sales promotion are communication efforts to inform and persuade buyers and others involved in the purchase decision. Each communication medium has certain assets and limitations. Management's task is to shape a promotion mix using the available elements. A key issue is selecting the role and objectives of advertising and personal selling in the marketing program. Once this is resolved the remaining decisions in advertising and sales force strategies are those shown in Exhibit 1.

CONCLUDING NOTE

Developing a marketing program positioning strategy requires the blending of product, distribution, price, advertising, and personal selling strategies. Shaping this bundle of strategies is a major challenge to marketing decision makers. Here we have sorted out the issues involved in marketing programming and shown how programming is linked to the other two key aspects of marketing strategy: market-target selection and setting objectives.

As cases are studied, you should keep in mind several characteristics of the marketing mix variables. They are both supplementary and complementary in nature. Some must work together, such as using advertising to develop product awareness. Other elements can to some extent serve as substitutes for each other. For example, pricing can be used in a promotional role through the use of promotional pricing (e.g., cents-off coupons). However, recall that each mix component may set some constraining guidelines for those decisions that remain.

CASES AND APPLICATIONS
FOR PART 4

The 10 cases and 5 applications in Part 4 focus on marketing program positioning strategy.

Cases

Zayre Corporation (Case 4–1) has experienced substantial growth in sales and profits in recent years. Its stock increased 600 percent in value between 1978 and 1985. The question now facing management is, "How should the corporation be positioned for continued success in the future?"

In Case 4–2, Seanav Corporation is a new firm formed to manufacture and market marine navigation equipment. A detailed business plan has been developed but the extensive market data has not been used to formulate a clear marketing strategy. Management must reexamine the market information and develop a concise and realistic marketing plan. The plan must be completed within five days.

Frank W. Horner Ltd. (Case 4–3), is a manufacturer of ethical and over-the-counter drug products. The marketing manager is planning the level and allocation of his communication budget for a recently introduced product.

Case 4–4, Norsk KJEM A/S, describes a 25-year-old chemical company with headquarters in Larvik, Norway. One product marketed by the firm is a "wetting agent" used to promote the retention and distribution of various industrial liquids. Johan Sunde, product manager for the firm, wants to develop a better definition of the target customers for the wetting agent and assess various aspects of the distribution strategy for the product.

Case 4–5, Screen Print Display Advertising, focuses on a Canadian firm that designs and produces point-of-sale displays and advertising products and services used in retail stores. Andy Smith, general sales manager, is contemplating a marketing strategy for entering the U.S. market with 4-foot by 8-foot ultraviolet ink murals.

The Nebon Medical Products, Inc. (Case 4–6), describes a situation where expansion into technical products has resulted in inadequate product coverage by the general-line sales force. Several product managers have recommended that the sales force be reorganized. Other situations requiring attention are also described.

Case 4–7, Newell Furniture Company, is concerned with the efforts of a medium-size, family-owned furniture company to reposition itself in the market after a decade of problems. Management wants to reduce the company's dependence on mass merchandisers.

Case 4–8, Airwick Industries, focuses on the marketing strategy for a product called Carpet Fresh, a rug and room deodorizer. Mike Sheets, president of Airwick, and Wes Buckner, executive vice president of the Consumer Products Division, are interested in developing a plan to increase sales and maintain the brand's competitive position.

S. C. Johnson and Son, Ltd. (Case 4–9), a Canadian subsidiary of S. C. Johnson and Son, Inc., markets industrial cleaning chemicals to government and business accounts. Recently some competitors have engaged in aggressive price discounting. A rebate proposal has been developed as a means to counteract competition. Several important decisions must be made within the next three weeks.

The final case in Part 4, J. W. Thornton, Ltd., concerns a British manufacturer and retailer of high-quality chocolate and sugar confectionery. Fluctuations in the fortunes of the company have made the board of directors aware that the company needs a longer-term strategy to give firmer direction to the business.

Applications

The Holly Farms Corp. application (4–11) provides an interesting analysis highlighting the difficulties of launching a new chicken product. Apex Chemical (4–12) presents a new-product introduction situation requiring a decision on which product(s) to introduce. The Tandy Corp. application (4–13) examines the potential impact of new technology on the market for recorded music. Apple Computer, Inc. (4–14), describes the firm's strategic focus under John Sculley's leadership. Supersonic Stereo, Inc. (4–15), presents a profitability analysis exercise in a field sales organization.

CASE 4–1

Zayre Corporation (B)

Soon after Mr. Maurice Segall became CEO of Zayre Corporation, . . . he instituted a number of changes which repositioned Zayre Corporation in its various marketplaces. Critical corrections were made quickly, but "without a bloodbath."

The entire retail environment shifted rapidly in 1978. As the Iranian revolution brought on a tripling of oil prices, rapid inflation and the highest interest rates in history hit the United States. Many discounters did not survive this difficult period. In 1978 there were over 65 discount chains with volumes over $100 million. Five years later, one-third of them did not exist. But Zayre's sales soared to $3.1 billion in 1985 with profits of $80.3 million (see Exhibit 1). Bradlee's, Caldor, and K mart moved toward higher-income customers. Zayre Stores stayed with its traditional customers and became one of the few successful chains selling to "center city" populations. Many such areas had strong ethnic preferences. As one Zayre executive said, "We had to solve the problem of maintaining the advantages of chain retailing, yet cater to the needs of individual locations, a really difficult task."

Case copyright © 1985 by James Brian Quinn. Research associate, Penny C. Paquette; research assistant, Barbara Dixon. The generous cooperation of the Zayre Corporation is gratefully acknowledged.

EXHIBIT 1

Zayre Corporation Financials: Selected Financial Data (dollars in thousands except per share amounts)

Fiscal Year Ended Last Saturday in January:	1985	1984	1983	1982	1981 (53 Weeks)
Summary of operations:					
Net sales	$ 3,123,008	$ 2,613,667	$ 2,139,616	$ 1,797,139	$ 1,594,235
Cost of sales, including buying and occupancy costs	2,372,467	1,986,559	1,616,889	1,361,753	1,209,179
Selling, general and administrative expenses	574,599	486,053	425,991	365,611	327,683
Interest costs:					
Debt	17,970	19,709	25,812	25,162	20,950
Capital leases	7,270	7,609	7,095	6,987	7,434
Total expenses	$ 2,972,306	$ 2,499,930	$ 2,075,787	$ 1,759,513	$ 1,565,246
Income before income taxes	$ 150,702	$ 113,737	$ 63,829	$ 37,626	$ 28,989
Provision for income taxes	70,386	52,311	28,653	15,479	11,415
Net income	$ 80,316	$ 61,426	$ 35,176	$ 22,147	$ 17,574
Number of common shares for earnings per share computations:					
Primary	20,108,771	19,254,852	16,286,334	14,335,790	13,795,560
Fully diluted	20,186,983	19,257,456	17,197,673	15,406,211	15,374,975
Net income per common share:					
Primary	$3.99	$3.19	$2.16	$1.53	$1.26
Fully diluted	$3.98	$3.19	$2.05	$1.46	$1.18

Stores in operation—end of year:					
Zayre Discount Department Stores	**290**	275	264	258	248
Hit or Miss	**401**	356	267	245	240
T.J. Maxx	**156**	118	86	64	43
Other financial data:					
Net income as a percent of sales	**2.57%**	2.35%	1.64%	1.23%	1.10%
Current assets	**$ 697,750**	$ 563,591	$ 449,246	$ 398,829	$ 347,646
Current liabilities	**381,006**	298,825	193,735	191,991	148,844
Working capital	**316,744**	264,766	255,511	206,838	198,802
Total assets	**1,108,889**	908,005	747,649	643,444	560,737
Long-term obligations, including capitalized leases	**217,824**	193,434	248,446	245,128	232,426
Shareholders' equity	**468,071**	395,457	294,762	199,232	174,110
Long-term debt-to-equity ratio, excluding capitalized leases	**.31 : 1**	.31 : 1	.58 : 1	.87 : 1	.90 : 1
Post-tax return on average equity	**18.60%**	17.80%	14.24%	11.86%	10.62%
Capital expenditures, excluding capitalized leases	**$ 98,518**	$ 76,279	$ 63,658	$ 54,914	$ 48,279
Number of common shares outstanding at year-end	**19,779,981**	17,953,297	8,393,173	5,411,615	5,209,166
Equity per common share	**$23.66**	$20.02	$15.96	$13.70	$12.39
Dividends per common share	**$ .39**	$ .27	$ .18	$ .15	$ .12

All per-share data and number of common shares for earnings-per-share computations reflect the 10% stock dividend paid May 31, 1984; the two-for-one stock split paid June 29, 1983; and the 20% stock dividend paid June 10, 1982.

Source: Zayre Corporation, Annual Report, 1984.

EXHIBIT 1 (*continued*)
Selected Information: Zayre Corp. Major Business Segments (in thousands)

Fiscal Year Ended:	January 26, 1985	January 28, 1984	January 29, 1983
Net sales:			
Discount department stores	$2,195,740	$1,902,146	$1,615,999
Specialty stores	927,268	711,521	523,617
	$3,123,008	$2,613,667	$2,139,616
Operating income:			
Discount department stores*	$ 122,246	$ 90,847	$ 55,059
Specialty stores	64,156	54,768	46,945
	$ 186,402	$ 145,615	$ 102,004
General corporate expense†	17,730	12,169	12,363
Interest expense	17,970	19,709	25,812
Income before income taxes	$ 150,702	$ 113,737	$ 63,829
Identifiable assets:			
Discount department stores	$ 744,630	$ 609,748	$ 555,268
Specialty stores	293,987	257,705	143,843
Corporate (cash and market- able securities)	70,272	40,552	48,538
	$1,108,889	$ 908,005	$ 747,649
Depreciation and amortization:			
Discount department stores	$ 28,754	$ 25,702	$ 24,371
Specialty stores	11,375	8,054	4,007
	$ 40,129	$ 33,756	$ 28,378
Capital expenditures:			
Discount department stores	$ 63,932	$ 43,848	$ 36,331
Specialty stores	34,586	32,431	27,327
	$ 98,518	$ 76,279	$ 63,658

* The discount department stores use the last-in first-out (LIFO) method of valuing hardgoods inventories. (See Note B to the consolidated financial statements for further information.)
† Expense in fiscal 1983 includes a $1.7 million reserve for certain notes receivable. In fiscal 1984 the company recovered $1 million of the amount reserved. The net results of the company's test of a new prototype, a wholesale warehouse outlet, are included in general corporate expense.

Source: Zayre Corporation, *Annual Report*, 1984.

EXHIBIT 1 (continued)
Zayre Corporation—Segment Information ($millions, except number of stores)

Fiscal Year Ending January:	1985	1984	1983	1982	1981	1980
Zayre Corporation						
Sales volume	3123	2614	2140	1797	1594	1550
Number of stores	847	749	620	567	531	528
Zayre Disct Dept Stores*						
Sales volume	2196	1902	1616	1433	1348	1345
Identified assets	745	610	555	506	463	443
Capital expenditures	64	44	36	41	41	37
Number of stores	290	275	264	258	248	254
Zayre Specialty Stores*						
Sales volume	927	712	524	364	246	205
Identified assets	294	258	144	115	61	41
Capital expenditures	35	32	27	14	8	4
Number of stores	557	474	353	309	283	274
T.J. Maxx	156	118	86	64	43	30
Hit or Miss	401	356	267	245	240	244

* Security analysts estimated that Zayre Stores units averaged about 72,000 ft^2 of space and had sales of about $8 million. They estimated T.J. Maxx averaged some 24,000 ft^2 and $5 million per unit, while Hit or Miss averaged only 3,500 ft^2 and $750,000 per unit.

Source: Zayre Corporation, *Annual Report*, 1984, 1983, 1981.

EXHIBIT 1 (*concluded*)
Store Locations—January 1985

State	Zayre Stores	T.J. Maxx	Hit or Miss	State	Zayre Stores	T.J. Maxx	Hit or Miss
Alabama	7	6	2	Mississippi	1	0	0
Arizona	0	0	3	Missouri	0	0	1
Colorado	0	3	7	Nebraska	0	1	0
Connecticut	5	8	12	New Hampshire	7	1	1
Washington, D.C.	0	0	2	New Jersey	0	5	32
Florida	63	11	19	New York	7	3	35
Georgia	14	4	12	North Carolina	10	6	7
Illinois	35	16	36	Ohio	17	16	25
Indiana	12	2	7	Oklahoma	0	1	3
Iowa	1	1	4	Pennsylvania	13	8	24
Kansas	0	1	0	Rhode Island	8	1	6
Kentucky	4	3	4	South Carolina	0	2	5
Louisiana	0	2	5	Tennessee	9	5	10
Maine	11	1	4	Texas	0	7	28
Maryland	8	0	12	Vermont	4	0	1
Massachusetts	35	14	38	Virginia	11	7	16
Michigan	2	15	25	West Virginia	0	0	2
Minnesota	0	2	7	Wisconsin	6	4	6
				Total	290	156	401

Source: Zayre Corporation, *Annual Report,* 1984.

BARRACUDAS OR FOSSILS

By 1983, Chicago was Zayre Stores' biggest market, and sales in the lower-middle income "southside" had grown from $25 million to $100 million in only five years. The original remodeling and upgrading budget for Zayre Stores had grown to $100 million. Change was constant during this period. As Malcolm Sherman, Zayre Stores president said, "If ever there was an industry that responds to Darwin's theory of survival of the fittest, it's retailing. A new retailer starts as a young barracuda, and can end up as a fossil 10 years later."

In this respect, off-price merchandising was to the early 1980s what discount stores had been to the 1960s and early 1970s. Off-price chains sprang up all over, specializing in women's apparel, family apparel, shoes, housewares, linens and domestics, and so on. These stores had a special appeal to the "white collar market" to whom brand names and styles were more important. T.J. Maxx boomed in its markets and by 1985 had become the second largest (to Marshall's $1.2 billion) retailer of off-price, brand name apparel in the United States according to *Standard & Poor's Corporate Descriptions,* December 1984. By 1985 the increased number of Maxx stores had called for a 300,000 ft^2 distribution center in Worcester, Mass., to supplement its original 450,000 ft^2 complex.

Although performance of off-price chains was highly variable, the best such chains achieved some $200 sales per square foot, with an 8–10 times inventory turnover, and net profits before taxes of 5 percent of sales. *Chain Store Age* estimated total off-price sales of some $17 billion by 1990. Unlike other retail trends started by entrepreneurs, the off-price chains all had big money behind them. U.S. Shoe, Melville, Dayton Hudson, and Zayre were among the big players. In addition to competing with more prestigious retailers such as Marshall Field and Lord & Taylor, off-price stores competed directly with the private brands sold by Sears, J.C. Penney, or Montgomery Ward—often made by the same manufacturers to the buyers' specifications. At first, buyers obtained off-price merchandise strictly from manufacturers' overruns, closeouts, returns, previous season's merchandise, irregulars (etc.). But increasingly, buyers could obtain excellent prices on large orders placed directly with manufacturers.

Hit or Miss had changed too. It now targeted mid-to-better-income females who wanted recognized merchandise at a lower price. It offered current season, first-quality women's sportswear (casual pants, shirts, blouses, etc.) and ready-to-wear dresses, coats, and suits in both brand names and private labels at about 50 percent off regular prices. (Reed Hunter was one of H or M's private labels.) The store focused on the somewhat conservative, youthful, professional, career-minded woman, who was very fashion conscious but had to watch costs. Although Hit or Miss had been "repositioned" extensively from 1978–85 and expanded to 356 units in 31 states, the chain seemed to lack a distinctive personality or loyal clientele and was still not a roaring success in 1985.

THE NEW ZAYRE

By 1985, Zayre Corporation had changed markedly. Even with Zayre's powerful recent growth and strong balance sheet (see Exhibit 1), Mr. Segall was still pointing for new horizons. His goal was a 20 percent per year compounded growth rate. Despite his easy-to-meet style and great personal charm, he was described by *Forbes* as "all business, clearly a workaholic, but he had to be to bring about such major changes [from 1978–84]. . . .

Clear thinking, tough decisions, well executed"[1] were said to be his hallmark. Mr. Segall described his style somewhat differently:

> I want growth in a disciplined fashion. . . . Everyone in this company knows what our goals are. We stand up once a year and I talk to 1,500 people—from mail clerks to executive VPs—and they know what our goals are. We don't keep secrets here. We continue to refine our mission statements, our target customers, and so on. We introduced three-year plans, which were tied to clear three-year income, sales, ROI, and operating objectives. . . . I don't want anything left to chance. I want us to be in control. All of us must execute the basics—not only with the highest of standards, but better than our competitors.
>
> We have business plans for each segment of the business which pull all these together in a consistent way. We have also developed extensive incentive plans tied directly to these. I believe in incentive plans. Everyone has incentive plans, but ours can be very generous (see Exhibit 2). Although I'm well paid, our key people can also make a lot of money, and we have made some millionaires. . . . I think that's great as long as the stockholder makes out better as a result.

Zayre's policy was to pay competitive base salaries, while putting significant emphasis on variable forms of compensation. The exact mix of salary, incentives, and other compensation varied, based upon the manager's organization level and job responsibilities. Three objectives underlay the Zayre compensation program: (1) to pay competitive basic and total compensation scales; (2) to reward exceptional individual performance, and (3) to ensure that the compensation program was cost effective by closely tying it to well-communicated business plans. Exhibit 2 summarizes Zayre's basic incentive plans.

In addition, Zayre used four types of long-term incentives to retain and reward its key executives: stock options, career shares, restricted stock, and long-term cash bonuses. Key executives could buy career shares for book value with a company-provided loan. Sale and conversion restrictions lapsed on these at 20 percent per year. A tax-free conversion to common shares could occur on this schedule at a predetermined exchange ratio. Zayre's Long Range Management Incentive Plan (LRMP) was a three-year cash incentive plan tied to company results for those who could influence intermediate-term performance. At the beginning of each three-year period, a three-year target was established for net income (75%) and net income/sales (25%) at divisional levels and net income (75%) and ROI (25%) at corporate levels. Incentives peaked sharply in a fashion similar to those set forth in Exhibit 2.

---

[1] "Making Money at the Low End of the Market," *Forbes,* December 17, 1984, p. 42.

Hits and Questions

While T.J. Maxx and Zayre Stores were growing and profitable in 1984–85, Hit or Miss still had problems. Mr. Segall said, "We're not executing properly there. We are currently struggling with the division's real mission. I'm still persuaded there is a market for our kind of store for the career-oriented young woman between 20 and 40. But we need a much better distinctive concept and better execution for our present target market. In 3,500 ft^2 you have very little room to make a statement, and we're making too many statements."

"In the case of T.J. Maxx, we're very pleased with the execution to date, but we're facing a different competitive environment. The T.J. Maxx concept was really designed eight or nine years ago. By definition, that design has to be obsolete now. The problem is how to position this excellent chain for the 1990s and execute that positioning effectively."

Other Ventures

By 1985, Zayre's management had begun to ask itself some very basic questions about the future. "Where do we go from here as a total corporation? What kind of company should we be in the 1990s? Should Zayre start some new ventures or acquire some? We started exploring a wide range of opportunities. When all was said and done we decided to take a crack at BJ's Wholesale Club, which was our version of the Price Club on the West Coast. But this is only the beginning."

Self service, cash-and-carry "wholesale clubs" (or warehouses) like BJ's offered a "limited membership" (of small businesses) access to name-brand goods at genuine wholesale prices. For an annual fee, a business could buy at posted wholesale prices. Noncommercial buyers could buy under a group membership which involved no annual fee, but required purchase prices 5 percent above posted prices. The key to wholesale club operations was abnormally low merchandise margins, extremely efficient operations, in a bare-bones, pseudo-warehouse environment. Mr. Segall noted, "In this kind of operation, there is no room for error. But the concept offers low prices and sound values; and that is what retailing is all about." Sumner Feldberg commented, "It isn't as if we are discovering America here; it happens to be a form of retailing developed over the course of the past few years with which some people have had great success. I'm very impressed with these operations by the remarkable volume they can generate." Sales per square foot of Price Club units were estimated at well over $500.

The Price Club in California had opened its first "wholesale club" warehouse store in 1976 and by 1983 grossed some $630 million and was widely imitated. (See Exhibit 3.) Experts thought this concept would grow to at

EXHIBIT 2
Zayre Corporation—Example Incentive Plans, 1985

Recipient	As Percent of Salary Target/Maximum	Performance Criteria	Below Goal Performance/ Award	Over Goal Performance/ Award	Administration
Store manager Assistant store manager	20%/100% 10%/40%	Controllable Income	99%/95% 98%/80% 95%/30% 90%/0	101%/104% 110%/140% 120%/180% Above = 6% for each 1% improvement	Adjusted for every 1% change in performance
Zone manager Zone merchandising manager Zone personnel manager	30%/45% 25%/50% 20%/40%	New income and NI/sales for zone and individual goals	Same as store managers	+6% for every 1% over goal until 110% perf. Then +8% per 1% change to 115% perf.	Award adjusted upward or downward by 6% of the target award per 1% var. in NI/sales vs. NI beyond a 5% range, but <2x target award. 50% in financial goal, 50% on individual.

Position						
Senior merchandising manager Buyer	21%/42% 15%/100%	Sales 25% + Gross profit 75% + Inventory levels	−16% per −1% sales variance, −11.1% per −1% gross profit variance	+16% per +1% sales variance, +11.1% per +1% gross profit variance	Sales award max 106% of goal. Gross profit award max 109% of goal. Adj. by −2.5% per +1% var. in year-end inventory goal if <5%. Max. penalty = 25%.
Zayre Stores division management: President Managers	32.5%/65% 15%/30%	85% 75% NI 25% NI/S 15% indiv. perf. goals	−5% per −1% NI below goal	+6⅔% per +1% NI above goal	Adjusted for NI/sales on same basis if <90% or >105% of goal. Adjusted by performance appraisal vs. individual goals.
Zayre corporate management	100%/115−120%	85% 75% NI 25% ROI 15% indiv. perf. goals	−5% per −1% NI below goal, −8⅓% per −1% of ROI goal	+5% per +1% NI above goal, +8⅓% per 1% ROI above goal	Awards apply outside ±3% limits on ROI. Adjusted by performance vs. individual goals.

Source: Company records.

EXHIBIT 3
Wholesale Membership Clubs: Comparative Data 1984

Company	Current Locations	Proposed Locations	Membership Policy	
			Wholesale	Retail
BJ's Wholesale Club (Zayre)	Hialeah, Fla. Medford, Mass. Johnston, R.I.	Hartford, Conn.	$30 annual fee—up to 2 additional memberships $10 each	5% markup
Club Wholesale (Elixir)	Boise, Idaho Las Vegas, Nev.	2 locations	$25 annual fee	5% markup
Costco	Anchorage, Alaska Clearwater, Fla. Fort Lauderdale Tampa Bay West Palm Beach Portland, Ore. Seattle (3) Spokane Tacoma Salt Lake City	Honolulu (10–12 units)	$25 annual fee	5% markup
Metro Cash & Carry of Illinois	Chicago (3)	No expansion plans	No fee	5% markup
Money's Worth	Greensboro, N.C.	1 in North Carolina	$25 annual fee	5% markup

Pace	Denver (2) Colorado Springs Tampa/St. Petersburg	Denver Tampa/St. Petersburg (2) Jacksonville Atlanta (3) Augusta Des Moines Omaha Greensboro, N.C. Raleigh Chattanooga Knoxville	$25 annual fee	5% markup
Price Club	Phoenix Mesa, Ariz. Tucson Los Angeles (5) Orange County, Calif. Sacramento (2) San Diego (4) San Francisco (2) Norfolk, Va. Richmond	Albuquerque	$25 annual fee	$15 fee +5% markup
Price Savers Wholesale Club	Anchorage, Alaska Salt Lake City Seattle Tacoma	Honolulu	$25 annual fee	5% markup
Sam's Wholesale Club (Wal-Mart)	Birmingham, Ala. Jacksonville, Fla. Kansas City, Mo. St. Louis Oklahoma City Charleston, S.C. Dallas (2) Houston (3)	Atlanta Wichita Louisville Tulsa Knoxville Memphis Nashville	$25 annual fee	5% markup

EXHIBIT 3 *(concluded)*

Company	Current Locations	Proposed Locations	Membership Policy	
			Wholesale	*Retail*
Warehouse Club (joint partnership W.R. Grace)	Chicago Akron Columbus Dayton Pittsburgh	Detroit	$25 annual fee	5% markup
Wholesale Club	Indianapolis Cleveland Milwaukee	Detroit (4) Cleveland	$30 annual fee	5% markup
Wholesale Plus	Fort Lauderdale	—	$25 annual fee	5% markup
Value Club	Austin El Paso San Antonio (3)	—	$25 annual fee	$5 fee +5% markup

Source: Reprinted by permission from *Chain Store Age Executive,* November 1984. Copyright © 1984 by Lebhar-Friedman, 425 Park Avenue, New York, NY 10022.

least \$20 billion by 1990.[2] Minimum volumes for early stores were \$25 million to \$30 million, but some units were selling annual volumes of over \$100 million. At first, estimates were that each store needed 400,000 to 600,000 people in its market area to be profitable, but this could drop as the concept caught on and operations were "debugged." A typical store operated on 10 to 11 percent merchandise margins and sold a major portion of its volume to smaller businesses, restaurants, groceries, drugstores, offices, etc. BJ's units opened with \$3 to \$4 million in inventory each and sought break-evens within one year. Most chains sought 60/40 business/group sales. BJ's Mervin Weich, an MIS data processing expert, noted that inventory turn-over goals would be some 16X per year—based on the Price Club experience. Parking for some 400 cars was *de rigueur*, with start-up costs of \$5 million to \$8 million per store being common. Most wholesale chain clubs targeted staffing levels per store at 70 to 200 people.

"Deep discounting" at 40 to 60 percent off suggested retail prices was also spreading rapidly in drug items, foods, auto parts, books, stationery, and so on. There were some 200 such units in 1985, but 1,000 were expected by 1990. They operated in 20,000 to 30,000 ft^2 formats with very restricted lines and inventories purchased mainly on "deals" from suppliers. Direct-mail selling was also growing at 10 to 15 percent per year. And Zayre was actively expanding its direct-mail operation, Chadwick's, begun in 1983. Sumner Feldberg said, "The first catalog effort was terrific and the customer response was excellent. But Chadwick's is primarily viewed as a means for the company to gain experience in mail order, something we have not been in before, as opposed to our long experience as chain-store operators."[3]

1985 COMPETITION

What did Zayre's main competitors look like in 1985?

Sears Roebuck.   With \$38.8 billion in sales, Sears was still the largest retailer by far with a continuing mission "to provide customers with more quality goods and services than any other organization of its kind." Sears sales consisted of \$29.5 billion in merchandise, \$9 billion Allstate Insurance, \$2.5 billion Dean Witter financial services, and \$1 billion from real estate and world trade activities. Sears had developed its "Store of the Future" concept with expanded product lines, more exciting displays and an emphasis on modernized and improved service levels at the point of sale. It had shifted its merchandise mix more to upscale apparel and home furnish-

---

[2] "Membership Retailing Trend Taking Off," *Chain Store Age Executive*, November 1984, p. 17.

[3] "Sumner Feldberg: Maxx-imizing Potential," *Chain Store Age Executive*, January 1984, p. 19.

ings, with relative deemphasis on hard-good lines. It was experimenting with smaller (8,000 to 30,000 ft²) stores to sell its own franchised products. Sears had also added some specialty stores (100 Business Centers and 4 Paint and Hardware Centers). Its total number of stores was down to 792 from 831 in 1982 with 391 full-line, 355 medium-line, and 52 hard-line stores.

K mart. Zayre's closest competitor was K mart with sales of $21.1 billion from 2,400 general merchandise discount stores and 1,120 specialty outlets. K mart discount stores operated in 48 states with an average 57,000 ft² format. Its stated strategy was "to provide a broader offering of brand names, larger assortment of high-value goods, and a more contemporary presentation of merchandise" because customers wanted better-quality merchandise at lower prices. Its customer mix had moved slightly upscale since 1977. K mart had diversified *within* retailing into: *Designer Depot*, an off-price family apparel chain following the Marshall's and T.J. Maxx format; *Waldenbooks*, at 900 stores and 5 discount units the largest book retailer in 50 states (acquired for $300 million and expected to sell $1 billion in 1990); *Builders Square*, large (80,000 ft²) warehouse home centers for contractors and do-it-yourselfers (15 outlets acquired for $88 million); *Pay-Less Drug Stores*, one of the largest retail drug chains (104 units plus discount outlets acquired for $500 million); *Financial Services*, available in 275 K marts with 1,000 projected by 1990; *Cafeterias*, 158 units in 2 chains expected to be $1 billion in sales by 1990; and *K mart Trading* for export of U.S.-made goods.

J.C. Penney. In metropolitan areas Penney's now had 564 department stores averaging 157,000 ft² representing 60 percent of its sales, and 205 soft-line stores having 7 percent of sales. It also had 801 small-town stores averaging 25,000 ft² (13 percent of sales), catalog sales (14 percent), and drug stores (14 percent). It was continuing to expand in fashions using its own designer labels and remodeling its stores accordingly. It was closing down its food, hardware, and car accessory departments.[4] Penney's financial services subsidiary, while still small and primarily involved in insurance sales (now through over 200 in-store centers), also operated the J.C. Penney National Bank and five Financial Centers in California. It had $22 million in net income.

Wal-Mart. Wal-Mart had grown to $4.7 billion in sales with 642 stores in 20 states. Its average store now had 50,000 ft² and plans called for 100 new stores in 1985. *Forbes* still showed Wal-Mart as first in its key financial return statistics (see Exhibit 4). Wal-Mart's basic strategy was

---

[4] "New Fangled Stores for Fussy Buyers: American Retailing," *Economist*, April 30, 1983.

EXHIBIT 4
Comparative Chain Performance

	K mart Corp.	Wal-Mart Corp.	Zayre Corp.
Sales ($ millions)			
FY ending 1/85	21,096	6,401	3,123
1/81	14,204	1,643	1,594
1/77	8,382	479	1,161
Net income ($ millions)			
FY ending 1/85	499	271	80
1/81	261	56	18
1/77	262*	16*	10*
Total assets ($ millions)			
FY ending 1/85	9,262	2,205	1,109
1/81	6,089*	592	561
1/77	3,983*	168*	435*
Merchandise inventory ($ millions)			
FY ending 1/85	4,588	1,104	603
1/81	2,846	280	296
1/77	1,738	89	211
Number of stores			
FY ending 1/85	3,365[c]	756[a]	847
1/81	2,327[c]	330	531
1/77	1,646	153	451[b]
Square feet of space (millions)			
FY ending 1/85	131.5[f]	41.9[d]	26.6[g]
1/81	114.5[c]	15.5	19.7
1/77	80.3	6.5	19.5

* Restated from original reported figures in later years' annual reports.
[a] 1984 figure includes 3 wholesale clubs; 1985 figure includes 11 clubs.
[b] Figures include On Stage/Nugent/Bell and Beaconway stores but exclude supermarkets and gas stations.
[c] Figures include shoe stores, Designer Depots, Waldenbooks, and Builders Square stores but exclude cafeterias.
[d] Figures include wholesale club space.
[e] Figures include only general merchandise space.
[f] Figures include both general merchandise and specialty store space.
[g] Rough estimates based on information provided in Annual Reports concerning Zayre Stores, Hit or Miss, and T.J. Maxx.

Source: Various years' Annual Reports for Wal-Mart Corp., K mart Corp., and Zayre Corp.

EXHIBIT 5
Selected Productivity Measures by Retailer Classification, 1983–1984

1983 Estimated Sales per Labor Hour*

	Total (105) %	Discount (17) %	Drug (18) %	Super-market (26) %	Depart-ment (18) %	Home Center (16) %	Specialty (10) %
Less than $25	8	—	6	4	6	6	40
$25–$50	24	29	28	12	33	25	20
$51–$75	15	18	22	4	6	31	20
$76–$100	19	12	17	42	11	6	10
$101+	5	6	—	12	—	6	—
Refused comment	13	12	6	15	17	19	10
Don't know/no answer	16	24	22	12	28	6	—
(MEAN)	$(60.3)	(61.1)	(55.5)	(80.2)	(48.6)	(57.5)	(40.9)

1983 Estimated Sales per Net Square Foot*

	Total (78) %	Discount (14) %	Drug (14) %	Super-market (10) %	Depart-ment (27) %	Home Center (6) %	Specialty (7) %
Less than $50	8	—	14	40	—	—	—
$51–$100	13	36	7	—	7	33	—
$101–$150	28	29	29	—	41	17	29
$151–$200	15	14	21	—	18	17	14
$201–$250	5	—	7	10	4	17	—
$251–$300	3	—	—	10	4	—	—
$301–$350	—	—	—	—	—	—	—

	Total (83) %	Discount (13) %	Drug (19) %	Super-market (16) %	Depart-ment (13) %	Home Center (11) %	Specialty (11) %
$351–$400	—	—	—	—	—	—	—
$401+	5	7	—	10	—	—	29
Refused comment	14	14	7	20	11	17	29
Don't know/no answer	9	—	14	10	15	—	—
(MEAN)	(151.5)	(139.6)	(127.7)	(158.6)	(145.0)	(135.0)	(265.0)

1983 Estimated Sales per Gross Square Foot*

	Total (83) %	Discount (13) %	Drug (19) %	Super-market (16) %	Depart-ment (13) %	Home Center (11) %	Specialty (11) %
Less than $50	10	—	5	38	—	—	9
$50–$100	13	23	5	—	15	46	—
$101–$150	24	46	37	6	23	9	27
$151–$200	11	—	21	—	8	18	9
$201–$250	4	—	10	6	8	—	—
$251–$300	2	—	5	—	—	—	9
$301–$350	4	8	5	—	—	—	18
$351–$400	2	—	—	—	—	—	9
$401+	5	—	—	12	—	9	18
Refused comment	17	15	5	19	31	18	—
Don't know/no answer	8	8	5	19	15	—	—
(MEAN)	(160.8)	(130.0)	(161.2)	(159.0)	(132.1)	(144.4)	(235.0)

* For chains using this system.

Source: *Chain Store Age Executive*, September, 1984. Reprinted by permission of *Chain Store Age Executive*. Copyright 1984 by Lebhar-Friedman, 425 Park Avenue, New York, NY 10022.

EXHIBIT 6

Sales and Earnings for Quarter Ended in September or October

	Sales ($ millions)		Percent Change
	1984	1983	
Chain—General Merchandise			
Sears[1]	$6,463	$6,190	4.4%
K mart	4,993	4,331	15.3
J.C. Penney	3,211	2,914	10.2
Federated	2,266	2,071	9.4
Dayton Hudson	1,868	1,659	13.0
Woolworth	1,404	1,353	3.8
Wal-Mart	1,584	1,167	36.0
May	1,133	1,003	13.0
Macy	1,011	929	8.8
ADG	951	905	5.0
Allied	932	883	5.5
CHH[2]	906	758	20.0
Zayre	777	659	17.8
Supermarkets and Convenience Stores			
Safeway	4,584	4,300	6.6
Kroger	4,623	4,505	2.6
Southland	3,085	2,430	26.9
Lucky	2,191	2,027	8.1
Winn-Dixie	1,732	1,648	5.1
A&P[3]	1,377	1,192	15.5
Drug Chains			
Walgreen	684	595	15.0
Jack Eckerd	637	543	17.3
Revco	511	453	12.6
Longs	328	291	12.7
Specialty Stores			
Melville	1,066	985	8.2
Tandy	596	583	2.1
U.S. Shoe	416	375	10.9
Limited	349	271	29.0
Toys "R" Us	322	221	45.7
Edison[4]	269	249	7.8
Zale	217	198	9.6

[1] Sears Merchandise Group sales only. Operating profits from this group amounted to $163.8 million, or a 3.1% increase over the $158.9 million of a year earlier.

[2] Actual earnings increased 59%. Earnings per share declined because of actions taken by CHH to fight off a takeover attempt by Limited Inc.

[3] Before extraordinary credits in both years.

[4] Without a nonrecurring after-tax gain from the sale of Handyman Store properties in Texas and Oklahoma, earnings per share would have been 73¢ in the 1984 quarter, a 28.8% decrease.

Source: *Chain Store Age Executive*, January 1985. Reprinted by permission of *Chain Store Age Executive.* Copyright 1985 by Lebhar-Friedman, 425 Park Avenue, New York, NY 10022.

unchanged, but it had moved into 11 wholesale clubs in 1985, opened its first drug discount store, and was testing a 25,000 ft^2 format for even smaller towns.

The Second Cluster

Among the second cluster of discounters, variety and diversity were most notable. Gemco-Memco stores in California grossed an amazing $23 million per store, including foods. And Target Stores owned by Dayton Hudson averaged $12 million per store. Elsewhere there were numerous local "pi-perack retailers" who could be successful for short periods of time by selling what the industry considered "schlock" merchandise. These units were very successful in specific locations, but Zayre was distinctly differentiated from these, and was by far the most successful chain with minority customers in the central cities of the United States. See Exhibits 4, 5, and 6 for some comparative data on various chains.

WHERE IS THE FUTURE?

Retailing would undoubtedly undergo many more changes in the late 1980s. See Exhibit 7 for data on some selected trends. Key executives at Zayre added some broad perspectives on how these might fit into their company's future.

Mr. Segall said, "We're all going to have to be sensitive to the extraordinary acceleration in the birth, growth, maturity, and decline cycle of American retailers. The pace is just incredible. The old-line retailer is gone, and today's successful patterns will be tomorrow's disasters. For us any aspect of retailing is fair game. The only thing we preclude is nonretail—no steelmaking, no broadcasting. Retailing will always be one of the largest business segments in our economy."

But excess capacity and market saturation was a real problem as each major company continued to expand. By 1985 retailing was characterized by "intertype marts with a pharmacy in the rear. Grocery stores carried both pharmacy and general merchandise items. Sears had moved out into financial services, as had K mart and some J.C. Penney units. And so on. Meanwhile specialized flea markets, off-price catalogs, house-to-house selling, party plans, and telemarketing were expanding at wild rates. And specialized discount retailers—such as Toys "R" Us and Bata (shoes)—were establishing a clear presence in their markets.

In March 1985, Mr. Segall noted, "One of the most exciting developments in U.S. retailing in 50 years is the potential purchase by Americans of $100s of billions worth of electronics in the years to come. Increased household formations, a bulge in the educated 25–45-year-old group, more use of the home as an entertainment base, the growth of cable communica-

EXHIBIT 7 Trends in Retailing

Sales by Store Classification (yearly sales in $ millions)

Type of Store	1972	1976	1977	1979	1980	1981	1982	1983
Food store	100718	144912	157941	195710	219399	242763	268352	278427
Supermarket	93298	134534	147758	183860	206121	227756	252094	261732
Eating/drinking establishment	36885	56852	63276	76751	87310	96417	107484	118935
General merchandise store	65065	94748	93948	112400	123157	135518	139654	147354
Department store	51056	75247	76965	93620	106698	111561	115969	120686
Appliance/accessory store	24741	36796	35564	43103	44999	48849	50593	54648
Furniture/home furnishing/appliance store	22534	34790	33177	40823	44162	47124	46105	52188
Furnishing/home furnishing store	14059	21239	20320	25049	26627	28754	27725	30895
Automotive dealer	90029	123417	149952	175508	169808	182841	172669	203052
Gasoline service station	33655	47513	56468	72122	93801	103447	107540	107978
Building materials/hardware store	23844	33081	38859	50506	49381	53818	52711	59410
Drugstore	15599	21529	23198	28668	31986	34075	37232	39124
Total retail sales	459031	661749	723134	887519	965746	1056107	1100750	1186387
Effective Buying Income		1176240		1618643	1814167			2329210

Sales by Product Classification (yearly sales in $ millions)

Product	1972	1976	1977	1979	1980	1981	1982	1983
Men's/boys' clothing	14999	22161	23057	26854	29656	32417	33497	35743
Women's/girls' clothing	25923	38110	37055	46278	47612	52052	53758	57502
Footwear	7677	11348	10941	13762	14120	15336	15916	17026
Audio equipment/musical instruments/supplies			9575		12733	13696	13718	15172
Television	8174	12291	4386	15014	5834	6296	6327	6952
Major household appliances	7341	11022	9565	13661	12773	13816	14019	15210
Health and beauty aids			11593		15813	17171	18407	19367
Drugs	15660	22021	12703	29175	17475	18710	20257	21362
Total Retail Sales	459031	661749	723134	887519	965746	1056107	1100750	1186387

Source: Compiled from Sales and Marketing Management, *Survey of Buying Power Data Service,* various years.

tion, new technologies, home computers, etc., mean this is the largest single-growth category in U.S. retailing." Marketing Science Institute estimated that home appliance, radio, TV, and electronic store sales would grow from $12 billion in 1980 to $52 billion in 1990.

All of these opportunities were being eyed by well-heeled, well-managed, aggressive, large corporations looking for new entries. Mr. Segall said, "Never before have so many professionals surveyed so many new kinds of developments, ready to pounce on the attractive ones with huge war chests for financing." But each new retailing approach was also reaching maturity faster than ever before, creating ever greater pressure for precise timing, positioning, and care in choosing what directions to pursue.

Macro-Trends

J. Sheth in the *Journal of Retailing* cited other macro trends in the field:

1. The United States was becoming a very affluent, diverse, adult-oriented society with highly individualistic life-styles in which time—rather than money—had become the scarce resource.

2. Competition in retailing was becoming more global in both sourcing and distribution. And a changing focus toward deregulation was allowing very large oligopolistic companies to exploit this trend.

3. The single middle-class U.S. society was becoming more a dual class, 25 percent affluent and 60 to 70 percent average-income society whose basic functional needs were easily met; demand was shifting to psychological satisfactions in products over sheer functionality—to wants over needs.

4. With the emergence of nontraditional households with dual or multiple incomes, more goods were being demanded at individualistic, rather than shared levels—with foods, leisure items, clothing, and services all being heavily affected.

5. For demographic and technological reasons, it would be increasingly common not to separate the time and place of work, home, and shopping activities.

6. As technology dropped the relative price of many appliances, the distinction between shopping goods and convenience goods would blur, and customers would increasingly depend on manufacturers as their guarantors of quality.[5]

Another source referred to these trends as "life-style retailing" tailored to the life-styles of specific target markets, rather than "supplier-driven" retailing. Demographically, the 35 to 45-year-old population and the over-80 population were growing most in percentage terms, while the under-20 group was falling in the late 1980s. This bulge represented the best-edu-

---

[5] J. Sheth, "Emerging Trends for the Retailing Industry," *Journal of Retailing,* Fall 1983, p. 6.

cated, most affluent, and culturally diverse population in U.S. history. During the past 10 years the black U.S. population had grown 17 percent and the Hispanic population had grown 61 percent.[6] But Mr. Stanley Feldberg pointed out that there were strongly divergent regional and local trends. For example, the Northeast industrial investment and production base had radically declined and its relative working population had decreased. But the emergence of new companies and service industries—and transfer payments by governments—had given Zayre strong Northeastern sales even in areas where major shutdowns had occurred. He observed, "Our total marketplace is so complex and rapidly changing that we must be constantly ready to adapt to new modes of retailing and specific customer needs as they develop. I doubt that we—or anyone else—can analyze now exactly what the customer will want and what new retailing structures will provide in the early 1990s."

The Retail Revolution

The Retail Revolution cited other powerful trends. Mass advertising and computerized technologies seemed to provide such overwhelming advantages to large retailers that its authors thought that—with few exceptions—the small independent retailer could soon be doomed. Both forces tend to create enormous barriers to entry and to affect margins so substantially that large scale becomes a prerequisite to competitiveness. Large-scale and high technologies were already affecting employment skill levels, management sophistication, and organizational and cost structures in profound ways—and were likely to be more important in the future. Government policies originally designed to protect small retailers through resale-price-maintenance agreements (allowing producers to fix retail prices on their goods) and Robinson-Patman regulations (producers must be able to justify price differences to customers on the basis of differential costs) had perversely created the very price umbrellas that made bigness possible and indeed essential. All these forces had significantly impacted both the supplier and distribution structure of the retail industry. *The Retail Revolution* ends with a query as to whether these forces will lead in the next 15 years to a point where "a handful of mammoth corporations will be left to constitute the distributive network in the nation. . . . Behind the glitter and glamour of modern department stores is a saga of dramatic change and adaptation that we are only beginning to comprehend."[7]

---

[6] Blackwell and Talarzyk, "Life-Style Retailing: Competitive Strategies for the 1980s," *Journal of Retailing,* Winter 1983.

[7] Bluestone, et al., *The Retail Revolution.* Boston: Auburn House Publishing Co., 1981.

ZAYRE IN THE FUTURE

As Mr. Segall looked to the future he said, "Zayre is almost 30 years old, a maturing young company in its prime. I have tried hard to generate a spirit in the company about itself and the future. This business is all people, and I have a lot of confidence in the people in this company. For the outside world, I only state a few objectives. One is that we are intent on achieving a 20 percent profit growth per year for many years to come. We intend to keep saying that and to posture ourselves accordingly. Our second goal is the image and reality of a well-administered organization and a thoughtful merchant. We must not ever rest on our laurels, but continue to progress with our customers and markets—and to administer competently. The next 5 to 10 years at Zayre will be exciting, interesting, and challenging. That I can promise you."

Appendix A—Some Organizational Terms in Retailing

Merchandising embraces the entire group of decisions and tasks involved in determining what merchandise is offered, acquiring it, and having it available in the right assortments at the right places to maximize the store's marketing objectives. In many retail operations, merchandising includes the functions of buying, receiving, marketing, and handling all merchandise as well as controlling inventory levels and mixes in the stores. In some large or complex chains, some of these activities may be split off as specialized functions or be decentralized regionally.

Buying is a major line activity in retailing. Buying decisions include what merchandise should be purchased, in what quantities, at what prices, under what terms, and when it should be purchased and received. In some stores the buyer also determines prices, markups, markdowns and closeouts, and plans and coordinates a department's special sales. Buying can be organized according to the class of merchandise purchased, store type, or location served. In most department stores buyers are in charge of all merchandising for their particular departments as well as directing the sales forces in these departments. In some decentralized operations, buying and local sales force management may be separated.

Operations includes all those activities necessary to maintain the quality and appearance of the physical facilities of the enterprise. In some highly decentralized retail concerns, these activities—as well as supervision and control of local salepeople and inventory-handling functions—are the responsibility of Operations. Service and support activities locally may report either to Operations or directly to other centralized line or administrative functions.

Sales is the face-to-face presentation of the product to the customer and the first recording of that transaction on the store's books through the cash register, sales slip, or electronic charge system. In some cases, salespeople report to the buying or merchandise heads; in others they are separated from these functions and report either through Operations or a centralized sales unit.

Promotion generally includes advertising, publicity, displaying of merchandise, and any tactics (other than merchandise selection and pricing) which will induce profitable sales volume. Special attraction techniques such as store signs, catalogs, premiums, trading stamps, and nonrecurring interest breaks are considered promotions. Store layout, design, traffic flow planning, rack displays, wall and floor coloring, lighting presentations, etc. are important aspects of in-store promotion which clearly impact the effectiveness of all other line activities.

Case 4–2

Seanav Corporation

Paul Wilson was elated. He had just received word that Seanav Corporation had been granted $30,000 in start-up funds from the federal government. This, along with the financing supplied by the founders, would enable the firm to survive until Seanav received a further injection of capital from its private investors.

Wilson was convinced that Seanav had unmatchable engineering strength and a head start on its potential competition. Private investors had also expressed interest in the newly formed high-technology company. It seemed certain that Seanav would now become a viable firm in the marine electronics industry. Its product was navigation equipment that gave a ship's position with greater accuracy than had been previously available. The equipment was also usable worldwide—a significant advantage over earlier systems.

The initial feedback from the accounting firm assisting Seanav in obtaining funding was also good. The detailed (130-page) business plan that had been developed over the last four months had enabled the accounting firm to develop a financial model of the company covering the next seven years. The problems with the business plan were in the market analysis; there was a great deal of detail, but Seanav's marketing strategy was not

This case was written by D. Joseph Irvine, University of Ottawa, Ottawa, Ontario, Canada, under the supervision of Roger C. Bennett, Associate Professor, McGill University, and David S. Litvack, Assistant Professor, University of Ottawa, Ottawa, Ontario, Canada. It is based upon the activities of a Canadian corporation. Names and some data are disguised. Reprinted by permission.

clear. Paul realized he had to reexamine the market information and develop a concise and realistic market plan, within the next week, in time for meeting with the accounting firm and potential investors. Paul sat back to review the market information before calling a meeting of his board of directors.

THE COMPANY

Born as an idea in the minds of a couple of engineers, Seanav was incorporated in August 1983. On the basis of the expertise of one of the principals, an exhaustive business plan was developed that encompassed the engineering, marketing, and administrative aspects of the company for a seven-year period. By early January 1984, it had become apparent that Seanav had a great deal of potential. On the basis of favorable reactions to the business plan by a major accounting firm, Seanav was able to open offices and a research laboratory in a high-tech industrial park.

The board of directors of Seanav consisted of three engineers and a lawyer. Mike Ruby was an aerospace engineer with 10 years of experience with navigation systems. Ruby had been involved in new-product development in the high-technology areas of the electronics industry, both as a product manager and, more recently, as the president of a marketing and engineering consulting firm. Ruby's entrepreneurial skills had been utilized by a number of international firms both in North America and in Europe. He acted as the marketing consultant for Seanav.

Louis Hurteau had over 25 years of engineering experience in the avionics and electronics industries; his main area of expertise was in systems analysis and design. As vice president of engineering, Hurteau was responsible for all engineering operations and program planning for Seanav.

John Richardson was a lawyer whose practice had focused on small and medium-size businesses for the purpose of patents and trademarks, taxation, letters of incorporation, and shareholder's agreements. Richardson's experience in the private sector would assist him in his role as secretary/treasurer of Seanav.

Wilson, the company's president, was a physicist with eight years of experience in the design and engineering of navigation systems. Wilson had been a key participant in several high-technology engineering projects, both in North America and Europe.

THE NAVIGATION INDUSTRY

Electronic navigation systems had become standard by the early 1980s because they provided clear economic and safety benefits to their users. The most evident economic benefit of an accurate navigation system was the fuel savings generated. An efficient navigation system reduced fuel consumption by allowing for frequent or continuous position fixing, thereby enabling the most direct route to be followed. In 1983 and 1984, fuel management packages were being developed to utilize continuous position-fixing data from satellites.

Another economic benefit of navigation systems was the time savings resulting from efficient route utilization and increased precision in position fixing. Additional economic benefits resulting from precise, all-weather navigation information reduced risk of environmental pollution (caused by collisions, etc.).

Navigation and positioning systems provided a number of safety benefits. It was, however, difficult to quantify the dollar savings resulting from these benefits. As transportation traffic increased, there was a greater need for accurate navigation and positioning information. This would facilitate traffic control and decrease the risk of collision. As the need to minimize costs and to capture economies of scale in the transportation business grew, the size of the craft increased and its maneuverability decreased. Accurate positioning information was required to compensate for this disadvantage. In the marine transportation sector, hazardous cargoes (oil, gas, chemicals, etc.) were being carried in greater volumes. Casualties (such as collision, grounding, and ramming) involving these vessels posed grave dangers to the environment and the public. Increased accuracy in navigation systems would offset this growing risk of environmental damage.

Historically, vessel navigation was performed by observing its course, or heading, relative to physical references. These references took the form of the heavenly bodies (such as Polaris and the sun) and the magnetic field of the earth. During the eighteenth and nineteenth centuries, worldwide navigation became possible through the use of sextants, chronometers (for longitude), and magnetic compasses. By estimating the direction and speed of the ocean current, the velocity of the vessel through the water, and the heading of the vessel relative to magnetic or true north, the captain could dead reckon his position with acceptable accuracy for deep ocean navigation. As ports and sea lanes became more congested, the importance of having more accurate information became apparent. In particular, the need to know true headings became vital.

The development of the ship's gyrocompass in the early 20th century was thus of such importance to the safety of the merchant fleet that many ships equipped themselves with the system immediately. By the 1980s, most vessels had an electromechanical gyrocompass providing a continuous indication of true heading of the vessel on a continuous basis, and free of the anomalies and inconsistencies of traditional heading determination techniques.

Modern vessels still relied upon gyrocompasses for heading determination, and many high-value vessels contained two for reliability. At a cost of many tens of thousands of dollars per system, these electromechanical devices were still deemed necessary for navigation and control purposes.

Because of the self-contained nature of gyrocompasses, it was not possible to standardize and regulate their use. Hence, models had proliferated over the preceding 40 years, and this form of navigation system became the most widely accepted for merchant-marine applications.

Many other navigation aids had been developed over the years in order to make transportation systems safer and more efficient, and to improve the overall effectiveness of military operations. This section discusses the major systems in order to set the stage for an introduction to the NAVSTAR Global Positioning System.

The OMEGA system was established to meet U.S. Department of Defense requirements for a worldwide general navigation capability. The system consisted of eight transmitting stations situated around the world. The system provided information that allowed a ship or other vessel to pinpoint its location with an accuracy of between two to four miles, depending on location, the selection of the stations in current use, the validity of the correction through propagation delay and the time of day of operation. It was doubtful that OMEGA would be accepted as a primary navigational aid in domestic air traffic systems, because the accuracy would not provide navigation precise enough for narrow lanes.

LORAN C was a system that was developed to provide the Department of Defense with a capability for greater range and accuracy. As with most radionavigation systems, LORAN C was developed by the Department of Defense but had found widespread acceptance with commercial users (more than 160,000 in maritime applications). The range of operations was limited to the U.S. coast, the continental United States, and selected overseas areas.

TRANSIT was the major existing satellite navigation system in use in 1983. The system was originally conceived to provide accurate navigation updates to U.S. Navy ships' navigation systems. But by the early 1980s, TRANSIT was a widely used commercial system as well (commercial users constituted 85 percent of the total user community). The system used six satellites placed in low polar orbits. Because the relative motion between the satellite and the user was used to determine position, users had to know their own speed relative to the earth's surface. The main disadvantage of TRANSIT was the time required to establish a low-quality position solution. The process took six minutes; thus, the user who moved a significant distance during those six minutes tremendously reduced the accuracy. TRANSIT provided worldwide coverage, but this coverage was periodic, and the interval between positional fixes could be as much as 90 minutes. The Department of Defense planned to totally phase out TRANSIT, beginning in 1987 and ending possibly as early as 1992. This would have a major impact on civil marine users, of which over 50,000 operated TRANSIT receivers.

THE NAVSTAR/GPS PROGRAM

In the early 1970s the Department of Defense recognized the need for a global, common-grid positioning and navigation system to increase both the availability of current weapon systems and their accuracy (particularly during adverse weather or at night). In response to these needs, the NAVSTAR program was in full-scale development, with the initiation of production of 18 satellites by Rockwell International (see Exhibit 1). (NAVSTAR was the program's initial name; later, it became more generally referred to as the Global Positioning Service [GPS].)

A competitive posture was taken by the department for the development and production of NAVSTAR user equipment. It was recognized as early as 1973 that continuation of the NAVSTAR program would depend largely on the availability of accurate but inexpensive user equipment.

In 1982 the Pentagon announced that NAVSTAR's signals would be available at an accuracy level of 100 meters instead of the previously announced 500 meters. This revised policy would attract thousands of civil users worldwide, as the civilian GPS would now meet all published civil navigation requirements except precision aircraft landing and maritime harbor entry.

Furthermore, as a result of the Korean Air Lines incident in September 1983, the president of the United States announced that NAVSTAR satellite signals would be made available free of charge to the worldwide naviga-

EXHIBIT 1
NAVSTAR satellite constellation

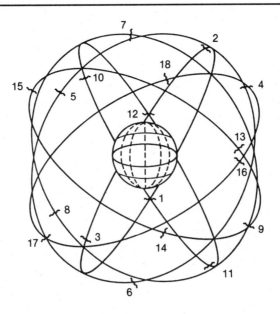

EXHIBIT 2
Navigation Systems Features*

Feature	LORAN C	OMEGA	TRANSIT	NAVSTAR/GPS
Predictable accuracy	0.25 NM	2–4 NM	500 m	25 m horizontal 30 m vertical
Repeatable accuracy	18–19 m	2–4 NM	50 m	25 m horizontal 30 m vertical
Relative accuracy	18–19 m	1–2 NM	38 m	10 m horizontal 8 m vertical
Fix rate	25/sec	1/10 sec	30–100 min	Continuous
Coverage	U.S. coast and selected areas	Near global (90%)	Worldwide (noncontinuous)	Globally continuous
Availability	99+%	99%	99% (when satellite in view)	99%

* Compiled from the Federal Radionavigation Plan (March 1982).

tion community to avert future airspace violations as a result of navigation error.

The value or utility of navigational signals depends on a number of technical and operational criteria, of which coverage and positional accuracy are the most evident to the user. Exhibit 2 lists the features of the LORAN C, OMEGA, TRANSIT, and NAVSTAR/GPS navigation systems. Although no one system met all the accuracy requirements of all navigation users, NAVSTAR/GPS was clearly the optimal system. The continuous coverage and fix rate of GPS, along with its increased accuracy, ensured that NAVSTAR would meet or exceed the requirements of most users.

The long-term growth prospects for the NAVSTAR market were excellent. It was expected that NAVSTAR would be adopted as a navigation system at a rate similar to that observed for the adoption, by civilian users, of TRANSIT. Exhibit 3 displays the growth in commercial users of the TRANSIT system. In 1983, the TRANSIT market was still growing exponentially, and there was no indication that this growth would slow in the near future. A similar growth curve or rate of adoption for NAVSTAR technology was forecast for the following decade. The Department of Defense had conservatively projected that the world marine market for NAVSTAR would grow to 10,000 users by 1990 and 20,000 users by 2000, and would reach 80,000 users by the year 2020. NAVSTAR industry experts believed that realistic estimates would be three to four times those figures.

EXHIBIT 3
Growth of TRANSIT System Users (1974–1982)

Year	Number of users
1974	600
1975	860
1976	2,399
1978	5,820
1980	16,255
1982	45,555

The federal radionavigation plan (FRP) outlined plans and policies for the federal government's radionavigation services. The FRP reflected the unique combination of responsibilities of the Department of Transport and the Department of Defense: public safety, transport economy, and national security. The plan covered government-operated systems having a high degree of common use (either military/civil or between different transportation modes). The radionavigation systems discussed included OMEGA, LORAN C, TRANSIT, and NAVSTAR/GPS.

The FRP focused on three aspects of planning: the efforts to improve existing systems, the development required to improve existing systems, and the ability of existing and proposed radionavigation systems to meet future needs. The FRP included extensive descriptions of existing radionavigation systems and requirements. The plan also included criteria to be used in, and the process for, selecting future radionavigation systems. It stated that a national radionavigation policy should "make NAVSTAR/GPS continuously available on an international basis for civil and commercial use at the highest level of accuracy consistent with national security interests." It also included the following statements about the future of existing radionavigation systems:

1. The Department of Defense currently uses LORAN C; however, this use will phase down as NAVSTAR/GPS becomes operational.
2. The military use of OMEGA will be phased out by the Army and the Air Force by 1992. The Navy intends to re-evaluate its use of OMEGA . . . when NAVSTAR/GPS becomes fully operational.
3. Phase-out by military TRANSIT users in favor of NAVSTAR/GPS is planned to begin in 1987 and end in 1992.

Although the military would begin the phase-out of LORAN C and other navigation systems as NAVSTAR/GPS became operational, civilian use of these systems would be dependent on the cost of the user equipment.

The FRP made the following statements about future civilian use of existing navigation systems:

1. The LORAN C system for coastal areas is expected to continue in operation at least until the year 2000.
2. OMEGA has been certified by the FAA for use on the North Atlantic by several airlines.
3. Commercial vessel use of the TRANSIT system has far outpaced Department of Defense use.
4. The degree of NAVSTAR/GPS acceptance for civil use will be especially sensitive to the successful design of low-cost user equipment.

THE MARINE MARKET

The world marine fleet consisted of three major categories of ships: the merchant marine fleet, the coastal vessel fleet, and pleasure craft. Exhibit 4 shows the five-year fleet forecasts for each of these categories. The merchant marine fleet, which included tankers, bulk (and other) carriers, and cargo vessels, operated under all-weather conditions and in all four phases of marine navigation (open ocean, coastal, inland waterways, and harbors). This class of vessel was larger than 100 gross registered tons (grt). The coastal vessel fleet included fishing and work boats of less than 100 grt. These vessels operated in coastal waters, harbors, and inland waterways,

EXHIBIT 4
World Marine Fleet Forecasts

Vessel Class	Thousands of Vessels (1988)	Average Annual Growth Rate
Merchant fleet: Large commercial ships (>100 grt)*	80	1–2%
Coastal vessel fleet: light commercial ships (<100 grt)	1,300	2–3%
Recreational vessels: yachts and pleasure craft	27,000	2–3%
Total world marine fleet	28,300	2%

* The merchant marine fleet consisted of large commercial vessels over 100 grt. This included tankers, bulk carriers, and cargo ships. Exhibit 5 lists these vessels and their numbers as of mid-1982.

mainly during acceptable weather conditions. The recreational fleet included yachts and small boats that could operate in all phases of marine navigation under good or acceptable weather conditions.

Merchant Fleet

The merchant marine fleet consisted of large commercial vessels over 100 grt. This included tankers, bulk carriers, and cargo ships. Exhibit 5 lists these vessels and their numbers as of mid-1982.

Navigation equipment could be purchased when a ship was being constructed, or it could be retrofitted. When a vessel costing tens of millions of dollars was ordered, the difference in price between the standard navigation

EXHIBIT 5
World Merchant Fleet by Ship Type*

Vessel Type	Number	Gross Registered Tonnage
Oil tankers	7,021	166,828,416
Liquified gas carriers	722	8,785,230
Chemical tankers	774	2,963,886
Miscellaneous tankers (trading)	128	279,669
Bulk/oil carriers		
(including ore/oil carriers)	418	26,030,013
Ore and bulk carriers	4,529	93,268,040
General cargo ships:		
Single deck	11,005	19,579,023
Multi-deck	11,237	59,898,492
Passenger/cargo ships	245	1,064,225
Container ships (fully cellular)	718	12,941,690
Lighter carriers	34	809,358
Vehicle carriers	245	2,485,130
Fish factories and carriers		
(including canneries)	866	3,672,380
Fishing (including factory trawlers)	21,081	9,363,785
Ferries and passenger vessels	3,526	7,684,483
Supply ships and tenders	1,687	1,276,423
Tugs	6,939	2,106,708
Dredgers	721	1,428,918
Livestock carriers	106	370,593
Icebreakers	94	423,722
Research ships	596	696,358
Miscellaneous (nontrading)	2,459	2,785,140
Totals	75,151	424,741,682

* Ships of 100 grt and over as of mid-1982.

Source: Compiled from *Lloyd's Register of Shipping Statistical Tables* (1982).

equipment and state-of-the-art equipment was negligible and could readily be justified in terms of the "new construction" budget. The retrofit decision, however, required that the purchase be justified over and above the current navigation equipment, and it required that the funds be removed from the owner's operations budget.

It could be quite difficult to convince a financial manager that a ship that had been navigating safely for years now required a capital outlay of $30,000 to ensure that it navigated safely in the future. Therefore, the "new construction" or shipbuilding segment of the merchant fleet was the most likely candidate for state-of-the-art navigation equipment.

There were other reasons why the most likely candidates for a NAV-STAR maritime set acquisition were ships under construction. The merchant market was resistant to innovation; as a result, many shipowners would wait until NAVSTAR had proven itself in other commercial applications before considering its installation. The combination of the total construction cost and the lead time required prior to launch allowed for state-of-the-art technology to be used in navigation systems purchase. In late 1983 the world merchant fleet was growing at a rate of about 1 percent per year. However, this growth rate was expected to increase by 1986 or 1987, when a post-recession shipbuilding boom was expected. This increase would be particularly noticeable in the tanker fleet. The shipbuilding market represented the largest single segment of the merchant market. Summarizing this analysis, Exhibit 6 indicates the possible total market for NAVSTAR equipment over the 10-year forecast period.

Aside from the inceased accuracy and coverage of NAVSTAR, a $30,000 receiver could replace the systems currently in use. Its price in 1979 was $91,000.

Coastal Fleet

The coastal vessel fleet consisted of light commercial vessels of less than 100 grt. This fleet included small fishing boats and small work boats that generally operated within 50 nautical miles of land. This group included all

EXHIBIT 6
Merchant Fleet Market for NAVSTAR/GPS*

Segment/Year	1984	1985	1986	1987	1988	1989–93
Retrofit	15	45	190	350	550	3,330
New construction	10	75	200	400	500	2,750
Total market units	25	120	390	750	1,050	6,080

* Aside from the increased accuracy and coverage of NAVSTAR, a $30,000 receiver could replace the systems currently in use (price in 1979: $91,000).

vessels operating beyond the sight of land but not requiring the expensive installations of multiple navigation systems typical of large oceangoing vessels. Expenditures on navigation equipment in the coastal vessel market were generally less than half of the capital outlay of the larger merchant ships.

The largest benefit to coastal vessels of a maritime set NAVSTAR GPS receiver was the improved performance/cost ratio. A receiver selling for approximately $25,000 would allow for worldwide positioning information to an accuracy of 100 meters. This would enable more efficient operations and perhaps increased fishery yields as a result of this accurate positioning information. The largest potential market for NAVSTAR receivers was in the oceangoing Japanese and Korean fishery fleets; unfortunately, this market was not readily available to North American manufacturers. Japanese shipbuilders would subcontract navigation equipment out to Japanese manufacturers unless they were given specific instructions to do otherwise. In the tradition-rich Japanese business world, this rarely occurred.

As with the larger merchant vessels, the new construction market for NAVSTAR receivers would be more significant than the retrofit market. As NAVSTAR came into operation and was used by the merchant fleet, it was believed that a lucrative market would unfold. Although slower to develop, the coastal vessel market, because of its relative size, would represent a larger sales volume than the marine market by the early 1990s. Competition was expected to be fierce in this market, as the NAVSTAR program would be fully implemented and the large merchant vessels would have demonstrated the reliability of this navigation aid. Exhibit 7 shows the estimated market size for the coastal vessel market, assuming less than 25 percent early adoption by the market segment within the 10-year forecast period. This is because most navigation system users would wait until the mid-1980s, when lower-cost, second-generation equipment would be made available.

Recreational Fleet

The recreational vessel fleet consisted of all private pleasure craft, yachts, and small boats. These craft generally operated in coastal areas, harbors,

EXHIBIT 7
Coastal Fleet Market Potential for NAVSTAR/GPS

Segment/Year	1984	1985	1986	1987	1988	1989–93
Retrofit market	—	50	125	250	400	6,500
New construction market	10	20	50	100	250	5,000
Total coastal market	10	70	175	350	650	11,500

and inland waterways, although some of the larger pleasure craft could be oceangoing. These vessels operated only under good weather conditions and seldom beyond sight of land.

In the early 1980s only a small percentage of these craft carried significant radionavigation equipment. This market, however, had an enormous potential for rapid growth. The expected availability of low-cost navigation systems during the early 1990s offered owners of these small craft a navigation capability they could use whenever they wanted or needed it.

The two main benefits of NAVSTAR/GPS to this segment would be safety and prestige. For the ocean-cruising vessels in this fleet, NAVSTAR provided worldwide availability with 100-meter accuracy at a relatively low cost. For a certain fraction of this market, the prestige of using the state-of-the-art navigation equipment would encourage the purchase of NAVSTAR receivers.

Exhibit 8 is a forecast of the recreational vessel market for the following 10 years. The segment would experience a great deal of growth. In earlier years many of these smaller craft would never install any more navigation equipment than a magnetic compass. However, as the cost of radionavigation equipment decreased, some of the larger and more fully equipped for these craft were expected to become a significant market for radionavigation equipment during the next decade.

Radionavigation Equipment Manufacturers

Companies actively involved in developing and promoting radionavigation equipment for the marine market were the slowest to commit to major GPS development programs at this time. A number of companies did have programs in the offing. For example, Magnavox was known to be spending approximately half a million dollars per year in the development of the Spartan set, a low-cost GPS marine navigator that would focus on merchant vessel and coastal vessel markets. Because of the success Magnavox had encountered with its other products in the marine market, the company would probably capture a large portion of the marine market as a result of its early development program. Some activities were taking place in Japan, with Mitsubishi and Japan Radio in the process of developing low-cost sets. Their emphasis would be primarily on the Japanese merchant and fishing fleets, although these companies were also reasonably successful in selling

EXHIBIT 8
Recreational Fleet Market for NAVSTAR/GPS

Segment/year	1984	1985	1986	1987	1988	1989–93
Market potential	—	—	25	50	100	750

EXHIBIT 9

Radionavigation Equipment Manufacturers in the Marine Market

	Market Segment			Product Type				
	Merchant	Coastal	Recreational	MARISAT	LORAN C	SATNAV	RADAR	GPS
1. Anritsu Electronics	X	—	—	X	—	—	—	—
2. Data Marine International	—	X	X	—	X	—	—	—
3. Digital Marine Electronics	—	X	X	—	X	—	—	—
4. Dornier	X	—	—	X	—	—	—	—
5. Elektrisk Bureau	X	—	—	X	—	—	—	—
6. EPSCO Marine	—	X	X	—	X	—	—	—
7. Furuno U.S.A.	—	X	X	—	X	—	—	—
8. Internav Ltd.	—	X	—	—	X	—	—	X
9. Japan Radio Co. Ltd.	X	X	X	X	X	X	—	—
10. King (Marine) Radio	—	X	—	—	—	—	X	—
11. Kingsberg N.A. (Robertson)	X	X	—	—	—	—	X	X
12. Magnavox	X	X	—	X	X	X	—	X
13. Micrologic	—	X	X	—	X	—	—	—
14. Mitsubishi	—	X	—	—	—	—	—	X
15. Motorola	X	X	—	X	—	—	—	—
16. Navidyne	X	X	—	X	X	X	—	—
17. N.C.S.	X	X	X	X	—	—	—	—
18. Racal-Decca Marine	X	X	X	—	X	X	—	—
19. Raytheon Marine	—	X	—	—	X	X	X	—
20. Sperry Marine	X	X	—	X	—	—	—	—
21. Toshiba	—	X	—	—	—	X	—	—
22. Tracor	—	X	—	—	X	X	—	—
Number of firms in each area	11	19	8	9	12	7	3	4

their products on an international basis. However, because of size, financial backing, and expertise of these firms, Seanav could expect fierce competition from such established companies.

Exhibit 9 lists the 22 major radionavigation equipment manufacturers in the marine market. Only four firms had established a GPS development program. The majority of the rest of the companies in the marine market were analyzing the GPS potential and its ramifications for their existing product lines.

THE BOARD MEETING

Paul Wilson began the meeting by summarizing the events of the past few days. He said, "I am happy to inform you that we have received our federal grant. We can now even afford to pay off some of our debts! However, the accountants have given us a strict deadline for the revision of our market plan. All the financial data, including our component cost estimates, our margins, and our operating expenses, are reasonable. The problem is that we now have only five days to develop our marketing strategy. Before I turn things over to Mike, I believe that John has a few words to say."

John stated, "As Paul has mentioned, we have a tight deadline. The reason for this is the federal government's changing of the R&D tax incentives. If our investors are to receive the maximum benefit from this change in legislation, they must act quickly. Seanav is not the only high-tech company that is trying to woo these investors."

Mike Ruby wasn't really listening to what was going on. He still had not finalized his strategy for Seanav. A number of alternatives were going through his mind. He had just returned from a business trip for another of his clients and had had only two hours to review the business plan and to develop alternatives. All of a sudden he realized that Paul was talking to him: ". . . since we've got the budgets finalized. New let's find out the best marketing strategy for Seanav's success," Paul said.

Case 4–3

Frank W. Horner Ltd.

In April 1978 Peter McLoughlin, marketing manager for over-the-counter (OTC) products at the drug company of Frank W. Horner Ltd. of Montreal, was planning his 1978–79 communications strategy for Fevertest with the assistance of Robert Kyba of the market research department. Described by McLoughlin as "our first real consumer-type promotion," Fevertest consisted of a thin plastic strip which, when applied to the forehead, indicated whether or not an individual had a fever. Between early November 1977 and the end of March 1978, factory shipments amounted to 317,000 units. McLoughlin and Kyba wondered whether they could improve upon this level of sales by investing in television advertising, an approach which had not been used during the initial promotional campaign.

COMPANY BACKGROUND

Frank W. Horner Ltd. was founded in 1912 by a nephew of Andrew Wyeth, the artist. By 1977, sales in Canada had reached $15 million. An additional $5 million in export sales were handled by the international division of Carter Wallace N.S. Horner distributed a variety of ethical and over-the-counter (OTC) pharmaceutical products[1] to 4,000 pharmacies across Canada through a sales force of 65 persons. Only 10 percent of sales volume was distributed through wholesalers. The product line included antacids (Diovol), antinauseants (Gravol), analgesics (Atasol), and tonics (Maltlevol). Prior to 1973, dollar sales of ethical products exceeded those of OTC products. However, by 1977 approximately 65 percent of Horner's dollar volume was derived from OTC products.

THE PRODUCT CONCEPT

An individual's temperature is commonly measured orally, though rectal temperature is a closer measure of body or core temperature. There is usually a three-degree centigrade difference between oral temperature and

---

This case was written by Assistant Professor John A. Quelch, of the Graduate School of Business Administration, Harvard University. Copyright © 1978, The University of Western Ontario.

[1] Ethical products are usually available to the consumer only by prescription, while OTC products, as the name implies, may be purchased over the counter by the consumer without a prescription.

skin temperature measured on the forehead. A further complication, irrespective of method of temperature measurement, is that there is no absolute figure for normal temperature. Normal temperatures vary among individuals. In addition, an individual's body temperature may vary as much as one-half degree centigrade during the course of the day. Despite these variations, doctors generally agree that a temperature of 38°C. or more indicates a definite fever.

In 1976 Horner executives were investigating acquisition of the Canadian distribution rights to a new type of fever indicator developed by Eurand, the Italian subsidiary of NCR. The indicator consisted of a thin strip which, when applied to the forehead for 15 seconds, showed an N if the person's temperature was normal and an NF if the person had a fever. The strip contained microencapsulated liquid crystals which changed color with changes in temperature. The temperature at which each color change occurred and the sequence of color changes were invariable. The microencapsulation process, on which North American patents had been acquired by NCR in 1969, shielded the liquid crystals from contamination and provided both greater reliability and longer effective life. The temperatures at which particular color changes occurred are illustrated in Exhibit 1.

EXHIBIT 1
Temperature-Color Change Relationships

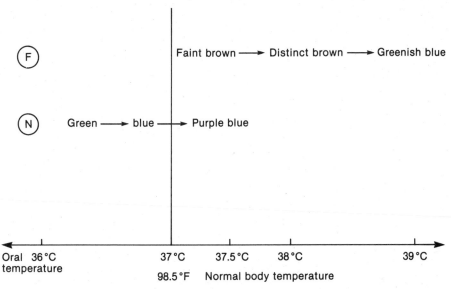

Note: the Fevertest strip included both an N and an F. As the temperature changed, the color of each letter changed as indicated in the chart. At or below normal temperature, the F was not visible.

Source: Company records.

Horner executives learned that the accuracy of the indicator could be jeopardized if it was soaked in water or alcohol; if it was not allowed to cool for 30 seconds between uses; or if it was not applied to a clean, dry forehead. The indicator could not be used reliably after sunbathing or strenuous exercise, since the normal temperature relationship between forehead and mouth would be interrupted. In addition, usage on children under two years was not recommended due to the immaturity of the body's thermal regulating systems.

PRELIMINARY RESEARCH

Despite the questionable accuracy of the indicator, both in general and under special circumstances, Horner executives decided to undertake the program of technical and market research outlined in Exhibit 2. The main highlights of the program were:

Consumer Group (May 1976). On the basis of a focus group interview[2] with 15 consumers in Quebec, women were found to be more interested in the product concept than men. The main concerns expressed related to the product's accuracy and its ability to sustain its effectiveness despite long periods of nonuse. Nevertheless, 12 of the consumers stated that they would buy the product if it were on sale at a pharmacy for a price between $1.75 and $2.00. Because consumers commented that the product appeared fragile and easy to mislay, Horner executives decided that product packaging would be important to provide protection and to convey an impression of quality to support a $2 price level.

Physician Survey (June 1976). Horner was not seriously interested in selling the product to physicians but, as an ethical drug company, was concerned that the product should not detract from the company's reputation with the medical profession if introduced. The physicians reacted positively to the product as a means of readily establishing if a patient had a temperature above 38°C. Positive reactions increased after the physicians tried the product. In the view of several of the group, the product's ease of usage made it appropriate for the many consumers who did not know how to use a thermometer correctly.

First Hospital Trial (August 1976). The indicator supplied by Eurand was tested in Horner laboratories and in-house by Horner employees. Next a field trial was conducted involving the staff of Montreal General Hospital. Fifty nurses were asked to measure patient temperatures with

---

[2] In a focus group, a trained interviewer typically spent one to two hours moderating a consumer discussion with the objective of exploring the current products or seeking reactions to new product concepts.

EXHIBIT 2
Summary of Technical and Market Research Program

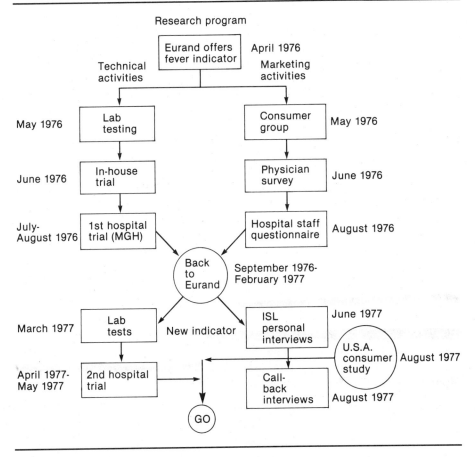

Source: Company records.

both the fever indicator and a thermometer. In replying to a staff questionnaire, they were somewhat negative regarding the product's accuracy, reporting that the indicator showed an F at a variety of temperatures between
37°C and 38°C. In addition, the indicator was not regarded as a time-saving
device. Although a glass thermometer took twice as long to register a patient's temperature, the nurse could attend to other duties while the reading was being taken, whereas the fever indicator required the nurse to hold
it in position. Some nurses also perceived a hygiene problem in using the
same indicator on several patients. In summary, 38 percent of nurses surveyed agreed that the accuracy of the indicator made it suitable for hospital
use. Thirty percent stated that they had experienced difficulty using the

EXHIBIT 3
Percentages of Consumers Interested in Ownership of Fever Indicator

	Total Sample (n = 200)	Mothers with Children 2–10 Years Old			General Public (n = 100)
		Total (n = 100)	English (n = 50)	French (n = 50)	
After seeing point-of-sale display	53%	69%	74%	64%	37%
After opening package and reading concept	65	79	64	94	49
After testing product	72	84	76	92	58
Immediate purchase at $1.75	45	68	42	94	21

Source: ISL Consumer Survey, June 1977.

product. Sixty-six percent believed that a fever-screening device could play a useful role in hospitals, particularly in chronic care and pediatric wards.

Second Hospital Trial (April 1977). Following the initial trial, Horner asked Eurand to supply a more accurate product. A second batch of improved fever indicators was used in another hospital trial at Montreal General. The second version of the product proved to be more sensitive, indicating an F at only 37.6°C. or 37.7°C., rather than across a range of temperatures between 37°C. and 38°C. Acceptance of Fevertest as a useful fever-screening device by members of the hospital staff increased significantly beyond the level recorded in the first hospital survey.

Consumer Survey (June 1977). A survey was conducted with three groups: 50 English-speaking mothers with children 2 to 10 years old; 50 French-speaking mothers with children 2 to 10 years old; and 100 members of the general public, half male, half female.[3] Each subject was first shown a point-of-sale display for the product. Next each subject was invited to open a product package and read about the product. Finally, each subject was asked to try the product. After each stage, consumer reactions to the product were elicited, and interest in ownership of the product was measured. Consumers reacted favorably towards the ease with which the product could be used, particularly when taking the temperatures of children. Favorable comments regarding the speed with which the indicator registered increased significantly after consumers tried the product. The unbreakable nature of the product also prompted favorable comment. Negative reactions

---

[3] Among approximately 7 million Canadian households, there were 1,340,000 English-speaking households with children 2 to 10 years old, and 360,000 similar French-speaking households. There were an additional 900,000 households with children 11 to 15 years old.

centered on the questionable accuracy of the indicator and the fact that it did not provide numerical temperature values. Exhibit 3 presents the percentages of each sample subgroup either very or fairly interested in the ownership of a fever indicator after each of the three stages of inquiry and, in addition, the percentages prepared to pay $1.75 on the spot for the indicator. The consumer survey also established that 85 percent of the sample had

EXHIBIT 4
Usage Instructions for Fevertest

≡FEVERTEST™

INSTRUCTIONS

NORMAL/NORMALE

FEVER/FIÈVRE

How to use.
Hold FEVERTEST strip by the clear ends, and apply to a clean, *dry* forehead, mat (dull) side against the skin. Keep in place for 15 seconds (even though results may appear in just 5 seconds). Liquid Crystals react best indoors between 18°–30°C (65°–86°F). Do not use immediately after sunbathing or exposure to extreme heat. Do not wash FEVERTEST strip with any substance.

How to read.
N — normal temperature
NF (brownish F) — transition phase
NF (green/blue F) — definite fever
The transition phase indicates either:
  1) the onset of a fever
or 2) a high forehead temperature.
If a distinct 'F' appears and you'd like a more precise reading, use a glass thermometer.

Note.
In children under 2 years of age, the body's thermal regulating system may still be immature. Therefore, it is preferable to use a glass thermometer for very young children.

How to store.
After each use, return FEVERTEST to its package and store away from sunlight, dampness and heat.
Do not wash FEVERTEST strip with any substance.
Properly cared for, your FEVERTEST strip may be used thousands of times.

Mode d'emploi
FEVERTEST. En le tenant par ses extrémités transparentes, appliquer l'indicateur sur un front propre et sec, en prenant soin d'appuyer la partie mate contre l'épiderme. Le laisser sur le front pendant 15 secondes, quoique la lecture puisse quelquefois se faire en 5 secondes. Les cristaux liquides réagissent le mieux dans la maison, entre 18° et 30°C (65°–86°F). Il ne faut pas l'employer immédiatement après un bain de soleil ou une exposition à une chaleur extrême, ni le laver ou le nettoyer.

Interprétation
N: état normal
NF: (F brunâtre) état de transition
NF: (F bleu/vert) état fébrile certain.
L'état de transition révèle soit:
  1) le début d'une fièvre

ou 2) une température frontale élevée.
Si vous constatez l'apparition nette du F et désirez connaître le degré exact de fièvre, utilisez un thermomètre ordinaire.

À noter
On remarque chez les enfants de moins de 2 ans un certain déséquilibre du système de régulation thermique. Il est donc préférable de se servir d'un thermomètre à mercure ordinaire pour les très jeunes enfants.

Mode de rangement
Après l'emploi, il faut replacer le FEVERTEST dans son étui de présentation et le tenir à l'abri du soleil, de la chaleur et de l'humidité. Il ne faut pas laver, ni nettoyer le FEVERTEST. Si vous vous conformez aux instructions, vous pourrez vous servir de l'indicateur de température des milliers de fois.

⊕HORNER
Montréal Canada

no difficulty comprehending the product concept and 89 percent did not find the concept difficult to believe. However, the survey results indicated that some consumers did not realize that the product was reusable. As a result this characteristic was highlighted in subsequent point-of-sale material. A substantial majority of consumers in the sample selected Fevertest from among several names as being most appropriate for the product.

Finally, Horner executives had information from a French company which had been selling the microencapsulated fever indicator since the end of 1976 at a price close to $2 each. Sales results indicated that close to 1 million units would be sold during the first year in France, a country of approximately 20 million households.

On the basis of this evidence and domestic consumer research, Horner executives decided to launch the fever indicator under the brand name Fevertest. The product was packaged in a blue plastic wallet with the comprehensive usage instructions reproduced in Exhibit 4.

INITIAL COMMUNICATIONS STRATEGY

Fevertest was launched early in November 1977 to coincide with the cold and flu season. The product was distributed through the Horner sales force at a price of $1.35 to pharmacies. A retail price of about $2 was recommended, thereby giving the pharmacy a margin of 33 percent. Details of the price and cost structure for Fevertest are presented in Exhibit 5. Due to the uniqueness of the product, the sales forecast of 550,000 units between November and April 1978 was regarded as somewhat speculative. This figure represented sales of 458 cases of 2 dozen units per sales territory. Because of production capacity constraints, a maximum allocation of 120 cases per territory was available in November.

The communications budget for the product launch is summarized in Exhibit 6. An automatic shipment of one case of two dozen Fevertests was sent to the most important 3,100 of 4,000 pharmacy accounts across Canada.[4] The pharmacies were invoiced on a 90-day payment basis for $32.40 each. Accompanying each case was a free Fevertest strip to be used by the pharmacist as a demonstrator, and a letter explaining the product concept, emphasizing the space efficiency of the product, and indicating the manner in which the case could be used as an effective display device. Executives believed that drugstores would be receptive to the automatic shipment

---

[4] Horner's reputation for successful new-product introductions was such that most pharmacies were prepared to receive and merchandise a case of Fevertest shipped automatically from the factory rather than in response to an order. In addition the Horner sales force had indicated that the trade would be receptive to an automatic shipment of Fevertest.

EXHIBIT 5
Fevertest Cost and Price Structure

Selling price per case ($1.35 each) 24/case	$32.40
Cost of goods	12.53
Gross margin	$19.87
Distribution, marketing, and administrative cost allocation	2.59
Sales commission (4 percent of selling price)	1.30
Available for communications budget and profit	$15.98

Handwritten annotations: 1.35 / 52¢ @ / 83¢ cont mg / .11 / .05 / .67 profit = 49% of 1.35

Source: Company records.

because of the novelty of the product together with Horner's long-standing reputation for distributing quality salable products. A promotional flyer illustrating the product and the display case is reproduced as Exhibit 7.

The case was designed in the form of a display which could be shelved in the thermometer section of the drugstore or placed on the dispensary counter where the pharmacist could discuss and demonstrate the product. The second approach was also believed likely to result in less theft. In addition to the displays, point-of-sale posters for doors, windows, and cash registers were distributed to the 3,100 pharmacies. Total point-of-sale promotion costs were $20,000.

As part of the sell-in-effort, Horner offered a cooperative advertising allowance of $15 to those stores which purchased 10 cases of Fevertests. It was estimated that about 650 stores might take advantage of this offer, for a total promotion expense of approximately $10,000.

EXHIBIT 6
Communications Budget for Fevertest Launch, 1977–1978

Unit objectives	500,000
Dollar objectives (at $1.35 each)	$675,000
Communications budget:	
Public relations	$ 15,000
Promotion to physicians	10,000
Journal advertising	8,000
Consumer print advertising	75,000
Point-of-sale displays	18,000
Selling sheets	2,000
Case allowances for cooperative advertising	10,000
Television advertising (January 1978)	18,000
	$156,000

Source: Company records.

EXHIBIT 7
Promotional Flyer for Fevertest

Trade advertising involved a full-page insertion in *Drug Merchandising* and *Le Pharmacien* (combined circulation of 12,000) at a cost of $8,000. A sample Fevertest was affixed to the advertisement in each copy of the magazine to facilitate trial among readers.

Consumer advertising included a full-page four-color advertisement in the December 1977 and January 1978 issues of *Reader's Digest* (circulation

1,256,000), *Selection* (31,000), *Homemakers* (1,232,000), and *Madame Au Foyer* (268,000). One-third page advertisements were inserted in the Views on Value section of *Reader's Digest/Selection* in February, March, and April, and in the Product Idea Unit section of *Homemakers/Madame Au Foyer* in March, April, and May. Exhibit 8 presents one of these print advertisements. Total costs for the advertising campaign were $75,000.

At a cost of $10,000, a Fevertest sample was mailed to 12,500 doctors. The accompanying product description emphasized that the product was not intended to replace the thermometer but to act as a screening device. It was

EXHIBIT 8
Print Advertisement, 1977–1978

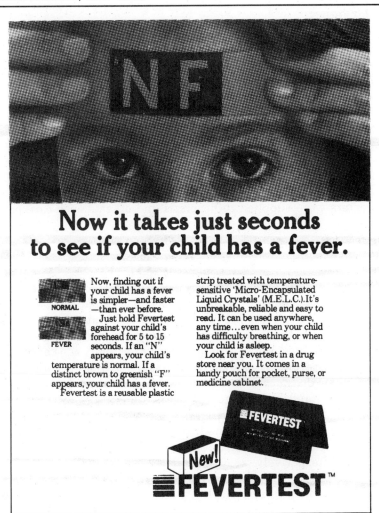

Now it takes just seconds to see if your child has a fever.

NORMAL

FEVER

Now, finding out if your child has a fever is simpler—and faster —than ever before.

Just hold Fevertest against your child's forehead for 5 to 15 seconds. If an "N" appears, your child's temperature is normal. If a distinct brown to greenish "F" appears, your child has a fever. Fevertest is a reusable plastic strip treated with temperature-sensitive 'Micro-Encapsulated Liquid Crystals' (M.E.L.C.). It's unbreakable, reliable and easy to read. It can be used anywhere, any time...even when your child has difficulty breathing, or when your child is asleep.

Look for Fevertest in a drug store near you. It comes in a handy pouch for pocket, purse, or medicine cabinet.

New!

≣FEVERTEST™

suggested that patients might check their temperatures more often with a Fevertest and that, as a result, some unnecessary calls to physicians might be eliminated.

Public relations kits tailored to different media were mailed to all radio stations, television stations, daily newspapers, women's editors, and medical journals. Once again, a free sample was included for demonstration purposes. The cost of 278 public relations mailings was $8,000. Other expenses associated with the public relations drive amounted to $7,000. The public relations material aroused such immediate interest that some announcements were made in the media before initial distribution of the product had been completed.

COMPETITION

Some druggists perceived Fevertest to be in competition with the glass thermometer. However, Horner executives believed that the calibrated thermometer would be used after the Fevertest if the indicator showed positive. Consumer research indicated that 84 percent of consumers would follow up an indication of fever on the Fevertest with a thermometer reading. Thus they viewed the glass thermometer and the Fevertest as complementary rather than as substitutes. Horner estimated the 1977 glass thermometer market (rectal and oral thermometers) at 4.4 million units. Of these, 2.6 million with a manufacturer's value of $3.25 million and a retail value of $6.5 million were sold to consumers. The remaining 1.8 million thermometers were supplied to hospitals and other health-care organizations.

Products similar to Fevertest were on sale in the United States, including Clinitemp, Fever Tester, and Fever Meter. These products were manufactured by small companies and sold at retail prices between $1.95 and $2.49. None of these indicators was microencapsulated. Despite the consequent accuracy and reliability problems, one of the products was calibrated in degrees and purported to provide an exact temperature reading. Promotional material for these indicators included appeals such as "space-age concept," "hospital-tested," "every member of the family can carry one," and "keep one at home, one in your car, one in your vacation first-aid kit." In all cases the target market appeared to be mothers with children.

McLoughlin and Kyba were uncertain whether the manufacturers of these fever indicators would attempt to distribute in Canada and, if so, what channels they would use. Too small to afford a direct sales approach, the competing companies could attempt to use drug wholesalers to distribute to pharmacies. Alternatively they might try to reach the consumer through mass merchandisers and supermarkets rather than through drugstores. The costs of new packaging and display materials to meet bilingual requirements were thought unlikely to be a sufficient deterrent to entry.

McLoughlin and Kyba were concerned about such potential competition, because the poorer quality of the competing indicators might reduce the credibility of the product concept and therefore adversely affect Fevertest sales. To differentiate Fevertest on the basis of microencapsulation would, it was believed, pose a difficult communications task. The threat of competition was highlighted early in 1978, when reports were received that a calibrated fever indicator, Stik Temp, was being distributed through drug wholesalers in British Columbia. Nevertheless, company estimates indicated that Fevertest held 95 percent of the Canadian fever indicator market.

TELEVISION ADVERTISING TEST

Horner executives were sufficiently satisfied with sales volume during the product launch to become interested in the possibility of using television to promote Fevertest. Television advertising held an advantage over radio and print advertising in that Fevertest could be demonstrated as part of the commercial. At the same time, Horner had little experience in consumer advertising, and there was a fear that any money spent in television advertising would benefit similarly named competitive products as much as Fevertest and might, in addition, attract further competition into the market.

Consequently Horner decided to conduct several experiments testing the effectiveness of television advertising in selected markets. A storyboard illustrating the content of the television commercial used in the tests is presented in Exhibit 9. During the period January 2–29, 1978, Horner spent $17,650 for advertising time on three Vancouver television stations with the goal of targeting women 18 years or older. Exhibit 10 shows the number of WRPs (women rating points)[5] achieved and the distribution of cost on a biweekly basis.

Weekly case sales for Fevertest during the introductory period both in total and for three major markets are presented in Exhibit 11. The results indicate that Vancouver sales were at an average level of 40 cases per week prior to the advertising effort. During the eight-week period after the campaign started, approximately 1,150 cases were sold, but by March 10, sales out of the Vancouver depot had returned to the preadvertising level. Horner executives saw no reason not to attribute the sales increase to television advertising, since Montreal and Toronto sales appeared to taper off during the same period.

---

[5] Weekly WRPs represent the percentage of women aged 18 to 49 in the Vancouver market who would be reached at least once by the television advertising during one week, multiplied by the average number of times (frequency with which) each such woman would be exposed to the advertising during the week.

EXHIBIT 9
Television Commercial Storyboard

EXHIBIT 10
Advertising on Three Vancouver TV Stations

	Weekly WRPs	Average Weekly Cost	Cost per Rating Point	Total Cost
January 2–13	113	$4,735	$41.90	$ 9,470
January 16–29	102	4,090	40.10	8,180
				$17,650

EXHIBIT 11
Fevertest Weekly Case Sales, 1977–1978

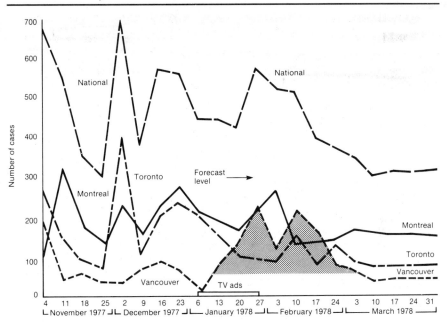

At the end of January, a comparative test of Fevertest awareness was conducted in Vancouver and Calgary. An awareness level of 77 percent was recorded in Vancouver, 45 percent in Calgary. Among Vancouver consumers 73 percent cited television commercials as their source of information, while 16 percent cited drugstores. The corresponding figures in Calgary, where no television advertising had been conducted, were 24 percent and 30 percent.

THE 1978–1979 COMMUNICATIONS STRATEGY

Before they could formulate the communications strategy for Fevertest, McLoughlin and Kyba were faced with the problem of whether or not to broaden distribution of the product beyond pharmacies. Supermarkets, for example, were thought likely to be interested in Fevertest because of its high margin per square foot relative to other products. Though Horner had no experience selling to supermarkets, moving into this channel could forestall potential competition and generate substantial sales volume. There was concern, however, about the effects of such a move on Horner's reputation with its pharmacy accounts and the degree to which they would withdraw support from Fevertest, particularly if supermarkets sold the product at a lower price. Furthermore, some Horner executives believed that the supermarkets might promote Fevertest as a novelty or gimmick item, thereby detracting from the desired image of usefulness and excellence of quality.

Sales forecasts suggested that 500,000 Fevertests would be sold in 1978–79 if the company continued to restrict sales to pharmacies. Depending upon the size of the communications budget, Horner executives believed that as many as 1.5 million Fevertests might be sold to the general public if distribution was broadened.

The distribution issue prompted Horner executives to wonder whether the original target market of mothers with young children should be broadened. The institutional market presented an additional opportunity to generate increased sales volume. It was believed that widespread usage of Fevertests in hospitals could be used by Horner to distinguish Fevertest from competing indicators when promoting the product to consumers.

In light of decisions regarding target market and message strategies, Horner executives recognized that the level and allocation of the communications budget would soon have to be finalized. In addition to the range of promotional activities in which Horner had invested during the 1977–78 year, four additional options were available:

Television Advertising.   The Horner advertising agency advised that an advertising objective of at least 100 WRPs was necessary for Fevertest. Exhibit 12 indicates the weekly cost of meeting this objective in 18 markets over 100,000 population. While the cost of year-long advertising in all of these markets was prohibitive, some executives belived that short flights of advertising in selected markets (similar to the Vancouver test) might prove to be a profitable investment. For example, one proposal was made to schedule three four-week flights in all 18 markets at a cost of $400,000.

Cooperative Advertising.   If a store purchased a minimum of 10 cases and featured Fevertest in its advertising, Horner was prepared to offer a cooperative advertising allowance of $1 per case. Horner executives estimated that 2,000 stores might purchase 10 cases and that half of these might take up the offer for a promotional cost of $10,000.

Tie-In Promotion.   Information about Fevertest could be disseminated either on or inside the package of another Horner product at no additional cost. McLoughlin was considering such a tie-in promotion with Atasol, a Horner analgesic.

Point-of-Sale Displays.   At a cost of $200,000, 1,000 motorized units to be used as counter displays could be produced. The unit would play a videotape showing how a consumer should use a Fevertest, and would be offered to pharmacies or other outlets as an attention-getting device. An additional $10,000 would be needed for accompanying point-of-sale mate-

EXHIBIT 12

Projected Fevertest Television Costs, 1978

Commercial length: 30 seconds.
Weekly weight: 100 women rating points (WRPs).
Markets: Population 100,000 plus.

	WRP Weekly Objective	Spill-In	Original WRP Weekly	Weekly Cost ($)	Weekly Reach (percent)	Average Weekly Frequency
St. John's/Corner Brook	100	0	100	$ 560.00	63%	1.6
Halifax/Sydney	100	0	100	1,290.00	63	1.6
Saint John/Moncton	100	0	100	600.00	63	1.6
Chicoutimi/Jonquiere	100	0	100	235.00	65	1.5
Montreal (English)	40	0	40	2,460.00	23	1.7
Montreal (French)	60	0	60	2,544.00	37	1.6
Quebec City	100	0	100	1,420.00	64	1.6
Kitchener	100	59	41	885.60	53	1.9
London	100	40	60	966.00	54	1.9
Ottawa (English)	80	0	80	1,792.00	48	1.7
Ottawa (French)	20	0	20	253.00	10	2.0
Sudbury	100	0	100	685.00	64	1.6
Thunder Bay	100	0	100	245.00	59	1.7
Toronto/Hamilton	100	0	100	8,500.00	55	1.8
Winnipeg	100	0	100	1,620.00	59	1.7
Regina	100	0	100	545.00	64	1.6
Saskatoon	100	0	100	555.00	64	1.6
Calgary	100	0	100	1,450.00	59	1.7
Edmonton	100	0	100	1,800.00	59	1.7
Vancouver/Victoria	100	0	100	4,160.00	58	1.7
				$32,595.60		
Plus 15 percent reserve for rate increases				4,889.34		
Total cost				$37,484.94		

Source: W. R. Kitching Associates Limited.

rial, including mirrors attached to the case displays to enable potential purchasers to see the color changes occurring when they applied the sample Fevertest to their foreheads.

Within the coming week, McLoughlin and Kyba had to finalize the Fevertest communications strategy for the 1978–79 year beginning June 1.

CASE 4–4

Norsk Kjem A/S

In the summer of 1984, Mr. Johan Sunde, product manager at Norsk Kjem A/S, commented, "Although Nick, Per, and I spend many weeks visiting distributors and customers around the world, it is difficult to feel that we really know what is going on in the promotion and the many different applications of our products. It is difficult to make our distributors put any effort behind our products as we have very little control over what they do. However, our product group broke even for the first time last year and we would like to start making our 20 percent target return."

Norsk Kjem A/S (NK) was an integrated chemical company situated in Larvik, Norway. The company had been in business for 25 years and it had an excellent reputation throughout the world. The company was organized into three major divisions as shown in Exhibit 1. The NK Chemicals Division marketed more than 100 different chemicals and each chemical had many different applications. The division was organized into five product groups according to basic input chemicals such as polymers, alcohols, and sulphates.

SULPHATES

In 1978, NK had taken out a license from an American company on a process for converting a by-product from one of the main processes into a salable chemical usually employed as a wetting agent. A wetting agent is used in many processes to promote the retention and even distribution of liquids.

The case was prepared by Professor Kenneth G. Hardy. The case was supported by the Research Associates Plan for Excellence. Any use or duplication of the material presented in this case is prohibited except with the written consent of the School of Business Administration. The author thanks the North European Management Institute for its cooperation. Copyright © 1974. The University of Western Ontario. Reprinted by permission. Revised 1976, 1986.

EXHIBIT 1
Simplified Organization Chart

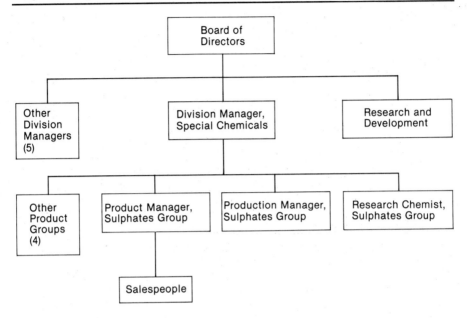

Prior to taking out the 1978 license and investing in the necessary plant and equipment, the market for wetting agents had been thoroughly researched by Mr. Nick Deveny. Mr. Deveny had visited many applicators in Europe and they had said, "give us a product equal to what we get from the United States and we will be interested." Mr. Deveny's estimates of demand by industry and country are shown in Exhibit 2.

In 1978, a product manager and two technical salespeople had been hired to launch the wetting agents. Mr. Nick Deveny, who had made the original market survey, was one of the two salespeople employed. All three people held university degrees in chemistry or engineering. Together, they named the original product and subsequent offshoots, prepared technical literature, designed packages, and established a distribution system.

In setting up distributors, the product manager and his salespeople used the following criteria of (1) establish only one distributor per country, (2) use established chemical distributors owned by nationals, and (3) try to get distributors that serve the concrete, dyeing, and pesticide industries because these end users seemed to have the largest potential. Subsequent to establishing the distributors, the product manager discovered that the Norwegian products had to have demonstrable advantages before end users would risk a switch to a new ingredient. From 1976 to 1980, sales of the two major products were very disappointing.

The original product manager in the Sulphates Group had established

EXHIBIT 2

Norsk Kjem A/S Estimated Potential as of 1976 for Chemical Products (by application and country; in tons)

Country	Textile Dyestuff	Carbon Black and Pigments	Pesticides	Concrete	Plaster-Board	Total
Benelux	200–360	0–100	1000–2000	1200–1600	0	2400–4060
England	1600–3000	240–320	4000–6000	6000–7000	0	11,840–16,320
France	2200–3000	100–300	4000–6000	4000–8000	100–600	10,300–16,900
Italy	800–1600	200–400	4000–8000	2000–4000	20–100	7020–15,100
Israel	0	0	200–1000	400–1000	0	600–2000
Scandinavia	0	100–200	200–400	200–600	100–200	600–1400
Spain	100–300	100–200	200–400	200–400	0	600–1300
Switzerland	3000–6000	100–200	200–1000	1000–4000	0	4300–11,200
Germany	4000–6000	500–1000	2000–6000	2000–6000	600–1000	9100–20,000
Total	11,900–20,200	1400–2800	15,800–30,800	17,000–32,600	800–1900	46,760–135,100

distributors on many different arrangements. Some carried inventory and others did not, some took title to the product and others left the transaction between NK and the end user. For example, the German distributor was wholly owned by NK. The United Kingdom distributor kept inventory, whereas Holland was handled by direct shipments. Distributor margins ranged from 5 to 8 percent of their selling price.

In the establishment of the distributors the original product manager had considered the "hungry" versus the "established" and had gone with the established special chemical distributors because of a bad experience with an overeager distributor and because he felt that a distributor would have to invest three or four years of market development with NK sulphates before he could expect a reasonable financial return.

Most of the distributors were old family-owned companies and all of them carried many other lines, but none that were directly competitive with Sulphates Group products. The margins and required selling effort were the same for NK sulphate products as they were for other manufacturer's products. Special chemical distributors usually had some technical expertise but the wide variety of applications taxed their abilities. The distributors employed from 2 to 100 salespeople and in Mr. Sunde's judgment, all of them needed technical service and backup.

In 1980, NK underwent a major reorganization. A new product manager, Mr. Sunde, was appointed and he reported to Mr. Andreas Hoxmark, general manager for the Chemicals Divisions. Mr. Hoxmark had been one of the two corporate planners at Norsk Kjem and he had excellent education and experience in chemistry.

Just before the reorganization, the previous product manager had decided to buy a second license from the United States company which had sold the rights to the first process. A new series of light-colored wetting agents was launched and the plant was expanded at a cost of $800,000. The

new wetting agents were tailor-made for three specific applications: pesticides, concrete, and textile dyestuffs.

Shortly after his appointment, Mr. Sunde decided that he should tell all
his customers and potential customers about the many applications of the
three new agents as well as the original products. To do this, he prepared a
master brochure which showed all five wetting agents and where they applied in 10 different major applications. Then a detailed brochure was prepared for each of the 10 applications and the appropriate brochures were
sent to the customers who had been coded according to their current applications. A response card and a letter from Mr. Sunde were sent out with the
brochures. The distributors received quantities of all literature in the appropriate language. Mr. Sunde commented, "The response was only fair. The
big seller turned out to be one of the new products but mainly to two accounts in Switzerland and Germany, a contract which was arranged even
before we bought the license to make the new products."

Between 1980 and 1983, Mr. Sunde and his two salesmen, Mr. Deveny
and Mr. Per Wiencke, spent a great deal of time traveling with distributors
in order to meet customers and to give out samples. Mr. Sunde called on
distributors in Switzerland, France, and Denmark, while Mr. Deveny took
Germany, Eastern Europe, Finland, Israel, and Italy. The second salesman,
Mr. Wiencke, called on distributors in the United Kingdom, Benelux, Spain,
Norway, Sweden, and all others. Exhibit 3 shows the sales volume and
arrangement with each distributor in 1983.

In September 1983, Mr. Sunde took a leave in order to study industrial
marketing but he kept in touch with his colleagues at NK. When he returned in the summer of 1984, the research people had redeveloped the
product line so that it was more than completely competitive in terms of
quality. Exhibit 4 shows sales, costs, and contribution for 1982 and 1983.

CUSTOMERS

In making any first purchase of a new wetting agent, the technical people in
a client company would require samples for testing. In large companies,
their recommendation would go to a purchasing agent and production manager, but in small companies, the owner/manager would make the final
decision. Mr. Hoxmark considered that it was very important to develop a
close rapport with customers. He encouraged contact between customers
and R&D people in the Chemicals Division in order that R&D personnel
could hear customer wants at first hand. He observed that small companies
often preferred small suppliers regardless of nationality. Most customers
kept open two sources of supply because delivery was just as important as
technical support.

There were 110 end users buying from Sulphates-Group distributors.
Nearly 80 percent of the Sulphates-Group volume was taken by 20 percent

EXHIBIT 3

Norsk Kjem A/S Sales, Products, Commission Structure, and Inventory of Exclusive Distributors in Each Country in 1983 ($000)

Country	Sales Tons	Sales $ Value‡	Commission	Inventory	Industries Served	Notes
Switzerland*	2,000	$ 450	5% fab	Yes	Textile dyestuff	Small company manager looks after sulphates, good connections in textile dyestuff
Holland	100	400	n.a.	No	Pesticides	
Germany*	2,200	400	3% fob	No	Textile dyestuff, carbon black, concrete and plasterboard	Norsk Kjem Sales Company, Norwegian chemist sells sulphates
U.K.*	800	320	7% cif	Yes	Textile dyestuff, carbon black, pesticides	2 people buy in 20-ton lots
France†	400	160	5% fob	Yes	Pesticides, plasterboard	Large dealer, 100 employees and 8 offices
Japan	300	160	n.a.	No	Textile dyestuff	
Italy†	100	160	n.a.	Yes	Concrete	Medium-size dealer
Eastern Europe	4,400	128	n.a.	No	Animal feed	
Scandinavia	4,246	120	. n.a.	Yes	Animal feed, concrete	
Spain†	600	120	n.a.	Yes	Concrete, plaster	Small- to medium-size dealer
Australia	1,200	90	n.a.	No	Pesticides, concrete	
Belgium	1,200	60	n.a.	No	Pesticides	
Kuwait	300	60	n.a.	No	Concrete, plasterboard	
Israel	270	54	n.a.	No	Concrete, plasterboard	
Others	2,000	160	n.a.	No	Miscellaneous	
Total	20,116	$2,834				

* Dependent on Sulphates Group or Norsk Kjem for accounts or financing.
† Mr. Sunde was dissatisified with the performance of these distributors.
‡ Norwegian Kroner have been converted to American dollars at the prevailing rate of exchange.
n.a. = Not available.

EXHIBIT 4
Norsk Kjem A/S Sales, Costs, and Contribution for 1982 and 1983 ($000)*

	1982		1983	
Sales		$1,852		$2,834
Variable cost		746		1,058
Contribution		1,106		1,776
Fixed manufacturing costs	$914		$1,180	
Promotion costs	212		262	
Corporate and division overhead	104	1,230	150	1,592
Net profit before tax		$ (124)		$ 184

* Norwegian Kroner have been converted to American dollars at the prevailing rate of exchange.

of the distributor's customers. Exhibit 5 shows the customers and their annual volume by application for 1983.

Small companies were numerous but not easily identified as potential customers. Compared to larger organizations, small companies tended to have more first-time applications, less information on competitive offerings, less technical expertise, less sensitivity to price, and smaller order quantities. Switching chemicals posed a substantial production risk, especially for large companies.

Differences by Industry

There were some differences in purchasing criteria by industry. The *textile dyestuff* manufacturing industry was dominated by large multinational corporations which used a wide variety of auxiliary chemicals. The distribu-

EXHIBIT 5
Norsk Kjem A/S Ton Volume per Customer (by application, 1983)

Applications	Total Number of Customers	Tons per Customer						Total Sales (Tons)
		<10	10–19	20–49	50–99	100–499	>500	
Textile dyestuff	17	7	—	6	—	3	1	5,160
Carbon black and pigments	14	8	3	2	1	—	1	480
Pesticides	18	7	2	5	3	1	—	1,176
Concrete	5	1	1	—	1	1	1	2,088
Plasterboard	8	1	2	4	1	—	—	516
Industrial cleaning	2	2	—	—	—	—	—	16
Animal feed	9	1	—	4	—	1	3	9,744
Miscellaneous	37	17	13	7	—	—	—	936
Total	110	44	21	28	6	6	5	20,116

tor's salesperson first called on lab and production personnel in the user companies in order to have the NK products tested. If lab and production people approved the products, the distributor's salesperson could discuss price, delivery time, and packaging with the purchasing agent. NK products were priced competitively. The entire process of first visit, discussing test results, and arranging an order could take from six months to more than one year.

The buying procedure in the pesticide and herbicide manufacturing industries was similar to the textile dyestuff industry. However the manufacture of pesticides and herbicides called for some additional physical criteria of the product. Moreover, multinationals and small formulators were prevalent in these manufacturing industries.

The *industrial cleaning* market was particularly price competitive. The same products were used in the *plasterboard* market where a good wetting agent could reduce water requirements and drying costs. Multinational corporations dominated the manufacture of plasterboard.

In making *concrete*, a good wetting agent could provide better distribution of all particles which would lead to increased compression strength. Small- and medium-size companies were prevalent in the manufacture of concrete.

Distributor Policies

North Carolina Chemical was Mr. Sunde's toughest competition. Despite having only one distributor for all of Europe, North Carolina Chemical had tied up almost all the big dye houses. As one example of their promotional methods, North Carolina sponsored a technical conference for all the people involved in the textile dyestuff industry.

Mr. Deveny told the casewriter, "We have to support the distributor heavily in the introduction period when a customer is trying our product. After that, there is little maintenance required. Our total sales depend heavily on our marketing effort because we can do research in each market and tell the distributors what to do. We are trying now to work on key users with good volume and fair prices. We are a long way from saturating the market but almost none of our distributors are scanning customers for new end users. Furthermore, there are a lot of sample requests as a result of our advertising but there is little follow-up from the distributors. We inform them of the sample request and some call on the customer, some do not."

Mr. Sunde had tried to institute a system of field reports from the distributors but they did not fill in the reports. As a result, Mr. Sunde and his salespeople relied on their own observations during their periodic field trips. In each country their itinerary was set up by the local distributor. Mr. Sunde would visit France, for example, two weeks a year and see 20 end customers in each of those weeks.

Mr. Sunde talked about some experiments with their distributors. First of all, the German subsidiary was developing sales faster than any other distributor. Mr. Sunde ascribed this to the large German market, the German technical sophistication and willingness to try new products, and "the fact that we have a good man there working only with our products." Mr. Sunde had just fired the United Kingdom distributor and shifted the business to two of the distributor's former salespeople. In France, the distributor had hired a product manager who grouped customers, established potentials and sales goals for salespeople and helped the salesperson look for new possibilities and pushed them. The result was a big increase in sales for the French distributor. Mr. Sunde had tried to woo the French pesticide industry with price concessions but the French distributor would only partly go along with the plan. The distributor would have been obliged to take a small reduction in his margin.

Marketing Options

The first option which Mr. Sunde had considered was to drop all the distributors and replace them with either a Norwegian-based sales force or one NK salesperson located in each major market. One field office would cost $100,000 per year for a salesperson's salary, travel expenses, secretarial and other expenses. The extra travel and communication expense from Norway would bring the cost of a Norwegian-based force up to the same cost of $100,000 per person.

The second major option was to help the distributors. In major markets, Mr. Sunde would share 50 percent of the cost of a distributor's salesperson if the salesperson would spend half his time on NK sulphates. Most distributor salespeople earned about $50,000 in salary and commissions. In smaller markets, an NK man might do missionary work for part of the year on a split (50–50) commission basis.

Another option would be to delineate selling tasks such as identifying prospects, developing the application, selling the customer, maintaining inventory, and after-sale servicing. Possibly the tasks could be divided between NK and the distributors. To compensate for the performance of these tasks, some sort of commission points or fee structure could be developed.

A fourth option was to assign additional NK salesmen to train the distributor's salespeople. It would take at least a month for one NK salesperson to thoroughly train one of the distributor's people. The likely sales response would vary considerably, depending on the market potential and the skill of the distributor's salespeople. ↓ the *alotted to product*

A fifth option was to work with the distributors, using existing resources. Some sort of management-by-objectives system might serve to motivate and guide the distributors. Mr. Sunde was well aware that the difficult part of a management-by-objectives system was the implementation of the system. The distributor reaction could range from enthusiastic cooperation to rejection of the NK sulphate line. Mr. Sunde had considered hiring more than one distributor per country but generally he felt that the sulphate business was too narrow to support more than one distributor.

In order to get more effort from his distributors, Mr. Sunde had considered the alternative of raising margins from the 5 to 8 percent range up to approximately 15 percent. But he was not sure that this would evoke sufficient extra effort to reach profit targets, given the competitive prices offered by the company.

However, before he could make any of these decisions, Mr. Sunde felt there was a more basic decision of target customers and priority of country/application. He was not sure that Mr. Deveny's 1976 survey of potential sales still held for his products. However, Mr. Hoxmark had asked for a report on distribution strategy and policy by the end of the month.

CASE 4–5

Screen Print Display Advertising Limited

In early 1982, Mr. Andy Smith, general sales manager of Screen Print Display Advertising Limited (Screen Print) of Brantford, Ontario, was contemplating a marketing strategy for entering the American market with the company's four-color 4-foot by 8-foot point-of-purchase murals that were produced with ultraviolet (U.V.) inks.

Because of the combination of its unique machinery and accumulated production experience in the Canadian market, Mr. Smith concluded that Screen Print had a competitive advantage with this product and decided to exploit this advantage in the United States. Mr. Smith had to decide what would be the most effective way to approach potential customers in order to convince them of their need for the giant murals for in-store decor.

Industry Background

Within the retail in-store decor market in North America, there were numerous point-of-sale display and advertising products such as flyers, posters, department-identification signs, and murals. The manufacturers and marketers of these graphic art products represented an important sector servicing this market. Some of the most widely used methods for produc-

---

This case was prepared by Susan Fleming, Research Assistant, at the University of Western Ontario, under the direction of Professors Terry H. Deutscher and Kenneth G. Hardy. Development of this case was supported by the Canadian Studies Program of Canada's Secretary of State. Copyright © 1986, The University of Western Ontario. Used with permission.

ing these products were (1) photographic enlargement, (2) lithographic printing, and (3) screen printing.

Photographic enlargement was a process of enlarging a photographic negative to many times its original size. A North American directory listed more than 2,000 professional color labs which had the capability to produce "photo decor" by a photographic enlargement process. Compared to other processes, prints produced with enlargement were believed to be less sharp in color and tone, and the prints faded more quickly over time.

Lithography, which was considered one of the simplest forms of graphic art, and which dated back to the 1790s was also used by thousands of companies. It was defined as "the impression of a picture reproduced from a specially treated surface of stone or other material." The image of a photograph negative was transferred to a sensitized metal printing plate by light exposure. The surface of the plate was then dampened with water, and a greasy ink was rolled on it. The ink adhered to the design only in those parts that were not dampened, because the grease attracted the ink and repelled the water. From the plate, the image was then transferred to the surface being printed. Litho printing was most frequently used in graphic artwork which required large quantity (i.e., hundreds of prints) runs and fine detail such as that found in books and catalogs. Although litho printing could be used for producing large 4' × 8' prints, the press required for the large murals would cost $3 to $4 million.

Another method, *screen process printing*, used a silk, nylon, or metal screen containing an image. A squeegee forced ink through the screen to form an image on paper or other material. Early screens were made by painting the image on silk with a fluid that was resistant to ink. Masking materials blocked out any unwanted printing areas. Modern techniques involved hand-cut stencils or photomechanical means used in screen-process work. Screen printing was used in graphic work that required short runs and not so fine detail. While lithographers were skilled craftspeople who typically had invested up to four years to learn their craft, individuals could become proficient in screen printing in approximately three weeks. As a result, there were several thousand companies in North America experienced in screen printing.

Conventional inks used in the litho and screen-printing processes were inks dried by a heat process involving evaporation of solvents. More specialized inks used within the industry were U.V. inks which were manufactured from automotive-grade pigments. These inks were cured by U.V. radiation, and when initially introduced to the industry, the radiation was seen as a potential source of skin cancer. As a result, the majority of printers had been cautious about getting involved with the U.V. inks. Printers who did use U.V. inks were very careful, and no cancer cases were attributed to this curing process.

The use of U.V. inks in screen printing gave printed material a brilliance, dimension, color retention, and print quality that was not obtainable by photographic enlargements and conventional inks. Although U.V. inks were not new to the printing industry, producing large 4′ × 8′ prints using U.V. inks was a relatively new concept. Printers had been using the U.V. inks for small, detailed prints, and few people had identified worthwhile markets for larger prints. In addition, an estimated $800,000 would be required for presses, screens, and other equipment to produce large prints.

Company Background

Screen Print was a privately owned company which designed and produced a full line of point-of-sale display, and advertising products and services for use at the retail-store level. A wholly owned subsidiary, Screen Print Display Advertising (Western) Limited, operated in Winnipeg.

The company (originally called Dominion Signs) began operations in 1908 for the purpose of making handmade signs. In the course of close to 80 years, Screen Print had been involved in a range of businesses from manufacturing highway signs and billboards to producing the sophisticated wall graphics of the 1980s. Segments of the company's diversified product mix included a comprehensive lithography line; custom fabrication of retail fixtures (e.g., counter and display cabinets) incorporating metal, plastic, and screen process printing; and merchandise showrooms.

Screen Print passed the $2 million sales mark in 1971 and continued steadily upward to become a business with sales of approximately $10 million which employed 200 full-time employees by 1982.[1] The trend to large shopping centers was thought to be instrumental in the corporation's growth in the 1960s and 1970s. The company's product mix consisted of screen printing (40 percent of sales), litho printing (25 percent), woodworking (25 percent), and custom fabricating with plastics (10 percent). Screen Print sold its flyers, posters and other products to numerous retail chains, including Beckers (a chain of convenience stores), Tim Horton Donuts (a chain of doughnut shops), and I.G.A. (an association of independent grocery stores).

In 1977, the company bought an ultraviolet ink-curing unit and started experimenting with U.V. inks in its screen-printing process. Shortly after acquiring this equipment, Screen Print was able to secure a contract to supply department-identification murals for over 100 Woolco stores across Canada. On the one hand, Screen Print had not yet accumulated much experience with the U.V. inks, and management was not certain how they would fulfill the contract. On the other hand, they were confident that the company had identified and could create a viable market for large prints

---

[1] All data concerning corporate sales and margins are disguised, but essential relationships have been maintained.

produced from U.V. inks. In addition, management knew that the company had good technical people and excellent production equipment. Therefore, they were eager to accept the challenge to supply murals to the Woolco chain. As a result, Screen Print was given the opportunity to experiment with U.V. inks to produce large four-color murals.

Because Screen Print's presses at the time were only large enough to produce 50″ × 40″ prints, and the murals required were 50″ × 60″, a number of small panels had to be put together to produce one large mural. It was often difficult to match colors consistently across the multiple panels. Therefore, the panels were split with black lines in order to keep a consistent design throughout the stores. Although Mr. Smith believed that the black lines detracted from the finished look of the murals, the Woolco contract had given Screen Print a chance to develop the knowledge and experience for producing large murals.

Shortly following the Woolco project, Screen Print was approached by Don Watt & Associates, an international design house operating out of Toronto, to prepare large, custom 4′ × 8′ U.V.-ink murals for the Loblaws supermarket chain. Given the chance to perfect their new product, Screen Print accepted the challenge and quickly developed a reputation as the only North American company capable of producing the giant murals.

Over the next few years, Screen Print was able to obtain contracts from a number of retail chains across Canada for large custom U.V.-ink murals. Steinberg's, K mart, I.G.A., Laura Secord, and MM Muffins stores all became customers for the large murals. As a result of its accumulated experience, Screen Print was able to produce large murals without having to separate panels with black lines. Management at Screen Print, rather than the company's 22 person sales force, had been responsible for identifying and securing customers for the large U.V.-ink murals. They had been able to do so through attending trade shows (the major show being the Food Marketing Institute [F.M.I.] held annually in Dallas), using existing contacts within the industry, and making cold calls. Once a potential customer had been identified and contacted, Mr. Smith believed that "the murals sold themselves." Customers' primary concerns were what other chains were using the murals in a particular area, how they could be different, and how much the murals cost. Mr. Smith estimated that 10 to 15 percent of customers that were called on had purchased the murals.

After receiving an order for the murals, Screen Print would arrange to photograph the subject material to be printed on the murals. When the photographs were approved, color separations were done. *Color separation* was a process of dividing a colored photograph negative into its basic four colors—red, yellow, blue, and black. These four colors, when mixed together in different proportions, produced every other color. The color-separation process was both time-consuming and expensive.

When separated, the film size was only 16″ × 20″, and the separated film had to be enlarged to the required printing size. The film was then trans-

EXHIBIT 1
Canadian Grocery Chains, 1982

Number of Stores in Chain	Number of Chains	Total Number of Stores	Percent of Grocery Sales
4 to 9	46	264	7.3%
10 to 49	20	383	5.4
50 to 99	10	636	15.0
100 to 249	5	757	32.7
250+	5	2,109	39.6
Total	86	4,149	100.0%

Large Canadian Grocery Chains

Company Name	Number of Stores	Sales ($000s)
1. Bantam Stores	55	$ 16,000
2. Canada Safeway Ltd.	197	1,300,000
3. Dominion Stores Ltd.	380	2,000,000
4. Great Atlantic & Pacific Co.	200	1,100,000
5. Kelly, Douglas & Co. Ltd. (Super-Valu Stores)	55	1,710,000
6. Loblaws Ltd.	225	4,490,000
7. Miracle Food Mart	69	550,000
8. Oshawa Group (Food City, IGA Stores)	200	2,100,000
9. Overwaitea Foods	46	200,000
10. Provigo	102	350,000
11. Westfair Foods Ltd. (subsidiary of Kelly, Douglas & Co. Ltd.)	66	889,000
12. Woodwards	20	505,000
13. Zehrmart Ltd. (subsidiary of Loblaws Ltd.)	33	100,000

Source: Thomas Grocery Register, 1980.

posed on a screen and, beginning with a yellow ink, the print was produced. When the printer was satisfied that the color density was correct, the desired number of prints were run. This same process was then repeated for each of the remaining three colors. A high level of skill was required to produce large U.V.-ink mural-quality prints.

Post press operations included mounting the prints (if required) and packaging and transporting them to the customers. After an initial sell-in, there was virtually no servicing required on the murals. Customers used the murals as part of their in-store decor package. The murals, which attractively depicted the stores' product and service line, were generally placed on the walls throughout the stores as department-identification markers.

By 1981, approximately 3 percent of the company's sales was accounted for by large U.V.-ink murals. Mr. Smith thought Screen Print had as much Canadian business with this product as was possible at this time because of a "me too" problem. He knew that retail chains like to present a unique interior design to customers as part of a competitive package. If a number of chains were using the large murals in their decor schemes, other chains would avoid using the mural concept for fear of becoming a "me too" store. This concern seemed reasonable, considering the concentrated nature of the Canadian grocery industry. Twenty large grocery chains operated almost 85 percent of all grocery stores, and accounted for 87 percent of all grocery sales in Canada (see Exhibit 1). He believed, however, that a significant opportunity might exist in the United States for the large U.V.-ink murals, and he wanted to assess the market potential and prepare a plan to capitalize on the opportunity.

THE UNITED STATES MARKET

Competition

According to Screen Print management, there were no other companies in Canada or the United States that could produce large murals with U.V. inks. Mr. Smith believed that his company had a strong advantage because it already had the large press required for the murals, and it had accumulated production experience in Canadian markets. There were, however, hundreds of companies that produced large murals by photographic enlargement and several that used conventional screen printing.

There were also firms experienced in U.V. printing, but only for smaller-size prints than those produced by Screen Print. To make the large murals, these companies would have to invest approximately $800,000 for the larger press and other equipment. Because most printing companies involved in screen printing were typically small operations employing three to four individuals, Mr. Smith believed that an investment of this size was beyond the means of most printing companies. In addition, he believed that the market was too small to interest the few large printing companies that did exist. Therefore, as a medium-sized firm, he believed that Screen Print was in a strong, competitive, position regarding the large murals. There were, however, a few European companies that had the technical capability and the experience to challenge Screen Print in the United States market. Fortunately, Screen Print management believed that these companies lacked Screen Print's in-depth knowledge of the North American culture, the retailing industry, and the public's shopping behavior.

Market Size

Mr. Smith had derived a rough estimate of the total market potential in the United States by identifying the number of stores that might use the murals. In general, chains with 15 to 20 stores were considered the minimum size which could afford large custom-made murals. The United States supermarket industry was a very fragmented industry. According to one industry source, "Although bigness is the order of the day, the grocery business is still regional, and the industry is not headed to the point where it might be run by a few large companies." There were over 190,000 grocery stores in the United States, and, of those, 365 supermarket chains operated 33,550 stores. The top 100 chains operated approximately 30,000 of those stores. Exhibit 2 provides data on the leading United States supermarket chains. These firms often became members in voluntary and cooperative group-wholesaler organizations in order to increase their buying power and to compete more effectively against the large chains.

Assuming that 10 to 15 percent of the top supermarket chains adopted the large mural concept within a five-year period, and that the average cost of prints per store was $10,000 for a store of 50,000 square feet, the total potential sales was estimated at $6 to 9 million annually, taking into account only the supermarket industry. The supermarket segment was

EXHIBIT 2
Top U.S. Supermarket Chains, 1981

Rank	Company	Sales ($000)	Grocery Stores Operated
1	Safeway Stores (California)	$16,580,318	2,477
2	The Kroger Co. (Ohio)	11,266,520	1,258
3	Lucky Stores (California)	7,133,676	541
4	American Stores (Pennsylvania)	7,096,590	1,122
5	Winn Dixie (Florida)	6,760,000	1,222
6	A & P (New Jersey)	6,226,755	1,055
7	Southland Corp. (Texas)	5,734,160	7,099
8	Jewel Companies (Illinois)	5,107,614	768
9	Grand Union (New Jersey)	4,137,447	732
10	Albertson's (Idaho)	3,480,570	412
11–20		14,437,907	1,268
21–30		6,797,239	2,812
31–40		4,416,262	577
41–50		2,706,736	2,438
Total		$101,881,794	23,781

Source: Company records.

EXHIBIT 3
Top 25 Drug Chains in the United States

Drug Chain (Headquarters)	Volume ($ billions)	Total Stores
1. American Stores (Salt Lake City)	$2.6	395
2. Jack Eckerd (Florida)	2.3	1,325
3. Walgreen (Illinois)	2.3	941
4. Revco D.S. (Ohio)	1.8	1,696
5. Jewel Cos. (Chicago)	1.8	485
6. Rite Aid (Pennsylvania)	1.3	1,095
7. Longs Drug Stores (California)	1.2	176
8. Thrifty (Los Angeles)	1.2	537
9. Pay'n Save (Seattle)	1.1	140
10. Pay Less NW (Oregon)	0.8	147
11. People Drug Stores (Virginia)	0.8	576
12. SupeRx (Cincinnati)	0.8	586
13. CVS (Rhode Island)	0.6	495
14. Thrift Drug (Pittsburgh)	0.6	361
15. Gray Drug Fair (Cleveland)	0.5	403
16. Supermarkets General (New Jersey)	0.5	126
17. K & B (New Orleans)	0.3	120
18. Hook Drugs (Indianapolis)	0.3	296
19. Dart Drug (Maryland)	0.3	n.a.
20. Adams Drug (Rhode Island)	0.3	425
21. Fay's Drug (New York)	0.3	101
22. Perry Drug Stores (Michigan)	0.3	126
23. Genovese Drug Stores (Massachusetts)	0.2	n.a.
24. Medi Mart (Massachusetts)	0.1	n.a.
25. Medicare-Glaser (St. Louis)	0.1	104

n.a. = Not available.

Source: Chain Drug Review, 1981.

thought to have the highest potential for large murals because the subject matter (i.e., food) did not change over time. However, there was also potential to exploit other markets, including food courts in shopping centers and specialty food, drugstore, general-merchandise, and fast-food chains (see Exhibits 3 and 4). Mr. Smith thought the possibility for large murals in these markets could be as large as that of the supermarket industry, although the sales potential was more speculative because Screen Print had very little experience in these markets, even in Canada.

An indication of the potential market could also be obtained by extrapolating the results of the company's Canadian sales experience. Based on the 10:1 ratio of gross national products (GNPs) of the two countries, the total potential United States market would be approximately $4 million per year,

EXHIBIT 4
Top 25 General Merchandise Chains

Rank	Chain	Volume $billions (U.S.)	Stores
1.	Sears	$18.8	831
2.	K mart	16.8	2,370
3.	J.C. Penney	11.4	2,053
4.	Federated	6.4	390
5.	Dayton Hudson	5.7	980
6.	Montgomery Ward	5.5	389
7.	F.W. Woolworth	5.1	5,124
8.	May Dept. Stores	3.7	1,468
9.	Wal-Mart	3.4	541
10.	Allied Stores	3.2	533
11.	Assoc. Dry Goods	3.2	311
12.	Carter Hawley Hale	3.1	1,026
13.	R.H. Macy	3.0	92
14.	Household Merch.	2.9	3,768
15.	Wickes	2.6	n/a
16.	BATUS	2.4	178
17.	Zayre	2.1	617
18.	Lucky	2.1	1,029
19.	Tandy Corp.	2.0	8,518
20.	McCrory Corp.	1.7	1,792
21.	Best Products	1.6	202
22.	Belk Stores	1.5	360
23.	Mercantile	1.4	84
24.	Melville	1.4	1,697
25.	W.R. Grace	1.3	613

Source: Chain Store Age, General Merchandise Edition.

assuming the Company was to confine its activities to supermarket chains. Mr. Smith believed that this method of estimating the total potential in the United States might be somewhat conservative because there were proportionally more noncompeting regional chains in the United States than in Canada.

Customers

According to preliminary research findings, the final decision to purchase large murals was made by general and merchandising managers because it involved a retail chain's corporate image and strategy. Key influencers within the retail chain were senior personnel within the construction group of the chain.

Major changes to in-store decor were usually made as part of a new building program or a major redecoration effort of older stores. Approximately 10 to 15 percent of stores in a chain were remodeled, replaced, or refurbished in any one year. According to one grocery-chain executive:

> When we do a plan for remodeling, we look at the long range; that is, five years. We work on the assumption that all strategies eventually will become obsolete.

Screen Print management believed it was unlikely that a chain could be convinced to adopt murals if it were not already contemplating a change to in-store decor. Mr. Smith believed that design houses had become increasingly important in recent years as retail chains attempted to reduce staff costs and eliminate "tunnel vision" that sometimes developed from designers who worked exclusively for a single company. It was estimated that four-fifths of the large supermarket chains used outside design houses, although many of them also had in-house designers who were often responsible for relatively routine projects.

Wholesalers and architects often provided store supplies, including point-of-purchase advertising materials to smaller chains and independents. Since the decision to utilize large murals was time-consuming, involved many people, and was of great significance to a retail chain, Mr. Smith concluded that Screen Print would have to be at the "right time" and "right place" in order to exploit the identified United States potential for large U.V.-ink murals.

Opportunities/Threats

Mr. Smith believed that the quality of Screen Print's large U.V.-ink murals was superior to those murals produced by photographic enlargements or printing with conventional inks, and that customers would be willing to pay a 20-percent premium for the U.V.-ink murals over these two competitive techniques. The product's advantages had been cited as brightness and life-like quality. In addition, the murals did not fade over time.

Other positive aspects of the United States opportunity included management's belief that, in the United States grocery industry, compared to Canada, there was an increased focus on merchandising, packaging, displays, promotion, etc., rather than on cost controls. There was also a heightened awareness that consumers considered supermarket stores "dull," "boring," and "unimaginative." Screen Print executives believed that this perception, coupled with the emergence of the "warehouse" type of supermarket, was conducive to the marketing of large murals. They believed that these products could be used for department identification markers, could lessen the "hangar-feeling," and could draw customers' attention to the walls rather than the often unfinished ceilings.

In addition, the increased size of stores expanded the available market for large murals. The larger products were better suited for larger stores since they tended to overwhelm the consumer in smaller outlets. The minimum economic size for conventional new supermarkets was generally considered 35,000 square feet, while it had once been 20–25,000 square feet. Stores with areas of 80,000 square feet were being built, and some designers envisioned outlets of 125,000 square feet.

One of the major concerns among potential users of large murals was thought to be the cost of custom-produced murals. Mr. Smith estimated that fixed start-up costs to retail chains, including photography, and color separations for each mural subject (i.e., ice cream, poultry, fresh produce, etc.) were $2,000—before any prints were actually run on the press. The average chain would use approximately 50 subjects throughout its stores. These fixed start-up costs were similar to those for screen printing with conventional inks.

On the other hand, printers were able to achieve economies of scale when printing with a screen-printing process, and screen printing became less expensive than photographic enlargement when producing a quantity of prints. For example, one photographic enlargement would cost retailers approximately $300, and 20 enlargements would cost $6,000 ($Canadian). Screen printing using U.V. inks, on the other hand, would cost retailers approximately $4500 for 20 prints (including $2,000 for photography and color separations) of the same subject on a custom-order, low-volume basis. Mr. Smith estimated that an average-size store of 50,000 square feet would use approximately 200 4' × 8' U.V.-ink murals (50 subjects), and that this quantity would cost retailers $10,000, or $50 per print on a large-volume commitment.

Another concern was that widespread use of large murals would result in homogenization in inside decor among supermarket chains, thus dispelling the competitive advantage enjoyed by early adopters of the large murals. Although the murals were produced on a custom basis, some people believed that the murals would develop a generic look as the subject material was similar from one supermarket chain to another. As well, potential United States customers expressed some concern about being supplied by a Canadian firm. They viewed importing as inevitably more complicated, requiring longer lead times than being supplied by a domestic manufacturer. Screen Print would also have to pay a 3.3 percent-of-selling-price import tariff for bringing its murals to the United States market. Mr. Smith did not believe that a tariff of this size would significantly affect his company's ability to compete with United States printing companies. The Canadian dollar was trading at about $0.75 U.S., which provided a pricing advantage to Canadian suppliers.

Alternative Penetration Strategies

Mr. Smith identified a number of alternative routes for penetrating the United States market with large U.V.-ink murals. Screen Print could sell their custom murals directly to end users, or they could enlist the aid of interior-design houses and/or wholesalers who served large retail chains in marketing the murals. If Screen Print sold direct to end users, they could offer a complete decor package centered around the large murals, or they could attempt to sell this one product idea only. Alternatively, they could use a combination of these penetration methods. Whichever option was chosen, Screen Print would also have to make decisions on sales force requirements, market segments to approach, selling price, and overall budget.

Design Houses.   Mr. Smith had identified 500 design houses in the United States with experience in supermarkets, and/or other chain retail stores and shopping centers. About 25 percent of these design houses specialized in the supermarket industry, although they also serviced other retail accounts if necessary. The 19 major firms serving this industry are listed in Exhibit 5. Mr. Smith believed that, on average, a design house employed 15 to 20 people, including one or two sales representatives, and it serviced any number of retail outlets, ranging from 8 to 300 accounts. Its accounts also ranged in size—from clients with two to three retail stores to clients with large retail chains. One design house could service accounts all across the country as there were virtually no regional boundaries. Design houses were professional service firms, and very few were manufacturers of

EXHIBIT 5

U.S. Design Houses with Experience with Supermarkets, Other Chain Retail Stores, and Shopping Centres*

> Decor and Graphics (Detroit)
> Programmed Products Corp. (Chicago)
> CDI Designs Inc. (Riverdale, N.Y.)
> Off The Wall Company Inc. (Sellersville, Pa.)
> The Doody Co. (Columbus, Ohio)
> Arnold Ward Studios Ltd. (Glen Cove, N.Y.)
> Herb Ross Associates (New York)
> Commercial Interior Products (Fairfield, Ohio)
> ISD-Kanden Co. Inc. (Los Angeles)
> Hambrecht Terrell Intl. (New York, N.Y.)
> Norman Rosenfeld, A.I.A. Architects (New York)
> Bernard Vinick Associates Inc. (Hartford)
> McClelland, Cruz, Gaylord & Associates (Pasadena)
> Maxwell Starkman (Beverly Hills)
> Mike Sanchez and Associates (Pasadena, California)
> Jarob Design (Grand Rapids, Michigan)
> George Taylor & Associates (Coral Gables, Florida)
> Space Design International (Cincinnati)
> Shaw & Slavsky (Detroit)

* Design houses listed were identified by Screen Print, desk research, and by interviewees in the course of the field work.

the items they used. Mr. Smith believed that the key to a design house's financial viability was maintaining the lowest possible level of fixed costs. He believed that design houses had a relatively low level of financial resources and that even the "large" ones had significantly less than $10 million in sales.

Mr. Smith also faced an issue of how many design houses to allow to distribute the murals. Although he believed that exclusive distribution arrangements would reduce Screen Print's penetration of the United States market, he knew that there would be little competitive advantage to an individual design house if the murals were available through a large number of design houses.

If Screen Print used design houses to penetrate the United States market, it would have to convince these designers that large U.V.-ink murals were important tools in serving retail clients needs. Since design-house personnel were artistically and aesthetically oriented, Mr. Smith believed they would have to be provided with visually attractive material. Therefore, he wanted to send letters of introduction to design houses and include samples of the actual product (although not the large size) with the letters. He was also considering developing a store model for illustrating alternate ways of using the murals, and/or producing a video film describing Screen Print. Design houses could then use some or all of this material to convince end users of the desirability of using the murals.

An advantage of using design houses was that designers had the capability to integrate Screen Print's murals into the overall design package of retail stores. This overall design concept could lead to quicker acceptance of the product. Designers also had frequent contact and established relationships with potential end users of large murals. When it secured a design contract with a retail chain which incorporated the large murals, a design house could recommend Screen Print to the retail chain as the contractor to produce the murals.

On the other hand, Screen Print would lose a certain amount of control by employing design houses in its United States market-penetration plans. It would not have direct contact with the customer. Furthermore, design houses would inevitably concentrate on their own retail-chain clients with limited time and resources to expand beyond an existing client base. In addition, designers who were selling a total decor scheme, not just large U.V.-ink murals, might not necessarily recommend the Screen Print product over one of many decor products they carried.

Mr. Smith believed that one concern among design houses would be the high cost of custom-made murals. Many design houses serviced smaller retail clients in addition to their clients with large retail chains, and the cost of custom-made murals might be prohibitive to these smaller customers. Mr. Smith reasoned that the availability of a number of stock items could increase a design house's willingness to employ the large murals in order to service these smaller clients. He estimated that 50 stock items, including 25 food images and 25 nonfood images would be sufficient to allow design houses and end users to experiment and tailor the murals to their particular needs at a reasonable price.

The development of a number of stock items would be a significant departure from the way Screen Print had serviced the market. Furthermore, it would require a significant investment of approximately $100,000—including photography and color separations. Although Mr. Smith thought it would be desirable to have design houses coinvest in an expansion of a stock line, he realized it was unlikely that design houses would share in product development costs. Such an investment could cause conflict between a design house's desire to sell the murals and its need to satisfy its clients' best interests. Design houses usually set their prices by doubling the cost of any item to achieve a 50 percent margin on their selling price to the end customer.

Mr. Smith knew, however, that if a design house incorporated murals into the design package of a client who operated only two or three stores, only a minimal number of murals would be required to service that account. Because of the fixed up-front costs per subject, production of the murals was more economical for Screen Print for a large order of murals. Therefore, Mr. Smith believed that Screen Print would have to ask a design house to commit itself to a larger number of murals than would be needed at any one time. This commitment would require that a design house carry an inventory of the stock murals, which could be stored at Screen Print's facilities for a minimal storage fee.

Direct to End Users.   A second alternative was for Screen Print to sell its large murals directly to end customers, either alone or as part of a complete in-store design package. By selling direct to end users, Mr. Smith was certain that his company would retain greater control of the marketing efforts for the large murals. He thought that pricing should be consistent with the achievement of an average gross margin of 35 percent of selling price.

If Screen Print sold its murals direct to retail chains, one option was to offer a complete decor package centered around the murals. With this option, Screen Print could be both a design house and a manufacturer. Mr. Smith knew the company had traditionally been capable of good "jack-of-all-trades" skills, as its services included photography, fabrication of retail fixtures, woodworking, etc. Therefore, he concluded that it should not be too difficult to acquire the necessary interior-design capabilities. Mr. Smith estimated that three or four people with store interior-design backgrounds would be required, at approximately $75,000 each.

In Canada, Screen Print sold the murals directly to end users, and the sales force had been able to establish good relationships with senior executives in the major supermarket chains. In the United States, however, the company had fewer personal contacts and the industry was much larger and more fragmented than in Canada. Mr. Smith wondered how seriously this situation would affect Screen Print's ability to sell direct to end users.

He estimated that two sales representatives would be required at approximately $100,000 each (salary and expenses) to identify potential customers—through attendance at trade shows, and through familiarizing themselves with trade magazines and trade directories. Letters of introduction could be sent to potential customers, along with a sample of the actual product (though not necessarily the large size). There were literally dozens of magazines that catered to the United States retailing and related industries, though very few such periodicals had a large circulation. (Two of the largest related periodicals, *Progressive Grocer* and *Supermarket News*, had circulations of 83,000 and 58,000, respectively.) Mr. Smith believed that advertising in a small number of the key magazines, with a budget of $50,000, would allow Screen Print to create awareness among potential users who would not have been approached directly by the sales representatives. He also estimated that 5 to 10 percent of his time would be required to assist the sales representatives in selling the large murals.

At present, Mr. Smith did not believe there would be any need to establish a physical presence (e.g., sales office or warehouse) in the United States to serve the market. He believed that shipping the murals directly to the purchasers would be a satisfactory distribution practice. However, if it did become necessary to open a United States office just to escape any apparent discrimination against a Canadian company, Mr. Smith estimated the cost to be between $70,000 and $80,000 annually, including rent, a toll-free telephone line, and a person to manage the office.

Design Houses and Direct Sales.   Mr. Smith realized Screen Print could penetrate the United States market more quickly if it sold its murals direct to end users and at the same time convinced design houses to incorporate the murals in their in-store design packages. However, he was concerned that design houses would be hesitant to compete directly against Screen Print, and he realized that Screen Print would not always be aware of what end users the design houses would be calling on. As a result, Screen Prints' efforts could overlap those of a design house.

If marketing efforts were targeted both to end users and design houses, Mr. Smith realized that advertising and promotional efforts would have to have a "push" effect in order to introduce the product to design houses who may, in turn, incorporate the murals in their design packages. Advertising and promotion would also have to have a "pull" effect in order to create awareness among potential end users.

Conclusion

Screen Print was willing to commit a significant level of resources (over $500,000 annually) to develop the identified business potential in the United States. This budgeted figure included salaries for individuals involved in United States sales ($200,000), travel expenses ($100,000), promotional material, ($100,000) and other sales expenses ($50,000), as well as additional indirect labor costs ($50,000).

Although he did not believe there was any immediate competitive threat in the United States market, Mr. Smith thought it was important for Screen Print to act quickly to capitalize on this opportunity. While market receptivity to the mural concept currently appeared to exist, tastes in in-store decor did change quickly. In addition, the longer Screen Print delayed in undertaking a concentrated marketing effort, the more likely it was that someone else would try to establish a presence. He believed that by 1986 there would probably be a handful of competitors in the market producing large U.V.-ink murals for retail chains. Therefore, he was anxious to establish his company as the only North American producer of giant 4' × 8' U.V.-ink murals. Once Screen Print was recognized in the United States as a dependable, quality manufacturer for point-of-purchase display and advertising products, Mr. Smith was sure that even greater opportunities could be created for Screen Print in the United States.

CASE 4–6

Nebon Medical Products, Incorporated

Nebon Medical Products (NMP) in Milwaukee, Wisconsin, is one of the top manufacturers of life-support medical equipment and surgical pharmaceuticals. In 1980, NMP recorded sales of $230 million (see Exhibit 1). Over the past five years sales have been increasing at an annual rate of 15 percent. The company currently employs 175 sales representatives, including a separate sales force of 40 that handles the company's pharmaceutical line exclusively. As the result of a recent staff reorganization a decision was made to realign the sales department to meet the future goals of the company better.

Three years ago Nebon's president retired, and the top position was filled by the executive vice president, Christopher John. Subsequently several other major changes occurred in the executive staff hierarchy. The most important were the elimination of the executive vice president position and the creation of the position of vice president, marketing and sales. Reporting to the new vice president would be the current vice president of sales, service, and distribution; the four marketing managers; the director of market research; and the director of promotion (see Exhibit 2).

The vice president of marketing and sales, destined to be one of the most powerful positions at NMP, was ultimately filled by Earl Callahan.

This case was prepared by Bonnie J. Queram, MBA, University of Wisconsin at Madison.

EXHIBIT 1
1980 Sales ($000)

Patient care		$ 84,270
Anesthesia equipment	$40,100	
Anesthesia disposables	20,450	
Nursing products	13,720	
Infant care	10,000	
Respiratory therapy		40,418
Architectural products		35,980
Pharmaceuticals		50,055
Other (government, OEM, service, military)		20,000
Total		$230,723

Callahan had previously held the top marketing job in a firm that manufactured medical products unrelated to those sold by Nebon. Filling this position with an "outsider" generated noticeable discontent among several executives who had been considered as top contenders. Shortly after he began
work, Callahan was pressured by John to have a revised sales organization
chart completed prior to Nebon's new fiscal year beginning July 1. After
reviewing Nebon's current organization charts, sales figures, and marketing plans for new products, Callahan realized there were several major
problems.

EXHIBIT 2

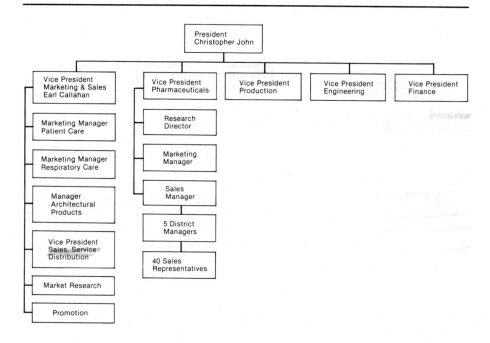

MARKETING ACTIVITIES

Nebon's marketing function was divided into four separate product areas. The patient-care group consisted of anesthesia equipment and disposables, nursing equipment, and infant-care supplies. The anesthesia line accounted for the greatest dollar volume, with 1980 sales of $60 million. With new products as the primary growth factor, sales were expected to be $115 million by 1985. Product prices range from a few cents for disposables to several thousand dollars for equipment.

The respiratory therapy line accounted for $40 million in sales in 1980. The line had experienced only slight growth over the last few years but was expected to generate $58 million by 1985 with the introduction of one major new respirator, priced as high as $35,000 with all accessories. The prime market for this do-everything machine was the small to medium-size hospital. Although Nebon was the leader in the anesthesia field, it did not enjoy the same position in respiratory care. In fact, due to several major failures with new products during the last 10 years, the Nebon name was still associated by many therapists with inferior quality, poor product design, and inadequate service.

The architectural product line, composed of pipelines and gas outlets, had sales of $36 million in 1980, while the pharmaceutical line, sold by a separate sales organization, accounted for $50 million. The major product was a liquid that, when converted to gas, was used to anesthetize patients for surgery.

SALES ACTIVITIES

The general-line sales force, consisting of 135 representatives reporting to 19 district managers, and six regional vice presidents (see Exhibit 3) were currently expected to call on four major departments in each hospital: anesthesia, respiratory therapy, nursing, and infant care. Additionally, they were expected to keep in contact with purchasing and, if one existed, with the biomedical engineering department. The latter, usually present only in larger hospitals, was often responsible for reviewing and testing potential new equipment. Biomedical engineers were becoming instrumental in the purchase of sophisticated electronic devices. Also, the sales force was expected to sell gas and electrical pipeline equipment to new hospitals or those being remodeled. This required that they work very closely with architects and construction contractors, usually a very time-consuming endeavor ranging from several months to over one year. The pharmaceutical sales force called on the anesthesia staff exclusively. Close and frequent contact was necessary in most cases. The sales force, all with chemical backgrounds, was expected to keep abreast of technological developments in the field. Some sales representatives were formerly anesthetists.

EXHIBIT 3

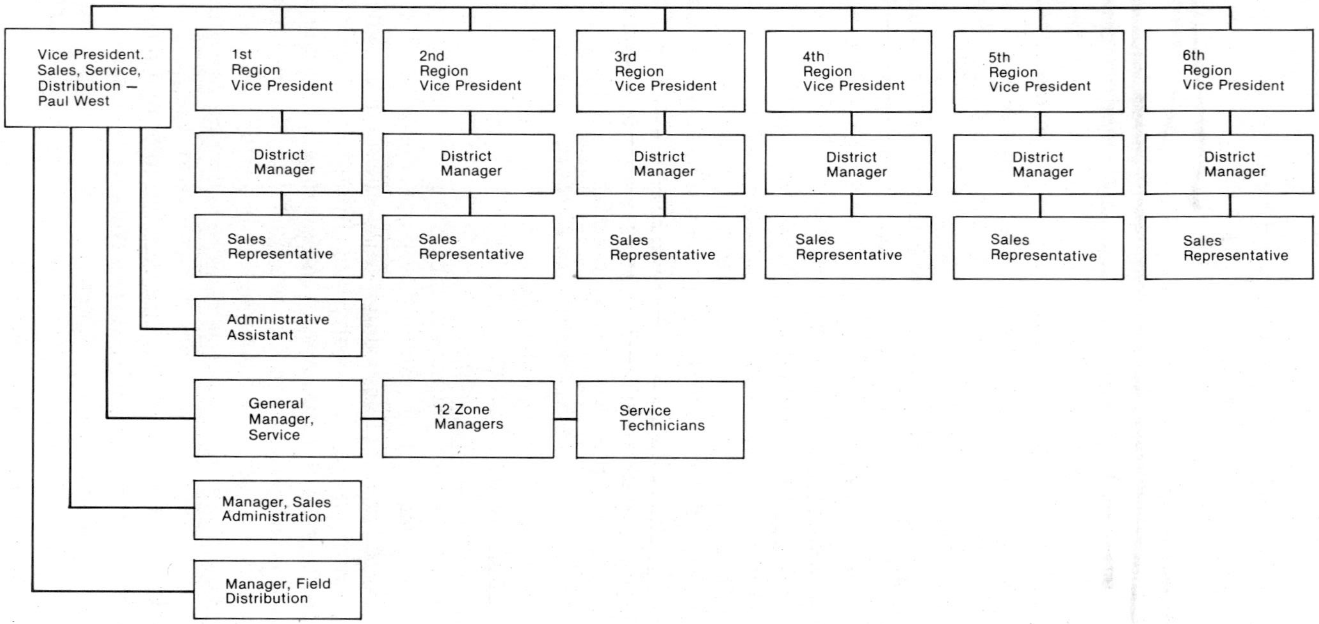

Organization chart (rotated 90°):

- **Vice President, Sales, Service, Distribution — Paul West**
  - 1st Region Vice President
    - District Manager
      - Sales Representative
  - 2nd Region Vice President
    - District Manager
      - Sales Representative
  - 3rd Region Vice President
    - District Manager
      - Sales Representative
  - 4th Region Vice President
    - District Manager
      - Sales Representative
  - 5th Region Vice President
    - District Manager
      - Sales Representative
  - 6th Region Vice President
    - District Manager
      - Sales Representative
  - Administrative Assistant
  - General Manager, Service
    - 12 Zone Managers
      - Service Technicians
  - Manager, Sales Administration
  - Manager, Field Distribution

Although Nebon's products covered a wide variety of medical applications and necessitated sales calls to many different departments, the general-line sales force had, to date, handled the lines very well. Callahan felt that one primary reason they had done so well was that the majority of Nebon's products were not particularly complicated and the sales force could be adequately trained by the product managers when new products were introduced. Additionally, although Nebon sold several thousand items, which realistically is a line much too broad for a sales representative to handle effectively, Callahan knew that many products sold with little or no sales effort because of the Nebon name and strong dealer network. Most dealers handled low-cost, easy-to-sell products, although some of the very large dealers sold high-priced equipment. Callahan also felt, however, that this would not continue in the future, because many products planned for market introduction in the next five years were complicated, state-of-the-art electronic pieces of equipment. Most of these products were in the anesthesia line. Nebon's lack of experience in the medical electronics field would mean that an intensive sales effort would be required to enter the market profitably, as there were several formidable competitors controlling the market.

Unfortunately it was generally known that perhaps as many as half of Nebon's sales representatives did not have the training or experience to sell these kinds of products. In view of the need to deal with hospital biomedical engineers on a very technical level, in the long run, Callahan surmised, it would be better to use only sales personnel experienced in selling electronic equipment rather than attempt to train the entire force. Besides, he knew from personal conversations that quite a few representatives had no interest in learning about or selling the new equipment. Thus he wondered about the feasibility of a separate sales group to handle electronic products exclusively.

OTHER INFORMATION

For the last year the marketing manager in respiratory care, Bill Griese, had been attempting to convince Callahan that in spite of the line's history real growth potential existed in respiratory therapy. He wanted the company to spend more time and money pursuing this market. Griese had also indicated that to sell and service the products adequately—particularly the new, very technical respirator—the line should be handled by a separate sales force. He argued that because most of Nebon's products were in the anesthesia field, the representatives were spending a disproportionate amount of sales time in that area. Thus Nebon's relatively poor sales and image in respiratory therapy were perpetuated.

Callahan knew that Jeff Hardy, marketing manager for patient care, would lobby for a separate sales group for the anesthesia products, since that line represents one quarter of the company's sales. Apparently this request had been made several times over the past five years. One proposal had included plans for the pharmaceutical sales force to also handle the anesthesia equipment because both were sold to the same department. Another proposal had called for a separate anesthesia equipment force altogether. Callahan felt that drugs and equipment required substantially different sales techniques and that one force could not adequately handle both. But he also had reservations about two different representatives calling on the same customer, as was currently the case. On the other hand, a separate anesthesia force would result in substantially more sales time spent on respiratory products by the general-line force.

PHARMACEUTICAL SALES ORGANIZATION

Approximately 10 years ago, Nebon's chemical research department discovered a revolutionary new drug to anesthetize patients safely for surgery. Following two years of testing for the Food and Drug Administration, the drug was approved and successfully introduced to the marketplace. It is currently used on 60 percent of all surgical patients, and it continues to capture market share. The drug has a very high gross margin, and in 1980 it had profits of $37 million on sales of $50 million. Its patent runs through 1990.

To develop the surgical drug market fully and lead the marketing and sales activities, a vice presidential position was created at the time of discovery of the new drug. Ronald Hagen was hired for this position. He in turn put together a separate sales organization with 45 persons by 1980. Most of the sales representatives were hired away from other pharmaceutical companies and thus demanded and were paid salaries and commissions substantially higher than those paid to Nebon's general-line salesman (see Exhibit 4).

EXHIBIT 4
Sales Compensation Plans

	General-line Representatives	Pharmaceutical Representatives
Base salary	$ 1,500–1,850	$ 1,650–2,100
Commission on sales up to quota	3/4%	1%
Commission on sales over quota	2%	2%
1980 salary range	$24,200–35,800	$29,800–42,750

*breed[?]
hostility
up/
them
in same
co.*

Hagen is very proud of his organization, believing that his sales representatives are a cut above the general-line organization. Consequently he wants no part of any plans to join the two forces. Besides, another new drug scheduled for introduction in 1983 will provide the drug sales group with a sufficient product load for several years into the future.

GENERAL-LINE SALES ORGANIZATION

The general-line sales organization, reporting to Paul West, consisted of 135 representatives, 9 district managers, and 6 regional vice presidents. The service department, also under West, consisted of a total of 150 technicians reporting to 12 zone managers.

West was initially quite upset about the apparent demotion of his position as a result of the reorganization; he had reported directly to John before Callahan was hired. Knowing that further reorganization was imminent, West felt he would ultimately lose control of the service and distribution areas. Although this would narrow his responsibilities somewhat, West was not particularly concerned. In fact, because of the need to update both the service organization and the distribution organization to handle the new electronic products, those areas had been commanding a disproportionate amount of his time for the last few months. West would prefer to hire a general manager for service and distribution and have that new individual, reporting to him, handle most of the responsibility in those two crucial areas. He intended to propose this to Callahan.

In the meantime, West was most interested in studying the sales force reorganization and conveying his ideas to Callahan. West had always been interested in developing a separate sales force for anesthesia equipment and disposables. He felt there was sufficient sales volume to support it and customers would be receptive to the extra attention and service. When selling this equipment, the representative would call on the anesthesia staff, a group typically more difficult to deal with and more technically oriented than personnel from other hospital departments. Often the sale also involved the hospital's biomedical engineers, which was not true of Nebon's other products. A separate force could be more intensely trained, thus ensuring better customer service.

West also felt that a strong case could be made for putting architectural products under the mandate of a small but specialized sales force. General-line sales representatives tended to ignore architectural products because their sale consumed so much time and involved contact with nonhospital personnel.

If a separate anesthesia force were developed, the remaining general line would be left with nursing, infant-care, respiratory-therapy, and architectural products. This seemed reasonable because many of these products were sold in the same hospital departments even though they were categorized in different product lines. West also felt that the dealers should be encouraged to handle more low-cost products, giving the general-line sales force more time for other products.

The real problem with splitting out the anesthesia products, West thought, was that each group would remain responsible for the new electronic products. West thought further, however, that since each force would be responsible for a smaller number of the new products, they could be sufficiently trained to do this work. Since most of the new electronic products were in the anesthesia area, the selection of this group would come from those with the most training and experience with electronics products. Additionally West felt there was a strong case to be made for having "electronic specialists" in both sales groups. These persons would handle all the products of their groups but would place more emphasis on the new equipment and would be available for dual sales calls with their colleagues who were not so well versed in the items.

At a recent convention, West briefly discussed his ideas with Tom Reinke, the western regional vice president and one of West's closest friends. Reinke had at one time worked for a company that manufactured sterilization equipment for hospitals. Following the development of a new, very sophisticated unit, it had divided the sales organization into two groups. One handled the existing line, and the other group specialized in the new equipment. Reinke indicated the sales force division proved disastrous, leading to duplicate sales calls, customer confusion, and increased expenses. He felt the same would occur with West's electronic specialists. He recommended that Nebon should hire more technically qualified personnel for the general-line sales force. West left the convention somewhat less enthusiastic about his sales force proposal.

CASE 4–7

Newell Furniture Company

Robert Bending, sales vice president of Newell Furniture Company, slowly removed the conference materials from his attaché case, sorted them out, carefully placed them on his desk, and then sat down deep in thought. He had just returned from a two-day seminar called "Strategic Marketing Strategy." While in many ways he had felt he could ill afford the time away

---

This case was prepared by Earl R. Sage and Thomas H. Stevenson of the University of North Carolina at Charlotte. Reprinted, by permission of the publisher, from *Management for the 1980s*, by William F. Christopher, p. 48. © 1980 AMACOM, a division of American Management Associations, New York. All rights reserved.

from the office and the pressing problems facing him there, he had hoped the seminar might spark some ideas for new approaches to these problems.

Heaven knows, new approaches were needed; things had not been going well with the company for some time, and he was well aware of the growing dissatisfaction of the company president, Steven Clayton, with recent sales performance. This, of course, was Bending's direct responsibility.

Bending had come to Newell a little more than a year and a half ago from the Holden Company, one of Newell's many competitors in the furniture business, where he had been director of marketing. The sales vice president position at Newell was open at that time due to a resignation. It was general knowledge that the resignation of the former vice president was submitted under pressure. The company conducted a search for a successor with a strong background in furniture marketing. Mr. Clayton, having learned through his acquaintances of Bending's performance record with Holden, had contacted him personally to discuss the position at Newell. Negotiations proceeded to mutually satisfactory arrangements on salary and other benefits, and Bending decided to join Newell.

At that time Mr. Clayton himself had only been with the company approximately one year. Prior to his arrival the company had been managed by members of the Newell family. Due to company problems and increasing frictions it had been decided by family members that outside professional management was needed. When Clayton joined the company as president he knew he faced a number of challenges but was confident he would be able to show positive results.

Bending glanced over the seminar materials. The seminar had stressed the development of a consistent marketing program: definition of the business, determination of the mission of the total business, the formulation of functional strategies, delineation of target segments, and the development of products, communications, channels, and pricing policies for reaching those segments. These were familiar themes to him, of course, since his undergraduate major had been in marketing and he had made a conscientious effort to keep up with the significant writings in the area, but he was becoming increasingly concerned with whether he had moved Newell's marketing program in the right direction. Sales and profit figures had been disappointing during the first year he had been with Newell (see Exhibits 1 and 2), but he was not then seriously concerned, because he knew time would be required to make the necessary changes to bring about an improvement. And too, a decision had been made by Mr. Clayton to bring the company's scope of operations to a lower level of sales as a new base for growth, starting the first year Bending was with the company. He was now well into his second year, and results continued to be disappointing. Sales for the first two quarters of 1980 were up only 8 percent over the previous year. Actual sales for the six-month period were $24 million versus a target of $28 million. Due to increases in cost of goods sold, there had been a decrease in gross margin and a resulting net loss for the half which was

EXHIBIT 1
Percent Distribution of Sales

	1979	1978	1977	1976	1975
Retail establishments:					
Retail stores	78.8%	69.4%	61.2%	48.0%	48.0%
Mass merchandisers	21.2	29.0	37.0	52.0	50.0
Government	—	1.6	1.8	—	2.0
	100.0	100.0	100.0	100.0	100.0

three times greater than that of the previous year. This was naturally a matter of great concern to Mr. Clayton and all of company management.

Bending sat back, considering his situation. For the first time in his working life he wondered if he was in a job he could not handle. He was disturbed by statements made privately by a former family member of management, who acknowledged:

> We made a lot of mistakes. We drifted and acted on impulse rather than on the basis of orderly planning. With the rise of the mass merchandisers—Levitz, Wickes, Penney's, Sears—we succumbed to the lure of volume, just as many manufacturers in other lines did. To reduce our prices to them, among other things we reduced our advertising, since they argued, reasonably enough, that sales to them did not require advertising. We gave less attention to our traditional customers and reduced our quality under the constant pressure to re-

EXHIBIT 2
Income Statement Summary ($000)

	Year Ending December 31				
	1979	1978	1977	1976	1975
Net sales	$43,300	$40,128	$50,134	$65,180	$68,750
Cost of goods sold:					
Materials	18,058	16,808	21,455	27,073	28,792
Direct labor	11,606	9,747	12,336	17,417	16,830
Overhead	9,121	10,082	11,229	15,120	16,140
Total	38,785	36,637	45,020	59,610	61,762
Gross profit	4,515	3,491	5,114	5,570	6,988
Interest expense	675	623	681	720	630
Total sales and general administrative expense	3,891	4,030	5,020	6,046	8,062
Net profit before taxes	(51)	(1,162)	(588)	(1,196)	(1,704)
Income taxes	—	—	—	—	—
Net profit after taxes	$ (51)	$(1,162)	$ (588)	$(1,196)	$(1,704)
Units sold (000)	358.4	359.1	455.8	620.8	667.5

duce prices. We were forced to carry more inventory to provide quick delivery, and this cost more money than we had. We neglected to realize that we had neither the size nor the strength to be a large-volume producer, yet we tried to act like one. Clayton, of course, recognizes this and is taking steps to correct it, but the adjustment will be painful because this is a rough time for our industry.

INDUSTRY

The broad category of home furnishings includes consumer purchases of furniture, mattresses, kitchen and household appliances, tableware, carpeting, and various other durable and semidurable products. Consumer expenditures for home furnishings were $77.6 billion in 1978, $85.7 billion in 1979, and were projected in Standard & Poor's *Industry Surveys* to increase 14 percent to an estimated $98 billion (in current dollars) in 1980. In recent years these expenditures have accounted for approximately 5.5 percent of disposable income.

The household furniture industry is a part of this overall industry. Three of the major segments are: wood household furniture (1980 shipments estimated by *Predicasts* at $5.2 billion), upholstered furniture ($3.9 billion), and metal furniture ($1.5 billion).[1] It is a highly competitive industry made up of small and medium-size businesses, many of which are still family-controlled. In 1977, according to the Bureau of the Census, there were 2,982 wood furniture manufacturing establishments, and over 70 percent of these establishments had fewer than 20 employees.[2]

The industry was originally located in the New England/Middle Atlantic states but then spread to the Middle West as the population moved in that direction. In the 1930s the Carolinas and Virginia became the center of the industry because of the abundance of lumber, cheap labor, and a large national market for low-priced furniture. This area of the South continued to be the center, with the majority of the top manufacturers located in a 150-mile belt running from Lenoir, North Carolina, to Bassett, Virginia.

The demand for household furniture has historically been related to disposable personal income, residential construction, existing home sales, and interest rates. Housing starts declined 40 percent in 1980 compared to the previous year, and existing home sales were down 20 percent. Higher interest rates influence not only home purchases but home furnishings as well, since approximately two-thirds of all retail furniture purchases are made through credit. Other factors include demographic changes, such as

---

[1] *Predicast Forecasts* (Cleveland, Ohio: Predicasts, Inc., 1980), SIC 250, pp. B166–67.

[2] U.S. Department of Commerce, Bureau of the Census, "Household Furniture," *1977 Census of Manufacturers* (Washington, D.C.: Government Printing Office, 1977), SIC 2511, 12, 14, 15, 17, 19. Industry Series MC 77–1–25A.

the maturing population in the United States, increase in the number of two-income families, and changing life-styles. The demand for furniture has declined to an annual "growth" rate of −3 percent over the past three years as a result of these influences, and the long-range forecast indicates at best a return to modest annual growth rates in the coming decade.

Furniture demand has over the years been style and price sensitive. Therefore furniture manufacturers must cope with low margins while at the same time they must commit substantial funds to product development. As competitive pressures increase during periods of reduced consumer buying, manufacturers are forced to generate new styling and distribution to stimulate sales.

Product lines for the coming season are shown several times during the year at wholesale trade exhibits. The major markets are in High Point, North Carolina, and Chicago, Dallas, and San Francisco. These shows are attended by buyers from major retailers ranging from furniture specialists to mass merchandisers. It is not unusual for a regional buyer to shop many of the trade shows across the country, since design and styling are very dynamic.

Also important to buyers is quick delivery. Consequently, the ability to carry an inventory for quick response to orders is a hardship, particularly for the smaller producers.

COMPANY HISTORY

The Newell company was founded by Mr. Harold Newell in 1935 in Seymour, North Carolina. Mr. Newell had been a salesman for a small furniture manufacturer in nearby Wayland, North Carolina. From a small beginning, the company developed into a successful concern with a reputation for quality and craftsmanship in both case goods (wood furniture) and upholstered furniture. During World War II, the majority of the company's output was taken up by sales to the government. After the war, the company expanded to meet the pent-up postwar demand for furniture. They continued to emphasize quality products at the middle to upper end of the price line. The company prospered and enjoyed steady growth until Mr. Newell's death in 1969, at which time management was taken over by other members of the Newell family.

Mr. Newell's death marked the turning point in the company's fortunes. Early in the 1970s the company decided to switch emphasis away from its traditional dealers, full-line furniture stores, toward mass merchandisers (such as Wickes and Sears). Newell's management reasoned that the big retailers seemed likely to capture a huge share of the furniture market.

By 1976 mass merchandisers accounted for more than 52 percent of Newell's net sales (see Exhibit 1), but these volume sales did not produce profits (see Exhibit 2). Newell offered these biggest customers exclusive lines of furniture in addition to the regular product lines at lower prices than its other dealers. As a result the traditional dealer base, which had peaked at approximately 5,200 dealers in the early 1960s, dropped to 2,180 dealers in 1976. With this dramatic decline Newell found itself heavily dependent on its new low-margin customers. Sales to traditional outlets had permitted a gross profit of approximately 20 percent in the past, but sales to mass merchandisers produced somewhat less than half that, with continuing pressure to reduce margins even further. They had also begun exerting increasing influence on product design and inventory plans.

NEWELL'S MARKETING PROGRAM

Starting in 1976 and in the ensuing years, Newell changed approaches a number of times, both in styling and distribution. In 1977 Newell entered the so-called designer market, engaging a well-known designer to develop a distinctive line of upper-middle–priced furniture meant to respond to what the company believed was a promising trend. This line was sold primarily to department stores and style stores. Although the line was received well by the press and by exclusive retailers and interior designers, its life was short due to production inefficiencies and the lack of final consumer acceptance.

During this time they followed a major program to reduce reliance on mass merchandisers as outlets.

In 1977 the company decided to emphasize case goods and other wooden furniture designed for the mass market at the medium retail price point. Each product line was reviewed, and as much as 50 percent of each was restyled with the aim of providing a broader appeal to the 25–44 age group, which represents the prime furniture-purchasing group. At the same time, the company broadened its offering of casual styling for the rapidly growing family-room market. Altogether, 48 new pieces were introduced at the fall show that year.

In 1978 a company spokesman announced that Newell's marketing approach would change considerably in the coming year in terms of styling, price points, and distribution of its products. There would be reduced emphasis on "trendy" merchandising programs and more concentration on basic styles considered to have broad appeal to both the retailer and the consumer. This would enable the company to "achieve an efficient volume, by merchandising basic products for the mass market and important middle retail points."

At the beginning of 1978 the company sold its upholstered furniture line to one of the Newell family members (see Exhibit 3). Arrangements were made for him to continue to produce the line under the Newell name. This action was taken because the line had long been considered unprofitable and the sale provided badly needed cash. At the 1978 shows, the company introduced only 22 new offerings.

EXHIBIT 3
Approximate Percentage of Net Sales by Product

	1979	1978	1977	1976	1975
Wood living room, bedroom, and dining room furniture	98	97	89	79	78
Upholstered furniture	—	—*	8	18	20
Other	2	3	3	3	2
	100	100	100	100	100

* Discontinued

EXHIBIT 4
Newell Company Balance Sheet ($000)

	1979	1978	1977	1976	1975
Assets					
Current assets:					
Cash	$ 2,100	$ 3,100	$ 785	$ 2,850	$2,000
Marketable securities	1,750	2,005	—	—	—
Accounts receivable .	7,200	4,759	7,546	9,980	10,010
Inventories	6,767	4,700	9,500	9,204	9,725
Prepaid expenses ...	721	520	830	650	200
Total current assets	18,538	15,084	18,661	22,684	21,935
Property and equipment (net of depreciation).............	9,200	12,100	13,005	12,300	11,520
Total assets	$27,738	$27,184	$31,666	$34,984	$33,455
Liabilities and stockholders' equity					
Current liabilities:					
Notes payable	$ 6,750	$ 6,200	$ 7,510	$ 9,000	$ 7,875
Accounts payable ...	2,180	2,150	2,630	3,180	3,250
Accruals	2,005	1,980	2,510	3,200	2,530
Total current liabilities......	10,935	10,330	12,650	15,380	13,655
Long-term debt	3,000	3,000	4,000	4,000	3,000
Stockholders' equity:					
Common stock......	10,600	10,600	10,600	10,600	10,600
Retained earnings ...	3,203	3,254	4,416	5,004	6,200
Total...........	13,803	13,854	15,016	15,604	16,800
Total liabilities and stockholders' equity .	$27,738	$27,184	$31,666	$34,984	$33,455

In recent months suggestions had been made that the company might profitably respond to a new trend, the marketing of unfinished, highly crafted furniture kits for the do-it-yourselfer. This had appeal, for it would utilize production capacity which was idle and available due to the decrease in volume occasioned by the move away from the mass merchandisers.

Development of an appropriate pricing strategy had been a continuing problem. Shortly after he joined the company, Bending had requested historical cost and profitability information by product line (there were approximately 480 different items of furniture being produced in 1978), but Frank Powers, financial officer of the company said he was unable to provide information at that level of detail. Powers himself had only been with the company since 1977. He acknowledged the desirability of such information, but the cost system in existence only provided summary information, primarily by manufacturing operation, and it would require some time (perhaps two years) to develop a new system. No specific action had been taken as yet. Bending felt strongly that Sears and other buyers were buying selectively on the basis of price and Newell was then left with inventories which were difficult to sell. Partly as a result of this the company opened an outlet store in Gaffney, South Carolina, in 1979 to dispose of these inventories at discount prices to the public. Gaffney is a well-known consumer outlet center.

Mr. Clayton in 1979 established an overall gross margin objective of 15 percent. Although 15 percent was below the industry average of 25 percent, it was considered to be a realistic interim target. Clayton also urged that accounts be required to buy complete product lines to avoid the selective buying which damaged profitability, but this was met with resistance by the company sales representatives.

Promotion is a key marketing element in the industry. Trade shows are the primary means by which product awareness is built at the retail level. Newell has always followed the industry in this respect and has maintained relatively large exhibit spaces. Because of declining volume, in recent years three of the spaces have been vacated in regional exhibits; however, Newell continues to attend all major home furnishings shows.

Newell has increased its advertising expenditures in line with its strategy of expanding its traditional dealer base (see Exhibit 5).

EXHIBIT 5
Advertising Expenditures/Net Sales

	1979	1978	1977	1976	1975
Advertising dollars (000)	$ 2,122	$ 1,765	$ 1,554	$ 1,304	$ 825
Percent of sales	4.9%	4.4%	3.1%	2.0%	1.2%
Net sales	$43,300	$40,128	$50,134	$65,180	$68,750

Brand loyalty is fairly strong in the furniture industry, so Newell has attempted to strengthen brand identification through dealer cooperative advertising. Dealer participation has been somewhat unenthusiastic, however. A Newell company salesman said "retailers have the impression that Newell is a name from the past." He remarked that this was undoubtedly due to reduced advertising which occurred during the mass-volume days of the company.

Bending, after considerable deliberation about where the advertising dollars should go, decided upon 50 percent for trade shows, 25 percent print media, and 25 percent on miscellaneous promotional and display materials. This had been the historical pattern for the company, and Bending concluded he had no good reason to change it.

Direct selling to retail establishments is important in the industry. Newell's sales force is organized on a regional basis, with assigned territories in each region. Although sales dropped nearly 40 percent from 1976 to 1978, the sales force was only reduced from 49 to 42 people. However, they are paid on a straight commission basis, so this does not represent a cash drain for the firm. Bending had hoped to institute a formal sales-performance evaluation system, but thus far he has been unable to do so.

In a year-end meeting with company management, December 1979, Mr. Clayton had stated that several key elements of Newell's competitive strategy would receive increasing attention: product development, quality, and speed of delivery. Although Bending was aware of these statements, his two-day marketing seminar made him wonder whether these were *the* critical considerations.

CASE 4–8

Airwick Industries: Carpet Fresh

In late fall of 1982, Mike Sheets, president of Airwick Industries, and Wes Buckner, executive vice president of the Consumer Products Division, were considering what to do next to strengthen the profitability, competitive position, and sales of Carpet Fresh.

This case was developed by Holly Gunner of Management Analysis Center, Inc., in collaboration with Professor Philip McDonald, College of Business Administration, Northeastern University, Boston, Massachusetts. It was prepared as a basis for class discussion rather than to illustrate either effective or ineffective handling of a situation. Copyright © 1983 by Northeastern University. Reprinted by permission.

PRODUCT BACKGROUND

Carpet Fresh, a rug and room deodorizer, was one of the most successful products in Airwick's history, far exceeding even optimistic sales expectations when it was first introduced in 1978. Used to freshen the smell of a rug and room when sprinkled on a carpet and vacuumed up during household cleaning, it had created an entirely new household product category. From a market size of zero before its launch in June 1978, the rug and room deodorizer category had grown to approximately $74 million in 1982 (Exhibit 1).

Retail sales in 1978 of $20.2 million belonged entirely to Carpet Fresh, which then enjoyed 100 percent market share. The market grew rapidly in 1979 but increased very slowly afterwards. After 1979, unit sales grew between 6 and 7 percent per year. Airwick's market share in 1982 was expected to be 48 percent (Exhibit 2) because several competitors entered the market after Airwick had pioneered the category. Airwick's share consisted primarily of Carpet Fresh sales, although one-eighth of the sales was accounted for by Glamorene Rug Fresh, a lower-priced, unadvertised brand that Airwick introduced in May 1979 to counter competitive entries.

At about $32 million in revenues (at the manufacturer's selling price), Carpet Fresh accounted for almost 30 percent of Airwick's consumer product sales in 1982. The brand also enjoyed the lowest cost of goods of any Airwick

EXHIBIT 1
Total Rug and Room Deodorizer Market

	Dollars (millions)*	Units (millions of ounces)†	
		Ounces	Change (%)
1977	$ 0.0	—	—
1978	20.2	—	—
1979	70.2	546	—
1980	68.5	584	+7.0
1981	66.1	628	+6.9
1982‡	74.0	666§	+6.1§
1983‡	80.0	—	—

* Food stores sales, at retail prices.
† Food store sales.
‡ Estimated.
§ Based on data as of 6/26.

Source: Airwick Industries (9/82).

EXHIBIT 2
Airwick's Rug-and-Room Deodorizer Market Share*

Year	Carpet Fresh	Glamorene Rug Fresh	Total
1978	100.0	—	100.0
1979	65.4	8.4	73.8
1980	46.9	8.3	55.2
1981	42.9	5.8	48.7
1982	42.2	5.6	47.8

* Percentage of retail grocery store dollar sales.

Source: Airwick Industries (3/83).

product and was a substantial contributor to company profits. Determining how to increase sales and maintain the brand's competitive position was thus a critical decision for Mike Sheets and Wes Buckner.

COMPANY BACKGROUND

In its early years Airkem, Inc. (Airwick Industries' original name) had focused its internal R&D and marketing efforts on sanitary maintenance items for industrial and institutional markets. Airwick Liquid, an odor-controlling consumer household product, had been marketed for Airkem by outside companies until 1963. When Ciba-Geigy acquired the company in the second half of 1974, Airwick had three major business lines: institutional, consumer, and aquatic (swimming-pool treatment chemicals).

Shortly after the acquisition, each line of business accounted for roughly one-third of Airwick's $47 million in sales. The Consumer Brands Division's sales in 1973 were highly dependent on air freshener products (Airwick Solid, Airwick Liquid, and Airwick Spray), which accounted for 97 percent of that division's net sales. All the division's profits came from Airwick Solid and Liquid. In late 1974 the patent on Airwick Solid ran out, and competitors S.C. Johnson and Drackett soon introduced solid air-freshener products that, according to one Airwick executive, "nearly put us out of business in 1975." The company ended 1975 with a loss and was saved only by the financial strength of Ciba-Geigy, its new parent.

Against this backdrop Mike Sheets was recruited in May 1975 to head the Consumer Product Division. Ciba-Geigy had acquired Airwick with the express purpose of diversifying into the consumer products (particularly household products) market. Mike had been vice president of marketing at the R.J. Reynolds Food Division and previously had held management positions with Gardner Advertising and McCann-Erickson, specializing in consumer packaged goods accounts. Mike perceived his marching orders as a mandate to "build the business," and he recognized the urgency of developing new product ideas that would successfully expand the division's narrow product line and diversify its exposure to competitive threats. He sensed that Ciba-Geigy was disappointed in what it had bought, but that it still had a very supportive attitude and was willing to provide the financial backing necessary to turn the business around. Nonetheless, Mike knew that the division had to get some home runs by 1980, or it would be divested.

Before there could be any home runs, Mike found he had to deal with the prior problem of simply fielding a team. Because of its historical emphasis on commercial and institutional products, the existing Airwick R&D group lacked the experience to develop materials highly suitable to the consumer market, and there was a dearth of viable consumer product concepts. Most of the ideas were aimed simply at adapting existing commercial products to sizes and forms thought suitable for household use. The one exception was Stick-Ups, another air freshener product that was successfully launched in late 1976 and helped the company finally achieve black ink for 1977.

Mike worked with Wes Buckner, vice president of marketing in the division (who came to Airwick from Ciba-Geigy's Madison Labs in late 1974) to create an R&D/marketing team that could get the job done. First, they engaged two well-known advertising agencies. Then they brought in Jim Smith to build a new R&D department, initially composed of one chemist with consumer product experience. Jim had once worked for Lehn & Fink, a competitor. Finally, Mike and Wes recruited one product manager, Dick Bankart, from outside the company. Together they set out to develop a product that would turn the division around. Standard practice in the industry was to have marketing people develop the product concept and then turn it over to R&D for physical development. But Mike believed strongly that the best products grew out of a collaborative effort between the two functions. "There's no reason why a chemist can't have marketing insights just because he's a chemist," he said.

SELECTION OF CARPET FRESH

Before considering various product ideas, strategic selection criteria were set. To pass the screen, a product would have to do the following:

> Incur delivered costs (variable manufacturing, freight, warehousing, and royalties) no greater than 40 percent of sales, to provide enough gross margin for advertising and promotion expenses.

Achieve minimum annual sales of $10 million and a maximum of $100 million, to be big enough to sustain advertising and interest the trade, but not so big as to bring Airwick into direct competition with industry giants such as Proctor & Gamble.

Be protectable by a patent.

Fill a specialized niche in the household or health product class.

Be differentiable in a meaningful way to the consumer, not a "me too" entry.

Entail a new application of known chemistry.

The group considered and eliminated several product ideas, including liquid floor cleaners, other air freshener ideas, and a pot-and-pan soaker. They generated a lot of ideas and checked them out using consumer group interview techniques; but they recognized that the small size of their group meant they had to place their bets on just one or two product candidates.

In May 1976, shortly after Jim Smith was hired, he had a friend from the Center for New Product Development (a small entrepreneurial firm) bring in a powdered substance that had been around for several years—and which had been rejected at one point or another by almost every company in the household products industry. The fragranced powder could be sprinkled on a rug and vacuumed up, thus freshening both the rug and the air in the room, as air was exhausted from the vacuum. Wes, Mike, and Jim were attracted by the idea because it constituted a new product category that was void of competitors, yet it fit well with Airwick's existing business. Nonetheless, they realized that consumers had no recognition of odors in rugs, the primary reason that other companies had rejected the product in the past. "We had a great answer to no problem," commented Mike. But there were no other good ideas, either, and time was ticking away. The team felt that this product might present a real opportunity, and so decided to pursue the idea.

POSITIONING CARPET FRESH

Product Concept

Concept testing to determine how best to position the product began in July 1976 and continued until a solution was reached in March of the next year. Through a market research technique of one-on-one interviews with 450 consumers responding to two different videotaped commercials, the team tried different ways to position the product. By using Airwick secretaries to act in the videotaped commercials, the team was able to modify the commercial messages rapidly as new information and problems came to light. Ad

agency, marketing, and R&D people watched the interviews together behind a one-way mirror and collaborated in solving each problem that surfaced. In this way the group was able to fine-tune the product by using
consumers' reactions to its physical characteristics (scent and texture),
package design, name, and attributes.

Two primary concepts were developed and tested. One—the "single-
minded" concept—characterized the product simply as a rug and room deodorizer. The other—the "three-way" concept—described it as deodorizing
the rug and room, decreasing static electricity, and keeping carpets clean
longer. One problem encountered was finding a way to get homemakers to
recognize that rugs picked up odors and held them. This was essential in
order to build a perceived need for a rug and room deodorizer. Homemakers
thought primarily in terms of cooking, smoking, and other odors in the air.
Another problem was to move consumers away from the idea that the product was a rug cleaner, as rug cleaners abounded and Carpet Fresh didn't
really clean rugs.

After nearly nine months of commercial and concept testing, a correlation was found in March 1977 between pet ownership and positive reaction
to the product by homemakers in the research sample. This suggested a
solution to both problems: use the single-minded concept, show odor sources
on the rug, and then show odors in the air. As June was the date targeted for
beginning a market test, this solution came none too soon.

Packaging and Shelf Position

While concept testing was going on, some needed modifications were made
in the product's physical characteristics, and a packaging consultant was
brought in to help design a package that would support the concept. The
team thought it important to use a novel shape and a color that would
convey the idea that this was neither a rug cleaner nor an air freshener, but
a totally new and serious product. (Exhibit 3 depicts one package the team
considered and also shows the one actually chosen.) In addition, the package
chosen was of sufficient height to place the brand next to Lehn & Fink's $75
million Lysol Spray, a "serious" product with a high shelf price that was
comparable to the price of Carpet Fresh. Lysol Spray was a fast-moving
product normally placed on store shelves very near, but not in the middle of,
air fresheners. The team did not want Carpet Fresh to be shelved directly
alongside air fresheners, since this would undermine the concept of a totally
new "rug and room deodorizer" product category, and price comparisons
would also have been very unfavorable. Nor did they want Carpet Fresh to
be shelved with rug cleaners, for the same reason. Furthermore, associating
Carpet Fresh with rug cleaners was to be avoided because rug cleaners were
purchased only once or twice a year.

EXHIBIT 3
Carpet Fresh Packaging

Considered   Chosen

Name and Price

The team believed the product also needed a highly descriptive name to help
consumers understand what this novel product did. After considering the
possibility that a very descriptive name would run the risk of being too
generic, eventually weakening the value of the trademark, the name "Carpet Fresh" was selected. It was decided to introduce 9-ounce (aimed at initial
purchases) and 14-ounce sizes and to price them for the market test at a
retail price of $1.29 and $1.79, respectively. While the field market test was
in progress, a laboratory test conducted by Yankelovich, Skelly & White
gauged consumer attitudes and reaction to three sets of price points (Exhibit
4). The highest price evaluated—$1.99 for the 14-ounce size—was set not to
exceed the price of Lysol Spray. In April 1977, prior to field testing, sales
and profit levels were projected for a national introduction in March 1978 of
the 9-ounce and 14-ounce sizes priced at $1.29 and $1.79, respectively, as
shown in Exhibit 5. Retail prices tested included a 28 percent trade margin,
standard for similar household product categories.

EXHIBIT 4

Date: June 20, 1977
To: W. Buckner
From: F. La Ronca
Subject: Yankelovich Lab—Carpet Fresh Trial

The trial phase of the Yankelovich lab is complete, and the results are very encouraging, as the table shows:

	Respondent Base	Trial	Rate (%)
Cell 1: High price ($1.39/1.99)	250 (coupon)	113	45
Cell 2: Regular price ($1.29/1.79)	175 (coupon)	90	51
	175 (no coupon)	70	40
Cell 3: Low price ($.99/1.39)	253 (coupon)	136	54
Total	853	409	48

Yankelovich is hesitant to give a normative range because there are significant variations by category and nothing directly comparable to Carpet Fresh. However, a 48 percent unfactored laboratory trial[1] is considered very healthy.

The coupon had a positive effect at all three price levels. However, the 40 percent trial rate with no coupon at the regular price is still very strong.

Carpet Fresh is seen to be price sensitive but not to a significant degree among the three ranges tested. Focus groups revealed that consumers did not consider the price too high and accepted the pricing, as there is no direct base of comparison. The repeat phase will be key to determining whether the brand could be more profitabily marketed at the higher price level.

Steve Rose is scheduled to discuss results to data in more detail the week of 6/20.

[1] "Unfactored laboratory trial" is the total rate of consumer trial for all price levels, with and without coupons.

Capital Request and National Launch Target Date

In the April 1, 1977, marketing plan that Mike and Wes prepared to request capital funds from the Ciba-Geigy Executive Committee, a recommendation was made to commit $440,000 for manufacturing equipment that Airwick would provide to outside production contractors. Excerpts from the plan follow.

Ideally, because of the market factors still to be checked out, we should not commit capital resources on Carpet Fresh until we have at least the controlled laboratory test market readings.

EXHIBIT 5
Carpet Fresh Projections (4/1/77)

Year	Cases (thousands)*			Annual Profit ($MM)	Gross Sales ($MM)
	Total	9 oz.	14 oz.		
1978 (9 mos.)	676	434	242	$(1,501)	$ 8.6
1979	871	560	311	478	11.1
1980	950	610	340	2,189	12.1

* 1 case = 1 dozen packages.

Source: Airwick Industries (4/77).

However, the critical path to product availability for a national launch, once the investment decision is made, is currently estimated at 52 to 57 weeks.

If we were to make an investment decision by April 18, 1977, on the basis of information now available, we would be able to launch the product nationally sometime between April 15, 1978, and May 20, 1978.

If, on the other hand, we were to wait until September 5, 1977, after availability of Yankelovich information, our national introduction date would be sometime between September 1, 1978, and October 6, 1978. Since we would be introducing the product just before the Halloween/Thanksgiving/Christmas period, we might be well advised, under this alternative, to delay introduction until early 1979.

A delay in the national introduction of Carpet Fresh until late 1978 or early 1979 would not seem to be consistent with the urgent need for the Airwick Products Division to bring successful new products to the national market with all practical speed.

Also, we know that a major competitor is working on a possibly related product. For maximum Carpet Fresh success, it is vital that we are the first rug and room deodorizer on the market.

In view of these considerations, we propose that we accept the significant business risk and make the decision to commit, on or before April 18, 1977, the necessary resources to proceed on the critical path to a national product launch.

This investment decision is estimated to amount to $440,000.

On about September 1, 1977, we will have controlled, laboratory test-market readings on the product. If at that time there would be reason to interrupt or terminate development of the capital equipment, it is estimated that approximately 33 percent, or $138,000, of the original commitment could be recovered.

During the early months of the field market test, an industry market intelligence service included a description of the Carpet Fresh product, price points, and market test in one of its reports.

THE MARKET TEST

A 36-week field market test was conducted for Airwick by AdTel in two test markets, Bakersfield, California, and Quad Cities (Davenport, Moline, Rock Island, East Moline), beginning at the end of May 1977. AdTel was a market research firm that set up actual market tests in cities where it had established relationships with grocery stores. It could arrange for shelf space in those stores and track product sales. AdTel also had an ongoing arrangement with 2,000 families in each test market city to keep diaries of monthly purchases of all products. From the diaries, AdTel could determine trial and repeat purchase cycles.

A primary objective of the Carpet Fresh market test was to gauge consumer acceptance of the product. Another key objective was to see if the positioning and advertising strategies would work to produce strong enough sales to project a target sales level of $8.6 million (based on the $1.29 and $1.79 price points) for the first nine months of the national launch in 1978. A target market share was also set at 12.3 percent of the air freshener category ($106 million in 1977), as there was no rug and room deodorizer category to use as a yardstick.

Shelf space in 81 grocery stores was obtained directly by AdTel without going through food brokers, as Airwick would do if it decided to introduce the product later. This method was chosen in part because going through food brokers would add three or four months to the waiting period before test data would begin to come in. Heavy TV advertising support was scheduled, with 19 spot commercials per week to be shown at four-week intervals. Because of the need to educate consumers about an unfamiliar product, 60-second spots were required rather than the more standard 30-second spots. In addition, 30¢-off coupons were to be sent by direct mail to stimulate trial. The coupons were sent to households that, according to market research studies, were heavy users of household products.

The Yankelovich laboratory market test was initiated at the same time. It could provide information on buyer demographics and price-point effects. Most importantly, the laboratory test could yield data by September 1977.

Market test results went far beyond even the most optimistic expectations. In September 1977, Wes reported on results through August of both the AdTel market test and the Yankelovich laboratory test. During the first 14 weeks of the AdTel test, two flights of TV advertising had been aired and 30¢-off coupons had been mailed. Average weekly sales were running at 142 percent of Airwick's original goal for the market test. The original target for Carpet Fresh's share of the air freshener market after national introduction

EXHIBIT 6

Yankelovich Laboratory Test—Consumer Trial of Carpet Fresh

Price Points (dollars)	Consumers Who Purchase (%)
$1.39/1.99	45
$1.29/1.79	51
$ .99/1.29	54

had been 12.3 percent, but results indicated that it had actually garnered a 43.5 percent share of the test market. In addition, the size of the air freshener market in the test area had expanded by 90 percent. In one test period, Carpet Fresh had even topped sales of fast-moving Lysol Spray by 16 percent!

The Yankelovich test results provided some positive signs as well. Consumers expressed high intent to repurchase the product after initial trial, in comparison to other household products. Price sensitivity for initial pur-

EXHIBIT 7

Combined Bakersfield and Quad Cities Test Markets: Carpet Fresh Monthly Unit Sales (40 panel stores)

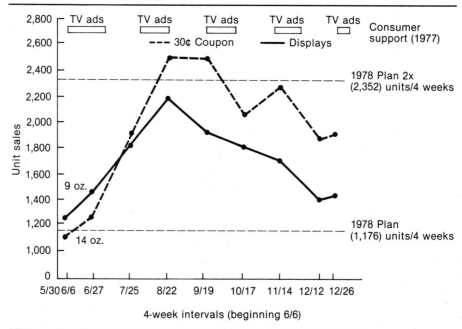

chase after viewing the commercial was not very strong, as illustrated by the test results in Exhibit 6.

The laboratory test also showed that the 14-ounce package obtained a larger-than-expected percentage of initial purchases. This fit with data from the AdTel test, in which the 14-ounce size accounted for 52 percent of total sales. Initial expectations were that the 9-ounce size would account for 54 percent of sales.

On the basis of these early results, Wes increased the unit sales volume projections for 1978, the year of national introduction, to 1,408,000 cases, more than twice the original plan (646,000 cases). Given the additional revenue this volume would yield, he also increased the planned advertising expenditure to $6.6 million from $3.7 million.

AdTel results through the end of 1977 are shown in Exhibit 7 in relation to the original 1978 sales plan projections. The exhibit also shows the

EXHIBIT 8

Date: October 18, 1977
To: W. Buckner
From: J. Goren
Subject: Carpet Fresh Out-of-Stocks in Test Markets

This summarizes the information provided by Ken Robb concerning out-of-stocks in the Carpet Fresh test markets.

Conclusions

The Brand believes the moderately depressed Carpet Fresh volume levels, especially on the 14-oz. size, exhibited in the test markets for the weeks ending 9/26 and 10/3 can be attributed to retail out-of-stocks.

Indicated Action

1. The Brand will work closely with R&D, Marketing Services, and Manufacturing in an attempt to avoid test market out-of-stocks.
2. The out-of-stock conditions in the test markets for the weeks ending 9/26 and 10/3 will be taken into consideration in The Brand's evaluation of the Carpet Fresh test market.

Findings

1. Quad Cities
   a. Audit stores: During the week ending 9/26 (9/19 to 9/26), 5 of the 20 audit stores were temporarily out of stock, primarily on the 14-oz. size.
   b. Distribution stores: No deliveries were made to distribution stores during the week ending 9/26. This contributed to 12 of the 24 stores in this panel being out of stock on at least one size of Carpet Fresh for most of the week.
2. Bakersfield: No out-of-stocks have been reported in the Bakersfield test market during the week ending 9/26.
3. Market Audits believes that a residual out-of-stock effect would be expected in at least the Quad Cities test market for the week ending 10/3.

timing of TV ads, coupon mailings, and special in-store displays. Exhibits 8 and 9 provide additional information on the AdTel and Yankelovich tests.

Given the strong, positive test results, a decision was made to prepare for a national launch, and a late March 1978 date for initial shipments was announced to the trade. Airwick did not have a strong position with brokers. The company had historically distributed its products in only a few regional markets, and the volume of Airwick products had never been a very important factor to brokers. For these reasons the team expected difficulty in gaining broker acceptance for Carpet Fresh. Broker commissions for Carpet

EXHIBIT 9

Date: October 21, 1977
To: M. Sheets
From: W. Buckner
Subject: Carpet Fresh Test Market Data

We have just received some top-line information from the Carpet Fresh test markets that is extremely encouraging. The table (below) outlines the top-line data from the consumer attitude and awareness study that was conducted among current Carpet Fresh users in the two test markets. This is the first consumer information that we have from people who have actually purchased the product in the stores in the market. The study was conducted in mid-September, and by that point, we had a total of seven weeks of advertising.

There was a trial level of 9 percent and an awareness level of 55 percent. Both scores are good but not outstanding. The unaided awareness score of 97 percent among users is extremely high. The 55 percent is the awareness of the brand among all the people that were contacted in order to find 200 users and 200 "aware but nonusers."

The purchase intent scale showing 82 percent for the top two boxes is extremely high. The research company indicated that in the 15 years that it has been conducting this type of market research, the 52 percent top box is the highest score it has ever received. The 82 percent purchase intent is deemed exceptional.

The likes and dislikes about the product are also shown in the table and are concerned primarily with the fragrance, the pleasant odor, and the effectiveness of Carpet Fresh. The dislikes are extremely low.

All of these data are very consistent with the previous work on Carpet Fresh that has been done during the past year, including the "one-on-ones," the consumer product use test, and the Yankelovich laboratory test.

It is the opinion of the research company that with the extremely high purchase intent we have achieved, additional advertising money would probably double the trial level and increase the awareness from 55 percent to 85–90 percent. In other words, we have a product that delivers satisfaction; therefore, one of the primary goals is to obtain a higher level of trial and

EXHIBIT 9   *(concluded)*

awareness in a shorter period of time in order to "preempt" this market from any competitors.

These data very definitely confirm our decision to increase the advertising expenditure from the original plan.

Carpet Fresh Awareness/Usage/Attitude Study*

Trial	9%	
Awareness	55%	
Unaided awareness among users	97%	

Purchase intent:		Among users
Definitely will buy		52%
Probably will buy		30 } 82%
Might or might not		9
Probably not		4
Definitely not		5

Likes:	Triers	Aware nontriers
Pleasant odor/clean fresh smell	64%	31%
Eliminates odor	45	48
Easy to use, convenient	21	10
Brightens/freshens carpet look	8	8

Dislikes:		
Smells too strong	8	
Too expensive/used up too fast	8	
Odor not last	5	
Hard to shake out	4	
No dislikes	66	

* Top-line data from study conducted mid-September 1977, seven weeks of advertising, starting June 1977.

Fresh would be 5 percent of net sales (manufacturer's selling price), standard in the industry for household products of this type.

MANUFACTURING

Larry Graf, senior vice president of Operations, and Rich Roscelli in Manufacturing were given the job of scaling up to produce large quantities of Carpet Fresh. Airwick's policy was to use outside companies to produce and package new products and to gradually develop in-house manufacturing capacity once the product was established. Producing commercial quantities of Carpet Fresh involved locating outside fillers and blenders, ordering tooling for plastic bottles and caps, ordering labeling equipment, and arranging for transportation of chemicals to powder producers, raw plastic material to molders, packaging to fillers, and finished cases of the product to distribution points. The logistics were complex, as manufacturing locations were dispersed in New Jersey and Ohio. Outside contractors had to be located near freight and warehouse facilities.

Roscelli described the situation faced by the Operations group at the time. Carpet Fresh was "totally beyond anything we had ever dealt with before." It involved the biggest scope of materials handling ever for Airwick. "It was staggering to see how many million pounds of powder we needed. Most of our products before were liquid, mostly water. . . . Scaling up for the test market involved only small quantities, and the problems we would run into for the national launch never really surfaced." The national launch was, in fact, delayed by two months. It was not possible to get all the equipment delivered to Airwick's outside contract manufacturers and have it running properly in time to build up the minimum inventory level required—enough to fill the pipeline and have 25 percent of projected first-year sales on hand in each warehouse. "We would have liked to delay it even longer to build a more comfortable inventory level, but a date had been announced to the trade, and we had to go ahead."

For the first six weeks after national introduction in June 1978, sales levels were not very encouraging. Then 30¢-off coupons were mailed to consumers, and demand took off. Roscelli later recalled that "it was a struggle for the first six to nine months because we had only about 10 people in our group to cope with the need for speeding up production and increasing capacity, even before the national launch." These people worked full-time on Carpet Fresh for several months, but they also had responsibility for other products. They worked 12 to 14 hours a day, and several were in Ohio during the worst winter in its history. "The roof literally blew off one manufacturing facility, and we were snowed in for four days," Roscelli recalled.

Sales projections were constantly being increased (see Exhibit 10), beginning after the AdTel test started, and they continued to be increased well after the market launch. Before the test Marketing had projected 676,000 cases for 1978, with one-third in the 14-ounce size and two-thirds in the 9-ounce size. Year-end sales for 1978 were actually 1,867,000 cases, and the mix of sizes was roughly two-thirds 14-ounce and one-third 9-ounce. Molding machines for each package size differed. Actual case sales for 1979 were 2,341,000, with a backlog of 400,000 cases; 2,000,000 cases were originally projected for 1979. The response of brokers to Carpet Fresh had been unexpectedly positive, particularly because Carpet Fresh gave them substantial new product sales volume without cutting into the sales of products they already carried. Airwick's position with existing brokers improved markedly, and a new group of more aggressive brokers developed an interest in handling Carpet Fresh.

Once sales took off in the summer of 1978, Manufacturing managers had to work very hard to provide Marketing people with information on product availability and location so that the sales department could allocate

EXHIBIT 10
Carpet Fresh Sales Projection Revisions

	Cases (thousands)			
Projection	9 oz.	14 oz.	Total	($000)
Original (4/1/77)				
1978 (9 mos.)	434	242	676	8,589
1979	560	311	871	11,064
1980	610	340	950	12,071
Revised (9/13/77)				
1978 (9 mos.)	n.a.	n.a.	1,408	18,755
1979	n.a.	n.a.	2,000	27,504
1980	n.a.	n.a.	2,100	28,879
Revised (9/19/77)				
1978 (9 mos.)	n.a.	n.a.	1,872	n.a.
1979	n.a.	n.a.	2,000	n.a.
1980	n.a.	n.a.	2,100	n.a.
Revised (8/18/78)				
1978	814	853	1,667	n.a.
1979	n.a.	n.a.	2,000	n.a.
1980	n.a.	n.a.	2,100	n.a.
Revised (10/78)				
1979	n.a.	n.a.	4,675	78,915
1980	n.a.	n.a.	4,647	79,000
Revised (11/78)				
1979	n.a.	n.a.	3,375	57,000
1980	n.a.	n.a.	n.a.	n.a.

n.a. = Not available.

Source: Airwick Industries internal memoranda.

whatever was available to the most critical markets. Larry Graf explained, "We learned a useful lesson from the Carpet Fresh experience because we had only a manual system for keeping track of product at the time. Today we have an automated MIS system to provide faster updates." Airwick also increased its capacity to produce Carpet Fresh (eventually brought in-house) to a level of 7.5 million cases per year for a total capital investment of $2.1 million. Actual sales in 1982 were just under 2 million cases, requiring a 3-million-case capacity to meet peak demand.

COMPETITIVE ENTRIES

Before launching Carpet Fresh nationally, the team tried to anticipate which competitors would enter the market and how. An early and strong response was expected from S.C. Johnson, the makers of Glade air freshener. They were the biggest in the business, and very aggressive, Drackett, with its Renuzit air-freshener brand, was viewed as the second potential threat. There was also a possibility that Boyle-Midway (makers of the Wizard air-freshener brand) might enter with a rug and room deodorizer product.

There seemed to be two likely ways to position competing entries: with a lower price and with fragrances. The team considered how it would respond to each of these. A decision was made to stay with just the regular Carpet Fresh scent, to avoid becoming "just another air freshener" and to avoid diluting the "serious" Carpet Fresh image by adding different fragrances. To prepare to meet price competition, in November 1978 Mike came up with the idea of launching another, less expensive "fighting" brand, which would not be associated with Carpet Fresh. Because Airwick had recently bought the Glamorene brand name, it was decided to introduce a rug and room deodorizer product called Glamorene Rug Fresh in a plain, cylindrical, 15.5-ounce package priced at $1.59. The brand would be supported by trade deals but no advertising. The Glamorene line in 1978 included a few household products (a rug cleaner, aerosol upholstery cleaner, and drain opener) that together accounted for less than $1 million in sales, plus Spray 'N' Vac, with $10 million in sales. The Glamorene name was well known, but its image was not that of an innovator.

Airwick had planned to introduce a 22-ounce size of Carpet Fresh on May 1, 1979, requiring additional tooling and production capacity. Because production executives were already working feverishly just to fill current demand for existing sizes (each day of stockouts cost $30,000 in lost contribution), a decision was made to postpone the 22-ounce introduction until October 1979 and to concentrate instead on tooling up for a May 1 introduction of Rug Fresh. Word had reached Airwick that Lehn & Fink, makers of Lysol Spray, were preparing to launch a rug and room deodorizer product, and the race was on to beat it to market. The Production personnel redoubled their efforts and managed to get Rug Fresh into production by March 1979. Lehn & Fink's brand, Love My Carpet, reached the market at the very end of April, and Rug Fresh was out on the shelves within a few days after. Love My Carpet was priced slightly less than Carpet Fresh in comparable sizes. Later that year, Wizard came out with a brand in floral and herbal fragrances priced at $1.29. The Wizard product had little advertising support. In 1980 Love My Carpet, holding to the same sizes, introduced two additional fragrances and added a third in 1982. By late 1982 the fragranced segment had grown to 17 percent of the total rug and room deodorizer market, and Love My Carpet had reduced Wizard to 3 percent of total market share. At one point Renuzit market tested a product but opted not to introduce it nationally. S.C. Johnson, originally thought to be the most likely competitor for Carpet Fresh, never entered the rug and room deodorizer market. Mike and Wes eventually learned through the trade press that S.C. Johnson was making major investments in health and beauty aids rather than in household products.

In August 1981 Arm & Hammer came out nationally with a baking-soda "Carpet Deodorizer" in a square, orange shaker box, with this message: "Absorbs odors with no cover-up perfume." The 21-ounce size was priced at 99¢, compared to Carpet Fresh's price of $2.19 for the 14-ounce size. Private label brands also entered the market in that year. In 1982 Arm & Hammer began regional market testing of a "light scent" version of its product, and it added a 30-ounce size. Carpet Fresh prices in 1982 were $1.49 (9-ounce), $2.09 (14-ounce), and $2.99 (22-ounce).

Exhibit 11 shows competitors' price points, product and size characteristics, sales, dollar-and-ounce market share, advertising expenditure levels, and percent penetration of grocery stores. Exhibit 12 provides information on Carpet Fresh income and expenditures. Total product category advertising by all companies in 1979 was $20 million but was reduced to $10 million

EXHIBIT 11
Competitive Situation in 1981

	Sales*		Share (percent)		Advertising		Percentage of Grocery Store Distribution
Competitor	Year	($millions)	Ounces	(Dollars)	Year	($millions)	
Love My Carpet							
12 oz., $1.35	1979	$13.9	20.2	$20.4	1979	$4.8	12-wk. SARDI (4/3/81)
20 oz., $2.08	1980	19.9	30.9	29.8	1980	4.8	
	1981	16.3	25.3	26.2	1981	3.5	Brand total 89%
Regular, Floral, Citrus	1982	13.8	21.4	22.3	1982	3.2	Regular 12 61%
(pricing strategy is to	1983	12.0	18.6	19.3	1983	3.0	Regular 20 45
slightly undersell							Citrus 12 25
Carpet Fresh on a							Citrus 20 14
unit basis)							Floral 12 32
							Floral 20 14
Arm & Hammer	1979	0	0	0	1979	0	n.a.
21 oz., $.99	1980	0	0	0	1980	0	Estimated 65% based
30 oz., $1.35 (est.)	1981	4.1	14.5	6.5	1981	2.4	on test market;
Pricing strategy is to	1982	5.1	18.0	8.1	1982	.5	dual size may be
undercut all competi-	1983	3.4	12.0	5.4	1983	.5	higher.
tors by holding 21							
oz. under $1.00 while							
maintaining a pre-							
mium to regular							
baking soda.							
Wizard	1979	3.4	4.9	4.8	1979	1.3	
Super (20 oz.),	1980	6.7	9.6	9.3	1980	2.7	
$1.99	1981	3.6	5.0	4.8	1981	.5	
Floral (12 oz.),	1982	2.9	4.0	3.9	1982	.3	
$1.29	1983	2.0	3.0	2.9	1983	.1	Brand total 41%
Super, Floral, Herbal							SF 11½ 7%
pricing strategy is to							SF 17½ 8
claim 25% more than							Herbal 11½ 9
the leading brand.							Herbal 17½ 11
							Super 17½ 21

* SAMI sales expanded by ±35 percent to account for nonfood and discounted by 25 percent margin.
n.a. = Not available.

Source: Airwick industries (1981). Figures for 1982 and 1983 are projections.

EXHIBIT 12

Carpet Fresh Profit-and-Loss Statements (thousands of dollars)

| | 1978 | | 1979 | 1982† |
	Plan*	Actual	Actual	Actual
Gross sales	$ 8,589	$27,224	$50,619	$32,271
Less: discounts, rebates, and allowances	1,365	3,830	6,173	4,791
Net sales	$ 7,224	$23,394	$44,476	$27,791
Variable manufacturing costs	2,444	$ 6,663	12,480	6,400
Gross margin	$ 4,780	$16,731	$31,966	$21,391
Variable expenses:				
Freight and warehousing	631	1,534	4,097	1,920
Royalties and commissions	696	1,818	3,048	2,880
Variable contribution	$ 3,453	$13,379	$24,821	$16,591
Marketing expenses:				
Advertising	$ 3,700	$ 5,884	$13,692	$ 6,000
Consumer promotion	570	1,441	1,083	320
Trade promotion	45	230	47	1,600
Selling and merchandising aids	50	44	47	32
Other marketing	125	54	166	320
Contribution before overhead expenses	$(1,037)	$ 5,726	$ 9,786	$ 8,319

Note: Exhibits 12 and 13 can be used to calculate what the gross margin and variable contribution would be at different levels of unit sales. The variable contribution is the amount available for marketers to use in stimulating product purchase. It is also possible to speculate about the effect on unit sales of various price levels and to see their impact on variable contribution—hence the amount available to stimulate purchase.
* Original plan, April 1, 1977.
† 1982 figures are estimated.

by 1981. In the first six months of 1982, category advertising expenditures were at an annual level of $12 million. Airwick planned to spend $6 million on advertising for the year and another $1.5 million on promotion. In analyzing the competitive situation, Airwick executives indicated that Love My Carpet, because of its name, was able to generate a higher level of consumer awareness than Carpet Fresh at one-third the advertising expenditure. Market share trends are shown in Exhibit 13.

Between 1979 and 1982 Airwick adjusted its marketing approach in response to various competitor moves (see Exhibit 14 for unit sales and selling price). In April 1979 it was decided to emphasize the "antisoil" properties of Carpet Fresh in order to differentiate it from Love My Carpet. The words "patented anti-soil formula" were added to the label, although the patented ingredient had always been part of the product. Television com-

EXHIBIT 13
Room and Rug Deodorizers' Dollar Share of Market* (percentage)

	1979	1980	1981	Year to Date† 1982
Carpet Fresh	65.4	46.9	42.9	41.1
Love My Carpet	20.4	29.8	29.0	30.3
Arm & Hammer	—	—	7.8	10.0
Glamorene Rug Fresh	8.4	8.3	5.8	5.3
Private label	—	4.0	6.5	7.4
All other	5.8	11.0	8.0	5.9

* Retail grocery store sales.
† Period ending 1/8/82–6/26/82.

Source: Airwick Industries (8/82).

mercials were developed to support this approach, but the product was not really a cleaner, and the shift from "deodorizer" to a "cleaner" message proved confusing to consumers. However, later that year Airwick brought suit for patent infringement against Lehn & Fink, to prevent its claims that Love My Carpet also had anti-soil properties. In 1981 Airwick concentrated its marketing funds on fending off competition.

EXHIBIT 14
Carpet Fresh Unit Sales and Manufacturer's Selling Prices

Size	Unit Sales (cases)*		
	1978	1979	1982
9 oz.	907,467	1,066,439	379,564
14 oz.	944,506	2,035,929	1,057,942
22 oz.	—	129,265	286,109

Size	Manufacturer's Selling Price†		
	1978	1979	1982
9 oz.	$12.00	$12.00	$12.86
14 oz.	17.16	17.16	18.88
22 oz.	—	22.32	25.92

* One case = 12 packages.
† Per case, before discounts, rebates, and allowances.

Source: Airwick Industries.

THE NEXT STRATEGIC DECISION

After Arm & Hammer's 1981 introduction, Wes and Mike began to wonder if this low-price brand might serve to expand the market by stimulating trial of the category among consumers who would subsequently trade up to Carpet Fresh. Because by 1982 only a fraction of all potential consumers used a rug and room deodorizer, one issue was whether Airwick should avoid marketing tactics that might interfere with Arm & Hammer's potential to expand the market as a whole. Alternatively, Airwick might try a tactic of its own to stimulate primary demand by positioning either Carpet Fresh or a line extension to bring in new buyers. Market Research on homemakers' use of rug and room deodorizer products provided the following data:

- 45 to 50 percent had never used the product.
- 35 percent had used the product in the last year.
- Of the 35 percent who used it in the last year:
  1. One-third used one can per year.
  2. One-third used two or three cans per year.
  3. One-third used more than three cans per year, (accounting for approximately 50 percent of unit sales).

Another option was for Airwick to extend its line into fragrances or to lower Carpet Fresh prices to fend off further share erosion by Love My Carpet and Arm & Hammer. Alternatively, Airwick could assume that market growth was virtually over for the category and gradually reduce advertising expenditures to make funds available for other products.

CASE 4–9

S. C. Johnson and Son, Ltd.

Four months ago, in November 1980, George Styan had been appointed division manager of INNOCHEM, at S. C. Johnson and Son, Ltd. (SCJ),[1] a Canadian subsidiary of S. C. Johnson & Son, Inc. INNOCHEM's sole product line consisted of industrial cleaning chemicals for use by business, institutions, and government. George was concerned by the division's poor mar-

---

Copyright © 1982, The University of Western Ontario, School of Business Administration, by Professor Roger More.

[1] Popularly known as "Canadian Johnson Wax."

ket share, particularly in Montreal and Toronto. Together these two cities represented approximately 35 percent of Canadian demand for industrial cleaning chemicals but less than 10 percent of INNOCHEM sales. It appeared that SCJ distributors could not match the aggressive discounting practiced by direct-selling manufacturers in metropolitan markets.

Recently George had received a rebate proposal from his staff designed to increase the distributor's ability to cut end-user prices by "sharing" part of the total margin with SCJ when competitive conditions demanded discounts of 30 percent or more off the list price to end users. George had to decide if the rebate plan was the best way to penetrate price-sensitive markets. Moreover he wondered about the plan's ultimate impact on divisional profit performance. George had to develop an implementation plan for the rebate proposal or draft an alternative to unveil at the 1981 Distributor's Annual Spring Convention, three weeks away.

THE CANADIAN MARKET FOR INDUSTRIAL CLEANING CHEMICALS

In 1980 the Canadian market for industrial cleaning chemicals was approximately $100 million at end-user prices. Growth was stable at an overall rate of approximately 3 percent per year.

"Industrial cleaning chemicals" included all chemical products designed to clean, disinfect, sanitize, or protect industrial, commercial, and institutional buildings and equipment. The label was broadly applied to general-purpose cleaners, floor maintenance products (strippers, sealers, finishes, and detergents), carpet cleaners and deodorizers, disinfectants, air fresheners, and a host of specialty chemicals such as insecticides, pesticides, drain cleaners, oven cleansers, and sweeping compounds.

Industrial cleaning chemicals were distinct from equivalent consumer products typically sold through grocery stores. Heavy-duty industrial products were packaged in larger containers and bulk, and marketed directly by the cleaning chemical manufacturers or sold through distributors to a variety of end users. Exhibit 1 includes market segmentation by primary end-user categories, including janitorial service contractors and the in-house maintenance departments of government, institutions, and companies.

Building Maintenance Contractors

In Canada maintenance contractors purchased 17 percent of the industrial cleaning chemicals sold during 1980 (end-user price). The segment was growing at approximately 10 to 15 percent a year, chiefly at the expense of other end-user categories. *Canadian Business* reported: "Contract cleaners have made sweeping inroads into the traditional preserve of in-house janito-

EXHIBIT 1
Segmentation of the Canadian Market for Industrial Cleaning Chemicals

End-User Category	Percent of Total Canadian Market for Industrial Cleaning Chemicals (end-user value)	Product Category	Percent of Total Canadian Market for Industrial Cleaning Chemicals
Retail outlets	25%	Floor care products	40%
Contractors	17	General-purpose cleaners	16
Hospitals	15	Disinfectants	12
Industrial and office	13	Carpet care products	8
Schools, colleges	8	Odor control products	5
Hotels, motels	6	Glass cleaners	4
Nursing homes	5	All others	15
Recreation	3	Total	100% = $95 million
Government	3		
Fast food	2		
Full-service restaurants	2		
All others	1		
Total	100% = $95 million		

rial staffs, selling themselves on the strength of cost efficiency."[2] Maintenance contract billings reached an estimated $1 billion in 1980.

Frequently, demand for building maintenance services was highly price sensitive, and since barriers to entry were low (small capitalization, simple technology), competition squeezed contractor gross margins below 6 percent (before tax). Variable-cost control was a matter of survival, and only products bringing compensatory labor savings could command a premium price in this segment of the cleaning chemical market.

A handful of contract cleaners did specialize in higher-margin services to prestige office complexes, luxury apartments, art museums, and other "quality-conscious" customers. However, even contractors serving this select clientele did not necessarily buy premium cleaning supplies.

In-House Maintenance Departments

Government. In 1980, cleaning chemical sales to various government offices (federal, provincial, and local) approached $2 million. Typically a government body solicited bids from appropriate sources by formally advertising for quotations for given quantities of particular cleaning chemicals. Although bid requests often named specific brands, suppliers were permitted to offer "equivalent substitutes." Separate competitions were held for each item and normally covered 12 months' supply, with provision for

---

[2] "Contract Cleaners Want to Whisk Away Ring-around-the-Office," *Canadian Business,* 1981, p. 22.

delivery "as required." Contracts were frequently awarded solely on the basis of price.

Institutions. Like government bodies, most institutions were price sensitive, owing to restrictive budgets and limited ability to "pass on" expenses to users. Educational institutions and hospitals were the largest consumers of cleaning chemicals in this segment. School boards used an open bid system patterned on the government model. Heavy sales time requirements and demands for frequent delivery of small shipments to as many as 100 locations were characteristic.

Colleges and universities tended to be operated somewhat differently. Dan Stalport, one of the purchasing agents responsible for maintenance supplies at the University of Western Ontario, offered the following comments:

> Sales reps come to UWO year-round. If one of us (in the buying group) talks to a salesman who seems to have something to say—say, a labor-saving feature—we get a sample and test it. . . . Testing can take up to a year. Floor covering, for example, has to be exposed to seasonal changes in weather and traffic.
>
> If we're having problems with a particular item, we'll compare the performance and price of three or four competitors. There are usually plenty of products that do the job. Basically, we want value—acceptable performance at the lowest available price.

Hospitals accounted for 15 percent of cleaning chemical sales. Procurement policies at University Hospital (UH), a medium-size (450-bed) facility in London, Ontario, were typical. UH distinguished between "critical" and "noncritical" products. Critical cleaning chemicals (i.e., those significantly affecting patient health, such as phenolic germicide) could be bought only on approval of the staff microbiologist, who tested the "kill factor." This measure of effectiveness was regularly retested, and any downgrading of product performance could void a supplier's contract. In contrast, noncritical supplies, such as general-purpose cleaners, floor finishes, and the like, were the exclusive province of Bob Chandler, purchasing agent attached to the Housekeeping Department. Bob explained that performance of noncritical cleaning chemicals was informally judged and monitored by the housekeeping staff: "Just last year, for example, the cleaners found the floor polish was streaking badly. We [the Housekeeping Department] tested and compared five or six brands—all in the ballpark pricewise—and chose the best."

Business. The corporate segment was highly diverse, embracing both service and manufacturing industries. Large-volume users tended to be price sensitive, particularly when profits were low. Often, however, cleaning products represented such a small percentage of the total operating budget that the cost of searching for the lowest-cost supplier would be expected to exceed any realizable saving. Under such conditions the typical industrial customer sought efficiencies in the purchasing process itself; for example, by dealing with the supplier offering the broadest mix of janitorial products (chemical, paper supplies, equipment, etc.). Guy Breton, purchasing agent for Securitech, a Montreal-based security systems manufacturer, commented on the time economies of "one-stop shopping."

> With cleaning chemicals, it simply isn't worth the trouble to shop around and stage elaborate product performance tests. . . . I buy all our chemicals, brushes, dusters, toweling—the works—from one or two suppliers. . . . Buying reputable brands from familiar suppliers saves hassles—backorders are rare and maintenance seldom complains.

DISTRIBUTION CHANNELS FOR INDUSTRIAL CLEANING CHEMICALS

The Canadian market for industrial cleaning chemicals was supplied through three main channels, each characterized by a distinctive set of strengths and weaknesses:

1. Distributor sales of national brands.
2. Distributor sales of private-label products.
3. Direct sale by manufacturers.

Direct sellers held a 61 percent share of the Canadian market for industrial cleaning chemicals, while the distributors of national brands and private-label products held shares of 25 and 14 percent, respectively. Relative market shares varied geographically, however. In Montreal and Toronto, for example, the direct marketers' share rose to 70 percent and private labelers' to 18 percent, reducing the national brand share to 12 percent. The pattern, shown in Exhibit 2, reflected an interplay of two areas of channel differentiation: discount capability at the end-user level and the cost of serving distant, geographically dispersed customers.

Distributor Sales of National-Brand Cleaning Chemicals

National-brand manufacturers, such as S. C. Johnson and Son, Airkem, and National Labs, produced a relatively limited range of "high-quality" janitorial products, including many special-purpose formulations of narrow market interest. Incomplete product range combined with shortage of manpower and limited warehousing made direct distribution not feasible in most cases. Normally a national-brand company would negotiate with distributors that handled a broad array of complementary products (equipment, tools, and supplies) by different manufacturers. "Bundling" of goods brought the distributors cost efficiencies in selling, warehousing, and delivery by spreading fixed costs over a large sales volume. Distributors were therefore better able to absorb the costs of after-hour emergency service,

EXHIBIT 2
Effect of Geography on Market Share of Different Distribution Channels

Supplier Type	Share Nationwide	Share in Montreal and Toronto
Direct marketers		
Dustbane	17%	
G. H. Wood	13	
All others	31	
Total	61	70%
Private-label distributors	14	18
National-brands distributors		
SCJ	8	
N/L	4	
Airkem	3	
All others	10	
Total	25	12

frequent routine sales and service calls to many potential buyers, and shipments of small quantities of cleaning chemicals to multiple destinations. As
a rule, the greater the geographic dispersion of customers and the smaller
the average order, the greater the relative economies of distributor marketing.

Comparatively high gross margins (approximately 50 percent of wholesale price) enabled national-brand manufacturers to offer distributors
strong marketing support and sales training along with liberal terms of
payment and freight plus low minimum-order requirements. Distributors
readily agreed to handle national-brand chemicals, and in metropolitan
markets, each brand was sold through several distributors. By the same
token, most distributors carried several directly competitive product lines.
George suspected that some distributor salesmen only used national brands
to "lead" with and tended to offer private labels whenever a customer proved
price sensitive or a competitor handled the same national brand(s). Using
an industry rule of thumb, George estimated that most distributors needed
at least 20 percent gross margin on retail sales to cover their salesmen's
commission of 10 percent on retail sales, plus delivery and inventory expenses.

Distributor Sales of Private-Label Cleaning Chemicals

Direct-selling manufacturers were dominating urban markets by aggressively discounting end-user prices—sometimes below the wholesale price
national-brand manufacturers charged their distributors. To compete

against the direct seller, increasing numbers of distributors were adding low-cost, private-label cleaning chemicals to their product lines. Private labeling also helped differentiate a particular distributor from others carrying the same national brand(s).

Sizable minimum-order requirements restricted the private-label strategy to the largest distributors. Private-label manufacturers produced to order, formulating to meet low prices specified by distributors. The relatively narrow margins (30 to 35 percent of wholesale price) associated with private-label manufacture precluded the extensive marketing and sales support national-brand manufacturers characteristically provided to distributors. Private-label producers pared their expenses further by requiring distributors to bear the cost of inventory and accept rigid terms of payments as well as delivery (net 30 days, FOB plant).

In addition to absorbing selling expenses normally assumed by the manufacturer, distributors paid their salesmen higher commission on private-label sales (15 percent of resale) than national brands (10 percent of resale). However, the incremental administration and selling expenses associated with private-label business were more than offset by the differential savings on private-label wholesale goods. By pricing private-label chemicals at competitive parity with national brands, the distributor could enjoy approximately a 50 percent gross margin at resale list while preserving considerable resale discount capability.

Private-label products were seldom sold outside the metropolitan areas where most were manufactured. First, the high costs of moving bulky, low-value freight diminished the relative cost advantage of private-label chemicals. Second, generally speaking, it was only in metro areas where distributors dealt in volumes great enough to satisfy the private labeler's minimum-order requirement. Finally, outside the city, distributors were less likely to be in direct local competition with others handling the same national brand, reducing the value of the private label as a source of supplier differentiation.

For some very large distributors, backward integration into chemical production was a logical extension of the private-labeling strategy. Recently several distributors had become direct marketers through acquisition of captive manufacturers.

Direct Sale by Manufacturers of Industrial Cleaning Chemicals

Manufacturers dealing directly with the end user increased their gross margins to 60 to 70 percent of retail list price. Greater margins increased their ability to discount end-user price—a distinct advantage in the price-competitive urban marketplace. Overall, direct marketers averaged a gross margin of 50 percent.

Many manufacturers of industrial cleaning chemicals attempted some direct selling, but relatively few relied on this channel exclusively. Satisfactory adoption of a full-time direct-selling strategy required the manufacturer to match distributors' sales and delivery capabilities without sacrificing overall profitability. These conflicting demands had been resolved successfully by two types of company, large-scale powder chemical manufacturers and full-line janitorial products manufacturers.

Large-Scale Powder Chemical Manufacturers. Economies of large-scale production plus experience in the capital-intensive manufacture of powder chemicals enabled a few established firms, such as Diversey-Wyandotte, to dominate the market for powder warewash and vehicle cleansers. Selling through distributors offered these producers few advantages. Direct-selling expense was almost entirely commission (i.e., variable). Moreover powder concentrates were characterized by comparatively high value-to-bulk ratios and so could absorb delivery costs even where demand was geographically dispersed. Thus any marginal benefits from using middlemen were more than offset by the higher margins (and associated discount capability) possible through direct distribution. Among these firms competition was not limited to price. The provision of dispensing and metering equipment was important, as was 24-hour servicing.

Full-Line Janitorial Products Manufacturers. These manufacturers offered a complete range of maintenance products, including paper supplies, janitorial chemicals, tools, and mechanical equipment. Although high margins greatly enhanced retail price flexibility, overall profitability depended on securing a balance of high- and low-margin business, as well as controlling selling and distribution expenses. This was accomplished in several ways, including:

- Centering on market areas of concentrated demand to minimize costs of warehousing, sales travel, and the like.
- Increasing average order size either by adding product lines which could be sold to existing customers or by seeking new large-volume customers.
- Tying sales commission to profitability to motivate sales personnel to sell volume, without unnecessary discounting of end-user price.

Direct marketers of maintenance products varied in scale from established nationwide companies to hundreds of regional operators. The two largest direct marketers, G. H. Wood and Dustbane, together supplied almost a third of Canadian demand for industrial cleaning chemicals.

S. C. JOHNSON AND SON, LTD.

S. C. Johnson and Son, Ltd. was one of 42 foreign subsidiaries owned by the U.S.-based, multinational S. C. Johnson & Son, Inc. It was ranked globally as one of the largest privately held companies. SCJ contributed substantially to worldwide sales and profits and was based in Brantford, Ontario, close to the Canadian urban markets of Hamilton, Kitchener, Toronto, London, and Niagara Falls. About 300 people worked at the head office and plant; another 100 were employed in field sales.

INNOCHEM DIVISION

INNOCHEM (Innovative Chemicals for Professional Use) was a special division established to serve corporate, institutional, and government customers of SCJ. The division manufactured an extensive line of industrial cleaning chemicals, including general-purpose cleaners, waxes, polishes, and disinfectants, plus a number of specialty products of limited application, as shown in Exhibit 3. In 1980 INNOCHEM sold $4.5 million of industrial cleaning chemicals through distributors and $0.2 million direct to end users. Financial statements for INNOCHEM are shown in Exhibit 4.

EXHIBIT 3
INNOCHEM Product Line

For all floors except unsealed wood and unsealed cork:	
Stripper:	**Step-Off**—powerful, fast action.
Finish:	**Pronto**—fast drying, good gloss, minimum maintenance.
Spray-buff solution:	**The Shiner Liquid Spray Cleaner**
	or
	The Shiner Aerosol Spray Finish.
Maintainer:	**Forward**—cleans, disinfects, deodorizes, sanitizes.
For all floors except unsealed wood and unsealed cork:	
Stripper:	**Step-Off**—powerful, fast stripper.
Finish:	**Carefree**—tough, beauty, durable, minimum maintenance.
Maintainer:	**Forward**—cleans, disinfects, deodorizes, sanitizes.
For all floors except unsealed wood and unsealed cork:	
Stripper:	**Step-Off**—for selective stripping.
Sealer:	**Over & Under-Plus**—undercoater-sealer.
Finish:	**Scrubbable Step-Ahead**—brilliant, scrubbable.
Maintainer:	**Forward**—cleans, disinfects, sanitizes, deodorizes.
For all floors except unsealed wood and cork:	
Stripper:	**Step-Off**—powerful, fast stripper.
Finish:	**Easy Street**—high solids, high gloss, spray buffs to a "wet look" appearance.

Maintainer:	**Forward**—cleans, disinfects, deodorizes.
	Expose—phenolic cleaner disinfectant.
For all floors except unsealed wood and unsealed cork:	
Stripper:	**Step-Off**—for selective stripping.
Sealer:	**Over & Under-Plus**—undercoater-sealer.
Finishes:	**Traffic Grade**—heavy-duty floor wax.
	Waxtral—extra tough, high solids.
Maintainer:	**Forward**—cleans, disinfects, sanitizes, deodorizes.
For all floors except asphalt, mastic, and rubber tile (Use sealer and wax finishes on wood, cork, and cured concrete; sealer-finish on terrazzo, marble, clay and ceramic tile; wax finish, only on vinyl, linoleum, and magnesite)	
Sealer:	**Johnson Gym Finish**—sealer and top-coater cleans as it waxes.
Wax finishes:	**Traffic Wax Paste**—heavy-duty buffing wax.
	Beautiflor Traffic Wax—liquid buffing wax.
Maintainers:	**Forward**—cleans, disinfects, sanitizes, deodorizes.
	Conq-r-Dust—mop treatment.
Stripper:	**Step-Off**—stripper for sealer and finish.
Sealer:	**Secure**—fast bonding smooth, long lasting.

EXHIBIT 3   (concluded)

Finish:	**Traffic Grade**—heavy-duty floor wax.
Maintainer:	**Forward** or **Big Bare**
Sealer-finish:	**Johnson Gym Finish**—seal and top-coater.
Maintainer:	**Conq-r-Dust**—mop treatment.
General cleaning:	**Break-up**—cleans soap and body scum fast.
	Forward—cleans, disinfects, sanitizes, deodorizes.
	Bon Ami—instant cleaner, pressurized or pump, disinfects.
Toilet-urinals:	**Go-Getter**—"Working Foam" cleaner.
Glass:	**Bon Ami**—spray-on foam or liquid cleaner.
Disinfectant spray:	**End-Bac II**—controls bacteria, odors.
Air freshener:	**Glade**—dewy-fresh fragrances.
Spot cleaning:	**Johnson's Pledge**—cleans, waxes, polishes.
	Johnson's Lemon Pledge—refreshing scent.
	Bon Ami Stainless Steel Cleaner—cleans, polishes, protects.
All-purpose cleaners:	**Forward**—cleans, disinfects, sanitizes, deodorizes.
	Break-up—degreaser for animal and vegetable fats.
	Big Bare—heavy-duty industrial cleaner.
Carpets:	**Rugbee Powder & Liquid Extraction Cleaner.**
	Rugbee Soil Release Concentrate—for prespraying and bonnet buffing.
	Rugbee Shampoo—for powder shampoo machines.

	Rugbee Spotter—spot remover.
Furniture:	**Johnson's Pledge**—cleans, waxes, polishes.
	Johnson's Lemon Pledge—refreshing scent.
	Shine-Up Liquid—general-purpose cleaning.
Disinfectant spray:	**End-Bac II**—controls bacteria, odors.
Air freshener:	**Glade**—dewy-fresh fragrances.
Glass:	**Bon Ami**—spray-on foam or liquid cleaner.
Cleaning:	**Break-up**—special degreaser designed to remove animal and vegetable fats.
Equipment:	**Break-up Foamer**—special generator designed to dispense Break-up cleaner.
General cleaning:	**Forward**—fast-working germicidal cleaner for floors, walls, all washable surfaces.
	Expose—phenolic disinfectant cleaner.
Sanitizing:	**J80 Sanitizer**—liquid for total environmental control of bacteria. No rinse necessary if used as directed.
Disinfectant spray:	**End-Bac II Spray**—controls bacteria, odors.
Flying insects:	Bolt Liquid Airborne, or Pressurized Airborne, P3610 through E10 dispenser.
Crawling insects:	Bolt Liquid Residual or Pressurized Residual, P3610 through E10 dispenser.
	Bolt Roach Bait.
Rodents:	Bolt Rodenticide—for effective control of rats and mice, use with Bolt Bait Box.

EXHIBIT 4
Profit Statement of the Division ($000)

Gross sales	$4,682
Returns	46
Allowances	1
Cash discounts	18
Net sales	4,617
Cost of sales	2,314
Gross profit	$2,303
Advertising	75
Promotions	144
Deals	—
External marketing services	2
Sales freight	292
Other distribution expenses	176
Service fees	184*
Total direct expenses	$ 873
Sales force	592
Marketing administration	147
Provision for bad debts	—
Research and development	30†
Financial	68
Information resource management	47
Administration management	56
Total functional expenses	$ 940
Total operating expenses	1,813
Operating profit	$ 490

* Fees paid to SCJ (corporate) for corporate services.
† A portion of a research chemist's cost to conduct R&D specifically for industrial products.

INNOCHEM MARKETING STRATEGY

Divisional strategy hinged on reliable product performance, product innovation, active promotion, and mixed channel distribution. Steve Remen, market development manager, maintained that "customers know our products are of excellent quality. They know that the products will always perform as expected."

At SCJ, performance requirements were detailed and tolerances precisely defined. The Department of Quality Control routinely inspected and tested raw materials, work in process, packaging, and finished goods. At any phase during the manufacturing cycle, Quality Control was empowered to halt the process and quarantine suspect product or materials. SCJ maintained that nothing left the plant "without approval from Quality Control."

"Keeping the new-product shelf well stocked" was central to divisional strategy, as the name INNOCHEM implies. Products launched over the past three years represented 33 percent of divisional gross sales, 40 percent of gross profits, and 100 percent of growth.

INNOCHEM had a sales force of 10 that sold and serviced the distributor accounts. These salespeople were paid almost all salary, with some bonus potential up to 10 percent for exceptional sales volume increases. The company had also recently committed one salesperson to work with large direct accounts. The advertising budget of $75,000 was primarily allocated to trade magazines and direct-mail advertisements directed at large segments of end users such as maintenance contractors. Sales promotions, by contrast, were directed mainly at distributors and consisted largely of special pricing and packaging deals to get distributors to bid Johnson products more aggressively in offers to end users.

Mixed Distribution Strategy

INNOCHEM used a mixed distribution system in an attempt to broaden market coverage. Eighty-seven percent of divisional sales were handled by a force of 200 distributor salesmen and serviced from 50 distributor warehouses representing 35 distributors. The indirect channel was particularly effective outside Ontario and Quebec. In part, the tendency for SCJ market penetration to increase with distances from Montreal and Toronto reflected Canadian demographics and the general economics of distribution. Outside the two production centers, demand was dispersed and delivery distances long.

Distributor salesmen were virtually all paid a straight commission on sales and were responsible for selling a wide variety of products in addition to Johnson's. Several of the distributors had sales levels much higher than INNOCHEM.

For INNOCHEM the impact of geography was compounded by a significant freight cost advantage: piggybacking industrial cleaning chemicals with SCJ consumer goods. In Toronto, for example, the cost of SCJ to a distributor was 30 percent above private label, while the differential in British Columbia was only 8 percent. On lower-value products, the "freight effect" was even more pronounced.

SCJ had neither the salesmen nor the delivery capabilities to reach large-volume end users who demanded heavy selling effort or frequent shipments of small quantities. Furthermore it was unlikely that SCJ could develop the necessary selling and distribution strength economically, given the narrowness of the division's range of janitorial products (industrial cleaning chemicals only).

The Rebate Plan

The key strategic problem facing INNOCHEM was how best to challenge the direct marketer (and private label distributor) for large-volume, price-sensitive customers with heavy service requirements, particularly in markets where SCJ had no freight advantage. In this connection, George had observed:

> Our gravest weakness is our inability to manage the total margin between the manufactured cost and end-user price in a way that is equitable and sufficiently profitable to support the investment and expenses of both the distributors and ourselves.
>
> Our prime competition across Canada is from direct-selling national and regional manufacturers. These companies control both the manufacturing and distribution gross margins. Under our pricing system, the distributor's margin at end-user list on sales is 43 percent. Our margin (the manufacturing margin) is 50 percent on sales. When these margins are combined, as in the case of direct-selling manufacturers, the margin becomes 70 percent at list. This long margin provides significant price flexibility in a price-competitive marketplace. We must find a way to attack the direct marketer's 61 percent market share.

The rebate plan George was now evaluating had been devised to meet the competition head-on. "Profitable partnership" between INNOCHEM and the distributors was the underlying philosophy of the plan. Rebates offered a means to "share fairly the margins available between factory cost and consumer price." Whenever competitive conditions required a distributor to discount the resale list price by 30 percent or more, SCJ would give a certain percentage of the wholesale price back to the distributor. SCJ would sacrifice part of its margin to help offset a heavy end-user discount. Rebate percentages would vary with the rate of discount, following a set schedule. Different schedules were to be established for each product type and size. Exhibits 5, 6, and 7 outline the effect of rebates on both the unit gross margins of SCJ and individual distributors for a specific product example.

The rebate plan was designed to be applicable to new incremental business only, not for existing accounts of the distributor. Distributors would be required to seek SCJ approval for end-user discounts of over 30 percent or more of resale list. The maximum allowable end-user discount would rarely exceed 50 percent. To request rebate payments, distributors would send SCJ a copy of the resale invoice along with a written claim. The rebate would then be paid within 60 days. Proponents of the plan maintained that the resulting resale price flexibility would not only enhance INNOCHEM competitiveness among end users but would also diminish distributor attraction to private labels. As he studied the plan, George questioned whether all the implications were fully understood and wondered what other strategies, if any, might increase urban market penetration. Any plan he devised would have to be sold to distributors as well as to corporate management. George had only three weeks to develop an appropriate action plan.

EXHIBIT 5
Distributors' Rebate Pricing Schedule (an example using Pronto Floor Wax)

Code: 04055	Product Description: Pronto Fast Dry Finish	Size: 209 Liter	Pack: 1	Effective date: 03-31-81 Resale list price 71 613.750 — *price to end user* Distributor price list 74 349.837 — *price to distrib*

Percent Markup on Cost with Carload and Rebate

Discount (1)	Quote (2)	Rebate (3)	Rebate (4)	2% Net (5)	2% Markup (6)	3% Net	3% Markup	4% Net	4% Markup	5% Net	5% Markup
30.0%	$429.63	8.0%	$ 27.99	$314.85	36%	$311.35	38%	$307.86	40%	$304.36	41%
35.0	398.94	12.0	41.98	300.86	33	297.36	34	293.86	36	290.36	37
40.0	368.25	17.0	59.47	283.37	30	279.87	32	276.37	33	272.87	35
41.0	362.11	17.5	61.22	281.62	29	278.12	30	274.62	32	271.12	34
42.0	355.98	18.0	62.97	279.87	27	276.37	29	272.87	30	269.37	32
43.0	349.84	18.5	64.72	278.12	26	274.62	27	271.12	29	267.63	31
44.0	343.70	19.0	66.47	276.37	24	272.87	26	269.37	28	265.88	29
45.0	337.56	20.0	69.97	272.87	24	269.37	25	265.88	27	262.38	29
46.0	331.43	20.5	71.72	271.12	22	267.63	24	264.13	25	260.63	27
47.0	325.29	21.0	73.47	269.37	21	265.88	22	262.38	24	258.88	26
48.0	319.15	21.5	75.21	267.63	19	264.13	21	260.63	22	257.13	24
49.0	313.01	22.0	76.96	265.88	18	262.38	19	258.88	21	255.38	23
50.0	306.88	23.0	80.46	262.38	17	258.88	19	255.38	20	251.88	22
51.0	300.74	24.0	83.96	258.88	16	255.38	18	251.88	19	248.38	21
52.0	294.60	25.0	87.46	255.38	15	251.88	17	248.38	19	244.89	20
53.0	288.46	26.0	90.96	251.88	15	248.38	16	244.89	18	241.39	19
54.0	282.33	28.0	97.95	244.89	15	241.39	17	237.89	19	234.39	20
55.0	276.19	30.0	104.95	237.89	16	234.39	18	230.89	20	227.39	21

(1) Discount extended to end user on resale list price.
(2) Resale price at given discount level (includes federal sales tax).
(3) Percentage of distributor's price ($613.75) rebated by SCJ.
(4) Actual dollar amount of rebate by SCJ.
(5) Actual net cost to distributor after deduction of rebate and "carload" (quantity) discount.
(6) Effective rate of distributor markup.

441

EXHIBIT 6

Effect of Rebate Plan on Manufacturer and Distributor Margins (example of one 209-liter pack of Pronto Floor Finish retailed at 40 percent below resale list price)

Under Present Arrangements

Base price to distributor	$349.84
Price to distributor, assuming 2 percent carload discount*	342.84
SCJ cost	174.92
SCJ margin	$167.92
Resale list price	613.75
Resale list price minus 40 percent discount	368.25
Distributor price, assuming 2 percent carload discount	342.84
Distributor's margin	$ 25.41

7%

Under Rebate Plan

Rebate to distributor giving 40 percent discount off resale price amounted to 17 percent distributor's base price	$ 59.47
SCJ margin (minus rebate)	108.45
Distributor margin (plus rebate)	84.88

24.8%

Competitive Prices

For this example, George estimated that a distributor could buy a private-brand "comparable" product for approximately $244. vs. 368.29

* A form of quantity discount which, in this case, drops the price the distributor pays to SCJ from $349.84 to $342.84.

EXHIBIT 7
Effect of End-User Discount Level on Manufacturer and Distributor Margins under Proposed Rebate Plan (example of one 209-liter pack of Pronto Fast Dry Finish)*

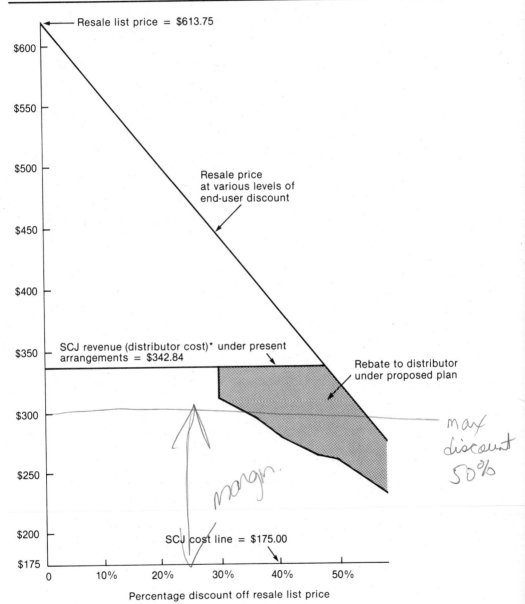

* Assuming 2 percent quantity (carload) discount off price to distributor.

CASE 4–10

J. W. Thornton Ltd.

"Business is going great—I wish I knew why," laughed Peter Thornton, joint managing director of J. W. Thornton Ltd., a leading manufacturer and retailer of high-quality confectionery. Certainly there appeared reasons for his good humor; while the dismal economic situation in the United Kingdom was causing most retailers to show little volume growth and declining margins, four months into the financial year Thornton's sales from its 148 shops were 4 percent up on budget, and profits were even further ahead (Exhibit 1).

Nevertheless there were many decisions that needed to be taken on how to move the business forward. In particular it was not obvious how many new stores the company should aim to open, whether franchising offered an effective method of long-term growth, or whether the company should seek to manufacture confectionery for a broader range of retailers at home and overseas. Further, while the current situation looked satisfactory, in the recent past it had appeared much less rosy, and the directors felt that major

EXHIBIT 1
Some General U.K. Economic Indicators, 1970–1980

Year	Retail Sales	Sales of CTNs*	Company Profits†	Cost of Living Index
1970	100	100	100	100
1971	108	107	113	109
1972	133	121	126	117
1973	151	131	150	128
1974	175	155	160	148
1975	208	191	171	184
1976	238	223	219	213
1977	271	257	265	251
1978	310	285	300	274
1979	345	297	397	311
1980	389	351	468	360

* Retail sales of confectioners, tobacconists, and newspaper shops.
† Before providing for depreciation and stock appreciation.

Source: *U.K. Annual Abstract of Statistics.*

Prepared by Peter Doyle, Bradford University, England. Copyright © 1981 by Professor P. Doyle. Reproduced with permission.

mistakes had been made on pricing policy, advertising, and overhead cost control which had significantly curtailed profit performance. The board of directors, in discussing these issues, had identified the need for a corporate strategy to provide a longer-term perspective than that of the annual budget. Mr. Peter, as he was known in the company, had agreed and had offered to present a paper for the next meeting outlining his ideas about the strategic direction for the business.

COMPANY BACKGROUND

The company was founded in 1911 by J. W. Thornton, who began making hard-boiled sweets in a coke stove in the basement of his shop in Sheffield. He was soon joined by his two sons Norman and Stanley, who remain on the board to this day. In the years that followed, the company opened more shops and gradually expanded its product range. In 1925 the company's Special Toffee was developed which is still the shops' best-selling product. Another milestone was Stanley and Norman's decision to develop a really high-quality range of chocolates. During a continental holiday in 1953 the brothers visited the Basle School for Swiss Chocolatiers and recruited one of the top students. The result was the Thornton range of Continental Chocolates, which now sells 600 tons annually. By 1939 Thornton's had expanded to 35 shops in the Midlands and North of England. Further rapid growth followed the end of confectionery rationing in 1952, and advertising and seasonal promotions gradually increased consumer awareness of the Thornton name. By 1980 the company had over 1,000 employees, two factories, and 148 shops.

The company had always emphasized certain features. Most important was the commitment to product freshness and quality. Unwillingness to hazard the business's hard-won reputation in these areas accounted for management's long reluctance to sell confectionery outside their own shops despite many requests from interested retailers. This philosophy, together with the desire to develop a distinctive specialist confectionery image, also made them increasingly reluctant to buy products for their shops other than those produced from their factories. Bought-in goods (mainly greeting cards) now account for only five percent of shop turnover. A consequence was that the shops continued with a narrow range of products—three basic lines: chocolate, toffee, and hard-boiled sweets represented over 90 percent of sales.

The company has continued to emphasize traditional values. The shops have changed relatively little over the years, and there has been no major product introduction since the range of Continental Chocolates over 25 years earlier. Advertising made much of the products being "all made in the good old-fashioned way." Finally it remained very much a family business; all the shareholders and all eight members of the board including the presi-

EXHIBIT 2
J. W. Thornton Ltd., Selected Performance Data (£000)

Financial Year	Sales (excluding VAT)	Gross Profit	Pretax Net Profit	Total Assets*	Stock-holders' Funds	Number of Shops
1969–70	£ 2,262	£1,240	£237	£1,218	£ 809	107
1970–71	2,222	1,177	270	1,305	885	110
1971–72	2,783	1,517	336	1,503	1,043	122
1972–73	3,461	1,869	544	1,896	1,241	126
1973–74	4,270	2,263	581	2,373	1,488	130
1974–75	5,653	2,802	576	2,931	1,735	128
1975–76	7,091	3,824	709	3,425	2,002	130
1976–77	8,821	4,455	552	4,228	2,217	130
1977–78	10,887	5,532	704	4,749	2,661	132
1978–79	12,826	6,714	946	6,201	2,594	138
1979–80	15,551	8,360	668	7,515	3,113	148

* Assets valued on historic cost basis.

Source: Annual reports.

dent, the chairman, the two managing directors, and the company secretary were Thorntons. Hence the practice within the company of calling the directors Mr. Tony, Mr. Peter, etc., was not just quaint; it was necessary.

After the mid-1960s Mr. Norman's three sons Tony, Peter, and John, together with Mr. Stanley's son Michael, took an increasingly large part in running the business. In 1979 Peter and John became joint managing directors when Tony moved up from managing director to chairman. Previously both Peter and John had shared responsibility for the manufacturing side of the business. Under the new structure Peter's main sphere of responsibility covered marketing and retail, and John looked after manufacturing and product development. Stanley and Norman remained on the board as president and consultant, respectively.

Until the mid-1970s the company had seen almost uninterrupted progress (see Exhibit 2). Probably the peak year was in 1973, when the company earned a pretax margin of 16 percent and a return on net worth of 44 percent. Then, like many other retailers, business got more difficult as the slower growth of consumer expenditures and the rapid rise in inflation hit margins and cash flow.

RETAILING IN THE UNITED KINGDOM

The postwar years saw remarkable changes in the pattern of retailing in the United Kingdom. A number of forces created the stimuli for change. Car registrations grew from 2.5 million in 1950 to 13.5 million in 1973 when the majority of households had a car, which both increased their mobility and enabled them to carry more shopping in one trip. A second feature was the dispersal of population from major towns. While the drift to the suburbs was less dramatic than in the United States, it did result in a noticeable shift in retail buying power from the inner urban areas to the outer suburbs. A third factor was the rise in female employment, which increased the pressure for longer shop-opening hours and for facilities for shopping with the family. Finally, the overall level of spending rose sharply as a result of both a larger population and, more importantly, rising income levels. Real disposable income doubled between 1950 and 1980.

The most important responses to these stimuli were:

1. The growth of self-service across many sectors of retailing. Self-service offered savings both to the retailer and the shopper. In food, for example, supermarkets increased from only 500 in 1950 to over 30,000 in 1973.

2. A trend toward fewer, larger shops. The total number of food shops, for example, fell by one-half between 1960 and 1980, but the development of self-service in particular meant that on average the newer shops had much larger floor space.

3. Economies of scale in buying and marketing led to increased concentration in retailing. The major chains increased their share of trade at the expense of independent shops in all sectors of retailing.

4. A consequence of this greater retailing concentration was increasing bargaining power over manufacturers. Manufacturers' margins were squeezed as the larger retailers demanded their own private brands and larger discounts.

5. The extension of intertype retailing competition, or "scrambled merchandising." Retailers sought to strengthen their margins by broadening their merchandise assortments. Food retailers diversified into nonfoods, and nonfood businesses added on food lines.

6. The development of out-of-town retailing and the growth of new types of shops, such as supermarkets, shopping mall boutiques, discount stores, and catalog showrooms. Many innovations took place during this period and grew rapidly at the expense of retailers which had reached the maturity state of the institutional life cycle.

7. Working wives, greater car ownership, and new types of mass merchandising encouraged the trend toward once-weekly one-stop shopping, increasingly at the large suburban superstore with ample parking.

After 1973, competition in retailing toughened noticeably, and retailers' profit margins halved between 1973 and 1980. The causes were the stagnation in consumer spending after 1973 and the rapid escalation in inflation. Larger retailers responded to the lack of market growth by price cutting to expand or maintain market shares, pressuring manufacturers even further for discounts and financial support, and boosting advertising budgets in an effort to strengthen the competitive position of their shops. During this period independent retailers had great difficulty in surviving, and several major retail groups ran into difficulties as they were squeezed by newer and more aggressive forms of retailing.

THE CONFECTIONERY MARKET

British confectionery consumption per capita, at almost 8½ ounces per week, is the highest in the world. The British eat twice as much candy as the Americans and French and four times as much as the Italians. Retail sales in 1980 exceeded £2,000 million [£2 billion] and amounted to over 700,000 tons.[1] The market is divided about equally in tonnage terms between chocolate and sugar confectionery, though chocolate's price makes that sector twice as valuable. Since 1960 there has been little difference in the volume or value growth [revenue] rates between the two sectors. A more detailed breakdown is given in Exhibit 3.

While overall market size has trebled in money terms between 1970 and 1980, there has been little volume growth: volume in 1980 was still marginally below the 1973 peak of 717,000 tons. This lack of growth is blamed on the recession, the sharp rise in cocoa and sugar prices, and the imposition of the value added tax (VAT) of 8 percent in 1974 (which rose to 15 percent in 1979). Unlike the United States, where consumption had been declining for many years, there was little evidence that diet or dental concerns were significantly affecting the market.

Confectionery manufacturing is fairly concentrated; seven companies account for 52 percent of sales strongly biased toward chocolate, while over 200 companies fight for the remaining 48 percent biased toward sugar. Cadbury's, Rowntree Mackintosh, and Mars are the three leading groups. Competition is fierce in advertising and brand development, especially in the filled chocolate bar/count line segment, which was the most buoyant and valuable sector of the whole confectionery market in recent years. Around £40 million was spent on advertising in 1980, making confectionery the most highly advertised of all product groups. There are many brands; the top 40 account for about 40 percent of the market. Other than Thornton's (which ranks about 16th), no major manufacturer is integrated forward into retailing.

Distribution of confectionery is extremely wide through a great variety of retailing outlets. The main channel, however, is still the mass of largely

---

[1] £1 = 100p (pence). In 1980 £1 = $2.00 (U.S.) approximately.

EXHIBIT 3
U.K. Confectionery Tonnage by Product Group, 1974–1979*

	Tons (000)		
	1974	*1977*	*1979*
Chocolate:			
Milk chocolate bars with fruit, nuts, etc.	27	15	18
Plain chocolate bars	47	40	38
Count lines†	153	159	186
Chocolate assortments (including boxes)‡	65	51	51
Straight lines	51	47	47
Easter eggs novelties	18	20	21
Total	361	332	361
Sugar:			
Hard-boiled‡	95	87	75
Toffee, caramel, and fudge‡	66	75	68
Gums, jellies, pastilles	41	42	41
Liquorice	20	18	16
Chewing gum	15	16	14
Medicated	13	12	8
Other	78	71	72
Total	328	321	294

* U.K. sales by U.K. manufacturers only. Approximately an additional 50 tons of confectionery were imported in 1979.
† Count lines are items sold for individual consumption rather than by weight or quantity. Well-known examples are Kit Kat and Mars Bar, each with annual sales of over £40,000.
‡ Main sectors in which Thornton's competes.

independent small confectioner/tobacconist/news agents (CTNs). Around 45,000 of these account for 38 percent of confectionery sales. But the number of CTNs has declined sharply in recent years, and their share of confectionery sales has dropped from 55 percent in 1960. Increasingly important are the large grocery supermarkets and superstores which have expanded their confectionery share from 20 to 32 percent since 1960. Other important outlets are cinemas, departments stores, and variety chains.

Women are the main purchasers of confectionery although children are the largest per capita consumers, especially in sugar. Women buy about 67 percent, men 20 percent, and children 13 percent. Fifty percent of purchases are made on Fridays and Saturdays. The average amount spent on each purchase occasion was about 33 pence in 1980. The gift market is very important, especially for Christmas, Easter, and Mother's Day. About 40 percent of spending is for gifts, mainly women for children and, secondly, men for women. A recent survey shows that among adult "heavy users" of confectionery women consume more than men and that they are predominantly in the lower (C2D) income groups.[2]

THORNTON'S CHANNELS AND PRODUCTS

The company now had 148 shops controlled by a sales manager supervising 16 area managers. While in recent years shops had been opened in Scotland and the South of England, the majority of them were in the Midlands and North of England. Virtually all shops were in town centre shopping areas. Most of the shops were very small, the majority having under 300 square feet of selling space, although the company had tried to open somewhat larger units in recent years. The shops were not self-service, and queuing was a significant problem at peak periods. In 1980 the average turnover per shop was £110,000, though some of the better shops were doing two or three times this figure.

After 1974, under Mr. Tony's lead the company began to sell its confectionery through other shops. The real stimulus for this change in direction was the alarming rise in high street-shop rents, which if continued threatened to make many of Thornton's shops unprofitable. The most significant move was the decision to allow other shops (generally small CTNs) to sell Thornton's confectionery as part of their range on a franchise basis. In return for a small fee, franchisees could buy Thornton's at 25 percent off retail price. During its first five years franchising showed considerable growth (see Exhibit 4). Currently there were 45 shops with a Thornton franchise. The second important development was the request by Marks and Spencer, Britain's most successful variety store group, to sell Thornton's chocolate under its own private label. Currently this exceeded £800,000 in sales. Besides franchising and Marks and Spencer, small amounts were sold to a few other U.K. chains, and some £167,000 worth was exported to distributors in 14 countries overseas.

Thornton's was represented in product groups accounting for only about one-third of the chocolate market (mainly assortments, straight lines, Easter eggs, etc.) and about two-thirds of the sugar market (boiled, toffee, jellies, etc.). In particular they were not represented in "count lines" and filled chocolate bars, which made up the most profitable segment of the chocolate market. Besides confectionery the shops sold small amounts of bought-in

---

[2] Survey researchers classify households and adults by social class. Broadly, A refers to upper middle-class households (3 percent of all households); B middle-class (13 percent); C1 lower-middle (22 percent); C2 skilled working-class (33 percent); D working-class (21 percent); E lowest levels of income (8 percent).

EXHIBIT 4

J. W. Thornton Ltd., Sales by Selected Channels of Distribution (£000, including VAT)

Financial Year	Thornton Shops	Franchise	Marks & Spencer	Other Chains	Export
1974–75	£ 6,049	£ 1	£ 3	£ 3	£ 3
1975–76	7,023	92	255	136	11
1976–77	8,351	392	661	167	24
1977–78	9,933	1,002	636	172	149
1978–79	11,845	1,303	462	205	184
1979–80	14,753	1,259	868	205	167

greeting cards (£500,000 in 1979–80) and ice cream (£200,000). Percentage gross margins averaged 60 percent for sugar confectionery, 57 for chocolate, 50 for cards, and 30 for ice cream.

THE THORNTON'S CONSUMER

When Mr. Peter took over responsibility for the marketing operation in 1979, his lack of experience was balanced by an enthusiasm to get the business moving ahead again. He was critical that many important decisions had been neglected in the past due to differences of opinion and priorities on the board. In an early memorandum he said that product standards had dropped; production convenience was taking precedence over marketing needs; shortages at peak times were resulting in lost business; and shop display, hygiene, and stock control standards were all declining due to insufficient investment in shopfitting and management.

Peter inherited Tucker Advertising, a Manchester advertising agency appointed by Mr. Tony some months earlier. The agency convinced Peter of the need to undertake some research into Thornton's consumers and the confectionery market before a marketing strategy could be developed. Until then the company had undertaken little market research. But from Tucker's research and that conducted by the two agencies succeeding it, a fairly complete picture had been developed. The main research findings were:

1. In socioeconomic terms the Thornton's shopper profile was close to the average profile of confectionery buyers: AB 15 percent, C1 26 percent, C2 38 percent, D 18 percent, E 3 percent.

2. In areas where Thornton's had shops, 71 percent of confectionery eaters shop at Thornton's at least occasionally. The average expenditure per shopper was 70–99 pence in October 1978 and somewhat higher for the AB socioeconomic group.

3. Thornton's shoppers had very positive attitudes to the shops. A sample of 544 Thornton shoppers found 42 percent mentioning product quality as the most attractive feature; 21 percent, good service; and 11 percent, window displays. Only 20 percent of respondents could think of anything unattractive about the shops. Of the negative responses, "too small" and "queuing" were most frequently mentioned.

4. Price did not appear a problem. Respondents thought generally that Thornton's products were a little more expensive, but they believed the products to be of higher quality and good value for the money. This was especially true of chocolate, but boiled sweets were seen as neither more expensive nor of better quality than elsewhere. Chocolate and toffee were seen as of very good value by over 90 percent of Thornton shoppers.

5. Most Thornton customers bought more confectionery from other outlets than from Thornton's. As the agency noted, this is not surprising. "However good the product and reputation, however conveniently located the outlets, Thornton's accounts for a tiny proportion of confectionery distribution. When heavily advertised, well-established products are available at the checkout of a supermarket that Thornton's customers have to visit to buy groceries, it is not surprising that they purchase competitive brands. Customers typically buy a wide range of confectionery from a variety of outlets." Thornton's 148 shops competed with 127,000 other outlets selling confectionery.

6. Non-Thornton customers appeared to be much younger, to be often heavy confectionery eaters, especially of count lines (i.e., market leaders like Mars Bars, Kit-Kat, Yorkie), and to be more downmarket. Thornton's products appeared to appeal to older customers, especially women.

7. Gift purchasing was very important in confectionery, especially for boxes of chocolates. The majority of boxed chocolates were bought for family or friends. Self-consumption was more frequently the purchase motive for loose chocolates, toffee, and boiled sweets. Toffees and boiled sweets were the most favored purchases for children.

The advertising agencies came up with various proposals based on their research findings. Tucker Advertising recommended targeting on C1–C2–D housewives aged over 25 and focusing on increasing awareness of Thornton's traditional product quality. Penelope Keith, a well-known television comedy actress, was used in humorous TV and radio commercials to communicate the product benefits. Beaumont, Robock and King (BRK), a leading London agency which won the account early in 1979, defined the primary target as the "heavy confectionery purchaser" who was female, aged 16–34, in the C2–D–E groups with two to three children, and whose life-style might be summarized as "laugh and grow fat." Their creative approach was again humorous and traditional, based around singing confectionery workers at Thornton's factory. The creative proposition was aimed at expressing Thornton's shop as a "treasure trove" of high-quality confectionery and "a family firm making your family favourites." The Cundiff Partnership, a small London agency which gained the account in mid-1980, decided to target on "medium" confectionery buyers who were younger and more up-market (A–B–C1–C2) than the typical Thornton's consumer. Creatively they concentrated on telling straightforward product quality stories about the brands and linking with main gift-giving occasions, such as Christmas and Easter.

THORNTON'S MARKETING ORGANIZATION

In 1978 Mr. Tony asked Dr. John Riley, a professor of business administration at a local university, to take an overall look at the company's operation. Riley's report showed that profitability had significantly declined since 1970. He argued that this was due mainly to external factors: little market growth; the changing pattern of retailing, and high rates of inflation eroding margins. But he also suggested the problem had been worsened by (a) management cutting back on marketing investments, (b) falling shop volume, and (c) a switch in the product mix toward less-profitable items. On the positive side, he noted the remarkable growth of franchising, the success of Continental Chocolates, good cost control, and the margin protection the shops offered ("unlike other manufacturers Thornton's is not easily squeezed by the buying power of the major retail groups").

Mr. Peter accepted most of the points in the Riley report and began to attack these problems quickly. One difficulty he faced immediately was the lack of retail experience of his two senior managers: Joe Royston, the marketing manager, and Len Andrews, the sales manager. After much exasperation with his inability to get information and implementation from his marketing and salespeople, he hired a retail manager, Colin Shaw, in June 1980. The new man was not a retailer, but Peter felt that he was young and bright and that his experience in brand management would be very valuable. Andrews resigned around the same time, and Peter was hoping to find an experienced successor quickly.

Dr. Riley also drew attention to the need to improve the management information and planning procedures. Peter agreed that most of the information the directors received was still production oriented. A vast amount of information was available on manufacturing costs and standards but it was not easy to determine sales and profit performance trends of the products, channels of distribution, and shops. Evaluating price and promotional changes on different parts of the business was virtually impossible. One of the problems, he felt, was forcing the accounting department to give a greater priority to providing better information.

Thornton's had never undertaken formal longer-term planning. In recent years, however, the accountant had developed a useful annual budget, although it often did not appear until a few months into the financial year (beginning June 1). Another problem was that sales appeared as a residual rather than an output from a marketing forecast. Generally, overhead costs for the forthcoming year were taken as "given"; target net and gross profits were then agreed by the board; and turnover was subsequently defined as that level needed to balance these assumptions. It was perhaps not surprising that the sales volume figures generally proved optimistic. In the 1979–80 financial year this budgeting procedure had, however, produced more serious consequences (see Exhibit 5). Overhead costs in the budget had been allowed to escalate by a heavy commitment to advertising and a decision to introduce a new layer of management to strengthen the manufacturing team; but the level of sales needed to cover these costs proved to be much too high, and net profit suffered severely. The directors were determined not to let this mistake be repeated, and in future they were sure that budgeted cost increases would be checked by realistic or even pessimistic budget sales forecasts.

EXHIBIT 5

J. W. THORNTON LTD.
Income Statement and Budget
1980–1981
(£000)

	Actual 1978–79	Actual 1979–80	Budget 1980–81
Sales (excluding VAT)	£12,826	£15,551	£18,250
Direct costs	6,112	7,191	8,760
Gross profit	6,714	8,360	9,490
Wages and salaries......................	2,947	3,942	4,335
Pension scheme	94	116	125
Distribution	266	321	404
Repairs...............................	354	405	460
Rent and rates........................	625	821	1,000
Postage, telephone, travel	166	240	267
Power................................	225	294	343
Legal and finance charges...............	242	307	284
Advertising...........................	153	503	253
Display	48	52	53
Miscellaneous	90	147	149
Depreciation	508	553	650
Total trading overheads............	5,718	7,701	8,323
Trading profit........................	996	659	1,167
Nontrading net income (expense)..........	(50)	9	(26)
Pretax profit.........................	£ 946	£ 668	£ 1,141

BUSINESS AND MARKETING STRATEGY ISSUES

In thinking about the longer term, Peter felt that there were a number of areas where fundamental strategic decisions needed to be made. Getting these choices right would determine whether the business would have a successful future or not.

Shop Operations

This was perhaps the area where the most crucial decisions were needed. There were a number of obvious questions. Should Thornton's continue to see the shops as providing the vast majority of sales and profits? How many shops should they have? Where should the shops be located? What image should the shops aim to present to the public? Peter initially concluded that Thornton's own shop should be the dominant form of growth rather than outside sales. He argued, "In this age of the superstore and self-service with impersonal indifference, there is a demand for a specialist with a unique proposition. We are in a position to fill this role with our unique business. We have a fine manufacturing plant, involved people, strong street sites, and quality products to build on." He argued for opening as many shops as the company could afford, probably 10–20 a year.

Another area of concern was the shop image. Several observers believed that the stores were not right and that their appearance was confusing, lacking in impact, and old-fashioned. Over the years, the board had experimented with various piecemeal modifications to layout and window display, but there had been no real fundamental changes for many years. Worse, many of the older shops were now much in need of refitting and modernization. Peter, influenced by the successful remodeling ventures of a number of leading British retailers, became convinced that Thornton's shops needed a comprehensive repositioning guided by experts. After interviewing all the top retail designers, he commissioned Fitch and Company, the largest and most experienced of these organizations, to develop a complete shop redesign and corporate identity program for the group. Fitch's past clients included many of Britain's largest and most successful retail organizations. In October 1979 Fitch produced their models which proposed to completely redesign the shops, merchandising methods, packaging and company image. A program for implementing these changes at a cost of about £25,000 per shop was also defined in detail.

During the following six months, experience and changed circumstances led to some rethinking. One problem was that sales and profit were less buoyant than expected. Another was that rising costs of rents and staff and the failure of the advertising campaign to boost shop volume made the race to open new ones look very risky. In particular, the shops opened in new types of off-center locations—at the Tesco, Carrefour, and Fine Fare shopping mall complexes, for example—proved highly disappointing. Finally, there was the view on the board that while the Fitch proposals contained some good ideas, the complete shop redesign they proposed was really not the type of atmosphere that would appeal to Thornton's traditional customers.

Franchise Operations

Both Tony and Peter were less than enthusiastic about the Thornton franchise operation, and in 1978 they had agreed to halt further growth despite many requests for franchises. All the franchisees were independent CTN shops which sold Thornton's lines as part of their general ranges of tobacco, newspapers, other confectionery, and miscellaneous merchandise. Thus the shops retained their old names and trading formats, only agreeing to give a portion of their selling space (averaging 20–40 percent) over to the Thornton range. In general Peter believed that the profit potential was insufficient to attract people to devote their entire shop to the Thornton range. The limited commitment which resulted left Thornton's unhappy with the franchise business. The board felt these outlets generally failed to display the products properly and kept stock too long, threatening Thornton's quality image as well as its exclusivity. Finally, franchised confectionery offered a lower gross margin than through Thornton's own shops.

But both felt that now this attitude should be reconsidered. Average shop volume was slipping marginally nearly every year. Further Dr. Riley had pointed out that while the gross margin was higher in their own shops, when average shop operating costs were allowed for, the margin on franchise sales appeared to be at least as good. A report the directors had received the previous week from Mr. Michael and the company accountant supported this analysis. Their analysis estimated the gross and net trading margins as follows.[3]

	Gross Margin (percent)	Trading Profit (percent)
Thornton's shops	55%	6%
Franchise sales	45	14
Marks and Spencer	37	7
Other home sales	35	3
Export sales	33	−6

Two other points also counted. First, Thornton's franchise operation had developed too fast and without proper understanding of the problems involved. The directors felt they now had the experience to develop a much better control system which would overcome many of the past weaknesses. Second, with only 45 franchises there was undoubtedly vast sales growth potential from expanding the number of franchised outlets.

---

[3] Some of the financial data in this case are disguised.

Marks and Spencer

With 255 stores in the United Kingdom and a turnover approaching £2 billion, Marks and Spencer is generally regarded as one of Britain's best-managed retailers. Since 1975 its business had become very important to Thornton's, M&S merchandising policy was based on developing very close, durable relationships with a small number of high-quality British manufacturers in each product field. Manufacturers had to follow M&S's exacting quality standards in supplying M&S with exclusive products sold under the "St. Michael" brand name. Thornton's was approached when M&S diversified into food and confectionery in the mid-1970s. In 1979–80 M&S purchased around £870,000 of Thornton's boxed chocolates and was also beginning to take Special Toffee and fudge on a trial basis.

Tony and Peter had always been hesitant about the M&S business. One reason was that the markup M&S required, exceeding 25 percent, meant it was a lower gross margin business for Thornton's. Profitability of the whole business was affected too, they believed, because M&S was reluctant to accept price increases not justified by corresponding manufacturer's cost increases. This was making it difficult to increase margins, and since Thornton's was not willing to be undercut in prices by M&S, the whole of Thornton's margin was held back. There were also strategic issues, M&S offered such large potential that Thornton's might risk becoming too dependent upon them in the future. In addition the directors asked: What is the differential advantage of a Thornton shop if the customer can buy its confectionery at Marks? M&S also interfered with Thornton's flexibility in other directions. They were unwilling to allow it to sell the products M&S bought to competitive retailers, severely limiting diversification options, though it was possible this objection could be overcome by introducing minor product differences which could differentiate the M&S range. Finally, M&S made life difficult for the factory: they could cancel or significantly increase orders with little notice. For example, in 1978–79, M&S purchases dropped substantially when for tax reasons they ceased to supply their Canadian stores with Thornton's confectionery. Finally, M&S orders were generally at peak times when capacity was already fully stretched. Nevertheless, in 1980–81, M&S orders were expected to top £1 million.

Export and Other Commercial Sales

The board believed there were many other exciting growth opportunities. In 1979–80 they exported some £167,000 of products to 14 countries, mainly through overseas distributors. While the volume was small, with sufficient management attention they felt it was possible to achieve major expansion, perhaps through overseas franchising. Thornton's toffee and chocolate had gained much favorable comment, many inquiries from interested buyers, and a number of prizes for quality at international confectionery exhibitions over the years. The board felt in many overseas markets Thornton's confectionery could offer a unique combination of very high quality at prices which were affordable by the average consumer.

At home, too, a large number of enquiries continually came into Thornton's from large department stores, supermarket groups, and other retailers interested in the lines. In recent years small customer accounts had been built up with a few retail groups, the largest being the Waitrose supermarket group, which in the last year had bought £70,000 of fudge and chocolates for sale under the Waitrose label. The Marks and Spencer constraint and the board's doubts about whether this was the right direction had restricted growth in this direction. Finally, in the last year, mainly under the enthusiastic direction of Joe Royston, Thornton's had begun selling by mail order, with sales reaching around £4,000 over the period.

Product Line

On reflection Peter admitted that what Thornton's sold was largely based on tradition ("what we have always sold") and what the factory people thought they could produce rather than on much consideration of market opportunities. But even without a changed strategy, the market was shifting the nature of Thornton's business. In recent years it had become much more a chocolate and gift retailer. Volume sales of chocolate through the shops had increased by 40 percent since 1970, while sugar confectionery had dropped by over 10 percent. The highest growth was in boxed chocolates, which had almost doubled over the decade: the weakest area was the traditional boiled sweet, which had almost halved (Exhibits 6 and 7). Chocolate products now represented 43 percent of retail volume and over 61 percent of revenues.

This change had not helped profits. Hard-boiled sweets in particular had high profit margins and a relatively low cost of sales. Further, the new growth areas that had compensated (i.e., chocolate boxes) had required additional investment which adversely affected return on assets and net profit. But there was probably little that could be done, since Thornton's hard-boiled, unlike its chocolate, had few distinctive features and the factory could not compete in unit cost with the large modern facilities of the major competitors.

Tony and Peter spent considerable time thinking about what products the shops should carry and "what business we are in." But defining the customer "need" or "want" Thornton's served in operational terms was not easy. The shops had sold at various times cigarettes, lemonade, and more recently greeting cards and ice cream. But the current view was that such extensions were inconsistent with the image of a unique specialist that Thornton's wished to create. However, they did not rule out certain complementary lines (e.g., cakes) in the future. Another possibility was broadening the confectionery lines carried by adding bought-in ranges to complement their own products. This had not been done in the past, Peter said, partly

EXHIBIT 6
Thornton's Shops: Confectionery Tonnage by Product Group, 1974–1980*

	Tons			
	1974	*1977*	*1979*	*1980*
Chocolate:				
Continental and other boxed chocolates	523	566	704	773
Continental—loose	241	250	282	279
Other chocolate—loose	567	458	489	491
Easter eggs, novelties	79	74	94	127
Misshapes	124	159	99	78
Total	1,534	1,507	1,668	1,748
Average price per ton	£1,850	£2,603	£3,884	£4,660
Sugar:				
Hard-boiled	620	529	421	409
Toffee	1,619	1,481	1,551	1,396
Fudge	185	190	219	179
Jellies	92	75	67	80
Total	2,516	2,275	2,258	2,064
Average price per ton	£1,031	£1,473	£1,862	£2,141

* Thornton shops only. Sales through other outlets amounted to 927 tons in 1980 (Exhibit 7).

because there was a tendency in the company for the shops to be seen as an outlet for the factory.

John Thornton had a committee which met on a regular basis to consider new product development in the factory. Thornton's past advertising agencies had been eager to push the company into producing a count line or filled chocolate bar like Yorkie or Cadbury's Fruit and Nut to compete in those sectors representing up to 50 percent of the chocolate market and where Thornton's was unrepresented. But Thornton's felt this was unrealistic, since these often massively advertised products relied on virtually uni-

EXHIBIT 7
J. W. Thornton's Sales by Product and Channel, 1980 (tons)

	Shops	*Franchise*	*M&S*	*Other*	*Export*
Chocolates:					
Boxed	773	145	183	25	28
Other	975	115	50	15	16
Hard-boiled	409	80	0	16	13
Toffee and miscellaneous	1,655	127	70	24	20

versal distribution and impulse purchasing for their sales. However, Thornton's was thinking about new lines. Additions and replacement items to the basic ranges of boiled sweets, toffee, and chocolates were being made continually. Up to 12 different centers or flavors might be introduced in a year. Four years ago "Traditional Assortment" had been introduced on a trial basis. This was a new range of super-quality, hand-finished chocolates selling at almost twice the price per pound of the Continental range. This was now in some 40 shops and generated a turnover last year of around £100,000. Other items on trial included additions to the children's confectionery lines and a small range of confectionery for diabetics.

Pricing Strategy

Like other retailers, Thornton's margins had been hit by the acceleration of inflation after 1973 and government price controls. But now they believed margins were under much better control. Peter said pricing strategy was based on the recognition that Thornton's products were high priced (e.g., a half-pound box of Continental was around 20 percent more expensive than a box of best-selling Cadbury's Dairy Milk) but that the consumer recognized their superior quality, and this allowed them to be perceived as good value for money. On the other hand, he believed that where their products were not unique they must be priced competitively. Recent experience, he believed, had proved his view. The Continental line had been unaffected by fairly steep price increases, whereas boiled sweets had shown impressive volume gains after a price cut—although he admitted that fudge had not shown a similar increase after the same policy had been applied.

Advertising and Promotion

During his first 12 months as managing director, Peter had spent an enormous amount of time with the advertising agency attempting to formulate a decisive marketing and advertising campaign. Between 1975 and 1978 Thornton's had tried to hold up net profit margins by restricting the growth of advertising and promotional expenditures. On taking over, Peter had felt this lack of investment had been a material cause of Thornton's recent sluggish performance. In 1979 Peter appointed BRK, a large London advertising agency, to handle this account. The advertising budget was trebled to over £500,000, and BRK developed a campaign employing television and a wide range of media to boost Thornton's image as a traditional and special type of confectionery shop. But the results were disappointing, and net profit was severely affected. In 1980 Peter began a serious reconsideration of advertising's role in the business.

He felt that a business of Thornton's size could not compete in advertising terms with Cadbury's or Rowntree's, which spent over £1 million supporting an individual brand. He also felt that broad "image" advertising for

Thornton's was not the way. Instead he believed that advertising should be tailored to support Thornton's brands with the strongest identity—Special Toffee and Continental Chocolates—and to help build new ones.

A new agency, the Cundiff Partnership, was appointed in mid-1980 with a much reduced budget. Local radio was chosen as the prime medium on cost-efficiency grounds, with local press as a "top up." Advertising was targeted around the main gift seasons—Christmas, St. Valentine's Day, Mother's Day, and Easter. In addition a Special Toffee promotion was scheduled for October 1980 to restimulate volume.

With his new retail manager Colin Shaw, Peter was also seeking to strengthen Thornton's public relations. Thornton's retained the services of a local PR consultant at a reasonable fee and was also considering retaining Harry Shepherd's new PR consultancy in London. Mr. Shepherd had worked for 30 years as head of PR at Marks and Spencer and had recently resigned to start his own business. Peter felt that they were now on the right track as far as advertising and PR were concerned.

Marketing and Organization

The directors were fairly happy with the current situation. Important decisions were being taken, and there were some favorable features in the environment. For example, while in the late 70s Thornton's had been squeezed by rising commodity prices, cocoa was now trading at record lows. This year the price had dropped by £400 a ton, and since Thornton's was buying 1,000 tons annually, this was having a significant effect on profitability.

Besides changes in marketing strategy, Tony and Peter knew that changes in marketing organization were also needed. Currently, Colin Shaw was retail manager looking after advertising and promotion; Joe Royston was now responsible for exports, Marks and Spencer, and franchise and other home sales; and a new sales manager responsible for the shops was to be appointed. The last was felt to be particularly important, since there was much to do in the area of sales control and supervision. Training was poor, and the manuals detailing expected behavior from retail staff were now out of date and not used. Peter knew from experience that strategy would never be implemented properly without the right people and organization.

APPLICATION 4–11

Holly Farms Corp.

Holly Farms Corp. thought it had created the Cadillac of poultry with its roasted chicken.

The fully cooked bird seemed just the ticket for today's busy consumers: a modern, more convenient alternative to raw chicken. It scored big in a year of test marketing.

The company began phasing in national distribution of the product last fall. But it fared so dismally that the planned expansion into more markets was halted so Holly Farms could reconsider its marketing strategy.

One analyst, Bonnie Rivers of Salomon Brothers Inc., cites the blunder as a major reason she recently slashed her estimate for Holly Farms' profit for the year ending May 31 by 22 percent, to $2.25 a share from $2.90. Higher feed and persistently low chicken prices also contributed to the lower profit projection, she says. In fiscal 1987, the Memphis, Tenn.-based poultry and food concern earned $71.7 million, or $4.31 a share, on revenue of $1.42 billion.

Company executives acknowledge that the roasted chicken product will hurt fiscal 1988 earnings, but they won't make any projections. "We're just losing a lot of business," says John Creel, Holly Farms' senior director of sales and marketing. Grocers are buying far less of the product than Holly Farms had hoped, he says, because they believe it doesn't last long enough on the shelf. Until this problem is solved, Holly Farms decided not to expand distribution of its roasted chicken, now available in about 50 percent of the nationwide market.

Holly Farms' experience is a classic example of how a food company can stumble in launching a product. While the extensive test marketing identified strong consumer support for the product—22 percent of Atlanta women surveyed said they had tried it, and of those, 90 percent said they would buy it again—the company failed to detect the concerns and resistance of its front-line customer, the grocer.

Several grocers concur that the problem isn't with the roasted chicken itself. Ray Heatherington, meat merchandising manager for Safeway Stores Inc.'s Northern California division, calls the product—which comes in Cajun, barbecue and original flavors—"outstanding." But his stores dropped it after several weeks, because of the short shelf life.

Holly Farms says the chicken's quality lasts for a good 18 days. So to be safe, it marks the last sale date 14 days after the chicken is roasted. But it can take as long as nine days to get the chicken to stores from the North

Source: Arthur Buckler, "Holly Farms's Marketing Error: The Chicken that Laid an Egg," *The Wall Street Journal,* February 9, 1988, p. 34.

Carolina plant, which Holly Farms spent $20 million to build just for the roasted chicken product. That doesn't give grocers much lead time. To avoid being stuck with an outdated backlog, many are waiting until they run out before reordering.

In the case of raw chicken, shelf life isn't a factor because the product's high volume means it is sold in the first few days after delivery and grocers know from experience how much to stock.

A general suspicion of new products also has probably hurt the effort. "It's a hard sell to get into the supermarket, particularly if you've got a new product that the consumers and retailers haven't seen before," says Joe Scheringer, an editor at Grocery Marketing magazine. The meat department is probably the most resistant to change, he adds.

Some competitors believe Holly Farms didn't do enough preliminary groundwork with retailers. Holly Farms acknowledges it probably didn't go far enough to tailor its marketing program to each supermarket chain or spend sufficient time educating meat managers.

But it plans to mend fences soon. Hoping to lengthen the shelf life by five to 10 days, Holly Farms is developing a system to pack the chickens using nitrogen instead of air. To shorten delivery time, the company is considering giving the product its own distribution system, instead of delivering it along with raw poultry.

Holly Farms also plans to shift a hefty portion of its marketing budget out of television and radio and into the grocery store in the form of promotions, coupons, consumer demonstrations, and contests for meat managers. Nearly two-thirds of Holly Farms' roughly $14 million in fiscal first-half marketing expenditures for the product went to media advertising; that proportion is being lowered to about one-half, the company said.

Holly Farms still believes the roasted chicken product will be a blockbuster. So does Salomon Brothers' Ms. Rivers, who says: "I definitely agree with what they're doing and why they're doing it."

At least one competitor is reserving judgment: Tyson Foods Inc. of Springdale, Ark., which is test marketing a similar chicken product in Indianapolis, says it has no immediate plans to broaden distribution, in part because of Holly Farms' experience.

Discussion Questions

1. Was Holly Farms' fully cooked chicken venture customer-driven or production-driven? Discuss.
2. Did Holly Farms' management follow a sound new-product planning process for the new chicken product?
3. Critically evaluate the positioning strategy used to introduce the new chicken product.
4. What strategy do you recommend that management adopt, based on the experience to date?

APPLICATION 4–12

Apex Chemical Company

The Executive Committee of Apex Chemical Company—a medium-size chemical manufacturer with annual sales of $60 million—is trying to determine which of two new compounds the company should market. The two products were expected to have the same gross margin percentage. The following conversion takes place among the vice president for research, Ralph Rogovin; the vice president for marketing, Miles Mumford; and the president, Paul Prendigast.

VP–RESEARCH: Compound A–115, a new electrolysis agent, is the one; there just isn't any doubt about it. Why, for precipitating a synergistic reaction in silver electrolysis, it has a distinct advantage over anything now on the market.

PRESIDENT: That makes sense, Ralph. Apex has always tried to avoid "me too" products, and if this one is that much better . . . what do you think, Miles?

VP–MARKETING: Well, I favor the idea of Compound B–227, the plastic oxidizer. We have some reputation in that field; we're already known for our plastic oxidizers.

VP–RESEARCH: Yes, Miles, but this one isn't really better than the ones we already have. It belongs to the beta-prednigone group, and they just aren't as good as the stigones are. We *do* have the best stigone in the field.

PRESIDENT: Just the same, Ralph, the beta-prednigones are cutting into our stigone sales. The board of directors has been giving me a going over on that one.

VP–MARKETING: Yes, Ralph, maybe they're not as good scientists as we are—or think we are—but the buyers in the market seem to insist on buying beta-prednigones. How do you explain that? The betas have 60 percent of the market now.

VP–RESEARCH: That's your job, not mine, Miles, If we can't sell the best product—and I can prove it *is* the best, as you've seen from my data and computations—then there's something wrong with Apex's marketing effort.

PRESIDENT: What do you say to that, Miles? What *is* the explanation?

VP–MARKETING: Well, it's a very tricky field—the process in which these compounds are used is always touch-and-go; everyone is always trying something new.

VP–RESEARCH: All the more reason to put our effort behind Compound A–115, in the electrolysis field. Here we know that we have a real technical breakthrough. I agree with Paul that that's our strength.

PRESIDENT: What about that, Miles? Why not stay out of the dogfight represented by Compound B–227, if the plastic oxidizer market is as tricky as you say?

VP–MARKETING: I don't feel just right about it, Paul. I understand that the electrolysis market is pretty satisfied with the present products. We did a survey, and 95 percent said they were satisfied with the Hamfield Company's product.

Source: Edward C. Bursk and Stephen A. Greyser, *Cases in Marketing Management,* 2nd ed., 1975, pp. 204–7, 208–10. Reprinted by permission of Prentice-Hall, Inc., Englewood Cliffs, N.J.

PRESIDENT: It's a big market, too, isn't it, Miles?

VP–MARKETING: Yes, about $10 million a year total.

PRESIDENT: And only one strongly entrenched company—Hamfield?

VP–MARKETING: Yes, I must admit it's not like the plastic oxidizer situation—where there are three strong competitors and about a half-dozen who are selling off-brands. On the other hand, oxidizers are a $40 million market—four times as big.

PRESIDENT: That's true, Ralph. Furthermore our oxidizer sales represent 25 percent of our total sales.

VP–RESEARCH: But we've been losing ground the past year. Our oxidizer sales dropped 10 percent, didn't they, Ralph? While the total oxidizer market was growing, didn't you say?

VP–MARKETING: Well, the electrolysis field is certainly more stable. Total sales are holding level, and as I said before, Hamfield's share is pretty constant, too.

PRESIDENT: What about the technical requirements in the electrolysis field? With a really improved product we ought to be able. . .

VP–MARKETING: Well, to tell you the truth, I don't know very much about the kind of people who use it and how they . . . you see, it's really a different industry.

PRESIDENT: What about it, Ralph?

VP–RESEARCH: It's almost a different branch of chemistry too. But I have plenty of confidence in our laboratory men. I can't see any reason why we should run into trouble. . . . It really does have a plus-three-point superiority on a scale of 100—here, the chart shows it crystal clear, Miles.

VP–MARKETING: But aren't we spreading ourselves pretty thin—instead, of concentrating where our greatest know-how. . . . You've always said, Paul, that. . . .

PRESIDENT: Yes, I know, but maybe we ought to diversify, too. You know, all our eggs in one basket.

VP–MARKETING: But if it's a good basket. . .

VP–RESEARCH: Nonsense, Miles, it's the kind of eggs you've got in the basket that counts—and Compound A–115, the electrolysis agent, is scientifically the better one.

VP–MARKETING: Yes, but what about taking the eggs to the market? Maybe people don't want to buy that particular egg from us, but they would buy Compound B–227—the plastic oxidizer.

PRESIDENT: Eggs, eggs, eggs—I'm saying to both of you, let's just be sure we don't lay any!

Discussion Questions

1. If you had to choose one of these two products, which would it be?
2. What criteria (and what ranking on each criterion) would you use in making this decision?
3. Could you, on the basis of this brief glimpse of Apex, give it any guidelines for product strategy that would help it to do more effective developmental or pure research?

APPLICATION 4–13

Tandy Corp.

Tandy Corp.'s plan to market relatively inexpensive compact disk players that can both record and erase music is almost certain to usher sweeping changes at all levels of the music industry.

Tandy's machines present menacing new competition for digital audio tape, the stereo industry's latest darling, just as that new technology struggles for a foothold in the $5.6 billion recorded music market. For record companies, it may well mean skimpier profits, possibly causing major changes in the way these companies manage their stables of artists. And for music-loving consumers it will mean studio-quality home recording for less than $500, and perhaps a much simpler choice in buying stereo equipment.

"This could be the format that finally satisfies every (consumer)," says Michael Riggs, editor-in-chief of *High Fidelity* magazine. Adds Terry Worrell, president and chief executive officer of Sound Warehouse Inc., a retailer of recorded music, "Never have I thought we would be as close to (a compact disk recorder) at this kind of cost. It's unbelievable."

But the recording industry itself is far from satisfied with the prospect of the new recorder, even though it's two years away and may yet prove unworkable, experts say, because of the powerful laser needed to burn digital code into the disk for recording. "It poses significant problems for us," says Jason Berman, president of the Recording Industry Association of America. "Any device that is an invitation for people to copy music without compensation is a problem."

The trade group—which says the industry already loses $1.5 billion a year in sales to home taping—fears that a compact disk recorder will only worsen such troubles. Ultimately, Mr. Berman says, that could limit the range of music record companies will support.

Records, cassettes and compact disks each have their advantages—and limitations. Records are cheap, but they're bulky and they wear out. Cassettes work great in the car, are easily portable and allow home taping, but the sound quality suffers, especially over time, as tapes tend to stretch or even break.

Digital tape offers state-of-the-art sound quality, but players are expensive, complicated machines that may be prone to break down. Compact disks have near perfect sound, are portable and nearly indestructible, but affordable home recording in the format seemed impossible—until Tandy's announcement last week.

Source: Paul Duke, Jr., "CD Recorder Poses Upset for Industry," *The Wall Street Journal,* April 26, 1988, p. 6.

EXHIBIT 1
Changing Market for Recorded Music*

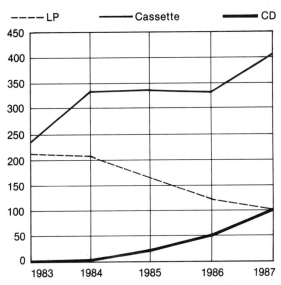

* Sales of LP records, compact disks, and cassettes (in millions of units).

Source: *Recording Industry Association of America.*

The new machines being developed by Tandy offer almost all of the advantages of records, cassettes, digital tape and compact disks, without any of the drawbacks. The affordable new technology, which Tandy intends to license to other stereo makers, will sweep records and cassettes off music store shelves, industry observers predict.

The most immediate impact will fall on digital tape recorders, a technology with great promise that has been stymied for months in the U.S. by record industry lobbying groups, who fear the machines will spur a boom in home taping.

Although almost two years away from introduction, the prospect of relatively cheap compact disk recorders reaching U.S. consumers could deliver digital tape makers a knock-out blow. "If they can get this (technology) into the market faster . . . we can kiss digital audio tapes goodby," says rock musician Frank Zappa.

Such digital tape recorder makers as Sony Corp. of Japan and Dutch electronics giant N.V. Phillips are gambling that buyers will be willing to brave high prices—digital tape players now cost $1,000 and up—for super high-quality tape recordings. A Sony spokesman notes that digital tapes are even smaller than cassette tapes and can record up to two hours of music.

Compact disks are limited to about 74 minutes. And digital tape is almost sure to get a market push from CBS Records, which was bought by Sony last year for $2 billion.

But compact disk recorders will bring a big asset to the battle that digital tape doesn't have yet: momentum. Digital tape players—not recorders—are just hitting the U.S. market, and prerecorded music in digital tape form is almost nonexistent. Meanwhile, compact disk sales have zoomed from 800,000 units and $17.2 million in 1983 to 102.1 million units and $1.59 billion in 1987.

Mr. Riggs of *High Fidelity* thinks the sturdy compact disks have succeeded because they answered consumers' gripes about records that soon were marked with unlistenable scratches, "but people aren't really upset with cassette decks, which is what (digital tape) would like to replace."

A digital tape recorder is a complicated machine—it uses a mechanism similar to a videocassette recorder—full of whirring metal and delicate parts. Compact disk players are comparatively simple, mostly a motor to spin the disk and a fixed laser to read it. Tandy's recorder would probably be somewhat more complex than a simple player, with a stronger laser to burn in digital code.

David Moran, president of the Boston Audio Society, says he worries that digital tape could have big problems with the heat and dust of car interiors. "Cars are a dangerous environment for a digital tape player," he says. Sony says, however, that it has developed units that can keep out the heat and dust. Compact disk players themselves have had mixed results in cars, but newer models reportedly have solved vibration problems.

Tandy's innovation isn't the only factor in the possible triumph of compact disks. To truly dominate the market, prices for prerecorded disks, now about $11 to $16 for new releases, will have to come down to challenge record prices, which are about $6 to $8. The price of a blank compact disk for recording, still unknown, will have to compete with blank cassettes, which cost about $2.

And even if compact disks vanquish digital audio tape, they'll face a formidable foe in the recording industry lobby. One of its arguments against the new recorder: More taping will steal profits and make record companies less willing to take risks and encourage new acts. Superstars like Michael Jackson and Bruce Springsteen are copied most, says a spokesman for CBS Records, but profits from their hits are "used to locate, record and market new artists."

The industry association's Mr. Berman says his group erred in not getting involved with digital tape recorder makers years ago, as they set design standards. Digital tape "got ahead of us," he says. "We're going to move more quickly on this."

Mr. Berman said the trade group would seek to meet with Tandy as soon as possible to discuss the industry's concerns. "Any technology that permits copying should be accompanied by some kind of royalty."

Discussion Questions

1. Define the product-market structure and analyze the market opportunity for Tandy's compact disk player that can both record and erase music.
2. Develop a marketing strategy for the new product.
3. What marketing strategy should the producers of digital tape recorders adopt to counter the potential competitive threat from Tandy's new recorder product?

APPLICATION 4–14

Apple Computer Inc.

The grainy televised image of a smiling John Sculley fades from the 20-foot screen, while the real thing, standing at the lectern on the stage below, nods and beams at the crowd. The last clatterings of a standing ovation die down.

Then, as Apple Computer Inc.'s president and chairman leaves the stage, a throng of autograph-seeking educators surrounds him. Some brandish copies of his book, *Odyssey: A Journey of Adventure, Ideas and the Future*. All are buzzing about his stirring speech and gee-whiz videos depicting a brave new world for computing and education.

Michael Mount, an Apple regional sales director, marvels at the scene here at the National Educational Computing Conference. "He's a star now, just like Steve Jobs was," he says, recalling Apple's charismatic, mercurial cofounder and previous chairman, who quit after a power struggle with Mr. Sculley three years ago. "An event like this is worth a million dollars to Apple."

Giving rousing speeches, signing autographs and waxing philosophical about how personal computers will change life in the 21st century are all in a day's work for Mr. Sculley nowadays. That is a far cry from five years ago when, as chief executive of PepsiCo Inc.'s Pepsi-Cola unit, he battled Coca-Cola Co. over tenths of a percentage point of market share.

But it is still marketing. In fact, Mr. Sculley's transformation from a shy, somewhat-wooden executive who knew little about computers into a high-profile, high-tech visionary strikes many observers as one of his greatest marketing coups. Besides becoming a glamorous spokesman for Apple's resurgence, the 49-year-old official has become a leader in his industry and a luminary beyond the business world, much like Chrysler Corp.'s Lee Iacocca or major league baseball's Commissioner Peter Ueberroth.

Source: Brenton R. Schlender, "Celebrity Chief: Shedding His Shyness, John Sculley Promotes Apple—and Himself," *The Wall Street Journal*, August 18, 1988, pp. 1, 14.

"This is the age of the celebrity CEO, and John Sculley is up there with the best of them," says John C. Dvorak, a newspaper columnist who critiques the personal-computer industry. This fall, in fact, Mr. Sculley and his wife will appear, along with Malcolm Forbes and Elizabeth Taylor, on Robin Leach's "Lifestyles of the Rich and Famous" television series.

To some critics both inside and outside Apple, Mr. Sculley's transformation goes beyond marketing and into the realm of hype. Some cite the egotism suggested by his book and his image-conscious management style. Technical people, including some Apple engineers, doubt the depth of such rhapsodic visions of the future of computing coming from an executive who admits not knowing how to use a financial spreadsheet on his own PC. Others deplore how, in an industry that often promises more than it can deliver, Mr. Sculley relies on slick video dramatizations of imaginary computers to illustrate where Apple's technological prowess *might* lead.

"There's no question John Sculley has become a business hero, but I worry that the same hype and egotism that got Apple into trouble a few years ago could happen again," says Richard Shaffer, the publisher of *Technologic Computer Letter*. Apple is selling "yesterday's products with flash and smoke and tomorrow's promises," he adds, noting that the hot-selling Macintosh computer is the legacy of the Jobs years. "We don't know what the 'new' Apple can really do yet."

Nevertheless, Mr. Sculley's emergence has brought much visibility and restored some credibility to the company. It coincides with Apple's own transformation from a troubled supplier of computers to schools and hobbyists into a thriving provider of business computers—and into one of the industry's most profitable companies. And despite reorganizing Apple to its core, Mr. Sculley has preserved much of the idealism that provides its shine.

"John has managed the difficult challenge of making Apple reassuring and inoffensive to the business world and yet not bland," says Jean-Louis Gassee, Apple's senior vice president for research, development, and product marketing. "Inside Apple, he is giving the company a new sense of self after losing its founder."

Celebrity executives, technological visionaries, and showboating special effects are nothing new at Apple, of course. Almost from the day Mr. Jobs helped found the company in 1976, he cultivated a larger-than-life public image of the youthful, idealistic entrepreneur bringing high technology to the masses. And it was Mr. Jobs who first jazzed up public appearances with projections of his own image on giant screens, a technique borrowed by Mr. Sculley and ironically reminiscent of Apple's chilling "Big Brother" TV commercial in 1984.

Although Mr. Sculley is neither a computer nerd nor an entrepreneur—he is an architect with an MBA from the University of Pennsylvania's Wharton School—he felt he had no choice but to become an industry leader after Mr. Jobs left in 1985. "What's different about heading Apple is that you are not an icon for just Apple but for the whole world of technology and computing beyond Apple," he says.

Mr. Sculley took his time stepping into the spotlight, however. At first, he explains, "I was perceived as a bad personality, if anything," held responsible for many of Apple's failings as well as for dumping Mr. Jobs. Moreover, "I still didn't know enough about the computer industry to feel comfortable talking about it" as a major spokesman, he concedes.

An advertising man recalls watching Mr. Sculley at a news conference shortly after Mr. Jobs left. "You could almost see the muscles move from the tension when he answered more-technical questions," says Steve Hayden, an executive vice president in charge of the Apple account at BBDO International Inc. "Then, somebody asked him about the Coke Classic and New Coke controversy, and he lit up like he'd met an old friend."

Only last year did Mr. Sculley assert himself as an industry leader. By then, Apple's sales and profits were growing again. In addition, the company had introduced two new Macintoshes and a novel program called Hypercard, a pet project of Mr. Sculley's that expanded the Macintosh's information-handling capabilities. Explaining the change in his approach, Mr. Sculley says: "It was like learning a new language. Suddenly, it all came together—my understanding of the technology, some new products with my imprint, and my book."

The book, written with the help of a *Business Week* editor, was the main vehicle for Mr. Sculley's coming out. "Odyssey" was part autobiography, tracing his experiences at Pepsi and Apple, and part treatise on management theory and future technology, expounding on "third-wave corporations," executives as "technology impresarios" and multimedia computers.

"Odyssey" also smacked of marketing and image-building, some contend. "There was a bit of a gilding of the lily in that book," says Victor Bonomo, PepsiCo's retired executive vice president, who adds, "John has always done a very good job of promoting himself." Mr. Bonomo says, and others at Pepsi agree, that "he took too much credit for some things that many people had a hand in," including the "Pepsi Challenge" marketing campaign in the 1970s that helped catapult U.S. Pepsi sales past Coca-Cola's.

"But what struck me most about the book was the way he laid his guts out on the matter of his showdown with Jobs," Mr. Bonomo adds. "That was very uncharacteristic of John, who I've always known to be a very private person."

As a publishing venture, it wasn't exactly a blockbuster. It drew mixed reviews and so far has sold fewer than 100,000 copies in the United States, plus more than 7,000 purchased by Apple for its employees. Lee Iacocca's *Iacocca*, in contrast, has sold about 6.5 million copies worldwide. People close to Mr. Sculley say he was hurt by the reviews and disappointed by the sales. "I'm not so sure if he knew then what he knows now that he would've written it," says Albert E. Eisenstat, senior vice president, company secretary, and Mr. Sculley's closest friend on Apple's executive staff.

Mr. Sculley still maintains that writing the book "helped me focus my thoughts and ideas," especially regarding Apple's future. He believes, however, that the book would have sold better had it been marketed differently, and he implies that it was a lack of egotism—not a surplus—that hurt sales. For one thing, "I didn't allow the publishers to put my picture on the cover because I didn't want it to look like just another CEO's ego experience," he says. "In hindsight, it probably would've sold better if we had." (His picture covers the back of the dust jacket.)

Nevertheless, some critics think Mr. Sculley let his egotism show when he had Apple buy copies for its employees. And recently, he had the company distribute copies of a Fortune magazine that featured his picture on the cover and a flattering synopsis of his views on the industry. The cover photo reflected Mr. Sculley's penchant for favoring imagery over reality: He is holding a plastic mock-up of the "Knowledge Navigator," a futuristic, multimedia laptop computer.

Since the publication of *Odyssey*, Mr. Sculley has spent more and more time in his public role. In recent months, he personally delivered a Macintosh to Moscow for Mikhail Gorbachev and another to the King of Thailand; he called on scientists such as Paul Chiu, who won a Nobel Prize last year for his work on superconductors; and he cruised the South China Sea on Mr. Forbes's yacht to film the episode of "Lifestyles of the Rich and Famous."

In between, he has stepped up his flashy, multimedia appearances at trade shows, universities, and events such as the educational-computing conference in Dallas. He was appointed by the Soviets to an international commission to explore peaceful uses of high technology and has become an outspoken advocate of educational reform. Recently, however, he got away for a much-publicized six-week "sabbatical" granted to all Apple employees after five years of employment.

All this leads some of Mr. Sculley's peers in the computer industry to suggest he may be spending too much time away from the job of running the company.

Of course, others think that Mr. Sculley's public roles are nothing more than good, free publicity for Apple. "I think he's doing exactly what's needed," says Marc Canter, the president of MacroMind Inc., a Chicago vendor of animation software for Macintosh computers. "Apple needs to be perceived as having a grand vision."

"I'm a marketing person," Mr. Sculley explained following his speech to the educators in Dallas, "and whenever I do this, I'm marketing Apple. The way we look at it, everything and everybody at Apple can be marketed if it helps the company."

The same goes for his crowd-pleasing, special-effects-laden video featuring the Knowledge Navigator, which Mr. Sculley asserts "isn't a product announcement but isn't science-fiction, either." Nor is it an original idea. It draws liberally from the brainstorms of Alan Kay, an Apple computer scientist who is one of several people credited with pioneering the idea of the personal computer in the late 1960s.

The video depicts a college professor using the Knowledge Navigator to pull together a last-minute lecture, complete with animated visual aids, merely by speaking to it. Meanwhile, the device also handles the professor's telephone calls and reminds him of a surprise birthday party for his father. Apple is planning a series of public premieres of Navigator videos in what it terms "vision rollouts," as opposed to product rollouts. At a Boston trade show for purveyors of Macintosh-related products last week, Mr. Sculley unveiled a video featuring a fictitious future business computer he calls the "Grey Flannel Navigator."

"Sure, things like the Knowledge Navigator are pure show business," concedes Alan Brightman, Apple's education marketing manager. "But I don't care if people hoot at it. They'll remember it."

Nobody can hoot at Apple's corporate performance, though. In the three years under Mr. Sculley's undisputed control, Apple has stormed back to the forefront, by most measures, of the personal-computer industry (see Exhibit 1). Its competitors—even International Business Machines Corp.—are scrambling to replicate the Macintosh's snazzy graphics and ease of use. Apple's gross margins, consistently above 50 percent, are the envy of the industry. And few multibillion-dollar high-tech companies can match Apple's nearly 50 percent annual growth rate since 1986; in the fiscal year ending Oct. 1, the company's revenue will total about $4 billion. Since mid-1985, the price of Apple shares has grown nearly sixfold.

Along the way, he reorganized the company twice. He hired a slew of seasoned executives from rival computer companies to complement a handful retained from the Jobs era. And he brought discipline to product-development efforts that previously had relied mainly on engineers' adrenalin to get products out.

"Most people underestimate the difficulty of changing the direction of a company," says Edward Esber, the chief executive of Ashton-Tate Co., a big PC-software concern. "John is leading Apple on a second wave, forging alliances with other companies—all with the end of having Apple become a company that has something to offer to business customers. They're not just trying to kill the Blue giant [IBM] anymore."

He gets high marks as a manager, too. He is at his best one-on-one, learns quickly and has a remarkable memory for details, colleagues say. Despite rumors about problems with highly independent managers, such as the outspoken Senior Vice President Gassee, he finds ways to defuse personality clashes. "Jean-Louis likes to talk in poetry and metaphors," Mr. Sculley says. "One of the secrets to get me and him on the same wavelength was to get him to write down his thoughts instead of talking."

But occasionally, things boil over, as in the messy falling out with Mr. Jobs. Last fall, Nanette Buckhout, Mr. Sculley's secretary of more than 10

EXHIBIT 1

How Apple Recovered under John Sculley

Revenue Picked Up. . .
(in $billions, years ending Sept. 30)

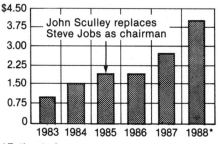

*Estimated.

Gains Came in a Vital Market . . .
Apple's share of PC's sold to businesses

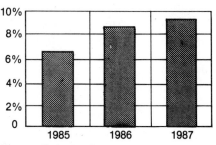

Source: Dataquest.

. . .New Income Rebounded. . .
(in $millions, years ending Sept. 30)

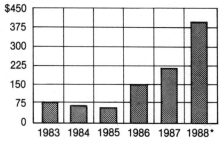

*Estimated.

And Its Stock Turned Higher
Apple versus S&P 500, Dec. 31, 1982 = 100

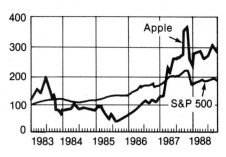

years, both at Apple and Pepsi, abruptly quit. It was surprising. Mr. Sculley had warmly praised her in his book as "an important confidant and partner" who had "provided the sanity and balance that helped me through some of the most difficult moments" at Apple. He even escorted her down the aisle at her wedding in 1986.

Insiders say Mr. Sculley's wife, Leezy, had trouble dealing with Ms. Buckhout. (Leezy, who previously was married to another Pepsi executive, is Mr. Sculley's third wife; she doesn't give interviews.) Mr. Sculley tried to reassign Ms. Buckhout to another job, but she declined, and she is said to have received a generous severance package for dropping a threat to sue. Mr. Sculley says only that her resignation was "one of those things."

Mr. Sculley's strength still lies in marketing. Despite delegating a lot of day-to-day responsibility for other aspects of Apple's operations, he still plays an active role in formulating advertising campaigns, frequently vetoing specific packages and making detailed suggestions. He also has tinkered a lot with Apple's marketing division. Since joining Apple in 1983, he has hired and then reassigned four different marketing vice presidents. The last reorganization, earlier this year, put product marketing in Apple's research and development organization rather than leaving it a stand-alone division. It is an unusual arrangement that acknowledges the primacy of product-development teams at Apple despite the company's penchant for slick marketing.

Mr. Sculley, the management theorist, probably will continue putting his imprint on Apple's organizational chart. The executive staff is busy planning a comprehensive reorganization aimed at preparing for Apple's next major revenue milestone—$10 billion a year—sometime in the early 1990s.

"Apple has no vice president of strategic planning because we're all expected to do that now," says Deborah A. Coleman, the chief financial officer. "But John has been the invisible hand. Apple is being reinvented through his leadership."

Although Mr. Sculley may be reinventing Apple, it isn't clear whether his organizational changes and newfound vision will result in new breakthrough products. So far, the company has been making the most of the Macintosh and Apple II lines, both offspring of the Jobs years. However, Mr. Sculley has been adept at "repositioning" the Macintosh for business users.

"There's more to being a visionary than seeing the future and having the vision," cautions Stewart Alsop, an industry consultant who publishes PC Letter. "To be truly successful, you have to have both the vision and the ability to implement it—to know how to get from here to there. Jobs was enough of an engineer that he knew what the technology would allow, and could tell people what had to happen and in what order to come up with great computers," Mr. Alsop continues. "I'm not so sure Sculley can do that."

Most high Apple executives expect Mr. Sculley to stick around until the $10 billion revenue milestone is met, and that should be long enough to find out whether he can indeed shepherd innovative products into the marketplace. Mr. Sculley says he isn't interested in running any other company or in public office. He earned $2,140,000 in salary and bonuses last year, and he has options on 767,000 shares of Apple stock at $7.75 a share, for an indicated profit, at the $42-a-share close yesterday, of about $26 million. He now owns 158,771 shares.

"My ultimate goal, if there really is one beyond what I'm doing now," he says, "is to be an Apple Fellow"—a title granted to a few well-known computer scientists who get free rein and lots of money to explore new technologies. "I'm not trying to pretend I'm an engineer," he adds, "but I feel comfortable being with engineers and talking about technologies."

Apple's best-known Fellow, Mr. Kay, doesn't think that goal is too high. "John is someone who can rise to any occasion, and that doesn't mean he's a phony," he says. "He has a first-class brain, he has a more inquiring mind than most engineers, yet he likes to build structures that work. He could be a terrific computer scientist."

Mr. Kay, who meets weekly with Mr. Sculley for freewheeling discussions on topics ranging from music to art to education to computer graphics, believes that the executive has only begun to leave his mark on Apple. "What drives Apple is basically romance. Everybody here wants a CEO who believes that," he says. "The great thing is, that even after making this a more businesslike company, John has come to embody the spirit and romance of Apple even more than Steve did."

Discussion Questions

1. Identify and discuss important business and marketing strategy issues that Apple's top management should incorporate into the firm's strategies during the 1990s.
2. Analyze and evaluate Apple's targeting and positioning strategies.
3. Critically evaluate Apple's personal-computer distribution strategy. Compare the strategy with key competitors, including IBM, Tandy, and Compac.
4. Recommend a marketing organizational design for Apple Computer.

APPLICATION 4–15

Supersonic Stereo, Inc.

"At this rate, I'll be looking for a new job," thought Bob Basler, sales manager of Supersonic's Atlanta district. "Our sales are stagnant, and what's worse, our profits are down." Sales and profit results for the last five years did not measure up to objectives established for the Atlanta district (see Exhibit 1). Basler knew that very shortly he would be hearing from Pete Lockhart, Supersonic's national sales manager and that the same question would be asked: "When are you going to turn the Atlanta district around?"

Bob was faced with another problem that added to his worries. One of his sales representatives, Charlie Lyons, was very upset and was threatening to quit unless he received a substantial salary increase. Lyons felt that since he led the district in sales volume, he should be amply rewarded. "I have to find out what's happening in the Atlanta district before I go and make recommendations for salary increases," Basler thought. "Besides, if I make such a recommendation, Pete will think that I have taken leave of my senses. He will not approve any salary increases for anybody as long as the Atlanta district's performance is so weak."

Source: Gilbert A. Churchill, Jr., Neil M. Ford, and Orville C. Walker, Jr., *Sales Force Management* (Homewood, Ill.: Richard D. Irwin, 1985), pp. 689–94.

EXHIBIT 1
Total Sales and Profit for the Atlanta District, 1980–1984

	1980	1981	1982	1983	1984
Total sales	$2,641,081	$2,445,120	$2,610,029	$2,514,113	$2,638,340
Net profit	13,873	14,050	15,381	16,511	14,383

Supersonic Stereo, Inc., is one of the country's leading manufacturers of stereo equipment. Since its formation in 1962, Supersonic has experienced rapid growth, based largely on its reputation for high-quality stereo products. Prices were competitive, although some dealers engaged in discounting. Supersonic distributed its stereo equipment on a selective basis. Only those dealers who could provide strong marketing support and reliable servicing were selected by Supersonic. Dealers were supported by Supersonic's national advertising campaign. Advertising averaged 5 percent of sales, somewhat more than what other stereo manufacturers spent for this item.

Supersonic's sales force was compensated with salary plus commission of 6 percent based on gross margin. Gross margin was used to discourage sales representatives from cutting prices. Accounts were assigned to sales representatives based on size. New sales representatives were usually assigned a number of small accounts at first. As they progressed they were assigned larger accounts. The more experienced sales representatives were assigned the larger, more desirable accounts. In some cases, a sales representative would have only three or four accounts, each averaging $250,000 a year.

The average base salary for the sales force reached $26,500 in 1984. Commissions averaged $9,500 in 1984. Total average sales force compensation was $36,000 in 1984. Travel expenses were paid by Supersonic. The total package was considered by one executive to be too plush. This executive, Stella Jordan, felt that not enough was expected from the sales force. "I know of one sales representative who calls on three accounts and in 1983 earned $38,563," she stated at a recent meeting. "If we want to improve our profits, then we need to either reduce our base salaries or cut back our commission rate."

Jordan's suggestion was not favorably received by Basler, who felt that such a move would have a disastrous effect on sales force motivation. Stella countered by pointing out that motivation must be lacking, since the Atlanta district's performance is so poor. "If salaries or commissions cannot be reduced, at least let's not raise them," she suggested. "Maybe we should consider raising quotas and not pay commissions until sales representatives exceed their quotas. Or," she continued, "maybe a management-by-objectives approach should be developed."

Basler knew that Jordan's comments demanded a response. He also knew that she was talking about Charlie Lyons when she mentioned a sales representative with three accounts earning $38,563. Basler suggested that he should be allowed time to do a complete cost analysis by sales representative before adopting any corrective action. Jordan agreed and offered her assistance. Salaries for the others were: Sand $24,500, Gallo $27,500, and Parks $26,000.

Basler's first activity was to identify available information for his district. He was able to secure a profit and loss statement for the Atlanta district (see Exhibit 2). Jordan suggested that since Basler was interested in sales force profitability, his next step should be to allocate the natural accounts in Exhibit 2 to their appropriate functional accounts. Exhibit 3 shows the results of this step.

"If we are going to do an analysis by sales representative, we need much more information," Stella indicated. To help in this regard, she compiled product sales data (see Exhibit 4).

Basler provided data for each sales representative, showing number of sales calls, number of orders, and unit sales by product line (see Exhibit 5). The next step would be to compile the data to develop a profitability analysis by sales representative.

The problem with Charlie Lyons is still there, mused Basler. He wants more money, and Stella Jordan thinks he is overpaid and underworked. Since Charlie Lyons is something of a focal point, we ought to do a profitability analysis for each of his customers. Basler's next step was to compile data by customer. Exhibit 6 presents customer data for each of Lyon's three accounts.

Preparing guidelines for allocating costs to sales representatives and customers was Basler's next task. Based on his review of several distribu-

EXHIBIT 2
Profit and Loss Statement, Atlanta district, 1984

Sales		$2,638,340
Cost of goods sold		2,014,485
Gross margin		$ 623,855
Expenses:		
Salaries	$177,000	
Commissions	37,431	
Advertising	131,915	
Packaging	43,642	
Warehousing and transportation	76,374	
Travel expenses	59,340	
Order processing	770	
Rent	83,000	
Total expenses		609,472
Net profit (before taxes)		$ 14,383

EXHIBIT 3
Allocation of Natural Accounts to Functional Accounts, Atlanta district

Natural Accounts		Functional Accounts					
		Selling, Direct Costs	Selling, Indirect Costs	Advertising	Order Processing	Warehouse and Transportation	Packaging
Salaries	$177,000	$106,500	$47,500		$12,000		$11,000
Commissions	37,431	37,431					
Advertising	131,915			$131,915			
Packaging	43,642						43,642
Warehousing and transportation	76,374					$ 76,374	
Travel expenses	59,340	57,340	2,000				
Order processing	770				770		
Rent	83,000	18,500			4,500	40,000	20,000
Total expenses	$609,472	$201,271	$60,000	$131,915	$17,270	$116,374	$74,642

EXHIBIT 4
Product Line Sales and Costs

Product	Selling Price per Unit	Cost per Unit	Gross Margin per Unit	Number Sold in Period	Sales in Period	Advertising Expenditures	Packaging
Receivers	$250	$212	$38	3,151	$ 787,750	$ 40,000	$ 6,302
Turntables	85	64	21	12,079	1,026,715	50,000	24,158
Speakers	125	87	38	6,591	823,875	40,000	13,182
				21,821	$2,638,340	$130,000	$43,642

EXHIBIT 5
Sales Calls, Orders, and Units Sold, by Salesperson

Salesperson	Number of Sales Calls	Number of Orders	Number of Units Sold			
			Receivers	Turntables	Speakers	Total
Paul Sand	85	60	668	2,652	1,534	4,854
Diane Gallo	105	85	823	3,270	1,582	5,675
Kathy Parks	110	60	816	3,131	1,578	5,525
Charlie Lyons	170	75	844	3,026	1,897	5,767
	470	280	3,151	12,079	6,591	21,821

EXHIBIT 6
Customer Activity Analysis for Charlie Lyons

Customers of Charlie Lyons	Number of Sales Calls	Average Time Spent on Each Call (minutes)	Number of Orders	Number of Units Purchased			
				Receivers	Turntables	Speakers	Total
American TV	65	55	40	422	1,513	854	2,789
Appliance Mart	55	45	15	337	1,058	569	1,964
Audio Emporium	50	45	20	85	455	474	1,014
	170	50*	75	844	3,026	1,897	5,767

* Average.

EXHIBIT 7
Guidelines

Functional Cost Item	Basis of Allocation
Direct selling	Number of calls times average time spent with each customer.
Commissions	6 percent of gross margin.
Travel	Total travel costs divided by number of calls; this figure is then multiplied by individual salesperson calls or customer calls.
Advertising	5 percent of sales dollars.
Packaging	Number of units × $2.
Warehousing and transportation	Number of units × $3.50.
Order processing	Number of orders × $2.75.

tion cost and analysis textbooks and further conversations with Stella Jordan, Basler developed the guidelines shown in Exhibit 7.

Basler's next step is the development of the necessary accounting statement which will permit a detailed analysis of each sales representative's profitability. From there he will proceed to a customer profitability analysis for Charlie Lyons's customers.

Discussion Questions

1. Prepare a profitability analysis for each sales representative.
2. Prepare a profitability analysis for Charlie Lyons' customers.
3. Do you agree with the way functional costs were allocated? What changes would you recommend?
4. How would you handle Charlie Lyons' request for more money?
5. Sales representatives may be paid too much. If this is true, how would you lower their total compensation?
6. Should the sales force be paid according to their contribution to profit instead of gross margin?
7. What are the implications of paying commissions only after quota has been reached?

PART 5

DEVELOPING
MARKETING PLANS

The major steps in the strategic marketing planning process are shown in Exhibit 1. Step 1, the marketing situation analysis, consists of product-market definition, customer analysis, key competitor analysis, environmental analysis, and marketing strategy assessment. Building on the findings of the situation analysis, Step 2 determines the market-target strategy. In Step 3, objectives for each market-target are formulated. Step 4 determines the marketing program positioning strategy for each market target. Coordinated strategies are developed for product, distribution, price, and promotion. Step 5 considers the organizational design and the allocation of responsibility for the activities included in the plan. In Step 6, the plan is assembled and the supporting financial budget is proposed. The plan is put into action in Step 7. Finally, in Step 8, the plan is evaluated and adjusted.

Exhibit 2 is a topic outline of a marketing plan prepared for a home furnishings products company. Although the plan is probably not directly transferable to another company, it is reasonably complete and provides a framework adaptable to the specific needs of other firms.

EXHIBIT 1

Steps in Preparing and Implementing the Strategic Marketing Plan

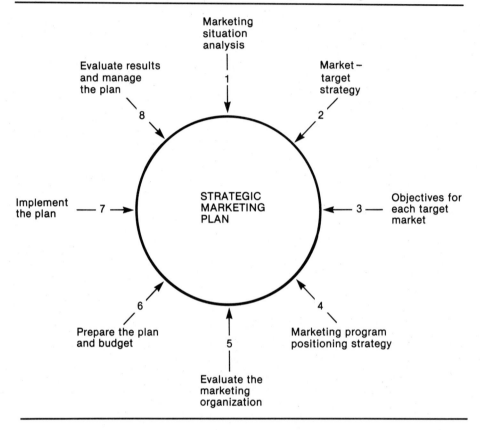

Source: David W. Cravens, *Strategic Marketing*, 2nd. ed. (Homewood, Ill.: Richard D. Irwin, Inc., 1985), p. 570.

EXHIBIT 2

A Product-Line Marketing Plan for a Home Furnishings Products Company

  I. Product policy statement

    State briefly but explicitly the price range, quality level, distribution policy, and brand strategy being used to reach the line's intended consumer markets.

 II. Marketing backgrounds

    1. Definition of consumer markets

      Describe the consumer markets in which each product line has been sold

      a. Characteristics of significant consumer groups. Show populations and per capita purchases by:

          Intended use of purchase (own use, gift, etc.)

          Family status and size

          Family income

EXHIBIT 2 *(continued)*

   Geographic region
   Other significant consumer characteristics
  b. Known or assumed consumer preferences and buying habits
   Product feature preferences
   Shopping habits
   Motivations for purchases (rank by importance)
    Product features
    Brand awareness
    Price
    Advertising
    Promotion
    Packaging
    Displays
    Sales assistance
    Other
  c. Significant consumer market trends: size, characteristics, and
   buying habits
   Recent trends
   Expected changes
 2. Market size and sales statistics
  a. Market trends (past five years)
   Industry sales
   Product-type sales
   Price index
  b. Distribution trends
   Industry sales by type of outlet (i.e., retail, premium, and Institu-
    tional) and further by major types of outlets within each broad
    area (i.e., department store, chain store, specialty store, etc.)
   Product-type sales by type of outlet
   Product-type sales by method of distribution (direct or wholesale)
  c. Product-line sales trends
   Sales dollars
   Sales dollars by type of outlet
   Share of total market
   Share of product-type market
   Share of key outlet distribution
   Sales dollars by method of distribution
   Price index
 3. Product-line profit and cost history (five years)
  a. Profit history
   Net profit dollars
   Net profit as percent of sales
   Return on investment
  b. Manufacturing cost history
   Gross profit dollars
   Gross profit as percent of sales
  c. Marketing cost history (five years)
   Show how marketing money has been spent and with what results
   Advertising cost
    Dollars by type (i.e., national, cooperative, and trade)
    Percent of sales
    Share of advertising versus share of market

EXHIBIT 2 *(continued)*

Promotion, display, and fixturing cost
Dollars
Percent of sales
Fixtures placements versus potential
Distribution cost (includes distributor discount, transportation, warehousing, inventory carrying costs, and the cost of distributor selling aids)
Dollars
Percent of sales
Distribution coverage versus potential
Kinds of accounts
Number of accounts
Sales potential of accounts
Field selling costs
Dollars
Percent of sales
Direct account coverage versus potential
4. Competitive comparison
Highlight significant differences between company and its competition.
Product-line composition and acceptance
Distribution methods and coverage
Field selling methods
Consumer marketing programs
5. Conclusions
Summarize the major problems and opportunities requiring action based on analysis of background information. Consider:
Consumer and trade market penetration
Distribution coverage
Product-line needs
Price revisions
Cost reductions
New market and product opportunities
III. Primary marketing and profit objectives
1. Marketing objectives
Sales dollars
Market share by major type of outlet
2. Profit objectives
Gross profit dollars
Gross profit as percent of sales
Net profit dollars
Net profit as percent of sales
Return on investment
Note external qualifying assumptions such as business cycle trends, industry trends, changes in size and characteristics of consumer market segments, distribution trends, competitive activity, price levels, import quotas, and factory capacity.
IV. Overall marketing strategy
State of strategic direction to be followed in order to achieve primary product-line marketing and profit objectives.
1. Consumer and trade market emphasis
2. Trademark and product feature emphasis
3. Marketing mix emphasis

EXHIBIT 2 *(continued)*

4. Functional objectives
Establish the contribution needed from each functional area in order to implement the overall strategy and to achieve primary objectives.
   a. Field selling
       Distribution objectives expressed in number, size, quality, and type of wholesale, retail, premium, and institutional accounts needed to meet the sales volume objectives
   b. Product development
       New product objectives expressed in numbers, types, introductory dates, sales volume, and profit contributions from new products
   c. Advertising
       Identify markets to be reached
       Communication objectives (nature of message and retention level sought by consumers and trade customers)
       Trade participation objectives in cooperative advertising programs
   d. Promotion and fixturing
       Sales objectives for major promotions
       Fixture placement and sales volume objectives
   e. Merchandising
       Objectives for the number and types of new merchandising programs and for trade participation in the company's programmed merchandising
   f. Business operation
       Customer delivery service objectives
       Inventory turnover objectives
       Product line composition and size objectives
       Pricing objectives
V. **Pro forma financial statements and budgets**
   1. Marketing budgets
      a. Field selling expense
      b. Advertising expense
         National
         Cooperative
         Trade
      c. Promotion expense
         Consumer
         Trade
      d. Fixturing and display expense
      e. Product development expense
      f. Market research expense
      g. Distribution expense
      h. Administrative and allocated expense
   2. Pro forma financial statements
      a. Annual profit and loss statement (expense detail as shown above)
         Next year pro forma by quarter
         Current year budget by quarter
         Last year actual by quarter
      b. Annual revision of five-year pro forma
         Profit and loss statement (expense detail for broad categories)
VI. **Action plans**
   1. Product-line plans
      a. New-product objectives

EXHIBIT 2 *(continued)*

    b. New-product positioning versus identified product needs of consumers

    c. New-product specifications
        Style, weight, size, finish, etc.
        Manufacturing cost
        Selling price

    d. New-product budgets
        Exploration and screening
        Development
        Market introduction

    e. New-product event schedule
        Design releases
        Designs complete
        Market tests complete
        Production releases
        Advertising planned and scheduled
        Selling aids complete
        Distribution achieved
        Commencement of consumer advertising, promotion, and selling

    f. Planned deletions and accompanying phaseout programs

2. Advertising plans

    a. National advertising (by individual campaign)
        Definition of consumers and their buying motivations
        Message theme and objectives
        Reach and frequency objectives
        Budgets
        Preparation and execution schedules
        Creative plans
        Media plans

    b. Cooperative advertising programs
        Trade participation objectives
        Budget
        Relationships to other marketing programs
        Preparation and execution schedule

    c. Trade advertising (by individual campaign)
        Message and audience objectives
        Budgets
        Preparation and execution schedules
        Creative plans
        Media plans

    d. Trademark changes

3. Sales promotion and display plans

    a. Consumer and trade promotion objectives

    b. General description of promotion programs, budgets, and calendar

    c. Fixturing programs and budgets

4. Major packaging plans

5. Trade selling plans

    a. Description of significant changes in distribution policy
        Approval outlets
        Distribution methods

    b. Distribution coverage objectives

    c. Account coverage objectives

    d. Selling expense budgets

EXHIBIT 2 *(concluded)*

---

    e. Specific new account targets
    f. Special trade merchandising programs and calendar
    g. Field selling programs and calendar
    h. New services for trade customers
        Delivery service
        Inventory backup
        Selling support or the like
    i. Sales quotas for each representative by product line
6. Special market research projects
   Include a general description of each project, its objectives, budget, and
   timetable.
7. Pricing recommendations
8. Special cost reduction programs
   Include a general description of each program, its expected dollar savings, and an assignment of responsibilities.

Source: Reprinted by permission from David S. Hopkins, *The Marketing Plan*, Report No. 801 (New York: Conference Board, 1981), pp. 113–18.

CONCLUDING NOTE

Preparation of the strategic marketing plan is one of the most demanding management responsibilities of the chief marketing executive. It requires folding together many different information-gathering and analysis activities into a comprehensive and integrated plan of action. Following a step-by-step approach in building the strategic plan will ensure that all components of the plan are covered and that their important interrelationships are recognized. The starting point is understanding the corporate strategic plan since the marketing plan is one of a bundle of functional strategies that must be combined to achieve corporate and business unit objectives.

Four important characteristics of the strategic marketing plan should be apparent. First, a logical process can and should be followed in developing the plan. Second, when the planning process raises relevant questions, management must supply the answers; decision makers develop strategic plans. Third, strategic marketing planning is a continuing activity that is adjusted and revised to take advantage of opportunities and avoid threats. Finally, marketing planning forms the leading edge of planning for the entire business unit. Marketing plans must be closely coordinated with research and development, operations, financial, and other business functions. Corporate and business unit objectives and strategies provide important marketing planning guidelines.

CASES AND APPLICATIONS
FOR PART 5

The eight cases and five applications in Part 5 continue the emphasis on program positioning strategy developed in Part 4. They also focus on strategic planning.

Cases

The first case concerns a company, Coastal Plastics, that has been experiencing a loss for the past year and a half. Top management of the parent organization, Arnol Corporation, has directed Alan Buford, general manager of Coastal, to develop a specific marketing strategy which will stop the losses of the division as soon as possible and provide a base for continued growth in the future.

The Needlework Company (Case 5–2) was founded in 1971 as a publisher of leaflets for the needlework trade. The company has added other products, and profits have increased rapidly. The company's new marketing manager has been assigned responsibility for preparing the company's first strategic plan. The case deals with this assignment.

Bavaria Manufacturing International (BMI), located in Munich, Germany, manufactures water faucets. Case 5–3 presents background information on the company's products, the industry, and the market. The marketing manager for BMI has been instructed to submit a final marketing plan for a new product line by the end of the next week.

Case 5–4, Cantel, Inc., describes a recently formed Canadian company that has just been granted a license from the Department of Communications to provide a national air network for a new mass communications technology: cellular radio communications. The firm must develop a marketing strategy for the cellular air network.

Thompson Respiration Products, Inc. (TRP) (Case 5–5), is a small manufacturer of portable respirators. Victor Higgins, executive vice president, has posed several short-term strategic issues to consider over the weekend. He also recognizes that broader questions regarding TRP's market target, marketing objectives, and positioning must be addressed in its strategic marketing plan.

Rosemount, Inc. (Case 5–6), is in the process of developing the annual marketing plan for its industrial instruments. Several important questions regarding products, markets, and overall strategy remain to be answered.

In case 5–7, Paper Mate focuses on whether or not to introduce a revolutionary new pen containing truly erasable ink. Derek Coward, vice president of marketing, must weigh several risks and trade-offs before making a final recommendation to the division's president.

Robinson Chemical Company (the final case in Part 5) manufactures specialty chemicals—high-performance engineering resins. The director of the firm's research labs is concerned about three products that have recently become available to the market. A marketing plan for the new resins is needed.

Applications

The L'Oreal application (5–9) targets the market for cosmetics that benefit aging skin. Color Tile (5–10) presents an interesting analysis of the floor-covering market and plans for expansion into new markets. The MADD application (5–11) describes the controversy surrounding a marketing strategy for a nonprofit organization. Nixdorf Computer AG (5–12) is a successful German computer manufacturer with a continuing commitment to customer satisfaction. Minute Maid Orange Juice (5–13) profiles the highly competitive, mature orange-juice market.

CASE 5–1

Coastal Plastics Company

Mr. Alan Buford, manager of the Coastal Plastics Company, a division of the Arnol Corporation, was considering a directive he had just received from top management of the parent organization. He was told by Arnol management that he was to come up with a specific marketing strategy and plan designed to stop the losses of the division as soon as possible and to provide a base for continued growth in the future.

COMPANY BACKGROUND

Coastal Plastics, located in the Puget Sound area of the state of Washington, is a plastic pipe extruder serving the Pacific Northwest. The company began operations in the early 1950s. The firm was acquired in 1967 by the Arnol

---

This case is produced with the permission of its author, Dr. Stuart U. Rich, Professor of Marketing, and Director, Forest Industries Management Center, College of Business Administration, University of Oregon, Eugene, Oregon.

Corporation, a large company in an unrelated field. Sales of the Coastal Plastics Company had grown from $60,000 during its early years to $2,000,000 in 1969, making it the second largest extruder in the Pacific Northwest. Profits, however, had declined, and the company was operating at a loss.

The management staff at Coastal Plastics consists of Mr. Buford, who acts as both general manager and sales manager; Mr. George Timkin, the plant manager; Mr. Alan Britt, the plant engineer; and a plant foreman.

INDUSTRY BACKGROUND

Thermoplastic pipe is made from four types of plastic resins: polyvinyl chloride (PVC), rubber-modified styrene (styrene), acrylonitrile butadiene styrene (ABS), and polyethylene (poly). The resins differ in chemical and physical characteristics, such as resistance to acids and bases, strength, melting point, and ease of extrusion. These plastic resins are bought from the large national petrochemical suppliers.

Plastic pipe competes with iron, aluminum, and asbestos-cement pipe in the Northwest market. In comparison with the other materials, plastic pipe is considered superior in terms of lower cost, ease of installation and maintenance, and lack of deterioration from environmental influences. Plastic pipe is considered inferior to the other materials in terms of crushability, strength, and melting temperature. Plastic pipe cannot be extruded in sizes greater than ten inches in diameter and also has a high degree of thermal expansion that restricts its use in some applications.

A machine called an extruder is used to form plastic pipe by heating the resin to near its melting point, forcing the fluid mass through a die, and then cooling the formed pipe in a water bath. A relatively unsophisticated plant to manufacture plastic pipe can be built for approximately $150,000. In fact, one of the successful competitors in the ABS market in the Northwest, the PJ&J Company, has what is called a "backyard operation" and operates out of a converted garage.

The different resins can all be satisfactorily extruded on the same machine, with the possible exception of PVC, which requires a stainless steel die instead of the usual milled steel die. All that is required to change resin type is to change the resin fed into the machine. A die change to make different-size pipe is even simpler. The extruder can be left hot and the pressure relieved so that the die could be changed.

COASTAL PLASTICS'S EXTRUDED PIPE

In time, all four thermoplastic resins were being converted by Coastal Plastics into plastic pipe ranging from one-half inch to eight inches in diameter. The final product has pressure ratings from 80 psi to 600 psi. The company's pipe was of standard quality and was comparable to that produced by competing pipe extruders.

Coastal Plastics later completed capital expenditures for new resin-blending and pipe-extrusion equipment that executives described as "the most technically advanced in the industry." The company then had a plant investment of over $2 million. In view of Coastal's unprofitable operating performance, it was considered doubtful that the Arnol Corporation would agree to additional capital expenditure appropriations for Coastal. Coastal owned and operated four modern pipe-extruding machines as well as three older machines. In spite of the modern production setup, a production problem arose from the firm's inability to maintain adequate control over pipe-wall thickness. Pipe production used 7 percent more resin material than was theoretically required to ensure a minimum pipe-wall thickness. The plant engineer was in charge of quality control, but, due to a substantial workload, he had spent little time on the costly material waste problem.

When corporate management imposed tight limits on finished goods inventories, Coastal Plastics aimed at minimizing inventories. Rush orders, which frequently could not be filled from inventory, necessitated daily extrusion machine changeovers. A relative cost study conducted by the plant engineer showed that Coastal could conceivably hold a much larger finished goods inventory and still not reach the point where costs of holding inventory would exceed machine changeover costs. Coastal Plastics averaged seven machine changeovers per day, at an average loss to contribution to fixed overhead of $25 per changeover.

PLASTIC PIPE MARKET SEGMENTS

In a time when Coastal Plastics was producing some 200 separate pipe products of varying sizes and resin types to supply 11 market segments, Mr. Buford felt that, in order to utilize plant capacity to the utmost, Coastal had to reach all of these end-use segments. Coastal's sales volume was highest in water transportation markets for PVC and styrene pipe. The company's total pipe production by resin type (in pounds) for the first six months of the year was as follows:

Poly	450,000
PVC	3,871,000
ABS	769,000
Styrene	1,032,000
Total	6,122,000

Arnol Corporation market researchers had concluded that demand for plastic pipe would increase during the next five years in all market segments in the states served by Coastal Plastics—that is, in Oregon, Washington, Idaho, and northern California. A summary analysis of each market segment follows, including the current consumption estimates and five-year growth projections for Washington alone and for the four-state region including Washington.

Agriculture Irrigation

This segment was the largest volume plastic pipe market in the Pacific Northwest. Plastic pipe, however, accounted for only 11 percent of all pipe used for agriculture irrigation. Newly developed plastic component systems, particularly plastic-component sprinkler irrigation systems, were replacing many open-ditch and metal-pipe water transportation systems. Arnol market researchers, in describing growth potential for this plastic pipe market, stated that the "pendulum is swinging from metal to plastic pipe as the primary water transportation method." PVC resin pipe was used almost exclusively to supply this segment. Total plastic pipe consumption in Washington was now 8.25 million pounds. Total for the four-state market area (Washington, Oregon, Idaho, and northern California) was 16.5 million. Estimated growth for the next five years for Washington, as well as for the whole region, was 17 percent.[1]

Private Potable Water System Market

Building codes continued to favor copper and aluminum and to exclude plastic pipe from use for home water-supply systems. Although public utilities were utilizing PVC plastic pipe for public water systems, plumbing contractors shied away from using polyethylene pipe in private systems. Total plastic pipe consumption for Washington was 145,000 pounds. For the Northwest region it was 350,000 pounds. No growth was forecast for the next five years.

Mobile Home Market

Most ABS plastic pipe sold to this segment was used in plumbing fixtures. Most mobile home manufacturers sought to buy plastic fixtures on a national contract basis. It was a rare occasion when one of these national concerns purchased pipe from a local or regional extruder. Washington plastic pipe consumption was 130,000 pounds; regional consumption was 1.4 million pounds. A 90 percent growth figure was forecast for Washington, and 75 percent for the region.

---

[1] Growth figures are for the five-year period. They are *not* annual growth rates. Therefore, a five-year growth figure of 61 percent is equivalent to a 10 percent average annual growth rate.

Public Potable Water

Some public water utilities were using PVC plastic pipe for water service lines that connect households to main water-distribution lines. Styrene pipe had given way in recent years to the stronger, less brittle, more inert PVC pipe. Washington consumption was slightly over 2 million pounds, and regional consumption over 5 million pounds. A 100 percent growth figure was projected for both the state and the region.

Industrial Market

Plastic pipe applications in processing, material supply, transfer, and waste disposal were severely limited in this segment. According to Mr. Buford, it was due to thermoplastic pipe's sensitivity to steam, sparks, and hot fluids. The most prominent industrial application was in copper mining, with minor applications in pulp and paper manufacturing, food processing, and sea water transfer. Total consumption in Washington was 600,000 pounds; for the region, slightly over one million pounds. Growth was projected at 45 percent for both the state and the region.

Turf Irrigation Market

Turf irrigation included applications such as public and private lawn-watering systems. Small-diameter PVC pipe was generally used by this market segment. Consumption in Washington was 3 million pounds; in the region it was 5.9 million. The projected five-year growth was 66 percent for Washington and 57 percent for the region.

Drain Waste and Vent Market

DWV was defined as all plumbing pipe running from and venting sinks, toilets, and drains to the structure drain. ABS pipe accounted for 86 percent to 90 percent of the market, with the remaining amount held by PVC. Plumbing unions had opposed the use of plastic pipe in favor of traditional materials, apparently due to the easy installation of plastic pipe with its resultant labor savings. Yet, the unions claimed the traditional steel and iron pipes were superior. Consumption in Washington was slightly over 1 million pounds; regional consumption was 1.75 million. Washington growth was projected at 27 percent; regional growth at 35 percent.

Conduit

Electric conduit was used primarily to protect and insulate electric power lines and telephone lines, both underground and in the buildings. Competitive materials included the traditional aluminum metals. Major users in this market were large contractors and utilities that bought on a competitive bidding system. Consumption in Washington was 465,000 pounds; regional consumption was 1 million pounds. A 75 percent growth figure was projected for Washington and 50 percent growth was forecast for the region.

Sewer and Outside Drain

This market segment used plastic pipe for connections from house to septic tanks and sewer systems, downspout drainage, water drainage, and septic tank drainage. The primary resins used were styrene and PVC. The major competitive materials were asbestos fibers, cast iron, and vitrified clay; however, they were generally competitive only in the large sizes used in a public sewer system. The FHA had recently approved plastic pipe for rural homes. Washington consumption was 1.4 million pounds, and regional consumption was 2.8 million. A 90 percent growth was forecast for Washington, and 78 percent growth was predicted for the region.

Gas Transportation Market

Plastic pipe in this segment was used to distribute low-pressure natural gas from major terminals through distribution mains to residences, businesses, and industrial users. Gas companies, which bought the pipe in large lots or on a yearly basis, had tested the plastic pipe and were not entirely pleased with the results. They favored the traditional steel pipe and the new epoxy-coated steel pipe that combined the inherent advantages of both plastic and steel. Washington consumption was 123,000 pounds; regional consumption, 300,000 pounds. The growth projection was marginal.

Water Well Service and Stock Water

Plastic pipe was used in rural areas to bring water from the individual farm wells into the home and to distribute it to outlying farm buildings to water livestock. The primary resins used were PVC and polyethylene. Washington consumption was 400,000 pounds, and regional consumption was 900,000 pounds. Relatively little growth was projected.

Adaptability to Uses

The four types of plastic pipe varied in their adaptability to use in the various markets just described. It depended on the physical attributes of the resin type as well as cost advantages needed for low-grade applications. PVC was the most versatile and was used in all market segments. Poly was suitable for use in all markets except sewer and outside drain, mobile homes, and drain waste and vent. ABS was adaptable for use in six of the eleven markets: public potable water, private potable water, turf irrigation, mobile homes, drain waste and vent, and gas transportation. Styrene was used for the most part in sewer and outside drain, drain waste and vent, and conduit markets.

PROMOTION AND SALES

Coastal Plastics used a limited amount of advertising in promoting its plastic pipe, preferring to rely on personal selling as its main promotional device. In the past the company had advertised in trade journals and in agriculturally oriented magazines such as *Pacific Farmer*. It also sponsored early-morning farm radio programs on local stations, and utilized the usual product information folders and catalogs.

Recently, Coastal had used a mailer soliciting inquiries on a "spike sprinkler" coupling for irrigation. The spike sprinkler was a device to position a sprinkler in the field, and it was considered a superior pipe coupling. The company had contracted for exclusive distribution of the coupling to be used with its pipe, but did not itself produce the device. Coastal had mailed 1,000 of the product folders and had received 200 inquiries. Mr. Buford was enthusiastic about the response and planned to increase mailer promotion in the future.

The company salesmen were assigned by geographic area, and they called on pipe distributors and large end-users in each area. They were responsible for sales of all company products in their respective areas. The three main sales areas were the Seattle–Puget Sound area, the Portland and eastern Oregon–eastern Washington area, and the southern Oregon–northern California area. Each of these areas was covered by one salesman. In addition, Mr. Buford had a number of working contacts and made visits to major accounts. This was relatively simple because most of the major distributors were located within short distances of the division office.

In addition to the field salesmen, there was one in-house salesman who handled small "drop-in" business, short-notice orders, and customers requiring a quote on an order of pipe. Often, a distributor would phone in an order asking for a price quote and delivery at the end-user's site the next day. If the company was not capable of meeting a price and delivery schedule, the customer would take his business elsewhere. The company tried its best to provide service on these accounts so that it could maintain plant capacity, even if it meant machine changeovers to produce the order.

Since the salesmen were assigned one to an area, they were responsible for missionary, maintenance, and service selling. They were compensated, according to corporate policy, by straight salary with no commissions paid for different product sales. They called on distributors and large end-users and were expected to educate distributors on product knowledge and use and to handle field complaints. Often these complaints emanated from a do-it-yourself end-user who had not followed the directions for joining pipe sections together correctly. At times the salesmen tried to stimulate sales by going to the end-user and providing technical service such as product specification and pipe-system design.

DISTRIBUTION

Coastal sold the majority of its plastic pipe through distributors, with 20 percent of the accounts contributing 75 percent of gross revenues. Only in the case of large end-users such as utilities and major contractors did the company try to sell directly. In such cases, the company paid the regular commission to the area distributor only if the distributor managed to learn of the sale and the distributor was of some importance to the company. Marketing terms were 2/10 net 30.

Pipe distributors, who were paid a commission of 5 to 10 percent of sales, performed several major functions: (1) they broke bulk and sold to many retailers in their area; (2) they used the pipe along with many other components in the piping systems that they installed, such as agricultural irrigation systems, plumbing systems, and turf irrigation systems; and (3) they provided financing and inventory service for their customers. Distributors held preparatory inventory in seasonal markets such as agricultural irrigation. In preparation for the seasonal demand, Coastal would deposit "dated" shipments at the distributor's warehouse.

Pipe distributors in most market segments considered price to be the most important factor determining from whom they bought pipe. Most distributors agreed that one pipe was as good as another; they considered delivery service to be the next most important factor. They did not feel that technical service offered by the manufacturer was very important in their choice of suppliers. In fact, some distributors were very ambivalent about the usefulness of manufacturer's salesmen. They did not feel that technical service by the manufacturer was very important in the sale of pipe. Some felt that the best thing salesmen could do was stay out of the field. They disliked pipe salesmen "muddying the water" at the end-user level and making promises to the end-user that the distributor was unable or unwilling to fulfill. Other distributors, however, felt that pipe salesmen could and did help by providing product knowledge to the distributor salesmen. Under no circumstances did any of the distributors favor having pipe salesmen contact the end-user.

Distributors generally viewed the price competition within the industry with disfavor. One reason was the lowered profit margin on sales of the pipe. Since distributors usually made a fixed percentage on sales, their income was reduced by lowered prices. Another reason was the distributor's concern that when he was making a bid on a system including plastic pipe, his competitor might get a more favorable quote on plastic pipe and therefore be able to quote a lower bid. The distributors wanted plastic pipe prices stabilized so that their bids could be based on their own competence and economic situation rather than on the pricing practices of the pipe manufacturers.

Although distributors disliked price competition, they were glad to see that Coastal and other producers had lowered the price to the point where imported pipe was not a major source of market supply. Many were reluctant to handle shipload quantities of imported pipe with its resultant inventory and handling problems. They much preferred a convenient source of supply, which the local producers could provide.

Although some distributors had considered making their own plastic pipe, they did not at the time consider such production attractive. For the time being, they were content to buy pipe from suppliers. Coastal had been a factor in this decision by improving service and by lowering prices.

In view of the continuing poor profit situation of his division, Mr. Buford had considered trying to integrate forward and capture the distributor's margin. One of the salesmen had felt that Coastal salesmen could do as good a job selling plastic pipe to end-users as the distributors did.

TRANSPORTATION

Approximately 75 percent of Coastal's annual volume was shipped via common carrier, with the remaining 25 percent being delivered by company-leased trucks or through factory "will-call" by customers. Because of competitors' practices, most of Coastal's shipments were either prepaid to Northwest destinations, or comparable freight allowances were made from gross sales price when pipe orders were picked up at the plant by customers. Because plastic pipe was so bulky, shipping costs averaged about 15 percent of the selling price. This meant that each competitor had a substantial advantage in selling in his own home market.

PRICING POLICY

Mr. Buford looked over the profit summary report (see Exhibit 1) and wondered whether changes in the present pricing policy might lead to improvements in the profit picture of his division. The present policy of "meeting or beating the price offered by any other supplier" had been initiated in 1968. It was during that year that the Japanese began exporting large quantities of plastic pipe to the Pacific Northwest. Due to lower raw material costs and a suspected dumping policy, they were pricing their products below local suppliers. Even though there were disadvantages in the sales agreements offered by the Japanese (such as order sizes of shipload quantities only), the Japanese were able to capture a significant portion of the market due to their low price.

EXHIBIT 1

Coastal Plastics Company—Profit Summary Report (per-pound basis, first six months of the current year)

	Poly	PVC	ABS	Styrene
Gross sales price	.3625	.2760	.3648	.2762
Less: Discounts, freight, allowances	.0710	.0138	.0378	.0377
Net sale price	.2915	.2622	.3270	.2385
Less: variable cost (raw materials and conversion)*	.3050	.2230	.3392	.2110
Direct margin (contribution to fixed cost)	−.0135	.0392	−.0122	.0275
Less: fixed cost	.0397	.0375	.0501	.0314
Profit	−.0532	.0017	−.0623	−.0039

* *Text authors' note:* For analysis purposes, treat conversion as *changeover costs* only. Other labor costs are included in fixed-cost figure.

The effects of the Japanese entry into the Pacific Northwest market were immediately felt by Coastal Plastics, since the Japanese were marketing PVC—the major resin type produced by Coastal. At that time, Mr. Buford reasoned that the size of the Pacific Northwest market could not accommodate another supplier of plastic pipe. He felt that steps must be taken immediately to drive the Japanese out of the Pacific Northwest.

To achieve this goal, Coastal adopted its present pricing policy, thus forcing the Japanese to compete on terms other than price, such as speed of delivery, where the Japanese were at a strict disadvantage. Soon after this, other suppliers followed suit. The average price levels gradually eroded from 28 cents per pound down to 26 cents per pound. With the decreased price the Japanese left the Pacific Northwest market, and Mr. Buford felt that they would not reenter it until the price came back to 28 cents per pound.

The Sierra Plastic Pipe Company had been the major competitor supplying southern Oregon and northern California. Then its plant burned to the ground, and a number of the other suppliers, including Coastal, increased their plant capacity in anticipation of taking over the accounts that they were sure Sierra would lose. To prevent the loss of its accounts, Sierra bought plastic pipe on the open market and was thus able to maintain its customers while its plant was being rebuilt. Because Sierra was able to remain in business, and because the growth of the Pacific Northwest market was not up to expectations, a considerable overcapacity on the part of all suppliers soon developed in the Pacific Northwest. This overcapacity was estimated at 30 to 40 percent, but some suppliers were continuing expansion.

Because of the overcapacity and the desire on the part of executives to maintain market share, Coastal had continued its present pricing policy. It was reasoned by Mr. Buford that a reduction in price would increase market share, which would increase production and narrow the gap between plant capacity and the production level, thus minimizing fixed cost per unit.

In evaluating the present pricing policy, Mr. Buford came to two conclusions. First, the profit picture for his division was most likely quite similar to that of the other regional suppliers. Secondly, while the distributors enjoyed the low price that was resulting from the fierce price competition, they were unhappy with the volatility of the price levels that was also generated.

COMPETITION

Domestic competition in Coastal's marketing area came from six regional manufacturers and five to eight major national producers. The number of national producers varied because some of them moved in and out of the Northwest market, depending on economic conditions. The regional manufacturers had about 75 percent of the market, while the larger national firms and a few import firms controlled the rest. Three of the regional firms controlled 60 percent of the Northwest market. Sierra Plastics was a leader, although Coastal and Tamarack Pipe closely followed. The three companies produced essentially the same products.

Tamarack Pipe was within 50 miles of the Coastal Plastics plant and was a strong competitor in the Portland, Oregon, market and the Puget Sound market. Due to its location in southern Oregon, Sierra Plastics had a strong competitive position in the southern Oregon–northern California market, resulting from its lower transportation costs in this area compared with those of Coastal and Tamarack.

Coastal Plastics had tried to differentiate its product in the past, but had met with limited success. In an attempt at differentiation, Coastal had changed the color of its PVC pipe from gray to white. Other competitors, especially the nationals, had made some progress in differentiating their products. Babbit Corporation, a national supplier of pipe and piping systems to industry, had added plastic pipe to its product line and advertised in such nationwide periodicals as *Chemical Engineering*. Babbit was very strong in the industrial segment of the market. Cable Company had distinguished its pipe by application to sump pump installations and had a virtual monopoly in this specialized application. PJ&J in northern California was the chief supplier of ABS pipe in the Pacific Northwest, primarily through being the least expensive marketer. For example, Coastal was able to buy PJ&J pipe and resell it at less cost than Coastal could produce comparable pipe.

In recent months, Coastal salesmen had reported that Tamarack had begun to concentrate more on the agricultural irrigation market, while

Sierra was concentrating on being the primary supplier of plastic pipe for conduit. Even though this market was small, it was anticipated to mushroom as the housing market resumed its growth. The large national firms had concentrated on the mobile home industry and appeared to have the greatest number of manufacturers, since contracts are negotiated on a countrywide basis.

The large national manufacturers were either owned by or affiliated with national petrochemical companies. These companies usually adjusted to the prevailing market conditions and were a stabilizing influence in the market.

The competitive conditions that had prevailed in the Northwest had depressed the financial conditions of some of the smaller independent firms, and it was not known how much longer they could continue operations. The larger independent firms, although experiencing losses, were as well financed as Coastal and were still battling for increased market share.

CONCLUSION

Mr. Buford realized that a number of changes were needed in many parts of his company's marketing program. He saw that some of these changes were interrelated; for example, decisions on pricing strategy might have an important impact on product policy, and vice versa. Certain decisions had to be made very soon if the company's profit position were to be improved, whereas other decisions could be postponed for a while.

Mr. Buford felt that his planning task was made more difficult by the limited size of the management staff in his division. Although the parent corporation provided help in market research and some coaching in general planning procedures, the actual planning and strategy determination was Mr. Buford's responsibility. Because of the need to keep division overhead expenses down to a minimum, Mr. Buford knew that no additional management staff could be hired at the present time.

As he walked into his office, pondering what to do first in the way of planning, his phone rang and the in-house salesman asked him to okay a price quote on a drop shipment for the next day. Mr. Buford okayed the quote, and then sat down muttering, "How can I find time to plan for the months and years ahead when daily operating problems demand so much of my time?"

CASE 5–2

The Needlework Company (A)

The Needlework Company was founded in early 1971 as a publisher of instructional leaflets for the needlework trade. Soon afterward the company also began to distribute books of other publishers in addition to certain supplies (e.g., yarn and fabrics) as well as tools and accessories (e.g., scissors, hoops, and needles). After a modest beginning, company sales and profits experienced rapid growth—particularly for the period 1979–81 (see Exhibit 1 for the company's income statement for this period). In late 1981 the company hired a new marketing manager, Robert Fisher, who in addition to his other duties was assigned the responsibility for preparing the company's first strategic plan.

The needlework skills which the company targeted with respect to its line of instruction leaflets were quite varied. The more popular ones included counted cross-stitch, crewel, crocheting, cross-stitch, embroidery, knitting, needlepoint, preworked needlepoint, and stamped cross-stitch. Exhibit 2 provides a glossary of these terms.

EXHIBIT 1
Company Sales and Profits, 1972–1981 ($000)

| | | | | | Profit | |
| | | Cost | | | --- | --- |
Year	Net Sales	Goods Sold	Gross Profit	Expenses	Before Tax	After Tax
1972	$ 166	$ 113	$ 53	$ 97	$ (44)	—
1973	648	431	217	240	(33)	—
1974	1,352	814	538	495	43	$ 41
1975	3,087	1,627	1,460	1,117	343	202
1976	3,981	1,913	2,068	1,638	430	239
1977	4,430	2,088	2,342	1,823	519	281
1978	6,097	2,814	3,283	2,360	923	481
1979	8,406	4,110	4,296	2,992	1,304	702
1980	14,250	7,330	6,920	4,753	2,167	1,187
1981*	28,393	14,605	13,788	9,048	4,740	2,494

* Estimated.

This case was written by Harper Boyd, professor of business administration, University of Arkansas. Reprinted from Stanford Business Cases 1983 with permission of the Publishers, Stanford University Graduate School of Business, ©1983 by the Board of Trustees of the Leland Stanford Junior University.

EXHIBIT 2
Glossary of Needlework Terms

Counted cross-stitch: A form of cross-stitch embroidery worked on an un-marked even-weave fabric base, using a coded design chart to determine color changes. The size of the finished embroidery is defined by the number of threads per square inch of the fabric and the "stitch count" of the charted design. Commonly used materials are embroidery floss and Aida cloth.

Crewel: Surface embroidery worked with wool or woollike yarn.

Crocheting: The creation of an interlocking fabric by using yarn and a single hooked tool.

Cross-stitch: Simple embroidery form whereby two stitches of the same length are used creating an x when completed.

Embroidery: Fabric decoration created with a needle and thread. Distinctive from sewing in that the primary purpose is embellishment rather than joining.

Knitting: The creation of an interlocking fabric by using yarn and two needles.

Needlepoint: An embroidery form utilizing yarn on an open-weave mesh canvas base to create a very durable fabric.

Plastic canvas: A needlepoint canvas, usually seven mesh (threads per inch) molded from a plastic material rather than woven on a loom. The canvas is stable yet flexible, making it easy to create three-dimensional projects.

Preworked needlepoint: A partially completed canvas on which the design has been embroidered, but the background has not. Most commonly used for furniture pieces such as chair seats. Also known as prefinished or preembroidered needlepoint.

Stamped cross-stitch: A form of cross-stitch embroidery in which the design is preprinted on the fabric surface.

Surface stitchery: Any of a variety of embroidery techniques used to embellish a fabric and/or canvas base by drawing a needle threaded with yarn through the base.

The company's goal or mission was "to become the dominant supplier of noncommodity products to the U.S. needlework industry."[1] To accomplish this the company felt it must provide the retail trade with a full line of products including both proprietary (own label) or jobbed items. The former could be manufactured by the company or produced to specifications by an outside source. In the case of jobbed items, the company simply served as a distributor.

To date, the company had produced over 300 leaflets (instructional manuals). The production process starts with a design prototype (the end-use product) usually submitted by a free-lance designer. If accepted by the company's product management staff, it is then placed in production, which involves reworking the instructions that accompany the prototype, testing

---

[1] The biggest commodity-type product (in sales) was acrylic yarn, which was purchased by fiber specification and color—rarely by brand name.

EXHIBIT 3
Sales of Major Lines Carried, 1980 versus 1981 ($000)

	1980	1981
Proprietary		
1. Leaflets/books.	$ 5,962	$ 8,989
2. Plastic canvas kits . . .	657	4,653
Subtotal	6,619	13,462
Jobbed/distributed		
1. Leaflets/books.	$ 3,080	$ 5,681
2. Thread/floss.	2,595	5,206
3. Fabric.	805	1,882
4. Needles	445	843
5. Total/accessories . . .	706	1,139
Subtotal	7,631	14,751
Net sales	$14,250	$28,393

them, and designing the leaflet cover and interior in terms of graphics and color. The last step is the actual printing, which is done by a large local printer.

Shortly after its founding, the company began to job floss, fabrics, and a variety of tools and accessories. By the end of fiscal year 1981 the company had in excess of 5,000 stockkeeping units, all of which were warehoused in a single location. Recently the company began to produce and market kits. The basic difference between an instructional leaflet and a kit, according to Mr. Fisher, "is that the customer buys all the material needed to accomplish the pattern, while with kits, all the materials are already assembled." The kits contained plastic needlepoint canvas as opposed to the more traditional cotton canvas. Different lines of kits were made for chains and the specialty store trade. Kit lines were produced for the fall and spring seasons as well as for Christmas. The distribution of company sales by product line for the year 1980–81 is shown in Exhibit 3. As might be expected, margins varied substantially, with proprietary products (leaflets and kits) averaging substantially above 50 percent versus 30 percent for jobbed items.

The company sold its product line to about 14,500 needlework specialty shops (called the regular trade) and about 75 chain organizations—all located in the United States.[2] The company sold only its proprietary lines (leaflets and kits) to the chains.

---

[2] The company also sold a relatively small amount to large Canadian distributors.

THE MARKET

The company's end-user market consisted of women and a relatively small number of men who knit/crochet and/or do surface stitchery. In 1981 the company commissioned a telephone survey of some 2,300 households distributed randomly throughout the United States. Its purpose was to provide quantitative data at the consumer/household level which could be used as a check on industry sales estimates provided by the trade. In addition it provided company management with certain demographic information about those individuals who were interested in the various needlework skill areas. Exhibit 4 contains a summary of the findings obtained from this research.

EXHIBIT 4
Market Research Survey

In 1981 the company commissioned a telephone survey of 2,300 households distributed randomly throughout the United States. Its purpose was to provide quantitative data at the consumer level which could be used as a further check on the industry estimates provided by the trade. The major findings from this study are as follows:

1. Some 36 percent of all U.S. households (77 million) had one or more individuals who had knitted, crocheted, done needlepoint, or cross-stitch during the past 12 months. This totaled 28 million households; of the individuals involved, 92 percent were female and 8 percent were male.
2. About half of the adult females who practiced some sort of needlework during the past 12 months also practiced other needlework-related skills such as crewel and embroidery.
3. Of the 28 million practicing households, 28.2 percent had someone who had knitted/crocheted, 16.1 percent had someone who had done needlepoint, and 9 percent had someone who did counted cross-stitching.
4. The demographics of those who have practiced some kind of needlework skill during the past 12 months are summarized as follows:
   a. Ninety-two percent were female, and 12 percent were under 18 years of age.
   b. Eight percent were males, and nearly half (48 percent) were under 18 years.
   c. The median age of females practicing knit/crochet was 45 years versus 38 years for needlepoint and 36 for counted cross-stitch.
   d. There was considerable variation of needlework skill by region of the country with knit/crochet highest in the West North Central region, needlepoint in the South Atlantic, and counted cross-stitch in both of these regions.
   e. Forty-two percent had some college or were college graduates versus 34 percent for the total population.
   f. The median income was $17,280 versus $15,150 for the total population.
5. The sources used most often for instructions/designs were:

EXHIBIT 4 (continued)

	Those Practicing:		
Source	Knit/Crochet	Needlepoint	Counted Cross-Stitch
Leaflets/booklets	32.2%	10.6%	31.0%
Magazines	18.6	6.9	8.8
Hard/soft-cover books	9.5	8.5	7.1
Complete kits	7.7	42.4	36.6
Did own design	2.8	11.2	3.1
Other person	11.8	0.6	4.1
Other	2.8	—	3.6

6. The usual supply source for instructions/designs was:

	Those Practicing:		
Source	Knit/Crochet	Needlepoint	Counted Cross-Stitch
Specialty stores (regular trade including department stores)	52.7%	77.8%	84.1%
Chains	47.3	22.1	15.9

7. The usual supply source for yarn/thread use:

	Those Practicing:		
Source	Knit/Crochet	Needlepoint	Counted Cross-Stitch
Specialty (regular trade)	40.1%	72.6%	63.2%
Chains	59.9	27.4	36.8

8. The usual supply source for needles/hooks was:

	Those Practicing:		
Source	Knit/Crochet	Needlepoint	Counted Cross-Stitch
Specialty stores (regular trade)	39.1%	67.2%	n.a.
Chains	60.9	32.8	n.a.

9. The usual supply source for complete kits was:

	Those Practicing:		
Source	Knit/Crochet	Needlepoint	Counted Cross-Stitch
Specialty stores (regular trade)	69.0%	78.4%	81.9%
Chains	31.0	21.6	18.1

EXHIBIT 4 (continued)

10. Twice as many females crochet than knit.
11. Knitters and crocheters made the following items during the past 12 months.

	Knitters			Crocheters		
Item Made	Percent	Number of Items*	Cost*	Percent	Number of Items*	Cost*
Sweaters	63	2	$21.00	9.3	2	$15.00
Afghans/quilts/ blankets	33	2	23.00	65.0	2	25.00
Baby items	18	5	16.00	16.0	4	14.00
Hats/caps/ scarves	17	4	8.00	9.8	3	4.00
Mittens	8	4	4.00	.5	1	2.00
Pillows/pillow covers	6	4	6.00	12.0	3	8.00
Slippers	10	5	9.00	6.0	5	10.00
Toys	3	6	6.00	6.0	5	7.00
Vests	3	1	6.00	2.0	3	7.00

* Average number of items made and average cost of materials used.

12. The major sources of design/instructions for knitters and crocheters were as follows:

Source	Ever Used	Used Most Often	Most Enjoy
Subscription or newsstand needlework magazine	44.7%	17.3%	18.1%
Instructional leaflet	62.4	31.3	27.9
Hard/softcover books	26.5	9.3	8.8
Complete kits	33.2	7.5	7.1
Other magazines	2.7	0.9	1.8
Other person	15.5	11.5	10.2
Made myself	4.9	2.7	3.1
Other	3.1	2.7	1.8
Don't know	14.6	16.0	21.0

13. The best-known knit/crochet leaflets were those published by the yarn companies. The awareness of the company's name among knitters/crocheters was as follows:

Leaflets Published by*	Leaflets on Hand	Leaflet Companies that Come to Mind (unaided)	Total Awareness (unaided and aided)
Needlework Company	3.1%	1.8%	27.0%
Coats/Clark	8.8	12.8	83.6
Columbia-Minerva	7.5	4.4	48.2
Bernat	6.2	7.1	43.4
Brunswick	1.3	2.2	53.5

* All but the Needlework Company are basically yarn companies which prepare and sell leaflets as a way of promoting their brand of acrylic yarn. The company does not sell such yarn, because it is basically a commodity sold by the yarn companies either direct or through distributors.

EXHIBIT 4 (concluded)

14. Over the next year, the level of knitting/crocheting activities was expected to increase. The figures below do not take into account those who will enter the market.

Expected Activity in Next Year

Will do more	27.2%
Will do less	15.6
Will do same	54.7

15. Pictures and wall hangings are the most popular needlepoint projects, at an average cost of $15.

Item Made	Percent Making	Number of Items*	Material Cost per Item*
Pictures/wall hangings	52.7%	2	$15.00
Pillows/pillow coverings	32.3	2	19.00
Chair covers	11.4	2	24.00
Christmas items	8.0	5	11.00
Household items	5.0	7	9.00
Purse/tote bags	4.5	3	13.00
Samplers	2.5	1	16.00
Animals/toys/trains	3.5	—	—
Bell pulls	1.0	1	14.00
Miniatures	.5	10	3.00

* Average number of items made and average cost of materials used.

16. Of those who had done needlepoint during the past 12 months, 15 percent were familiar with the company's kit brand. Some 2.5 percent had purchased such a kit, and all indicated satisfaction with their purchase(s).
17. Counted cross-stitch was done by 9 percent of all U.S. households. Of those practicing this skill, 40 percent had done so for less than a year.
18. Those doing counted cross-stitch currently do not expect to increase the level of their activity over the next 12 months.
19. Projects done in counted cross-stitch are similar to items done in needlepoint; that is, pictures/wall hangings, pillows, and Christmas items.
20. While only 5.4 percent of those doing counted cross-stitch recall (on an unaided basis) the Needlework Company as a publisher of instructional leaflets, nearly 50 percent do so on an aided/unaided basis.

THE INDUSTRY

The company sold its products both to chains and to the regular trade. The former consisted of such well-known retail organizations as K mart, Wal-Mart, Target, Woolworth, Ben Franklin, and TG&Y. The company estimated that several thousand chain-store units carried their leaflets and kits. Sales to chains represented about 15 percent of total company sales. Chains sold these products at about the same price as the regular trade. In the past, chains had purchased mostly knit and crochet leaflets but in recent

EXHIBIT 5
1981 Market Potential by Product Line: Chain versus Regular Trade

	Market Size ($000)	Company Sales ($000)	Share	Average annual Growth Rate*
Regular trade				
Leaflets/books	$ 24,790	$10,856	43.8%	20%
Plastic canvas kits	9,006	4,653	52.0	25
Thread/floss	33,810	5,206	15.4	15
Fabric	19,600	1,882	9.6	15
Needles	17,560	843	4.8	10
Tools/accessories	27,780	1,139	4.1	20
Total†	$132,546	$24,571	19.0%	—
Chains				
Leaflets/books	$ 8,150	$ 3,814	46.8%	15%
Plastic canvas kits	3,440	0.0	0.0	25
Thread/floss	13,760	0.0	0.0	15
Fabric	1,750	0.0	0.0	20
Needles	18,920	0.0	0.0	10
Tools/accessories	‡	0.0	0.0	—
Total†	$ 46,020	$ 3,814	8.0%	—

* Next five years. Includes annual inflation of 10 percent.
† Does not include yarn and specialty/miscellaneous products.
‡ Less than $1 million in sales.

months had evidenced strong interest in the company's surface stitchery leaflets.[3] The sale of kits depended for the most part on the buyer's reaction to a kit line. The company produced several new lines each year, since a given line was popular for only a few months.

The regular trade consisted of small independent specialty stores which sold instructional leaflets/books, yarn, fabric, thread/floss, needles, kits, and tools/accessories. Most were small with sales of less than $100,000 a year. They existed, to a considerable extent, because of the owner's interest in needlework. Some were even located in the owner's home. About 10 to 15 percent turned over annually. A recent analysis revealed that some 20 percent of the company's regular trade accounts brought in excess of $2,000 of company merchandise annually and accounted for over 70 percent of sales to the regular trade. At the other extreme lay those stores (some 50 percent) buying $500 or less annually, which represented less than 10 percent of sales. Company sales and share data are presented in Exhibit 5.

[3] This is an umbrella term which includes a variety of embroidery skills used to embellish a fabric and/or canvas base by drawing a needle threaded with yarn through the base. See Exhibit 2 for more specifics relating to the skills involved.

Regular trade outlets tended to keep minimum inventories and to maintain little stock control. They relied heavily on suppliers—including local distributors—to maintain backup stocks. Retailer studies consistently showed a high out-of-stock condition on many items. For the most part such stores did not engage in price promotions and followed the retail prices suggested by their suppliers, which on an average provided margins of between 40 and 50 percent.

The regular trade was mostly serviced by a large number of small suppliers. In the leaflet/book area, there were over 100 companies selling to the regular trade. Some 16 companies dominated the fabric market, while 6 did much the same with thread and floss. The latter was dominated by a French company (DMC) which accounted for over 60 percent of total category sales. Needles were supplied primarily by only two companies—both American (Boye and Bates). As might be expected, there were a large number of companies selling tools and accessories—several hundred, of which a number were European. There were also a large number of kit companies. While there were but a few acrylic yarn producers, there were several hundred small specialty yarn sellers.

Manufacturers typically used distributors and/or sales reps to sell the regular trade. Only a very few used direct selling, and most of these used a dual system in which company salesmen handled only the very large accounts. Small manufacturers often had a difficult time gaining access to the market, since sales reps typically did not carry competing lines. Thus they were forced to rely on small local jobbers of which there were several hundred. The latter operated on margins in excess of 30 percent but found it difficult to inventory a full line of products. The Needlework Company, with jobbed sales in excess of $14 million and an inventory in excess of 5,000 stockkeeping units, was the nation's largest distributor of needlework products.

THE MARKETING DEPARTMENT

The company had a traditional organizational structure consisting of five departments—marketing, finance, accounting, personnel, and operations. Marketing contained sales (both regular trade and chain), product management, leaflet preparation (including art), marketing research (including sales analysis), merchandising, and order receipt/customer service. Operations included receiving and shipping (referred to as warehouse operations), kit manufacturing, building maintenance, and the computer. Purchasing reported to finance. All departments reported directly to the president.

The company had two sales forces—one each for chains and the regular trade. Both were headed by vice presidents. The former consisted of six men, five of whom had in excess of 15 years' industry experience each. As indicated earlier, all chain sales were made direct. All chain salesmen were paid a salary plus bonus (as well as expenses) with salary representing about 70 percent of total compensation. The bonus was based on actual sales versus target and was tailored for each man, depending on his contribution to meeting the target. Thus, in effect, each man had a quota to meet, and his bonus depended in large measure on the extent to which he exceeded this target. The bonus of the vice president in charge of chain sales (who also handled several large accounts) was based on the target set for his accounts and total chain sales. In 1981 he was expected to receive about $135,000 in salary and bonus, while the average of the other chain salesmen would be around $85,000.

Sales to the regular trade were handled by 37 sales reps (32 men and 5 women) who also handled other noncompeting lines. It was estimated that company sales accounted for better than 80 percent of their total sales. Each rep had an exclusive territory and was expected to call on all key accounts (defined as purchasing annually in excess of $1,000 from the company the prior year) at least every three months. Because of the independent nature of these middlemen, the company did not receive any call reports on their activities. The vice president in charge of regular trade sales estimated, however, that his sales force concentrated on the upper 30 percent of stores and called on them three to four times a year. The balance of the accounts were handled via regional and national trade shows; periodic general mailings (three to four times a year) mostly pertaining to price changes, new items, and discontinued items; telephone calls to and from customers; and leaflet automatics (new leaflet shipments five times yearly). The latter was on a subscription basis. About 27 percent of the regular trade (mostly larger stores) had signed up for this service.

Sales reps received a commission on their sales the size of which depended on the product line's gross margin. Thus proprietary products (leaflets and kits) provided higher commissions than did jobbed items. In 1980, commissions averaged about 7 percent. The reps received commissions on all sales to their territory (except for chains) regardless of whether they solicited or serviced the business. Sales from leaflet automatics, trade shows, unsolicited accounts, and phone/mail orders received directly from retailers were credited to their account. Sales reps paid their own travel expenses and were primarily concerned with product placement and therefore tended to focus on new products. Even so, informal field studies showed that product placement was weak, especially with respect to jobbed items. The sales manager thought that this would always be a problem, given that the company carried some 5,000 such items. "After all," he said, "we can't expect them to average more than two to three calls a day, given the geographical dispersion of their accounts. They probably can't spend more than two hours with a customer, and a lot of this is waiting time since the store manager has to handle customers while he's there." He also noted that because of the long industry experience of most of his reps, a considerable amount of time was spent in answering questions about industry trends and the trade's acceptance of new products.

The company did not hold national sales meetings. These were not thought necessary in view of the fact that each rep was visited twice a year by either the sales manager or his assistant, met with company officials at one or more trade shows each year, and talked to the home office frequently by phone. A newsletter was sent out monthly summarizing industry trends and reporting on average company sales to date by product line. In addition each sales rep received an individualized monthly statement showing sales and commissions for the month as well as year to date. A computerized sales-by-account report was sent to each rep quarterly. Information concerning special promotions, new products, product deletions, and price changes was sent out as they occurred. In 1980 there had been over 100 such announcements. Sales reps were expected to keep their own product files, which for the most part contained four-color product information sheets (8½ × 11). The company had some 14 order forms (1 for each major line), which also served as price listings. The cost of a complete set of order forms was 58 cents. A set was inserted with each customer shipment.

The sales organization had experienced little turnover over the years. Of the six who had left during the past four years, only one departure had been initiated by the company. Most had dropped other lines to concentrate more on the sales of company products.

The company received an average of over 1,600 orders daily, of which 83 percent were by phone and mostly customer originated. In terms of the regular trade, the sales force submitted 7 percent of all orders, which represented 18 percent of sales. Better than 95 percent of all orders received were shipped within 72 hours. To minimize backorders, the company maintained high inventories (the average inventory for 1981 was $3.8 million).

The Marketing Department's product management group consisted of three product units—one each for knit and crochet leaflets, surface stitchery, and kits. Each unit comprised a manager and several assistants, including instruction writers. In 1981 the company published 16 knit and crochet leaflets, 28 surface stitchery leaflets, and 4 different kit lines which contained a total of 63 individual items.

The merchandising group consisted of a manager and two assistants. They studied sales trends by products and made recommendations to the product managers and the purchasing unit regarding the addition and deletion of items, what leaflets to consider producing, and what inventories to carry on major items. In addition the unit was charged with the development of special in-store displays although, to date, only a few had been prepared. The merchandising manager was also the chairperson of the new products committee, which met weekly to discuss product additions and deletions.

The art unit took the instructional material and turned it into the finished product. Thus the manager and her 10 artists and production people were responsible for all design, layout, and photography work plus managing the printing operation, which was contracted to a local supplier. A considerable amount of time was spent in proofing and checking quality at each stage in the process. In addition this unit prepared all the packaging and instructional materials for the kit line.

What little marketing research was done was initiated by the marketing manager. He typically determined what information was needed and how it was to be obtained, before turning it over to an outside contractor. All sales analysis was done by the assistant sales manager, who was assisted by one clerical employee. They did both chain and regular trade analyses, although the latter dominated the time spent on this activity.

OPPORTUNITIES AND THREATS

One of the major reasons for the company's increase in sales had been the strong market demand for its surface stitchery products. There was, however, substantial disagreement among company managers as to the total market growth rates for such products over the next three years. For example, the president forecast a market growth rate over the next three years of 50 percent/25 percent/0 percent versus 25 percent/0 percent/0 percent by the marketing manager.

To confound and aggravate the problem, the surface stitchery forecasts impacted not only on leaflets but also on those for yarn, fabrics, and many accessories. Thus overall differences of many millions of sales dollars were involved depending on what growth rates were assumed. Since the company produced its own surface stitchery leaflets and also jobbed substantial quantities, there was the question of how much should be invested in company leaflets versus simply selling leaflets produced by other companies.

It was also difficult to forecast the sales of kits, since much depended upon the consumer's response to both the product concept and the design. Some kits appeared to have faddish overtones and thus could impact strongly on primary demand. The company was considering selling the same kit line to both chains and regular trade. Such a move would save considerable monies and add about 10 percentage points to the line's gross margin. In the past the company had produced separate and distinctly different lines for chains versus regular trade in an effort to minimize any discontent on the part of the latter.

The president was concerned about the company's future mix of proprietary and jobbed items and its impact on margins and costs. In recent years the sale of distributed products had increased faster than that of the company's own products, thereby impacting gross margins. Further, such a shift increased the company's vulnerability versus local jobbers who for the most part sold the same products and brands as the company. The president wondered if the company should move toward private labels.

Yet another problem was the effect of growth and inflation on the company's cash flows, capital requirements, and costs. The company's accounts receivable were $4,800,000, and the 1981 average collection time was 63 days. Notes payable were $2,101,000. The company paid no dividends, and its stock was closely held.

In looking to the future, the marketing manager suggested that the company's economic objective should be to achieve a five-year compounded annual growth rate (real dollars) of 20 percent in sales and 22 percent in earnings. The president argued for a 30 to 35 percent compounded increase in sales and 33 to 38 percent in earnings. Both men felt that at least 70 percent of total revenue should come from the regular trade and that the company should become an increasingly important supplier of proprietary needlework products.

CASE 5–3

Bavaria Manufacturing International (BMI)

In April 1976 the president of Bavaria Manufacturing International (BMI) met with members of the company's new products task force at the firm's Munich head office. The purpose of the meeting was to discuss the European market introduction of the company's newest product line (see Exhibit 1). Present were BMI's marketing, production, sales, and engineering managers. At the meeting the president made the following statement:

> BMI has traditionally been one of the most profitable companies in the Winchester group. Winchester is looking for big things from us this year, and we are staring down at red figures on our income statement. They are pressing us to introduce the Titan faucet line now. As there is no immediate end in sight to the recession in the construction industry across Europe, we must find new ways of increasing sales. Accordingly I am moving the Titan introduction date up from January 1977 to September 1976. I think we all believe in this product, and we must make every effort to get it to market as soon as possible. Our

---

This case was written by Lawrence M. Rumble, research associate, under the supervision of Professor Christopher Gale, Copyright © 1978 by IMEDE (Institut pour l'Étude des Méthodes de Direction de l'Entreprise), Lausanne, Switzerland.

EXHIBIT 1
Titan

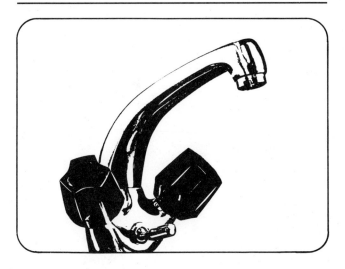

objective is to sell DM25 million worth of Titan in the first 12 months. . . .[1]
Karl, I must have your final marketing plan by the end of next week.

This last statement was addressed to Karl Schonfeld, BMI's marketing manager. Schonfeld, a recent MBA graduate from an internationally known Swiss business school, felt all eyes on him. He sensed that the successful introduction of this economy faucet line at this time of need for the company was an opportunity for him to make his mark at BMI.

After the meeting Schonfeld retired to his office to begin work on the plan. He began by reviewing materials on the company, the industry, and the market. He then set about examining aspects of the new business that BMI was about to enter.

THE COMPANY

BMI was one of the major water faucet manufacturers in Europe. Begun as Bavaria Manufacturing in 1924 by two brothers, Hans and Otto Weidemann, the company started producing faucets for consumer and commercial use and never significantly diversified. It grew as a family business, survived World War II, and by the 1970s was considered to be one of the "big five" faucet manufacturers in Europe. In 1976 BMI marketed a full line of

---

[1] The average exchange rate during 1976 was US$1 = DM2.48.

EXHIBIT 2
BMI Products and Parts Diagram

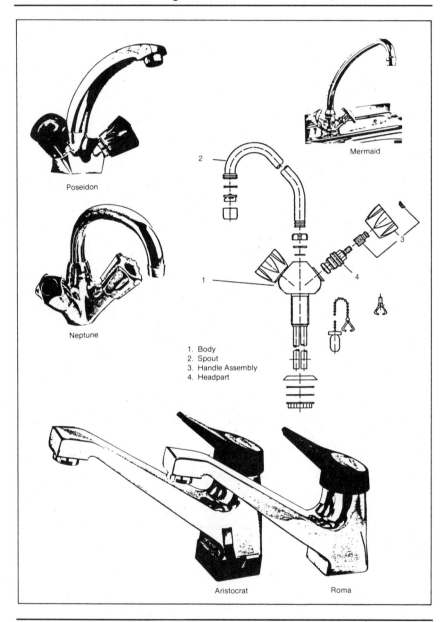

Poseidon

Mermaid

Neptune

2

1

3

4

1. Body
2. Spout
3. Handle Assembly
4. Headpart

Aristocrat

Roma

Source: Company publications.

classical faucets as well as lines of "one-hand mixers"; thermostatically controlled faucets for use in homes, institutions, and hospitals; bathtubs; and other accessories for the bathroom (see Exhibit 2). Faucets comprised 96 percent of its sales.[2]

BMI's head office was in Munich, and all its factories were located in West Germany. The company distributed its products through marketing subsidiaries in Europe and through agents around the world. In 1958 the Weidemann family sold 60 percent of the company to Winchester Holdings of London, England, and it was renamed Bavaria Manufacturing International. The Weidemanns retired from active management in 1961.

BMI had built its business on the basis of a high-quality product backed up by good service. Over the years, its faucets had gained a reputation for their ease of installation and their durability. Many plumbers tended to use BMI faucets because they had apprenticed on them. Among plumbers it was commonly said, "If it's BMI, it's *quality.*"

The company had traditionally been an innovator. For example, it had pioneered faucets which used fewer connections than older products, to facilitate installation. However, in recent years the industry had matured, and BMI's competitors had matched the company's innovations. By the 1970s BMI manufactured products for the upper and middle segments of the faucet market, stringently maintained its reputation for quality, and sold its products at premium prices. It held 14 percent of the European market for faucets.

THE FAUCET INDUSTRY: THE BIG FIVE ET AL.

The faucet industry in Europe was not highly concentrated, with the five largest producers controlling only 50 percent of the market. (See Exhibit 3 for data on sales and industry structure. Exhibit 4 presents data on market share held in selected markets by major competitors.) Aside from BMI the major producers were as follows:

Grohe. Grohe was unquestionably the industry leader. A full-line German producer specializing in high-quality faucets for the upper end of the market, it was a family concern which had been in the faucet business for 50 years. Grohe, like BMI, was an innovator; its one-hand mixer had

---

[2] There were two general classifications in the faucet industry: classical faucets and one-hand mixers. Classical faucets had two separate mounts for hot and cold water controls, and either two separate spouts or a common spout into which both hot and cold water were fed. One-hand mixers were single-spout faucets in which hot and cold water were mixed in preset amounts selected by turning a single faucet handle. These were a recent innovation and represented a rapid-growth segment of the market.

EXHIBIT 3
1975 Sales of Major Faucet Manufacturers

Company	Base	Total Sales (DM millions)	Sales of Standard Faucets (DM millions)	Relative Price Index	Unit Sales (standard faucets)
Grohe	Germany	DM150	DM 42	100*	1,300,000
BMI	Germany	125	30	100	1,000,000
Hansa	Germany	62	19	100	550,000
Pangaud	France	60	28	70	1,000,000
CEC	France	52	20	75	750,000
Ideal Standard	Germany	32	10	100	300,000
Mamoli	Italy	24	12	70	700,000
Kludi	Germany	23	18	70	800,000
Damixa	France	22	0	0	0
Porcher	France	19	12	70	600,000
Venlo	Holland	15	5	85	200,000
Buades	Spain	13	8	65	400,000
SGF	France	12	5	70	200,000
Zuchetti	Italy	12	5	70	200,000
Rocca	Italy	10	5	70	200,000
Rapetti	Italy	10	5	70	200,000
Seidl	Austria	8	3	90	100,000
Schmidl	Germany	7	12	90	100,000
Others		214	86	70	4,000,000
Total		DM870	DM325	80	12,600,000

* This column represented management's judgment of the relative price levels for similar faucets, where the most expensive product in the market was assigned a value of 100.

Source: Company records.

been one of the first marketed in Europe. The company's 1975 sales were estimated at DM150 million. Grohe was strong in classical faucets, one-hand mixers, and hospital fittings. It maintained an in-house sales force and subsidiary sales and service organizations in Great Britain, Spain, France, Italy, Holland, Japan, and the United States.

Hansa. Hansa was a full-line, family-owned German producer of high-quality faucets, with a particular strength in one-hand mixers and medium-priced classical faucets. It maintained its own sales force. Hansa exported faucets all over Europe, but the firm had no really dominant position in any country other than Germany. Its sales were estimated to be DM62 million.

Pangaud. Pangaud was a privately held, full-line French producer. This firm had its own sales force but was a strong factor primarily in France,

EXHIBIT 4
Market Shares of Manufacturers in Major European Markets

		West Germany	France	Italy	Spain	Total Europe
Grohe	Standard	22 %	4 %	2 %	7%	13%
BMI	Standard	19	4	1	2	9
Hansa	Standard	6	.5	—	4	6
Pangaud	Standard	1	5	1	18	9
	Substandard	—	2	—	4	3
CEC	Standard	—	5	—	14	6
	Substandard	—	1	—	3	2
Ideal Standard	Standard	2.5	0.5	0.5	5	3
Mamoli	Standard	—	0.5	12	1	3
	Substandard	—	—	3	6	3
Kludi	Standard	4	—	—	—	5
Porcher	Standard	—	7	—	—	4
	Substandard	—	2	—	—	2
Venlo	Standard	0.5	—	—	—	—
Buades	Standard	—	—	—	12	2
	Substandard	—	—	—	36	11
Total	Standard	55 %	26.5%	16.5%	63%	61%
	Substandard	0	5	3	49	21

Source: Company estimates.

particularly in the low–medium-quality segment of the classical faucet market. Its sales in 1975 were DM60 million.

   CEC. CEC was a union of several French producers which offered a full range of faucets from low-priced classical faucets up to thermostats. This group was a major factor in the French market but had no significant position outside that country. It maintained a small sales force. Its sales were DM52 million in 1975.

   One German manufacturer, Ideal Standard, a subsidiary of the U.S. giant, American Standard, was a fast-growing firm which had recently introduced a popular one-hand mixer. All of these firms concentrated almost exclusively on the production of water faucets for the European and export markets.

   The remainder of the market was supplied by some 200 smaller manufacturers, many of which operated on a regional basis. In Italy alone there were more than 100 faucet manufacturers, many of them low-overhead operations catering to local markets. These manufacturers specialized in cheaper-quality products and supplied much of the "substandard" segment of the market.

THE MARKET FOR FAUCETS

Faucets were a DM870 million business in Europe in 1976.[3] The market could be divided up according to the following price segments:

Medium- and high-price segment	DM130,000,000
Thermostats and hospital fittings	225,000,000
Standard products	325,000,000
Substandard products	90,000,000
Accessories and spare parts	100,000,000
Total	DM870,000,000

The "standard" segment was defined by BMI management as that part of the market where function and price were the main factors affecting the brand decision and where quality (durability) and service were important considerations. Style and general appearance were less important than in the medium- and high-price sector. Management defined the "substandard" segment as that part of the market where products were below normal German government standards with respect to noise and flow control and where price was a major consideration and quality and service were less important. However, these segments were not clearly distinct from each other. Certain products could be considered to be in the standard sector in one European country and in the substandard sector in another, because different countries had different accepted norms with regard to sanitary fitting installations.

Markets could also be classified according to whether they were residential or insitutional. Approximately 90 percent of faucets were sold for residential buildings, while the remaining 10 percent went to the institutional market (hospitals, offices, hotels, etc.). On average a residential dwelling unit had five faucets, while the number of faucets in an institutional building varied according to its function. In the residential sector approximately 45 percent of the fittings were purchased for new construction and 55 percent for the repair and replacement (R&R) market. Of those fittings purchased for new construction, 50 percent were for individual units, and 50 percent were for collective residences (apartments and condominums). These estimates represented averages, as the rate and type of construction in individual countries varied according to economic structures and domestic government policies (e.g., with regard to social housing projects).

There was an increasing trend in the wealthier countries of Europe, such as Germany, for families to undertake construction of their own homes. In approximately 60 percent of new private home construction, a family or individual financed the project. The remainder was developer financed. The

---

[3] 1976 estimate at factory wholesale prices, excluding the United Kingdom.

social housing (state-financed) segment of the residential new construction market was virtually all collective housing and represented 70 percent of all collective housing construction. The remainder was financed by private sources.

In the residential repair and replacement (R&R) market half of the sales were for use in collective housing units and half for use in individual dwellings. There was a broad tendency toward upgrading the quality of the fittings used when replacement was needed, especially when the owner was also the occupant.

In the institutional market approximately 70 percent of faucets were purchased for new construction and the remainder for the R&R market. Approximately 10 percent of new construction was state financed (hospitals, administrative buildings), and 90 percent was privately financed (hotels, offices, factories, clinics). In old institutional construction the sales of faucets were spread proportionally between state-constructed and privately constructed buildings.

During 1975 there was a near collapse of the construction market across all of Europe. In 1974, 714,000 new dwelling units were constructed in Germany; in 1975 this number dropped to 500,000, and predictions for 1976 hovered around the 400,000 mark. The recession occurred in most European countries to a comparable degree. It affected faucet manufacturers to the extent that they were tied to the construction sector and at a time when many were planning capacity expansions. The decline was attributed primarily to overspeculation in real estate during the early 1970s. This applied especially to units being built by private sources for investment purposes. Social housing was virtually unaffected.

DISTRIBUTION

Ninety-five percent of all faucets in Europe were sold through sanitary wholesalers. Normally, a wholesaler would carry the complete range of products of one or two of the major faucet manufacturers, along with products of three or four local suppliers. The wholesaler did not normally enjoy an exclusive franchise from a manufacturer to sell its products in a particular area. A wholesaler stocked some 30,000 separate plumbing items, of which faucets represented between 2 percent and 8 percent of DM sales. His inventory thus represented a substantial capital investment. There were 4,000 wholesalers in the EEC. Though there was a diversity of size among companies in this trade, an average wholesaler would do a sales volume of DM4,500,000 per year.

Wholesalers sold primarily to plumbers, installers, and building contractors. An independent plumber would generally buy a faucet for a specific application and install it directly. In making his selection, he would take into consideration the type of building requiring the faucet, the characteristics of the plumbing attachments, and the owner's wishes. In residential housing, the owner might prefer an expensive and attractive unit or a cheap, functional one. The plumber preferred to work with faucets which were easy to install and would not need service or repair for as long as possible.

Installers were businessmen who employed a number of plumbers and took on larger plumbing contracts. They would characteristically buy a number of faucets for a contract and would be concerned about the profit margins on these, the volume discounts, and the quality of the products themselves. The majority of the installers' business was in new residential and institutional construction. An installer would generally take into consideration the opinions of his plumbers when making purchase decisions, if he were allowed a free choice when purchasing faucets. However, the faucets to be used on a given contract would often be specified by the contractor himself.

Building contractors undertook construction projects independently, for private developers, or under government contract. On a small project, a contractor/developer would commonly make purchase decisions on faucets himself or delegate it to the installer with certain guidelines. The contractor would take price, quality, and appearance into consideration according to the type of building being constructed. On a larger project, the developer would usually approve the faucets the contractor or installer selected. Occasionally an architect would specify a certain brand of faucet for his building, though these did not generally occupy a significant part of his attention because they did not represent significant construction costs.

On government contracts, a government specifier would commonly select the faucets to be used by the contractor, with occasional input from an architect. Government specifiers were primarily concerned with the price and quality of a faucet. In the social housing sector it was important that a faucet meet price restrictions and the government norms in terms of noise and flow control. BMI management felt that of these two considerations, price was probably more important.

While "quality" was an important consideration among many purchasers, BMI management felt that it was difficult to define precisely. BMI marketing executives believed that quality was closely related to the amount of hand polishing and brass (by volume) in a faucet but that these characteristics were not easily apparent to all users. However, plumbers and installers generally stated that they "could tell quality when they saw it and felt it."

COSTS, PRICES, AND MARGINS

Production costs of faucets varied according to how much brass was used in a given unit, the quality of the headpart (see Exhibit 2), the amount of hand shaping and polishing which was required, the types of handles used, and the quality of the chrome plating. With so many variables, production costs would fluctuate considerably according to the unit produced and the corporate structure of the company producing it. Full-line manufacturers would manufacture several faucet lines of varying qualities and market them at varying prices.

A manufacturer would generally sell to wholesalers at a price which would allow him an average contribution over variable factory costs of 33⅓ percent. In turn, a wholesaler generally priced in order to enjoy a 16⅔ percent markup on his selling prices to plumbers, installers, and contractors.

The individual plumber or installer dealing with the public would sell the faucet at a price which would allow him a 26 percent markup.

As no two manufacturers produced faucets of exactly the same quality or appearance, prices for competing products could vary considerably. In this regard BMI tended to price its products high relative to the prices of its competitors.

BMI—PRODUCT LINES

BMI produced and sold three classical faucet lines in 1974—the Poseidon, Neptune, and Mermaid. In addition it produced the Aristocrat and Roma lines of one-hand mixers, a line of thermostatically controlled fixtures for home use, and another for institutional use. The classical faucet lines were differentiated as follows:

Poseidon Line. This was BMI's top line and was characterized by its elegant shape, distinctive styling, and brilliant (transparent plastic) handles. The Poseidon line had been introduced three years earlier and was aimed at the luxury market for sanitary fittings. It was available in both chromium- and gold-plated editions. A representative chrome faucet in this line sold for approximately DM60 to wholesalers. The Poseidon line comprised approximately 3 percent of BMI's sales.

Neptune Line. The Neptune line was BMI's middle line, had equally distinctive styling but used slightly less brass than the Poseidon, and had attractive metal handles. A representative faucet from this line sold for DM40 to wholesalers. The Neptune line had been introduced eight years earlier and accounted for 8 percent of BMI's sales.

Mermaid Line. The Mermaid line was BMI's only entry in the standard faucet market. It was of comparably high quality but was of a more economical design than the Poseidon and Neptune. A representative faucet from the line sold for DM30 to wholesalers. Although the Mermaid line was over 20 years old, it was still BMI's top seller, comprising 24 percent of total company sales.

Each of the product lines included—in addition to the basic faucets, spouts, and shower heads—attachments to adapt the faucets to various plumbing installations. Differing specifications in each of the countries of Europe (e.g., the distance between hot and cold water pipe centers) and abroad required that those producers that exported make available a larger number of attachments with each line. Thus, although there was some commonality, BMI's product lines generally consisted of some 150 separate manufactured parts made from 500 to 600 component parts.

THE TITAN PROJECT

The Titan line was BMI's newest line of classical faucets. It was an economic faucet line (EFL) aimed at the low-cost and public housing markets, where BMI had no market offering.

The product had been conceived as early as 1973. At that time management was becoming increasingly concerned about the number of small firms which imitated BMI designs and undersold it in the marketplace. These "copycat" producers would modify BMI's basic design, manufacture a cheaper-quality product which looked similar, and sell it for 30 percent to 40 percent less. These producers had for some time been making inroads into BMI's markets, especially into sales of the Mermaid line. The EFL was BMI's response to this threat.

The impetus to turn the EFL concept into a reality was provided by the recession in the construction industry. BMI, along with most of its competitors, had not anticipated the drop in demand and was caught with excess manufacturing capacity on its hands. The search for new market opportunities caused the company to again turn its eyes to the "low end" of the market. An internal study was done which indicated that the copycat products eating into BMI's sales generally used less brass by volume than did BMI's products. It also indicated that over 30 percent of the labor costs of BMI's faucets were in the hand-polishing operations, and 20 percent to 30 percent in the handles. The study recommended that BMI design a line which could be produced entirely by automated processes and which would use an amount of brass comparable to the amount used in the imitation products. Costs could thereby be reduced by approximately 25 percent. BMI would then be able to drop its prices so as to be competitive with the copycat products and would break into the social housing and substandard markets it had thus far been excluded from.

As originally conceived, the EFL was to have replaced the existing Mermaid line. It was to have been marketed under the BMI name as a high-quality, low-cost faucet line. Sold at prices 20 percent below the Mermaid, it would rely on BMI's reputation for quality, and BMI's service and distribution organization would assure its acceptance in the marketplace. BMI expected the EFL—now dubbed Titan—to pick up Mermaid's sales and take market share away from competitors in the low-price standard and substandard faucet markets.

Product Development

Product development began in August 1975 with the formation of a task force comprising BMI's marketing, sales, production, and engineering managers. This was BMI's first experience with such group management. The production manager, Mr. Rolf, was chosen to head the force, as it was his responsibility to bring the Titan into production and achieve necessary cost reductions. The engineering manager was instructed to design an EFL which looked distinctly different from existing BMI lines but which maintained BMI's standards of quality. He was to sacrifice design for function and economy where this became necessary. The marketing manager, Schonfeld, was to develop a detailed marketing plan for the EFL, to be approved by Winchester. The sales manager was to work with Schonfeld on marketing aspects of the line.

In September 1975 the first drawings were received from the engineering department. These were shown to the managers of various BMI subsidiaries across Europe to indicate the exact specifications and physical characteristics of the new line. Some of the managers indicated different specifications which would be required in their home markets. BMI engineering staff made it clear that lower costs had been achieved not by diminishing the quality of the product but by developing a line from standard parts. The development of a completely new line which used the smallest possible number of standard parts would enable the company to achieve economies of scale on long production runs.

By October, models were produced for costing, and by November the first prototypes were ready. These deadlines were all met in record time for BMI product development. Among the members of the task force there was a shared commitment to the project which was manifested in a strong feeling of confidence about the future of the line.

Consumer Testing

Once the prototypes were received from engineering in November, two consumer surveys were conducted. Schonfeld wished to use these to pinpoint any problems with public acceptance of the Titan. Any alterations in the product would have to be incorporated in the near future if the EFL was to meet its target introductory date.

In the first test, 150 people selected at random were invited into BMI's factory showroom in Munich to examine the prototypes. The Titan line was displayed alongside similar lines of French, Austrian, and Spanish manufacture. All lines were unmarked. After allowing each respondent time to view and test the faucets, BMI staff interviewed him or her in order to record perceptions of the products. Each interview took up to one-half hour, and the results were recorded on survey sheets.

The results of the first consumer test did not reveal any particular bias for or against the Titan line. It was noted that the consumer apparently judged the quality of a faucet by the handles and that his or her overall response to the appearance was also clearly related to perception of the appearance and feel of the handles. The only notable finding in the report was that respondents commonly indicated a preference for one line over another based on color. Since the handles on most, but not all, faucet sets were chrome and not colored and since the hose and head of the shower sets were either black or white, it was not altogether clear what this meant. The problem was further compounded by the fact that Titan had plastic handles which were of a dark green color but which could easily be mistaken for black.

The BMI board of directors discussed the research results and could not come to any firm conclusion. Since it was known from experience in a past consumer test that the characteristics of the faucet handles strongly influenced consumer perception, it was decided to remove the variable from the test data. Accordingly, a second consumer survey was run, only this time all the faucets tested were supplied with identical chrome handles. Thus the only color differences were in the hose and head of the shower sets.

The results from the second survey were again inconclusive. Although there seemed to be some preference for shower sets with a white hose over those with a black hose, there was still not clearly stated consumer preference for the Titan line (with black hose) over its competitors or for any of the competitors over Titan. From this, Schonfeld and the task force felt that the only reasonable conclusion they could draw was that there was no particular feature of the Titan which would incline the consumer to select another faucet in preference to it when the consumer was presented with an alternative choice. Armed with this information, and mindful of the approaching introductory date, Schonfeld set about making up his marketing plan.

SIZE-UP

Schonfeld began by accumulating relevant data on the countries of Western Europe (see Exhibit 5). He quickly eliminated Britain from the list of available markets because he knew its plumbing installations were so different from those of continental Europe as to make that market totally inaccessible to continental manufacturers. In order to account for differing European faucet standards, he divided prospective countries where the Titan could be

EXHIBIT 5
Statistics on European Market, 1975

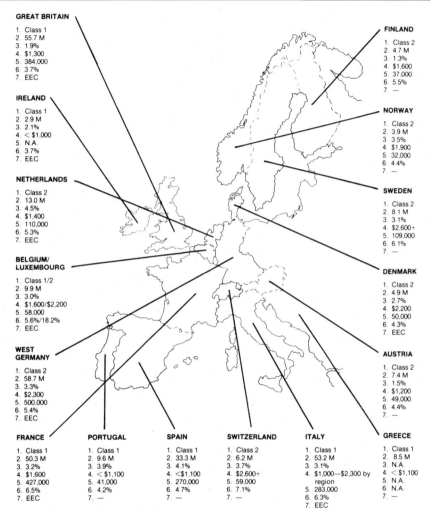

GREAT BRITAIN
1. Class 1
2. 55.7 M
3. 1.9%
4. $1,300
5. 384,000
6. 3.7%
7. EEC

IRELAND
1. Class 1
2. 2.9 M
3. 2.1%
4. <$1,000
5. N.A.
6. 3.7%
7. EEC

NETHERLANDS
1. Class 2
2. 13.0 M
3. 4.5%
4. $1,400
5. 110,000
6. 5.3%
7. EEC

**BELGIUM/
LUXEMBOURG**
1. Class 1/2
2. 9.9 M
3. 3.0%
4. $1,600/$2,200
5. 58,000
6. 5.6%/18.2%
7. EEC

**WEST
GERMANY**
1. Class 2
2. 58.7 M
3. 3.3%
4. $2,300
5. 500,000
6. 5.4%
7. EEC

FINLAND
1. Class 2
2. 4.7 M
3. 1.3%
4. $1,600
5. 37,000
6. 5.5%
7. —

NORWAY
1. Class 2
2. 3.9 M
3. 3.5%
4. $1,900
5. 32,000
6. 4.4%
7. —

SWEDEN
1. Class 2
2. 8.1 M
3. 3.1%
4. $2,600+
5. 109,000
6. 6.1%
7. —

DENMARK
1. Class 2
2. 4.9 M
3. 2.7%
4. $2,200
5. 50,000
6. 4.3%
7. EEC

AUSTRIA
1. Class 2
2. 7.4 M
3. 1.5%
4. $1,200
5. 49,000
6. 4.4%
7. —

	FRANCE	PORTUGAL	SPAIN	SWITZERLAND	ITALY	GREECE
1.	Class 1	Class 1	Class 1	Class 2	Class 1	Class 1
2.	50.3 M	9.6 M	33.3 M	6.2 M	53.2 M	8.5 M
3.	3.2%	3.9%	4.1%	3.7%	3.1%	N.A.
4.	$1,600	<$1,100	<$1,100	$2,600+	$1,000–$2,300 by region	<$1,100
5.	427,000	41,000	270,000	59,000	283,000	N.A.
6.	6.5%	4.2%	4.7%	7.1%	6.3%	N.A.
7.	EEC	—	—	—	EEC	—

Legend:

1. BMI's market classification.
2. Population.
3. Growth in population over five years.
4. Per capita income.
5. Housing completions in 1975.
6. Housing as a percentage of GNP.
7. EEC member or not.

Note: There were no tariffs on faucets in the EEC. Tariffs in other countries averaged 5 percent.

Source: *Business Atlas of Western Europe, 1975.*

sold into Class 1, 2, and 3 markets. He then outlined these classifications in a memo:

> **Class 1.**   Class 1 countries include France, Italy, Spain, Portugal, and Greece. These are countries where there is a substantial market for substandard faucets. In total volume the substandard market represents DM84 million and the standard market DM52 million at factory prices. BMI's sales in the standard section of Class 1 countries amounted to some DM12.4 million in 1975.
>
> **Class 2.**   Class 2 markets are those in which few, if any, substandard products are sold, and include Germany, Austria, Belgium, Holland, Luxembourg, and the Scandinavian countries. The total standard market size in these countries is estimated to be DM265 million in 1976, or which DM111 million will come from Germany. BMI's sales into this sector were DM22.5 million in 1975.
>
> **Class 3.**   Class 3 countries, of which the Middle East and Eastern Europe are prime examples, are those in which all products, be they standard or substandard, are sold at roughly the same price. Total market size is estimated to be DM100 million. BMI sales (Mermaid only) amounted to DM5 million in 1975. Large portions of this market are protected by government policies or trade treaties and are therefore inaccessible to BMI.

Since the Titan line was intended to allow BMI to penetrate the substandard markets, Class 1 countries were to be a major focus of the marketing effort. The Titan would be positioned as close as possible to the low-priced competition in these countries. Schonfeld was aware that the product line had to be positioned in all markets in such a way as to maximize *incremental* sales to BMI and to minimize cannibalization of other lines. The president's remarks at the task force meeting had underlined this, since overall corporate sales were slumping substantially.

However, this was a complex issue, since a management decision had recently been made not to withdraw the Mermaid line from the market. Senior management at BMI believed that since the Titan was intended to enable BMI to penetrate markets it had previously been excluded from, it could be positioned in such a way as to pick up incremental sales without cannibalizing Mermaid's sales in the market segment where it was still selling strongly. The Titan line was clearly differentiated from the Mermaid and other BMI lines on the basis of appearance alone, and it was felt that it could be priced sufficiently below Mermaid so as to be considered an addition to the BMI family of products.

The pricing issue was highly influenced by the economics of the investment, however. Schonfeld had recently received a report from the production department which stated that the target reduction of 25 percent on variable Mermaid costs was no longer attainable. He had had reports to suggest this in the past, but this latest one indicated that costs of the Titan line were unlikely to be more than 10 percent below those of the Mermaid. Schonfeld was disturbed by this. Earlier predictions of rises in costs had been based on the fact that the production department had been unable to cast two faucets in a single mold as planned (something BMI had been unsuccessful at on previous occasions), because hand-polishing operations could not be fully eliminated, and because fully automatic production (i.e., the purchase of some major machinery) would not be feasible until substantial sales volume materialized. These factors had resulted in predictions of costs 17 percent below Mermaid. However, the new cost increases were based on the increased tooling, setup, operating, and working capital costs associated with increased parts requirements to meet specifications in Class 1 countries such as Italy and Spain. In fact the number of product variations for the line had expanded from the 20 originally envisaged to 80 to cover French, Italian, and Spanish plumbing specifications.

Schonfeld was aware that to date DM2,975,000 had been invested in the Titan project. Of this, DM1,740,000 had been spent on product development, DM750,000 on production machinery, and DM485,000 on tooling. One thousand prototype Titan faucet sets had been produced for test market purposes. The expected costs per unit submitted in the latest report were based on assumed unit sales of 1 million to 2,500,000 faucets per year. If sales were 10 percent below the 1 million mark, costs per unit could be expected to rise 5 percent. This trend would continue down to a sales level of 500,000 units, after which per unit costs would escalate rapidly. If sales were only 800,000 units, therefore, costs would be equal to those of the Mermaid line.

The basic faucet from the Titan line would have to be sold to wholesalers at DM24 in order to be 20 percent below Mermaid in price. However, in light of the new cost figures, variable manufacturing cost at this price increased from the originally projected 69 percent to 75 percent. This was before expected variable packaging and shipping costs of some DM2.5 per unit. Schonfeld was thus caught in a cost-price squeeze and had to decide whether or not to risk raising the price of the Titan. If he did raise the price, he wondered by how much this should be done and in what markets. He estimated that at DM24, Titan sales would be 1 million units and that Mermaid sales would drop from 1 million to 800,000 units. He estimated that Mermaid sales would drop by 4 percent below 800,000 for every 5 percent decrease in Titan prices below DM24 and that Titan sales would increase by 7.5 percent for every 5 percent drop in price. If he raised the price of Titan, he estimated that sales would decrease by 10 percent for each 5 percent increase over DM24 but that Mermaid sales would remain virtually unaffected. This was due to his belief that Titan and Mermaid would be perceived as different brands. Finally, Schonfeld did not believe that the market would accept a price increase on Mermaid.

He also had to wonder if cost reduction strategies might be employed. The most obvious one would be to recommend full automation immediately. However, this would take time and would require a further capital outlay of DM1 million. The degree to which costs would be further reduced was uncertain. From the data available to him, he estimated that full automation might reduce Titan's costs by 3 to 4 percent. Another alternative would be to reduce the number of countries the Titan would be introduced in, in order to curb the proliferation of variations (estimated at an incremental 20 for each of Spain, France, and Italy).[4] A further option involved implementing a cost reduction program on the handles of the Titan line. He believed that by moving to a plain handle, costs on this item could be reduced by 5 percent to 8 percent. However, he believed that the plain handles would be less attractive to end consumers than the existing plastic Titan handles.

Because of the cost-price issue and the positioning issue, the countries in which Titan was to be distributed assumed paramount importance. From the beginning it had been intended that the line would be targeted at the social housing sectors of the French and Italian markets. However, Schonfeld had to consider how many additional markets would be required to enable BMI to reach its sales target. Germany itself was BMI's stronghold, where it held the greatest market share and had the best distribution, highest reputation, and best relations with the trade. Spain was the other market for which parts were already available. However, Spain and Austria were not EEC members, and wholesalers would have to pay a tariff of 5 percent of the landed cost of the faucet in these countries. (There were no tariffs on faucets in the EEC. Tariffs in Class 3 countries averaged 10 percent of the landed cost of the units.) Schonfeld knew that BMI's distributors provided good market coverage in all European countries with the exception of Great Britain and Ireland. He also had to consider the possibility of selling Titan through innovative marketing channels such as "do-it-yourself" retail outlets. These were expanding rapidly in some countries such as Germany and Switzerland.

Branding was also an important issue. Schonfeld had considered selling the Titan under a brand name other than BMI in order to avoid cannibalization of Mermaid sales. It would thus be clearly differentiated in the eyes of BMI's traditional customers and could be marketed to the substandard, standard, and social housing sectors of European countries, perhaps at a price higher than the price at which it could be sold under the BMI name. If, on the other hand, the BMI name were used, customers would be assured of the quality of the product. Schonfeld considered some compromise positioning, where Titan would be sold as a "subsidiary brand" to the BMI family of products.

SCHONFELD'S MARKETING PLAN

Schonfeld decided to recommend to the production department that cost-reduction measures be investigated, but knew he would have to work with

---

[4] There would be few incremental product variations required if Titan were sold in more Class 2 countries.

EXHIBIT 6
Company Assessment of Target Groups and Factors They Consider in Selecting Standard Faucets

| | Potential Customer | | | | | | |
| | | | | | | | |
Concerns	Whole-saler	Plumber	Installer	Developer/Contractor	End User	Government Specifier	Architect
Quality	X	X		X		X	X
Price			X	X	X	X	
Function		X	X	X	X	X	X
Appearance				X	X		X
Profit	X	X	X				
Ease of installation		X	X				
Brand	X	X					

Source: Derived from company records.

the figures presently available to him. He took one last look at the results of an attitude survey which had been conducted by BMI in Germany the previous year (Exhibit 6) and proceeded with his task. With time pressures mounting he did not have available to him the results of the Titan test market which had been under way for several weeks in Vienna.

After a week he felt he had a workable proposal. Titan would be sold as a BMI line, using the BMI sales force, and would be backed up by the BMI service organization. It would be positioned at the low end of the BMI product range and distributed through wholesale channels exclusively. The EFL would be sold in Germany, France, Italy, and Spain in the introductory 12 months. Schonfeld decided to add Austria to the list of introductory markets, as there was already a full test market being conducted there.

After much deliberation, he had elected to raise the factory price of the Titan by an average of 15 percent in order to assure the profitability of the line. However, he concluded from talks with salesmen in the field that buyers were more price sensitive in Class 1 markets than in Class 2, where the name BMI on Titan would probably be perceived as a genuine opportunity to buy BMI quality at a lower price than Mermaid. Accordingly he decided on a three-tier pricing scheme whereby Titan prices were raised by 10 percent in Class 1 markets, to DM26.50, and by 17 percent in Class 2 markets, to DM28; on average, Class 3 price (excluding tariffs) was to be DM30. This would optimize the overall margin for the product (see Exhibit 7 for Schonfeld's sales projections and expected cannibalization of Mermaid sales over the next two years).

In order to minimize cannibalization of other lines, Schonfeld decided on a direct-mail campaign for promotional material, aimed at specifiers and buyers for "standard" and "low-quality" building projects. Brochures advertising the Titan line would be directed to clients who were not likely to

EXHIBIT 7

Titan's Projected Sales and Cannibalization of Mermaid if Titan Is Sold for an Average Price of DM27.6/Unit (DM millions)

	1976 Mermaid	1977 (1st year of Titan)		1978 (2nd year of Titan)	
		Mermaid	Titan	Mermaid	Titan
France	DM 2.1	DM 2.0	DM 6.1	DM 1.6	DM 9.7
Italy	1.5	1.1	3.0	0.8	5.5
Spain	0.9	0.5	2.3	0	2.8
Austria	0	0	0.7	0	0.9
Germany	16.4	14.6	8.4	7.0	18.1
Other	4.6	3.8	0	2.6	0
Class 3	5.0	0	4.5	0	5.0
Product total	DM30.0	DM23.0	DM25.0	DM12.0	DM42.0
Total sales	DM30.0	DM48		DM54	

Source: Company records.

consider purchasing another line of BMI faucets (specifically Mermaid) and would bypass those buyers who would normally purchase Mermaid. The promotional message in these brochures would be: "Titan: BMI quality at an attractive price."

The selling emphasis, in comparison with Mermaid, would be as follows:

	Titan	Mermaid
Plumbers	20%	50%
Wholesalers	20	30
Planners, architects, specifiers	60	20
	100%	100%

The total promotional budget was DM1,250,000.

Schonfeld finished with a summary of his plan for achieving his first-year objectives (see Exhibit 8). After completing it, he sat back and reflected that, if his reasoning were correct, this would be one of the most successful new products in BMI's history. He noted that the first test results had come in from Vienna. The report stated that there had been no complaints whatever with any of the Titan faucets which had been installed in the two months since the test began. It also reported that Titan was selling well in the test market area. Schonfeld was pleased by this but did not wish to be overly optimistic.

Before turning in his plan, Schonfeld decided to go over it one more time. He knew that it would be scrutinized carefully by executives at Win-

EXHIBIT 8
Summary of Schonfeld's Marketing Plan

1. First-year sales objectives: DM25 million.
2. Brand name: Titan—One of the BMI Family of Products.
3. Distribution channel: Sanitary wholesalers.
4. Markets:

Market	Sales
France	DM 6,100,000
Italy	3,000,000
Spain	2,300,000
Austria	700,000
Germany	8,400,000
Class 3	4,500,000
Total	DM25,000,000

5. Pricing:

Class of market price	
1.	DM26.50
2.	28.00
3.	30.00

6. Positioning: Social housing and substandard and low end of standard markets.
7. Promotion: Printed material (leaflets) aimed primarily at architects, specifiers, and wholesalers; specially trained sales support—total budget DM1.25 million.
8. Message: "Titan: BMI quality at an attractive price."

chester House, in addition to BMI top management in Munich. He would have to explain why he had elected to proceed as he had and what alternatives he had considered. If he were called to London, he knew he would have to defend his proposal in front of the Winchester senior management committee.

CASE 5–4

Cantel Inc.

In December 1983, a recently formed company, Cantel Inc. of Montreal, had just been granted a license from the Canadian Department of Communications to provide a national air network for a new mass communications technology, cellular radio (cellular) communications. The Cantel Management Team faced what they considered a "marketer's dream" as they contemplated how Cantel should market its cellular air network. Specifically, they questioned whether the company should be involved in the provision of a complete cellular package, including the promotion, sales, installation, and maintenance of both cellular telephones and network subscriptions. In addition, they were considering a number of alternative distribution channels for bringing cellular to potential end users, and pricing and promotional programs were not yet finalized.

CELLULAR RADIO COMMUNICATIONS

The Cellular Concept

Cellular radio was a new form of wireless communications that connected to telephone systems through radio frequencies instead of telephone wires. The concept was a combination of radio, telephone, and computer technologies that made possible portable, cordless telephones.

The term cellular referred to the division of urban centers into a number of small geographic sectors or cells, each of which had several radio channels. A radio channel was defined as a frequency band for the transmission of radio signals. The development of this high-capacity mobile radio system had been referred to as the mass communications technology of the 1980s. Some industry observers suggest that it would do for mobile telephony what cable and satellite technologies had done in expanding the choice of television programming with pay television, while others suggested that the technology could ultimately replace the ordinary telephone.

The "radio" part of cellular involved several low-powered radio antennae that sent and received messages over the air, just as in home radio or

Case material of the School of Business Administration is prepared as a basis for classroom discussion and it may not be reproduced without the written consent of the School. This case was prepared by Susan Fleming, Research Assistant, under the direction of Professors Terry H. Deutscher and Kenneth G. Hardy. Development of this case was supported by the Canadian Studies Program of Canada's Secretary of State. Copyright © 1985, The University of Western Ontario. Reprinted by permission.

television. Cellular networks allowed for full duplex communication, that is, the transceiver transmitted on one frequency and received on another frequency. With duplex communication a cellular telephone user could talk and listen without having to switch between "send" and "receive" channels.

How It Works

The "cellular" part of the technology involved dividing a city or geographic area into cells varying in size from 2 to 25 kilometers in diameter. Each cell was connected to radio antenna; when callers made a call, the signal from their automobile was transmitted to the radio antenna. The radio antenna was connected to a base unit linked to a central computer that, in turn, connected the cellular telephone to other cells within the cellular network and also to the regular wired telephone network (see Exhibit 1). The master computer kept track of which calls were using which frequencies and when. As callers drove through a city, their calls were transferred or "handed off" from cell to cell by the switching device, a process that would not interfere with reception.

The system operated on a low-power output, and the same channels could be used in nonadjacent cells, allowing many callers to take advantage of the system at the same time. For example, in Toronto a conventional mobile phone system could accommodate only 24 callers at once, while the new cellular network was capable of handling thousands of calls simultaneously.

"Roaming" on the cellular network was the act of traveling with one's cellular telephone to a cellular service area which was not one's home service area. It was beneficial to long-distance drivers or those people who used their portable telephones on airplane or train trips. All American and Canadian cellular systems were compatible, roaming was possible between all in-service American and Canadian cities—more than 70 cities in total.

The History of Cellular

The early generations of mobile phones were first introduced in 1921 and were operated by a single high-powered radio antenna that served a large geographic area but could provide relatively few channels. As a result, complaints of busy circuits, lack of privacy, and poor reception were frequent. In addition, there were often long waiting lists to subscribe. By 1983 there were 35,000 mobile telephone subscribers in Canada. Although new mobile-telephone equipment cost about $5,000 per unit, it was much cheaper than cellular to operate.

Cellular radio communication was initially invented and developed by Bell Labs in the United States in the 1960s to solve frequency congestion problems of conventional mobile telephony. As one cellular company executive put it, "The difference between the old mobile system and cellular is the

EXHIBIT 1
The Cellular System

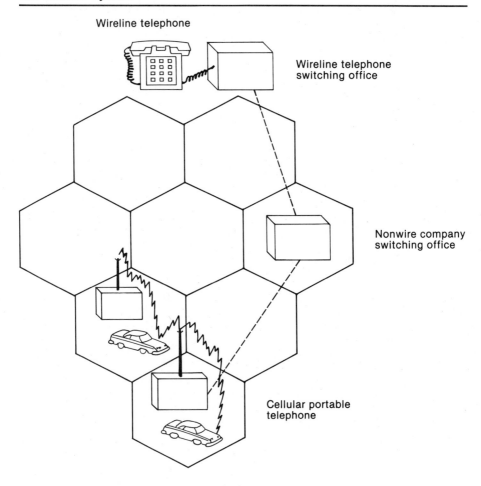

Wireline telephone

Wireline telephone
switching office

Nonwire company
switching office

Cellular portable
telephone

difference between a busy signal and a conversation." The service became
available in the United States in 1979 with an experimental service for
2,000 customers in Chicago.

In 1983, the central body for regulating telephone companies in the
United States, the Federal Communications Commission, ordered the
break-up of telephone monopoly American Telephone & Telegraph Company (AT&T). As a result, when cellular went commercial in 1983, licenses
were awarded on a city-by-city basis to nonwire companies to compete directly with wireline companies in the Bell system. This move created a
duopoly in each cellular market. Within the first year of introduction there
were more than 18,000 cellular subscribers in the United States and the
cellular market in North America was projected to be worth $12 billion total
by 1990—generated equally from the sale of telephones, the usage charges

for the cellular network, and the sale of equipment to operate the cellular network. Cellular had also been successfully launched in a number of other countries including parts of Europe, Asia, and South America.

The Cellular User

Traditionally the mobile-telephone market was composed of corporate executives and high-income entrepreneurs. Use of cellular, however, was not intended to be restricted to people with high disposable incomes, but rather any company or individual who was concerned with improved customer service, competitive edge, increased productivity, better use of resources, and improved accessibility. According to research studies conducted in both Canada and the United States, resource-based industries, construction firms, and services showed the highest level of interest among businesses (see Exhibit 2). In addition, companies with annual sales between $250,000 and $50 million and with more than 10 employees showed a high interest in cellular telephones. Other important findings in the customer profile included above-average appeal to individuals under 45 years of age whose interest in the concept increased as income increased. Managers, professionals, and salespeople showed high interest, and there was an above-average interest in cities with a population of one million or more.

Sales representatives, for example, could make active use of cellular when caught in traffic. They could use their cellular telephone to check for messages back at the office, give directions to secretarial and service support staff, or call a client, lawyer, or accountant, just as if they were actually

EXHIBIT 2
Potential Cellular Users

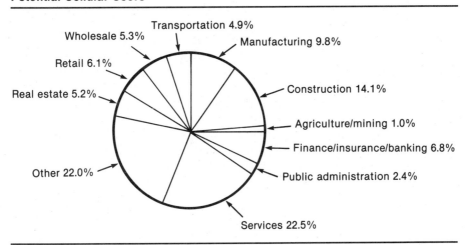

Source: Research Data on Chicago Cellular Market.

in the office. Chartered accountants, who spent considerable time driving between clients' and their offices and who generally billed by the hour, were also identified as potential cellular users. The cellular telephone would allow them to turn driving time into billable time. Similarly, lawyers and consultants could benefit from cellular.

CELLULAR IN CANADA

Size of the Market

In October 1982, the Canadian federal government's Department of Communication (DOC) invited proposals for firms interested in operating a cellular network in any of the 23 cities in Canada which had been identified as cellular markets. Later, the DOC decided to offer a national license rather than a per city license, but limited the first-year market to the 17 million people in Ontario and Quebec; the remaining eight provinces would be available at the beginning of the second year. At stake was a market estimated at approximately $100 million by 1986. Canadian cellular research indicated that penetration rates at maturity could approach the standard American forecast of 1.4 percent of the population. The research also indicated that the number of units per subscriber would average 2.11 for business and 1.49 for households, while the number of calls per day per subscriber was expected to be 7.38 to 10.12 for businesses and 5.63 for households, with an average duration of 2.9 minutes. In addition, the research indicated that the cellular market would reach maturity five years after the system had been launched.

Still the future of cellular in Canada was uncertain. According to a DOC radio policy director in Canada, "We don't know if it's a cash cow or a bust for four or five years down the road." Said another industry spokesperson, "It's only when the general public can afford cellular that cellular (cellular network) operators will start making money." One of the "wireless" companies was predicting 100,000 subscribers in five years, while a "wire" company was predicting only 42,000 subscribers for the same period. Many industry watchers consider even the latter figure inflated, given the high costs to subscribers, the limited population and geographic diversity of the Canadian market.

At $40,000 to $60,000 per channel, setting up a Canadian cellular network would cost $150 million. Even though it was a highly capital-intensive business, competition for the cellular network license was intense.

The DOC License

The federal government had decided that a national scope would be critical for gaining acceptance of the cellular service. However, within the Canadian telecommunications industry, there was no single telephone company that served the entire country. The existing wire telephone companies offered service in regional areas only. Bell Canada, for example, served the Ontario and Quebec markets, and in other regions the telephone service was provided by various provincial and municipal telephone companies such as the British Columbia Telephone Company.

Therefore, to promote competition, the DOC adopted the American policy of granting two licenses in each region—one to an established telephone (wireline) company and another to a nontelephone (nonwire) company. After reviewing applications from numerous companies, a five-year license to establish a cellular network was awarded in December 1983 for a start-up in July 1985. After five years, the DOC would review the operations of the licensee and either renew the license or take it away from the licensee. Each licensee was assigned different frequency blocks, and each cellular geographic area had 666 duplex channels divided equally among the competing networks. Cantel, a new nonwire company was licensed as the only national cellular service provided. The existing wireline telephone companies were granted licenses to establish competing provincial air networks in their respective regions.

Cantel Background

Cantel was incorporated in 1983 by three major Canadian companies, specifically to be in the cellular business. The combined assets of the three partners, Rogers Telecommunications Ltd. of Toronto, First City Financial Corporation of Vancouver, and Telemedia Enterprises Inc. of Montreal, exceeded three billion dollars. Cantel planned to have assets and capital worth $50,000,000 within two to three years. In addition, the company planned to offer all-Canadian technology and all-Canadian ownership with combined experience in communications, administration, finance, and leasing. The company employed 162 people, and was organized into three regions—western, eastern, and central Canada.

In December 1983, Cantel was chosen by the federal Department of Communications to provide a cellular network in 23 major cities across Canada by the end of 1986. According to a Cantel spokesperson, "We believe no significant market exists today in Canada for cellular. The market for cellular must be created." The company's overall marketing/sales objectives, therefore, were to create a market for cellular, penetrate that market, and grow with it. Just as important were the objectives to be profitable and to beat the competition by attaining 50 to 70 percent market share in each product market.

Another of Cantel's objectives was to avoid the problems which resulted when cellular was introduced in a number of states in the United States. As one member of the Management Team recalled:

> Everything looked great in the United States after the first few months' operations. Suppliers could not meet the demand, the dealers were quoting six to eight weeks to get a phone installed, the press were calling it the goldrush of

the '80s. Then all of a sudden the order rates slowed. One month, two months, three months passed. What happened? It came as quite a shock to all observers and everyone had their own explanation. Why did the bottom drop out? What actually happened was that people were not out selling, and those who were buying were the early adapters, the so-called pent-up demand. The companies within the industry soon regrouped, restrategized, hit the street, and started selling. They are just now, after one year, finally back on track selling at the rates they had originally projected in the first place.

Competition

Cantel decided to begin its task of creating a national cellular network in the Toronto and Montreal markets. In these markets, Cantel competed directly against Bell Cellular Inc. (Bell), a division of Bell Communications Systems Inc. The system design, distribution, and cost of both Cantel's and Bell's cellular networks were expected to be similar. Bell Cellular had arranged for Northern Telecom and Canadian General Electric Company Ltd. to design its system, while Cantel had chosen NovAtel Communications Ltd. of Calgary and Ericsson Inc. of Sweden.

Both Bell and Cantel had tried to create "roaming" agreements with other cellular companies in order to expand the geographic scope for their subscribers. Bell was able to obtain connecting rights with 40 American cities, while Cantel obtained rights with 60 American cities.

The rates charged for use of the cellular network also were expected to be similar for Bell and Cantel. Early evidence indicated that Bell subscribers would choose from three rate plans including a $4.95 per month service charge, plus a per-minute charge of $.60 in peak hours (7 A.M. to 8 P.M.) and $.30 at other times. Alternatively, Bell subscribers could choose a monthly base price of $49.95 plus $.25 per minute. Rates being considered for Cantel's network were a $15.00 monthly service charge, plus a per-minute charge of $.50 for the first 130 minutes, $.35 for the next 170 minutes, and $.25 for any time over 300 minutes each month. Off-peak hours (7:00 P.M. to 7:00 A.M.) were to feature time rates at 33 percent off.

Because of the similarities between the two companies (although the Management Team believed that Cantel's policy of building in excess capacity with more cell sites made its network demonstrably superior in performance), the buyers' choice of a cellular air network was expected to be based more on personal preference than on the actual performance of the network (see Exhibit 3). Each company, therefore, faced the task of loading their cellular networks with subscribers before the other one did.

Although the Management Team believed cellular would eventually become a consumer product, the high costs to subscribers would initially attract more business subscribers than household subscribers. A subscriber had to rent, lease, or purchase the hardware; have it installed; get a license from the DOC; get the service started; pay for air service; and secure annual

EXHIBIT 3
Likely Subscribers' Preference for Their Current Telephone Company

Among Businesses

Percent of Respondents Who:	Montreal	Toronto	Vancouver
Prefer present company (Bell/BC Telephone)	22%	20%	25%
Have no preference	58	65	75
Prefer private company (Cantel)	20	15	18

Among Households

Percent of Respondents Who:	Montreal	Toronto	Vancouver
Prefer present company	12%	21%	15%
Have no preference	61	59	55
Prefer private company (Cantel)	27	30	30

equipment maintenance. Total expenses incurred by subscribers before they could make their first cellular telephone call were expected to be similar regardless of which network they chose.

MARKETING CELLULAR

Extent of Operations

In December 1983, as the Management Team contemplated how Cantel could load its cellular network with subscribers, they also considered whether the company should be involved in the provision of a complete cellular package including the promotion, sale, installation and maintenance of cellular telephones.

Members of the Management Team reasoned that cellular consumers had two sets of needs—subscriber equipment needs and cellular service needs (see Exhibits 4 and 5). These needs could be satisfied by some or all of the various business functions required to provide cellular services to consumers; that is, operating the system, manufacturing equipment, selling, installation and maintenance, and financing.

EXHIBIT 4
Consumers' Cellular Needs: Subscriber Unit

Need	Explanation
Information	Benefits of cellular, unit features, where to subscribe, training
Competitive price	Low price through low costs, cooperative buying, reduced margin
Enhanced services	Capability of unit to provide special services, e.g., call-forwarding
Variety	Different models, features, colors
Reliability	Good reception, little downtime
Warranty	Insurance against design defects or poor workmanship
Installation and maintenance	Assurance of quick and reliable installation and maintenance anywhere
Inventory	Ability to take possession of unit immediately
Order processing	Ability to purchase or rent unit
Financing	Ability to spread payment over time
Flexibility	Avoidance of being locked in to potentially obsolete unit

Source: The Canada Consulting Group Inc.

EXHIBIT 5
Consumers' Cellular Needs: Air Service

Need	Explanation
Information	Benefits of cellular, system features, where to subscribe
Competitive price	Low price through low costs, reduced margin requirements
Access to system	Phone number, capacity
Coverage	Ability to use cellular over a wide area
System reliability	Good reception, ability to complete calls
Enhanced services	System software capable of blocking incoming calls if desired or restricting numbers accessed
Complaint handling	Courteous and speedy rectification of system problems
Order processing	Ability to gain quick access to system
Billing	Accurate and documented invoicing

Source: The Canada Consulting Group Inc.

Cantel could simply offer connection to the cellular network, billing, and maintenance services. Alternatively, Cantel could be a full-service competitor, by including telephone sales and telephone-installation services in the above cellular package. Exhibits 6 and 7 provide some assumptions about the way cellular telephone usage would increase, as well as assumptions on pricing of units, and installation and maintenance. Based on extrapolations from American estimates and from Canadian research, 190,000 units were expected to be operating in 23 markets in Canada within five years.

There were a number of options open to Cantel that would have Cantel buy telephones from manufacturers. If one of these options was selected, Cantel would likely sign exclusive agreements with up to six manufacturers of cellular hardware, including Mitsubishi Electric Corporation, a Japanese electrical and electronic giant. Such a decision would ensure that the same

EXHIBIT 6
Growth Assumptions in Penetration of Cellular Telephones (23 markets)

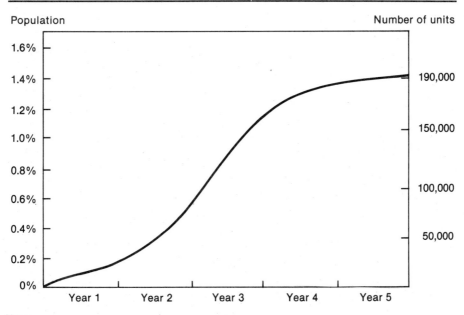

Notes:
  1.4 percent penetration at maturity is based on American estimates and Canadian research.
  Chart assumes all 23 cities start up at the same time, which is unrealistic for Cantel; however, in any individual city, this pattern should apply once cellular service is available from Cantel or the Telco.

Source: The Canada Consulting Group Inc.

EXHIBIT 7
Assumptions on Air Usage, Pricing of Units, Installation and Maintenance

	Year 1*	Year 2	Year 3	Year 4	Year 5	Comments
Number of air min-utes per unit per month	275	275	275	275	275	As more units are in use, mobile–mobile calls will increase air usage. Increasing business use offset by growing importance of infrequent house-hold use.
Unit retail price:	High $2,500 Low 2,000	$2,300 1,500	$2,100 1,000	$1,900 750	$1,700 500	Both sets of estimates based on Motorola Canada, various re-ports, American expe-rience, discussions with cellular unit manufacturers.
Installation revenue	200	150	125	125	125	3 hours installation time.
Maintenance revenue	100	100	100	100	100	Annual parts and labor.

Other assumptions:
  Successive modifications in subscriber units will come on stream during the first five years—these will be acquired both by new subscribers and by current subscribers to replace existing units.
* Year 1 begins January 1985.

Source: The Canada Consulting Group Inc.

product line would be available to all customers. It would also enable Cantel to put together a standard promotion package. Management was also aware, however, that any decision that required Cantel to own inventory would incur inventory holding costs of about 20 percent a year.

Price/Demand Considerations

The selling price of cellular telephones was expected to have a substantial impact on the volume of telephones sold, and therefore on the volume of cellular network subscribers. If telephones were sold to subscribers, Cantel anticipated initial difficulties in loading its cellular network with subscribers. Exhibit 10 (later in this case) shows price/demand data obtained through a survey of 2,400 businesses in the United States. Respondents were asked to indicate their level of interest in leasing cellular telephones at a given monthly price. The curve shows a substantial increase in demand, from 5 percent to 40 percent, as price decreases from $250 per month to $60

EXHIBIT 8
Marginal Income from Cellular Service

Item	Annual Values	Assumptions
Marginal:		
Service	$ 300	$25/month
Usage	825	25¢/minute avg. 275 min/mo.
Total	$1,125	
Marginal costs:		
Bell interconnect	$ 237	Cantel estimate
Customer service	70	2.00/month billing + 20 min./ month inquiries
R&D	21	1.9% revenues per application
Bad debt	16	1½% industry standard
Bell block numbers	14	$117/month for purchasing 100 numbers from Bell
DOC charge	4	$80/channel/year; 20 subscriber/ channel
Depreciation on capital equipment	47	$705 incremental capital/subscriber 15-year depreciation straight line
Total	$ 409	
Actual marginal income per subscriber	$ 716	

Source: The Canada Consulting Group Inc.

EXHIBIT 9
Gross Margin from Each Subscriber Unit

Item	Average Costs to Cantel	Projected Margins As a Percentage of Selling Price
Telephone unit*	$1,300	48
Installation	100	50
Service initiation	10	75
Annual DOC license	36	—
Annual maintenance	40	60

* Technological change made it difficult to predict closely the market life of the telephone unit. Estimates ranged from three to seven years.

EXHIBIT 10
Price/Demand Curve

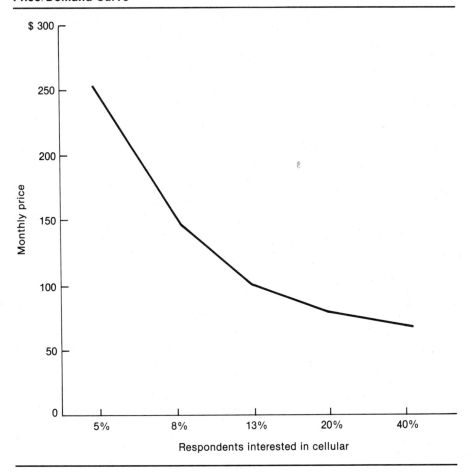

Source: U.S. market estimates.

per month. Cantel's management team knew that one option was to get involved in leasing cellular telephones. They also realized that this option would require a heavy investment in telephones.

Advertising and Promotion

Members of the Management Team believed that, like most new technologies, cellular would require a major marketing effort to create awareness of the technology and understanding of the benefits it provided. They classified potential cellular users as either A, B, or C prospects. 'A' prospects were the early adapters—those people who were usually the first on the block to buy anything new. These people were the ones who would buy products and services they wanted, before they could immediately relate the benefits of the product and services to their needs. As a result, they were not believed to be price sensitive.

'B' prospects were the group of people who had the need but were either not aware of the product or did not see its benefits. The Management Team believed this group was the key one to focus attention on. Another sector of the 'B' group were the people who were aware of the product and its benefits, but could not see the value of the product relative to its cost. This sector had to be sold on the cost/value relationship of cellular.

'C' prospects were the price-sensitive group, whether they had a need for cellular or not. They were the people who would hold off buying until they thought the price was the lowest it would ever be. The Management Team believed this group represented the long-term potential for cellular, but they also believed that cellular as a consumer retail product was "several years away."

With this classification in mind, the Management Team was contemplating several advertising and promotion campaigns in order to convince prospective buyers of their want and need for cellular from Cantel. One campaign being considered was an early subscription bonus. People who became subscribers in February 1985 (five months before the system went live in July) would get their first five months' basic service charge waived, plus 100 minutes of local call charges free for each of the first five months after their numbers were activated. Those people signing in March would receive the same benefits for four months; April for three months, and so on. In addition, a planned direct marketing campaign was expected to generate leads for Cantel. Letters were to be mailed to the presidents of 5,000 firms in Toronto and Montreal, as well as the 100,000 companies which had been identified as prime prospects (that is, construction, manufacturing, and service firms).

The Management Team was also planning a four-stage advertising program. The first stage (starting in early 1985) was geared to introducing Cantel—what it was and what it did. Second, commencing around March 1985, Cantel would attempt to develop the market by advertising the potential benefits of cellular. Advertising customer promotions, the third stage, was expected to generate leads and maximize competitive opportunities to reinforce Cantel's leadership position. This stage, which would include pre-start bonus programs, would commence in May 1985. Finally, an on-line service launch campaign starting in July 1985 was aimed at convincing customers that now was the time to buy. Members of the Management Team did not expect Bell to be equally aggressive in their advertising and promotion efforts. Rather, they believed Bell would allow Cantel to initially take the leading role in developing the cellular market.

DISTRIBUTION

Requirements

Another concern of the Management Team was how Cantel could most effectively distribute cellular to potential end-users. They knew Cantel's distribution system had to be extensive and in place quickly. A quick start-up was considered essential to convert early adopters, especially companies who already had some form of mobile communications. Therefore the distribution system had to have access to companies who currently owned or rented pagers, radio telephones, answering machines, etc.

Another critical element of the distribution strategy was wide coverage of target markets in order to provide education, information, demonstration, and installation. This element required a large network of salespeople who were professional, knowledgeable, and aggressive. In addition, installation facilities which were conveniently located, fast, and reliable would be required. Other important elements of a distribution strategy included an ability to convert successfully from equipment sales to Cantel subscriptions; a continued presence for after-sales service, promotion of added features, and complaint handling; and an ability to remain flexible with distribution agents in order to sell through retail outlets as their importance increased.

In addition, an approach was needed to understand the consumer in each market through research data. Cantel profiled potential cellular users over the first five years in each of the 23 markets. Using demand calculations based on surveys conducted in North American marketplaces of all types of businesses and occupations, Cantel executives were able to determine the probability of a specific business, and even specific occupations within that business, buying cellular. By taking the aggregate of all businesses and occupations for a total marketing area (such as the city of Montreal), the total potential for cellular in that area was calculated.

Postal codes were then overlaid onto this market area to further define the demographics within that postal code. The company was able to determine the demand projection for each postal code area. The total market area was divided into a number of territories that were equal in terms of potential cellular customers and potential dollar value. The number of potential territories was determined by using the five-year projections of demand and the number of salespeople and facilities required to satisfy this demand. The Toronto market, for example, was broken into 12 potential territories.

The list of businesses and occupations in a specific territory was then broken out by SIC code (Standard Industry Classification Codes) such as construction, manufacturing, real estate, transportation, services, etc. The SIC code allowed Cantel to channel direct mail and selling activities to a specific occupation or business group. Using the SIC code, prioritized lists of various target market groups could then be developed.

A specific target market group such as construction was defined as a vertical market. Members of the Management Team believed that a vertical market approach to marketing provided a better marketing appeal than a traditional horizontal approach where the market segmentation was based on income and occupation across a variety of industries and professions.

Distribution Options

The Management Team was considering several distribution options in which to bring cellular service and equipment to potential customers.

1. Established Outlets. One distribution alternative was to create a distribution channel which could be based on established dealers and/or retailers from a broad segment of cellular-related businesses. Retailers such as Sears, Canadian Tire, and Radio Shack had the advantage of competitive pricing and convenient locations. They also had a proven ability to merchandise products already understood by consumers. Dealers with direct sales forces (such as companies selling pager systems) had an established list of customers and a sales organization, as well as contacts with other buying groups. In addition they typically had the ability to provide installation, training, after-sales service, and information and education on product features.

The Management Team knew that a number of large retailers, such as major department stores and major automotive chains, had expressed interest in selling both the product hardware and the subscriptions through their retail outlets. They were not sure, however, how many outlets would be needed to ensure adequate market coverage.

2. Direct Sales Force. Another consideration was to sell direct to end-users with a Cantel sales force. The use of an outside sales force would increase the intensity of the cellular sales effort, but it would also result in substantial costs. Historical averages experienced in the United States for cellular indicated that sales representatives could average four to five calls per day on prequalified prospects. If one assumed that after the initial pent-up demand was met, as in some American markets, that it took three calls to close an order, based on a four-call-per-day rate, each sales representative would be expected to close one order per day, or approximately two hundred orders per year. At that rate, the Management Team realized that a substantial number of sales representatives (at considerable expense) would be required to penetrate Cantel's 23 markets. Each representative would cost Cantel between $50,000 and $100,000 annually in compensation, training, and expenses.

As they contemplated the forecasted growth in penetration of units over the next few years, members of the Management Team were concerned about whether Cantel could hire and train representatives fast enough to beat Bell and Bell affiliates to the market. On the other hand, the Management Team estimated that, in the United States, retailing of cellular accounted for less than 5 percent of all sales, and they believed that, in the early stages, direct face-to-face selling with demonstrations was the key to achieving sales goals.

3. Company-Owned Stores.   A third alternative under consideration was Cantel-owned and operated facilities which would sell both product hardware and subscription numbers, as well as provide installation and maintenance services. These facilities would provide valuable retail visibility in addition to total control in providing a complete cellular package.

However, Cantel lacked initial recognition among consumers, and, following the American example, retailing of units was expected to become very crowded with competitors. As a result, there was no guarantee that margins or market share would hold.

The Management Team estimated that an annual operating cost of $700,000 would be required for each company-owned facility, and that each facility would have to sell 871 units annually in order to break even (see Exhibit 11). This volume would represent 31-percent market share of a one million population market. Cantel's short-term priority was the establishment of its system and a wide distribution system. As a result, some members of the Management Team had some concern that setting up of retail operations could be a drain on management time and energy.

4. Franchise.   The Management Team was considering a "quasi-franchise" distribution channel. Franchises could be owned and operated by

EXHIBIT 11
Break-Even Sales Level for Cantel-Owned and Operated Retail Facilities

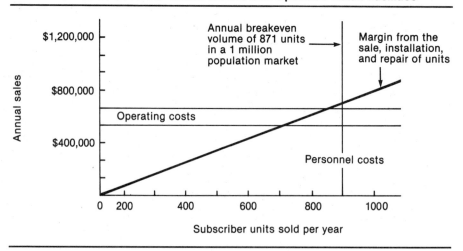

Source: The Canada Consulting Group Inc.

companies with a variety of backgrounds. Each company would bring to cellular a list of established customers. By setting up franchises apart from their major businesses, Cantel could be assured that cellular was receiving the full support and attention of the franchisees. Franchisees could provide parallel cellular distribution by selling to end-users through a direct sales force as well as through retail outlets.

Franchisees also could act as wholesalers by arranging for subagents (independent entities, often dealers, who would have contractual agreements with the franchisees) such as Radio Shack, Canadian Tire, or Sears, to distribute cellular equipment. A large, extensive network of subagents who could market telephones and subscriptions on the franchisee's behalf was considered the key to a successful franchise system.

With a minimum of two direct salespeople and a number of subagents, members of the Management Team believed that the franchise could average a minimum of 60 subscription and telephone sales per month. Higher sales representatives' yield rates and increased numbers of both direct and indirect sales representatives per franchise could increase production and profitability of each franchise.

There were disadvantages to this alternative as well. As a Cantel franchise would be unknown to consumers, considerable expenses would have to be incurred to communicate an unknown technology as well as an unknown franchise to the public. The Management Team estimated that $4 million would be required for advertising and promotion efforts for approximately 12 franchises in the Toronto and Montreal markets. In addition, conflicting interests could arise with franchisees supplying, as well as competing with subagents for end-users.

5. Resellers.   Another option was to follow the strategy of an American company of distributing cellular through resellers. A cellular network company sold blocks of telephone numbers to resellers (generally large companies) then acted as wholesalers of the company's service. They set up a distribution channel through retailers to end-users, and the reseller billed the customer directly. Members of the Management Team thought Cantel could load its air network more rapidly by providing incentives to resellers rather than by attempting to develop a customer base entirely alone.

Unfortunately the American system was not as successful as anticipated. The American company established its own dealer outlets as well as selling through resellers. This dual-distribution channel led to inconsistent billing practices as both the company and the resellers billed end-customers directly. In addition, the resellers often competed directly for end-users with the retailers it engaged.

Bell Cellular in Canada had chosen to distribute its cellular network equipment through exclusive arrangements with manufacturers of cellular telephones, including Canadian General Electric, Motorola Canada Inc., Brooktel Inc. and Tandy/Radio Shack. This route was chosen after the DOC had ruled that Bell Cellular could not use existing Bell telephone centers to carry cellular telephones. In choosing to distribute through manufacturers, Bell Cellular had argued that manufacturers could sell cellular telephones through the manufacturers' established distribution channels. Bell Cellular customers would be able to make arrangements for installation and maintenance, access the Bell Cellular Service network, and complete an application for the DOC license, all in one location.

Members of the Management Team, on the other hand, argued that the product and the manufacturing of the product were too new to lock into a distribution channel that put a company's total future in the hands of a few manufacturers. They also argued that following the American example, the retail role of the manufacturer would steadily decline. Since the inception of commercial cellular in the United States in October 1983, the number of retail sellers had proliferated, and manufacturers had become less important.

CONCLUSION

As the Management Team contemplated the situation they knew they had some difficult decisions to make. Those decisions would have to be made quickly in order to have time to implement any recommendations and in order to beat Bell to the early subscribers. As a young, unknown company competing against "Ma Bell," the Management Team realized Cantel faced an uphill battle, but failure to load the Cantel air network with subscribers could result in a loss of the DOC license in 1989. Without that license Cantel would be unable to exploit cellular, the "mass communication technology of the 1980s."

CASE 5–5

Thompson Respiration Products, Inc.

Victor Higgins, executive vice president for Thompson Respiration Products, Inc. (TRP), sat thinking at his desk late one Friday in April 1982. "We're making progress," he said to himself. "Getting Metro to sign finally

---

This case was written by Professor James E. Nelson and DBA Candidate William R. Woolridge, the University of Colorado. Some data are disguised. © 1983 by the Business Research Division, College of Business and Administration and the Graduate School of Business Administration, University of Colorado. Used by permission.

gets us into the Chicago market . . . and with a good dealer at that." Metro, of course, was Metropolitan Medical Products, a large Chicago retailer of medical equipment and supplies for home use. "Now, if we could just do the same in Minneapolis and Atlanta," he continued.

However, getting at least one dealer in each of these cities to sign a TRP Dealer Agreement seemed remote right now. One reason was the sizable groundwork required—Higgins simply lacked the time to review operations at the well-over 100 dealers currently operating in the two cities. Another was TRP's lack of dealer-oriented sales information that went beyond the technical specification sheet for each product and the company's price list. Still another reason concerned two conditions in the dealer agreement itself—prospective dealers sometimes balked at agreeing to sell no products manufactured by TRP's competitors and differed with TRP in interpretations of the "best efforts" clause. (The clause required the dealer to maintain adequate inventories of TRP products, contact four prospective new customers or physicians or respiration therapists per month, respond promptly to sales inquiries, and represent TRP at appropriate conventions where it exhibited.)

"Still," Higgins concluded, "we signed Metro in spite of these reasons, and 21 others across the country. That's about all anyone could expect—after all, we've only been trying to develop a dealer network for a year or so."

THE PORTABLE RESPIRATOR INDUSTRY

The portable respirator industry began in the early 1950s when polio-stricken patients who lacked control of muscles necessary for breathing began to leave treatment centers. They returned home with hospital-style iron lungs or fiber glass chest shells, both being large chambers that regularly introduced a vacuum about the patient's chest. The vacuum caused the chest to expand and, thus, the lungs to fill with air. However, both devices confined patients to a prone or semiprone position in a bed.

By the late 1950s TRP had developed a portable turbine blower powered by an electric motor and battery. When connected to a mouthpiece via plastic tubing, the blower would inflate a patient's lungs on demand. Patients could now leave their beds for several hours at a time and realize limited mobility in a wheelchair. By the early 1970s TRP had developed a line of more sophisticated turbine respirators in terms of monitoring and capability for adjustment to individual patient needs.

At about the same time, applications began to shift from polio patients to victims of other diseases or of spinal cord injuries, the latter group primarily a result of automobile accidents. Better emergency medical service, quicker evacuation to spinal-cord injury centers, and more proficient treatment meant that people who formerly would have died now lived and went on to lead meaningful lives. Because of patients' frequently younger ages, they strongly desired wheelchair mobility. Respiration therapists obliged by recommending a Thompson respirator for home use or, if unaware of Thompson, recommending a Puritan-Bennett or other machine.

Instead of a turbine, Puritan-Bennett machines used a bellows design to force air into the patient's lungs. The machines were widely used in hospitals but seemed poorly suited for home use. For one thing, Puritan-Bennett machines used a compressor pump or pressurized air to drive the bellows, much more cumbersome than Thompson's electric motor. Puritan-Bennett machines also cost approximately 50 percent more than a comparable Thompson unit and were relatively large and immobile. On the other hand, Puritan-Bennett machines were viewed by physicians and respiration therapists as industry standards.

By the middle 1970s TRP had developed a piston and cylinder design (similar in principle to the bellows) and placed it on the market. The product lacked the sophistication of the Puritan-Bennett machines but was reliable, portable, and much simpler to adjust and operate. It also maintained TRP's traditional cost advantage. Another firm, Life Products, began its operations in 1976 by producing a similar design. A third competitor, Lifecare Services, had begun operations somewhat earlier.

Puritan-Bennett

Puritan-Bennett was a large, growing, and financially sound manufacturer of respiration equipment for medical and aviation applications. Its headquarters were located in Kansas City, Missouri. However, the firm staffed over 40 sales, service, and warehouse operations in the United States, Canada, United Kingdom, and France. Sales for 1981 exceeded $100 million, while employment was just over 2,000 people. Sales for its Medical Equipment Group (respirators, related equipment, and accessories, service, and parts) likely exceeded $40 million for 1981; however, Higgins could obtain data only for the period 1977–80 (see Exhibit 1). Puritan-Bennett usually sold its respirators through a system of independent, durable medical equipment dealers. However, its sales offices did sell directly to identified "house accounts" and often competed with dealers by selling slower-moving products to all accounts. According to industry sources, Puritan-Bennett sales were slightly more than three-fourths of all respirator sales to hospitals in 1981.

However, these same sources expected Puritan-Bennett's share to diminish during the 1980s because of the aggressive marketing efforts of three other manufacturers of hospital-style respirators: Bear Medical Systems, Inc., J. H. Emerson, and Siemens-Elema. The latter firm was expected to grow the most rapidly, despite its quite recent entry into the U.S. market (its headquarters were in Sweden) and a list price of over $16,000 for its basic model.

EXHIBIT 1
Puritan-Bennett Medical Equipment Group Sales ($ millions)

	1977	1978	1979	1980
Domestic sales:				
Model MA–1 Units	1,460	875	600	500
Amount	$ 8.5	$ 4.9	$ 3.5	$ 3.1
Model MA–2:				
Units	—	935	900	1,100
Amount	—	$ 6.0	$ 6.1	$ 7.8
Foreign sales:				
Units	250	300	500	565
Amount	$ 1.5	$ 1.8	$ 3.1	$ 3.6
IPPB equipment	$ 6.0	$ 6.5	$ 6.7	$ 7.0
Parts, service, accessories	$10.0	$11.7	$13.1	$13.5
Overhaul	$ 2.0	$ 3.0	$ 2.5	$ 2.5
Total	$28.0	$34.0	$35.0	$37.5

Source: *The Wall Street Transcript.*

Life Products

Life Products directly competed with TRP for the portable respirator market. Life Products had begun operations in 1976 when David Smith, a TRP employee, left to start his own business. Smith had located his plant in Boulder, Colorado, less than a mile from TRP headquarters.

He began almost immediately to set up a dealer network and by early 1982 had secured over 40 independent dealers located in large metropolitan areas. Smith had made a strong effort to sign only large, well-managed, durable medical equipment dealers. Dealer representatives were required to complete Life Product's service training school held each month in Boulder. Life Products sold its products to dealers (in contrast to TRP, which both sold and rented products to consumers and to dealers). Dealers received a 20 to 25 percent discount off suggested retail price on most products.

As of April 1982, Life Products offered two respirator models (the LP3 and LP4) and a limited number of accessories (such as mouthpieces and plastic tubing) to its dealers. Suggested retail prices for the two respirator models were approximately $3,900 and $4,800. Suggested rental rates were approximately $400 and $500 per month. Life Products also allowed Lifecare Services to manufacture a respirator similar to the LP3 under license.

At the end of 1981 Smith was quite pleased with his firm's performance. During Life Products' brief history, it had passed TRP in sales and now ceased to see the firm as a serious threat, at least according to one company executive:

We really aren't in competition with Thompson. They're after the stagnant market, and we're after a growing market. We see new applications and ultimately the hospital market as our niche. I doubt if Thompson will even be around in a few years. As for Lifecare, their prices are much lower than ours, but you don't get the service. With them you get the basic product but nothing else. With us, you get a complete medical care service. That's the big difference.

Lifecare Services, Inc.

In contrast to the preceding firms, Lifecare Services, Inc., earned much less of its revenues from medical equipment manufacturing and much more from medical equipment distributing. The firm primarily resold products purchased from other manufacturers, operating out of its headquarters in Boulder as well as from its 16 field offices (Exhibit 2). All offices were stocked with backup parts and an inventory of respirators. All were staffed with trained service technicians under Lifecare's employ.

Lifecare did manufacture a few accessories not readily available from other manufacturers. These items complemented the purchased products and, in the company's words, served to "give the customer a complete respiratory service." Under a licensing agreement between Lifecare and Life Products, the firm manufactured a respirator similar to the LP3 and marketed it under the Lifecare name. The unit rented for approximately $175 per month. While Lifecare continued to service the few remaining Thompson units it still had in the field, it no longer carried the Thompson line.

Lifecare rented rather than sold its equipment. The firm maintained that this gave patients more flexibility in the event of recovery or death and lowered patients' monthly costs.

EXHIBIT 2
Lifecare Services, Inc., Field Offices

Augusta, Georgia	Houston, Texas
Baltimore, Maryland	Los Angeles, California
Boston, Massachusetts	New York, New York
Chicago, Illinois	Oakland, California
Cleveland, Ohio	Omaha, Nebraska
Denver, Colorado	Phoenix, Arizona
Detroit, Michigan	Seattle, Washington
Grand Rapids, Michigan*	St. Paul, Minnesota

* Suboffice.

Source: Trade literature.

THOMPSON RESPIRATION PRODUCTS, INC.

TRP currently employed 13 people, 9 in production and 4 in management. It conducted operations in a modern, attractive building (leased) in an industrial park. The building contained about 6,000 square feet of space, split 75/25 for production/management purposes. Production operations were essentially job shop in nature: Skilled technicians assembled each unit by hand on work-benches, making frequent quality control tests and subsequent adjustments. Production lots usually ranged from 10 to 75 units per model and probably averaged around 40. Normal production capacity was about 600 units per year.

Product Line

TRP currently sold seven respirator models plus a large number of accessories. All respirator models were portable but differed considerably in terms of style, design, performance specifications, and attendant features (see Exhibit 3). Four models were styled as metal boxes with an impressive array of knobs, dials, indicator lights, and switches. Three were styled as less imposing, overnighter suitcases with less prominently displayed controls and indicators. (Exhibit 4 reproduces part of the specification sheet for the M3000, as illustrative of the metal box design.)

Four of the models were designed as *pressure machines*, using a turbine pump that provided a constant, usually positive, pressure. Patients were provided intermittent access to this pressure as breaths per minute. However, one model, the MV Multivent, could provide either a constant positive or a constant negative pressure (i.e., a vacuum, necessary to operate chest shells, iron lungs, and body wraps). No other portable respirator on the market could produce a negative pressure. Three of the models were designed as *volume machines*, using a piston pump that produced intermittent, constant volumes of pressurized air as breaths per minute. Actual volumes were prescribed by each patient's physician based on lung capacity. Pressures depended on the breathing method used (mouthpiece, trach, chest shell, and others) and on the patient's activity level. Breaths per minute also depended on the patient's activity level.

Models came with several features. The newest was an assist feature (currently available on the Minilung M25 but soon to be offered also on the M3000) that allowed the patient alone to "command" additional breaths without having someone change the dialed breath rate. The sigh feature gave patients a sigh either automatically or on demand. Depending on the model, up to six alarms were available to indicate a patient's call, unacceptable low pressure, unacceptable high pressure, low battery voltage/power failure, failure to cycle, and the need to replace motor brushes. All models but the MV Multivent also offered automatic switchover from alternating

EXHIBIT 3
TRP Respirators

Model*	Style	Design	Volume (cc)	Pressure (cm H_2O)	Breaths per Minute	Weight (lbs.)	Size (ft.³)	Features
M3000	Metal box	Volume	300–3,000	+10 to +65	6 to 30	39	0.85	Sigh, four alarms, automatic switchover from AC to battery
MV Multivent	Metal box	Pressure (positive or negative)	n.a.	−70 to +80	8 to 24	41	1.05	Positive or negative pressure, four alarms, AC only
Minilung M15	Suitcase	Volume	200–1,500	+5 to +65	8 to 22	24	0.70	Three alarms, automatic switchover from AC to battery
Minilung M25 Assist (also available without the assist feature)	Suitcase	Volume	600–2,500	+5 to +65	5 to 20	24	0.70	Assist, sigh, three alarms, automatic switchover from AC to battery
Bantam GS	Suitcase	Pressure (positive)	n.a.	+15 to +45	6 to 24	19	0.75	Sigh, six alarms, automatic switchover from AC to battery
Compact CS	Metal box	Pressure (positive)	n.a.	+15 to +45	8 to 24	25	0.72	Sigh, six alarms, automatic switchover from AC to battery
Compact C	Metal box	Pressure	n.a.	+15 to +45	6 to 24	19	0.50	Sigh, four alarms, automatic switchover from AC to battery

n.a. = Not applicable.
* Five other models considered obsolete by TRP could be supplied if necessary.

Source: Company sales specification sheets.

EXHIBIT 4
The M3000 Minilung

M3000 MINILUNG

PORTABLE VOLUME VENTILATOR

What it can mean to the User....

The M3000 is a planned performance product designed to meet breathing needs. It is a significant step in the ongoing effort of a company which pioneered the advancement of portable respiratory equipment.

This portable volume ventilator sets high standards for flexibility of operation and versatility in use. The M3000 has gained its successful reputation as a result of satisfactory usage in hospitals, for transport, in rehabilitation efforts and in home care. This model grew out of expressed needs of users for characteristics which offer performance PLUS. It is engineered to enable the user to have something more than just mechanical breathing.

Now breathing patterns can be comfortably varied with the use of a SIGH, which can be obtained either automatically or manually.

Besides being sturdy and reliable, the M3000 can be adjusted readily.

Remote pressure sensing in the proximal airway provides for more accurate set up of the ventilator pressure alarms.

This model has the option of a patient-operated call switch.

AC-DC operation of the M3000 is accomplished with ease because automatic switch-over is provided on AC power failure, first to external battery, then to internal battery.

THOMPSON takes pride in planning ahead

See reverse for specifications

M3000 MINILUNG
Portable Volume Ventilator

SPECIFICATIONS

300 to 3000 ml adjustable volume

10 to 65 cm water pressure

6 to 30 breaths per minute

Automatic or Manual Sigh

Alarms
Patient operated call alarm
Low Pressure alarm and light
High Pressure alarm and light
Low Voltage light with delayed alarm
Automatic switch-over provided on AC power failure. first to external battery, then to internal battery
Alarm delay switch

Pilot lamps color-coded and labeled

Remote pressure connector

Self-contained battery for 2 hour operation—recharges automatically

Power sources
120 volt. 60 hz: 12 volt external battery: and internal battery

Size 12⅝ W × 11¼ D × 10¼ inches H

Weight 39 pounds (Shipping weight 48 pounds)

current to either an internal or an external battery (or both) in the event of a power failure. Batteries provided for 18 to 40 hours of operation, depending on usage.

Higgins felt that TRP's respirators were superior to those of Life Products. Most TRP models allowed pressure monitoring in the airway itself rather than in the machine, providing more accurate measurement. TRP's suitcase-style models often were strongly preferred by patients, especially the polio patients who had known no others. TRP's volume models offered easier volume adjustments, and all TRP models offered more alarms. On the other hand, he knew that TRP had recently experienced some product reliability problems of an irritating—not life threatening—nature. Further he knew that Life Products had beaten TRP to the market with the assist feature (the idea for which had come from a Puritan-Bennett machine).

TRP's line of accessories was more extensive than that of Life Products. TRP offered the following for separate sale: alarms, call switches, battery cables, chest shells, mouthpieces, plastic tubing, pneumobelts and bladders (equipment for still another breathing method that utilized intermittent pressure on a patient's diaphragm), and other items. Lifecare Services offered many similar items.

Distribution

Shortly after joining TRP, Higgins had decided to switch from selling and renting products directly to patients to selling and renting products to dealers. While it meant lower margins, less control, and more infrequent communication with patients, the change had several advantages. It allowed TRP to shift inventory from the factory to the dealer, generating cash more quickly. It provided for local representation in market areas, allowing patients greater feelings of security and TRP more aggressive sales efforts. It

EXHIBIT 5
TRP Dealer Locations

Bakersfield, California	Salt Lake City, Utah
Baltimore, Maryland	San Diego, California
Birmingham, Alabama	San Francisco, California
Chicago, Illinois	Seattle, Washington
Cleveland, Ohio	Springfield, Ohio
Fort Wayne, Indiana	Tampa, Florida
Greenville, North Carolina	Tucson, Arizona
Indianapolis, Indiana	Washington, D.C.
Newark, New Jersey	
Oklahoma City, Oklahoma	· Montreal, Canada
Pittsburgh, Pennsylvania	Toronto, Canada

Source: Company records.

shifted burdensome paperwork (required by insurance companies and state and federal agencies to effect payment) from TRP to the dealer. It also reduced other TRP administrative activities in accounting, customer relations, and sales.

TRP derived about half of its 1981 revenue of $3 million directly from patients and about half from the dealer network. By April 1982 the firm had 22 dealers (see Exhibit 5), with 3 accounting for over 60 percent of TRP dealer revenues. Two of the three serviced TRP products, as did two of the smaller dealers; the rest preferred to let the factory take care of repairs. TRP conducted occasional training sessions for dealer repair personnel, but distances were great and turnover in the position high, making such sessions costly. Most dealers requested air shipment of respirators, in quantities of one or two units.

Price

TRP maintained a comprehensive price list for its entire product line. (Exhibit 6 reproduces part of the current list.) Each respirator model carried both a suggested retail selling price and a suggested retail rental rate. (TRP also applied these rates when it dealt directly with patients.) The list also presented two net purchase prices for each model along with an alternative rental rate that TRP charged to dealers. About 40 percent of the 300 respirator units TRP shipped to dealers in 1981 went out on a rental basis. The comparable figure for the 165 units sent directly to consumers was 90 percent. Net purchase prices allowed an approximate 7 percent discount for orders of three or more units of each model. Higgins had initiated this policy early last year with the aim of encouraging dealers to order in larger quantities. To date, one dealer had taken advantage of this discount.

EXHIBIT 6
Current TRP Respirator Price List

| | Suggested Retail | | Dealer | Dealer Price | |
| | Rent/Month | Price | Rent/Month | | |
Model				1-2	3 or More
M3000	$380	$6,000	$290	$4,500	$4,185
MV Multivent	270	4,300	210	3,225	3,000
Minilung M15	250	3,950	190	2,960	2,750
Minilung M25	250	3,950	190	2,960	2,750
Bantam GS	230	3,600	175	2,700	2,510
Compact CS	230	3,600	175	2,700	2,510
Compact C	200	3,150	155	2,360	2,195

Source: Company sales specification sheets.

Current policy called for TRP to earn a gross margin of approximately 35 percent on the dealer price for 1–2 units. All prices included shipping charges by United Parcel Service (UPS); purchasers requesting more expensive transportation service paid the difference between actual costs incurred and the UPS charge. Terms were net 30 days with a 1.5 percent service charge added to past-due accounts. Prices were last changed in late 1981.

CONSUMERS

Two types of patients used respirators, depending on whether the need followed from disease or from injury. Diseases such as polio, sleep apnea, chronic obstructive pulmonary disease, and muscular dystrophy annually left about 1,900 victims unable to breathe without a respirator. Injury to the spinal cord above the fifth vertebra caused a similar result for about 300 people per year. Except for polio, incidences of the diseases and injury were growing at about 3 percent per year. Most patients kept one respirator at bedside and another mounted on a wheelchair. However, Higgins did know of one individual who kept eight Bantam B models (provided by a local polio foundation, now defunct) in his closet. Except for polio patients, life expectancies were about five years. Higgins estimated the total number of patients using home respirators in 1981 at 10,500:

Polio	3,000
Other diseases	6,500
Spinal cord injury	1,000

Almost all patients were under a physician's care as well as that of a more immediate nurse or attendant (frequently a relative). About 95 percent paid for their equipment through insurance benefits or foundation monies. About 90 percent rented their equipment. Almost all patients and their nurses or attendants had received instruction in equipment operation from respiration therapists employed by medical centers or by dealers of durable medical equipment.

The majority of patients were poor. Virtually none were gainfully employed, and all had seen their savings and other assets diminished to varying degrees by treatment costs. Some had experienced a divorce. Slightly more patients were male than female. About 75 percent lived in their homes, with the rest split between hospitals, nursing homes, and other institutions.

Apart from patients, Higgins thought that hospitals might be considered a logical new market for TRP to enter. Many of the larger and some of the smaller general hospitals might be convinced to purchase one portable respirator (like the M3000) for emergency and other use with injury patients. Such a machine would be much cheaper to purchase than a large Puritan-Bennett and would allow easier patient trips to testing areas,

EXHIBIT 7
Regional Spinal Cord Injury Centers

Birmingham, Alabama	Houston, Texas
Boston, Massachusetts	Miami, Florida
Chicago, Illinois	New York, New York
Columbia, Missouri	Philadelphia, Pennsylvania
Downey, California	Phoenix, Arizona
Englewood, Colorado	San Jose, California
Fishersville, Virginia	Seattle, Washington

X-ray, surgery, and the like. Even easier to convince should be the 14 regional spinal-cord injury centers located across the country (Exhibit 7). Other medical centers that specialized in treatment of pulmonary diseases should also be prime targets. Somewhat less promising but more numerous would be public and private schools that trained physicians and respiration therapists. Higgins estimated the numbers of these institutions at:

General hospitals (100 beds or more)	3,800
General hospitals (fewer than 100 beds)	3,200
Spinal cord injury centers	14
Pulmonary disease treatment centers	100
Medical schools	180
Respiration therapy schools	250

DEALERS

Dealers supplying home care medical products (as distinct from dealers supplying hospitals and medical centers) showed a great deal of diversity. Some were little more than small areas in local drugstores that rented canes, walkers, and wheelchairs in addition to selling supplies such as surgical stockings and colostomy bags. Others carried nearly everything needed for home nursing care—renting everything from canes to hospital beds and selling supplies from bed pads to bottled oxygen. Still others specialized in products and supplies for only certain types of patients.

In this latter category, Higgins had identified dealers of oxygen and oxygen-related equipment as the best fit among existing dealers. These dealers serviced victims of emphysema, bronchitis, asthma, and other respiratory ailments—a growing market that Higgins estimated was about 10 times greater than that for respirators. A typical dealer had begun perhaps 10 years ago selling bottled oxygen (obtained from a welding supply wholesaler) and renting rather crude metering equipment to patients at home under the care of a registered nurse. The same dealer today now rented and serviced oxygen concentrators (a recently developed device that extracts oxygen from the air), liquid oxygen equipment and liquid oxygen, and much more sophisticated oxygen equipment and oxygen to patients cared for by themselves or by relatives.

Most dealers maintained a fleet of radio-dispatched trucks to deliver products to their customers. Better dealers promised 24-hour service and kept delivery personnel and a respiration therapist on call 24 hours a day. Dealers usually employed several respiration therapists who would set up equipment, instruct patients and attendants on equipment operation, and provide routine and emergency service. Dealers often expected the therapists to function as a sales force. The therapists would call on physicians and other respiration therapists at hospitals and medical centers, on discharge planners at hospitals, and on organizations such as muscular dystrophy associations, spinal cord injury associations, and visiting nurse associations.

Dealers usually bought their inventories of durable equipment and supplies directly from manufacturers. They usually received a 20 to 25 percent discount off suggested list prices to consumers and hospitals. Only in rare instances might dealers instead lease equipment from a manufacturer. Dealers aimed for a payback of one year or less, meaning that most products began to contribute to profit and overhead after 12 months of rental. Most products lasted physically for upwards of 10 years but technologically for only 5 to 6: Every dealer's warehouse contained idle but perfectly suitable equipment that had been superseded by models demanded by patients, their physicians, or their attendants.

Most dealers were independently owned and operated, with annual sales ranging between $5 million and $10 million. However, a number had recently been acquired by one of several parent organizations that were regional or national in scope. Such chains usually consisted of from 10 to 30 retail operations located in separated market areas. However, the largest, Abbey Medical, had begun operations in 1924 and now consisted of over 70 local dealers. Higgins estimated 1981 sales for the chain (which was itself acquired by American Hospital Supply Corporation in April 1981) at over $60 million. In general, chains maintained a low corporate visibility and provided their dealers with working capital, employee benefit programs, operating advice, and some centralized purchasing. Higgins thought that chain organizations might grow more rapidly over the next 10 years.

THE ISSUES

Higgins looked at his watch. It was 5:30 and really time to leave. "Still," he thought, "I should jot down what I see to be the immediate issues before I go—that way I won't be tempted to think about them over the weekend." He took a pen and wrote the following:

1. Should TRP continue to rent respirators to dealers?
2. Should TRP protect each dealer's territory (and how big should a territory be)?

3. Should TRP require dealers to stock no competing equipment?
4. How many dealers should TRP eventually have? Where?
5. What sales information should be assembled in order to attract high-quality dealers?
6. What should be done about the "best efforts" clause?

As he reread the list, Higgins considered that there probably were still other short-term—oriented questions he might have missed. Monday would be soon enough to consider them all.

Until then he was free to think about broader, more strategic issues. Some reflections on the nature of the target market, a statement of marketing objectives, and TRP's possible entry into the hospital market would occupy the weekend. Decisions on these topics would form a substantial part of TRP's strategic marketing plan, a document Higgins hoped to have for the beginning of the next fiscal year in July. "At least I can rule out one option," Higgins thought as he put on his coat. That was an idea to use independent sales representatives to sell TRP products on commission: a recently completed two-month search for such an organization had come up empty. "Like my stomach," he thought as he went out the door.

CASE 5–6

Rosemount, Inc.

In January 1975 John Williamson, vice president of marketing at Rosemount, Inc., listens intently as marketing department personnel identify opportunities that might fit into the long-range strategy for the company's Industrial Products Division. The meeting is a significant one for Rosemount, as it must lead to a final version of a comprehensive marketing plan for 1975 that can shift attention from one product line (the Model 1151 series), which had provided dramatic growth for the company during the past five years, to new products and markets. The Model 1151 product line consists of expensive, high-precision electronic pressure transmitters.

Potential new products include (1) an original equipment manufacturer (OEM) offering the Model 1151, (2) an inexpensive electronic gauge pressure

This case was made possible through the cooperation of Rosemount, Inc. The case was prepared by William Rudelius, University of Minnesota, and Steven W. Hartley, University of Denver, as a basis for class discussion rather than for illustration of the appropriate or inappropriate handling of administrative situations. Copyright © 1982 by the Case Development Center, School of Management, University of Minnesota.

transmitter—the Model 1144, and (3) an electronic pressure transmitter designed for nuclear applications—the Model 1153. These products are all in late stages of development. A variety of new markets for current and new products are also under consideration. Rosemount has limited resources available to allocate to further research and development and to marketing efforts; therefore an assessment of the products and markets with greatest potential is vital to the company.

THE COMPANY

Rosemount, Inc., was a spin-off of the University of Minnesota. During the Korean War, the university's Aeronautical Engineering Department operated the Rosemount Aeronautical Research Laboratories at Rosemount, Minnesota. In these labs students and engineers from the University of Minnesota worked on projects for the rapidly growing aerospace industry. One Rosemount project, sponsored by the U.S. Air Force, developed a temperature sensor for military aircraft. Unable to find a manufacturer for the new design, the air force offered the original project members a contract to produce the sensor they had designed. Shortly thereafter, in early 1956, Rosemount, Inc., was formed—with one product and one customer.

Early Years. That first contract provided the means for Rosemount to gain expertise in manufacturing sensors for precise temperature measurement. This in turn enabled Rosemount's participation in the U.S. space program starting in the late 1950s. As the space program grew, the need for advanced space technology provided the opportunity for Rosemount to gain research, development, and manufacturing expertise in sensing devices. Engineering excellence became the basis for success and provided the foundation for growth. In 1960 pressure measurement technology developed by Rosemount allowed the company to introduce high-quality pressure sensors. Again, primary applications were in the space and aircraft markets.

By 1966 Rosemount's annual sales had reached $8.5 million. However, a severe problem was the overwhelming dependence on the U.S. space and defense programs. So in the late 1960s Rosemount tried to apply its unique temperature and pressure measurement technology to industrial markets. Several of these markets were growing and needed expensive, high-accuracy instruments.

Present Situation. Currently Rosemount provides its products to four primary markets—commercial aviation, defense and space, energy, and process and manufacturing. Sales during fiscal year 1974 were well distributed among the four markets, exceeding a total of $32 million (see Exhibit 1). Rosemount considers this recent diversification into four markets to be a key strength for the company.

EXHIBIT 1
Rosemount Financial Data ($000)

Summary of Earnings	1970	1971	1972	1973	1974
Net sales	$13,388	$15,324	$19,012	$23,977	$32,875
Cost of sales	7,628	8,382	10,278	13,296	18,315
Other expenses*.	4,911	5,366	6,466	7,889	11,098
Net income before taxes	849	1,576	2,268	2,792	3,462
Income taxes	393	757	1,194	1,393	1,895
Net income after taxes	456	819	1,074	1,399	1,567
Instrument sales by market:					
Commercial aviation	1,540	2,309	2,671	3,128	3,616
Defense and space	6,100	6,615	8,011	8,180	8,876
Energy	1,330	1,815	3,218	5,114	5,851
Process and manufacturing . . .	3,880	3,880	3,648	4,990	10,916
Total instrument sales	12,850	14,619	17,548	21,412	29,259†
Pressure transmitter sales	100	600	1,350	3,740	8,533†

* Marketing and sales personnel = 10 percent; advertising = 3 percent of selling, general, and administrative expenses.
† Figures include noninstrument sales, and instrument sales include nonpressure transmitter sales.

Source: Company financial statements.

PRODUCT LINES

John Williamson feels that now is the time for Rosemount to assess opportunities for its present and prospective product lines. He leans forward in his chair as George Mills, head of the Product Planning Group, and technical executives summarize opportunities for four key product lines.

Model 1151 Series. As with temperature-related products, Rosemount elected to concentrate on high-quality technology when developing the pressure-related products. Using electrical capacitance to measure changes in pressure, the Rosemount Model 1151 series of pressure sensors established new standards of accuracy and reliability in a wide variety of applications. Exhibit 2 shows advertising copy that describes many applications and design features of the Model 1151 series. Very simply, the basic function of the Model 1151 is to monitor pressure, convert the pressure to an electrical signal, and transmit the signal to a control or monitoring station. The primary component of any pressure measurement device, the sensor, is responsible for the first steps. Because a change in pressure is proportional to such properties as temperature, velocity, weight, force, and strain, many types of sensors are available. The Rosemount product uses a unique technique in which the capacitance, varying directly with pressure, is converted to an electrical signal.

Rosemount manufactures an entire series of Model 1151 transmitters that are used to measure different types of pressure. They include: differen-

EXHIBIT 2
Advertising Copy for the Model 1151

The one to measure up to...

Rosemount 1151 Transmitter In 1970 Rosemount introduced a unique solid-state pressure transmitter that changed the course of transmitter design. Today, the 1151 is the largest selling electronic DP transmitter in North America. It has become the performance standard against which all other transmitters are measured.

Rosemount 1151 Transmitters have been on the job, day in and day out, in the toughest applications customers can find. They have proven themselves in refineries, chemical plants, pulp mills, power plants and everywhere in-between.

Solid design features of the 1151 include: 0.2% accuracy, adjustable damping, integral elevation/suppression, a rugged two-compartment housing to keep the atmosphere out of the electronics, and a modular design that minimizes spare parts investment. These are just some of the reasons for the success of the 1151 Transmitter.

Next time you have to measure flow, level, or pressure, measure it with the transmitter that gives you reliability, stability, accuracy and simplicity that you can depend on, the Rosemount 1151 Transmitter. Call our field sales office nearest you, or contact Roger Thompson, Rosemount Inc., P.O. Box 35129, Minneapolis, MN 55435. (612) 941-5560.

Rosemount

Subsidiaries in Belgium, Canada, Denmark, England, France, Holland, Italy, Japan, Singapore, Switzerland and W. Germany.

---

tial pressure (difference in pressures at two different points in a pipe or system), gauge pressure (pressure in excess of atmospheric pressure), and absolute pressure (pressure above zero pounds per square inch). Of the many models, the differential-pressure type accounts for more than 80 percent of Rosemount pressure transmitter sales.

Now in 1975 the Model 1151 has become the standard product offering for Rosemount and also a standard of the pressure transmitter industry. In his presentation George Mills attributes the wide acceptance of the product and rapid growth in its sales to four key benefits: (1) high-quality performance, (2) ruggedness of design, (3) economical purchase and installation, and (4) reduced maintenance cost. Other benefits, such as specifications, materials of construction, and available options, also give the Model 1151 series a competitive advantage.

Model 1153 Series. In 1971 Rosemount initiated a program to develop a pressure transmitter qualified for nuclear applications—the Model 1153 series. One reason for this decision was the increased acceptance of the Model 1151 in the power-generating industry. Thus, extending the product line to include nuclear applications in the power-generating industry appeared to be an obvious move.

The design and manufacture of the sensor component of the Model 1151 and of the Model 1153 were very similar. But the transmitter component for the Model 1153 required major changes from the Model 1151 design. These transmitter changes were needed for the product to meet specifications established by the government for all instrumentation utilized in nuclear power facilities. Specifically the standards require rigorous aging, radiation, and seismic tests. During the past three years a large portion of Rosemount's research and development (R&D) resources have been allocated to this effort. Although some success has been achieved, additional work is required to "qualify" the product fully for nuclear applications. The estimated unit variable cost for the Model 1153 was $560.00. Rosemount hoped to achieve a 14 percent pretax-return-on-sales goal with this product.

Model 1144 Series.   The proposed Model 1144 pressure transmitter represents an inexpensive version of the more reliable Model 1151 gauge pressure transmitter. The Model 1144 would not have differential-pressure measurement capability. Preliminary design efforts indicated that the Model 1144, which would utilize pressure technology developed for the Model 1151, would meet most performance specifications of competitive products. The new design, which requires an additional $150,000 in research and development to reach the production stage, could also be priced below most other gauge pressure transmitters. However, because the Model 1144 would be similar in function to the Model 1151—an extremely successful product to date—several managers have expressed concern about further development of the inexpensive model. The primary concern was the possibility that Model 1144 sales would reduce those of the Model 1151—that is, the products would compete with, rather than complement, each other. The estimated unit variable cost for the Model 1144 was $280. An 8 percent pretax-return-on-sales objective was set for this product.

OEM Model 1151 Series.   The OEM Model 1151 series pressure transmitter would simply be a Rosemount Model 1151 pressure transmitter with a different color paint. These transmitters would then be resold by another firm for use with its own products. Such an arrangement would (1) allow Rosemount to estimate production needs (through OEM production contracts) and (2) gain sales in new markets. A disadvantage, again, would be the possibility that the OEM products would compete directly with regular Rosemount products. The estimated unit variable cost for the OEM Model 1151 was $345.00. An 18 percent pretax-return-on-sales objective was set for this product.

Support Costs

Each of the product line alternatives would require different levels of marketing, manufacturing, and R&D support. Mr. Mills had solicited rough estimates of these costs from various R&D, manufacturing, and marketing personnel and now presented them to John Williamson and the others in a summary table (see Exhibit 3). Although the information represented subjective judgments, George felt that it was important to get a "feel" for the

EXHIBIT 3
Estimated Financial Data on the Alternative New Products

Product	R&D	Manufacturing	Personal Selling	Advertising	Miscellaneous Marketing Support
			Incremental Fixed Costs		
OEM					
1151	0	$ 10,000	0	0	$40,000
1144	$150,000	50,000	$ 50,000	$60,000	40,000
1153	250,000	100,000	200,000	40,000	40,000

Source: Estimates made by case writers.

costs involved. In addition he noted that Rosemount achieved a 41 percent contribution margin and a 10.5 percent pretax return on sales in 1974 (see Exhibit 1).

COMPETITION

Number of Competitors

The number of competitors listed under the SIC heading of 3,823 "Industrial Instruments for Measurement, Display and Control of Process Variables and Related Products" was 119 in 1974. These companies manufacture a large number of products, including sensors, actuators, indicators, recorders, controllers, and transmitters.

Exhibit 4 depicts Rosemount's major competitors in the pressure transmitter market. Foxboro, the largest competitor, offers a range of products from individual instruments to integrated process management and control systems. Foxboro also offers customized control panels and a host of customer support services, including repair, maintenance, and training programs. Despite the dominance of Foxboro in the pressure transmitter market, Rosemount had been able to gain considerable market share over the past four years.

Competitive Products

Exhibit 5 provides information about competitive product offerings. For example, only Statham, Bourns, Bell & Howell, and Teledyne-Tavis offer a gauge pressure transmitter similar in price and performance to the Model 1144. All other competitors offer products that compete directly with the Model 1151. None of the companies currently offer both products. Informa-

EXHIBIT 4
Pressure Transmitter Market (percent market share of North American sales)

	1970	1971	1972	1973	1974
Fischer and Porter	10%	10%	10%	9%	8%
Foxboro	50	48	44	38	32
Statham	0	0	3	4	5
Honeywell	5	5	7	9	10
Leeds and Northrup	3	5	5	5	5
Rosemount	<1	3	6	12	20
Taylor	15	15	13	11	9
Other*	16	14	12	12	11
Total	100%	100%	100%	100%	100%
Market size ($ millions)	$15	$18	$20	$26	$32

* Includes Bourns, Barton, Bell & Howell, Westinghouse, Bailey, Robertshaw, and Teledyne-Tavis.

Source: Estimates made by case writers from company records.

EXHIBIT 5
Competitive Product Information and Prices

	Type of Pressure Transmitter			
Manufacturer	High-Priced	OEM	Low-Priced	Nuclear-Qualified
Bailey	Yes	No	No	No
Barton	Yes	No	No	No
Bell & Howell	No	No	Yes ($435)	No
Bourns	No	No	Yes ($450)	No
Fischer and Porter	Yes ($585)	No	No	No
Foxboro	Yes ($560)	No	No	Yes
Honeywell	Yes ($565)	No	No	No
Leeds and Northrup	Yes	No	No	No
Robertshaw Controls	Yes	No	No	No
Rosemount	Yes ($555)	? ($465)	? ($430)	? ($900)
	Model 1151	OEM 1151	Model 1144	Model 1153
Statham	No	No	Yes ($485)	No
Taylor	Yes ($600)	No	No	No
Teledyne-Tavis	No	No	Yes ($440)	No
Westinghouse	Yes	No	No	No

Source: Estimates made by case writers from company records and competitors' sales literature.

tion regarding competitors' developmental efforts is difficult to obtain; however, two important points have been raised by Rosemount personnel. First, with the exception of the nuclear-qualified transmitter, the new products being considered by Rosemount could easily be added by competitors. Second, several competitors are probably spending R&D resources on the development of a new "generation" of pressure measurement technology that, if successful, could greatly reduce the position of the Model 1151 series in the marketplace.

Annual Sales of Pressure Transmitters

Sales in the control instrument have been increasing at an annual rate of approximately 20 percent—reaching $1.5 billion in 1973. Instruments account for 60 percent of the industry sales, while 8 percent of the instrument sales are from electronic pressure transmitters. Currently the North American market (United States and Canada) represents 38 percent of all pressure transmitter sales. Pressure transmitter sales in the United States and Canada grew at a rate of approximately 20 percent during the past four years. Market forecasts indicated that sales will continue to increase at a rate of at least 20 percent through 1980. Overseas markets are also expected to grow, although foreign manufacturers are challenging the once-dominant U.S. firms. In fact, non–U.S. firms are even expanding in the U.S. market. These changes have been attributed to growth of the world market and increased technological and business skills in Western Europe and the Far East.

MARKETS

Although Rosemount has diversified into four major instrument markets, the majority of Rosemount and industry electronic pressure transmitter sales are to the energy and process-and-manufacturing markets (see Exhibit 6).

Energy

Rosemount shipments to the energy market rose 63 percent in 1973 over 1972. Because of significant long-term growth potential, development efforts directed at the energy market have been encouraged. The market consists of three submarkets—electrical power generation, oil and gas production and distribution, and oil and gas refining—that have varied sales records.

Electrical Power Generation.   The electrical power generation submarket consists of government- and investor-owned utilities. Rosemount's Model 1151 competes primarily with Foxboro, Leeds and Northrup, Bailey, and Westinghouse products for the fossil-fueled utilities, while only Foxboro

EXHIBIT 6
Pressure Transmitter Sales in North America by Market ($000)

Industry	1970	1971	1972	1973	1974
Process and manufacturing	$ 6,200	$ 7,900	$ 8,200	$12,900	$16,500
Pulp and paper	3,000	3,700	4,400	5,200	6,200
Chemical	3,200	4,200	3,800	7,700	10,300
Energy	8,600	9,900	11,300	12,900	15,000
Oil and gas production and distribution	5,300	6,100	6,700	7,700	9,000
Oil and gas refining	1,600	2,000	2,500	3,000	3,600
Electric utilities: fossil	1,600	1,700	1,900	2,000	2,100
Electric utilities: nuclear	100	100	200	200	300
Other	300	500	400	600	600
Total	$15,100	$18,300	$19,900	$26,400	$32,100
Rosemount					
Process and manufacturing	$100	$500	$ 580	$1,550	$4,140
Pulp and paper	0	200	260	620	1,240
Chemical	100	300	320	930	2,900
Energy	0	40	600	1,532	2,200
Oil and gas production and distribution	0	0	235	955	1,615
Oil and gas refining	0	0	65	162	195
Electric utilities: fossil	0	40	300	415	390
Electric utilities: nuclear	0	0	0	0	0
Other	0	0	20	38	60
Total	$100	$540	$1,200	$3,120	$6,400

offers a competitive product for the nuclear power utilities. Leeds and Northrup, and Bailey, currently dominate the fossil-fueled segment of the market, but marketing managers feel that the lower-priced Model 1144 would be very attractive to these customers.

Although electric utilities will continue to account for a major portion of the U.S. market for electronic transmitters, they will represent a steadily declining share as market growth decreases (see Exhibit 7). This growth pattern reflects a fundamental change in the demand for electric power in the United States; historically, demand grew at an annual rate of 7 percent. Moreover, now in 1975, the United States is just coming out of the 1973–74 international oil embargo, and energy experts expect a shift from fossil-fueled power generation to nuclear power generation. Each type of power plant requires approximately $150,000 worth of electronic pressure transmitters. Twenty percent of Rosemount's sales to the energy market are to electric utilities.

Oil and Gas Production and Distribution (Pipeline). The market for instrumentation utilized in the production and pipeline distribution of oil and gas is projected to have a favorable growth pattern of 15 percent annually through 1985. Underlying this growth pattern is an increasing level of capital expenditures to increase the production of oil and gas in the United States to make U.S. citizens less dependent on foreign oil. Although few new production fields are anticipated during the forecast period, modernization and upgrading projects for existing facilities as well as some

EXHIBIT 7
Projected Growth of Electrical Power–Generating Capacity (domestic and foreign)

	1975	1976	1977	1978	1979	1980	1981	1982	1983	1984	1985
Total power-generating capacity at peak (millions of kilowatts)	476	502	528	555	584	613	641	675	707	745	773
Annual growth (percent)	6.0	5.5	5.0	5.1	5.2	5.0	4.6	5.3	4.7	5.4	3.8
Plant construction:											
Fossil fuel:											
Number	37	39	39	38	35	31	29	27	26	21	26
Size (megawatts × 1000)	15.0	16.0	16.1	15.3	15.6	15.7	12.7	14.6	12.8	11.6	14.8
Nuclear:											
Number	5	7	8	6	11	11	12	15	16	20	12
Size (megawatts × 1000)	5.0	6.5	7.7	5.9	11.0	12.3	13.4	15.8	18.3	23.6	14.1

Source: Company estimates.

replacement projects will continue to be a substantial factor in future market growth. Similarly the number of new oil and gas pipeline installations will be limited. Pipeline expenditures will consist of small-scale projects direct at expansion, modernization, upgrading, and replacement.

Despite increased capital expenditures, Rosemount has not been extremely competitive in oil and gas production and distribution. Currently none of the pressure transmitter manufacturers dominate the submarket. However, because a production field can require up to 600 transmitters for use on injection and recovery wells, low-priced transmitters such as those offered by Bourns, Statham, and Bell & Howell have a slight competitive advantage. Exhibit 8 provides electronic pressure transmitter sales projections through 1985.

Oil and Gas Refining. The least successful submarket for Rosemount has been oil and gas refining. What was previously believed to be a shortage of refining capacity has actually become an excess. Uncertainties of supply, existence of government regulation, and reduced demand for gasoline all were contributing factors. This situation became apparent only recently as refineries trimmed, postponed, or canceled their expansion plans. Foxboro and Honeywell have become the major suppliers of pressure transmitters to this submarket by also selling supervisory control computers. Rosemount is not yet able to supply a control system and therefore cannot assume responsibility for an entire refinery. Taylor and Fischer and Porter also serve as secondary suppliers to the oil- and gas-refining market. The Fischer and Porter company has expressed interest in purchasing Rosemount transmitters as an OEM product. Several Rosemount marketing managers feel that this may be the best alternative for gaining access to orders requiring complete systems.

Process and Manufacturing

The combined market for measurement and control instrumentation in the process-and-manufacturing industry now exceeds $250 million in the United States alone. Although most sales are made to the chemical and pulp-and-paper industries, the market includes other industries such as

EXHIBIT 8

Projected Sales of Pressure Transmitters to Oil and Gas Markets (domestic and foreign; $ millions)

Sales	1975	1976	1977	1978	1979	1980	1981	1982	1983	1984	1985
In production and distribution	40.8	47.3	54.2	62.0	71.9	85.1	97.7	112.0	129.4	148.8	170.7
In refining	16.5	17.6	18.5	19.5	20.7	21.8	23.1	24.8	26.1	27.8	29.4

Source: Company estimates.

mineral processing and food and beverage. The products manufactured by these industries have little in common, but their requirements for control systems and instruments are quite similar. Because accuracy and stability are of great importance in process-and-manufacturing plants, buyers look for very high performance specifications.

Rosemount is not yet a dominant supplier in this market. In fact only recently has any progress been made against Taylor, Fischer and Porter, and Foxboro—the established competitors in the market. To encourage acceptance, Rosemount has adopted a "concentration" strategy that directs most marketing efforts at major, multinational companies (e.g., International Paper, Boise Cascade, Du Pont, Union Carbide). Small firms are contacted through system suppliers and original equipment manufacturers.

Rosemount's annual sales to the process-and-manufacturing market increased over 110 percent from 1973 to 1974. Marketing managers feel that the market has additional growth potential for Rosemount as long as capital expenditures are at a high level. Both the paper and chemical industries have focused on pollution abatement in recent years, absorbing many of the capital equipment resources. Thus, growth potential for the next two or three years appears favorable.

Pulp-and-Paper Manufacturers.   U.S. pulp and paper consumption has grown at a rate of about 4.5 percent over the past several years. Industry experts now believe that the pulp-and-paper industry is approaching 95 percent of capacity utilization. Significant increases in capital spending also indicate that plans for expansions and new plants are in progress. Although recent increases in consumption have brought the industry to record production levels, the rate of increase is declining. Growth rates are likely to continue to decline because domestic per capita consumption is already quite high, many markets appear to be saturated, and the population is increasing at a slower rate. Future growth will come from foreign markets where per capita consumption is still low.

Chemical.   Although capital expenditures in process and manufacturing have fallen somewhat below expectations, oil companies seem to be diverting funds from refining to petrochemical production. Several factors may account for this shift in spending. First, refining capacity is adequate. Second, worldwide shortages of petrochemicals (particularly feedstocks and fertilizers) were caused by the 1973 Arab oil embargo. Capital spending for 1975 is expected to rise to 15.3 percent of sales, or about $4.3 million.

CURRENT MARKETING STRATEGY

Despite Rosemount's recent growth and the apparent success of the Model 1151 series, Mr. Williamson feels that a marketing plan is essential for future growth. Historically the company has used over 50 percent of its research and development budget to develop new applications for current products, test competitive products, and investigate potential technical improvements to current temperature and pressure measurement technology. New-product efforts typically receive "project" status to be reviewed on an annual basis. Marketing resources are allocated to areas of potential growth. As the number of new-product and market alternatives increases, the need for an explicit allocation procedure increases. Focused marketing and research and development efforts seem increasingly important.

Appeals and Product Features Stressed

Company salesmen identify several factors that are critical in competing with other instrument manufacturers:

1. *Reputation.* Reputation is considered the strongest competitive factor. Users looked for reliable and fast service.
2. *Knowledge.* Thorough knowledge of the user's industry is considered critical. Users expect suppliers to know where instruments are required to maintain production efficiency or product quality and where instruments are unnecessary, thus reducing costs.
3. *Technology.* Product reliability and quality are extremely important to users, particularly in applications where product failure would shut down the factory or system or where production quality would be greatly reduced.
4. *Price.* Competitive bidding always plays a role in contract negotiations but is less important than other factors. In fact, many users do not even consider bids from unestablished suppliers.

Sales Efforts

Sales of new products or to new users are very difficult. Users of pressure transmitters are extremely loyal. If the requirement they have been using is reliable and functional, they are reluctant to change suppliers. Users are loyal because they feel the suppliers know their processes and needs. Reeducating a new supplier is too costly in terms of time and does not ensure that the new supplier will be reliable. Even a reputation for high-quality performance in one industry is rarely enough to make a sale to a user in another industry.

Because users expect salesmen to be knowledgeable about Rosemount products, competitive products, and industry applications, significant sales training is required. The marketing department (1) provides regular product-line education sessions for new salesmen and (2) distributes evaluations of competitive products whenever possible. Salesmen often develop expertise in particular industries or applications. Introducing new products or

ignificant implications in terms of marketing costs, as new
mation will be required or new customers will have to be

PLANNING MEETING

A corporate planning meeting is scheduled for the last week of January, and
Mr. Williamson must recommend and support specific resource allocations.
First, he must set goals for Rosemount's industrial trial products and markets for 1975. Second, he must identify the market segments on which
marketing effort must be focused and the product lines to which R&D effort
will be allocated.

CASE 5–7

Paper Mate

The vice president of marketing for the Paper Mate Division of the Gillette
Company, Derek Coward, was considering whether to recommend to top
management the commercialization of a revolutionary new pen. He had just
read the marketing plan presented by the product manager, David Melley,
which proposed that the new pen—code named "Delta"—be introduced to
the market. Delta represented a breakthrough in pen technology. It could be
the first pen on the market containing truly erasable ink. Earlier pens,
claiming erasability, had not sold successfully because the erasure resulted
from abrading away the paper rather than removing the ink.

    Paper Mate's technological breakthrough had been made several years
earlier by Henry Peper of the Gillette R&D Department, who was credited
as the author of the Paper Mate erasable ink patent. Mr. Peper described his
invention as "a complicated process based on a simple idea." The idea was to
combine ink with rubber cement. When erased, the ink adhered to the
rubber cement rather than to the paper. Erasure could be made for several
hours after writing, but after about 24 hours the ink became permanently
absorbed in the paper. Although the combination of a special ink with rubber cement remained the basic technical concept, years of additional research and development had been necessary to bring the pen up to consumer
use standards. To force the sticky fluid to flow around the ball point, for
example, compressed nitrogen was sealed inside the ink container.

This case originally appeared in Victor P. Buell, *Marketing Management: A Strategic Planning Approach* (New York: McGraw-Hill, 1984), pp. 619–25.

PAPER MATE HISTORY

In 1955 the Gillette Company acquired the Frawley Pen Company, maker of the Paper Mate brand of ball-point pens; this company formed the nucleus of what was to become the Paper Mate Division of Gillette.

The first commercially produced ball-point pen, developed by Milton Reynolds, had gone on sale at Gimbels' department store in New York City, October 29, 1945. Ten thousand pens were sold that day at $20 each. While the pens did not work too well, the potential advantages of the ball point versus the conventional fountain pen obviously had captured consumer interest. The Frawley Co. had introduced the Paper Mate brand of ball-point pen in 1949. This pen overcame the principal disadvantages of earlier ball-point pens and led to Gillette's interest in acquiring Frawley. Paper Mate's success over the years had come about because of both internally developed innovations and improvements on the innovations of others. With the addition of its Flair porous pen, the Paper Mate Division became the leader of the pen industry in terms of dollar sales. Paper Mate's divisional and division marketing organization charts are presented in Exhibits 1 and 2.

Paper Mate's parent, the Gillette Company, had net sales of $1.7 billion in 1978 and net profit after tax of $94.6 million. Percent of sales and profit contribution by major lines of business were as follows:

Business	Percent of Sales	Percent of Profit Contribution
Blades and razors	33%	72%
Toiletries and grooming aids	25	13
Braun products (electrical)	24	13
Writing instruments	8	6
Other	10	(4)
	100%	100%

EXHIBIT 1
Organization of the Paper Mate Division (July 1, 1979)

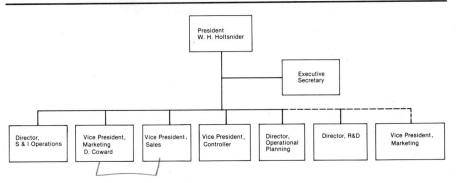

EXHIBIT 2
Marketing Organization, Paper Mate Division (effective February 15, 1979)

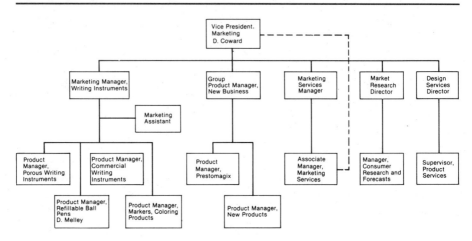

The Paper Mate Division accounted for sales of $141 million and profit contribution of $12.7 million. Sales growth had been at a faster rate than the industry.

THE WRITING INSTRUMENT INDUSTRY[1]

Total industry unit sales grew modestly from 2.2 to 2.7 billion units (23 percent) between 1972 and 1978. Dollar sales grew considerably faster, however, from $319 million to $582 million (82 percent), as can be seen in Exhibit 3. Industry sales follow an uneven year-to-year pattern. Sales show a close correlation with gross national product. Inflation was partly responsible for the more rapid rise in dollar sales, but a more important reason was a shift in consumer demand toward higher-quality products. Exhibit 4 presents the percent change by product type in units and dollars between 1972 and 1978.

Exhibit 5 shows the breakdown of industry sales by type in 1978. The leading product is the ball-point pen followed by the porous-point pen. Ball-point and porous-point pens combined accounted for 88 percent of industry unit sales and 67 percent of dollar sales. Exhibit 6 shows an industry breakdown of writing instrument sales by channels and market segments.

---

[1] As defined by the Writing Instrument Manufacturers Association, the industry is composed of fountain, ball-point, and porous-tip pens; markers; mechanical pencils; and desk pen sets.

EXHIBIT 3
Estimated Writing Industry Instrument Sales, 1972–1978

Year	Units (millions)	Percent Change	Sales (millions)	Percent Change
1972	2,159		$319	
1973	2,341	8.4%	353	10.7%
1974	2,344		370	4.8
1975	2,120	(9.6)	365	(1.4)
1976	2,295	8.3	474	29.9
1977	2,438	6.2	538	13.6
1978	2,742	12.5	582	8.1

Source: Writing Instrument Manufacturers Association, Inc.

EXHIBIT 4
Percent Change by Type of Writing Instrument, 1972–1978

	Percent Change in Sales	
	Units	Dollars
Refillable ball point	(1.2%)	67.1%
Nonrefillable ball point	32.7	43.5
Total ball point pens	16.1	57.8
Total porous pens*	36.1	52.4
Markers	84.0	35.9
Mechanical pencils	17.3	21.9
Fountain pens	(34.7)	60.1
Desk sets	(19.5)	47.9
Total industry	22.7%	82.3%†

* Not broken out by type in 1972.
† Includes products not available in 1972. When these are excluded, industry sales for the categories shown increased by 59° percent.

Source: Writing Instrument Manufacturers Association, Inc.

EXHIBIT 5
Percent of Industry Sales by Type of Writing Instrument, 1978

Instrument	Percent of All Units Sold	Percent of Total Dollar Sales
Refillable ball point	29.3%	29.6%
Nonrefillable ball point	34.7	16.1
Total ball-point pens	64.0%	45.7%
Porous-point writing	19.3	19.3
Porous-point coloring	4.8	1.5
Total porous-point pens	24.1%	20.8%
Markers	8.8	7.0
Mechanical pencils	2.6	8.4
Fountain pens	0.3	4.5
Desk pen sets	0.1	1.8
Other	—	11.7
Total	99.9%	99.9%
Total ball-point and porous-point pens	88.1%	66.4%

Source: Writing Instrument Manufacturers Association, Inc.

EXHIBIT 6
Percent of Manufacturer Dollar Shipments, 1977 (by channel of distribution)*

Retail	45.6
Export	19.3
Specialty advertising	15.9
Commercial-industrial	14.1
Government	2.9
Military	2.1
Miscellaneous	0.1
	100.0

* "Channel of distribution" is the heading used by the WIMA. Marketing students will recognize that some categories are user markets rather than channels.

Source: Special survey in 1977 for the Writing Instrument Manufacturers Association, Inc.

EXHIBIT 7
Distribution Channels for Writing Instruments

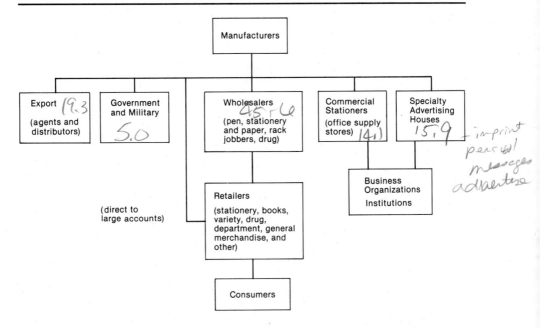

Imports in 1974 were $23.6 million, but represented something less than 6 percent of the dollar value of domestic sales. Imports, however, were growing at a faster rate than the domestic industry between 1970 and 1974.[2]

Writing industry distribution channels are shown in Exhibit 7. Nearly half of industry shipments reach domestic consumer through a variety of retail outlets. Retailers purchase primarily from the four types of wholesalers shown; larger retailers may also buy direct from manufacturers. Over 30 percent of industry shipments are purchased by business organizations and institutions through channels such as commercial stationery dealers and specialty advertising houses. The latter imprint pens with company names and advertising messages. Approximately a fifth of total shipments go into export channels, and the remaining 5 percent are sold to government and military installations.

---

[2] Source: *U.S. General Imports, Schedule A, Commodity by Country.* Bureau of the Census, U.S. Department of Commerce. Import data include categories of writing instruments not included in WIMA figures. For this reason imports probably were less than 6 percent if only the WIMA definition is used.

EXHIBIT 8
Market Share Rankings—Ball-Point and Porous-Point Pens (retail dollar value, 1978)

Ranking	Ball Point	Porous Point
1	Paper Mate and Bic (tied)	Paper Mate
2	Parker	Pentel
3	Cross	Sanford and Pilot (tied)
4	Sheaffer	Bic
5		Spree

Source: Market Research Department.

Market Shares. Exhibit 8 shows estimated market-share rankings of leading pen companies in 1978 based on dollar sales at retail prices. The information is reported separately for ball-point and porous-point pens. It should be noted that share data cover retail sales only.

In 1978 five companies accounted for nearly 90 percent of the dollar value of ball-point pens sold at retail. Paper Mate and Bic were tied for first place. Paper Mate led in the medium- and higher-price refillable pen segments, while Bic led in the lower-price nonrefillable segments. Consequently, Bic was the industry leader in terms of units sold. Six companies accounted for approximately 75 percent of the dollar value of porous-point pens sold at retail. Paper Mate was the clear-cut leader in this pen segment, with Pentel in second place.

NEW-PRODUCT PLANNING AT PAPER MATE

During the several years that the erasable ink pen, Delta, had been in technical research and development, the Market Research Department of Paper Mate had conducted several consumer research studies to try to measure the market potential for an erasable ink pen. The advantage of being able to make corrections when writing with an ink pen had seemed sufficiently obvious to justify continued investment in R&D in the early years. The question remained, however, whether the idea was powerful enough to create a new and profitable market.

The first consumer use studies confirmed that there was significant consumer interest in erasability, but that the writing quality of the pens tested was not acceptable. After R&D had made improvements in writing quality, Paper Mate continued with market research. Three projects which marketing management felt provided significant information are described briefly: (1) a consumer use test; (2) the B/EST test, which provided information on trial and draw; and (3) the Yankelovich Laboratory Test, which showed whether people would buy the new pen under simulated market conditions.

Consumer Use Test. This test was conducted by Market Facts—New York, Inc., who placed products with families in two national consumer mail samples for extended in-home testing. The samples were balanced with U.S. Census data with respect to geographic region, population density, sex, age (between 12 and 54), household income, number in household, and occupation and education of male head of household.

The Delta pen with eraser was placed in 400 households. A branded ball-point pen (the *control* pen) was placed in a separate but matched sample of 400 households. The control pen was a standard ball-point pen with no eraser. Some of the comparative results are shown in Exhibit 9. Respondents were questioned twice—April and June—to see whether there was a difference in response after longer use. For convenience in presentation the results of the two responses have been averaged. While attitudes toward the test pen were generally favorable, potential problem areas were revealed as well.

B/EST Test. This test is designed to give indications of the strength of a new product concept—i.e., will it change people's perception of the marketplace enough to cause them to buy. (A first purchase is called *trial* in marketing idiom.) The test was conducted with panels of 200 consumers in three different shopping malls. The participants were screened to ensure that the panels were balanced with the general population in terms of sex and age and that they were users of ball-point pens. Each panel was shown a display board of eight pens, one of which was Delta. The balance consisted of a cross section of well-known brands of ball-point pens of varying prices. For purposes of the test, Delta was named "Ink Manager." It was presented differently to each panel as follows:

> Panel A—$ .98 disposable
> Panel B—$1.29 disposable
> Panel C—$1.29 refillable

Respondents first read a description of each product and then were shown the display board containing the eight pens. Respondents were then given 10 tokens each, with instructions to choose the three products they would be most likely to purchase. Each product chosen was assigned a minimum of one token. The remaining seven tokens were to be distributed among the same three products to indicate intensity of purchase interest. The results for "Ink Manager" were as follows:

	Panel A, $.98 Disposable	Panel B, $1.29 Disposable	Panel C, $1.29 Refillable
Percent of respondents who assigned any tokens to "Ink Manager"	43%	38%	44%
Percent tokens assigned to "Ink Manager"	15	14	15

"Ink Manager" was the third choice of all panels. In addition to the third-choice ranking and the information on pricing, other findings were reported. Twenty-nine percent of respondents said they were willing to try "Ink Manager." Before exposure to the erasability feature, consumers rated this quality as unimportant, but raised it to important after learning that such a feature was available. The product drew from ball-pen, porous-pen, and pencil users. Purchasers were more likely to be female than male and more likely to be 40 or older.

Yankelovich Laboratory Test.   YLT is a market testing service for new products which attempts to simulate real-world market situations. It can be used by a company to determine whether to go to test market or as a partial substitute for test marketing where the company wishes to avoid market exposure of its new product to competition.

The YLT facility had interviewing rooms, a theater, an experimental store, and facilities for interviewing consumers by phone. Participants, drawn from various organizations such as PTAs and churches, visit the facility in groups. In all, 500 men and women aged 15 to 59 participated in the Delta test. Corrective factors were applied by YLT to compensate for demographic imbalances and biases introduced by the experimental technique. For purposes of this test Delta was named "Second Chance." It was presented in an attractive finished design as a refillable pen with an eraser on the top.

After obtaining demographic information on each participant—as well as the name, address, and phone number—the group saw a popular television show with its regular commercials, except that a commercial for the "Second Chance" erasable pen was also included. Following the show the participants were led into the convenience-type store and permitted to make purchases using their own money. However, all items were discounted proportionally to encourage buying. The store contained a pen section stocked with a representative sample of brands and included "Second Chance." After having the opportunity to shop, the group was broken into small focus groups for discussions about why the participants purchased what they did and why they rejected other brands. Consumers who bought "Second Chance" were contacted at home later by telephone at 30-day intervals to

EXHIBIT 9
Consumer Use Test—Delta versus Control Pen

| (a) Ratings Results | | | (b) Preference Compared with Previous Pen Used Most Often | | |

(a) Ratings Results

| | Percent of Users | |
Rating	Delta	Control Pen
Very good	56%	55%
Good	39	37
Total	95%	92%
Fair	4	7
Poor		1
Don't know	1	—
	100%	100%

(b) Preference Compared with Previous Pen Used Most Often

| | Percent of Users | |
Preference	Delta	Control Pen
Prefer test pen	78%	62%
Prefer previous pen	14	24
No preference	8	14
	100%	100%

(c) Positive and Negative Comments

Qualities Judged—Positive	Percent of Users Commenting Favorably		Qualities Judged—Negative	Percent of Users Commenting Negatively	
	Delta	Control Pen		Delta	Control Pen
Erasability	85%		Writing quality	50%	24%
Writing quality	34	76%	Physical characteristics	13	20
Physical characteristics	17	44	Erasability	6	
Writing immediacy and convenience	12	26	Writing immediacy and convenience	4	13

(d) Uses of Pens during Tests

| | Percent of Users | |
Used for	Delta	Control Pen
Making lists	90%	88%
Addressing envelopes, signing cards	69	72
Personal letters	67	68
Short notes or memos at work	62	61
Signing checks, legal documents	59	75
Working with a lot of numbers	58	48
Taking notes at classes, work or meetings	60	45
Writing lengthy reports	33	24
Homework	34	20

Source: Consumer use tests conducted by Market Facts–New York, Inc.

check for product satisfaction and willingness to repurchase at varying prices. The key results of the YLT were as follows:

1. 38 percent bought "Second Chance."
2. Of the people buying some type of writing instrument, 60 percent bought "Second Chance."
3. On the 30-day call back to purchasers of "Second Chance":
   a. 66 percent were completely satisfied.
   b. The main source of satisfaction was erasability, which had exceeded the expectations of most users.
   c. "Ink smearing/smudging" and "too light a writing line" were the primary performance negatives.
4. The willingness-to-repurchase rate was: after 30 days, 57 percent; after 60 days, 64 percent; and after 90 days, 64 percent.
5. Purchasers confirmed a willingness to pay between $1.50 and $2.00 for the product.[3]

THE PROBLEM

As Derek Coward reviewed the marketing plan for the erasable pen, he was mindful of the high proportion of promising new products that never attain commercial success. He was aware that Delta faced many of the types of risks and trade-offs characteristic of new-product introductions generally. For example:

1. The new product had disadvantages as well as advantages.
2. The favorable results of the consumer sales tests had been obtained under simulated rather than real market conditions.
3. Consumers traditionally are skeptical before trial as to whether a new product will work as claimed.
4. Consumers' purchase habits are not easily broken.
5. Bankers' attitudes toward erasable ink might have an unfavorable effect on consumer purchases.
6. Erasability might prove to be a novelty that would wear off quickly.
7. Erasable pen sales could be expected to draw ("cannibalize") sales from existing Paper Mate products. If it drew from Paper Mate products, however, it should also draw from product sales of Paper Mate's competitors. The question was to what extent in each case.
8. The large commitment of promotional funds that would be required to support the new-product introduction could have a disastrous effect on divisional profits if consumer purchases fell much below the sales forecast.

---

[3] For comparative purposes, the most popular ball-point refillable pens marketed under the Paper Mate brand name at that time ranged in price from $.98 to $1.49.

CASE 5–8

Robinson Chemical Company

THE FUTURE OF HPERS

Over the past seven years, John MacDougall, director of the research labs, supported research and development of high-performance engineering resins (HPERs) at the Chemical Division of the Robinson Company. Mr. MacDougall is concerned about the future of three products which have recently become available to the market. These products complement a specialty resin HPI–50, which in the past five years has found several applications. As head of the Plastics Business Group, Mr. MacDougall must now determine the best marketing approach for these resins for 1985 through 1987. Production estimates are needed due to the two-year lag between the time a capital request is granted and actual production begins. Bill Zerwiske, who is developing the market for these resins, also estimates a minimum of two years to get from the initial sampling of an engineering plastic to a commercial sale.

The HPER market has been targeted as a way for the Chemical Division to support the corporate financial objective of a 19 percent growth in earnings. But questions exist as to the performance of these resins against competitive products. Due to their recent development, little long-term performance data for these products is available. However, Mr. MacDougall feels confident in the products' acceptance if the correct markets can be identified. A survey of the competitors in this industry was obtained to help focus Robinson's future strategy (Appendix 1).

COMPANY BACKGROUND

In 1981 the Robinson Company was one of the top five industrial process and control equipment companies in the United States, with revenues of $1.2 billion from its industrial equipment segment. Corporate dollar sales and earnings have grown at 13.6 percent and 18.7 percent, respectively, compounded annually from 1977 to 1981. The chemical segment contributed 19 percent of 1981 sales ($324 million) to the parent company. This segment develops, manufactures, and sells isocyanates, polyurethane foams and elastomers, other specialty chemical intermediates, and metering and dis-

This case was prepared by Peter J. LaPlaca, School of Business Administration, University of Connecticut at Storrs.

pensing equipment used in the urethane foam industry. The chemical segment has evolved from a producer of a single product line based on one patented technology in the early 1950s into a vertically integrated specialty chemicals producer with a broad range of alternate technologies.

ISOCYANATE TECHNOLOGY

Isocyanates are derived from a complex reaction of petrochemical-based raw materials. Polyurethanes are formed by reacting the isocyanate with another liquid called a polyol in weight ratios from approximately 40:60 to 60:40. A diverse set of polyurethanes and modified urethanes is possible by using different isocyanates (Robinson produces 10 types), polyols (on the order of 100 industrywide), catalysts, and additives such as foaming agents. Urethanes can be either thermoset, where the product can neither be melted nor reused, or thermoplastic, where the product has a melt point and can be reprocessed by injection molding or extrusion, optionally with fillers or fibers.

Robinson markets isocyanates separately (drum or bulk quantity), systems which include both components, as well as pellets of the thermoplastic urethane (TPU—a key to the acronyms used in this case is given in Appendix 2), polyoplast, in 50-pound bags. Applications include rigid foam insulation, seat cushions, shoe soles, fascia in car interiors, and even the artificial heart. The urethane industry is becoming mature in regard to its mainstay markets of automotive and housing, with growth rates of 3 to 4 percent annually and high price competition.

Other isocyanate-based polymers include the high-performance engineering resins (HPERs) polyamide, polyimide, polyesteramide (all based on a 60 percent to 70 percent isocyanate), and the lastest entry, Superpoly, a high-performance TPU. A description of these products, their uses, properties, and target markets is given in Appendix 3.

ISSUES: THE CHEMICAL DIVISION

Since 1980, sales and earnings of the Chemical Division have followed the severe downturn in the economy. Urethane sales to the automobile and building construction industries fell over 25 percent from 1981 to 1982, with a net divisional loss of over $30 million in 1982. Although 1983 sales are expected to improve, recovery is closely tied to the economy. The present situation of soft prices for isocyanates will be further aggravated by new production capacity from Robinson's joint venture in Portugal, which came onstream at the end of 1982.

EXHIBIT 1
Organizational Chart, 1983

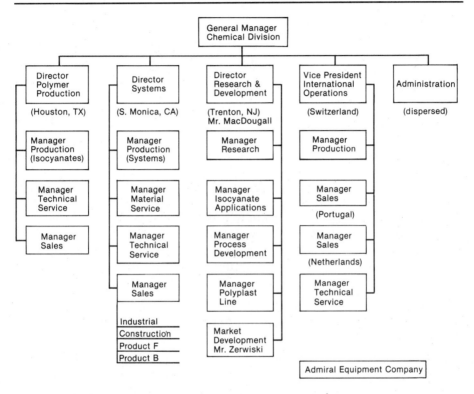

Another issue involves the structure of the Chemical Division (Exhibit 1). The geographic dispersion of customer functions involved in supplying urethanes creates problems in interdepartment communications, in overlapping functions, and in providing a single face to buyers. The subsidiary which manufactures urethane processing equipment (Admiral Equipment Co.) operates independently of the Chemical Division. Admiral's functions could potentially be integrated with the Chemical Division's toward a common goal—that is, to meet fully the customers' needs in order to sell isocyanates.

While it is a publicly traded corporation, the Robinson Company is closely held and strongly identifies with its history in the industrial equipment industry. The following table indicates research and development and capital expenditures as a percentage of divisional sales, and total allocation. Corporate policy implies less support for long-term growth in the Chemical Division, vis-à-vis the Industrial Equipment Division.

Division	Sales Revenue	Expenditure*	
		R&D	Capital
Industrial Equipment	65%	79% (10.7)*	76% (7.4)
Chemical	19	7 (3.1)	12 (4.2)
Agricultural	16	14 (7.5)	12 (4.8)
	100%	100%	100%

* Parentheses show percent of division sales.

Common marketing policies have been upheld for all divisions. Since equipment and controls are sold on quality, little market development has been needed. In selling industrial equipment and controls, high value added and little direction competition ensured high profit margins. During the 1970s these characteristics adequately described the Chemical Division. However, the competitive environment is rapidly changing for specialty chemicals. Intense competition puts pressure on prices; and growth in sales demands knowledge of market opportunities for new products.

PREVIOUS MARKETING STRATEGIES

With the objective of increasing isocyanate sales, Robinson's Chemical Division has developed various new applications for isocyanates. These new technologies provide a faster, more efficient process, greater flexibility in product design, or better performance-to-cost ratios than the existing technology. These are given in Exhibit 2, with their related industrial applications. Much of this technology is protected by patents but may be shared with prospective customers under written agreements.

The small size of Robinson's Chemical Division relative to other chemical companies does not hinder its efforts to support complete customer functions. Robinson provides research and development, production, technical service, and distribution. Although these functions are not physically consolidated, the technical resources are available.

Efforts are being made to improve the flow of communication between these groups. An ad hoc task force, consisting of members of the research, technical service, and sales segments was summoned to concentrate on product development problems, opportunities, etc. This task force was replaced by the Plastics Business Group, which involves market development, sales, and technical service representatives.

Due to Robinson's policy of promoting from within, most salespeople have experience in research or technical service. Specific knowledge regarding isocyanate technology allows the salespeople to field specific processing

EXHIBIT 2
Applications Served by Alternate Technologies

Applications served

Applications served	Laminated panel cores	Pour-in-place insulation	Structural foam	Flexible foam	Elastomers	Binder resin	Reinforcing fibers/fillers	Isocyanurates	Thermoplastics
Automotive: Bumpers/fascia					●				
Seating				●					
Body panels							●	●	
Building construction: Wall insulation	●	●							
Particle boards						●			
Carpet underlay					●				
Adhesives/sealants					●				
Bedding/furniture			●	●					
Sporting goods					●				●
Electrical/electronic: Wire coatings					●				
Business machine housings			●				●	●	
Connectors					●				
Refrigeration	●						●		

Alternate technologies

problems rather than returning to the research or technical service group for a solution.

Two approaches have been used to increase isocyanate sales. In an industry such as automotive or housing, the standard operating procedures and materials used have been established; high capital investments ensure the continuation of these operations. Therefore, to be sold on urethane bumpers or foam insulation, the industry must also be sold on the technology. Robinson has some background in the "nuts and bolts" side of the technology through its subsidiary, Admiral Equipment Co. Also, technical service provides the customer interaction necessary to increase the success rate. Quality control problems resulting from rushing the product through development have been identified, and appropriate corrective actions were taken. Technical service is crucial to solving these problems and protecting the company's image.

Most important for expanding the isocyanate markets is to achieve a final product which is superior to the present one, based on efficiencies gained in the process or final properties. Competitors in the urethane markets will emphasize one or two property improvements or a feature such as an internal release agent to sell a system. By integrating its function, the research group can request and test certain experimental isocyanates from the production facility. Salespeople can rely on technical service or research to try an idea which a customer suggests. This integration of functions has proven to be a useful strategic tool for developing isocyanate sales.

To reduce its dependence on the cyclical industries (automotive and building), Robinson supports product development in smaller, growth-oriented niches. These segments typically have low sales volume of 10–15 million pounds/year but provide high profit margins; additionally their specific needs require significant product innovation, which has contributed to Robinson's recognition as an innovator. Robinson has successfully targeted the sporting goods industry, among others, with its polyplasts line. Polyplasts are highly differentiated into systems that may have low-temperature flexibility (for ski boots), high abrasion resistance (for roller skate wheels), solvent resistance (for tubing), or high resilience (as membrane for the artificial heart).

PRODUCT INFORMATION

Two extremes of thermoplastic resins with different pricing and servicing strategies can be identified in order to differentiate the market: commodity resins and high-performance resins; however, there exists a continuum of products on this scale to sufficiently blur such a discrete categorization. Commodities are becoming highly specialized through developments in fiber reinforcement, additives, copolymer blends, etc., to match unique property requirements. Likewise, as the demand for high-performance engineering resins increases and proprietary knowledge becomes known to the industry, more competitors are drawn into the market. Keen competition and increasing volumes of high-performance engineering resins (HPERs) being sold create a market similar to that for the commodity resins. A definition proposed to simplify this situation is that high-performance engineering resins are not necessarily processed with fibers, fillers, or additives or otherwise blended to attain their outstanding properties.

COMMODITY PLASTICS

The commodity plastics, such as polyethylene, crystalline nylons, polypropylene, and polystyrene are available in grades ranging from general-purpose (GP) and impact grades to highly specialized resins for flexibility in processing techniques or to offer a specific property. For instance, polyethylene materials vary in physical properties from hard to soft, rigid to flexible, and tough to weak; it can be optically clear or opaque. Applications are equally diverse.

In this mature industry, commodity producers have striven to improve process technology, as this is the one point where they can exercise cost control. A company, such as Du Pont, which is integrated backward into energy and raw materials has a further advantage in cost control.

The similarity of each commodity resin across competitors means there are multiple sources. Price competition is keen. Price discounting in fractions of one cent per pound are common in truckload sales (40,000 pounds per truckload). Consumption of these resins is several billion tons annually, and growth rates are generally in the 4 to 7 percent range. An advance in technology, however, can offer substantial growth opportunity, as seen in linear low-density polyethylene (Exhibit 3). The technology for using these resins is well known, as they have existed for 20 years or more. Selling these

EXHIBIT 3
U.S. Commodity Resins

Resin	Consumption* (million)	Growth Rate* (1982–1985)	Price† (per pound)	Sample Application
Polycarbonate	256 pounds	7.0%	$1.62	Business machine housings; bumpers; structural foam
Polyethylene				
High-density	4893	6.9	.45–.48	Bags; gas tanks; 55-gallon drums
Low-density	7725	4.9		
LD (except LLDPE)	6094	−6.2	.28–.37	Films; coatings
Linear low-density	1631	27.7	.35–.39	Chemical tanks; high-strength film
Polypropylene	3783	7.9	.40	Food packaging; automotive parts
Polystyrene				
(except expandable)	2990	5.5	.45	Computer housing
Expandable	442	5.7	.45	Insulation
Polyvinyl chloride	5380	4.2	.52–.58	Vinyl siding; pipe; records

* *Predicast Forecasts* (SIC 282), January 1983.
† *Chemical Marketing Reporter,* March 28, 1983, p. 53.

EXHIBIT 4
Characteristics of Selected Unreinforced Engineering Resins

Properties[1] Resin/ASTM	Flammability (UL rating)[2]	Notched Izod Impact Strength (ft-lb/in)	Head Deflection Temperature (°F)	Load Bearing to 250°F	Moisture Absorption (D 570–A)	Optical Clarity
Acetal[4]	HB	1.4	277	Yes	0.25	No
6 nylon[4]	V–2	1.0	147	—[7]	1.6	No
Polycarbonate[4]	No	14.*	270	Yes	0.15*	Yes
Modified poly-phenylene oxide[4]	V–0	7.0*	190	Yes	0.07*	No
Polyethylene terephthalate[4]	No	1.7	145	No	—	Yes·
Polybutylene terephthalate[4]	V–0	0.5	135	No	0.09*	No
Acrylonitrile-utadiene-styrene	No	6.7*	180	No	0.3	No
612 nylon[5]	V–2	1.0	135	No	0.25	No
63T nylon	V–2	1.3	256	Yes	0.41	Yes
12 nylon	No	1.5	255	Yes	3.1[8]	Yes
Polyarylate[6]	V–0	4.2*	345*	Yes	0.27	Yes
Polyamide-imide[6]	V–0	2.5	525*	Yes*	0.28[8]	No
Polyetherimide[6]	V–0	1.0	392*	Yes	0.25	No
Thermoplastic polyurethane	No	22.*	194	No	0.17	No

* Superior performance.
[1] *Plastics Technology 1982/83,* mid-June, 1982.
[2] UL ratings:

94 HB   *a.* Not having a burning rate exceeding 1.5 inches/minute over a 3.0-inch span for specimens having a thickness of 0.120–0.500 inch.
       b. Not have a burning rate exceeding 3.0 inches/minute over a 3.0-inch span for specimens having a thickness less than 0.120 inch.
       c. Cease to burn before the flame reaches the 4.0-inch reference mark.

   V–0   *a.* Not have any specimen that burns for more than 10 seconds after either test flame application.
       b. Total combustion time is not to exceed 50 seconds for all 10 applications of the test.
       c. Not to have any specimen that burns to holding clamp.
       d. Not have any specimen that drips and ignites cotton 12 inches below.
       e. Not have any specimen with a glow time of more than 30 seconds after removal or second test flame.

Chemical Resistance	List Price[3] (per pound)	Sample Applications	Trade Name	Supplier
No	$ 1.55	Door handles; gears; appliances	Deirin 500	Du Point
Yes	1.73	Tubing; moldings; hot-melt applications	Capron 8202	Allied
No	1.64	High-clarity film; medicine; light fixtures; packaging	Lexan 121	GE
No	1.31–1.92	Business machine housings; electrical; appliances	Noryl 190	GE
No	0.62	Clear bottles; food/beverage packages	Kodar PETG	Eastman
No	1.36–1.70	Interior panels; moldings	Celanex 2012	Celanese
No	0.64	Telephones; plumbing; appliances	Lustran 648	Monsanto
Yes	2.98	Wire jacketing; cable fasteners	Zytel 158L	Du Pont
Yes	3.60	Chemical site glass; electrical connectors	Trogamid T	Kay-Fries
—[9]	3.61	Filter housings; electrical connectors	Grilamid TR55	Emser
No	4.00	Lighting fixtures; snap conn.; appliances	Ardel D-100	Union Carbide
No	17.00	Engine parts: piston, intake valve, push rod	Torlon 4203	Amoco
Yes	4.25	Under-the-hood automobile circuit boards	Ultem 1000	GE
Yes	1.93	Bumpers; agricultural equipment; gears; wheels	Isoplast	Upjohn

V–2 a. Not have any specimen that burns for more than 30 seconds after either test flame application.
b. Total combustion time is not to exceed 250 seconds for all 10 applications of the test.
c. Not have any specimen that burns to holding clamp.
d. Be permitted to have some specimens that drip flaming particles which ignite cotton 12 inches below.
e. Not have any specimen with a glow time of more than 60 seconds after removal of second test flame.

[3] Bulk list prices: *Plastics Technology,* January 1983.
[4] Represents low end of HPERs.
[5] Generally sold with fillers, additives, etc.
[6] Represents high end of HPERs.
[7] Intermittent load-bearing capabilities to 250 F.
[8] Long-term moisture absorption.
[9] Resistant to hydrocarbons, aromatic and aliphatic solvents. Not resistant to strong acids or bases.

Source: *Modern Plastics Encyclopedia,* 1983.

resins requires a minimal technical background or backup. In fact, with the current price/earnings squeeze in the chemical industry, fewer salespeople are selling to wider geographical areas to improve their overall productivity.

ENGINEERING RESINS

Engineering resins are characterized by superior performance in hostile environments. HPERs retain their strength at elevated temperatures and may offer higher impact strength at low temperatures, be especially resistant to chemical attack, or have low frictional properties. Their applications often replace metals. Electrical resistivity and flame retardance also open new electrical/electronic applications. An optically clear HPER will find additional, unique applications. Due to these qualities, HPERs maintain high prices and profit margins relative to the commodity resins. Selected engineering resins, their properties, and uses are shown in Exhibit 4.

Growth of engineering resins in the United States is projected at 9.5 percent annually through 1986, with 1.3 billion pounds to be consumed in 1986, as seen in Exhibit 5. Providing technical support is essential to sales of these resins as they are generally new to the customers. HPERs often demand extra care in processing (such as drying) in order to maximize properties. A strong technical service group, with access to the customer's

EXHIBIT 5
U.S. HPER Consumption and Growth

	Pounds Consumed (millions)		Percent Growth Rate
Product	1981	1986	(1981–1986)
Nylons	280	402	7.5%
PC	245	422	11.5*
MPPO	130	210	10.0
Acetal	97	130	6.0
PBT/PET	60	121	15.0
Polysulphone/PPS	18	25	7.0
	830	1,310	9.5%†

* *Plastics World*, November 1982: 7–8 percent growth through 1980s; *Predicasts Forecasts*, January 1983: 9.1 percent annual growth for polycarbonates.
† Average.

Source: *Chemtech* (12), American Chemical Society, 1982, pp. 552–55.

research and development, is essential for the "hand-holding" aspect of sales and to provide feedback to research for further product development.

The company that can provide three or four different resins, each differentiated within its line, stands a better chance of meeting customer needs by virtue of the breadth of specifications covered. Also, a discounting method is used in selling speciality resins where a buyer can combine purchases of several resins (weightwise) to sum to a truck load and thereby receive a discount in price.

INDUSTRY TRENDS

The engineering resin market has been characterized as risky due to a combination of high capital intensity and extended time period (e.g., 10–15 years) to achieve a positive cash flow. However, the HPER industry is seeing

EXHIBIT 6
Energy Requirements of Plastics and Metals

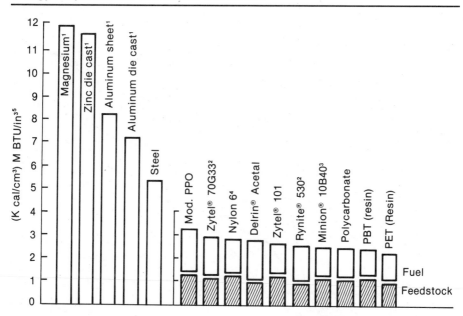

[1] Includes secondary metals usage of 34.5 percent for all sheet, 46 percent for die cast A1, 5 percent for Mg, 5 percent for zinc.
[2] Glass-reinforced.
[3] Mineral-reinforced.
[4] Includes energy credit for ammonium sulphate.
[5] Does not include energy to extract oil, gas, and coal from below ground.

Source: *Engineering Plastics News*, Du Pont Company, Marketing Communications Department.

more competition, as it is a very desirable investment over the long term. A marketing communication prepared by Du Pont indicates a significant cost and energy advantage of engineering plastics over metals, as shown in Exhibit 6. A projection of HPERs' and metals' prices of the same report shows engineering plastics maintaining a very substantial volumetric cost advantage over metals for the next decade and probably into the next century (see Exhibit 7).

EXHIBIT 7
Engineering Plastics and Metals Prices (Historical and Projected)

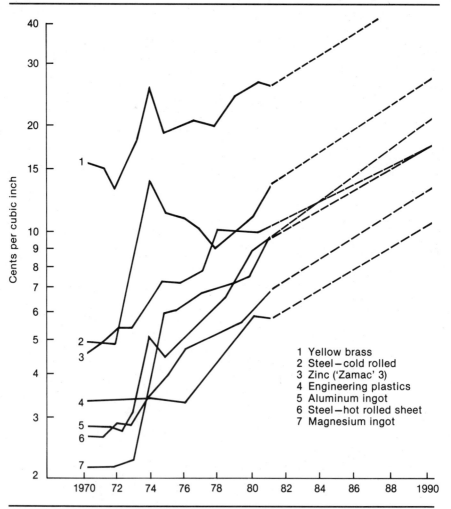

1 Yellow brass
2 Steel – cold rolled
3 Zinc ('Zamac' 3)
4 Engineering plastics
5 Aluminum ingot
6 Steel – hot rolled sheet
7 Magnesium ingot

Source: *Engineering Plastics News*, Du Pont Company, Marketing Communications Department.

As patents terminate, the industry gains access to proprietary knowledge, and the time element in developing new technology is reduced. With technological advances, commodity resins are developing into higher-performance resins. Product improvements have been attained through mineral fillers, glass-fiber reinforcement, flame-retarding additives, etc., and through alloys of two or more resins. These products achieve good price/performance balance with a minimal risk. Examples of this type of product differentiation are GE's Lexan and NORYL product lines. (Appendix 4 details these product lines.)

As trends suggest, price competition in the industry is growing. GE's strength in having NORYL protected by patents does not preclude price attacks, since many resins compete directly for the same application. Also, many applications for resins are concentrated in the automotive market, putting the resin producers at a bargaining disadvantage.

A strong trend in the industry is toward international research, production, and sales functions. Robinson's international operations are increasing due to present cost advantages overseas. Petroleum raw materials can be purchased in the international market for isocyanate production in Portugal and Japan. Distribution costs to the Japanese and European markets are minimized by these overseas operations. However, investments overseas are subject to risks or price controls, fluctuations in currency exchange rates, and differing rates of economic growth.

FUTURE DECISIONS

MacDougall is faced with the problem of identifying an appropriate marketing strategy for the Chemical Division in general and HPERs in particular. This strategy will include identification of target markets, research and development priorities, and pricing, distribution, and promotional strategies. MacDougall felt that the goals identified by corporate would be possible but, given the resource constraints in both R&D and capital expenditures, only if there were very tight controls imposed on a well-developed strategy.

Appendix A   Competitors in the HPER Industry

Exhibit 8 is a summary of the following competitors' strengths and weaknesses and other descriptive information.

E. I. du Pont de Nemours & Co.

As the leader of U.S. chemical producers for 1982, Du Pont is positioned with several strategic advantages. In 1982 the company diversified into energy and chemical feedstocks with the purchase of Conoco Company. This ensures a stable and relatively cheap supply of raw materials for its plastics business. The company is now

EXHIBIT 8

Company	Strengths	Weaknesses
Du Pont	Integrated into petro-chemicals and energy supplies Differentiated product line Pricing power Large commitment to HPERs	Undifferentiated sales force to market both commodities and specialty HPERs
General Electric	Full range of HPERs Backward integrated (phenols) Personal corporate interest High growth, investment plans	Diversified investment interests
Monsanto	Vertical integration backward (petro-chemicals and energy supplies) Vertical integration forward (fabricated products) High R&D commitments	Largely a commodity supplier Sales dependent on economic cycles Undifferentiated sales force
Union Carbide	Proprietary processes/products Excellent properties of HPERs	Largest buyer of ethylene Weak balance sheet Needs strategic approach to market HPERs
Celanese	Vertical integration within company divisions International production	Dependent on externally supplied feedstocks Nonproprietary products/process
Upjohn	Vertical integration backward into chemical feedstocks Worldwide production and sales functions	Little product differentiation within HPER line Needs strategic approach to market specialty HPERs
Emser	Broad specialty chemicals base Worldwide production and sales functions	Dependent on externally supplied feedstocks Small size of operations

EXHIBIT 8 (concluded)

Company	Strengths	Weaknesses
Huels	Vertical integration backward (petro-chemicals and energy supplies) Worldwide sales force	Must purchase (more) feedstocks from external supplies Customer functions based in West Germany
Kay-Fries	Producer of chemical intermediates Worldwide production facilities	Limited customer funds in United States Depends on external supply for feedstocks Undifferentiated sales force
Dow	Active in oil and gas recovery and production Vertical integration into chemical feedstocks	Largely a commodity producer No price leverage; dependent on economic cycles Inexperience in product/market development of HPERs Alternate investment opportunities

less vulnerable to cycles, resulting in a more stable stock. Also, Du Pont takes some of the cash generated by the mature fibers business and invests it in businesses that have more potential for growth, such as plastics.

Du Pont's strategy is founded on a strong technological base, with nearly $2 billion invested in R&D over the past three years. Research and development is aimed at cutting production costs and developing technically sophisticated products. Polymers such as Delrin (acetal resin), Sytel ST (the "world's toughest nylon"), and Kevlar (aramid reinforcing fiber) are examples. These products are used to replace metal parts and in electrical/electronic applications. Many of these compounds are patentable innovations which give substantial improvements over present products.

In the high-volume commodities, such as fibers, Du Pont competes on low cost, quality, and reliability. Capitalizing on the increased supply of raw materials, Du Pont recently announced its entry into high-density polyethylene.

Strategy in selling the high-performance polymers is based on developing niches with high value-in-use. Thus the highly differentiated product line. With 250 products in the high-performance polymer line, each application may consume only 10–15 million pounds/year but retain high profit margins due to this strategy. Sales depend heavily on technical service to educate the end user on processing techniques.

Du Pont promises to remain strong in the HPER industry, with plant additions noted for Hytrel (polyester elastomer) in Luxembourg and expanded production and marketing of Hytrel through a joint venture in Japan with Toray Industries. Production of Kevlar will triple to 45 million pounds/year with a $200 million investment in three U.S. plants, initiated this year. Kevlar is highly specialized, with prices ranging from $6 to $20 per pound.

One weakness noted is that Du Pont salespeople are responsible for the whole line of polymer products. Therefore they cannot be as responsive to individual property or processing needs. The sales force concentrates selling efforts on the high-volume commodities rather than the lower-volume, high-performance resins.

General Electric Co.

General Electric is a highly diversified manufacturer of consumer products, industrial equipment, aircraft engines, medical equipment, etc., with a strong commitment to innovation. The GE Credit Corporation has financed new products since 1943, although mostly from outside companies. With the sale of a natural resources interest in 1983, GE has $5 billion to invest in advanced technology such as factory automation, medical equipment, and man-made materials. The R&D budget of 3.0 percent of sales for 1982 supports this strategy.

GE wants to strengthen its one-third share of the worldwide $2.9 billion-per-year market for engineering resins. The company has a 20-year, $1.5 billion plan to expand, especially into foreign markets. GE is building a $105 million plant for NORYL in the Netherlands, for 1984 production. A $50 million joint venture in Japan will produce PPO resins. The company is building a $20 million technical center to expand the development and technical support capabilities of its plastics business. Recently GE expanded phenol production to assure a high-quality supply for several of its plastics. These plans have the personal support of the chairman and CEO, J. F. Welch, Jr., who rose through the engineering plastics operation to general manager of worldwide operations.

Today GE's line of engineering TPs includes polycarbonate, PPO-based resins, thermoplastic polyester, and the new polyetherimide, Ultem. Priced at $4.25 to $6.50 per pound, Ultem fills an intermediate position in the plastics spectrum in terms of price, properties, and processing.

Monsanto Company

As the largest U.S. chemical company in earnings for 1982, Monsanto's strength lies in its vertical integration. This includes oil and gas exploration and production, petrochemicals, plastic materials, and fabricated products. The commitment of $200 million to research and development (3.2 percent of sales) supports its technological efforts in the traditional areas, new materials, life science, and alternate energy sources. The strategy follows the pursuit of high-value businesses and maximum protection of foreign investments. This is seen in the divestiture of European fibers operations, including nylons (1978), polyesters (1980), and acrylic fibers (1983). Also, a polystyrene business was sold.

Monsanto agreed to join in a venture to produce nylon raw materials with an Italian company. An exchange of proprietary technology with Yoshino opens the Japanese market without a large investment.

Although Monsanto has flexibility in pricing, its position as a leading supplier of ABS and nylon is vulnerable to economic cycles. These products are dependent on the automobile and housing markets. Monsanto is tracking new opportunities in areas outside the acquired business.

Union Carbide Corporation

Union Carbide, number three in U.S. chemical producers' earnings for 1982, has recently completed a portfolio restructuring in an effort to insulate the corporation from cyclic fluctuations. Emphasis is on technological processing advantages of commodity monomers and polymers and some specialty chemicals. UCC is integrated from the basic products into value-added consumer products (e.g., Glad Wrap). It is not integrated into raw materials and is one of industry's largest purchasers of ethylene. Therefore UCC runs the risk of being denied adequate feedstocks during shortages. UCC's priority is to strengthen its balance sheet by trimming capital outlays (R&D expense is about 2.0 percent of sales) and through higher prices for its products.

UCC's entries in HPERs include polysulfone and polyarylsulfone, two specialty resins. The polysulfone capacity of 15 million pounds/year indicates a niche strategy. However, UCC must change its sales strategy to address the special applications suited for the polysulfones.

Celanese Corporation

Celanese is a diversified producer of fibers, petrochemicals, plastics, and specialty polymers, ranking eighth among U.S. chemical producers in 1982. Celanese Research Company performs basic research and development and advanced manufacturing technology. Celanese Mexicana is a multiproduct petrochemical producer. This plant and a proposed venture in Saudi Arabia would rely on local resources and turn out value-added products. Celanese Corporate is a major producer of bulk monomers and fibers. This company attempts to lead the market in reliability, manufacturing technology, or marketing.

Its high degree of vertical integration is apparent in the 19 percent of sales accounted for by other Celanese units. This company produces raw materials for Celcon (acetal copolymer) and nylon 6/6. Celanese also markets Celanex (PBT) and a PET resin, Petpac, for which it is dependent on external supplies for feedstocks. None of Celanese' products or processes are proprietary. Without a reliable supply of feedstocks, it is subject to shortages. Since the devaluation in Mexico, capital spending has been cut back in Celanese Mexicana.

Upjohn Co.

The Upjohn Co. is a diversified producer of pharmaceuticals, agricultural chemicals, and specialty chemicals. The Chemical Division produces the feedstocks and markets these feedstocks and complete systems for polyurethane foams, elastomers, and thermoplastics. As a small chemical company, relative to its competitors, Upjohn's strategy is to target unique opportunities for its specialty products. Manufacturing operations and sales are gaining a worldwide base. However, overseas sales were hurt last year by the strong U.S. dollar.

Over the last two years Upjohn added a high-performance polyamide and TPU to its polyurethane lines. The automotive and construction industries have been targeted in the past for the polyurethanes. In these mature markets, Upjohn competes on price rather than customer service. In order to be competitive with the new HPERs Upjohn, like UCC, must seek new markets for these resins and develop strong technical support.

Dynamit Nobel AG. (Kay-Fries, Inc.)

Dynamit Nobel AG. is a diversified West German company with interests in plastics, chemicals, and explosives. Worldwide sales for 1981 rank DN AG. fifth among U.S. chemical producers. As a recognized trendsetter, the Plastics Division supplies materials for building construction, semifinished products, and high-precision injection molded parts. Manufacturing facilities are worldwide, as are sales subsidiaries. The U.S. subsidiary Kay-Fries is responsible for selling specialty chemicals, intermediate products, and HPERs. Dynamit Nobel's HPERs include high-performance PVC, nylon 12 (Trogamid), and engineering fluoropolymers. Kay-Fries supplies limited R&D and technical service in the United States. The broad product line implies less expertise in targeting markets for HPERs.

Emser Industries Incorporated

The companies of Swiss-based Ems-Chemie Holding AG (EMS) produce and market engineering plastics, synthetic fibers, and agrochemicals; generate electric power (mainly for their own plants); and license, design, and build plants. EMS—Grilon Holding, Inc., in the United States has a production facility (EMS—American Grilon) and a sales company (Emser Industries).

For a relatively young and small company, EMS has high industry recognition in HPERs. EMS's engineering plastics include nylon 6, nylon 12 (Grilamid TR 55) copolyamids, epoxies, and polyester resins. Corporate strategy concentrates on specialty products that are "tailor-made" and therefore difficult to substitute. EMS stresses solid know-how, highly developed application technology, as well as innovative consulting and assistance in the processing of products.

Chemische Werke AG. (Huels)

Huels is a U.S. subsidiary of the West German chemical company, Chemische Werke AG. Chemische has business in raw materials, energy, trading, and petrochemicals. It is 89 percent owned by Vepa, which in turn has proprietary interests in Deminex, and energy exploration concern. Taking advantage of the energy and petrochemical feedstocks available, Chemische Werke manufactures PVC, nylon 6, 6/6, 6/12, and (since 1982) nylon 12. Huels was formed in 1979 specifically for worldwide sales of the HPERs. The 11-member group at Huels offers samples of the nylon 12 and technical assistance. U.S. companies might hesitate to invest in Huels' products due to the research being overseas and the uncertain price-to-performance of this new product.

Dow Chemical Company

Ranking first in revenues and second in earnings for 1982, Dow Chemical Company leads basic chemicals and commodity resins production. Dow has recently gone on a "fitness" program, cutting capital expenditures, shedding assets to retire debt, and selling unprofitable overseas ventures. To increase profitability, Dow acquired a prescription drug manufacturer and has an interest in specialty chemicals and polymers. Dow announced it will be supplying polycarbonates by 1984. Combining its strength in commodities, monomer supplies, and established distribution channels, Dow could become a price leader in the low-to-middle range of the HPER market.

Appendix B Key to Acronyms

ABS	Acrylonitrile-butadiene-styrene
GP	General purpose
HPER	High-performance engineering resin
MPPO	Modified polyphenyleneoxide
PA	Polyamide
PAI	Polyamide-imide
PBT	Polybutylene terephthalate
PC	Polycarbonate
PEI	Polyetherimide
PET	Polyethylene terephthalate
PI	Polyimide
TPU	Thermoplastic urethane

Appendix C High-Performance Engineering Resins

Four isocyanate-based polymers form Robinson's bid in the HPER market. Characteristics are given below:

1. Superpoly, a chemical-resistant, low-moisture absorption engineering resin has exceptional impact resistance. Superpoly competes most directly with other high-impact engineering resins such as PC, impact-modified nylon, and PPO-based resins. Potential end uses range from automotive parts (bumper components, lamp housings) to sports equipment such as skis and tennis rackets. Good weather resistance suggests agricultural applications. This resin is priced at $2.00/pound.

2. HPA–70 is an amorphous nylon which has toughness, strength, solvent and moisture resistance, and a favorable impact strength compared to other nylons. The first application for HPA–70 is a filter bowl housing for motor fuels, although its chemical and alcohol resistance should open up more opportunities in replacing metals and in the electronics segment. HPA–70 is priced at $3.25/pound for truckload sales.

3. Elastamid, a polyesteramid, has good abrasion resistance and solvent resistance at elevated temperatures. It is used with reinforcing steel cable as a motorcycle belt drive. It is priced about the same as Superpoly.

4. A 10-year-old product, HPI–50 has high strength and chemical resistance at extreme temperatures. This HPER serves highly specialized, small-volume

applications due to its price of more than $20/pound. HPI–50 is sold in pellet form, like the first three HPERs, or in a 20 percent solution. Recently a customer has developed a fiber-spinning process for the HPI–50 solution.

Appendix D   Product Differentiation in Engineering Resins

Two highly differentiated product lines GE offers are the PC, Lexan, and an MPPO, NORYL. Lexan is sold in 10 GP grades for optimum processing flexibility, two flame-retarded grades, one high-modulus grade for toughness and impact strength, two blow-molding grades, three glass-reinforced grades, and one high-heat grade. Another example is GE's modified phenylene oxide (NORYL) which includes 16 varieties and unlimited colors for total value versatility. Various grades of NORYL allow processing by injection molding, extrusion, and foam or thermoformed molding.

APPLICATION 5–9

L'Oreal

Chevilly-Larue, France—In a sprawling research complex here, a technician makes a plastic mold of the wrinkles around a woman's eyes. Soon, a computer prints out a graph of the hapless woman's crow's feet and calculates the patch of skin's "wrinkle coefficient."

Nearby, a computer screen displays a blowup of skin wrinkles and calculates the amount of shadow they cast—an approach inspired by a method sometimes used to measure craters on the moon. Armed with such data, scientists at L'Oreal S.A. measure the effect of potential wrinkle remedies.

As populations age around the world, the big French cosmetics concern thinks aging skin provides one of its hottest market opportunities. It says at least 50 of its scientists in this Paris suburb and elsewhere now devote full time to the wrinkle challenge.

This marriage of intensive research with marketing opportunity has helped L'Oreal prosper while its biggest American rivals, Avon Products Inc. and Revlon Inc., have slipped. Between 1979 and 1984, L'Oreal's earnings soared 120 percent (see Exhibit 1), while Avon's declined 28 percent and Revlon's declined 27 percent. In the past three years, L'Oreal has by-

---

Source: Roger Ricklefs, "France's L'Oreal, Now No. 2 in Cosmetics, Targets Lucrative U.S. Market for Growth." Reprinted by permission of *The Wall Street Journal.* © Dow Jones & Company, Inc., October 25, 1985. All rights reserved.

EXHIBIT 1
L'Oreal Earnings (in millions of dollars, converted at current rate)*

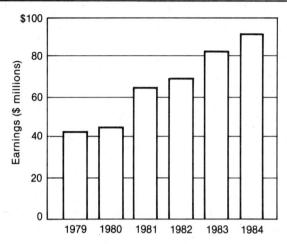

* Figures exclude investment reserves and capital gains and
losses on disposal of fixed assets.

Source: L'Oreal annual report.

passed Revlon and Japan's Shiseido to become the world's second largest
cosmetics concern, outranked only by Avon. Revlon is engaged in an intense
takeover defense against Pantry Pride Inc.'s $1.83 billion offer by attempt-
ing a leveraged buyout through Forstmann Little & Co., which plans to split
the company.

American companies will be seeing more of L'Oreal. "In the next five
years, the United States will probably be the country of greatest growth for
us," says Charles Zviak, L'Oreal's chairman.

Once known mostly for hair-care products, L'Oreal has turned into one
of France's hottest glamour companies. In the past five years, its stock has
more than tripled in value, giving L'Oreal one of the five highest stock
market capitalizations of all French corporations. The company's largest
shareholder, Liliane Bettencourt, is reportedly the richest woman in
France. L'Oreal's recently retired long-term chairman, François Dalle, is
one of President François Mitterrand's oldest friends.

L'Oreal, according to industry sources, spends about twice as much on
cosmetics research as Avon and Revlon. A chemist who concocted France's
first chemical hair dye in his kitchen sink and peddled it around Paris on a
tricycle founded L'Oreal nearly 80 years ago. A chemical engineer—Mr.
Zviak—runs the company today. L'Oreal says it employs 1,000 people in

cosmetics research. It makes the investment pay by applying their talent to everyday products that it thinks the market wants.

A research staff of 40 toiled eight years to give the world Preference, a hair-coloring product, says Mr. Zviak. Though costlier than rivals, Preference quickly captured about 30 percent of the U.S. hair-coloring market. Free Hold, a brisk-selling no-rinse foam that holds hair in place without the sticky rigidity of a spray took five years to develop, Mr. Zviak says. The patent for this everyday product ran to 139 pages.

The company also has at least 20 people toiling on the lipstick challenge. "Lipsticks are a perpetual problem," says Jean-Paul Boelle, an official at the laboratory here. If they are easy to apply, they tend to melt. If they shine nicely but aren't formulated just right, they tend to spread messily beyond the lips.

Besides pushing research, the company also has developed a reputation for marketing and market timing. It introduced the hugely successful Ambre Solaire suntan lotion in the 1930s—just before the government gave in to workers' angry demands for mandatory paid vacations.

After World War II, the company decided to talk the French into using a shampoo, instead of the traditional bar of soap, on their hair. "After the war, people started to see what went on in the United States, and we could see that the time was ripe," Mr. Zviak says. To make the French shampoo-conscious, L'Oreal even sponsored children's shampoo contests in local circuses, which played a big role in French life before television. The tyke who worked up the biggest lather in his hair—with L'Oreal's Dop shampoo—won a prize.

As it became dominant in French cosmetics, L'Oreal started hitting international markets. These markets accounted for about 60 percent of last year's sales of $1.95 billion. "There are very few French companies that are so well implanted in foreign markets," says Henri Sainte Opportune, an analyst with the Paris securities firm of Oddo Desache & Cie.

In the United States, L'Oreal operates through Cosmair, an agency owned by the biggest L'Oreal shareholders as well as the French company itself. Two years ago, Cosmair bought the cosmetics business of Warner Communications for $146 million. This added the Ralph Lauren, Polo and Gloria Vanderbilt fragrances to L'Oreal's U.S. product line, which also includes Lancome, L'Oreal brand cosmetics, Anais Anais perfume and other products. The acquisition also helped boost Cosmair's U.S. sales to $700 million last year, nearly double the figure three years earlier, Mr. Zviak says.

The U.S. operation helped L'Oreal benefit from the dollar's rise in recent years. But, as the company has expenses as well as sales in dollars, the recent decline of the American currency "isn't a big problem if the dollar stays around eight francs," Mr. Zviak says.

The company acquired a big foreign shareholder in 1974 when Mrs. Bettencourt, daughter of L'Oreal's founder, Eugene Schueller, sold nearly half of her L'Oreal stock to Nestlé, S.A., the Swiss food giant. Today, she holds 51 percent of a holding company that owns 58 percent of L'Oreal's stock. Nestlé owns the rest of the holding company. With about 5 percent of Nestlé's stock, Mrs. Bettencourt is also Nestlé's biggest shareholder.

For all of its success, L'Oreal has its share of problems and flops. A perfume named for designer Ted Lapidus fizzled and was withdrawn from the market. More significantly, a pharmaceutical operation has proved slow to develop. Its operating profit declined 12 percent last year to $9.5 million.

But Mr. Zviak says heavy research spending on pharmaceuticals should start paying off in two or three years. Overall, L'Oreal's earnings advanced 12 percent in the 1985 first half to $50 million from $44.8 million in the year-earlier period. Revenue for the half advanced 10 percent to $1.1 billion from $1 billion. Mr. Zviak predicts full-year sales and earnings will advance about 13 percent from last year.

Discussion Questions

1. Contrast and compare L'Oreal's product strategy with those of its competitors.
2. Discuss the advantages and risks associated with L'Oreal's targeting the market for aging-skin cosmetics.
3. Describe and evaluate L'Oreal's positioning strategy.

APPLICATION 5–10

Color Tile, Inc.

When you last tuned in, Fort Worth's Color Tile was concluding the final episode in a series of takeover bids.

Since becoming a subsidiary of Knoll International Holdings Inc. in a buyout engineered in October 1986 by Knoll and Color Tile executives, Color Tile has faded from view. Knoll's stock is not traded publicly and, even operationally, Color Tile has been quiet, adding no stores to the chain of 830 it has in the United States and Canada.

But that is about to change.

President Eddie Lesok, 39, says the company will open 50 stores in the next year, most of them in the Northeast, where its penetration is weak. Fifty more will open in 1989. And the company plans to keep up that pace into the 1990s.

Source: Tom Steinert-Threlkeld, "It's been a quiet few months for the company, but big changes are afoot at Color Tile," *Fort Worth Star Telegram*, April 19, 1988, pp. 3, 5.

And old stores will be made new. Soon 100 of the remaining stores will be redesigned and updated with new merchandising devices. Eventually, all will.

The aim: Improve market share in the home improvement field.

That may be a tall order, because, broadly defined, the home improvement field includes everything from Payless Cashways to your local spa dealer.

But narrowly defined, Color Tile already is faring well in market share. *Modern Floor Covering*, a trade publication, ranked Color Tile as the nation's largest retailer of floor coverings for 1987, surpassing Sears, the nation's largest retailer (see Exhibit 1).

This, even though Sears had more U.S. outlets, 759 to 665. This, even though Sears sells "soft surfaces" and Color Tile sells only "hard surfaces," in Lesok's terms.

EXHIBIT 1

Top 10 Floor Covering Companies (includes tile, vinyl and carpet sales, 1987)

Store	Retail Volume ($millions)*	Number of Locations
Color Tile Fort Worth, Texas	$335	665
Sears Chicago, Illinois	310	759
New York Carpet World Southfield, Michigan	306	99
Abbey Carpet Sacramento, California	166	269
Sherwin Williams Cleveland, Ohio	120	1,500
CarpetLand USA Munster, Indiana	115	57
Carpeteria Hollywood, California	95	67
Standard Brands Paint Torrance, California	75	136
ABC Carpets New York City	60	1
Carpet Fair Baltimore, Maryland	53	27

* Estimated.

Source: *Modern Floor Covering*, January 1988

The soft surface market is about 2.5 times as big as the hard surface market. Soft surface means carpeting; hard surface means ceramic tiles, vinyl and wood flooring.

No wonder Knoll International was interested in Color Tile. The company had become the No. 1 retailer of floor coverings competing with one hand tied behind its back, leaving the bulk of the market—carpeting—to others.

"Color Tile has enormous potential in a market where it was already dominant and could become more dominant through improved product offerings and customer support," Knoll Chairman Marshall Cogan says.

Customer support at Color Tile means doing such things as providing necessary tools for the job to customers rent-free and giving free advice on laying flooring—things competitors won't do.

"We're a fashion business," Color Tile Executive Vice President Larry Nagle says. "Part of our fashion is service. It's our luxury."

But more critically, it's also an opportunity to sell. An attentive salesperson gets the customer's ear. If that ear is attentive, other parts of the body may follow the instructions that are heard.

"You encourage them to do more and buy more," Cogan says succinctly.

Which has led, even in this seemingly dormant period for Color Tile, to substantial growth in the quiet world of unreported financial figures.

For the 12 months ended December 31 1987, Color Tile recorded $488 million in sales and an operating profit of $60 million (see Exhibit 2).

Those sales are about $100 million above sales reported in the last full year Color Tile was a public company, the 12-month period that ended June 30, 1986. Operating profits also were up nearly a third. Sales in that final fiscal year were $387 million, and operating profit was $45.8 million.

With growth like that without any new stores, "there's clearly great growth opportunity out there," Lesok says.

The push will be into the Northeast, where Lesok says the company's

EXHIBIT 2
Color Tile Sales and Profit ($millions)

Fiscal Year	Sales	Operating Profit*
6/30/83	$241.1	$32.4
6/30/84	282.8	35.7
6/30/85	347.2	45.9
6/30/86	387.1	45.8
12/31/87	488.0	60.0

* Profit before taxes, depreciation, interest.

Source: Color Tile, Inc.

market share is light, and urban areas, where Knoll Managing Director Judith Woodfin says some home improvement retailers fear to tread.

"There is a do-it-yourself market that resides in cities," she asserts.

Achieving name recognition in those markets probably won't be difficult. In a nationwide survey conducted in November by New York's Grey Advertising Inc., Color Tile registered almost universal recognition among respondents who either had undertaken a do-it-yourself project in the last year or were planning one in the next year. Fully 97 percent of those respondents, 27 percent of all those surveyed, knew the Color Tile name and recognized it as selling hard floor coverings.

Even though that may translate into relatively low recognition among the public, it's the do-it-yourselfers that count.

"The important thing is that Color Tile is a store that is basically synonymous with do-it-yourself tile and wall-covering among the people who are doing that," says Tim Teran, Grey's vice president and associate director of marketing and research.

Both the new and retrofitted stores also will take on a new merchandising look aimed at boosting individual store sales. Walls, not just tables, will be used to display tiles. Product sample areas will be expanded. Merchandise will be stocked in a back room so the front of the store can focus on sales.

All that, Lesok hopes, will in turn create "more efficient visual merchandising," which in turn "will attract a more upscale customer." Not that Color Tile's average customer is a slouch now, with a typical household income of $45,000.

At the same time, the company will try to drive down costs. Knoll's policy is to make its subsidiaries the low-cost producers in their fields. One of the ways that can be achieved is through volume purchasing. Other Knoll subsidiaries, such as General Felt Industries, also buy adhesives to attach flooring to floors, so they are buying adhesives jointly to drive down the purchase price.

And like its electronic brethren at Tandy Corp., Color Tile manufactures products when needed. Three U.S. and three Canadian plants manufacture 38 percent of what the company sells. Color Tile buys the rest both domestically and abroad, again using volume to drive down costs. In Italy, which is the fashion leader in ceramic tile, Woodfin says, Color Tile buys 25 percent of all the tile produced.

Talk of expanding Color Tile's offerings to carpet frequently is heard, particularly now that the company is part of Knoll, which has other subsidiaries involved in carpet cushion.

So far, Color Tile management continues to reject a move to soft surfaces. The worries: Competing properly in carpet would require a huge devotion of resources, as well as development of talents the company doesn't have. It also could hurt sales of the company's bulwark products.

Still, Barry Witt, senior vice president and chief financial officer, says the company may begin testing carpet sales in some stores in a few years.

In the meantime, it will expand its offerings of hard surfaces. The aim, of course, is to be the hard-surface superstore, even at 4,200 square feet per store.

For instance, Tony Greco, the company's group vice president for marketing, this year is trying a new, high-priced line of tiles, Armstrong's Century Solarian line. At $2.39 a tile, "that's a high price point" for Color Tile, he says, but "it's taken off like a rocket."

The reason, he thinks, is that customers increasingly are upgrading their homes, seeking more prestigious surfaces. Indeed, 10 years ago one of the company's hottest sellers was tiles of—you guessed it—carpet. Now ceramic tiles account for 35 percent of sales.

Still, the offerings have to be broad enough and the service strong enough to keep the customer from going to Home Depot.

"When you've seen what we have," Lesok says, "you've seen what is available in the marketplace."

Discussion Questions

1. Is Color Tile using a market segmentation strategy? Discuss.
2. Critically evaluate whether Color Tile should expand into other types of floor covering and/or other home improvement products.
3. Analyze Color Tile's strategic situation.
4. Develop a marketing strategy for Color Tile.

APPLICATION 5-11

MADD

A group of scruffy toughs on motorcycles drive up to an elegant Victorian mansion. As a butler greets them, they are transformed magically into well-groomed aristocrats.

Their drink: Harley-Davidson Wine Cooler. Uncapped, it roars like a motorcycle.

Commercials such as this one, which aired recently on television in California, are splitting the ranks of the five-year-old national crusade

---

against drunk driving. Some crusaders, health activists who say such ads perpetuate ties between drinking and driving, want to ban the ads or at least get equal time for anti-alcohol blasts. But the alcohol and broadcasting industries—with the notable support of Mothers Against Drunk Driving, or MADD—vehemently oppose those ideas.

The crusade is split on other issues as well. The health groups want to campaign against drunk driving to apply its considerable political muscle against alcohol problems broadly. Besides attacking ads, they seek health warnings on beer, wine, and liquor containers. They also seek higher taxes on alcohol, and tougher licensing laws that would limit sales of alcoholic drinks at concerts and other events where drivers are deemed likely to drink.

But others take less of a hard line on drinking hard stuff. "We aren't against drinking," says Donald Schaet, the executive director of MADD, which aims to attack alcohol abuse, not alcohol itself. "We are just trying to encourage responsible behavior."

MADD and allies have prompted many states to raise their drinking age and police and courts to crack down on drunk drivers. It gets most of its funds from grass-roots contributions. But MADD money also has come from Anheuser-Busch Inc., the mother of Budweiser beer.

Alcohol producers and broadcasters, fearing the imposition of even tougher anti-alcohol policies, are lending considerable support to the softer-stance crusaders. Anheuser-Busch has given at least $70,000 to MADD. Broadcasters also have courted MADD. The National Broadcasting Co. network televised a "docudrama" about the group's founder and former head, Candy Lightner, whose daughter was killed by a drunk driver. And the National Association of Broadcasters, a major trade group, featured Mrs. Lightner in public-service announcements against drunk driving.

Industry groups have also sought to ingratiate themselves with a MADD lookalike called SADD, or Students Against Driving Drunk. Anheuser-Busch has given SADD at least $200,000, a substantial part of the group's budget. Donald Shea, the president of the U.S. Brewers Association, is one of the most active members of SADD's board.

Like MADD, SADD says it isn't battling drinking per se, and it sees no reason to refuse industry money. Says Robert Anastas, SADD's executive director: "The guy who makes beer or crushes grapes isn't the devil."

But anti-alcohol hard-liners suggest that MADD and SADD are being co-opted. SADD's "contract," in which teenagers agree to call a parent for a ride if they get too drunk to drive, subtly supports teenage drinking, argues Allen Rice, the executive director of the Michigan Interfaith Council on Alcohol Problems, a church-financed group.

"SADD's message suggests that drinking itself is okay—a fact of life to be accepted by society," says Mr. Rice.

Especially upset about the approaches of MADD and SADD are the health lobbies, many of which have labored in obscurity for years. Says

James Mosher, an associate director of the Prevention Research Center, a California think tank: "If we are to prevent (drunk driving) we must do more than threaten, cajole or persuade individuals to act more responsibly."

Infighting among these groups has always existed, but it has worsened since last year when the split over anti-alcohol ads developed. MADD has drawn new fire by declining to join a coalition that is lobbying in Congress to require the television networks to carry "counter-messages" to alcohol commercials.

Its critics say MADD's posture stems from its ties to broadcasters. "I oppose alcohol advertising, and the broadcasters won't have anything to do with me," adds Doris Aiken, the president of Remove Intoxicated Drivers, a group that says it refuses alcohol-industry money.

MADD dismisses such criticism. Says the group's Mr. Schaet: "There don't seem to be any valid studies to show that advertising contributes to drunk driving."

While refusing to join the equal-time lobby, MADD has endorsed a "public-service announcement" prepared by Joseph E. Seagram & Sons, a U.S. liquor company owned by Seagram Co. of Canada. The message: Contrary to common belief, the "typical" serving of beer (12 ounces) contains as much alcohol as the "typical" serving of wine (five ounces) or spirits (1¼ ounces).

Seagram & Sons, which boasts about MADD's support, claims its spot helps reduce drunk driving by clearing up a misconception—that drivers are less likely to get drunk on beer or wine than on liquor. But the networks have refused to run the ad, saying it violates a long-standing ban on commercials for liquor (but not beer or wine). Seagram's spot does run on cable-TV channels.

Shaun Sheehan, an official of the National Association of Broadcasters and a member of MADD's board, defends MADD's backing of Seagram. "MADD's war is with the impaired driver," he says. "It isn't with people who choose to drink, or with people who have driver's licenses."

A broader war is called for, MADD's critics insist. Anti-alcohol groups contend that booze is tied so closely with social life, and social life so closely with the automobile, that narrow attacks on just drinking and driving won't work.

Alcohol-related deaths have declined to about 23,500 last year from 28,000 in 1980 when the push for tougher laws and education programs began. But analysts think about half the decline reflects a drop in the number of teen-age drivers. According to a federal estimate cited by Laurence Ross, a University of New Mexico sociologist, eight of every 10 drunk-driving deaths involve victims who were drunk themselves or were riding in cars driven by drunks. The threat of being caught doesn't adequately deter drunk drivers, Mr. Ross says.

Part of the solution is to change public attitudes so that people are less likely to get drunk in the first place, regardless of whether they drive, insists George Hacker, the director of alcohol programs for the Center for Science in the Public Interest, a self-financed group concerned mostly with health and nutrition.

A first step, he suggests, would be ending ads such as those for Harley-Davidson Wine Cooler. He says the ads encourage a casual attitude toward drinking and driving, by glamorizing alcohol and blurring the distinction between alcohol and soft drinks. "Riding a motorcycle is a symbol of masculinity in our society," he says. "The ad's message is that drinking the wine cooler is part of being a man, too."

Scooter Juice Inc., the California maker of the wine cooler, believes its ads are harmless enough. The company notes that the toughs it portrays don't drink until after they park their motorcycles. Says Eldon Killian, Scooter's sales manager: "We say the time to drink is when your kickstand is down."

Discussion Questions

1. Identify the organizations and groups that MADD should include in its analysis of the market and competition.
2. What are the marketing strategy issues that MADD's management should consider in the organization's strategic marketing plan?
3. Recommend a marketing strategy for MADD, covering the next three years.

APPLICATION 5–12

Nixdorf Computer AG

What does it take to compete with International Business Machines Corp.?

A sound strategy. A reliable product. And, if you're Nixdorf Computer AG, a bit of the unorthodox.

What else could explain why a computer-company chairman's knuckle is swollen twice normal size from a floor hockey game with fellow employees? Or why training for its salesmen includes a three-day survival course— without water or food?

"We've always been very competitive in our thinking," says Klaus Luft, Nixdorf's 46-year-old chairman. "We said we wanted to beat IBM when a lot of people said you cannot fight IBM. Sure you could."

Source: Thomas F. O'Boyle, "Nixdorf Uses Novel Strategy to Compete." Reprinted by permission of *The Wall Street Journal.* © Dow Jones & Company, Inc., March 16, 1988, p. 22. All rights reserved.

Nixdorf has been giving IBM and a lot of other rivals a run for their money. Founded in a basement workshop in 1952 by entrepreneur Heinz Nixdorf, who died two years ago, the company today is Europe's fourth-largest computer maker. In the past five years, a sluggish period generally for the industry, Nixdorf's sales grew an average 17 percent a year, while profits raced along at a 28 percent annual clip. The company, which according to one poll recently displaced Daimler-Benz AG as West Germany's most admired, predicts its 1987 sales of 5.1 billion marks ($3 billion) will double by the early 1990s.

Nixdorf's founder recognized early that businesses need "solutions"—reliable computer hardware and custom-designed software—rather than just computers. Half of Nixdorf's sales come from software, the programs that run computers, and other services. At IBM, computer hardware, which is more susceptible to competition, accounts for two-thirds of sales.

Nixdorf's success also stems from a feisty corporate sense of itself as the giant-killer doing battle with IBM. Of course, IBM is still a Goliath. IBM's sales last year were $54.22 billion, more than 18 times Nixdorf's. Its worldwide sales per employee of $139,000 last year were tops in the computer industry and higher than Nixdorf's $109,000. And IBM still dominates the U.S. market, where Nixdorf's presence is small.

But in Europe and particularly Germany, Nixdorf has been nibbling away at IBM's long-standing dominance. In some market sectors, Nixdorf now leads. Among small to medium-size computer systems, those costing less than $200,000, Nixdorf's 20 percent market share in Germany exceeds IBM's 15 percent, according to estimates by Quantum Group International, an electronics research firm. And Nixdorf's sales to European retailers in the past five years have grown twice as fast as IBM's.

"I don't think Nixdorf's products are any better" than the competition's, says a sales manager at a large European rival. "But they have had impressive growth and I think the main reason is their motivation. There's a lot of spirit in that company. They're also very good at making the customer feel he's important."

Nixdorf is also good at defying convention. For example, it has become a leading computer company from headquarters here in Paderborn, a remote town in northern Germany, rather than in Munich, the nation's Silicon Valley. It is Europe's second leading maker of money-dispensing automatic teller machines, though Germany has the fewest of them, per capita, of any country in Europe. It is also a company whose chairman's ground-floor office is the same size, with the same spartan decor—white walls, a desk, a computer terminal, an easel with a writing pad—as every other Nixdorf manager's office. There are no executive dining halls, no special parking spaces, no chauffeured limousines.

Quantum president Mirek Stevenson recalls talking some years ago to about 60 of Nixdorf's top managers in Kitzbuehel, Austria. "We broke for lunch," he says, "and all of a sudden . . . the Nixdorf people rose in unison, went outside, put on their cross-country skies and skied for an hour. I thought they were putting me on."

Customers, too, consider Nixdorf unique. Richard Parsons, director of data processing for one of Britain's largest retailers, Tesco PLC, recently awarded Nixdorf an $88 million order for computers at 180 of its stores. The reason, he says: Nixdorf was "hungrier" than IBM, Tesco's long-time supplier. Nixdorf asked him what he wanted, listened and designed a 60-lane check-out system that responded to his needs. IBM didn't. Nixdorf also wrote part of the software before it had the contract. IBM didn't. And Nixdorf offered a slight discount. IBM didn't.

Mr. Luft's visit to Tesco in December clinched the sale. "We were very impressed that he took the trouble to come," Mr. Parsons says. "He wasn't a figurehead like you get at some companies. He knew what he was talking about."

"A lot of companies claim they listen to customers, but Nixdorf really does," adds George Verghese, an electronics analyst at Deutsche Bank's securities research unit in London.

The company, for instance, doesn't merely attend the international electronics trade fair in nearby Hanover each March. The entire headquarters relocates there for two weeks, including all top executives, not just those responsible for sales and marketing. When Mr. Nixdorf died of a heart attack two years ago, it was on the dance floor at the Hanover Trade Fair.

Nixdorf's main customers are banks, retail stores, and government agencies. The computer systems it sells are tailored to meet customers' needs. But the main thing it sells is service. When changes in the German government's tax code went into effect in January, for instance, the Finance Ministry didn't have to lift a finger. Nixdorf created a program incorporating the changes. When a customer wants a new or renovated building for its computers, Nixdorf's architects provide blueprints—and, if needed, custom furniture.

"It reminds me of the way IBM used to be in the 1960s," says Michael Anderson, president of Nixdorf's U.S. subsidiary. The executive, who worked at IBM for 16 years until 1981, says the chief similarity is that Nixdorf is "a young, aggressive, fast moving, fun organization." Nixdorf hired almost 4,000 workers last year, bringing its world-wide work force to 30,000. The average employee's age is 31, the company average 20 years ago.

Nixdorf also appears to avoid the lack of flexibility common to German workers, young or old. Two years, ago, when Mobil Corp. unit Montgomery Ward & Co. bought Nixdorf cash register systems for all 292 of its department stores, Nixdorf needed volunteers to relocate to Chicago for a few years.

"The call went out," says senior vice president Dieter Wendorff, "and 24 hours later we had filled our quota."

Discussion Questions

1. Examine and evaluate the role of Nixdorf's corporate culture in guiding its business and marketing strategies.
2. Discuss Nixdorf's marketing advantages.
3. Critically evaluate Nixdorf's market targeting, indicating any changes that should be made in the strategy.
4. What positioning strategy is Nixdorf using to compete against IBM and other competitors?

APPLICATION 5–13

Minute Maid Orange Juice

An orange juice war is intensifying as major players try to squeeze bigger shares out of a crowded, softening market.

The greater competition comes in part from a drought in Brazil that has sharply driven up prices. As a result of those higher prices, some industry executives are predicting as much as double-digit drops in consumption this year in both the frozen and the chilled, ready-to-serve segments of the $3 billion market.

In an already difficult environment, Tropicana Products Inc.—acquired last month by Seagram Co. for a hefty $1.2 billion—is becoming increasingly aggressive. Tropicana, which has been the star of the fast-growing, ready-to-serve segment, is now rolling out its Tropicana Pure Premium Orange Juice on the West Coast where the brand, a big success story elsewhere, has been weak.

In certain cases, marketing consultants say competitors trying to cling to market share have greeted Tropicana's arrival with special price promotions.

"Competitors are not going to make it easy for Tropicana," says Michael Bellas, a consultant at Beverage Marketing Corp. "It will really have to earn its increased share." Adds Tom Pirko, president of Bevmark Inc., a Los Angeles consulting firm, "Competitors are trying to block the spread of Tropicana."

Both Procter & Gamble Co., which makes Citrus Hill, and Coca-Cola

---

Source: Alix M. Freedman, "An Orange Juice War Is Growing As Makers Vie for Fresh Markets." Reprinted by permission of *The Wall Street Journal.* © Dow Jones & Company, Inc., April 27, 1988, p. 28. All rights reserved.

Co., which makes Minute Maid, insist they aren't cutting prices, and Coca-Cola has recently raised prices about 15 cents a half gallon in selected markets.

Some observers say Tropicana, the second-biggest U.S. orange juice producer, has to make a focused expansion attempt in order to justify its purchase price.

"The war is escalating and spreading out of its traditional boundaries because Tropicana—paid for at an obscene price—has to do all kinds of things to generate income," says Joseph G. Smith, president of Oxtoby-Smith Inc., which does consumer research for Minute Maid.

But he adds: "The anticipation that Minute Maid will let itself be victimized is simply naive."

Minute Maid, the leading orange juice producer, is widely believed to be poised for a counterattack. In recent years, the brand has performed poorly as consumer preferences shifted away from the frozen juice segment, where it dominates with a 20.5 percent share. But consumers, particularly working women, perceive the ready-to-serve juices as fresher and more convenient. In this segment, Minute Maid has only a 17.7 percent share compared with Tropicana's 27.3 percent share. Procter & Gamble's third-ranked Citrus Hill has 9.3 percent of the frozen market and 9.1 percent of the ready-to-serve category.

Competitors believe Coca-Cola is about to introduce a new Minute Maid ready-to-serve juice, made from fresh oranges rather than concentrate, that will go head-to-head against Tropicana's premium product. Until now, Tropicana has boasted that it is the only company to make such a juice.

Tropicana executives profess not to be worried. "Who's chasing whom?" shrugs Martin Goodfriend, Tropicana's vice president of administration. Mr. Goodfriend points out that even in last year's flat market, Tropicana registered a 3.7 percent share increase in the ready-to-serve segment.

Coca-Cola won't confirm an imminent launch of a new juice, nor will it divulge specifics of its strategy. But George Woody, vice president for marketing at Coca-Cola Foods, acknowledges his company is struggling with how best to regain its momentum in a market now dominated by ready-to-serve products. "We have to grapple with that changed dynamic and how we market our product," he says.

Soon, Coca-Cola may make mass-marketed fresh juice even fresher. The company is said to be testing a Minute Maid automatic juice machine that would squeeze oranges right in store aisles. These machines, increasingly popular in supermarkets and specialty stores, until now have been sold on a limited basis by small entrepreneurs. And the juice they produce is usually sold at a premium to the regular packaged brands.

"The marketing thrust is to end-run Tropicana's premium product and establish the Minute Maid name as the gold standard," explains one source with close ties to Coca-Cola. But Mr. Goodfriend of Tropicana disparages the orange juice machines as a "novelty." "The quality swings of oranges are tremendous," he insists. "You can't provide a consistent, consumer-preferred product."

Tropicana is also about to unveil a new line of non-refrigerated orange-based drinks called Twisters. Offering "taste twists" like orange-straw-berry-banana, these products represent the company's first big move into the bottled juice drinks area where brands such as Mott's and Ocean Spray are entrenched.

"This is a category that has some clear leaders in it already," cautions Mr. Bellas of Beverage Marketing. "They are getting into another very competitive area." Adds Kevin Murphy, director of operations at Ocean Spray: "Tropicana is a formidable rival, but we have the lion's share of the business and will act to protect it."

Discussion Questions

1. Define and analyze the product-market structure which includes Minute Maid.
2. Define and evaluate Minute Maid's strategic situation.
3. Evaluate Minute Maid's targeting and positioning strategies (make any necessary assumptions).
4. Identify and discuss probable trends that will (may) affect the orange juice industry during the next three to five years. How should these opportunities and threats be considered in the development of Minute Maid's future marketing strategy?

PART 6

ORGANIZING, IMPLEMENTING, AND CONTROLLING MARKETING STRATEGY

Much of the actual work of managing involves strategic and tactical implementation, evaluation, and control of marketing operations. Successful performance of these activities relies heavily upon managers' understanding of the planning process. Strategic planning is a continuing cycle of making plans, launching them, tracking performance, identifying performance gaps, and then initiating problem-solving actions. In accomplishing strategic evaluation, management must select performance criteria and measures and then set up a tracking program to obtain the information needed to guide evaluation activities. When first establishing a strategic evaluation program (and periodically thereafter), a strategic marketing audit provides a useful basis for developing the program.

Strategic evaluation, the last stage in the marketing strategy process, is more aptly designated as the starting point (except perhaps in new-venture situations). Strategic marketing planning requires information from various ongoing monitoring and performance evaluation activities. Discussion of strategic evaluation has been delayed until this final part in order to have first examined the strategic areas that require evaluation and identified the kinds of information needed by the marketing strategist for assessing marketing performance.

FACILITATING IMPLEMENTATION

Plans, without proper implementation and control, are typically ineffective: A complete implementation plan should specify precisely:

- What activities are to be implemented.
- Who will be responsible for implementation.
- The time and location of implementation.
- How implementation will be accomplished.
- The performance measures and criteria to be used in evaluation.
- The nature and scope of the performance tracking program.
- How performance gaps will be identified.
- What actions will be taken under what circumstances.

Managers are important facilitators in the implementation process, and some are more effective than others. To be effective implementors, managers need:

- The ability to understand how others feel, as well as having good bargaining skills.
- The strength to be tough and fair in putting people and resources where they will be most effective.
- Effectiveness in focusing on the critical aspects of performance in managing marketing activities.
- The ability to create a necessary informal organization or network to match each problem that arises.[1]

The implementation of marketing strategy may partially depend on external organizations such as marketing research firms, marketing consultants, advertising and public relations firms, channel members, and other organizations participating in the marketing effort. These outside organizations present a major management challenge when they actively participate in marketing activities. Their efforts should be programmed into the marketing plan and their roles and responsibilities clearly established and communicated. There is a potential danger in not informing outside groups of planned actions, deadlines, and other implementation requirements. For example, the advertising agency account executive and other agency staff members should be familiar with all aspects of the promotion strategy as well as the major dimensions of the marketing strategy. Restricting information from participating firms can adversely affect their contributions to strategy planning and implementation.

---

[1] Thomas V. Bonoma, "Making Your Marketing Strategy Work," *Harvard Business Review,* March–April 1984, p. 75.

STRATEGIC EVALUATION AND CONTROL

The relationship between strategic planning and control is shown in Exhibit 1. Strategic planning is an ongoing process of making plans, implementing them, tracking performance, identifying performance gaps, and initiating actions to close the gap between desired and actual results. Management must establish performance criteria and measures so that information can be obtained for use in tracking performance. The purpose of evaluation may be to (1) find new opportunities or avoid threats, (2) keep performance in line with management's expectations, and/or (3) solve specific problems that exist.

Let us assume that we are concerned with establishing a strategic evaluation program for a business unit in which there has been no previous formal strategic marketing planning and evaluation program. Since evaluation essentially is comparing results with expectations, it is necessary to lay some groundwork before setting up a tracking program. The starting point is a *strategic marketing audit:*

EXHIBIT 1
Strategic Planning and Control Process

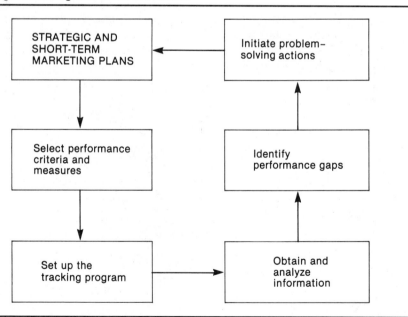

Source: David W. Cravens, Strategic Marketing (Homewood, Ill.: Richard D. Irwin, 1982), p. 413.

A strategic marketing audit is a comprehensive review and assessment of marketing operations. It includes a careful examination of the following:

1. Corporate mission and objectives.
2. Business composition and strategy.
3. Buyer analysis.
4. Competitor analysis.
5. Market-target strategy and objectives.
6. Marketing program positioning strategy.
7. Marketing program activities.
8. Marketing planning.
9. Implementation and management.

Examples of specific questions that should be addressed in examining each of these areas are shown in the appendix to Chapter 3.

There are other reasons for conducting a strategic marketing audit than its use in guiding the installation of a formal strategic marketing planning and evaluation program:

1. Organizational changes may bring about a complete review of strategic marketing operations.
2. Major shifts in business involvement such as entry into new product and market areas, acquisitions, and other alterations in the composition of the business may require strategic audits.

While there is no norm as to how often a strategic audit should be conducted, the nature of the audit and costs involved suggest that the time span between audits should be at least five years and perhaps more, depending upon the company situation.

CASES AND APPLICATIONS
FOR PART 6

The six cases and five applications in Part 6 focus on organizing, implementing, and controlling marketing strategy.

Cases

The first case, Donaldson Company, Inc. (DCI), describes the world's largest manufacturer of heavy-duty filtration equipment. While enjoying considerable past success, the company has experienced major losses recently. A major focus of the case is the problem of coordinating worldwide selling and customer service efforts within the Original Equipment Group of DCI.

Case 6–2, American Safety Razor Company (ASR), is an example of a business unit that a large corporation (Philip Morris) decided to eliminate. Eventually, a group of ASR executives purchased the business. After buying the company, the new management is faced with developing strategies to move ASR toward financial stability and profitable performance, operating against strong competitors such as Gillette.

Robert N. Maxwell Memorial Community Hospital (Case 6–3) is an established and well-known major hospital serving a large metropolitan area. The hospital's present marketing efforts are fractionalized and scattered among a number of people. Top management feels that the present marketing organization will be inadequate in the future.

Case 6–4, Aurora Lotion, describes a situation in which a Swiss subsidiary of a British company is plagued by parallel importing. The general manager of the Swiss subsidiary is concerned about the impact of this situation on sales force morale and profitability.

The Parke-Davis Professional Health Group case (6–5) examines the pharmaceutical market in Canada and the Parke-Davis sales-force strategy. Marvin Skripitsky, marketing director of the Professional Health Group, is considering several alternatives to deal with a perceived staffing problem.

Case 6–6, the Gillette Company—Safety Razor Division, provides an in-depth look at the giant in the razor industry. The case identifies the Trac II brand manager's concerns as he prepares to develop his annual marketing plan. The extensive data in this case provide an excellent opportunity for marketing analysis.

Applications

The Pratt & Whitney application (6–7) describes how the market leader in jet aircraft engines lost its competitive advantage. The Winkleman Manufacturing Company (6–8) presents an interesting pricing analysis situation. Time Unlimited, Inc. (6–9) considers a proposal to drop production of one of their models to concentrate on the other. In Application 6–10, Toys "R" Us considers the company's marketing situation and the future strategic opportunities and threats in the competitive market for toys. The Limited, Inc., application (6–11) profiles one of the world's most successful specialty retailers.

CASE 6–1

Donaldson Company, Inc.

By 1985, Tom Baden, vice president of the Donaldson Company, Inc. (DCI) was convinced that the rules of competition in the industrial air and fluid filtration industry had changed. Two years earlier DCI had experienced its first loss in 50 years. While the situation improved in 1984, Baden realizes that a decision about his group's organizational structure is essential.

Baden is vice president of DCI's Original Equipment Group (OEG), whose revenues in 1984 represented over 40 percent of DCI's 1984 annual sales of $250 million. Stated simply, Baden's task is to return OEG to financial performance levels of the 1975–79 period and establish a base for long-term growth in the markets served by OEG. Baden is also responsible for reinforcing DCI's corporate image as a high-quality, high-service provider of state-of-the-art products.

THE COMPANY

History

In 1915 Frank Donaldson, Sr., the original chairman of the company, invented the first effective air cleaner for internal combustion engines. Air is a necessary ingredient for the combustion process to occur. Before his inven-

---

This case was prepared by Shannon Shipp, M.J. Neeley School of Business, Texas Christian University. The U.S. Department of Education funded the preparation of this case under Grant #G00877027. Copyright © 1985 by the Case Development Center, University of Minnesota, School of Management, 271 19th Avenue South, Minneapolis, MN 55455.

tion, engines were extremely susceptible to "dusting out," or becoming inoperative due to excessive accumulation of dust entering the engine from unfiltered air.

In subsequent years, DCI led the industry in introducing new products, such as oil-washed filters, mufflers, multistaged air cleaners, and high-tech hydraulic filters. DCI became the world's largest manufacturer of heavy-duty air cleaners and mufflers and established a worldwide reputation for technology. Facilities grew from 200 square feet of manufacturing space in 1915 to more than 3 million square feet of manufacturing and office area worldwide in 1980.

Mission

By 1984 the company had broadly defined its mission: to design, manufacture, and sell proprietary products that "separate something unwanted from something wanted." The company's product line included air cleaners, air filters, mufflers, hydraulic filters, microfiltration equipment for computers, air pollution equipment, and liquid clarifiers. These products were developed, sold, and serviced by the organizational structure appearing in Exhibit 1. According to this exhibit, DCI has a functional organizational structure, with the nine worldwide support groups responsible for product development, manufacturing, administration, finance, and the four business groups responsible for selling and servicing products to their respective markets. The 1980 to 1984 sales of the four major business groups are listed in Exhibit 2. The fifth group listed, Microfiltration and Defense Products (MFD), was a part of the Business Development Group until 1984, when it was spun off to form a new business group.

1983–1984 Situation

In 1983 a peculiar set of external and internal causes combined to downgrade DCI's performance. Among external causes, sales of medium/heavy-duty trucks, buses, tractors and combines, construction equipment, and aftermarket replacement elements simultaneously hit five-year or all-time lows. These markets constituted the majority of sales for both the Original Equipment Group (OEG) and International. Although soft demand had been experienced in one or two of these markets before in a single year, never had all businesses declined so precipitously in the same year. Also, the strength of the dollar in 1982–84 was making DCI's customers less competitive in foreign markets. This in turn affected DCI's sales of replacement parts.

In 1984 DCI's operating results began to return to pre-1983 levels (see Exhibit 3). One reason was a success in the wet filtration area, particularly in high-stress environments. The primary reason was that sales by customers in DCI's worldwide markets, particularly heavy-duty trucks, began

EXHIBIT 1
DCI Organization Chart (1983)

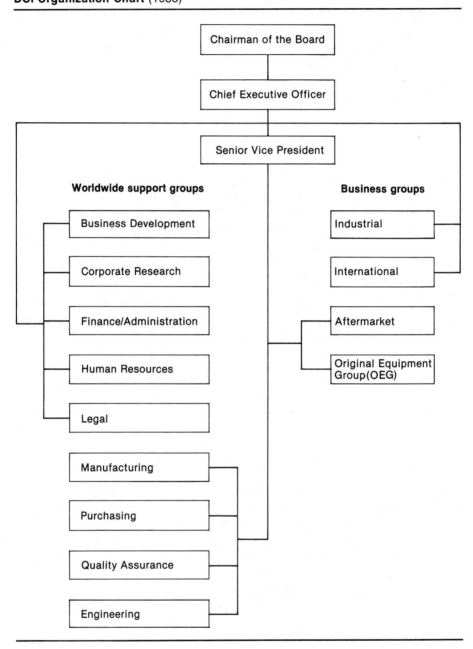

Source: Internal company documents.

EXHIBIT 2
DCI's Four Major Business Groups (annual sales, $ millions)

	1984	1983	1982	1981	1980
Original equipment group	$102.2	$ 63.9	$101.3	$104.6	$101.6
Aftermarket	22.6	17.6	20.5	20.1	17.0
Industrial	32.2	32.0	41.3	37.0	25.0
International	71.2	68.7	81.4	87.0	69.4
MFD	26.0	21.4	17.4	15.1	11.4
Total	$254.2	$203.6	$261.9	$263.8	$234.4

Source: DCI 1984 Annual Report.

EXHIBIT 3
DCI Operating Results ($000)

	1984	1983	1982
Net sales.	$254,052	$203,608	$262,018
Cost of sales	157,257	131,548	169,816
Gross earnings	96,795	72,060	92,202
Earnings (loss) before income taxes	20,238	(1,738)	12,805
Income taxes.	10,546	1,800	5,572
Tax rate	52.1%	—	43.2%
Net earnings	9,692	(3,358)	7,233
Depreciation	7,694	8,320	8,518
Interest	2,670	2,076	2,345
Financial Position			
Current assets	$ 97,425	$81,668	$ 82,109
Current liabilities	45,022	32,796	35,574
Current ratio	2.2	2.5	2.3
Working capital.	52,403	48,872	46,535
Long-term debt.	19,549	21,791	18,752
Shareholder's equity	90,232	84,880	91,637
Capitalization ratio	22.1	22.1	21.2
Return on average shareholder's equity . .	11.1	(4.0)	7.9
Return on average invested capital	9.0	(3.3)	6.4
Property, plant, and equipment (gross). . .	$118,663	$118,182	$114,465
Property, plant, and equipment (net). . . .	55,045	59,694	63,739
Total assets	$160,613	$148,083	$151,160

Source: DCI 1984 Annual Report.

to return to pre-1983 levels. Because of the external causes described previously, however, DCI management thought it unlikely that sales by its customers would return to pre-1980 levels. To counter the effects of the decline in worldwide demand for DCI's products, Tom Baden concluded that OEG must address several critical internal problems.

Some of the internal problems included an inability to coordinate customer service to multinational customers, inability to provide accurate cost figures for given production quantities, and—especially for its small customers—"being difficult to buy from."

DCI found it difficult to coordinate customer service efforts for those customers with multiple purchasing or production facilities in different countries. Although DCI had offices in all of the countries where high sales potential existed, (e.g., in West Germany, Brazil, and Mexico) lack of coordination among the offices caused spotty customer service. For example, customers were known to "shop" for the best prices among DCI offices. The different DCI offices were therefore competing against each other for the same business.

DCI was also unable to provide accurate cost figures for small production quantities. This hampered salespeople's efforts to quote prices that would cover DCI's costs, and yield profits. For example, setup costs in switching from producing one product to another were not factored into the costs of production runs, and hence omitted from the prices charged. Furthermore, account executives were measured primarily on sales rather than profits, thereby encouraging them to devote less attention to the costs of actually filling an order.

Although relationships with its largest customers were strong—based on its ability to work with those customers in solving problems—small customers complained to salespeople of slow response for engineering drawings and price quotes. They also complained of slow responses to questions about billing or order status. Very small customers (under $25,000 in annual sales) were not vocal with complaints about DCI because they were seldom contacted by DCI representatives.

ORIGINAL EQUIPMENT GROUP (OEG)

OEG Products and Markets

OEG constitutes the bulk of DCI's traditional businesses, such as heavy-duty trucks, and construction, mining, industrial, and agricultural equipment. It sells air and hydraulic filters, acoustical products (mufflers), and replacement elements to manufacturers and end users of heavy-duty mobile equipment in North America. OEG has not typically sold oil filters, as they are a commodity item and require much higher production runs than OEG traditionally makes. OEG is reviewing its position on producing oil filters because its customers often seek a single source for all their filter needs. About half of the annual worldwide sales of these products are in North America.

Current Organizational Structure for OEG

OEG is currently organized around the market segments it serves (see Exhibit 4). The construction, agriculture, industrial, and truck-bus market segments have their own market director and support staff that are responsible for all planning and administration as well as for maintaining good relations with the largest customers in the market. Each market group has outside salespeople who call directly on customers, as well as inside salespeople responsible for routing orders and customer service. A manager of marketing support is responsible for order-entry personnel and clerks. There are also two special project managers in OEG. The first special project manager coordinated the efforts of the worldwide action teams responsible for gathering information on competitors and customers. The second developed a marketing program to try to understand the needs of small original equipment manufacturers (OEMs) and the feasibility of using telemarketing to reach them.

EXHIBIT 4
OEG's Market-Based Organizational Structure

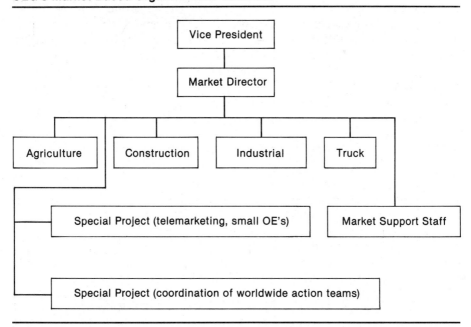

Source: Internal company documents.

OEG's Position Within DCI

OEG has primary worldwide responsibility to serve mobile heavy-equipment OEMs. The International Group supports OEG's efforts, while the Aftermarket Group competes with OEG for the same end-users. The International Group sells OEG's products in markets outside North America. Communication between OEG and International is crucial in providing high levels of customer service for multinational customers with plants in several countries. The Aftermarket Group competes with OEG by selling mobile heavy-equipment replacement elements under the Donaldson name through fleet specialists, heavy-duty distributors, and other outlets. These replacement parts compete with similar products sold by manufacturers' dealers supplied by OEG.

Within each market segment, customers are served by size. Large accounts (more than $250,000 in annual sales) are served by market directors or salespeople assigned to that account. Mid-sized customers (between $25,000 and $250,000 in annual sales) are called upon by a salesperson responsible for that territory. Small OEMs are served, if at all, by inside salespeople or order-entry personnel in the marketing support services group.

Organization by market segment offers a number of advantages to OEG, such as (1) easy tracking of changes in demand or customer usage characteristics and (2) an organizational structure similar to that in Engineering that facilitates good communications. Organization by market segment also has some problems, such as (1) some customers straddling several markets, making it difficult to assign the costs and profits from serving that customer to a specific market, and (2) an occasional inability to coordinate the engineering support for those customers who straddled market segments because an engineer from each of two market segments might be assigned to solve the same technical problem.

ACTION TEAM REPORTS AND ANALYSES

To regain OEG's previous market position, in early 1984 Tom Baden initiated a year-long strategic analysis to study all aspects of OEG operations. Reports were prepared by action teams from DCI offices around the world. These reports were the basis of a series of meetings that included all OEG executives and were used to obtain ideas for actions to improve OEG's organizational structure and marketing policies.

Baden must reach a decision on whether the existing marketing organization structure is best able to achieve OEG's goals or whether a new structure would be better. To make that decision, four elements of the year-long strategic analysis are considered: (1) competition, (2) customers, (3) marketing-mix strategies, and (4) telemarketing and global account management as alternatives to personal selling in reaching some customers.

Major Competitors

DCI is the traditional heavy-duty mobile-equipment market leader for heavy-duty filters. Major competitors include Fleetguard, Fram, Nelson, and Mann and Hummel. Other firms, such as Wix, Baldwin, Purolator, and AC/Delco, compete in certain market segments. In general, all of the competitors are on sound financial footing. Fleetguard and Fram have very healthy parent organizations (Cummins Engine and Allied/Bendix Corporation, respectively). Mann and Hummel and Nelson are healthy from good internal financial management. Research and development costs are generally lower for these organizations than for DCI because they tend to follow DCI's technological breakthroughs. Each competitor is strong in a particular market or through a particular channel, and most offer a full line of air and oil filters, which enables both customers and distributors to meet their filter needs through a single source.

OEG's Customers

OEG has over 600 customers, divided into three groups: large, mid-sized, and small.

Large Accounts.   OEG's large customers (more than $250,000 in annual sales), consisting of 46 original equipment manufacturer (OEM) accounts and their dealers, constitute more than 90 percent of OEG sales and more than 40 percent of DCI sales. Thirty of these customers are headquartered in the United States, eight in Europe, and eight in Japan. A partial list of these customers appears in Exhibit 5. These customers are all large, and most have sales offices and production facilities in more than one country.

The competitive environment for large OEMs is undergoing rapid change. Some large OEMs, such as Caterpillar and Ford, are experiencing reduced sales due to increasing competition from non–U.S. manufacturers. The large OEMs are coping with the reduction in sales by calling on suppliers to reduce prices. For example, Caterpillar announced a three-year program beginning in 1983 and terminating in 1985 that required its suppliers to maintain stable prices even though inflation was predicted to increase 22 percent for that period. The emphasis by large customers on cost containment is a major change from the 1970s (which emphasized product performance) and could squeeze OEG's margins and hurt DCI's performance.

According to meetings among salespeople and account executives, OEG's largest customers have common needs for filtration equipment. At a

EXHIBIT 5
Some Large Current or Potential Customers for OEG

	North America	Europe	Japan
	Ford	Daimler-Benz	Hitachi
	Caterpillar	IVECO	Isuzu
	Champion	Leyland	Komatsu
	Clark Equipment	Lister	Kubota
	Cummins	Lombardini	Mitsubishi
	Detroit Diesel	MAN	Nissan

Source: Internal company documents.

minimum, large customers desire state-of-the-art products at the lowest possible prices for products meeting specifications. Recent demand by large customers include:

1. Just-in-time deliveries.[1]
2. Long-term fixed source contracts.
3. Drop-ship arrangements to customers' dealers and/or manufacturing facilities for OE parts.
4. Worldwide availability of product.
5. The OE brand name on the product.
6. Electronic system tie-ins for improved order placement/followup and customer service and support.

These demands accompanied OEM efforts to consolidate their purchases to achieve stronger positions vis-à-vis their suppliers.

Large customers also perceive sales opportunities for replacement elements sales through their dealer networks. In North America, the large OEMs have 21,000 outlets, or original equipment dealers (OEDs), through which OEG could sell replacement elements. OEDs represent a new market opportunity for DCI. Traditionally, OEG has sold replacement elements to OEMs imprinted with the OEM's brand. Once the OEM takes title to the products, OEG expects the OEM to provide the necessary training and support to its distributors through which the products will be sold. Recently, OEDs are more actively looking for product lines to improve cash flow and profitability. Part of the impetus for the search for additional products is slow equipment sales. Service parts provide a logical line extension and source of steady cash flow for OEDs. To capitalize on the market in service parts, however, OEDs need extensive manufacturer support in terms of

---

[1] Just-in-time deliveries occur when the supplier and customer have devised a schedule to ensure the next shipment of parts or supplies is delivered when the customer is about to use the last unit from the previous shipment.

sales training, product knowledge, product literature, and merchandising, and complete lines of filters to service all makes of equipment, not just lines they represent.

Mid-Size and Small Accounts. Mid-size ($25,000 to $250,000 in annual sales) and small (less than $25,000 in annual sales) OEMs are offered only standard products from the OEG catalog. Custom engineering is rarely provided to these customers, unless they are willing to bear its full cost.

These smaller OEMs have different needs than large OEMs. In general, they desire state-of-the-art products but are willing to wait for a large OEM to install a new product first. They also desire consistent contact with OEG salespeople to keep abreast of changing filter prices (while realizing that they do not have the volumes to command the lowest available prices) and good product quality. Some OEMs often request the DCI name on the filters used in their equipment as a marketing tool, capitalizing on DCI's reputation for high quality among end users.

Marketing-Mix Strategies

Product and Price. DCI is known throughout the industry for its conservative management style, using strategic moves based on careful planning. OEG is no exception. OEG prefers serving selected, high-margin markets where customers are beginning to demand higher performance levels than those available from the products currently available. Pursuing these markets allows OEG to exploit its strengths of quality design and engineering, as well as allowing OEG to charge a premium price for its products. Price cutting is not a major component of OEG's market strategies.

Distribution. Distribution of OEG's products occurs through two primary channels. The first is directly to OEMs, which purchase products for installation on new equipment. In some markets, such as heavy-duty trucks and construction equipment, more than 70 percent of all new units shipped are factory-equipped with DCI products. OEMs depend on DCI as a reliable supplier of state-of-the-art products whose engineers design products for special applications or environmental conditions.

The second major channel is for replacement elements. These elements are often packaged and sold under the customer's name and logo and distributed through its dealer network. For example, OEG provides replacement elements for Caterpillar, International Harvester, J.I. Case, Freightliner, and Volvo, imprinted with their names and logos.

Promotion. OEG products are promoted several ways, including advertising, direct mail, trade shows, and promotional literature. A distribution of OEG's promotional expenditures for 1984 appears in Exhibit 6. DCI encourages direct communication between OEG engineers and technicians and their customer counterparts. While this is not reflected in the promo-

EXHIBIT 6
Promotional Budget (1984)

Item	Percent of Budget
Advertising	55%
Trade shows	16
Sales literature	13
Coop advertising	4
Photography	2
Public relations	2
Other sales materials	1
Advertising specialties	1
Audiovisual materials	1
Other	5
	100%

Source: Internal company documents.

tional budget, it is an important element in OEG's communications with its customers. Other off-budget promotional expenses include sending OEG engineers to attend professional meetings and guiding customers on tours of the research and testing unit that contains some of the most modern filtration research facilities in the world.

Selling Methods.   OEG has traditionally relied on face-to-face selling to provide information to and solicit orders from customers. Two major problems exist with heavy reliance on personal selling. First, it is not cost efficient for OEG to use personal selling to reach mid-size and small customers unless a standard product already exists to fit the customer's application. As a result, service to these customers is provided primarily by local distributors or through DCI's Aftermarket Group. The lack of direct customer contact with these accounts has resulted in OEG having a low level of knowledge regarding their needs. Second, for large customers with multiple purchasing and usage sites, it is difficult to coordinate the activities of salespeople assigned to customers geographically. This problem becomes acute when the customer has purchasing or usage sites overseas, served through the International Division. This means that salespeople's activities have to be coordinated across geographic regions as well as across divisions within DCI.

Alternatives to Personal Selling

Two selling methods, telemarketing and global account management, are being considered as substitutes or supplements to the current selling method.

Telemarketing. Telemarketing involves organized, planned telephone communication between a firm and its customers. Telemarketing ranges from salespeople simply calling prospective customers to set up appointments, to complex systems with different employees responsible for different parts of selling, such as prospecting or customer service.

One special project manager explored the feasibility of telemarketing to small OEMs. The study's objective was to profile small OEMs that had purchased OEG products. These firms were questioned about their use of OEG products, needs for additional OEG support, and overall satisfaction with OEG products and services. Four hundred and sixty-one small OEMs were contacted during the month-long study, none with more than $25,000 in purchases from OEG the preceding year. Some study results appear in Exhibit 7.

Global Account Management. Global account management (GAM) is a method of assigning salespeople to accounts. Sellers use GAM when customers are large, with multiple purchase or usage points. Under a GAM system an account executive is responsible for all the communication between the customer and the seller, including (but not limited to) needs analysis, application engineering, field support, customer service, and order processing. Depending on the account size, the executive might have several subordinates provide necessary services. GAM's major advantage is communication coordination. Since all seller and buyer contact is monitored by the account manager, miscommunication is unlikely.

Implementing GAM would involve assigning teams to OEG's largest customers to improve support. Account teams would be composed of salespeople and applications engineers, with the number of people on the account

EXHIBIT 7
Telemarketing Study Results

	Number	Percent of Responses
Literature requests	211	46%
Satisfied customers	102	22
Not qualified as customers	58	13
Follow-up phone calls	17	4
Orders	9	2
Quotes	8	2
Terminations	5	1
Unavailable (not listed) duplicates	51	11
	461	100%

Source: Internal company documents.

EXHIBIT 8
Global Account Management (sample organization chart)

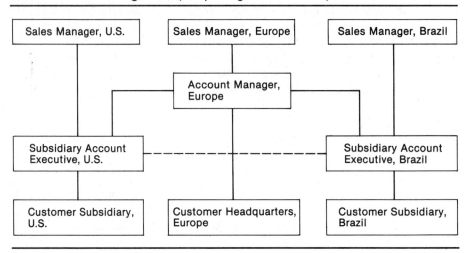

Source: Internal company documents.

proportional to its annual orders. Each team head, or Account Manager, would coordinate communications between all customer buying locations and OEG. Account managers would have worldwide profit and loss responsibility for their assigned customers. Sales representatives in district offices in other countries would report their customer activities to the lead account executive. Account executives are responsible for the subsidiaries of global customers in their geographic area. Account executives and sales representatives typically have multiple reporting relationships. A sample organizational chart appears in Exhibit 8. The boxes do not all represent people assigned full time to that account. For example, the account manager in Europe for Daimler-Benz would report to the sales manager in Europe. The Daimler-Benz account manager for Europe might also be a subsidiary account excecutive for Caterpillar in Europe, reporting to an account manager in the United States.

TOM BADEN'S DECISION

After attending the worldwide action team and OEG operations presentations, Tom Baden split OEG executives into two groups. Each group prepared a presentation explaining its vision for OEG's future corporate structure and marketing strategy.

Existing OEG Corporate Structure

One group maintained that the current organization structure (see Exhibit 4) would adequately meet the challenges posed by current external and internal problems. They believe that the 1983 problems were due to temporary forces and that the existing structure should not be changed.

Proposed New OEG Corporate Structure

Based on the results of the action team reports, the second group made several suggestions to improve OEG's performance. Two suggestions, global account management for large OEM's and telemarketing for small customers, were key features of the organizational structure proposed by the second group.

To incorporate these selling methods into OEG operations, the second group proposed the organization structure appearing in Exhibit 9 to replace the structure shown in Exhibit 4. The major difference is the replacement of the market groups (truck, agriculture, industrial, and construction) with the large-customer and mid-size and small-customer groups. The product/technical group is added to improve communication between engineering and marketing. Although this is a change from the current organizational structure, it is not a basis on which to accept or reject the new structure, since it could be appended to the current structure with little effort.

EXHIBIT 9
Proposed Structure—Original Equipment Group

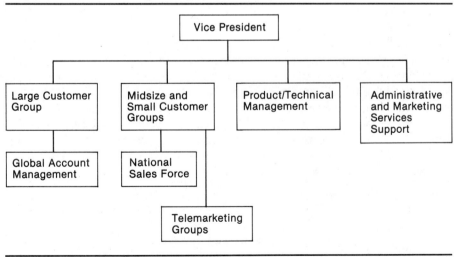

Source: Internal company documents.

The suggested organizational structure would offer a number of advantages. Service to multinational customers would be coordinated under a single account manager. Current problems with lack of coordination among DCI offices could be minimized. Small OEMs would receive more attention. Although little deviation from standard products would be permitted these customers, they would be contacted more frequently under telemarketing. Service to mid-size accounts would not change.

The proposed plan has several disadvantages as well. With fewer managers at the market director level, the number of workers each must supervise would increase. For the director of large accounts, that would involve 10 to 13 account managers for 30 to 40 accounts (some managers would be responsible for more than one account). Second, the reporting relationships (see Exhibit 8) grow rather complex under a GAM structure. This can obscure good and poor performance, making it more difficult to reward outstanding performance or detect poor performance. It could also make the saleperson's job more ambiguous as orders come from several bosses. Third, new-product development would be centered around applications for specific customers. With all salespeople focusing on specific customers, no one would be charged with maintaining a perspective on the market as a whole. Without a broad perspective on changing market conditions, it would be possible to miss a trend in customer usage characteristics, which could cause OEG to fail to become a technology leader in the new market. Narrow focus on a single customer's needs might also cause the salesperson or applications engineer to miss similar work performed for another account, thus duplicating effort.

THE DECISION

Baden must choose one of the two organizational structures to present to corporate management. Baden is aware that any organizational change inevitably causes staff upheaval, and he wants to ensure that the OEG structure chosen will remain in place for a long time. In deciding, he also must remember that the current organizational structure has been successful for many years and that any changes must be supported by sound reasoning. To help decide, he prepares the following questions to organize his presentation on the appropriate organizational structure to top DCI management.

1. How will customers react to both plans?
2. Which plan comes closest to solving the problems OEG faced in 1983?
3. Analyze the major strengths and weaknesses of each alternative. What conclusions can be drawn from the analysis?
4. Other than the alternatives presented, what organizational structures exist to accomplish the same goals? What dangers exist in suggesting an alternative organizational structure?

CASE 6-2

American Safety Razor Company

American Safety Razor Company's fight for survival was one of Virginia's biggest business news stories in 1977. Philip Morris, the parent company of American Safety Razor (ASR), had been seeking a buyer for the troubled subsidiary. However, sale was not easy because profits of ASR had declined each of the previous three years (see Exhibit 1). Philip Morris also insisted that prospective buyers guarantee to retain all 870 ASR employees. The Bic Pen Company had agreed to buy ASR; however, the Federal Trade Commission blocked the sale and claimed that such an agreement would be in restraint of competition.

Since no other purchase offers were considered acceptable, Philip Mor-

EXHIBIT 1

AMERICAN SAFETY RAZOR COMPANY
Five-Year Comparative Income Statement
($000)

	1973	1974	1975	1976	1977*
Net sales	$22,909	$26,089	$28,008	$27,917	$30,286
Royalties and other revenues	24	27	94	75	51
Total operating revenues	22,933	26,116	28,102	27,992	30,337
Less:					
Variable cost	8,768	9,692	9,924	9,965	11,225
Shipping expense	630	618	579	653	794
Fixed manufacturing	4,001	4,602	4,767	4,086	4,278
Available contribution margin	9,534	11,204	12,832	13,288	14,040
Operating expenses:					
Advertising	1,616	1,601	1,744	1,882	1,324
Sales force and promotion	4,503	5,571	7,451	8,070	8,462
Marketing research/marketing administration	379	449	453	417	346
General and administrative	1,290	1,320	1,720	1,397	1,479
Research and development	506	547	599	702	627
Total operating expenses	8,294	9,488	11,967	12,468	12,238
Operating profit	1,240	1,716	865	820	1,802
Interest expense	0	0	0	0	0
Other expenses	245	432	24	118	723
Profit before taxes	$ 995	$ 1,284	$ 841	$ 702	$ 1,079

* Amounts projected prior to management purchase in September.

This case was prepared by Joseph R. Mills, customer service manager of American Safety Razor Company, and Thomas M. Bertsch, associate professor of marketing at James Madison University. Confidential information has been disguised.

ris decided to close ASR. Manpower was reduced drastically as part of Philip Morris's liquidation plan. In operations alone, one-third of the work force was laid off. The national sales force was cut from 80 people to 30. Then, in September 1977, ASR's president John R. Baker and eight other company executives finalized an agreement to purchase ASR from Philip Morris. The executives paid $600,000 of their own money and $15 million which they had borrowed from two banks and a federal aid program.

COMPANY STRATEGY

Baker's initial marketing strategy after acquisition of ASR was to offer lower prices than Gillette and Schick and to expand ASR's share of the existing female market with the unique woman's razor, Flicker. From 1960 to 1976 ASR had focused on increased advertising expenditures, expansion of the sales force, greater consistency in product quality, competitive pricing, and development of new products. However, the new owners could not afford expensive, high-risk marketing strategies because of the financial strain of purchase and the need to pay off company debts that amounted to over $1 million a year in interest alone.

Baker expected ASR to "bounce back" and grow. He believed that ASR had an advantage over competition because the new owners were the company's managers and the existing work force was determined to succeed. However, management continued to search for ways to speed the improvement of company profits and market share.

COMPANY SALES COMPOSITION

As indicated in Exhibit 1, ASR's sales were approximately $28 million for the year prior to management purchase of the firm. Seventy percent of company sales were in the "wet shave" consumer market. Its own brands provided more than three-fourths of the dollars obtained by ASR from that market segment.

Industrial products provided the largest portion of ASR sales revenue. Twenty-seven percent of company business was in the industrial market segment. Sales growth since 1967 was attributed largely to the efforts of ASR to serve industrial consumers regardless of how unique the product might be.

The surgical blade market segment accounted for less than 5 percent of ASR's sales. Although the demand was not large, surgical blade sales were consistent in volume.

The remainder of company sales revenue came from foreign markets. By 1977 ASR's international sales had almost reached $2 million. Shaving blade products accounted for approximately 60 percent of the sales dollars from exports, and industrial products accounted for the rest.

BLADE MARKETS

Domestic Consumer Market

In 1977 the U.S. wet-shave market was estimated by the health and beauty aid industry to be $400 million per year at the retail level. That year, Gillette was holding 55 percent of the shaving blade market. Schick claimed 22 percent, and ASR held 11 percent. The remainder of the wet-shave market was divided between Bic and Wilkinson.

Little market growth was expected for at least the next 10 years because of the slow rate of population growth. Opportunities were increasing in the women's market segment because teenage girls were shaving at an earlier age and more frequently than they did during the early 1970s. However, males were shaving less frequently. Beards were more widely accepted in the late 1970s than they were in the early 1970s, and the popularity of the bearded look had increased. Very few electric-razor users switch to blades, so that market segment did not represent a significant area of possible growth for ASR. Firms in the blade industry expected most new domestic consumer business to come from either increasing market share of their company or opening up new markets.

Industrial Blade Market

The industrial blade market in the United States was estimated by industry leaders to be in the $40 million to $50 million range. ASR held about 20 percent of that market, which made it one of the largest manufacturers of industrial blades in the United States. Ardell Industries, Crescent Manufacturing, and Winsor Manufacturing had 10 percent, 5 percent, and 2 percent, respectively, of the industrial blade market. Exacto and Durham, which offered a limited product line, each had gross sales in the $5 million to $6 million range. Of the four major producers of shaving blades, only ASR competed in the industrial market.

Surgical Market

The surgical blade market was estimated at only $6 million. Bard-Parker was the sales leader with a 59 percent share of the market; ASR was a distant second with 29 percent, followed by Beaver with 8 percent. Proper, a foreign company that exports large quantities of blades to the United States, was next with 2 percent of the market. The surgical blade market was very small compared to the wet-shave consumer market.

International Market

The sales potential of foreign wet-shaving markets was estimated by one industry leader to be 10 times the actual dollar sales to the U.S. market. In 1977 Gillette accounted for between 80 and 90 percent of the foreign sales of

U.S. blades. Schick, Wilkinson, and ASR also competed in the overseas market, but Gillette had taken the lead in teaching people to shave.

ASR has had mixed results from its efforts to penetrate foreign markets. The company had approximately half of the shaving blade market in Puerto Rico. However, high labor costs forced closing of its production facility in Scotland, and its efforts in Brazil to provide technical assistance for blade manufacturing did not meet expectations. Even though setbacks were encountered in several foreign markets, the new owners of ASR still believed that some international markets could be highly profitable for ASR.

PRODUCT STRATEGY

ASR offers over 500 different versions of packaged shaving, industrial, and surgical blade products. See Exhibit 2 for a list of product line changes made by ASR.

Products by Gillette have become the industry standards for comparison. Therefore ASR's shaving blade products are judged against Gillette's products and are designed to meet those standards. However, ASR's shaving

EXHIBIT 2
Major Product Line Changes of ASR, as of 1977

Year Introduced	Product	Status
1875	Star safety razor	Replaced with Gem razor
1889	Gem safety razor	Continued, with modification
1915	Ever-Ready shaving brush	Continued
1919	Gem, Star, and Ever-Ready shaving blades	Continued
1933	Lightfoot soap	Discontinued in 1973
1934	Electric shaver	Discontinued in 1934
1935	Pile wire-carpet	Discontinued in 1977
1935	Surgical blades and handles	Continued
1947	Double-edge shaving blade	Continued
1948	Injector shaving blade	Continued
1963	Stainless steel coated blade	Continued
1969	Face Guard shaving blade	Continued
1970	Personna tungsten steel blades	Continued
1971	Flicker	Continued
1973	Personna Double II shaving system	Continued
1974	Personna Injector II blade	Continued
1975	Double Edge II	Discontinued in 1976
1975	Lady	Continued
1977	Single II shaving system	Continued

systems, such as Flicker and Double II, are designed to be distinctive in appearance.

Typically, major competitors in the blade industry denied that they developed products in response to the introduction of a new product by a competitor. Company representatives usually stressed that they were responding to consumer needs, not actions of competitors. The industry practice, though, was for major producers to follow quickly a competitor's innovative product with a competing product. When Wilkinson introduced its stainless steel blade in the early 1960s, all major competitors followed with similar products. In 1969 Gillette introduced its Platinum Plus blade, and competitors followed with versions of the platinum-chromium blade. Eighteen months after ASR introduced Flicker to the women's wet-shaving market, Gillette introduced Daisy. The time between introduction of a new type of product and introduction of a similar product by a major competitor is now only 10 to 12 months.

New product introductions are one way for a firm to increase market share. However, a new, better shaving blade product may not gain much market share. This fact became painfully clear to ASR soon after the introduction of twin-blade systems in 1971. Gillette's introduction in this product category was the Trac II. Schick called its introduction Super II. ASR decided that it had one of three choices: make no introduction, make the same design as Gillette and offer it under a different name, or make a slightly different product. ASR's management decided it had to make an introduction because of the large market potential involved. The ASR version came out eight months later and was called Double II.

Since ASR was late in entering this new consumer market segment, management chose to try a modified twin-blade system. The new version was a double-edge bonded blade system, which offered twice as many shaves as the Trac II and Super II. The shaving system uniquely featured a gap between the bonded blades that permitted the cut hair to be washed away. With discounts offered, the consumer could buy the ASR system at the same price as Trac II. ASR's new product was a good one, according to consumer tests, but Double II did not pick up the 16 percent market share expected (see Exhibit 3).

The major marketing emphasis in the industry since the middle 1960s has been directed toward the marketing of "shaving systems" versus razors and blades. One of the newest systems to be introduced is the disposable razor. Some market analysts estimated that the disposable razor category could build into a 20 percent segment of the estimated $400 million blade market. By 1978 Wilkinson and Schick had followed Bic and Gillette into the low-priced disposable razor market with their own versions of a disposable razor.

ASR offered industrial blades for the carpet industry, utility knife blades, and specialty blades for the food, textile, and electronic industries. There was also an industrial line of injector, single-edge, and double-edge

EXHIBIT 3
Market Performance of Twin-Blade Systems

Product	Date of Introduction	1971–1973 Advertising ($ millions)	January 1974 Share of Total Razor Blade Market	1973 Sales ($ millions)
Trac II (Gillette)	1971	$117	23.2%	$10.9
Super II (Schick)	1972	4	6.3	2.5
Double II (ASR)	1973	3	1.3	0.6

blades. The company had been able to convince its industrial customers that disposable blades mean a quality product and a reduction of machine downtime. The strategy of ASR was to find new industrial users for disposable blades, but the market was specialized, so customized orders were common.

ASR offers a full line of surgical blades and handles. Since competitors have not made any recent introduction of new products for this market, ASR has devoted its efforts to technological and quality improvements. Consistent processing effort is expended to improve the sharpness and durability of its surgical blades.

Although standard-brand shaving blade products and industrial blades were sold in the international market, many products were especially prepared for each market. For instance, in South America many double-edge blades are sold one at a time; therefore ASR individually wrapped and packaged each blade for that market. Package labels for Europe were printed in four languages: English, French, Portuguese, and German. In the Far East, a single-edge blade with an extra-thick back for easier handling was sold instead of the standard single-edge blade. Customized orders were accepted in the hope of building repeat business.

DISTRIBUTION STRATEGY

Most razors and razor blades in the United States were sold in retail groceries and drugstores. New retail accounts were solicited directly on the basis of their expected volume. ASR had decided to concentrate on large accounts. Therefore it used distributors to serve small accounts, but it sold direct to large accounts. Much of the industry was dominated by large accounts such as chain drugstores and supermarkets.

The company was hesitant to reject requests for dealer labels. Management felt that ASR could not compete unless its product offerings were in a dominant position on the shelf. This was particularly true of wholesalers and retailers, who were willing to push their own brand considerably more than a manufacturer's brand.

In general, demand for manufacturers' brands of blades was not growing significantly. However, ASR saw an opportunity to increase its market share in the dealer-brand segment of the market. A product was considered eligible for dealer labels if it had at least 8 to 10 percent of the branded market. All dealer label accounts were handled by a small corporate department which performed the necessary marketing functions. ASR held 75 percent of this growing market segment.

ASR sold its surgical blades through a national hospital supply company, which acted as exclusive distributor for the blades. The distributor was permitted by contract to ship to any location in the world. The 1976 contract between the two firms also included renewal clauses.

ASR's industrial products were sold to both users and distributors. Brokers were used to sell less than 20 percent of the products. ASR's industrial sales force concentrated its efforts on the large-volume customers and distributors. Many of the direct customers were manufacturers in the electronics, textile, and food industries.

The International Marketing Division utilized distributors in most countries because ASR did not employ an international sales force. ASR preferred to sell to many distributors within a country in order to obtain wide distribution and to avoid dependence on a single distributor; however, many foreign distributors had exclusive selling rights in their country. The most active accounts were in Latin America, Canada, and Japan.

PRICING STRATEGY

ASR's prices for unique products, such as Flicker and single-edge blades, were competitive with the prices of other shaving products in the market. If a retailer did any local promotion of ASR's brands of products, then cooperative advertising was arranged. ASR's double-edge, injector, and Double II products were priced less to retailers than similar items offered by competitors.

ASR was the price leader for industrial blades. Since dealer promotions and national advertising were not used for industrial blades, this market segment was a consistent contributor to profitability.

The company's surgical products were priced low in relation to competition. The national distributor established the resale prices, and the wholesale prices were renegotiated annually.

ASR's products were sold in foreign wholesale markets for approximately one-third less than they were sold for in the United States. Price quotes on export orders did not include shipping costs, although domestic prices included shipping charges.

PROMOTION STRATEGY

The amount spent by ASR on national advertising varied according to the newness of the product. Established products, such as single-edge blades, were not advertised. However, a product such as Flicker did receive attention. Flicker was both a relatively new product and one which was dominant in the market. Therefore ASR allocated $1 million for promotion of its Flicker ladies' shaving system in 1977.

Razors and razor blades were typically marketed with large expenditures for promotion. Gillette, for example, spent $6 million on promoting its new Good News! shaver in 1977. Gillette also planned to support its new Atra (automatic tracking razor) with a $7.7 million advertising campaign in 1977. Major competitors of ASR had spent large sums of money on consumer-directed advertising and promotion to maintain strong national brand preference.

The Bic Pen Company, which had been blocked from buying ASR, decided in 1976 to compete in the American branded blade market. It planned a large and expensive introductory marketing program for 1977, budgeting $9 million for sales and promotion of its single-blade, lightweight razor, which is completely disposable. Part of the promotional strategy was to give away a disposable razor and blade to 40 percent of the U.S. households.

Promotional methods used by major producers of blades included giveaways, rebates, cents-off programs, couponing, cooperative advertising with retailers, special displays, and volume discounts. The industry relied heavily on the use of TV advertising. However, several other advertising media were used, including full-page magazine ads and Sunday newspaper supplement ads.

MARKETING ORGANIZATION

Prior to the planned liquidation of ASR by Philip Morris, the marketing group consisted of brand managers, assistant brand managers, a marketing administrator, a single marketing researcher, and an assistant researcher. By 1978 the group had been reduced to the vice president of marketing, the director of product management, and the director of international marketing (see Exhibit 4). ASR's top management felt that the smaller marketing team could handle the reduced advertising budget and the target market segments.

Both the sales group and the marketing group were based in Staunton, Virginia. The vice president of sales reported to the company president. The directors of field sales, industrial products, and national accounts reported to the vice president of sales. Three field sales managers reported to the director of field sales. Twenty-four regional managers reported to the field sales managers. ASR had four selling divisions: Branded Products, Private Label Products, Industrial and Surgical Products, and International Marketing.

The sales force represented the only link between the company and large retail accounts, such as chain drugstores and supermarkets. Chain stores were very important since they represented the key strategic ap-

EXHIBIT 4
Marketing-Sales Organization

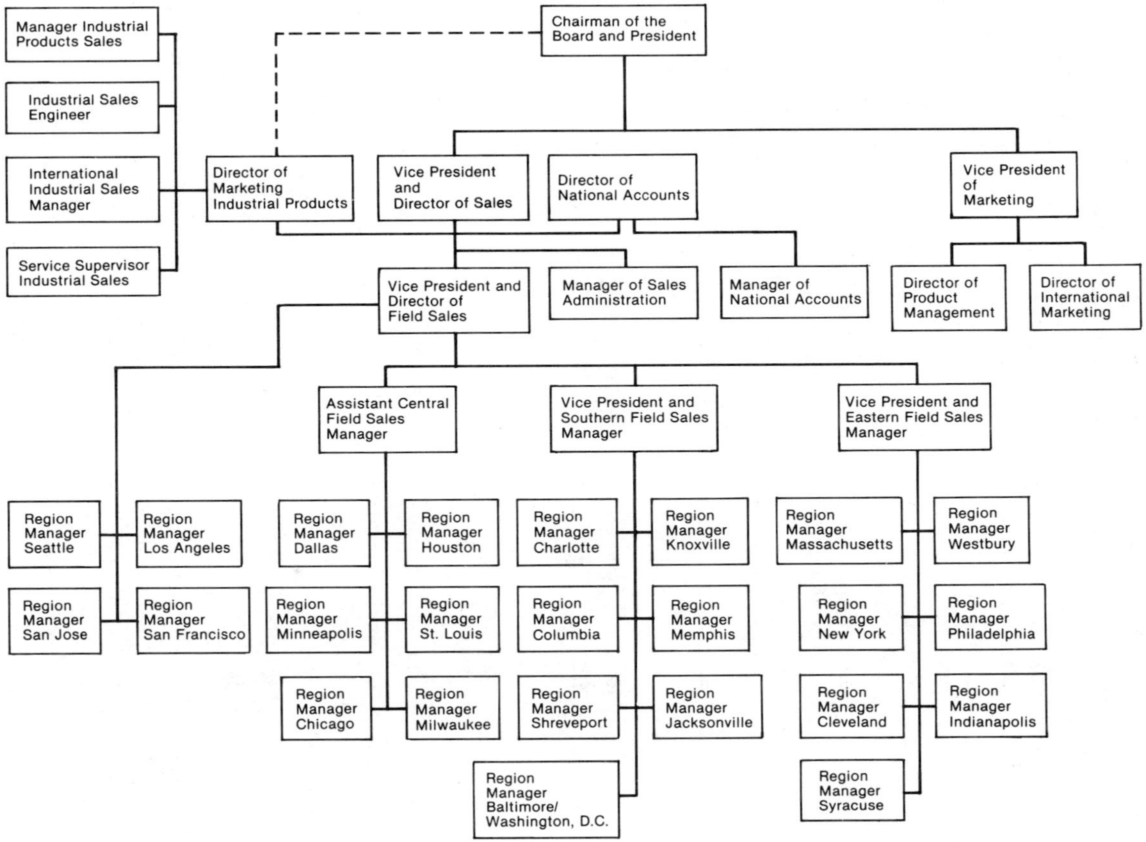

proach of the ASR shaving blade business. Each regional sales manager was expected to spend much of his time in developing sales to the big chains.

Until late 1974 ASR's field salespeople received a compensation package composed of straight salary plus fringe benefits. Then, in 1975, an incentive system was introduced which included a monthly commission, a semiannual incentive for participation in company promotional programs, and annual compensation opportunities related to regional profitability. The new compensation package was introduced to help both the sales managers and the salespersons. By 1978 the sales managers felt that ASR was attracting better quality, experienced salespersons and that the sales personnel liked the new incentive rewards.

CASE 6–3

Robert N. Maxwell Memorial Community Hospital

BACKGROUND AND HISTORY

The Robert N. Maxwell Memorial Community Hospital is a large 400-plus bed hospital serving a city of 842,000 in a county of 1,808,000 people. The hospital is one of eight major ones operating in the county and is ranked second in size in terms of number of beds and number of admissions per year. In addition, several small hospitals also operate in the county, but these are not considered to be major competitors.

The hospital has operated in the community for a number of years and is well known by area physicians and the community. Over 800 physicians are on the hospital's staff, and they provide the hospital with physician expertise in such areas as urology, pediatrics, OB–GYN, orthopedics, general practice, internal medicine, general surgery, neurosurgery, ophthalmology, ENT (ear-nose-throat), plastic surgery, proctology, thoracic medicine, and dental. Many of these 800 physicians are on the staffs of other area hospitals at the same time, but they do admit patients to Maxwell Hospital. It is common practice for many physicians to use more than one hospital, and thus a single physician could be on staff with a number of hospitals at the same time.

Originally the hospital had been called County General Hospital, but it

---

Reprinted from R. W. Haas and T. R. Wotruba, *Marketing Management: Concepts, Practice and Cases,* copyright © Business Publications, Inc., 1983, by permission of the publisher.

was renamed Robert N. Maxwell Memorial Community Hospital during World War II. Robert N. Maxwell had been the 24-year-old son of a member of the hospital's board of directors, Joshua Maxwell. The younger Maxwell had been an Army Air Corps P-40 fighter pilot who had been killed early in the war in the Philippine Islands. The hospital had been renamed in his memory and was now commonly referred to simply as Maxwell Hospital. Few people in the community actually knew who Robert N. Maxwell had been or the derivation of the hospital's name.

Howard Hartley is the associate director of the hospital and functions in the capacity of its chief operating officer. A graduate of a Midwestern university with an MBA degree, Hartley is a very able and respected administrator. He is responsible for a host of departmental and functional activities, one of which is marketing. He is chairman of the hospital's loosely defined marketing committee and is therefore considered the top marketing officer in the organization. Hartley, however, does not consider himself a marketing authority and in fact is somewhat concerned about this. He has held this position for a number of years, dating back to when the hospital was relatively small. In those days, competition was not as strong as it had become in 1980, and the hospital itself was not as complex. Marketing had not been considered a really important activity. By 1980, the picture had changed—competition was fierce, and the organization was large and sometimes unwieldy. In addition, Hartley was concerned about his own ability to manage the marketing aspects of the company, since he was responsible for so many other activities at the same time. He did not feel he could give marketing the attention it needed.

THE PRESENT HOSPITAL ORGANIZATION

Exhibit 1 depicts the present general organization of the hospital. Five individuals make up the organization's top management team.

Paul Cashman holds the position of executive director and is for all purposes the equivalent of the organization's president. Well educated, articulate, and gracious, Cashman is an ideal top officer. He relates well with physician groups, with various hospital association people, with the area's political leaders, and with the community in general. In addition, he is a good buffer between the hospital and its board of directors. He does not, however, take an active interest in the day-to-day operations of the organization but leaves that to his subordinates. He relies heavily on Hartley to keep him informed in this area.

As has been stated, Howard Hartley is the hospital's associate director and acts as the chief operating officer. Cashman looks to Hartley to actually run the hospital. As the organization chart shows, Hartley is involved in many areas, heading up seven departments and chairing five functional committees as well.

EXHIBIT 1
Organization Chart

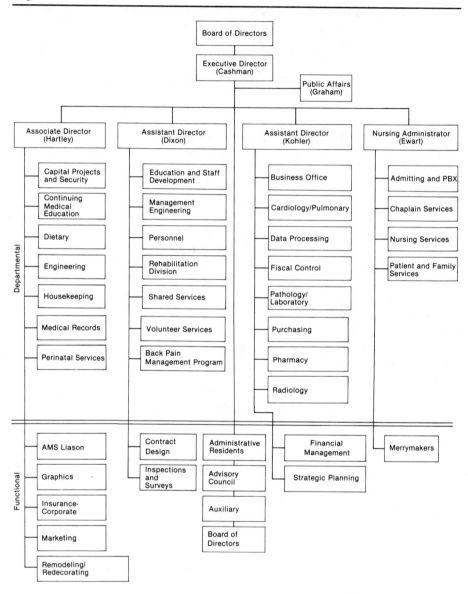

Andre Dixon is an assistant director and is considered the hospital's top personnel officer. A college graduate with a degree in personnel management, Dixon has little interest or expertise in marketing. As the chart shows, his primary area of responsibility is in training and personnel development, although he is also involved in the administration of the hospital's rehabilitation division and its back-pain management program. Both of these are medical programs headed by physicians. Dixon works closely with these physicians in the administration of these programs.

Terry Kohler is also an assistant director and is the organization's top financial officer. A recent MBA degree holder from an Ivy League university, Kohler is a financial, statistical, and data processing whiz. As the chart shows, his areas of responsibility are in fiscal control, purchasing, and data processing. He, like Dixon, is also involved in the administration of medical programs and departments, such as pathology and radiology. A very bright and able young administrator, Kohler is also responsible for the hospital's strategic planning program. In view of all his responsibilities, Kohler has little time for marketing activities although he does serve on the hospital's marketing committee.

The fifth top administrator is Nonny Ewart, the nursing administrator. Ms. Ewart has considerable nursing experience and is considered a very able nursing administrator. Well respected by her nurses, Ewart brings stability and professionalism to this important area of hospital administration. Her degree is in nursing, and she acknowledges openly that she has little awareness of what is involved in hospital marketing.

The primary marketing vehicle in the organization is the hospital's marketing committee. This committee is comprised of Dixon, Kohler, Ewart, and Hartley as chairman. Norman Graham, an outside consultant retained by the hospital, also serves on this committee. Graham heads the public affairs department which reports directly to Cashman as the chart indicates. This department is primarily responsible for publicity and public relations. Often, Paul Cashman attends committee meetings which typically take place on the first and third Thursdays of every month at 8:00 A.M. In addition, representatives from various departments, such as patient and family services, and public affairs, are often invited to attend. The committee meets to discuss marketing ideas and programs, and Hartley assigns various marketing activities to members when such activities are decided upon. This committee, while stretched thin, has fostered a genuine interest in strengthening the hospital's marketing orientation, which Hartley believes is a positive factor.

THE PROBLEM

A number of things are bothering Hartley regarding the hospital's marketing position.

First, the hospital's market share in terms of beds and admissions appears to be dropping. Hartley has analyzed these data between 1970 and 1980, and the decline is illustrated in Exhibit 2. Hartley is concerned that if these trends continue, Maxwell Hospital could be in trouble in the future.

EXHIBIT 2

Robert N. Maxwell Hospital's Share of Beds and Admissions among Major Hospitals in the County Area, 1970 and 1980

	Beds				Admissions*			
	1970		1980		1970		1980	
Hospital	Number	Percent	Number	Percent	Number	Percent	Number	Percent
Maxwell	352	16.0%	401	15.7%	16,679	18.8%	14,793	15.6%
Canyon†	175	8.0	195	7.6	1,569	1.8	6,882	7.3
Claybourne	99	4.5	150	5.8	6,057	6.8	4,082	4.3
Greymont	234	10.6	234	9.1	13,175	14.8	12,039	12.7
Mercyhurst	498	22.6	511	20.0	21,599	24.3	21,140	22.3
Peninsula‡	150	6.8	150	5.9	4,277	4.8	4,391	4.6
Bayside	240	10.9	363	14.2	10,745	12.1	12,994	13.7
Doctors & Nurses	219	10.0	250	9.8	5,738	6.4	4,387	4.6
North County	232	10.6	306	11.9	9,096	10.2	14,202	14.9
Total	2,199	100.0%	2,560	100.0%	88,935*	100.0%	94,910*	100.0%

* Admission figures do not represent maximum number of patients possible, but rather the number of patients actually admitted in those years.
† Opened in mid-1972.
‡ Opened in 1974.

Second, a study conducted on the staff physicians indicates that the hospital may not be attracting enough young physicians. Reviewing age distributions for general practice and internal medicine physicians between 1970 and 1980, Exhibit 3 shows the data observed. Since both types of physicians are important in generating referrals, Hartley feels that the trends are not favorable.

Third, this same physician study indicates that a definite heavy-user pattern exists with physicians on staff. This is shown in Exhibit 4 which reveals that 12.4 percent of the staff physicians (104 of 835) admitted 61.2 percent of the patients (9,053 of 14,793 in 1980). Hartley believes this statistic is important, but he is unsure of its marketing implications.

Fourth, Hartley is concerned because there is no marketing specialist

EXHIBIT 3

Age Distributions of Staff Physicians

	Percent of General Practice Physicians		Percent of Internal Medicine Physicians	
Age Groups	1970	1980	1970	1980
50 and under	69.6%	43.8%	81.3%	66.9%
51 and over	30.4	56.2	18.7	33.1
Total	100.0%	100.0%	100.0%	100.0%

EXHIBIT 4
Heavy-User Concept of Maxwell Hospital Physicians in 1980

Area	Total Number of Physicians	Number and Percent of Heavy Users		Patients Admitted by Heavy Users	
		Number	Percent	Number	Percent
Urology	37	6	16.2%	204	61.3%
Pediatrics	75	10	13.3	1,541	57.3
OB–GYN	94	16	17.0	2,942	57.1
Orthopedics	68	10	14.7	857	63.8
General practice	148	10	6.8	486	59.6
Internal	142	11	7.7	1,274	60.1
General surgery	93	10	10.8	751	62.9
Neurosurgery	18	6	33.3	256	92.6
Ophthalmology	59	6	10.2	156	88.1
ENT	26	5	19.2	249	83.3
Plastic surgery	16	5	31.2	55	84.4
Proctology	3	2	66.7	64	100.0
Thoracic	26	5	19.2	188	86.4
Dental	30	2	3.3	30	68.6
Total	835	104	12.4%	9,053	61.2%

or professional on the marketing committee or in the entire hospital. He has read many health-care journal articles whose authors impress the need for hospitals to market more effectively in the changing health-care environment. These same authors also stress the need for hospitals to employ health-care marketing professionals to manage their marketing operations. He is also intrigued by the want ad which he had read in a major metropolitan newspaper (see Exhibit 5). Hartley cannot help but wonder if Maxwell Hospital has arrived at that point where marketing should be handled as a primary as opposed to a secondary activity.

MARKETING OBJECTIVES

A major responsibility of Hartley and the marketing committee had been to develop marketing objectives for the hospital. This was required as part of Kohler's strategic planning program. The committee put in many long hours on this and defined three target markets:

1. *The Physician Market.* Since most hospital patients are admitted by physicians, focusing marketing efforts on physicians in the area seemed most appropriate.

2. *The Patient Market.* Since patients can and do influence physicians in their selection of hospitals, the committee felt some form of patient marketing was needed.
3. *The Community Market.* Since the hospital must operate as a part of its community, marketing effort to promote Maxwell Hospital as a good citizen was logical.

The marketing committee then established objectives in each of these three target markets.

Overall Objective

To increase overall utilization of Robert N. Maxwell Memorial Community Hospital as a major community hospital in the county.

EXHIBIT 5

DIRECTOR OF
HOSPITAL MARKETING

A unique, growth opportunity now exists with our young, rapidly expanding National Health Care Management Company, for a highly motivated individual having a solid record of achieving significant quantifiable results.

The Director's responsibility is to achieve increased utilization and increased revenue for the Emergency Department's ancillary services, and in-patient units of general acute hospitals. The successful candidate would have authority to achieve, with his staff, census improvement results through physician contacts, community relations activity, public service health education programs, open-houses, inter-agency affiliations, and any other suitable techniques with which she or he might be familiar or might innovate. The qualified candidate might come from any of a variety of career backgrounds, but must be thoroughly familiar with hospital procedures and interrelationships. Such a candidate might be a Hospital Administrator, a Registered Nurse Consultant, a Nursing In-Service Director, a Clinic Manager, an Operations Executive of a Hospital Management Company, or an individual who has successfully marketed and developed management contracts for Hospital Ancillary Services.

If you are an ambitious executive seeking an environment where your growth and reward are contingent only upon your own performance, starting with an excellent salary and liberal fringe benefits, this is the unlimited opportunity you have been seeking.

Send your resume and salary requirement to:

BOX D-005NA,   TIMES
An Equal Opportunity Employer M/F

Physician Market Objectives

- To attract and retain a growing number of heavy-user physicians to the hospital.
- To continue to develop areas of specialization which will in turn attract physicians to the hospital because of the quality of services offered. This is currently being done with cardiovascular services, perinatal services, and rehabilitation services. (These were termed Commitment Level I services.)
- To create an awareness, liking, and preference for Maxwell Hospital among younger physicians and those recently arrived in the county.
- To increase the number of primary physicians (e.g., general practice and internal medicine) and thereby increasing the hospital's referral potential for other physicians.
- To increase the identification by present physicians with Maxwell Hospital and thus foster a closer relationship between the hospital and physicians using the hospital.
- To increase awareness by physicians in the state and surrounding area of the hospital's services, particularly in its areas of specialization.
- To increase awareness of the quality of services provided by Maxwell Hospital to strengthen the preference for Maxwell Hospital among all types of physicians in the county.

Patient Market Objectives

- To continue to provide the highest quality of patient care possible to foster favorable word-of-mouth promotion by patients to potential patients and to physicians in the marketplace.
- To develop the image of Maxwell Hospital as a quality provider of first-rate acute health care to potential patients in the marketplace.
- To attract health maintenance patients as well as acute health-care patients.
- To develop a file of patients of record so that more of the market has an existing relationship with Maxwell Hospital.
- To establish Maxwell Hospital as a complete source of information on health-care services and their availability in the county area.

Community Market Objectives

- To increase the level of public awareness in the county, and to broaden the image of Maxwell Hospital as not only a highly specialized hospital but also a total community hospital.
- To provide assistance and services to health-related institutions and to other community organizations.

- To increase the level of public awareness in the state and surrounding region of Maxwell Hospital's Commitment Level I Services.
- To establish the image of Maxwell Hospital as a good corporate citizen that is concerned and involved with community issues and problems.

The committee does not see the three markets as equals but recommends that marketing efforts be devoted toward the three in these proportions: 70 percent to the physician market, 20 percent to the patient market, and 10 percent to the community market.

Hartley believes the committee has done a good job and that the objectives are valid. He doubts, however, that these objectives could be attained with the hospital's existing marketing organization. In particular, he does not believe the hospital possesses the necessary marketing expertise or resources to develop strategies and programs to reach these objectives. He wonders how the hospital might best be organized to attain these objectives and reverse the trends he feels are alarming. Advise Mr. Hartley.

CASE 6–4

Aurora Lotion

John Fairchild frowned as he hung up the telephone. He had just finished another conversation with Urs Brunner, the general manager of Produits Pour Femmes, SA (PPF), on a subject that had become increasingly troublesome over the last three years: how to respond to the problem of parallel importing of Aurora Lotion into Switzerland. Fairchild was the general manager of the Overseas Division of Smythe-Dabney International, Ltd., a British company which marketed Aurora and other women's cosmetics. A large portion of his job was devoted to offering information and recommendations to the managers of the subsidiary companies which made up the division.

The management of PPF, the Swiss subsidiary, had reported a growing rash of price cutting on Aurora Lotion, one of its most important products, by a group of independent distributors who were buying Aurora in England and bringing it to Switzerland themselves. This practice, which had been dubbed "parallel importing" or "black importing" in the trade, had put

---

This case was prepared by Thomas Kosnik, research associate, under the direction of Professor Christopher Gale. Copyright © 1978 by l'Institut pour l'Étude des Méthodes de Direction de l'Entreprise (IMEDE), Lausanne, Switzerland. Reproduced by permission.

PPF's gross margins under pressure and squeezed the company's return on sales. The situation had reached the point that Urs Brunner had asked John Fairchild to intervene and recommend a strategy to counter the threat, including a substantial reduction of PPF's selling price for Aurora if necessary.

SMYTHE-DABNEY INTERNATIONAL, LTD.

The parent company for PPF was Smythe-Dabney International, Ltd. (SDI), with headquarters outside London. In 1977 SDI's sales were £25.8 million and its trading profits were £2.6 million. In the last 10 years earnings per share had increased at the compound rate of 20 percent a year. Sir Anthony Carburton, the chairman of SDI, felt that the impressive record was the result of several factors, including the quality of the company's product, the energies and talents of a close-knit management team, and the ability to stay a step ahead of competitors in the marketplace.

From the earliest days with the introduction of Aurora Lotion, SDI had marketed only products of high quality and had stressed that theme in advertising and promotion campaigns. As a result the various SDI cosmetics, under the Aurora name and in several other well-known brand families, enjoyed widespread brand recognition and consumer loyalty.

A keen sensitivity to the needs of both the channels of distribution and consumers caused the company's directors to search continually for ways to make their products and services more competitive. They had defined the market they served as the women's beauty care market and had acquired a wide line of products that complemented each other and ensured efficient utilization of the sales force and marketing staff. They quickly learned that the ability to supply the trade was critical and earned a reputation for having the company's products in stock in a timely fashion, providing a valuable service for their distributors. They used extensive television advertising to stimulate demand, and point-of-purchase displays in retail outlets to make it easier for consumers to select the products they needed.

The objectives of the company for the next three years were to increase sales and earnings per share 20 percent a year and to maintain a pretax income/sales ratio of 10 percent. The basic guidelines the corporate management had drafted to reach those objectives were to:

1. Increase unit volume of sales in all product lines.
2. Maintain historic direct (gross) margins.
3. Keep corporate overhead expenses low by maintaining a lean home office staff.
4. Give management of subsidiary companies decision-making authority on all tactical matters, with consultation with corporate management on strategic issues.

THE OVERSEAS DIVISION

SDI was composed of the UK Division and the Overseas Division. In 1977 the Overseas Division sold £10.8 million worth of women's beauty products in continental Europe, North America, and the Far East. In Europe, SDI had company-owned subsidiaries in France, Germany, and Switzerland and marketed its products in other countries through independent wholesale distributors.

Both Fairchild and Carburton shared the view that the most promising markets for future growth were in Europe and North America. In 1977 much of the 20 percent growth in sales and profits projected for the company as a whole was expected to come from the Overseas Division.

PRODUITS POUR FEMMES, SA

PPF was responsible for the marketing of Aurora and other SDI products in Switzerland. Its reporting relationship in the Overseas Division is shown in Exhibit 1. The organization was small, with 14 people in all comprising a sales force, marketing department, accounting department, and warehouse crew.

Sales of the company in 1977 were SFr. 4.3 million, up 22 percent from the year before. Exhibit 2 shows PPF's income statement for 1976 and 1977.

Urs Brunner had recently taken over as general manager. He and his marketing manager were the key decision makers in day-to-day activities;

EXHIBIT 1
Smythe-Dabney International Ltd.—Overseas Division Organization Chart

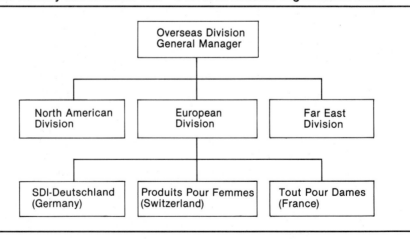

Source: SDI company records.

EXHIBIT 2

PRODUITS POUR FEMMES, SA DIVISION
Income Statement
1976 and 1977
(SFr. 000)

	1976	1977
Sales	3,525	4,300
Less: Cost of goods sold	1,160	1,720
Direct margin	2,365	2,580
Less:		
Advertising	405	403
Distribution	204	330
Promotion*	175	230
Other expenses†	55	70
Brand contribution	1,490	1,520
Less:		
Sales force expenses	410	430
General and administration	670	610
Trading profit (before tax)	410	480

* Does not include trade discounts on Aurora Lotion.
† Other expenses included marketing research, product research, public relations, depreciation, and inventory losses through obsolescence, damage etc.

Source: SDI company records (disguised).

John Fairchild and Dustin Cushman, the general manager for Europe, involved themselves with PPF only on matters of strategic importance.

THE PRODUCT

Aurora Lotion was a high-quality, all-purpose lotion for women. It was applied by being spread lightly over the skin of the face, arms, legs, and other parts of the body and then rubbing gently until the lotion was completely absorbed into the skin. The company stressed in its advertising that Aurora relieved dryness due to sun, wind, water, or detergents and made skin feel soft, clean, and gentle to the touch. It also stated that the effects of the lotion were longer lasting than those of many similar products. A single application of Aurora before bedtime each evening kept the skin "soft and beautiful," while it was necessary to apply other lotions as often as three or four times a day to get the same protection. The secret of Aurora's long-lasting effectiveness was a unique formula which allowed the lotion to penetrate the skin more completely than competing brands.

Aurora Lotion was the brand leader in a growing line of beauty products which included hand lotion, moisturizers, and bath preparations. Ex-

EXHIBIT 3

AURORA PRODUCT GROUP PPF
Brand Contribution Statement
1976 and 1977
(SFr. 000)

	1976	*1977*
Sales.	850	1,140
Less: Cost of goods sold	290	526
Direct margin.	560	614
Less:		
Advertising	94	106
Distribution expenses	50	55
Promotion*	74	150
Other expenses†	15	12
Brand contribution	327	291

* Does not include trade discounts on Aurora Lotion.
† Other expenses included marketing research, product research, public relations, depreciation, and inventory losses.

Source: SDI company records (disguised).

hibit 3 contains the Aurora product line's brand contribution statement to PPF. The company also marketed the full line of SDI products under other brands, including facial cosmetics, eye cosmetics, hair preparations, nail polish, and deodorants. In 1977 Aurora Lotion sales accounted for 20 percent of the total sales of PPF.

Over the years, Aurora Lotion had become increasingly familiar to women in many European countries. In fact, parallel importers capitalized on this brand recognition and easily sold Aurora Lotion in Switzerland that had been shipped directly from Britain, even though the directions for use of the lotion were in English. Fairchild and Brunner estimated that 120,000 bottles of Aurora were parallel-imported into Switzerland in 1977, compared with PPF sales of 200,000 bottles in the same period.

COMPETITIVE PRODUCTS

All-purpose lotions for women were available in great variety and a wide range of price and quality. However, they tended to cluster in three main groups.

1. High-priced products. These lotions were most often produced by companies making fashionable women's perfumes. They had the same scents as popular women's fragrances, so the consumer could use the lotion along with her favorite cologne or perfume. These lotions were sold for SFr.

20 to SFr. 50 in retail outlets, for bottles of 100 to 200 centiliters (cl). Some packages were annotated in grams rather then centiliters.

2. Medium-price lotions.   Many of these lotions were imported to Switzerland from France and England. They were attractively packaged and often made claims to characteristics that differentiated them from other lotions. Some were made by perfume houses to match less-expensive fragrances. They sold for between SFr. 7.50 and SFr. 15, and the most common bottle size was 200 cl.

3. Low-price lotions.   These products were the simple, functional answer to the everyday problems of dry, rough skin due to water, weather, and housework. Prices ranged from SFr. 3 to SFr. 6 for a plastic container of 240 cl to 450 cl.

Exhibit 4 provides examples of all-purpose lotions in the three price ranges. Aurora Lotion, with a suggested retail price of SFr. 15 for 200 cl, was positioned near the top of the middle range of lotions.

Consumers cited several problems that sometimes arose when using an all-purpose lotion. These related to the fragrance of the lotion and its ability to penetrate the skin. Some products had a heavy, sweet, or powerful scent that could potentially clash with or mask the fragrance of perfume. Some lotions left the skin feeling slippery, greasy, or wet after application, while

EXHIBIT 4
Sample of All-Purpose Lotions Available in Switzerland

Product	Size of Selling Unit	Retail Selling Price per Selling Unit
High-price:		
Caron	120 cl	SFr. 28.00
Chanel	80 g	24.50
Je Reviens	100 cl	22.50
Amnioderm	200 cl	30.00
Medium-price:		
Aurora Lotion	200 cl	SFr. 15.00
Bea Kasser	150 cl	14.50
Janine D	200 cl	13.50
4711	200 cl	9.50
Ma Garde	125 cl	7.50
Oil of Olay	200 cl	7.50
Fenjal	250 cl	7.50
Winston's	300 cl	8.40
Low-price:		
Rose Milk	240 cl	SFr. 5.90
Nivea	250 cl	4.95
Kaloderma	300 cl	4.50
Jana Lait de Toilette (Migros)	430 cl	3.50

Source: Field research at retail outlets, Lausanne, Switzerland.

others were not absorbed into the skin and washed off immediately upon contact with water. In the former case the lotion might stain clothing or furniture. In the latter case it was necessary to apply the lotion several times a day, after bathing, doing dishes, or returning from out of doors. The popularity of Aurora Lotion was due in large part to the fact that it had a light, clean scent that did not clash with perfumes and also that it penetrated deeply without leaving the skin slick or greasy.

THE BEAUTY CARE MARKET IN SWITZERLAND

Switzerland was a small, topographically rugged country in the center of Western Europe. The Swiss enjoyed a relatively high standard of living; the per capita GNP in 1975 was SFr. 22,500, the highest in Europe. The population was 6.4 million people, and the diversity of the Swiss was reflected in the fact that there were four official languages, as follows:

First Language	Percent of Population
German	65%
French	18
Italian	12
Romansh	1
Other	4
Total	100%

Source: Market research report, Swiss Federal Railway.

There were 3.28 million women in Switzerland who were distributed among the following age groups:

Age Group	Number of Women (000)
0–14	700
15–19	240
20–29	510
30–39	450
40–49	400
50–59	340
Over 60	640
Total	3,280

Source: *Consumer Europe 1977*.

Retail sales of all beauty products in Switzerland were SFr. 535.3 million in 1975. The per capita expenditure for the Swiss adult woman was nearly SFr. 210. The women's cosmetic market comprised several segments, which in 1975 accounted for the following percentages of the total retail sales:

Product Category	Percent of Beauty Product Sales
Face cosmetics	12%
Eye cosmetics	4
Hair preparations	22
Skin preparations	18
Fragrances	18
Deodorants	8
Bath preparations	4
Other	14
Total	100%

Source: *Consumer Europe 1977.*

Total sales of beauty products increased 12.6 percent from 1974 to 1975 in Switzerland. There were also changes in the structure of the market. Sales of fragrances and skin preparations, which included all-purpose lotions, rose sharply, while there was a decline in the volume of face and eye cosmetics and bath preparations.

According to some experts, the potential for the skin preparations market varied significantly among European countries. Sales levels depended not only upon the predominant skin types in a country but also upon the affluence of the women. Partly because of the standard of living in Switzer-

EXHIBIT 5
Swiss Market for Skin Preparations, 1975

	Retail Sales (SFr. million)	Unit Sales (packs)	Usership (million women)	Percent of Usership
Hand cream/lotion	SFr. 22.8	7.8	1.85	72
Body cream/lotion	12.2	2.5	0.98	38
Moisturizers	7.5	1.2	0.73	29
All-purpose lotions	34.0	6.4	1.74	67
Others	18.8	+	+	+
	SFr. 95.3			

Source: *Consumer Europe 1977.*

land and the fact that a relatively large proportion of the women were fair skinned, the expenditure per adult woman on skin preparations was higher than in every other Western European country but Germany. In 1973 the "average" Swiss woman spent about SFr. 37 on skin lotions of various types. Exhibit 5 gives a breakdown of sales and usership of various categories of skin preparations, including all-purpose lotions.

CHANNELS AND PRICING

Smythe-Dabney products reached the buying public through a variety of channels of distribution, each with its own pricing arrangement. Aurora Lotion was manufactured in England and then sold in the United Kingdom to independent wholesalers or large retail chains. In countries with an SDI subsidiary, such as Switzerland, Aurora was sold to the affiliated company, which then resold it to wholesalers and retail stores. SDI billed all customers in pounds sterling. Company-owned subsidiaries were charged a transfer price, which was the standard manufacturing cost of the product, including:

- Raw materials.
- Direct labor.
- Factory overhead.
- Handling and warehousing.

The senior management of SDI adopted this transfer pricing arrangement in order to give the managers of each subsidiary maximum discretion over margins and profits. The reasons for this strategy were:

1. The majority of marketing costs were, in fact, incurred in the country where the product was sold.
2. Advertising, price promotions, and sales force management decisions were under the control of the subsidiary's management.
3. The practice reinforced the SDI concept of division autonomy on day-to-day decisions and fostered good relationships between subsidiary managers and corporate officers.

SDI's price to independent customers in Britain was standard manufacturing cost plus a percentage of the cost for contribution to overhead and profit. All customers paid freight charges from factory to their warehouses.

SDI gave independent distributors in the United Kingdom a 3.75 percent discount for cash purchases and up to 6 percent volume rebate for purchases of large amounts of any product. In addition, each month, the company ran price promotions for groups of products in order to encourage British distributors to increase the volume of products they carried.

In England, wholesalers' markups on cosmetics were usually between 15 percent and 25 percent; retail margins were 35 percent to 45 percent of

EXHIBIT 6
Percentage of Retail Sales of Women's Beauty Care Products Sold through Various Outlets in Switzerland

Outlet	Description	Percent of Total Sales
Department and cosmetics stores	Cosmetic departments of large department stores and small shops and "parfumeries" specializing in cosmetics.	20%
Drugstores and pharmacies	Drugstores sold cleaning compounds, preparations, and parapharmaceuticals; pharmacies sold prescription drugs and other products.	40
Multiple stores/hypermarkets	Large chains selling food items as well as many nonfood products, from clothing to hardware to beauty products, often at discount prices (e.g., Migros and Carrefour).	25
Direct sales	Door-to-door salespersons.	3
Supermarkets/food outlets	Small and medium-size retail stores selling mainly food, with some nonfood lines.	9
Other		3
Total		100%

Source: *Consumer Europe 1977.*

the selling price to the consumer. On the other hand, wholesale margins for beauty products in Switzerland were between 40 percent and 55 percent of the selling price to retail outlets, and retail margins were 42 percent to 50 percent. In Switzerland, Aurora Lotion and other PPF products were sold at the retail level in a wide variety of outlets. Exhibit 6 shows the percentage of total sales of beauty care products that were sold through various outlets in 1975. While the data were incomplete, there was evidence of a rapid increase in the portion of total sales that were accounted for by hypermarkets in the last few years.

PARALLEL IMPORTS

Perhaps the biggest single problem that confronted the management of PPF was the parallel importing of Aurora Lotion. The difference in the wholesale price in Britain and Switzerland made it profitable for a distributor to send a buyer to England, purchase the product at the British wholesale price, and ship it to Switzerland for eventual resale to retail outlets. The process had become increasingly common in the last several years, and the management of PPF counted several large distributors who parallel imported Aurora Lotion among their main competitors in the marketplace. Although parallel importing was irritating to the sales force and management of PPF, it was not illegal and it was impossible to monitor.

There were three main reasons that the wholesale price of Aurora Lotion was lower in England than in Switzerland. First, retail prices were higher on the Continent than in Britain, reflecting a higher cost of living. Second, SDI conducted aggressive promotions in the United Kingdom each month, and the resulting average level of wholesale prices was lower than in Europe, where such promotions occurred less frequently. Finally, from 1972 through 1978 there had been a substantial decline in the value of the British pound against other currencies, including the Swiss franc. As a result of this trend, Swiss distributors had not had to increase the price of Aurora Lotion to the retail trade in five years, although SDI had hiked prices in Britain by as much as 25 percent a year in the same period. Since SDI billed its customers in pounds sterling, the fall of the pound against the Swiss franc had offset the British price increase.

Exhibit 7 contains a hypothetical example of the landed cost per bottle of parallel-imported Aurora Lotion.

A large British wholesaler purchased Aurora Lotion at £10.55 per case of 12 bottles. Normally the distributor was expected to take a 3.75 percent

EXHIBIT 7
Hypothetical Example of Parallel Importer's Cost per Bottle of Aurora Lotion*

SDI price/case.	£10.55
SDI price/bottle	0.88
Less: 3.75 percent cash discount	0.04
Net purchase	0.84
Less: 6 percent volume rebate	0.05
British distributor's cost	0.79
Add: 15 percent markup	0.14
Wholesale price	0.93
Add: transport cost at 6 percent	0.06
Landed cost/bottle.	£ 0.99
Landed cost/bottle†	SFr.3.70

* Figures have been rounded.
† Assumes 3.75 SFr./pound.

Source: Discussions with SDI directors.

cash discount and to be eligible for a volume rebate of 6 percent of his net purchases. When reselling these goods in large volume, he was content to receive a 15 percent markup.

A wholesale distributor or large retailer doing business in Switzerland sent a representative across the English Channel to buy from the British supplier. He paid £0.93 for each bottle and incurred additional freight charges at 4 percent to 8 percent of the cost of goods, depending upon the volume shipped to Switzerland. Assuming at the time of the transaction an exchange rate of 3.75 Swiss francs per pound, his cost for a 200 cl bottle of Aurora Lotion landed in Switzerland was SFr. 3.70. The price list for PPF recommended the following price structure for the 200 cl bottle of Aurora (including freight):

PPF suggested list price to distributors	SFr. 5.00
Distributor's suggested list price to retail outlets	8.70
Retailer's suggested list price to consumers	15.00

According to Urs Brunner, the retail price of Aurora Lotion had not declined in the last few years despite the parallel imports. Since the consumer was paying the same price, the channels were apparently enjoying higher margins.

It was difficult to assess the impact of parallel importing on PPF or SDI as a whole. On the one hand the average price of Aurora Lotion sold by PPF to the trade had declined over 20 percent in the past three years. Although PPF's list price for the product had not been reduced, the company had run a series of trade promotions which gave discounts to distributors, aimed at countering the competition from parallel imports. Exhibit 8 provides details in the trend of PPF's selling price for Aurora.

EXHIBIT 8

Trends in Average Selling Price and Landed Cost of Aurora Lotion (200 cl) by Produits Pour Femmes, SA, 1975–1978

	1975	1976	1977	1978*
Average selling price per bottle (SFr.)†	5.00	4.70	4.30	4.00
Average landed cost per bottle (pounds)	0.35	0.40	0.45	0.50
Average exchange rate (SFr./£)‡	5.40	4.05	3.95	3.75

* 1978 is average for the first quarter of the year.
† "Average price" is list price less discounts given in trade promotions.
‡ Average rate during fourth quarter 1975–77; during first quarter 1978.

Source: SDI company records (disguised).

Sales of Aurora Lotion had increased in units and in Swiss francs, and Fairchild was not sure whether the increases were in spite of the parallel imports or because of them. Probable effects of the activity had been higher market penetration of the product and increased brand recognition, both of which were beneficial to PPF. Besides, from SDI's point of view, the sales of Aurora parallel imported from England benefited the parent company by the contribution from the SDI sales to the British wholesalers.

Even if the practice had mixed results Fairchild knew that he could not shrug off the situation. It was clear from his conversation with Brunner that it had resulted in low morale in the Swiss subsidiary's sales force. Salespersons were rewarded for units sold and wanted to cut the price of Aurora to make them more competitive with the parallel importers.

ALTERNATIVES

John Fairchild reviewed the possible responses he had considered to the problem at hand. One alternative was to lower PPF's recommended selling price for Aurora Lotion to distributors. He was concerned about the possible financial consequences of such a price cut, both for PPF and for SDI. Moreover he wondered what steps he should take to ensure that trading profits would not be sacrificed. He believed that related options included cutting the subsidiary's advertising budget, trimming the sales force, and raising the prices of other products.

On the other hand, he wondered whether PPF could simply adhere to the policy that had been followed in the past. Such a strategy would continue to consist of three elements:

1. Avoid direct competition in published list prices.
2. Use trade promotions such as price-off discounts or "buy two, get one free" to respond to competitive pricing.
3. Stress the advantages provided by PPF to the trade, such as continuity of supply, advertising to stimulate demand, and a full line of related products.

Although the problem of what to do about the price of Aurora Lotion demanded action in the short run, it also had implications for the future of the subsidiary over the long term. Fairchild wondered whether the independent Swiss wholesalers would begin to parallel import more SDI products across the channel. Aurora Lotion, which accounted for 20 percent of PPF sales, might only be the first of a growing number of products on which the subsidiary would face increasing price competition.

Perhaps the existence of parallel importers was a signal that PPF was not an efficient channel of distribution. SDI might be better off to conduct its business directly with the independent distributors in Switzerland. This issue took on added significance because of SDI's plans to expand abroad in the future. The corporate directors would be faced with the decision of whether to set up a company subsidiary or to sell SDI products through existing independent wholesalers each time they entered a market in a new country or region.

A meeting with Sir Anthony Carburton and the other SDI directors was scheduled soon. Fairchild decided that this would be the best time to present his views on the situation at PPF and make his recommendations to the group.

CASE 6–5

Parke-Davis Professional Health Group

In May 1984 Mr. Marvin Skripitsky, the marketing director of the Parke-Davis Professional Health Group, was in the process of preparing the 1985 Strategic Plan recommendations for his group. A formal presentation of his recommendations was to be made to Mr. Robert Serenbetz, the president of Warner-Lambert Canada, at the end of May. As Mr. Skripitsky reviewed the Group's situation, he was convinced that the most pressing problem facing the Group was the lack of detailing capacity in the sales force. The Professional Health Group was planning to introduce a number of new products over the next three years and there appeared to be insufficient sales force time available to adequately present new and existing products (i.e., to "detail" the products) to the medical community. He viewed this inability to properly promote the Group's pharmaceutical products as the major barrier to meeting the Group's growth objectives. Mr. Skripitsky knew that he, in consultation with Mr. Malcolm Seath, the general manager of the Health Care Division, and Mr. Gerry Gibson, the Group's director of sales, would have to make specific recommendations for dealing with the detailing capacity problem at the presentation to Mr. Serenbetz.

COMPANY

Parke-Davis was the pharmaceutical affiliate of Warner-Lambert, a major U.S.-based multinational. With worldwide sales of over $3.1 billion (U.S.) Warner-Lambert manufactured a wide range of pharmaceutical, personal care, and other products, including such well-known brands as Listerine,

This case was prepared by Professor Adrian B. Ryans. Copyright © 1985, The School of Business Administration, The University of Western Ontario. Used by permission.

Chiclets and Schick. Parke-Davis had been founded in Detroit, Michigan, in 1866, and the company began operations in Canada in 1887, making it the second pharmaceutical company to operate in Canada. Over the years Parke-Davis had pioneered many significant health-care products including the first antidiptheric serum in 1893, Dilantin for the control of epilepsy in 1938, Benadryl the first antihistamine in North America in 1946, and in 1949 Chloromycetin the first wide-spectrum antibiotic to be discovered. Parke-Davis was acquired by Warner-Lambert in 1970. In 1979 Parke-Davis and Warner-Chilcott, the original pharmaceutical division of Warner-Lambert, were merged into one division to become the pharmaceutical component of Warner-Lambert Canada Inc. In 1983 Parke-Davis was merged with Warner Lambert's Personal Products business unit to form a new Health Care Division. In 1984 the Health Care Division was projected to have sales of $87 million with Parke-Davis accounting for $62 million of these sales.

Health Care Division

The mission of the Health Care Division was to be a Canadian leader in developing and providing pharmaceutical and personal care products for health and well-being while achieving steady growth in sales and profits. In the five-year strategic planning period beginning in 1985, the division was targeting for annual sales growth 4 percent above the level of inflation to achieve sales of approximately $133 million by 1989. Management of the Health Care Division believed that this objective was attainable, since the division enjoyed a number of major strengths, including a planned stream of major new products during the planning period, a broadly based product line that was not dependent on one or two major products or product categories, and a strong clinical trial and registration capability to expedite the approval of new pharmaceuticals and new claims for existing products. In addition, Parke-Davis had a strong image in the minds of consumers, pharmacists, doctors, and government. Most image studies placed Parke-Davis within the top five firms on almost every image criterion. This strong corporate image was useful in gaining access to doctors and the drug trade, and was helpful in developing and maintaining a consumer franchise for smaller nonprescription brands that could not support direct consumer advertising. While the broadly based product line was a strength in many respects, it also represented a weakness in that it made it difficult for the sales force to find the time to adequately detail all the products to the doctors. In addition, many physicians no longer viewed Parke-Davis as an innovator, since the product line was relatively old. A successful introduction of the planned new products was expected to correct this.

In Canada, the Health Care Division comprised two major groups: the Consumer Health Group and the Professional Health Group. Because both Warner-Chilcott and Parke-Davis had several big proprietary and OTC

EXHIBIT 1

Partial Organization Chart of the Health Care Division

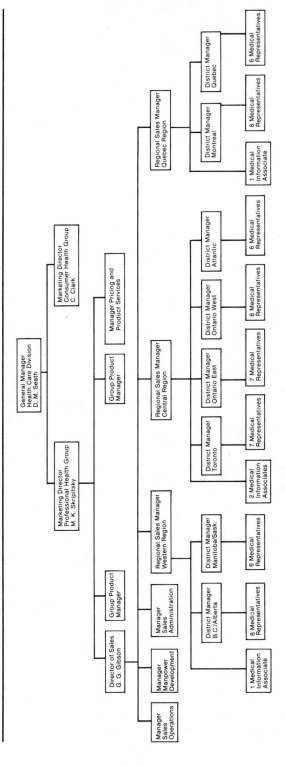

EXHIBIT 2
Parke-Davis Products

Anticonvulsants	Nardil
Prescription hemorrhoidals	Nicrostat
(Anusol)	Oral contraceptives
Amsa	Peritrate
Benadryl	Ponstan
Choledyl	Tucks
Chloro/Vira–A	Tedral
Colymycin	Thrombostat
Elase	Pyridium
Eryc	Mandelamine
Hose	Beben
Lopid	Vanquin
Mylanta	

pharmaceuticals in 1979, the merger resulted in the Consumer Health Group becoming the largest supplier of self-medication products in Canada, including such well-known brands as Benylin, Agarol, Sinutab and Gelu-sil.[1] These products were sold under the Parke-Davis name. The Consumer Health Group also marketed a wide range of personal care products (including Listerine, Bromo, Softsoap, Showermate, Schick, Topol, and Lensrins) that were distributed through drug stores and other convenient retail outlets. In addition to its extensive line of prescription ethical pharmaceuticals the Professional Health Group was responsible for promoting *selected* Consumer Health Group brands, such as Benylin, a major brand of cough syrup, to physicians. The general manager of the Health Care Division was Mr. Malcolm Seath.

Professional Health Group

The 1984 sales of the Professional Health Group were forecasted to be $33 million and the Group had an objective of increasing sales to over $50 million by 1989. Direct cost of goods sold and freight typically amounted to

---

[1] Pharmaceutical products were usually divided into ethical and proprietary categories, depending on how they were marketed by the manufacturer. Ethical products were marketed directly to the medical profession, whereas proprietary products were promoted directly to the consumer. Ethical products were commonly divided into two further categories: prescription pharmaceuticals and over-the-counter (OTC) pharmaceuticals. As the name implies, prescription pharmaceuticals were available only on a prescription written by a physician. OTC pharmaceuticals could be purchased by the consumer without a prescription.

about 25 percent of selling price. During this period the Professional Health Group hoped to increase its market share in ethical (prescription) pharmaceuticals from 1.8 percent to 2.2 percent. The Professional Health Group was headed by the marketing director, Mr. Marvin Skripitsky. Reporting to the marketing director were two group product managers and the director of sales, Mr. Gerry Gibson. A simplified organization chart for the Group is shown in Exhibit 1. By 1984 the sales force consisted of 56 medical representatives, 4 medical information associates, 8 district managers and 3 regional managers.

The Professional Health Group was responsible for the 24 products or product groups shown in Exhibit 2. The Professional Health Group planned to add 15 products to this product line over the next three years, with these products having potential sales of over $25 million by 1989.

INDUSTRY ENVIRONMENT

Management of the Health Care Division saw both threats and opportunities in the external environment. Health care costs were expected to continue to increase faster than the economy as a whole due to technological developments and an aging population. Although management felt that pharmaceuticals were the most cost-effective part of the health care system, they believed that pharmaceuticals would continue to attract the attention of politicians and others responsible for controlling health care costs. Some provinces had adopted "formularies" in an attempt to control pharmaceutical costs. In these cases the provincial government would only pay for pharmaceuticals listed in the formulary for people who were receiving government assistance in paying for pharmaceuticals. In addition, management believed that the increasing complexity of the health care system would force politicians to give more power to bureaucrats who would be perceived as "unbiased." In this environment access to key politicians and bureaucrats would be key.

Insurance companies, which paid at least some drug bills for 70 percent of Canadians, were expected to become increasingly important. Historically they had been passive participants in the health care system, paying whatever pharmacists charged for whatever pharmaceuticals were prescribed by doctors. Some were now attempting to restrict the choice of pharmaceuticals for which they would provide full reimbursement and in some cases they were attempting to force mandatory substitution of generic drugs.

On the more positive side there was a growing feeling in the industry that the federal government might change Canada's compulsory licensing laws to encourage more innovation in pharmaceuticals in Canada and to encourage more pharmaceutical firms to conduct more of their research in Canada. The compulsory licensing law in Canada required the patent-holding manufacturer to license patented products to other manufacturers.

Parke-Davis executives continued to believe that the keys to growth in the pharmaceutical industry in Canada would be the development of innovative new products and strong marketing of these products.

MARKET FOR PHARMACEUTICAL PRODUCTS IN CANADA

The total market for ethical and proprietary pharmaceutical products in Canada was more than $2.5 billion, with 17 percent of these sales being made to hospitals. The medical community in Canada comprised about 43,000 doctors and over 1,000 hospitals. There were also almost 5,000 retail pharmacies in Canada.

Competition

The overall pharmaceutical industry in Canada was highly competitive, with the largest company, American Home Products, having less than 8 percent market share of the combined ethical and proprietary pharmaceutical market sold through hospitals and drug stores. An additional 14 companies had market shares greater than 2 percent. The various divisions of Warner-Lambert had a combined market share of over 3 percent. Most of these companies were broad-line pharmaceutical companies. Competition in the industry seemed to be increasing, with the recent entry of major non-pharmaceutical companies through the acquisition of small pharmaceutical companies. Both Procter & Gamble and Dow Chemical had entered the market, using this mechanism, in the early 1980s.

By the end of 1983 there were a total of 55 pharmaceutical companies with sales forces operating in Canada. The number of medical representatives employed by these companies are shown in Exhibit 3. Some of the major competitors operated under more than one name and corporate structure. American Home Products operated under the Wyeth, Ayerst, and Whitehall names. Johnson & Johnson sold its products under the Ortho, Johnson & Johnson, McNeil, and Janssen names. Several companies, including both American Home Products and Johnson & Johnson, had more than one sales force. Merck Frosst, the company with the largest number of medical representatives in Canada had three different sales forces operating under different names, with almost 140 representatives at the end of 1983. When a company had more than one sales force, they usually operated under the names of different divisions (often the names of predecessor companies). Thus Johnson & Johnson had two sales forces operating under the McNeil and Ortho names individually. Earlier in 1984, one relatively small pharmaceutical company, Boehringer-Ingelheim, had added a second sales force. These two sales forces were using the same name, and the calling

EXHIBIT 3
Number of Medical Representatives Employed by Competitors in Canada

Size of Sales Force*	Number of Companies
0–10	3
11–20	4
21–30	9
31–40	4
41–50	15
51–60	13
61–70	6
71 or greater	1
Total number of sales forces	55

* Excludes managers and OTC representatives.

cards of the salespersons simply indicated that they were specialists in particular therapeutic classes. It was too early to measure the acceptance of this approach by the medical community. The large number of sales forces meant that the competition for a doctor's time was intense—Mr. Gibson estimated that some doctors could have as many as 40 to 50 medical representatives trying to see them in a given two-month period.

All the major brand name manufacturers of pharmaceuticals faced competition from generic manufacturers.

The Selling of Ethical Pharmaceuticals in Canada

Medical representatives (over 25,000 of them in North America alone) played a key role in the selling of ethical pharmaceuticals. Often called "detail men" (although they were increasingly women) for the details they provide doctors and pharmacists about pharmaceuticals, they played a key role in trying to convince doctors to prescribe their company's pharmaceuticals to the doctor's patients. Many market research studies concluded that doctors relied very heavily on medical representatives for information on prescribing pharmaceuticals. Some authorities suggested that the success of a new pharmaceutical could depend almost as much on the effectiveness of the medical representatives promoting the new product as on the product itself. The medical profession was faced with the difficult problem of keeping up with the flood of new pharmaceuticals that were continually becoming available. While the pharmaceuticals in major therapeutic product classes—such as those designed to treat heart disease—shared many similarities, the differences could be critical to the patients using the pharmaceutical. Detail men played a crucial role in providing the kind of information that would help a doctor decide whether a particular pharmaceutical was appropriate for a particular patient's condition. Many doctors, particularly harried general practitioners with a diverse practice, found it difficult to keep up with all the literature on the products that they might use in their practice, and they appreciated the information a detail man could provide. A well-trained detail man could provide the doctor with information on the chemical composition of the pharmaceutical, its possible side effects, and how it would interact with other medicines a patient might be taking. From the pharmaceutical company's point of view detail men provided a valuable feedback channel sometimes alerting the company to side effects that might not have been noticed before. Detail men also frequently organized symposia for groups of doctors, often bringing in outside medical authorities to help bring doctors up-to-date on current medical practice and pharmaceuticals. Major pharmaceutical companies regularly had their representatives set up displays in major hospitals in their territories. These displays of products and literature were staffed by the representative and many doctors dropped by after their morning rounds in the hospital or at the end of the working day.

One of the toughest jobs many detail men faced was getting past the receptionist or the nurse in a doctor's office, particularly when the office was crowded and the doctor was behind schedule. Increasingly, doctors were establishing rules that they would only see one medical representative a day. Parke-Davis representatives tried to make appointments with the doctor ahead of time, when this was possible. Even when the medical representative got into the doctor's office the doctor might keep the representative waiting and might be interrupted by a nurse or a telephone call during their conversation. The representative typically only had 5 to 10 minutes to make his presentation. During the presentation he might place primary emphasis on one or two products with brief reminders about one or two others. The pharmaceuticals presented to a particular doctor depended on the nature of the doctor's speciality and practice. Doctors frequently asked questions about products or might have questions about the appropriateness of particular products in a given situation.

Parke-Davis sales representatives were expected to make 5 to 6 calls per day on doctors, about two calls per day on retail pharmacies and perhaps one call every two days on a hospital. As did many other major pharmaceutical companies, Parke-Davis divided each year into six two-month sales cycles. A major planning issue was the decision as to which one or two products should get primary emphasis in each of these sales cycles for each medical specialty. Each medical representative attempted to call on all the doctors, retail pharmacies, and hospitals targeted by Parke-Davis at least once during each sales cycle. By 1984 Parke-Davis was targeting its sales

EXHIBIT 4

Coverage of Physicians and Retail Pharmacies by Parke-Davis Sales Force (by province)

	British Columbia	Alberta	Saskatchewan	Manitoba	Ontario	Quebec	Atlantic Provinces	Total Canada
Physicians:								
Total physicians*	5,180	3,310	1,410	1,870	15,900	12,470	3,340	43,480
Covered by Parke-Davis	1,750	1,400	700	700	6,300	4,550	1,750	17,500
Percent covered	33.8%	42.3%	49.7%	37.4%	39.6%	36.5%	52.4%	40.2%
Retail Pharmacies:								
Total retail pharmacies	593	559	229	285	1,648	1,079	502	4,965
Covered by Parke-Davis	400	320	160	160	1,440	1,040	400	4,000
Percent covered	67.5%	57.5%	53.5%	56.1%	87.4%	96.4%	79.7%	80.6%

* This includes all physicians registered in a province. Not all physicians registered in a province were active in a medical practice. For example, some were retired or employed in teaching, research, or administrative positions.

685

force at some 18,000 doctors out of the 43,000 in Canada, and at over 80 percent of the retail pharmacies. The approximate Parke-Davis coverage of physicians and retail pharmacies by province is shown in Exhibit 4.

THE PROFESSIONAL HEALTH GROUP SALES FORCE

Organization

The field sales force of 60 persons was divided into two groups: the 56 medical representatives and 4 medical information associates (MIAs). The medical representatives were organized into eight geographical districts, each headed by a district manager, and had responsibility for detailing the full Professional Health Group product line to the medical community in their geographical territories.

In 1983 top management of the Professional Health Group had become very concerned about the ability of the medical representatives to detail their large existing product line, and at the same time introduce the large number of sophisticated new products that were planned in the future. The introduction of a sophisticated new pharmaceutical often required that the medical representative focus on key specialists and other potential opinion leaders. Since the medical representatives had largely been trying to maintain sales of existing products rather than introduce new ones over the preceding three or four years, they often were not actively working these key specialists. To overcome this problem, management decided to add a small number of more sophisticated representatives with stronger medical and pharmacological training, and very strong communication skills. These representatives would specialize in launching new products and would do the initial follow-up with doctors after the launch of the product. Given their strong educational background and the fact that at any point in time they would be focusing on a very small number of new products, it would be possible to provide them with more in-depth knowledge about each new product than could be given to the medical representatives.

The company began to add the MIAs in 1983. They were also given geographical territories, but these territories were obviously much larger than those of the medical representatives, since four of them had to cover the whole of Canada. The four MIAs reported directly to the regional managers. Two were assigned to the Central Region and one each to the Quebec and Western Regions.

Recruiting and Selection

In selecting new representatives the Professional Health Group sought individuals with a strong background in one of the health sciences. Most recent recruits had Bachelor's degrees in Science, Nursing, or Pharmacy. Some were recruited directly out of university, but many had worked in the health care industry before joining Parke-Davis. One recent recruit was a registered nurse with several years of nursing experience in a hospital. Another was a pharmacist in his early 30s, who had become bored with the routine of dispensing pharmaceuticals and the long hours associated with operating a retail pharmacy.

Training

After joining Parke-Davis each medical representative attended two two-week training programs in Toronto. This training included material on Parke-Davis, and intensive training on biology and pharmacology, product information on the Parke-Davis product line, and some basic selling skills training. Between the sessions the representative was in his or her territory under the close supervision of the district manager. Training was a continuing process in any pharmaceutical company, with each representative receiving training in new products as they were introduced. When a major new product was introduced it was common to provide the representatives with programmed learning materials, followed by an intensive two-day training meeting in Toronto. Many salespersons were also continually trying to update their skills by reading textbooks and a variety of other medical and pharmacological information made available to them by their companies. About every two years all medical representatives come to Toronto for an intensive "refresher" sales training course.

Compensation

Parke-Davis compensated its representatives using a base salary plus bonus compensation plan. In 1984 base salaries for representatives varied from $21,000 for a new sales trainee with no experience to $36,000 for a senior sales representative. In addition, each representative was eligible for a regional bonus of up to 15 percent of base salary and an individual merit bonus of up to 10 percent of base salary. Thus a high-performing medical representative could earn as much as $45,000 plus fringe benefits and the use of a company automobile.

The regional bonus was based on the region's success in meeting sales objectives. For the purpose of calculating the regional bonus the product line was divided into A, B, and C brands. "A" brands were those that in the opinion of management were the most profitable and had the greatest potential for future growth. "B" brands included high-volume brands with less potential for growth, but whose sales should be maintained. "C" brands included all other brands, which were not typically actively promoted. Management established objectives for each of the three groups of brands for each of the three regions and performance against these objectives was measured. Approximately 55 percent of the bonus was applied to the achievement of the A objective, 30 percent to the achievement of the B objective, and 15 percent to the achievement of the C objective. If a region met exactly 100 percent of its objectives for each group of brands each member of the regional team would receive a bonus of 10.5 percent of base salary. If 102 percent or more of the objective for each group was met, the full 15 percent bonus was awarded. Management did not believe it was feasible to do this monitoring at lower than a region level due to the difficulty of establishing exactly which representative or even district was responsible for a given sale. It was not uncommon for a·prescription to be written by a doctor in one city, for the prescription to be filled at a retail pharmacy in another city, and for that pharmacy to have its drugs shipped from a warehouse in a different province.

The individual bonus was based on the district manager's judgment of the individual's contribution relative to others in the region. In order to make this judgment the district manager reviewed territory sales data, call activity and other activities, such as the number of symposia organized by the representative and the number of physicians who attended these symposia. The individual bonus decisions had to be reviewed and approved by the responsible regional manager and Mr. Gibson. District managers were in a good position to make this subjective judgment since they spent at least one day every month in the field with each of the representatives they supervised.

Performance Appraisal

Each representative was formally reviewed once a year by his or her manager. In this performance appraisal the district manager carefully reviewed the representative's achievements since the last review and any areas of concern. Particular attention was paid to the employee's skills in managing the work and in dealing with other people. The manager also focused on the individuals promotability and training and development needs. Each performance appraisal was reviewed by the regional manager and Mr. Gibson.

Motivation

A sales meeting was held once during each of the six sales cycles during the year. These meetings played an important role in the training and motivation of the sales force. Frequently these meetings would be held at the district level, but occasionally regional or national meetings would be held, particularly when a major new program or product was about to be launched.

THE DETAILING CAPACITY PROBLEM

In the strategic planning process for the Parke-Davis Professional Health Group in May 1984, Mr. Seath, Mr. Skripitsky, and Mr. Gibson viewed the Professional Health Group's lack of detailing capacity as its most pressing

EXHIBIT 5
Planned 1985 Medical Promotion Schedule (six two-month sales promotion cycles)

		1	2	3	4	5	6
General practitioners (GPs)	Primary	Lopid Benylin	Eryc Choledyl SA	Lopid Benadryl	Choledyl SA Lopid	Lopid Ponstan	Eryc Mylanta
	Reminder	Eryc Mylanta	Mylanta Anusol/Tucks	Ponstan Mylanta	Eryc Ponstan	Eryc Mylanta	Anusol/T Benylin
Surgeons	Primary	Mylanta Thrombostat	Anusol/Tucks	Mylanta Thrombostat	Mylanta	Thrombostat	Anusol/T
	Reminder	Hose	Hose	Anusol/Tucks Hose	Hose	Mylanta Hose	Mylanta Hose
Pediatricians	Primary	Benylin Choledyl Liquid	Benylin Choledyl Liquid	Benadryl Colymycin	Benadryl Vanquin	Choledyl Liquid Benylin	Benylin Choledyl Liquid
Obstetrics/ Gynecology (OB/GYNs)	Primary	Ponstan	Ponstan Mylanta	Ponstan	Ponstan	Mylanta Thrombostat	OC's Ponstan
	Reminder	Mylanta Tucks OC's	Tucks	Tucks OC's	OC's Tucks	Mylanta Tucks	Mylanta Hose
Internal medicine	Primary	Lopid	Lopid Nitrostat IV Eryc	Lopid Eryc	Lopid Nitrostat IV Eryc	Lopid Nitrostat IV	Lopid Eryc
	Reminder	Mylanta Eryc	Mylanta	Mylanta Benadryl	Mylanta	Mylanta Eryc	Mylanta Benylin
Hospital staff		Thrombostat Chloromycetin Mylanta	Nitrostat IV Benadryl Elase	Thrombostat Benadryl Mylanta	Nitrostat IV Elase	Thrombostat Chloromycetin Mylanta	Nitro IV Elase
Miscellaneous samples		Ponstan Hose	Hose Benylin	Hose Colymycin Eryc Anusol/Tucks	Benadryl Hose	Benadryl Hose Benylin	Ponstan Hose

problem. The Group had launched Eryc, a major new antibiotic, in December 1983 with a first-year sales objective of $600,000. While the MIA sales force had played a major role in the prelaunch and launch activities for the product and was actively involved in the follow-up, the medical representatives would have to support it aggressively in their detailing calls for the next 18 months or so, if it was to achieve its market potential. In May 1984, Lopid, a major new cardiovascular pharmaceutical, was introduced with a first-year sales objective of almost $500,000. Again, the MIAs were playing a major role in the introduction. With three more new products slated for introduction in 1985, seven more in 1986, and at least five more in 1987, the detailing capacity problem was critical.

The magnitude of the problem was evident to Mr. Skripitsky and Mr. Gibson as they looked at the tentative 1985 Medical Promotion Schedule for the year beginning January 1, 1985, shown in Exhibit 5. Eryc and Lopid, the two new products, would require much of the available primary detailing time. In the case of general practitioners (GPs), 6 of the 12 available spots were taken up by the two new products, with an additional 2 of the 12 spots taken up by Choledyl SA, another relatively new product introduced early in 1983. Increasingly the inclusion of new products meant that impor-

EXHIBIT 6

Advertising and Promotion Budget for Prescription Anusol in 1984 and 1985 (planned)

	1984 (estimated) ($000)	1985 (planned) ($000)	Percentage Change, 1984–85
Promotion:			
"Loss of revenue"*	$221	$242	10%
Medical promotion	8	10	25
Mailing of samples	15	15	0
Samples (cost of goods)	224	307	37
Total	$468	$574	23%
Advertising:			
Print	$ 78	$150	92%
Print production	0	12	—
Agency fees	24	26	8
Audits and surveys	6	7	17
Total	$108	$195	81%
Total advertising and promotion budget	$574	$769	34%
As percent of sales	18%	22%	

* "Loss of revenue" was the estimated cost of price discounts and free-goods (buy 11 and get 1 free) that would be offered to the retail drug trade.

tant "bread and butter" products, many with good growth potential, would have to be dropped from active sales force promotion.

One brand that would fall in this category was Anusol HC, a pharmaceutically elegant prescription hemorrhoidal preparation, that was targeted at general practitioners, family physicians, and surgeons. With projected 1984 sales of $3.1 million, a market share of almost 50 percent in a market with a real growth rate of over 5 percent, and a manufacturing contribution margin of over 60 percent it was a major contributor to Parke-Davis's sales and profits. In 1984 total advertising and promotional spending on the product was expected to be over $500,000, with about 40 percent of this for samples. A breakdown of the actual advertising and promotion budget for 1984 and the planned budget for 1985 are shown in Exhibit 6. A projected 34 percent increase in the budget to support a 10 percent increase in sales was a partial response to the decreased availability of detailing time for the brand.

Alternatives under Consideration

As the management team of the Professional Health Group grappled with the problem of insufficient personal medical detailing time it was apparent that there were several options open to them. The major options were:

1. Expand utilization of the MIAs to provide prelaunch, launch, and the entire postlaunch responsibility for new products for key specialists. This option would ensure that the new products would be very effectively detailed to the key potential prescribing specialists for a particular new product. The major disadvantage of this option was that the MIAs would be of little assistance in detailing the new products to general practitioners.

2. Increase the size of the regular sales force. This would allow the geographical territories to be smaller, permitting Parke-Davis to reach more doctors. However, management felt it was unlikely to increase the detailing time a salesperson could spend with key doctors for the Parke-Davis product line, since doctors would be unlikely to be willing to talk to the medical representative more than once during each two-month sales cycle. Thus the representative's capacity to detail more products to any one physician would not be enhanced.

3. Develop a second medical sales force for the Professional Health Group. The existing product line could be split between the two sales forces, perhaps with one sales force specializing in the cardiovascular and pulmonary products and the other sales force specializing in the anti-infective and anti-inflammatory products. If the few miscellaneous products in the Parke-Davis product line were also assigned to the second sales force, the two sales forces would have similar dollar volumes. Of the 15 new products planned for the 1985–87 period 6 would be in the first group of products and 9 in the second group of products. With this option many physicians, drug stores, and hospitals would be detailed by two Parke-Davis medical representatives, thus doubling the number of products that could be detailed in any two-month sales cycle. However, management was unsure how the medical profession would react to this strategy—would doctors agree to see two different Parke-Davis sales representatives during a given two-month sales cycle, or would they only see one in each sales cycle? Management were also unsure how competition might react to this strategy. While some other competitors did have more than one sales force, with the exception of the recent move by Boehringer-Ingelheim these different sales forces operated under different names—often the names of predecessor companies.

4. Make no changes in the sales force, but make adjustments elsewhere to reflect the detailing capacity problem. Some managers felt it would be possible to revamp the detailing schedule to maximize the number of products on promotion. Substantial increases in the advertising and promotion support to brands might also reduce the need for detailing time on some of the products. To handle the large number of anticipated new-product introductions, these introductions could be delayed to provide a minimum four to six months' interval between the introduction of new brands. The detailing load could also be reduced by licensing the new products with low sales potential to other pharmaceutical manufacturers.

The Second-Sales-Force Option

By far the most radical of the four options under consideration was the addition of the second sales force. It was viewed to be quite risky and if the decision to proceed with it was made there were several major implementation issues that would need to be addressed.

In "fleshing out" the two-sales-forces option for discussion purposes, Mr. Skripitsky and Mr. Gibson thought that they would require 49 representatives for each sales force organized as shown in Exhibit 7. Where feasible, district managers would be responsible for medical representatives from only one of the sales forces, although in the more geographically dispersed areas such as Manitoba/Saskatchewan, rural Quebec, and the Atlantic Provinces, the district managers would have medical representatives from both sales forces reporting to them. Mr. Skripitsky and Mr. Gibson envisioned the continuance of the MIA sales force with five representatives assigned to it. The MIAs would support both sales forces as needed. The 1985 incremental cost of adding salespersons, managers, and support staff and facilities was estimated to average about $57,000 per person in the field; that is, $2.4 million for the 42 incremental persons that would be required to staff the two sales forces. Sales-force costs were expected to rise about 7 percent per year during the rest of the 1980s.

If a second sales force was added the number of detailing slots available would be increased from 24 (four slots in each of the six sales cycles) to 48. In a preliminary look at the potential impact of this doubling of slots manage-

EXHIBIT 7
Proposed Sales Organization with Two Sales Forces

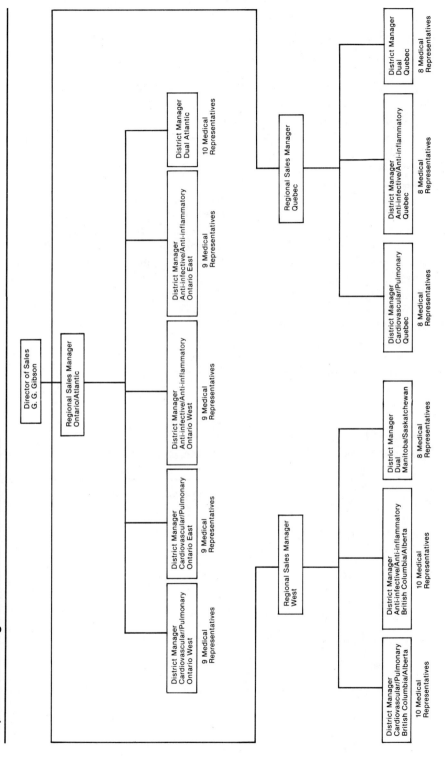

ment thought that the 1985 Medical Promotion Schedule for general practitioners might be modified as shown in Exhibit 8. This would allow several more products to be detailed, some of them at high frequencies. In consultation with the product managers for the various products involved, Mr. Skripitsky and Mr. Gibson estimated that under the two-sales-forces option sales might be $1.3 million higher in 1985 than they would be with the continuance of current policies. Incremental sales of $4.6 million, $5.6 million, $7.9 million, and $9.5 million were expected in 1986, 1987, 1988, and 1989, respectively. The sources of these incremental sales are shown in Exhibit 9.

If the decision was made to add a second sales force there were several major implementation issues that needed to be addressed. A major concern was the naming of the two sales forces. Two major options had been proposed. Some managers thought that both sales forces should operate clearly under the Parke-Davis name, with one sales force being called the Cardiovascular/Pulmonary Sales Group and the other the Anti-Infective/Anti-Inflammatory Sales Group. Others thought that the Parke-Davis name should be used but that the salespersons be represented as coming from two separate divisions. Suggestions for the division names included Research Laboratories Division of Parke-Davis, the Scientific Laboratories Division of Parke-Davis, and the Warner Laboratories Division of Parke-Davis. The chosen name would appear on the representative's calling card. Another issue was whether all medical representatives should be trained on the full

EXHIBIT 8

Change in 1985 Product Exposure to General Practitioners (GPs) with Second Sales Force

Product	Frequency on Detail Schedule		
	Current Plan	Plan with Second Sales Force	Change
Lopid	4	5	1
Benylin	2	4	2
Eryc	5	4	(1)
Mylanta	5	6	1
Choledyl	2	4	2
Anusol/Tucks	2	5	3
Benadryl	1	2	1
Ponstan	3	3	—
Hose	—	3	3
Oral contraceptives	—	6	6
Colymycin Otic	—	1	1
Procan	—	5	5
	24	48	24

EXHIBIT 9
Estimated Impact of Second Sales Force on Sales ($000)

	1985	1986	1987	1988	1989
Incremental sales from existing ethical products	$ 615	$1,215	$1,680	$2,440	$3,040
Incremental sales from Consumer Health Group products[1]	300	350	400	450	500
Incremental sales from new products	400	3,000	3,500	5,000	6,000
Total incremental sales	$1,315	$4,565	$5,580	$7,890	$9,540

[1] Consumer Health Group products sold under the Parke-Davis brand (e.g., Benylin and Gelusil).

Parke-Davis product line, or just on the part of the product line sold by their sales force. As more new products were introduced, training on the full product line would probably require that the sales training program be lengthened. Perhaps the major implementation issue was how to introduce the idea of two Parke-Davis sales forces to the doctor and his or her receptionist/nurse. A negative reaction on their part could jeopardize the whole two-sales-forces plan. A continuing problem would be the need for the two sales representatives serving a particular geographical area to coordinate their activities so that they didn't end up calling on the same doctors at about the same time.

Mr. Gibson also wondered how the sales force would react if a second sales force were to be introduced. He could imagine some salespersons being concerned that an additional salesperson in their territory would make it more difficult for them to see their doctors and to gain as frequent access to hospitals. Many would be concerned about how any changes would affect their compensation and would want assurance that they wouldn't be expected to generate the same absolute dollar increases in sales on a reduced business base.

Possible Test

If the decision was made to add a second sales force, Mr. Skripitsky and Mr. Gibson wondered if they should first test the concept in one part of Canada, prior to introducing it nationally. If they proposed a test, they would have to recommend how it should be conducted, where it should be conducted, and how long it should last. The choice of a test area would not be an easy one. Every province or region of the country had significant drawbacks. British Columbia was geographically large and the Vancouver area had a very high ratio of physicians to people. Alberta had the advantages of being a relatively isolated market with little government intervention and having the Parke-Davis Western Region office in Edmonton. The latter would facilitate monitoring of any test. On the negative side it was a market in which Parke-Davis did extremely well and might not be representative from that point of view. The Alberta economy was also depressed in 1984. Both Saskatchewan and Manitoba were isolated markets, but both provincial governments had very restrictive formularies making them unrepresentative of the rest of Canada. Ontario's major disadvantage was its size. With over 36 percent of Canada's population, it seemed too large for a test market. If only part of the province was used, monitoring the results of the test would be extremely difficult and expensive, given the potential spillover effects of marketing activity in one part of the province into other areas. Quebec was also large and was a market where Parke-Davis was having some problems in early 1984. In addition, while the company had the capability to train French-speaking representatives, the burden of training people for the test would fall heavily on the shoulders of one individual. The Atlantic Provinces were viewed as being somewhat unique in Canada from a pharmaceutical marketing prospective, and Mr. Skripitsky and Mr. Gibson did not feel that any results obtained there would necessarily be projectable to the rest of the country.

THE SITUATION IN MAY 1984

As Mr. Skripitsky sat down in late May to decide what sales-force recommendations should be included in the five-year plan he knew that he would have to deal with a number of key issues that Mr. Seath was likely to bring up. Mr. Skripitsky felt that Mr. Seath would have major concerns about the two-sales-forces option. One of his concerns would be the large, continuing, fixed costs that would be associated with a second sales force. Warner-Lambert considered itself a very "people-oriented" company, and there would be no question of dismissing members of the second sales force if it did not work out. The investment of resources in a new salesperson was also considerable. Mr. Skripitsky felt the company's investment in a new salesperson could add up to $50,000 in the first two years the representative was with the company. Mr. Seath would want to be convinced that any additions to the sales-force head count would be fully warranted and that the additions were meeting a permanent need, not a temporary one. While Mr. Skripitsky expected that the 15 new products would be introduced, there was always the possibility that some of the introductions might have to be delayed or canceled if unforeseen problems occurred, such as a failure to get regulatory approval for a product. Mr. Seath would also want Mr. Skripitsky's assurance that the older products would in fact respond to more detailing time.

Mr. Skripitsky also knew that a key element of Mr. Seath's strategy for the Health Care Division was the continuing establishment of the Parke-Davis name as a highly respected brand name in the medical community. Mr. Seath would need to be convinced that the addition of a second sales force would not lead to any dilution of the Parke-Davis name.

Before presenting his recommendations Mr. Skripitsky knew he'd have to develop a detailed set of recommendations for whichever option he chose. If he decided on the two-sales-forces option, he would have to have specific recommendations on its size, timing, the naming of the sales forces, whether or not to test market the concept, and a host of implementation issues. He realized he had a lot of work to do within the next week to prepare his recommendations.

CASE 6–6

The Gillette Company—Safety Razor Division

In July 1978 Mike Edwards, brand manager for TRAC II®[1], is beginning to prepare his marketing plans for the following year. In preparing for the marketing plan approval process, he has to wrestle with some major funding questions.

The most recent sales figures show that TRAC II has continued to maintain its share of the blade and razor market. This has occurred even though the Safety Razor Division (SRD) has introduced a new product to its line, Atra. The company believes that Atra will be the shaving system of the future and therefore is devoting increasing amounts of marketing support to this brand. Atra was launched in 1977 with a $7 million advertising campaign and over 50 million $2-rebate coupons. In less than a year the brand achieved a 7 percent share of the blade market and about one-third of the dollar razor market. Thus the company will be spending heavily on Atra, possibly at the expense of TRAC II, still the number one shaving system in America.

Edwards is faced with a difficult situation, for he believes that TRAC II still can make substantial profits for the division, provided the company

---

This case was prepared by Charles M. Kummel, research assistant, under the supervision of Associate Professor Jay E. Klompmaker, The University of North Carolina at Chapel Hill, School of Business Administration. Copyright © 1980 Jay E. Klompmaker.

[1] TRAC II® is a registered trademark of the Gillette Company.

continues to support the brand. In preparing for 1979 the division is faced with two major issues:

1. What is the future potential of TRAC II and Atra?
2. Most important of all, can SRD afford to support two brands heavily? Even if it can, is it sound marketing policy to do so?

COMPANY BACKGROUND

The Gillette Company was founded in 1903 by King C. Gillette, a 40-year-old inventor, utopian writer, and bottle-cap salesman, in Boston, Massachusetts. Since marketing its first safety razor and blades, the Gillette Company, the parent of the Safety Razor Division, has been the leader in the shaving industry.

The Gillette safety razor was the first system to provide a disposable blade which could be replaced at low cost and provided a good inexpensive shave. The early ads focused on a shave-yourself theme: "If the time, money, energy and brainpower which are wasted [shaving] in the barbershops of America were applied in direct effort, the Panama Canal could be dug in four hours."

The Pre–World War II Years

With the benefit of a 17-year patent, Gillette was in a very advantageous position. However, it wasn't until World War I that the safety razor began to gain wide consumer acceptance. One day in 1917 King Gillette came into the office with a visionary idea: present a Gillette razor to every soldier, sailor, and marine. Other executives modified this idea such that the government would do the presenting. In this way, millions just entering the shaving age would give the nation the self-shaving habit. In World War I the government bought 4,180,000 Gillette razors as well as smaller quantities of competitive models.

The Daily Shaving Development

While World War I gave impetus to self-shaving, World War II popularized frequent shaving—12 million American servicemen shaved daily. Thus there were two results: (1) Gillette was able to gain consumer acceptance of personal shaving, and (2) the company was able to develop an important market to build for the future.

The Post–World War II Years

After 1948 the company began to diversify through the acquisition of three companies which gave Gillette entry into new markets. In 1948 the acquisition of the Toni Company extended the company into the women's grooming aid market. Paper Mate, a leading maker of writing instruments, was bought in 1954, and the Sterilon Corporation, a manufacturer of disposable supplies for hospitals, was acquired in 1962.

Diversification also occurred through internal product development propelled by a detailed marketing survey conducted in the late 1950s. The survey found that the public associated the company with personal grooming as much as, or more than, with cutlery and related products. Gillette's response was to broaden its personal care line. As a result Gillette now markets such well-known brands as Adorn hairspray, Tame cream rinse, Right Guard antiperspirant, Dry Look hairspray for men, Foamy shaving cream, Earth Borne and Ultra Max shampoo, Cricket lighters, and Pro Max hairdryers as well as Paper Mate, Erasermate, and Flair pens.

Gillette Today

Gillette is divided into four principal operating groups (North America, International, Braun AG, Diversified Companies) and five product lines. As Exhibit 1 indicates, the importance of blades and razors to company profits is immense. In just about all the 200 countries where its blades and razors are sold, Gillette remains the industry leader.

In 1977 Gillette reported increased worldwide sales of $1,587.2 million, with income after taxes of $79.7 million (see Exhibit 2). Of total sales $720.9 million were domestic and $866.3 million were international, with profit contributions of $109 million and $105.6 million, respectively. The company employs 31,700 people worldwide, with 8,600 employees in the United States.

Statement of Corporate Objectives and Goals

At a recent stockholders' meeting, the chairman of the board outlined the company's strategy for the future:

> *The goal of the Gillette Company is sustained growth.* To achieve this, the company concentrates on two major objectives: to maintain the strength of existing product lines and to develop at least two new significant businesses or product lines that can make important contributions to the growth of the company in the early 1980s.
>
> In existing product lines, the company broadens its opportunities for growth by utilizing corporate technology to create new products. In other areas, growth is accomplished through either internal development or the acquisition of new businesses.
>
> The company uses a number of guidelines to evaluate growth opportunities. Potential products or services must fulfill a useful function and provide value for the price paid; offer distinct advantages easily perceived by consumers, be based on technology available within, or readily accessible outside, the company; meet established quality and safety standards; and offer an acceptable level of profitability and attractive growth potential.

EXHIBIT 1

Approximate Percent of Sales and Contributions to Profits of Gillette Business Segments, 1973–1977

Year	Blades and Razors		Toiletries and Grooming Aids		Writing Instruments		Braun Products		Other	
	Net Sales	Contributions to Profits	Net Sales	Contributions to Profits	Net Sales	Contributions to Profits	Net Sales	Contributions to Profits	Net Sales	Contributions to Profits
1977	31%	75%	26%	13%	8%	6%	23%	13%	12%	(7)%
1976	29	71	28	15	7	6	21	10	15	(2)
1975	30	73	30	15	7	5	20	8	13	(1)
1974	30	69	31	17	7	6	20	5	12	3
1973	31	64	32	20	7	5	22	10	8	1

Source: 1977 Gillette Company Annual Report, p. 28.

EXHIBIT 2
Gillette Company Annual Income Statements, 1963–1977 ($000)

Year	Net Sales	Gross Profit	Profit from Operations	Income before Taxes	Federal and Foreign Income Taxes	Net Income
1977	$1,578,209	$834,786	$202,911	$158,820	$79,100	$79,720
1976	1,491,506	782,510	190,939	149,257	71,700	77,557
1975	1,406,906	737,310	184,368	146,954	67,000	79,954
1974	1,246,422	667,395	171,179	147,295	62,300	84,995
1973	1,064,427	600,805	155,949	154,365	63,300	91,065
1972	870,532	505,297	140,283	134,618	59,600	75,018
1971	729,687	436,756	121,532	110,699	48,300	62,399
1970	672,669	417,575	120,966	117,475	51,400	66,075
1969	609,557	390,858	122,416	119,632	54,100	65,532
1968	553,174	358,322	126,016	124,478	62,200	62,278
1967	428,357	291,916	101,153	103,815	47,200	56,615
1966	396,190	264,674	90,967	91,666	41,800	49,866
1965	339,064	224,995	75,010	75,330	33,000	42,330
1964	298,956	205,884	72,594	73,173	35,500	37,673
1963	295,700	207,552	85,316	85,945	44,400	41,545

THE SAFETY RAZOR DIVISION

The Safety Razor Division has long been regarded as the leader in shaving technology. Building upon King Gillette's principle of using razors as a vehicle for blade sales and of associating the name "Gillette" with premium shaving, the division has been able to maintain its number one position in the U.S. market.

Share of Market

Market share is important in the shaving industry. The standard is that each share point is equivalent to approximately $1 million in pretax profits. Over recent history Gillette has held approximately 60 percent of the total dollar market. However, the division has put more emphasis on increasing its share from its static level.

Product Line

During the course of its existence Gillette has introduced many new blades and razors. In the last 15 years, the shaving market has evolved from a double-edged emphasis to twin-bladed systems (see Exhibit 3). Besides Atra and TRAC II, Gillette markets Good News! disposables, Daisy for women, and double-edge, injector, carbon, and Techmatic band systems (see Exhibit

EXHIBIT 3

Long-Term Summary of Gillette Razor Blades: Percent Consumer Blade Sales—Food/Drug Total, United States (estimated market share)

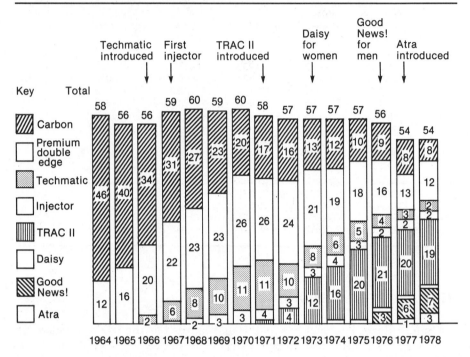

4). Within their individual markets, Gillette makes 65 percent of all premium double-edge blade sales, 12 percent of injector sales, and almost all of the carbon and band sales.

Marketing Approach and Past Traditions

During 1977 the Gillette Company spent $207.9 million to promote all its products throughout the world, of which $133.1 million was spent for advertising, including couponing and sampling, and $74.8 million for sales promotion. In terms of the domestic operation, the Safety Razor Division uses an eight-cycle promotional schedule, whereby every six weeks a new program is initiated. During any one cycle, some but not all products and their packages are sold on promotion. Usually one of the TRAC II packages is sold on promotion during each of these cycles.

> Gillette advertising is designed to provide information to consumers and motivate them to buy the company's products. Sales promotion ensures that these products are readily available, well located, and attractively displayed in re-

EXHIBIT 4
Safety Razor Division Product Lines, June 1978

	Package Sizes	Manufacturer's Suggested Retail Price
Blades:		
TRAC II	5, 9, 14, Adjustable 4	$1.60, 2.80, 3.89, 1.50
Atra	5, 10	1.70, 3.40
Good News!	2	0.60
Daisy	2	1.00
Techmatic	5, 10, 15	1.50, 2.80, 3.50
Double-edge		
Platinum plus	5, 10, 15	1.40, 2.69, 3.50
Super-stainless	5, 10, 15	1.20, 2.30, 3.10
Carbon		
Super blue	10, 15	1.50, 2.15
Regular blue	5, 10	0.70, 1.25
Injector		
Regular	7, 11	1.95, 2.60
Twin-injector	5, 8	1.40, 2.20
Razors:		
TRAC II	Regular	3.50
	Lady	3.50
	Adjustable	3.50
	Deluxe	3.50
Atra		4.95
Double-edge		
Super-adjustable		3.50
Lady Gillette		3.50
Super speed		1.95
Twin-injector		2.95
Techmatic	Regular	3.50
Three-piece		4.50
Knack		1.95
Cricket lighters:		
Regular		1.49
Super		1.98
Keeper		4.49

tail stores. Special promotion at the point of purchase offers consumers an extra incentive to buy Gillette products.[2]

In the past the company has concentrated its advertising and promotion on its newest shaving product, reducing support for its other, established lines. The theory is that growth must come at the expense of other brands. For example, when TRAC II was introduced, the advertising budget for

---

[2] 1977 Gillette Company Annual Report, p. 14.

other brands was cut such that the double-edge portion decreased from 47 percent in 1971 to 11 percent in 1972, while TRAC II received 61 percent of the division budget (see Exhibit 5).

A long-standing tradition has been that razors are used as a means for selling blades. Thus, with razors the emphasis is to induce the consumer to try the product by offering coupon discounts, mail samples, and heavy informational advertising. Blade strategy has been to emphasize a variety of sales devices—such as discounts, displays, and sweepstakes at pharmacies, convenience stores, and supermarkets—to encourage point-of-purchase sales. In spite of this tradition, razor sales are a very significant portion of division sales and profits.

At the center of this marketing strategy has been the company's identification with sports. The Gillette "Cavalcade of Sports" began with Gillette's

EXHIBIT 5
Approximate Gillette Historical Advertising Expenditures, 1965–1978*

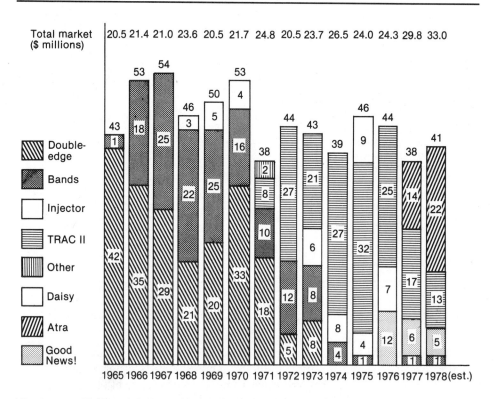

* Total market ($ millions) refers to the total dollars spent by all competitors for advertising in a given year. The numbers above and inside the bars refer to percentages of total market expenditures. For example, in 1965, double-edge advertising accounted for 42 percent of total market expenditures for advertising.

radio sponsorship of the 1939 world series and continues today with the world series, Super Bowl, professional and NCAA basketball, and boxing. During the 1950s and 60s Gillette spent 60 percent of its ad dollar on sports programming. Influenced by research that showed prime-time entertainment offered superior audience potential, in the early 1970s the company switched to a prime-time emphasis. However, in the last two years Gillette has returned to its sports formula.

Marketing Research

Research has been a cornerstone to the success of the company, for it has been the means to remain superior to its competitors. For example, Gillette was faced in 1917 with the expiration of its basic patents and the eventual flood of competitive models. Six months before the impending expiration, the company came out with new razor models, including one for a dollar. As a result the company made more money than ever before. In fact, throughout the history of shaving, Gillette has introduced most of the improvements in shaving technology. The major exceptions are the injector, which was introduced by Schick, and the stainless steel double-edge blade, introduced by Wilkinson.

The company spends $37 million annually on research and development for new products, product improvements, and consumer testing. In addition to Atra, a recent development is a new sharpening process called "Microsmooth" which improves the closeness of the shave and the consistency of the blade. This improvement is to be introduced on all of the company's twin blades by early 1979. Mike Edwards believes that this will help to ensure TRAC II's retention of its market.

At the time of Atra's introduction Gillette research found that users would come from TRAC II and non-twin-blade systems. This loss was estimated to be 60 percent of TRAC II users. Recent research indicates that with heavy marketing support in 1978, TRAC II's loss will be held to 40 percent.

THE SHAVING MARKET

The shaving market is divided into two segments: wet shavers and electric. Today the wet shavers account for 75 percent of the market. In the United States alone 1.9 billion blades and 23 million razors are sold annually.

Market Factors

There are a number of factors at work within the market: (1) the adult shaving population has increased in the past 15 years to 74.6 million men and 68.2 million women; (2) technological improvements have improved the quality of the shave and increased the life of the razor blade; and (3) the volume of blades and razors has begun to level off after a period of declining and then increasing sales (see Exhibit 6).

While the shaving market has increased slightly, there are more competitors. Yet Gillette has been able to maintain its share of the market—approximately two-thirds of the dollar razor market and a little over half of the dollar blade market.

Market Categories

The market is segmented into seven components: new systems, disposables, and injector, premium double-edge, carbon double-edge, continuous band, and single-edge systems. In the early 1900s the shaving market was primarily straight-edge. During the past 70 years the market has evolved away from its single- then double-edge emphasis to the present market of 60 percent bonded systems (all systems where the blade is encased in plastic). Exhibit 7 shows the recent trends within the market categories.

Competitors

Gillette's major competitors are Warner-Lambert's Schick, Colgate-Palmolive's Wilkinson, American Safety Razor's Personna, and BIC. Each has its own strongholds. Schick, which introduced the injector system, now controls

EXHIBIT 6
Razor and Blade Sales Volume, 1963–1979

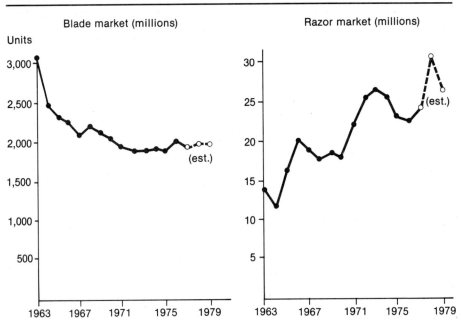

EXHIBIT 7
Recent System Share Trends

	1972	1973	1974	1975	1976	1977	First Half, 1978
Volume:							
New systems	8.8%	20.6%	28.8%	36.2%	39.9%	40.8%	43.8%
Injector	20.2	17.6	17.1	16.3	15.7	14.2	12.8
Double-edge							
Premium	39.4	34.9	30.8	27.4	24.5	21.1	19.0
Carbon	12.0	10.6	9.4	8.1	7.3	7.6	6.6
Bands	13.1	10.3	8.0	6.4	4.7	3.7	2.7
Disposables	—	—	—	—	2.5	6.9	9.7
Single-edge	6.5	6.0	5.9	5.6	5.4	5.7	5.4
Total market	100.0%	100.0%	100.0%	100.0%	100.0%	100.0%	100.0%
Dollars:							
New systems	11.8%	26.9%	36.9%	46.0%	50.1%	50.1%	52.1%
Injector	21.8	18.6	17.8	16.4	15.0	13.8	12.5
Double-edge							
Premium	41.5	34.2	28.7	24.0	20.8	18.1	16.1
Carbon	6.1	5.4	4.7	4.2	4.0	4.1	3.5
Bands	15.4	11.8	8.7	6.5	4.8	3.6	2.8
Disposables	—	—	—	—	2.8	7.5	10.5
Single-edge	3.4	3.1	3.2	2.9	2.5	2.8	2.5
Total market	100.0%	100.0%	100.0%	100.0%	100.0%	100.0%	100.0%

80 percent of that market. ASR's Personna sells almost all of the single-edge blades on the market. Wilkinson's strength is its bonded system, which appeals to an older, wealthier market. BIC has developed a strong product in its inexpensive disposable.

The competitive pricing structure is comparable to that of Gillette

EXHIBIT 8
New Product Introductions and Their Effects on the Market, 1959–1977

Year	Product Segment	Sales Blade/Razor Market ($ millions)	Change (percent)
1959	Carbon	$122.4	Base
1960	Super blue	144.1	+17.7 over 1959
1963	Stainless	189.3	+31.3 over 1960
1965	Super-stainless	201.2	+ 6.3 over 1963
1966	Banded system	212.1	+ 5.4 over 1965
1969	Injector	246.8	+16.3 over 1966
1972	Twin blades	326.5	+32.2 over 1969
1975	Disposable	384.0	+17.6 over 1972
1977	Pivoting head	444.9	+15.9 over 1975

within the different system categories. While all the companies have similar suggested retail prices, the differences found on the racks in the market are a function of the companies' off-invoice rates to the trade and their promotional allowances.

While it is not much of a factor at this time, private label covers the range of systems and continues to grow.

Market Segmentation

The success of Gillette's technological innovation can be seen by its effect on the total shaving market. While other factors are at play in the market, new product introductions have contributed significantly to market expansion, as Exhibit 8 indicates.

THE TWIN-BLADE MARKET

Research played a key role in the development of twin blades. Gillette had two variations—the current one, where the blades were in tandem; the other, where the blade edges faced each other and required an up-and-down scrubbing motion. From a marketing standpoint and the fact that the Atra swivel system had problems in testing development, TRAC II was launched first. The research department played a major role in the positioning of the product when it discovered hysteresis, the phenomenon of whiskers being lifted out and after a time receding into the follicle. Thus, the TRAC II effect was that the second blade cut the whisker before it receded.

Since its introduction in 1971 the twin-blade market has grown to account for almost 60 percent of all blade sales. The twin-blade market is defined as all bonded razors and blades (e.g., new systems: Atra and TRAC II; disposables: Good News! and BIC). Exhibit 9 shows the trends in the twin-blade market.

EXHIBIT 9
The Twin-Blade Market, 1972–1978 ($ millions)

	1972	1973	1974	1975	1976	1977	1978*	1979*
Razors	$ 29.5	$ 32.1	$ 31.4	$ 31.3	$ 31.5	$ 39.7	$ 53.8	
Disposables	—	—	—	—	14.5	41.5	64.9	
Blades	31.6	72.0	105.7	147.5	176.3	183.7	209.2	
Total twin	$ 61.1	$104.1	$137.1	$176.2	$222.3	$264.9	$327.9	
Total market	$326.5	$332.6	$342.5	$384.0	$422.2	$444.9	$491.0	$500.0

* Estimated.

During this period many products have been introduced. They include: 1971—Sure Touch; 1972—Deluxe TRAC II and Schick Super II; 1973—Lady TRAC II, Personna Double II, and Wilkinson Bonded; 1974—Personna Flicker, Good News!, and BIC Disposable; 1975—Personna Lady Double II; and 1976—Adjustable TRAC II and Schick Super II.

Advertising

In the race for market share the role of advertising is extremely important in the shaving industry. Of all the media expenditures television is the primary vehicle in the twin-blade market. For Gillette this means an emphasis on maximum exposure and sponsorship of sports events. The company's policy for the use of television advertising is based on the conviction that television is essentially a family medium and that programs should be suitable for family viewing. Gillette tries to avoid programs that unduly emphasize sex or violence.

As the industry leader, TRAC II receives a great deal of competitive pressure in the form of aggressive advertising from competitors and other Gillette twin-blade brands (see Exhibit 10). For example, the theme of recent Schick commercials was the "Schick challenge," while BIC emphasized its low cost and comparable clean shave in relation to other twin-blade brands. However, competitive media expenditures are such that their cost-per-share point is substantially higher than that of TRAC II.

Despite competitive pressures, TRAC II aggressively advertises too. As a premium product it does not respond directly to competitive challenges or shifts in its own media; rather it follows a standard principle of emphasizing TRAC II's strengths.

EXHIBIT 10
Estimated Media Expenditures ($000)

	1976	First Half, 1977	Second Half, 1977	Total 1977	First Half, 1978	Total 1978
Gillette	$10,800	$ 4,800	$ 6,400	$11,200	$ 8,100	$13,800
Schick	7,600	3,700	4,300	8,000	4,300	8,900
Wilkinson	2,700	1,400	2,200	3,600	1,400	2,200
ASR	2,600	700	200	900	200	800
BIC	600*	4,300	1,800	6,100	4,000	7,300
Total market	$24,300	$14,900	$14,900	$29,800	$18,000	$33,000
Brands:						
TRAC II	$ 6,000	$ 3,300	$ 1,700	$ 5,000	$ 2,400	$ 4,000
Atra	—	—	4,000*	4,000	4,500	7,500
Good News!	1,900	1,200	600	1,800	700	1,600
Super II	2,600	1,400	2,600	4,000	3,000	4,600

* Product introduction.

EXHIBIT 11
1976, 1977 TRAC II Media Plan ($000)

	Quarter				
	1 *JFM*	*2* *AMJ*	*3* *JAS*	*4* *OND*	*Total*
1976:					
Prime-time	$ 835	$ 575	$1,200	$ 550	$3,160
Sports	545	305	450	1,040	2,440
Network	1,380	880	1,650	1,590	5,600
Other	80	85	70	165	400
Total	$1,460	$ 965	$1,720	$1,755	$6,000
1977:					
Prime-time	$1,300	$ 900	$ 300	—	$2,500
Sports	500	400	400	400	1,700
Network	1,800	1,300	700	400	4,200
Print	—	—	200	200	400
Black	75	75	75	75	300
Military and miscellaneous	25	25	25	25	100
Total	$1,900	$1,400	$1,000	$ 700	$5,000

As Exhibits 11 and 12 indicate, the TRAC II media plan emphasizes diversity with a heavy emphasis on advertising on prime-time television and on sports programs. In addition, TRAC II is continuously promoted to retain its market share.

For 1978 the division budgeted $13.5 million for advertising, with Atra and TRAC II receiving the major portion of the division budget (see Exhibit 13). The traditional Gillette approach has the newest brand receiving the bulk of the advertising dollars (see Exhibit 5). Therefore it is certain that Atra will receive a substantial increase in advertising for 1979; whether the division will increase or decrease TRAC II's budget as well as whether the division will increase the total ad budget for 1979 is unknown at this time.

TRAC II

The 1971 introduction of TRAC II was the largest in shaving history. Influenced by the discovery of the hysteresis process, by the development of a clog-free dual-blade cartridge, and by consumer testing data which showed 9 to 1 preference for TRAC II over panelists' current razors, Gillette raced to get the product to market. Because the introduction involved so many people and was so critical to reversing a leveling of corporate profits (see Exhibit 2), the division president personally assumed the role of product devel-

EXHIBIT 12
1978 TRAC II Media Plan

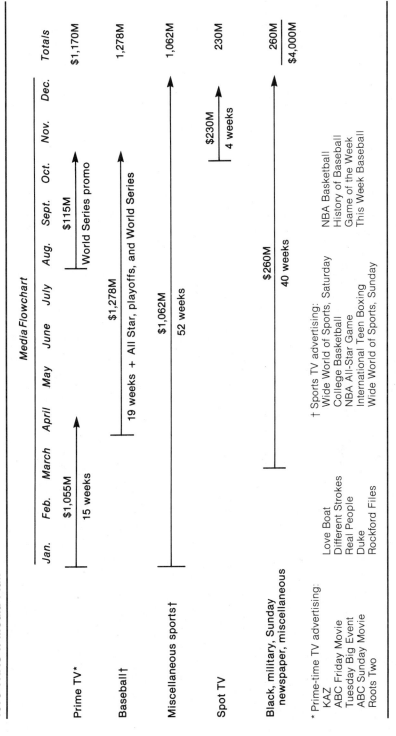

Media Flowchart

	Jan.	Feb.	March	April	May	June	July	Aug.	Sept.	Oct.	Nov.	Dec.	Totals
Prime TV*		$1,055M 15 weeks →							$115M World Series promo →				$1,170M
Baseball†				$1,278M 19 weeks + All Star, playoffs, and World Series →									1,278M
Miscellaneous sports†						$1,062M 52 weeks →							1,062M
Spot TV											$230M 4 weeks →		230M
Black, military, Sunday newspaper, miscellaneous							$260M 40 weeks →						260M
													$4,000M

* Prime-time TV advertising:
KAZ
ABC Friday Movie
Tuesday Big Event
ABC Sunday Movie
Roots Two

Love Boat
Different Strokes
Real People
Duke
Rockford Files

† Sports TV advertising:
Wide World of Sports, Saturday
College Basketball
NBA All-Star Game
International Teen Boxing
Wide World of Sports, Sunday

NBA Basketball
History of Baseball
Game of the Week
This Week Baseball

EXHIBIT 13
1978 Division Marketing Budget (percentages)

	Atra Line	TRAC II Line	Good News!	Double-Edge Blades	Double-Edge Razors	Techmatic Line	Daisy	Injector Line	Twin Injector	Total Blade/Razor
Marketing expenses:										
Promotion*	42.3%	69.4%	65.2%	92.2%	75.4%	52.7%	58.4%	77.5%	48.3%	60.7%
Advertising†	55.6	28.8	31.2	4.6	—	—	39.0	—	26.3	36.5
Other	2.1	1.8	3.6	3.2	24.6	47.3	2.6	22.5	25.4	2.8
Total	100.0%	100.0%	100.0%	100.0%	100.0%	100.0%	100.0%	100.0%	100.0%	100.0%
Percent line/total direct marketing	34.1%	38.4%	14.9%	7.6%	0.4%	0.3%	3.4%	0.2%	0.7%	100.0%
Percent line/total full-revenue sales	20.5%	41.8%	13.4%	16.8%	1.4%	2.1%	2.2%	0.6%	1.2%	100.0%

* Defined as off-invoice allowances, wholesale push money, cooperative advertising, excess cost, premiums, and contests and prizes.
† Defined as media, sampling, couponing, production, and costs.

opment manager and lived with the project day and night through its development and introduction.[3]

Launched during the 1971 World Series promotion, TRAC II was the most frequently advertised shaving system in America during its introductory period. Supported by $10 million in advertising and promotion, the TRAC II results were impressive: 1.7 million razors and 5 million cartridges were sold in October; and during the first year, the introductory campaign made 2 billion impressions and reached 80 percent of all homes an average of 4.7 times per week. In addition a multimillion-unit sampling campaign was implemented in 1972 which was the largest of its kind.

For five years TRAC II was clearly the fastest-growing product on the market, and it helped to shape the switch to twin blades. Its users are predominantly men who are young, college-educated, metropolitan, suburban, and upper income.

The brand reached its peak in 1976, when it sold 485 million blades and 7 million razors. In comparison, projected TRAC II sales for 1978 are 433 million blades and 4.2 million razors. During the period, TRAC II brand contribution decreased (see Exhibit 14).

Competitors' responsive strategies seem to be effective. The growth of Super II during the last two years is attributed to certain advantages that it has over TRAC II. Super II has higher trade allowances (20 percent versus 15 percent), has gained valuable distribution, has increased media expenditures, and has generally lower everyday prices.

In preparing the 1979 marketing plans the objective for TRAC II was to retain its consumer franchise despite strong competitive challenges through consumer-oriented promotions and to market the brand aggressively year-round. Specifically TRAC II was:

1. To obtain a 20 percent share of the cartridge and razor market.
2. To deliver 43 percent of the division's profit.
3. To retain its valuable pegboard space at the checkout counters in convenience, food, and drug stores as well as supermarkets.

In 1978 Mike Edwards launched a new economy-size blade package (14 blades) and a heavy spending campaign to retain TRAC II's market share. He employed strong trade and consumer promotion incentives supported by (1) a new improved product claim of Microsmooth; (2) new graphics, and (3) a revised version of the highly successful "Sold Out" advertising campaign.

Midyear results indicate that TRAC II's performance exceeded division expectations, as it retained 21.6 percent of the blade market and contribution exceeded budget by $2 million.

---

[3] For an excellent account of the TRAC II introduction by the president of Gillette North America, see William G. Salatich, "Gillette's TRAC II: The Steps to Success," *Marketing Communications*, January 1972.

EXHIBIT 14
TRAC II Line Income Statement, 1972–1978

	1972*	1973	1974	1975	1976(base)	1977	1978(est.)
Full-revenue sales (FRS):							
Promotional	28%	41%	71%	100%	100%	110%	112%
Nonpromotional	38	91	89	83	100	80	65
Total	32	60	78	93	100	99	95
Direct cost of sales:							
Manufacturing	63	77	93	111	100	88	83
Freight	51	80	91	106	100	82	80
Total	62	77	93	111	100	88	83
Standard profit contribution	26	56	75	89	100	101	97
Marketing expenses:							
Promotional expenses							
Lost revenue	26	39	72	100	100	114	126
Wholesale push money	455	631	572	565	100	562	331
Cooperative advertising	27	36	58	71	100	115	133
Excess cost	25	50	59	83	100	63	92
Premiums	3	29	16	28	100	78	217
Contests and prizes	7	21	110	115	100	215	109
Total	26	40	67	90	100	112	129
Advertising:							
Media	90	83	110	119	100	96	75
Production	96	128	130	104	100	196	162
Couponing and sampling	470	344	177	112	100	166	131
Other	19	120	68	78	100	54	54
Total	124	110	108	117	100	96	78
Other marketing expenses	108	120	847	617	100	242	86
Marketing research	122	65	47	34	100	134	91
Total assignable marketing expenses	67	69	87	102	100	106	108
Net contribution	14	53	81	85	100	100	94
Percent promotional FRS/total FRS	56	43	58	76	163	70	74
Percent promotional expenses/promotional FRS	15	16	16	15	11	17	20
Percent promotional expenses/total FRS	9	7	9	10	11	12	15
Percent advertising expenses/total FRS	28	13	10	9	7	7	6
Percent media expenses/total FRS	17	8	8	8	6	6	5

* Each year's data are shown as a percentage of 1976's line item. For example, 1972 sales were 32 percent of 1976 sales.

ATRA

Origin

Research for the product began in Gillette's United Kingdom Research and Development Lab in 1970. The purpose was to improve the high standards of performance of twin-blade shaving and specifically to enhance the TRAC II effect. The company's scientists discovered that instead of moving the hand and face to produce the best shaving angle for the blade, the razor head itself could produce a better shave if the razor head could "pivot" in such a way as to maintain the most effective twin-blade shaving angle. Once the pivoting head was shown to produce a better shave, test after test, research continued in the Boston headquarters on product design, redesigning, and consumer testing.

The name "Atra" came from two years of intensive consumer testing of the various names which could be identified with this advanced razor. The choice was based on its easiness to remember and on its communication of technology, uniqueness, and the feeling of the future. Atra stands for *Automatic Tracking Razor Action.*

Introduction

Atra was first introduced in mid-1977. The introduction stressed the new shaving system and was supplemented by heavy advertising coupled with $2 razor rebate coupons to induce trial and 50-cent coupons toward Atra blades to induce brand loyalty.

During its first year on the national market, Atra was expected to sell 9 million razors, although 85 percent of all sales were made on a discount basis. Early results showed that Atra sold at a faster level than Gillette's previously most successful introduction, TRAC II.

The Atra razor retails for $4.95. Blade packages are sold in 5 and 10 sizes. TRAC II and Atra blades are not interchangeable. Because of Gillette's excellent distribution system it hasn't had much problem gaining valuable pegboard space.

CURRENT TRENDS AND COMPETITIVE RESPONSES IN THE TWIN-BLADE MARKET

There has been quite a bit of activity in the shaving market during the first half of 1978. Atra has increased total Gillette share in the razor and blade market. During the June period, Atra razors have continued to exceed TRAC II as the leading-selling razor while the Atra blades' share was approximately 8 percent, accounting for most of Gillette's 4 percent share growth since June 1977. Thus the growth of Atra has put more competitive pressure on TRAC II.

In addition, the disposable segment due to BIC and Good News! has increased by five share points to a hefty 12 percent dollar share of the blade market. Combined with TRAC II's resiliency in maintaining share, competitive brands have lost share: Schick Super II, ASR, and Wilkinson were all down two points since June 1977.

In response to these recent trends, the TRAC II team expects competition to institute some changes. In an effort to recover its sagging share, Edwards expects the Schick muscular dystrophy promotion in October to help bolster Super II with its special offer. The pressure may already be appearing with Schick's highly successful introduction of Personal Touch for women this year, currently about 10 percent of the razor market, which has to draw TRAC II female shavers. In addition it appears inevitable that Schick will bring out an Atra-type razor. This will remove Atra's competitive advantage but increase pressure on TRAC II with the addition of a second pivoting-head competitor.

Continuing its recent trends, it appears that the disposable segment of the market will continue to expand. The first sign of this is the BIC ads which offer 12 BIC disposables for $1. Good News! will receive additional advertising support in the latter half of the year as well as the introduction of a new package size.

One of Edwards' major objectives is to emphasize the importance of TRAC II to upper management. Besides the Microsmooth introduction, a price increase on TRAC II products will be implemented soon. It is unclear whether the price change will have an adverse effect on brand sales.

In preparing the 1979 TRAC II marketing plan, Edwards realizes that Atra will be given a larger share of the advertising dollars following a strong year and that the disposable market will continue to grow. TRAC II share remains questionable and is dependent upon the level of marketing support it receives. Whether TRAC II will be able to continue its heavy spending program and generate large revenues for the division remains to be seen. All of these factors as well as the company's support of Atra make 1979 a potentially tough year for Mike Edwards and TRAC II.

1979 MARKETING PLAN PREPARATION

Edwards recently received the following memorandum from the vice president of marketing:

Memo to: Brand Group

From: P. Meyers

Date: July 7, 1978

Subject: *1979 Marketing Plans*

In preparation for the marketing plan approval process and in developing the division strategy for 1979, I would like a preliminary plan from each brand group by the end of the month. Please submit statements of objective, corresponding strategy, and levels of dollar support requested for the following:

1. Overall brand strategy[4]—target market.
2. Blade and razor volume and share goals.
3. Sales promotion.
4. Advertising.
5. Couponing and sampling.
6. Miscellaneous—new packaging, additional marketing research, marketing cost–saving ideas, etc.

See you at the weekly meeting on Wednesday.

In developing the TRAC II marketing plan, Edwards has to wrestle with some strategy decisions. To get significant funding, how should he position TRAC II? Can he enhance the likelihood of retaining current spending levels for TRAC II with the proper positioning strategy?

In addition, where do disposables fit into Gillette's overall marketing strategy? Are they a distinct segment? How does he convince the vice president that dollars are more effective on TRAC II than on Good News!? What is Atra's current positioning strategy, and does he anticipate changes? Given the strategies of TRAC II, Atra, and disposables, what problems will this create for the consumer and for the trade?

---

[4] Brand strategy means positioning the brand in such a way that it appeals to a distinguishable target market.

APPLICATION 6–7

Pratt & Whitney

In a stunning reversal of industrial fortunes, General Electric Co. has wrested huge segments of the global, multibillion-dollar market for commercial jet aircraft engines from United Technologies Corp.'s Pratt & Whitney group.

For more than 30 years Pratt & Whitney dominated the market. But in 1985 GE shipped more commercial-airliner engines than Pratt & Whitney for the first time. Since then it has increased its lead in shipments. In 1986 it overtook Pratt & Whitney in dollar sales, and its lead in new orders is growing (see Exhibit 1). Says Harry Gray, United Technologies' former chairman: "GE has been eating Pratt's lunch."

Pratt & Whitney is vigorously defending its market. It remains a strong competitor, industry officials say, and Pratt & Whitney executives vow to regain the No. 1 position. But the turnabout in the engine business, says Christopher Demisch, a First Boston Corp. securities analyst, locks Pratt & Whitney and GE into "a long, tough fight" for market share. A Pratt & Whitney comeback won't be easy, if only because airline customers, once having decided on engine orders for new planes, rarely switch suppliers.

The stakes are huge. In the next decade, global sales of commercial and military engines and spare parts will reach nearly $160 billion, according to a Pratt estimate. Though commercial sales will account for just under half that, they are far more profitable than military business.

The turnabout stems from a series of events, some stretching back years and some still unfolding. The story is one of corporate gambles that didn't pay and the deft exploitation of an opponent's weaknesses. During Mr. Gray's tenure at United Technologies, the company bet billions of dollars on two new engines that, so far at least, aren't paying off. Mr. Gray canceled a third engine project, leaving a gaping hole in Pratt & Whitney's line that fancy engineering footwork permitted GE to fill.

A recent record of slipshod service, especially tardiness in supplying spare parts, has also damaged Pratt & Whitney. No mere inconvenience, the late arrival of needed parts can disrupt airline maintenance and flight schedules, inflating costs and enraging passengers—and executives. Robert Daniell, the chairman of United Technologies recently got a blistering letter of complaint from Steven Rothmeier, the chairman of Northwest Airlines.

"We were living hand-to-mouth on spares from Pratt," Mr. Rothmeier

EXHIBIT 1
The Pratt-GE Jet-Engine Battle

	1982	1983	1984	1985	1986	1987
Airliner engines shipped:						
Pratt	480	384	455	360	432	425
GE	314	293	290	420	513	524
New orders:						
Pratt	n.a	409	482	484	494	467
GE	45	60	585	880	675	1,360
Civil and military engine sales (in $billions):						
Pratt	$5.3	$5.2	$5.4	$5.3	$5.5	n.a.
GE	$3.1	$3.5	$3.8	$4.7	$6.0	n.a.
Civil and military engine operating profits (in $millions):						
Pratt	$329	$284	$317	$373	$446	n.a.
GE	$344	$395	$460	$673	$869	n.a.

Note: GE figures include engines made in joint venture (50–50) with Snecma of France. n.a. = Not available.

says in an interview. "I told Daniell that we need a permanent fix for this problem, not just a Band-Aid."

Japan Air Lines executives also have been upset with Pratt & Whitney's service. At one point, because of a lack of Pratt & Whitney parts, not one of JAL's 40 spare engines for its 747 fleet could operate. "If you repeatedly let one of your best customers down," says a senior JAL official, "they go someplace else."

JAL hadn't bought a GE engine in 25 years. But in October, it switched to GE from Pratt & Whitney as its supplier for new 747 engines, partly because of the spare-parts problem. This was a major blow to Pratt & Whitney. JAL flies 60 of the big jets, the biggest 747 fleet in the world.

Pratt & Whitney entered the commercial jet age in the late 1960s with a near-monopoly on the engine business. Early Boeing and McDonnell Douglas jets used only Pratt & Whitney engines. But GE had pioneered some military jet engines and, using this technology, took on Pratt & Whitney in the commercial market. Britain's Rolls-Royce also made commercial jet engines and remains a distant No. 3.

Airline executives were skeptical of GE's early efforts. "Many of them thought of us only in association with light bulbs," says a GE official. GE nevertheless supplied the engine for the McDonnell Douglas DC-10, which sold widely, giving GE a broad beachhead.

Pratt & Whitney, meanwhile, faced agonizing decisions as the 1980s began. Boeing had launched production of an odd-sized plane, the 757. GE and Pratt & Whitney each were producing two basic engines: a big high-thrust engine and a small one. To power the 757, Pratt & Whitney had either to produce a new, midsize engine, requiring a manufacturing investment of nearly $1 billion, or abandon the market to Rolls-Royce. Mr. Gray heeded Boeing's predictions that the 757 would sell in huge numbers and took the risk. GE didn't follow suit.

Then Mr. Gray took another risk. GE had leapfrogged Pratt & Whitney in some technical areas, making GE engines cheaper to build. (Pratt & Whitney even bought a GE engine and tore it apart to see how GE was doing it.) So Mr. Gray decided to replace Pratt & Whitney's big engine with another brand-new engine, a second billion-dollar gamble. "We didn't have much choice—GE had left Pratt in the dust," Mr. Gray says, so far as bringing down manufacturing costs was concerned. He also concluded that the new engine would give Pratt & Whitney a sales edge with airlines; it would boast lower fuel consumption than GE's big engine.

To help finance his new engine projects, Mr. Gray stopped development of a new, small Pratt & Whitney engine. Pratt & Whitney just couldn't afford yet another gamble, he says. But the decision would haunt the company later.

In the past three years, Pratt & Whitney's new midsize engine has gone into service on Boeing 757 jets flown by carriers such as Northwest and Delta—but the engines have encountered a host of troubles.

Northwest has given Pratt & Whitney a list of 20 items to fix. The engines, for example, suck up sand spread on icy runways, causing premature wear and expensive engine removals for extra maintenance. "We've been vacuum-cleaning the runways," complains one Northwest man. Nor has it helped that the extra maintenance—requiring extra parts—has come just when Pratt & Whitney was falling behind in deliveries of spare parts.

To make matters worse for Pratt & Whitney, the anticipated huge market for its midsize power plant has failed to materialize. Sales of 757s have been tepid—partly because falling fuel prices have damped the allure of its engine's vaunted fuel savings. So far only 119 757s with Pratt & Whitney engines have been ordered.

For its part, Pratt & Whitney admits to some service lapses. Deliveries of spare parts, some of which are highly complex and take a year to produce, have been late, the company concedes. Pratt & Whitney has been swamped by the current boom in air travel, which has left airlines clamoring for supplies to maintain engines. At Pratt & Whitney, sales of commercial spare parts doubled to $1.6 billion last year from two years earlier. "There were times we couldn't make the parts fast enough," admits Arthur Wegner, Pratt & Whitney's president.

But surging demand was especially burdensome for Pratt & Whitney. Its 17,000 engines in service (triple GE's number) include 60 different models, multiplying the number and types of spare parts needed. Pratt & Whitney is scurrying to increase parts inventories. It also plans to streamline its hodgepodge of models so that it can stock more of fewer types of parts.

The company dismisses bugs in its midsize engine as the sort common to new engines and vows they will be fixed. The glitches, however, are hurting sales of its new big engine, which began service a few months ago on Pan American World Airways and Singapore Airlines jets. The big engine employs technology developed for Pratt & Whitney's midsize engine, and some airline executives worry that the same problems may crop up. This is a groundless worry, Pratt & Whitney says. "You can bet [that] everything I learn on [the midsize unit] I will instantly fix" on the big engine, says Selwyn Berson, a vice president of the company.

GE isn't saddled with new-engine worries. Instead of developing new engines, its engineers have been grinding away at improving older units. With break-in bugs eliminated long ago, GE salesmen have been touting their engines' reliability.

This was ultimately to give GE an edge in negotiations with Japan Air Lines, which in 1986 began shopping for an engine for a longer-range version of its 747 jumbo jet. At the outset, one JAL faction favored Rolls-Royce; another favored Pratt & Whitney. But GE's reliability pitch struck a responsive chord. "We are an island nation; we must have reliable aircraft to maintain links with the rest of the world," says one JAL man.

Safety questions also figured in the reliability discussions. The new 747 will have a two-man crew instead of the usual three, and JAL pilots worried about the prospect of handling in-flight engine failures with a smaller crew. The Japanese are ultrasensitive about safety anyway. "When JAL has an accident, somebody has to fall on his sword," says one U.S. engine salesman.

Sensing victory, GE executives revved up their sales campaign. Jack Welch, the chairman of GE, and Edward Hood, vice chairman, talked to JAL officials in Tokyo. Meanwhile, JAL officials were fuming over Pratt & Whitney's late spare-parts deliveries, which had repeatedly disrupted JAL maintenance work. Then the airline's powerful engineering group completed its technical evaluation of the competing engines. GE's came in first, Rolls's second and Pratt & Whitney's third, industry officials say. JAL gave its order to GE.

GE has also scored triumphs with its small engine. Built in a joint venture with Snecma of France, it sold poorly in the 1970s. But a few years ago GE engineers managed to squeeze it under the wing of the small Boeing 737 by designing a unique oval engine casing that permitted adequate ground clearance. New Boeing 737s powered by the GE engine have become the hottest-selling jets in the world. Nearly 800 have been sold.

Pratt & Whitney doesn't have a small engine to rival GE's, thanks to Mr. Gray's cancellation of the small-engine project. Belatedly, Pratt & Whitney is scrambling to fill this gap in its product line. With its financial and technical resources strained developing its midsize and big engines, Pratt & Whitney set up a joint venture with Rolls-Royce and other European and Japanese companies to develop a small engine, the V2500. But the section of the engine being built by Rolls doesn't run very well. In ground tests, parts keep fracturing and flying apart.

Pratt and Whitney officials are furious. "Incompetent," is the way one top Pratt & Whitney man recently described Rolls. But a spokesman for the joint venture says recent tests show that the Rolls section—redesigned for the third time—will work.

If it doesn't, it could mean delays for V2500-powered jets ordered by Pan Am and Lufthansa. At best, the engine already lags far behind GE's small engine in the sales race.

Yet the tide could turn in Pratt & Whitney's favor. As bugs are worked out of its new engines and if fuel prices soar, airlines may snap up its products. And there is no doubt Pratt & Whitney will fight to regain lost business. Says Mr. Wegner, the company's president: "The day we lost at JAL was the first day of our campaign to win JAL back."

Discussion Questions

1. Discuss the flaws in Pratt & Whitney's positioning strategy that apparently contributed to its loss of the dominant market position.
2. Was the company's analysis of the mid-size engine market faulty?
3. Examine the strategy implications of concentrating on product improvement (GE's apparent strategy) versus new-product development (Pratt & Whitney's strategy).
4. Discuss the role of marketing strategy implementation in the performance of Pratt & Whitney in the jet engine market.

APPLICATION 6–8

Winkleman Manufacturing Company

In a recent staff meeting, John Winkleman, president of Winkleman Manufacturing Company, addressed his managers with this problem:

> Intense competitive pressure is beginning to erode our market share in handhelds. I have documented 11 large orders that have been lost to Backman and Wiston within the past three months. On an annual basis this amounts to nearly 10,000 units and $1.5 million in lost opportunities. Within the last 18

This case was prepared by Jim Dooley, under the supervision of Dr. William L. Weis. Albers School of Business, Seattle University. Copyright © 1981 by Jim Dooley and William L. Weis.

months, at least 16 serious competitors have entered the market. Two-thirds of these DMMs have continuity indicators. The trend is the same for European and Japanese markets as well. Our sales of handheld DMMs in fiscal year 81 is forecast to grow only 1.7 percent. According to Dataquest projections, the handheld DMM market will grow 20.9 percent for the next five years. I think that figure is conservative. Our competitors are gaining attention and sales with added features, particularly at the present time with continuity indicators. Since a new Winkleman general-purpose, low-cost handheld is two years from introduction, it is important that something be done to retain the profitable position of market leader in our traditional direct and distributor channels. Next meeting I want some ideas.

The Winkleman Manufacturing Company is a major electronics manufacturer in the Northwest, producing many varied products. The three products that most concern Mr. Winkleman are the Series A handheld digital multimeters (DMMs). As an innovator in the field of handheld DMMs, Mr. Winkleman saw his business flourish over the last two years. But now, with his three most successful products in late stages of maturity and a recession in full swing, times are not looking as rosy.

The three multimeters of concern are model numbers 1010, 1020, and 1030. These three models form a complementary family line. The 1010 is a low-cost unit containing all standard measurement functions and having a basic measurement accuracy of .5 percent. The 1020 offers identical measurement functions but has an improved basic measurement accuracy: .1 percent. The top of the line is the 1030. In addition to a basic accuracy of .1 percent, the 1030 offers several additional features, one being an audible continuity indicator. (See Exhibit 1 for sales and projected sales of these three models.)

At the next staff meeting, one of the newer management team members, Dave Haug, presented his ideas for tackling the lost-market problem:

> What we need is a face-life of our existing product line to hold us over the next two years. Changes in color, a new decal, some minor case modifications, and most important an audible continuity indicator in the 1010 and 1020 should give us two more years of product life to tide us over. We can call this

EXHIBIT 1
Selected Sales and Projections (number of units)

Model	FY 80 (actual)	FY 81 (forecast)	Percentage
1020	67,534	61,800	−8.4%
1010	37,455	35,500	−5.5
1030	25,602	35,500	+39.0
Total	130,591	132,800	+1.7%

Series B to retain continuity in switching from the old to the new. As my analysis indicates, Winkleman's decline in 1010/1020 sales could be reversed and show a modest increase in market share over the next two years with the inclusion of the Series B features [see Exhibit 2]. Discussions with large-order customers indicate that Winkleman could have won 40–60 percent of the lost large orders that were mentioned at our last meeting if our entire handheld family featured audible continuity. As you well know, the popularity of continuity indication has been confirmed in several other studies conducted over the past two years.

An estimate of sales of Series B has been generated from inputs from field sales, distribution managers, and discussions with customers. Conservative estimates indicate that sales of Series B will increase 6.9 percent above current Series A levels, with a marginal revenue increase of $1.5 million at U.S. list and assuming the same list prices as the current Series A models. During this current period of tight economic conditions, the market is becoming increasingly price sensitive. I am aware that our normal policy dictates multiplying the factory cost by three for pricing purposes and that the added factory cost of an audible continuity indicator is $5.00; but for income purposes we should not tack this on to the current prices. My analysis indicates that an increase of $5.00 would reduce incremental sales by 20 percent, and an increase of $10.00 would reduce incremental sales by 80 percent.

Also remember that we must pay for some nonrecurring engineering costs (NRE) [see Exhibit 3]. These must come out of our contribution margin— which at Winkleman is calculated by taking the total dollar sales less the 28 percent discount to distributors less factory cost for those units. I believe that increasing these prices will reduce our margins significantly, hindering our ability to cover the NRE, let alone make a profit. Therefore I propose we go ahead with Series B and hold the line on prices.

Dennis Cambelot, a longtime Winkleman employee, spoke up with a comment on Dave's proposal:

Dave, I think this Series B idea shows a lot of potential, but pricewise you are way out of line. We have always added the standard markup to our prod-

EXHIBIT 2
Series A and B—Projected Comparison (number of units)

Model	Unit Price	Series A FY 81	Series B FY 81	Change (percentage)	Total Sales* (change *)
1020	$179	61,800	66,000	4,200 (+6.8%)	$11.81 (+.75)
1010	139	35,500	40,000	4,500 (+12.6%)	$ 5.56 (+.63)
1030	219	35,500	36,000	500 (+1.4%)	$ 7.88 (+.11)
Total		132,800	142,000	9,200	$25.25

* Dollars in millions.

EXHIBIT 3
Engineering Costs and Schedule

Objectives for Series B, Models 1010, 1020, and 1030:
  All case parts molded in medium gray
  New decal for all units
  Pulse-stretched beeper for 1010 and 1020
  Rubber foot on battery door
  Positionable bail
  Manuals updated as necessary
For these objectives, NRE costs will be:

Manual (updated schematics for 1010, 1020, along with instructions for operation of beeper; model number and front panel changes for all units)	$ 3,500
Battery door mold (add three units)	12,000
Battery door foot die	3,000
Decal	1,900
Bail improvement	8,600
Photo lab	250
PCB fab (prototypes)	500
Engineering labor (25 man-weeks)	81,000
Hard model run	6,000
Total	$116,750

ucts. We make quality products, and people are willing to pay for quality. The only thing your fancy MBA degree taught you was to be impractical. If you had gotten your experience in the trenches like me, your pricing theories would not be so conservative, and this company could make more money.

At the close of the meeting, Mr. Winkleman asked that each manager consider the Series B proposal. He directed that this consideration include: (1) whether or not to adopt the B series; (2) if yes, at what price level; (3) alternative suggestions.

Discussion Question

How would you respond at the next meeting?

Time Unlimited, Inc.

The Microcomputer Division of Time Unlimited, Inc., manufactures and sells two models of computers. The smallest one, the RAM–64, and 64K internal memory, two double-density 5½-inch floppy disk drives with 197K bytes each, a detachable full typewriter keyboard, and a 12-inch video display of 80 columns × 24 rows with scrolling capability. In addition, it includes as standard software a profit plan, a household budget program, a word-processing system, and two computer games of the customer's choice. It can be used either as a home computer or in a small business where the data-processing needs are not extensive. The other model, the RAM–128, is larger than the RAM–64 and has greater capacity, including two 8-inch double-sided, double-density disk drives holding over 700K bytes. In addition to the software package offered with the RAM–64, a complete accounting program and a sophisticated statistical analysis package are included as part of the standard software. However, it still is classified as a microcomputer. The RAM–128 is purchased by businesses that want a small computer with the additional data-processing capabilities that the smaller model does not offer. Time Unlimited, Inc.'s prices are higher than their competitor's because the RAM computers offer processing and programming features not available from competitors, as well as a superior warranty and service program. Time Unlimited usually announces any price changes after the competition has posted theirs for the year.

Late in 1981 the Computer Division managers held a meeting where the following discussion took place. In attendance were:

Jon Patric—marketing manager
Andrea Suzanne—chief accountant
Ross Edwards—vice president of the Computer Division
Jim Mathews—production manager

JON PATRIC: In a few months we are going to raise the price of the RAM–64 from $1,800 to $2,000 per unit, while our competition will be raising their prices from $1,700 to $1,850 per unit. In addition, the price of the RAM–128 will go from $13,500 to $15,000 per unit. By contrast, our competition is planning on raising their prices from $12,500 to $14,000. We project that our microcomputer sales division should sell at least 40,000 units of the RAM–64 at $1,800 per unit; at $2,000 per

Source: Professor Mary Ziebell, Seattle University, and Professor Don T. DeCoster, University of Washington.

unit we should sell at least 20,000 units. Our market studies also indicate that at $13,500 per unit we should sell at least 4,000 units of RAM–128, while at $15,000 per unit we project sales of at least 2,000 units. I'm very concerned about this decrease in our volume of sales and question the advisability of raising our prices at this time.

ANDREA SUZANNE: The reason we are increasing the prices of the RAM–64 and RAM–128, Jon, is due to the fact that labor and material prices have gone up about 12 percent over the last year. Our increase in price just reflects the cost of inflation. I have finished compiling some current data (Exhibit 1) through June of 1981, if anyone is interested. One idea to decrease cost would be to cut the 10 percent sales commission to 7 or 8 percent. That's all our competitors are paying their sales staff. Also our service warranty costs have increased from 4 percent to approximately 7 percent of sales. We really need to know the cause of this increase.

ROSS EDWARDS: Jon, if we kept both models at the current price, would the competitors keep their prices at the current level, or would they still raise their prices? We really need to know this. Also it seems from the attached income statement (Exhibit 2) that the RAM–128 line is not as profitable as the RAM–64 line. Perhaps we should be concentrating our marketing efforts on the RAM–64. It also seems to me we should seriously consider Andrea's suggestion on reducing sales commissions.

JON PATRIC: Our competition would probably raise their prices even if we kept ours the same, though perhaps not as much as originally planned, Ross. We are currently in a strong market position (Exhibit 3), and I would not like to see this market share lost. In response to Andrea's suggestion, I am certain that a decrease in the level of commissions would seriously affect our market share because of salespeople's decreased motivation.

JIM MATHEWS: From a product-line evaluation standpoint, we are not making much money on the RAM–128. Maybe we should drop it and produce only the RAM–64 or develop another model. I realize we cannot transfer all of the equipment that is used in manufacturing the RAM–128 to the manufacture of the RAM–64, but we can transfer the labor that is used to produce the RAM–128 to produce the RAM–64. However, your question on increasing warranty costs, Andrea, is harder to answer. Up through 1980 we have always considered 4 percent of the sales price of both the micros a reasonable estimate of our costs of servicing the computers under the one-year warranty, and this proved accurate in the past. But with the increase in parts and labor costs as well as some small problems in this year's production process, it's not surprising that warranty costs have increased. In fact I'm rather surprised the increase wasn't more. It is important, given our current marketing strategy, that we maintain the highest possible reputation in this area. At least that's what Jon is always telling me.

ANDREA SUZANNE: To get back to the idea of dropping the RAM–128 line, we really may want to give that further consideration. Our records show that the nontransferable RAM–128 equipment has a book value of $4,350,000. We should be able to sell this equipment for around $2 million. This would give us a good cash inflow, enough perhaps to develop a new product line.

EXHIBIT 1

Estimated Cost Comparisons of RAM–64 and RAM–128 at Different Production Volumes through June 1981

A. RAM–64

Expenses	Volume (units)				
	10,000	20,000	30,000	40,000	50,000
Raw materials	$ 144	$ 144	$ 144	$ 144	$ 144
Purchased parts	160	160	160	160	155
Direct labor	510	500	490	485	490
Departmental overhead					
Direct*	35	34	32	33	33
Equipment depreciation. . . .	144	72	48	36	29
Indirect†	235	120	80	60	48
General overhead‡	127	125	120	122	123
Production costs	1,355	1,155	1,074	1,040	1,022
Marketing and administration§ .	677	578	537	520	511
Total costs	$2,032	$1,733	$1,611	$1,560	$1,533

B. RAM–128

Expenses	Volume (units)				
	1,000	2,000	3,000	4,000	5,000
Raw materials	$ 1,450	$ 1,450	$ 1,450	$ 1,450	$ 1,450
Purchased parts	1,740	1,740	1,740	1,730	1,720
Direct labor	4,600	4,500	4,350	4,400	4,500
Departmental overhead					
Direct*	400	380	373	365	370
Equipment depreciation. . . .	870	435	290	218	174
Indirect†	1,305	652	435	326	261
General overhead‡	1,110	1,100	1,087	1,095	1,100
Production costs	11,475	10,257	9,725	9,584	9,575
Marketing and administration§ .	5,738	5,129	4,858	4,793	4,788
Total costs	$17,213	$15,385	$14,583	$14,377	$14,363

* Power, supplies, repairs.
† Supervision, interest, rent, property taxes.
‡ Allocated on the basis of 25 percent of direct labor.
§ Allocated on the basis of 50 percent of production costs.

JIM MATHEWS: Great idea, Andrea. Our current plant capacity is 50,000 units of the RAM–64 and 5,000 units of the RAM–128. With the cash from the sale of the RAM–128 equipment, we could expand our plant capacity to 70,000 units of the RAM–64. It would cost about $3 million for an additional building and equipment, give or take a little.

EXHIBIT 2

TIME UNLIMITED, INC.
Income Statement
For Year Ending December 31, 1980
($000)

	RAM–64*	RAM–128*	Total
Gross sales	$54,600	$40,500	$94,500
Expenses			
Raw materials	$ 3,880	$ 3,915	$ 7,795
Purchased parts	4,320	4,698	9,018
Direct labor	12,960	11,745	24,705
Direct overhead	864	980	1,844
Equipment depreciation	1,440	870	2,310
Indirect overhead	2,160	1,174	3,334
General overhead	3,240	2,935	6,175
Marketing and administration.	14,364	13,114	27,478
Total expenses	$43,228	$39,431	$82,659
Income	$10,772	$ 1,069	$11,841

* Sold in 1980: 30,000 units of RAM–64; 3,000 units of RAM–128.

EXHIBIT 3
Time Unlimited, Inc., Market Position

	Sales Volume		Price (per unit)	
Selling Year	Industry Totals	Time Unlimited	Competition's Average Price	Time Unlimited
RAM–64 model				
1978	40,000	5,000	$ 5,000	$ 6,000
1979	75,000	10,000	2,500	2,700
1980	150,000	30,000	1,700	1,800
1981	200,000	—	1,850	—
RAM–128 model				
1978	7,500	500	$20,000	$23,000
1979	15,000	1,500	15,000	16,500
1980	25,000	3,000	12,500	13,500
1981	35,000	—	14,000	—

ROSS EDWARDS: Well, I can see from our discussion that there are several options open to us. I do have an additional concern. After reviewing the data brought in by Andrea, I'm not exactly sure how much it is costing us to produce and sell either of our models. We really need this piece of information. And while you are thinking about that, please keep one important point in mind. Our divisional goal is an income of 12 percent of sales, so we should consider that when seeking solutions to the questions that were brought up in today's meeting. It is reasonably urgent that we come up with a suitable analysis as soon as possible. We are almost through the year now and must make some decisions for the coming year. I'll see you back here in one week.

APPLICATION 6–10

Toys "R" Us, Inc.

Last Christmas, a Florida newspaper ran a cartoon of a couple, laden with gifts, emerging from a Toys "R" Us store. "Broke 'R' Us," the caption read. Company executives liked the cartoon so much that copies now hang in their offices.

The toy industry may be in a slump, but not Toys "R" Us, Inc. Overall, toy sales have grown an average of just 2 percent the past couple of years, but sales at Toys "R" Us have increased a robust 27 percent annually. Last year, its cash registers rang up 20 percent of the $12.5 billion in toys sold in the United States, up from just 13 percent in 1984 (Exhibit 1).

"Every time a Toys 'R' Us moves in, our sales go down 20 percent the first year," laments Michael Vastola, chairman and chief executive officer of Lionel Corp., a competing toy-store chain.

But Charles Lazarus, who earned $60 million last year as the company's chairman and chief executive officer, mostly by exercising stock options, isn't satisfied. His goal: to sell half of all toys sold in the United States.

Helen Singer Kaplan, Mr. Lazarus's psychiatrist wife, kids him about having an "edifice" complex. "Why do you need to open so many stores?" she asks. "Because it's fun," Mr. Lazarus replies. "If permitted to sell in the Soviet Union, we would."

Securities analysts predict that by 1995 the retailing giant will be close to Mr. Lazarus's goal, selling 40 percent of the toys in this nation. Sean McGowan, vice president of research at Balis Zorn Gerard Inc., sums up Toys "R" Us approach: "Its strength isn't its product, but the way it sells it."

The giant retailer's strategy has remained essentially the same since it emerged from bankruptcy proceedings in 1978. It sells toys as if Christmas were always around the corner: Each store, stuffed to the rafters, offers 18,000 toys in convenient locations at low prices. The company's buying clout, and its use of computers to spot emerging hits, mean that it usually is

---

EXHIBIT 1
Growth Spurt at Toys "R" Us

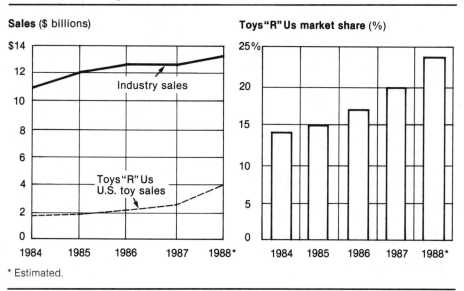

Sales ($ billions)   Toys "R" Us market share (%)

* Estimated.

Sources: Deutsche Bank Capital Corp.; Toy Manufacturers of America.

stocked with hot items even when other retailers aren't. It also tries to win over new customers by selling baby products, such as disposable diapers, at or below cost.

In the past couple of years, Toys "R" Us has fine-tuned the success formula. Last Christmas, for example, it installed scanners at its cash registers to speed up checkouts. And the company now also uses a computer to schedule work shifts to increase efficiency.

Perhaps as much as anything, growing customer loyalty explains its continued growth. "Look at these baseball cards," says a smiling Mary Lou Kuegler as she leaves a Toys "R" Us store in Dedham, Mass. "I got them for $4.50 apiece. Everywhere else they're six bucks." Ms. Kuegler, a Newton, Mass., housewife, says she drives seven miles past other discounters and department stores to do most of her toy shopping at Toys "R" Us.

Because of customers like Ms. Kuegler, Toys "R" Us sales for the first six months have increased 34.6 percent to $1.33 billion from the year-earlier period, and same-store sales rose 18.2 percent (see Exhibit 1).

Although some of Toys "R" Us' sales growth of late has come from an increase in the number of stores, much has come from existing stores at the expense of retailers that don't specialize in toys. K mart Corp. and Service Merchandise Co. have slowly shrunk the size of their toy departments, at least in part because Toys "R" Us has taken away business.

Discount and department stores, whose toy inventories must be slashed by December 26, simply can't compete very well by offering only 3,000 toys and occasional sales. "Seasonal sellers competing against Toys 'R' Us, is like amateurs going up against professionals," says Richard Nager, an analyst at Ladenburg Thalmann & Co.

Toys "R" Us also has managed, at least so far, to fend off imitators. Two chains—Child World, Inc., and Lionel—have designed almost identical stores. "But neither imitator has been able to carry out the concept better than the master," says Dorothy Lakner, an analyst for Deutsche Bank Capital Corp. One reason for Lionel's 56 percent profit decline in 1987 was competition from Toys "R" Us, says Jane Gilday, an analyst for McKinley Allsopp Securities.

While Toys "R" Us sells $330.80 of goods per square foot a year, Child World manages $221.70 and Lionel $193.10, Ms. Lakner says. Put another way, Toys "R" Us averages $8.4 million in sales a year per store, compared with $4.9 million for Child World and $4.4 million for Lionel—though their stores are about the same in size.

Toys "R" Us offers low prices, but it still could be vulnerable in a price war, analysts say. Late last year, Child World deliberately undersold Toys "R" Us in an effort to gain market share, and it worked. Child World's Christmas-season same-store sales rose 21.2 percent, compared with 12 percent for Toys "R" Us. But Child World dismissed the architect of the strategy, President Gilbert Wachsman, last February, apparently because the low prices reduced profits too much. "Both Toys and Lionel are resting easier now that Wachsman is gone," says Ms. Gilday of McKinley Allsopp.

Toys "R" Us also enjoys clout with toy makers and is able to get larger quantities of scarce toys, some say.

In the first quarter of this year, for instance, about half of the company's 19.6 percent increase in same-store sales was due to the popular Nintendo Entertainment System, according to Daniel Barry, an analyst at Kidder, Peabody & Co. Lionel would like to have more Nintendo games but can't get them. "Generally what's felt in the industry is that Toys 'R' Us gets a large share of shipment of everything," complains Mr. Vastola, Lionel's chief executive.

Toys "R" Us officials deny the company enjoys special favor with toy makers. Instead, they say, smart planning through computer surveys and the financial ability to buy toys earlier in the year, when supplies are more plentiful, enable the company's stores to be well stocked.

The way it's growing, Toys "R" Us is becoming even more formidable. The 314-store chain plans to open 45 stores this year in the United States. And, with 52 stores abroad, it is continuing its expansion overseas. Foreign countries, where mom-and-pop shops and department stores dominate the toy market, are ripe for a Toys "R" Us style of selling, analysts say. For example, 70 percent of the toys in Europe are sold at Christmas, which means Toys "R" Us can exploit the off-season market, Ms. Lakner of Deutsche Bank Capital says.

While Toys "R" Us doesn't give financial results for its overseas division, Ms. Lakner estimates that foreign sales totaled $200 million last year and will increase to $910 million by 1991.

After five years, the company's move into children's clothes with its Kids "R" Us stores is finally showing a profit, analysts add. Kids "R" Us— 112 stores and growing—sells brand-name clothes at a discount. Mr. Barry of Kidder Peabody estimates Kids "R" Us had sales of $200 million and earnings of about $7 million last year and should post sales of $400 million and earnings of $13 million this year.

Succeeding in the $15-billion children's clothing business is tougher than toys, both because there is more competition and because retailers have only about 10 weeks to sell merchandise before the change of season. But Kids "R" Us says it is more than holding its own. It sells 85 percent of its clothing at a profitable price, marking down just 15 percent—compared with an industry average of 22 percent—to clear inventory, says Michael Searles, president of Kids "R" Us.

Toys "R" Us has relatively little turnover among its middle and upper management ranks, analysts note. Through its employee stock option plan, more than 40 employees have become millionaires in the past 10 years. But, says Norman Ricken, Toys "R" Us president and chief talent scout, the company demands hard work in return. "I like to recruit people who like to work, not people who like to get rich," he says. "Toys 'R' Us is not a 9-to-5 but an 8-to-faint job," Mr. Ricken jokes.

"At Toys 'R' Us, we have a theory," he says. "If you're really dominant, no one can compete with you. Our goal is to be that dominant in the business."

Discussion Questions

1. Analyze and describe Toys "R" Us's competitive advantage. What further competitive threats should management guard against?
2. Analyze the market opportunity for toys during the period 1990–2000.
3. Evaluate the positioning strategy used by Toys "R" Us.
4. Assume that Child World and Lionel independently decide to launch a price war in order to increase their market share position. Recommend a marketing strategy for use by Toys "R" Us in countering this competitive threat.

The Limited Inc.

When R. H. Macy & Co. announced its $3.58 billion leveraged buyout last week, the Wall Street rumor mill soon had other major retailers up for sale. High on the list of rumored acquirers is Leslie H. Wexner, chairman of The Limited Inc.

Mr. Wexner, whose family controls 35.1 percent of Limited, won't comment, and he hasn't made any moves to satisfy the gossips. But the very appearance of his name indicates his stature and marks progress from just 18 months ago when Limited's unsuccessful bid to buy the much larger Carter Hawley Hale Stores Inc. shocked the market and triggered a wave of David and Goliath analogies.

Last week, however, the retailer capped its 2,400-plus store empire with the purchase of New York's Tony Henri Bendel shop, which Limited plans to expand internationally. That added the top layer to Limited's nationwide collection of specialty women's apparel stores, which include large-size apparel stores, Victoria's Secret lingerie shops and the trend-setting Limited chain for the 18-to-35-year-old set. Early next month the company will open a showpiece, seven-level Manhattan store in a restored landmark building on upper Madison Avenue.

Limited's prospects appear, well, unlimited. How did the company, which started 22 years ago as a single suburban store near this midwestern city, begin to set trends for others in the fiercely competitive and fickle fashion field? And, more importantly, can it keep it up?

Mr. Wexner, the 48-year-old billionaire founder, usually gets the credit for the company's success. (He also has gotten a lot of personal publicity, including a recent cover story in *New York Magazine* that described his life down to the color of his maroon socks.) But behind his oft-cited retail instinct is a management team executing a series of deliberate strategies that have enabled Limited to squeeze out or buy up many competitors.

To help keep a closer eye on the industry which Limited has said repeatedly it wants to lead, the company next year will move into a newly purchased townhouse on New York's Upper East Side that will serve as its corporate offices there. "We want to tap more into world resources," says Mr. Wexner, chatting recently in the study of his suburban Columbus mansion.

He and other top officers already spend 75 percent of their time in makeshift quarters at the Limited divisions based in New York. But the

---

Source: Julie Solomon, "Limited Is a Clothing Retailer on the Move: Chairman Cites Departure From 'Conventional Wisdom'". Reprinted by permission of *The Wall Street Journal.* © Dow Jones & Company, Inc., October 31, 1985, p. 6. All rights reserved.

company needs "a presence" in the city, albeit secluded and "low-profile," Mr. Wexner adds. The company will retain its extensive office and distribution facilities as its headquarters here. But the home-away-from-home also is intended to give the financial community more access to Limited.

So far, that community seems almost to worship Limited. "I'm always asking myself" where Limited could fall down, says Art Charpentier of Goldman, Sachs & Co. "It's very difficult to find any place that they seem vulnerable. What it says is that (if they trip up) it's going to be a bolt out of the blue. There'll be people who said they anticipated it."

About the only criticism competitors and other retail observers can muster suggests that Limited's corporate culture, while a strength, is so intense that it produces some management turnover. Also, the company's market domination alienates vendors who, analysts add, can't do much about it.

"Look what happened to those who tried to sue Limited" last summer when it abruptly canceled orders for its newly acquired Lerner division, says one industry executive, requesting anonymity because she is wary of Mr. Wexner's "power." Vendors backed off, she says. "They need to eat, too."

The acquisition of Lerner, which turned out to have serious inventory problems, added a note of rancor to Limited's story this year. Limited is in the early stages of a lawsuit against New York-based Rapid-American Corp., which sold the unit. The suit claims that Rapid-American failed to disclose accounting information on the inventory.

But analysts say Limited is ahead of schedule in turning Lerner around. And, despite the concern's frustrated attempt to buy Carter Hawley Hale, it rarely stumbles. Including the 751-store Lerner division, the company for the current fiscal year expects to report $2.5 billion in sales, up 87 percent from sales of $1.34 billion last year, on which the company earned $92.5 million, or 77 cents a share (see Exhibit 1). Analysts project full-year earnings of about $1.10 to 1.15 a share.

EXHIBIT 1
Limited Inc.'s Rapid Growth Since 1981 (years ending in January)

	Net Income ($ millions)	Per Share*	Sales ($ millions)	Number of Stores
1985	$92.5	77¢	$1,343.1	1,412
1984	70.9	59¢	1,085.9	937
1983	33.6	29¢	721.4	825
1982	22.4	20¢	364.9	430
1981	13.1	12¢	295.0	352

* Restated for stock split paid in 1985.

"The only thing that worries me is Les Wexner being hit by a beer truck," says Al Pennington, president of a consulting firm bearing his name.

But Limited's success can be traced to more than Mr. Wexner's fashion eye, manic devotion to work, and management touch. It also reflects, for example, Limited's intense ownership ethic (along with management, 25 percent of Limited employees own more than half of the company's stock) and an international manufacturing organization that, consultants say, gives Limited a critical edge over competitors in supply, pricing, and timing.

Add to that Limited's willingness to leverage itself repeatedly to grab more segments of the consolidating specialty retail market, suggests Phil Barach, chairman of U.S. Shoe Corp., a competitor, who says his company moves like a "turtle," compared with Limited.

At a retail seminar earlier this year, David Kollat, a Limited executive vice president, scoffed at projections of a no-growth decade ahead for women's apparel. "We'll grow at the expense of our competitors," listeners recall him saying.

Mr. Wexner bases the company's success on its departures from "conventional wisdom." He cites its refusal to rapidly rotate buyers the way department stores do, and even the flashy, American-style interior of its offices in Hong Kong, where, he says, most Americans opt to blend in with more subtle Oriental styles.

It is not that "Limited does anything different from the rest. They just do it better," says Chris Schwartz, vice president for corporate development at Dylex Ltd., a Toronto-based specialty retailer with 2,700 stores that recently bought such Limited competitors as the Foxmoor chain.

A case in point is Mast Industries, Limited's manufacturing and buying arm, whose purchase by Limited in 1978 was heavily criticized. Traditionally, says Martin Trust, who founded Mast and now heads it, many retailers have jumped into the retail supply cycle late, bought through third-party "hired guns"—often on a one-order basis—and depended on New York middleman suppliers along with the rest of the retail herd. "In the old days, it was OK to chase the market," says New York retail consultant Carol Farmer.

She says more retailers will begin to do as Mast does: Keep the retailer involved from the sewing machine on up. Mast helps Limited marketing people track and predict trends, locates countries and manufacturers, and will even set up in business a promising entrepreneur or buy machinery for a small, undercapitalized manufacturer. Full-time quota specialists try to stay ahead of the international protectionist game by buying up production "options." As a result, say industry sources, Mast has long-term relationships that speed delivery to its stores and preempt other retailers.

To illustrate Mast's power, competitors point to the "Shaker" sweater, a V-necked, brightly colored, oversize garment that Limited predicted, after test marketing last year, would be a must-have item for millions of young women.

Ms. Farmer, who worked for Lerner before Limited bought it, says Limited seemed suddenly to have "jillions" of the sweaters in its stores, forcing Lerner's and others into frantic, costly catch-up efforts.

The 20 percent of Mast's output that goes to outsiders, including some Limited competitors, helps keep Mast up-to-date on the rest of the industry, says Mr. Trust. But the 25 percent of Limited divisions' apparel that Mast supplies is the bulk of its projected $400 million in sales this year. By contrast, Dylex's product sourcing division, which some say also is very progressive, will do only $200 million.

Mast's quick production turnarounds fit what Robert Morosky, vice chairman, describes as an important Limited strategy: flexibility. More interested in controlling budgets and employees, he says, many retailers won't allow quick reversals or unexpected budget increases. Limited gives buyers and other employees the authority to make quick decisions without layers of approvals. Accounting employees, for example, can offer suppliers prepayment in exchange for discounts, an independence other retailers wouldn't grant to mere "bookkeepers," he says.

Dylex's Mr. Schwartz says the company has managed to maintain an unusual "entrepreneurial zeal." But the culture isn't for everyone. One top retail executive turned down a job with Limited, citing the company's single-mindedness, time demands and requirement that employees not stray outside Limited's very closed society. "I'm too old to join a monastery," the executive told Limited.

Whether the culture and systems can be maintained as Limited grows is an open question. "If they acquired (a big department store company) and got really leveraged, it could backfire," at least temporarily, says Mr. Pennington, the consultant.

But Mr. Morosky, the Mast vice chairman, says he is unfazed by leverage levels like the 121 percent of debt relative to equity that Limited recorded when it acquired Lerner. That figure is now down to 70 percent. And Mr. Wexner vows to get into the department-store business, either through acquisition or a joint venture.

He does concede that it is dangerous to see success as "a self-fulfilling prophecy." Goldman Sachs' Mr. Charpentier says he thinks Limited got that message back in the late 1970s when management problems hurt earnings.

Discussion Questions

1. What factors contributed to Limited Inc.'s extremely successful growth and financial performance?
2. Identify and discuss the strategic marketing opportunities and threats that Limited Inc. should consider in developing their strategic marketing plan.
3. Discuss the feasibility of Limited Inc. growing at the expense of its competitors in the no-growth decade for women's apparel expected to begin in 1985.
4. Outline a strategic marketing plan for Limited Inc. covering the period 1987–90. Make any reasonable assumptions necessary to complete your plan outline.

INDEX

INDEX OF CASES AND APPLICATIONS